Contemporary Approaches to Research on
Learning Environments
Worldviews

Contemporary Approaches to Research on
Learning Environments
Worldviews

edited by

Darrell L. Fisher

Science and Mathematics Education Centre
Curtin University of Technology, Australia

Myint Swe Khine

National Institute of Education
Nanyang Technological University, Singapore

 **World Scientific**

NEW JERSEY • LONDON • SINGAPORE • BEIJING • SHANGHAI • HONG KONG • TAIPEI • CHENNAI

Published by

World Scientific Publishing Co. Pte. Ltd.

5 Toh Tuck Link, Singapore 596224

USA office: 27 Warren Street, Suite 401-402, Hackensack, NJ 07601

UK office: 57 Shelton Street, Covent Garden, London WC2H 9HE

British Library Cataloguing-in-Publication Data
A catalogue record for this book is available from the British Library.

CONTEMPORARY APPROACHES TO RESEARCH ON LEARNING ENVIRONMENTS
Worldviews

ISBN 981-256-508-6
ISBN 981-256-511-6 (pbk)

Printed in Singapore by World Scientific Printers (S) Pte Ltd

Preface

Theo Wubbels
Institute of Education
Utrecht University
The Netherlands

Learning environment research is booming all over the world as can be seen by the high number of books that are being published and the many recent journal articles. These articles can be found, as can be expected, in the specialised journal *Learning Environments Research: An International Journal*, but also, and this is remarkable, we see more and more learning environment related studies in other journals. This book with contributions on a variety of important issues is further proof of the vibrant status of the field of learning environments research. Whereas 25 years ago the field of learning environments research was dominated by scholars from Australia and the USA, nowadays studies are reported from all over the world. Europe and even now Asia are centres of excellent research as can be seen from the contributions in this book.

The tradition of learning environments research goes back to the seminal work by Rudolph Moos in the seventies of the previous century. Based on his work with families, the quality of the learning environment became accepted as a crucial factor in education. Stern, Stein and Bloom (1956) distinguished the idiosyncratic view that each person has of the environment from the shared view that members of a group hold. Following this distinction, the student's individual perception of the learning environment was acknowledged as a mediating factor between characteristics of the learning environment and a student's learning. Nowadays we see complex analyses to unravel the relationships between the shared and individual perception and the influence of these perceptions on student learning. Further, to improve student achievement, improving the learning environment became the starting point of many reform movements. Based on extensive research, a variety of economical, valid and widely-applicable questionnaires is now available for help in such improvements. In addition, more recent research has produced practical qualitative instruments.

Methodologically the developments over the last 25 years have been tremendous. Early studies predominantly were quantitative in nature, but now we see a broad variety of approaches, from quantitative, to qualitative, mixed methods studies and in the last five years more and more intervention studies. Early studies usually belonged to one of the following two categories: studies investigating the relations between learning environment characteristics and student outcomes and studies from the impact of interventions, for example curriculum reforms, on learning environments. Nowadays we see a broadening from these descriptive studies to intervention studies and even action research. The question addressed then is how learning environment questionnaires and other instruments can be used to bring about improvement in the quality of learning environments. Research methods have not only developed considerably in the diversity of approaches, but also in the use of advanced statistical multilevel methods.

This book convincingly shows how broad the field is and what the variety of available research methods is. Important traditional issues are covered such as relations between learning environments aspects and student outcomes. The focus of the book is however on exciting new areas such as the development of technology rich environments and advanced new research methods. Hopefully this book will encourage and guide important future research into all aspects of learning environments.

Reference

Stern, G.G., Stein, M.J., & Bloom, B.S. (1956). *Methods in personality assessment*. Glencoe Ill.: Free Press.

From the Editors

Learning environment research has undergone considerable growth in the past thirty years and has now reached a stage of notable diversity and internationalisation. Earlier studies mainly used questionnaires to assess learning environments but today both qualitative and quantitative approaches are used. Many contemporary studies are a productive combination of these two approaches. Our first book *Technology-rich learning environments: A future perspective* has been well received by educators from all levels. This book is our second attempt at bringing together prominent educators and researchers from around the world to share their contemporary research on educational learning environments.

Our gratitude goes first to the contributors for responding to our invitation to share their work and making this book a reality. We thank our publisher, World Scientific, for taking up this project, particularly our editor, Juliet Lee who accepted this challenging task. We would very much like to thank our wives, Gail and Elizabeth, since without their encouragement and continuing support this book would not have been possible.

In the first chapter, Dorman, Fisher, and Waldrip report a study linking students' perceptions of learning environments and assessment with academic efficacy and attitude to science in Australian secondary schools. A specially validated instrument, the Students' Perceptions of Assessment Questionnaire, assessed five assessment characteristics: Congruence with Planned Learning, Authenticity, Student Consultation, Transparency and Diversity. Scales to assess attitude to science and one academic efficacy scale were employed as outcome measures. Multiple regression and structural equation modelling were used to study relationships among these variables and the extent to which a postulated model fitted the data. Results showed that classroom environment and student perceptions of assessment were significant positive predictors of academic efficacy and attitude to science.

In their chapter, Khine and Lourdusamy from Nanyang Technology University, Singapore address the issue of teachers' professional development in the area of interpersonal behaviour through reflective analysis of one's own behaviour and by getting feedback from students. By using the Questionnaire on Teacher-Student Interaction (QTI), the study investigated differences between the teachers' reflective analysis of their own behaviour and students' perception of the classroom interaction in Singapore schools.

The study described by Fisher, den Brok and Rickards in Chapter 3 provides information on a meta-analysis performed on a large Australian secondary student and teacher QTI data set. QTI dimension scores were examined against factors such as gender, class size and subject. To investigate separate and combined effects of variables, a hierarchical analysis of variance (distinguishing between the school, class and student level) was conducted with ML3E software. This chapter discusses the effect sizes and variance explained by these variables.

Avi Hofstein focuses on the science laboratory as a unique mode of instruction and learning environment in the fourth chapter and includes a review of the literature regarding the use of the SLEI in Australia and in Israel. Teachers' and students' perceptions of a science laboratory learning environment were measured. Research findings are presented that help us in improving the pedagogy and educational effectiveness of the laboratory.

In Chapter 5 Van Petegem and Donche write about learning environment research in higher education in Belgium. Their results show that individual differences in learning and teaching were present. Different learning patterns were also associated with different preferences for learning environments. Their studies also indicate that personal and contextual factors like learning orientations and types of education are associated with differences in learning patterns. In the final part of this chapter, an overview of possible research perspectives to elaborate their present research model is given.

From the Netherlands, den Brok, Bergen and Brekelmans discuss comparisons between students' and teachers' perceptions which are usable variables in investigating the teacher-learner process and the preparation and staff development of teachers. The study investigated divergence and convergence in perceptions for 72 teachers (from various subjects) and their classes (1,604 students) with the Questionnaire of Instructional Behaviour (QIB) and pertained to teacher control of student learning (strong, shared or loose), clarity of instruction and classroom management. Results showed that almost half of the teachers had higher perception scores than did their students, that no relationship existed between teacher experience and the amount of divergence, and that teaching style was related to the amount of divergence found. This suggests that more learning environment research is needed to explain convergence and divergence between student and teacher perceptions.

In Chapter 7, Kerr, Fisher, Yaxley and Fraser report two studies of student perceptions in science classrooms at the post-compulsory level. The first study used the College Science Classroom Environment Survey (CSCES) to investigate science students' perceptions of their actual and preferred psychosocial learning environments. The second study used the Technology-Rich, Outcomes-Focused, Learning Environment Inventory (TROFLEI) to assess ICT-rich psychosocial environments. Associations were examined between physical, psychosocial, and attitudinal data, and comparisons were made with results from the earlier study.

Waxman and Chang's Chapter 8 provides a very good example of the mixed method approach for examining classroom learning environments. This chapter also offers a summary of recent research that incorporates the mixed methods of survey research, such as student questionnaires, systematic classroom observation, and their application to investigate various aspects of classroom environments for educationally resilient (i.e., academically successful) and nonresilient (i.e., academically unsuccessful) students in urban elementary schools located in the USA. Importantly, the chapter addresses some of the implications of current mixed methods research for future research and teachers' professional development

Wahyudi and Treagust in Chapter 9 explore the status of science education in Indonesian lower secondary schools from a classroom learning environment perspective. They investigated how science education was delivered and how the students perceived their classroom-learning environment in both rural and urban schools. They reported that classroom observations confirmed that science teaching in urban schools was better than that in rural schools, reflecting students' perceptions of their classroom environments.

Chapter 10 by Saunders and Fisher deals with an action research approach with primary pre-service teachers to improve both university and primary school classroom environments in New Zealand. The study focused on the use of the CUCEI in a collaborative process that the lecturer and pre-service students used for examining and improving upon what was happening in their science education classes while at the same time considering their own learning environment. The study indicated that student teachers can be provided with strategies to examine, improve and reflect on the learning environment of their classrooms.

In Chapter 11, Koul and Fisher report the first ever large-scale study conducted in Jammu (India) where multiple research methods were used to explore the nature of classroom environments and student-teacher interactions. A sample of 1,021 students from 32 science classes in seven co educational private schools completed the questionnaires, What is Happening in This Class (WIHIC) and the Questionnaire on Teacher Interaction (QTI), as well as an attitude scale. The quantitative data provided a starting point from which other qualitative methods (interviews and observations) were used to gain a more in-depth understanding of the classroom environment. It is hoped that the information in this chapter will give readers an understanding of the existing learning environments in Jammu, India.

Wanpen and Fisher in Chapter 12 describe a case study conducted in a tertiary computer classroom in the northeast region of Thailand. The Constructivist Learning Environment Survey (CLES) was used with a large sample of students to determine its reliability for use in Thailand, and then administered to a class of students taking a computer course to find out their actual and preferred perceptions of their learning environments. These data were then used in a practical way to improve the class environment.

Templeton, Johnson, Lee and Guofang from the USA describe how they have investigated the factors that professional staff, faculty, and administrators in the College of Education and Human Services (COEHS) at Lake State University (LSU) described as conducive to an improved college (working, teaching and learning) environment. Participants completed the School-Level Environment Questionnaire. Their findings and a description of their interesting process are reported in Chapter 13.

In New Zealand, Falloon (Chapter 14) documents key findings of an eighteen-month case study into a learning environment involving Year 5 and Year 6 students at a suburban primary school. It examines the nature of teacher and student work practices in an environment where there was a ratio of one computer to approximately two students, and details the complexity of the interrelationship between teacher philosophy, curriculum design, and classroom organisational systems, that significantly impacted upon student work and social performance. It presents and discusses data captured using *Camtasia* video recording software, which enabled unique and unscripted "insider views" to be gained of the manner in which students worked with the teacher, each other, and the software, as they undertook their learning tasks.

Kyriakides from the University of Cyprus presents the results from a study attempting to show that teacher effectiveness research and research into teacher interpersonal behaviour can help us explain most of the student variance at classroom level. In this chapter the main findings of both teacher effectiveness research and research into teacher interpersonal behaviour are presented. A stratified sample of 32 primary schools in Cyprus was selected and two questionnaires measuring student perceptions of teacher behaviour in the classroom according to each research tradition were administered to all Year 6 students from each class of the school sample. It was found that the data collected from most of the scales of both questionnaires were associated with student achievement gains in both cognitive (Mathematics and Greek Language) and affective outcomes of schooling.

In Chapter 16, Hirata, Ishikawa and Fisher report on three studies describing associations between students' perceptions of their classroom environment and their individual characteristics in Japanese higher education. The first study involved the use of the CUCEI: College and University Classroom Environment Inventory and the Locus of Control Scale which were administered to 406 students. The analysis of data revealed that students' academic achievement and internal locus of control were associated with satisfaction from learning. The secondary study concerned the analysis of data from 100 students and clarified the relevance that existed between students' perceptions of actual and preferred satisfaction as well as innovation in learning. In the third study analysis of covariance structures, using structural equation modelling was involved. The results suggest that student perceptions of their classes are clearly relevant to individual student characteristics and needs.

Dorman, Aldridge and Fraser present their finding in the use of structural equation modelling to investigate associations between classroom environment and outcomes in Australian secondary schools. The 80-item Technology-Rich Outcomes-Focused Learning Environment Inventory (TROFLEI) was used to assess 10 classroom environment dimensions. A sample of 2,178 high school students from Western Australia and Tasmania responded to the TROFLEI and three student outcome measures: attitude to the subject, attitude to computer use and academic efficacy. Confirmatory factor analysis using LISREL supported the 10 scale *a priori* structure of the instrument. Multiple regression identified particular classroom environment scales that were significant predictors of three outcome scales. Structural equation modelling using LISREL revealed that teacher support and equity predicted attitude to subject and that differentiation, task orientation, computer usage and young adult ethos predicted attitude to computer use. Overall, the modelling indicated that improving classroom environment has the potential to improve student outcomes.

Lipponen, Lallimo and Lakkala from the University of Helsinki, Finland present their ideas on designing infrastructures for learning with technology in Chapter 18. They argue that the functionality, the implementation and use of technology in schools and in workplaces is based on, and requires the creation of, a set of interconnected structural elements. It is further explained that these interconnected structural elements, such as social practices, and educational use of technology form infrastructures that can be designed in a similar way as, for instance, technical infrastructures are designed. They call these infrastructures learning-oriented infrastructures. Learning-oriented infrastructures provide a framework for designing the entire structure of teaching and learning with technology. In this chapter, they analyse the characteristics of these infrastructures in complex learning environments by demonstrating how they are related, and support working with technology.

Chapter 19 deals with assessing the effectiveness of a blended web-based learning environment in an Australian high school. Chandra and Fisher present the findings of a study in which *Getsmart*, a teacher designed website, was blended into science and physics lessons at an Australian High School. It shows how the results of learning environments research were used in assessing the effectiveness of the approach from the students' perspective. The investigation also gave an indication of how effective *Getsmart* was as a teaching model in such environments.

From Taiwan, Huang describes in Chapter 20 the validation of the College and University Environment Inventory. The results of an application of the inventory revealed that, in Taiwan, most juniors had favourable relations with other students and with administrative staff, and perceived positively their library resources and emotional development. Student-faculty relations, university system support to student affairs, and language learning, however, may need to be improved. The implications of these findings are discussed in this chapter.

In Chapter 21, Wahyudi and Fisher describe the working environments in an Indonesian junior secondary school context. Using the Indonesian version of the School Level Environment Questionnaire (SLEQ), the study found that teachers view their school environments positively on all scales, except that of Staff Freedom. A comparison between actual and preferred perceptions showed statistically significant differences on all scales, except Staff Freedom and Work Pressure. It was also found that urban school teachers viewed their school environment less favourably than did their counterparts in rural and suburban schools. Statistically significant differences were found on the Participatory Decision Making and Work Pressure scales. This study suggests that these findings should be used as a starting point for improving working environments in rural, suburban, and urban schools in Indonesia.

Telli, Cakiroglu and den Brok investigated Turkish secondary students' perceptions of their classroom learning environment and attitude toward biology. The data were gathered from 1,983 ninth and tenth grade students from 57 biology classes at schools in two major Turkish cities. Data were collected with an adapted and translated version of the What is Happening in This Classroom (WIHIC) instrument and the Test of Science Related Attitudes (TOSRA). Correlation and regression analyses revealed that students' perceptions of their learning environment in biology were significantly associated with their attitudes. In addition, results of the study revealed that there were significant differences in gender and grade level. The authors discuss these findings in Chapter 22 and compare them with prior learning environment studies.

Quinton provides a critique on the possible future of learning in Chapter 23. He describes how the potential of the Internet and the technologies it inspires makes it feasible to not only access and manage information in productive and efficient ways, but also to create an environment in which we can deliver dynamically interactive, personalised solutions tailored to the needs and preferences of all learners. He presents the challenge to us of harnessing technological innovations in ways that will assist us to create learning environments in which we can deliver high quality learning outcomes relevant to the changing needs of learners.

In Chapter 24, Chai and Tan explain that Computer-Supported Collaborative Learning (CSCL) is an emerging field of research that has gained significant momentum in the past decade. For its relatively short history, it has been associated with three perspectives of learning: acquisition, participation, and knowledge creation. Their chapter focuses on CSCL for knowledge creation, particularly the Knowledge Building approach proposed by Bereiter and Scardamalia. It includes the theoretical foundation of Knowledge Building, its relevance in the Knowledge Age, some key research directions and methodologies, and discussion on some key challenges.

Chard in Chapter 25 describes how in recent times learning environment research has moved into distance and web-based learning environments, with new instruments being developed for the purpose of evaluating and improving these environments. This chapter discusses the development of learning environment instruments from their roots in psychosocial research to the current development of learning environment instruments for the evaluation of virtual learning environments including 3D virtual worlds designed for learning.

It has been a long process and a formidable task to compile the twenty five chapters for this book. But we are very pleased to see the final result from which we hope will establish a landmark in the history of learning environment research.

Darrell L. Fisher
Curtin University of Technology
Australia

Myint Swe Khine
Nanyang Technological University
Singapore

About the Contributors

Jill M. Aldridge is a Senior Lecturer at the Science Mathematics Education Centre at Curtin University of Technology, Perth, Australia. Her research is in the field of teaching and learning. Currently, her focus is on the integration of ICT into classrooms and whether this leads to more individualised and outcomes-focused learning environments.

Rosalyn Anstine-Templeton is Dean of the College of Education and Human Services at Marshall University in Huntington, West Virginia. Her research interests include studying learning environments in the field of at risk populations and higher education.

Theo Bergen is Professor of Educational Sciences, holding a chair in teacher performance at the Graduate School of Teacher Education of the Radboud University Nijmegen (The Netherlands). A central issue in his research interest is the learning of teachers in the context of innovation. Currently, his research focuses on how teachers' professional development can be stimulated by means of collegial coaching.

Mieke Brekelmans is Associate Professor in a teacher training and educational research group of the Institute of Education (IVLOS) at Utrecht University (The Netherlands). Her research is in the field of teaching and teacher education. Currently, her focus is on the relation between teacher thinking and action, and the development of teaching during the professional teacher career.

Perry den Brok is Associate Professor in a teacher training and educational research group of the Institute of Education (IVLOS) at Utrecht University (The Netherlands). His research is in the field of teaching and teacher education. Currently his focus is on multicultural and intercultural studies on classroom environments, and factors that explain differences in student perceptions of teaching.

Jale Cakiroglu is Assistant Professor at the Department of Elementary Education, Middle East Technical University, Ankara, Turkey. Her research interests include teacher efficacy beliefs, learning environments research and the nature of science.

Ching Sing Chai is a Lecturer in the Learning Sciences and Technologies Academic Group, National Institute of Education, Nanyang Technological University, Singapore. His areas of research interests are computer supported collaborative learning and using information technologies as cognitive tools.

Vinesh Chandra is a Senior Mathematics and Science Teacher at Mansfield State High School in Queensland, Australia. He graduated with his doctorate in science education from Curtin University of Technology in 2005. His research interests include classroom and online pedagogies, gender issues and applications of technology in science education. For his innovative approaches to teaching, he was awarded the prestigious Queensland Premiers Smart State Teacher Excellence Scholarship in 2002. In 2005, he received the Queensland Society of Information Technology in Education (QSITE) Teacher of the Year award.

Hui-Li Chang earned her doctorate degree in Mathematics Education at The University of Houston, USA. She was a Post-Doctoral Research Fellow at the USA Department of Education, Center for Research on Education, Diversity and Excellence (CREDE) where she directed the "Effective Teaching and Learning for Language Minority Students in Mathematics" project. She was also a principal researcher on the "Pre-service Teacher Education for Diversity Research Synthesis Project". Dr. Chang is currently teaching graduate research courses at National-Louis University in Illinois.

Susan M. Chard is a Senior Lecturer at Whitireia Community Polytechnic, Porirua New Zealand. Her research is in the field of web based learning. Currently, her focus is the development of web based 3D learning environments and the methods of evaluating these environments.

Vincent Donche is a Researcher of the Institute of Education and Information Sciences at the University of Antwerp, Belgium and works in the research group EduBROn [Counselling, Research & Development in Education] [www.edubron.be]. His research interests include learning styles, teaching styles, autonomous learning and constructivist learning environments. He is completing his doctoral degree focusing on student and teacher learning in higher education.

Jeffrey P. Dorman is a Reader in the School of Education at the Brisbane campus of the Australian Catholic University. His research interests include the study of learning environments and the use of structural equation modelling to analyse educational research data.

Garry Falloon is a Senior Lecturer at the Faculty of Education at the University of Auckland, but is presently seconded to the New Zealand Ministry of Education to develop and manage the Digital Opportunities Projects (www.digiops.org.nz). He recently completed doctoral research on student learning in a digital classroom environment, and has research interests in examining the efficacy of such organisational systems for supporting student learning, and in determining if, how, and where computers can best support overall student development.

Darrell L. Fisher is Professor of Science Education and Deputy Director of the Science and Mathematics Education Centre at Curtin University of Technology, Australia. His major research interests include classroom and school environments, and curriculum issues related to science, particularly curriculum evaluation. He has published and presented on these topics throughout the world. He is a Fellow of the Australian College of Education and the Regional Editor for Asia and Australia of *Learning Environments Research: An International Journal*. He is a world leader in learning environment research and co-author of the book published by World Scientific, *Technology-rich Learning Environments: A Future Perspective.*

Barry J. Fraser is Professor and Director of the Science and Mathematics Education Centre at Curtin University of Technology, Australia. He is co-editor of the 72-chapter *International Handbook of Science Education* published by Kluwer, and Editor-in-Chief of the Kluwer journal *Learning Environments Research: An International Journal.* He is a fellow of the American Association for the Advancement of Science, International Academy of Education, Academy of Social Science in Australia and Australian College of Education. He is the 2003 recipient of the Outstanding Contributions to Science Education through Research Award from the National Association for Research in

Science Teaching in the USA. He is an eminent scholar in learning environment research.

Sonomi Hirata is presently in the Faculty of Human Development at Hakuoh University in Japan. Prior to that, she held a position at the Department of Human Science at Waseda University in Tokyo. She received her BSc and MSc in Human Science, and a PhD from Waseda University. She has taught courses in teacher-training; educational psychology and in general subjects in psychology. Her work has been published in journals such as *Learning Environments*, an International journal, the Japanese *Journal of Counseling Psychology*, and the Japanese *Journal of Criminal Psychology* as well as in proceedings of several international conferences. Her research interests include examining the relation between classroom climate and student behaviour, and constructing psychological measurements for learning environment design.

Avi Hofstein holds a PhD in science education (chemistry) from the Weizmann Institute of Science in Israel. He is a Professor and Head of both the Chemistry Group and the *Science for All* programs in the Science Teaching Department at the Weizmann Institute of Science, Israel. He has been involved in all facets of the curricular process in chemistry namely development, implementation, and evaluation. He has conducted research in many areas of science education (e.g. learning environment, learning difficulties in science learning, professional development and laboratory work). In recent years, he has been involved in the development of leadership amongst chemistry teachers in Israel in order to promote reform in the way chemistry is taught in high schools in Israel.

Shwu-yong L. Huang is an Associate Professor at the Center for Teacher Education, National Taiwan University, and was formerly the Director of the Center at National Tsing Hua University. Prior to her return to Taiwan in 1999, she taught at the University of Houston, USA, and served as the principal of a Chinese school and as President of the Chinese American Educational Research and Development Association in the USA. Her research interests focus on school and classroom learning environments and on teacher education. She has received research awards in Taiwan and abroad. Currently, as a co-principal investigator, she is helping to establish a large-scale Taiwan Higher Education Data System.

Makoto Ishikawa works at the Center for Educational Research and Development, Joetsu University of Education in Japan. He received his PhD from Waseda University. He has taught courses in teacher-training; ICT for education, ICT for Teachers, and in other subjects in ICT. His research interests include evaluating computer-supported cooperative work and e-learning environments.

Celia E. Johnson is Associate Professor at Bradley University in Peoria, Illinois. Her research interests include studying learning environments in the field of at risk populations, special education and early childhood education.

Craig R. Kerr is a Science and Mathematics Teacher at The Don College in Devonport, Tasmania and a PhD graduate of Curtin University of Technology Australia. His research interests include the study of science learning environments, and particularly, the design and integration of ICT-rich learning areas. Currently, his focus is on the holistic study of psychosocial and physical aspects of ICT-rich learning environments, and associations between these factors and student satisfaction with learning.

Myint Swe Khine is Associate Professor and Coordinator of Master Degree Program at the National Institute of Education, Nanyang Technological University, Singapore. He received his Master degrees from the University of Southern California, USA and University of Surrey, UK; and Doctor of Education from Curtin University of Technology, Australia. He has co-authored and published books which include *Studies in Educational Learning Environments: An International Perspective* (World Scientific), *Engaged Learning with Emerging Technologies* (Springer), and *Technology-rich Learning Environments: A Future Perspective* (World Scientific).

Rekha B. Koul has taught high school students for a short time, followed by teaching at undergraduate level and has finally conducted over twelve years of research/extension activities aimed at women as main beneficiaries at the Agricultural University Kashmir, India. She obtained her Doctor of Science Education from Curtin University of

Technology, Australia. At present she is working on learning environment projects in Australia. Her most recent research has involved studies of classroom learning environments and teachers' interpersonal behaviour.

Leonidas Kyriakides is Assistant Professor in Educational Research and Evaluation at the University of Cyprus. His field of research and scholarship concerns the evaluation of educational effectiveness whether of teachers, schools or educational systems. Specifically his research interests are on the development of generic and differentiated model of educational effectiveness, the evaluation of pupil progress and the application of effectiveness research to the improvement of educational practice. He is the author of more than 35 research papers in international journals, five books and 18 chapters in books. His most recent book (with Campbell, Muijs and Robinson) is *Assessing Teacher Effectiveness: Towards a Differentiated Mode*, published by RoutledgeFalmer in 2004.

Jiri Lallimo is a Researcher at the Centre for Research on Networked Learning and Knowledge Building in the Department of Psychology of the University of Helsinki, Finland. His main area of research at the present concerns how psychological and sociocognitive viewpoints of organisational intelligence are embedded in knowledge sharing, and collective efforts for building and advancing knowledge.

Minna Lakkala has a background in general psychology and computer science. She has an extensive experience of teachers' training in the educational use of ICT. Her main research interest at present is teachers' pedagogical expertise in relation to collaborative inquiry learning. Lakkala has participated in large national and international research projects concerning the use of ICT at schools. She has participated in the development of educational ICT, and ICT-related user training as a consultant and educator from the beginning of the 1980s. Currently she is pursuing her doctoral studies at the Centre for Research on Networked Learning and Knowledge Building in the Department of Psychology at the University of Helsinki, Finland.

Hwa Lee is Assistant Professor at Bradley University in Peoria, Illinois. Her research interests include studying learning environments in the area of special education and early childhood education.

Lasse Lipponen is a Senior Lecturer in educational psychology at the University of Helsinki, Finland at the Department of Applied Educational Science. His main research area is collaborative and technology mediated practices of learning and working. Lipponen has considerable expertise in design, development, experimentation, and analysis of new technology-supported learning environments. During the past years he has been involved in several EU and nationally funded projects. Lipponen has taught at several Finnish universities and given numerous expert lectures on new technology and its use in education and working life. He has authored a number of articles on technology supported learning, and functioned as a referee in several conferences and journals.

Atputhasamy Lourdusamy is a Senior Fellow in the Learning Sciences and Technologies Academic Group, National Institute of Education, Nanyang Technological University, Singapore. His areas of research interests are teaching, learning and teacher education.

Peter Van Petegem is Professor and President of the Institute of Education and Information Sciences at the University of Antwerp, Belgium. He is the leader of the research group EduBROn (www.edubron.be). His major research interests include quality concern and school effectiveness, autonomous learning, learning styles and educational policies. Recently he also focuses on learning environment research that tries to integrate the above-mentioned topics.

Stephen Quinton is employed by the Division of Humanities at Curtin University, Australia as an Academic Researcher in the design and delivery of multi-modal learning environments. He is actively involved in several research projects that focus on the effective application of convergent technologies to educational practice. His current research activities include the development of a database managed learning objects framework as applied to the design of online learning environments and the adaptation of learning styles and multiple intelligences theory to the provision of customised learning solutions. The practical outcome will be to demonstrate how individualised learning strategies can be delivered in an online teaching environment.

Tony Rickards is a Senior Lecturer in science, mathematics and technology education at the Science and Mathematics Education Centre,

Curtin University of Technology, Australia. He has held posts at the University of Western Australia, in the Graduate School of Education, and the University of Southern Queensland, where he was founding Director of ITEL, an Information Technology Enhanced Learning research centre. He has over 20 years of teaching experience in computer education at all levels of education in Australia. His current research, publications and professional involvement center on teacher-student interpersonal behaviour in science, mathematics and technology-rich learning environments.

Kathryn J. Saunders is a Senior Lecturer in the Mathematics, Science and Technology Education Department, School of Education, University of Waikato, New Zealand and is currently completing her doctoral degree at Curtin University of Technology, Australia. Her research interests include the study of learning environments with a current focus in the area of pre-service education.

Seng Chee Tan is currently the Deputy Head of the Learning Sciences and Technologies academic group in the National Institute of Education, Singapore. He holds a concurrent appointment as an Assistant Director in the Educational Technology Division, Ministry of Education. One of his key roles is to bridge the research communities on educational technology between the two organisations. His research interests include using computers as cognitive tools and Computer-Supported Collaborative Learning, particularly in the area of knowledge creation.

Sibel Telli is a PhD Student in Secondary Science and Mathematics Education at the Middle East Technical University in Turkey. She has been a high school biology teacher for 11 years. Her PhD project focuses on learning environments research, in particular teacher-student interpersonal behaviour.

David F. Treagust a Professor of Science Education in the Science and Mathematics Education Centre at Curtin University of Technology, Australia. His primary research interests are related to understanding students' ideas about science concepts, and how these ideas contribute to conceptual change and can be used to enhance the design of curricula and the classroom learning environment. He is the author or co-author of over 120 science education articles in refereed journals and has presented over 200 papers at international, and at Australian national and state conferences. He has frequently consulted on projects in developing countries and has supervised many doctoral students from developing and transitional societies in Asia and Africa.

Guofang Wan is Associate Professor at Ohio University in Athens, Ohio, USA. Her research interests include studying learning environments in the field of language arts and English as a second language education.

Wahyudi is a Science Teacher of SMA Negeri 1 Banjarmasin — a state senior secondary school, Kalimantan Selatan, Indonesia. After completing his doctoral degree in the Science and Mathematics Education Centre, Curtin University of Technology, Australia, he is now pursuing his university teaching as Lecturer at the Faculty of Education and Pedagogy, Ahmad Dahlan University, Yogyakarta, Indonesia.

Supatra Wanpen is a Language and Computer Lecturer at Udon Thani Rajabhat University, Thailand. She has just completed a Doctor of Science Education degree at Curtin University of Technology in Australia. Her research interests include learning environments and technology in education. Her focus now is on improving learning environments in computer classes.

Bruce G. Waldrip is Associate Professor of Science Education at the University of Southern Queensland, Toowoomba, Australia. His research agenda has been varied yet focused on student learning. Past and present research include an investigation into students' reactions to assessment strategies; factors that effect students' perceptions of their classroom environment; implementation of a school and teacher change research project for both primary and secondary science teachers; students' worldviews; a study of cultural factors affecting students' learning; and Student understanding of concepts. He currently lectures on science education and research methodology.

Hersh C. Waxman is Professor of Educational Leadership and Cultural Studies in the College of Education at the University of Houston, USA; a Principal Researcher in the National Center for Research on Education, Diversity, and Excellence; and a Principal Investigator in the Mid-Atlantic Regional Educational Laboratory for Student Success. His research focuses on equity, excellence, and social justice issues, such as closing the achievement gap and improving the education of students at risk of failure. He has published articles on these topics in journals such as *Journal of Educational Research, Learning Environments Research: An International Journal, Journal of Education for Students Placed at Risk*, and *Urban Education*. Some of the books he has recently co-edited include: *Observational Research in USA classrooms: New Approaches for Understanding Cultural and Linguistic Diversity* (Cambridge, 2004); *Educational Resiliency: Student, Teacher, and School Perspectives* (Information Age, 2004); and *New Directions for Teaching Practice and Research* (McCutchan, 1999).

Bevis G. Yaxley is currently Director of the Institute for Inclusive Learning Communities, at the University of Tasmania, Australia. He has been an Adjunct Associate Professor, at the Key Centre for Science & Mathematics Education in Curtin University of Technology and Principal Science Education Officer, Department of Education, Tasmania. He was given the Outstanding Educator Award of the Tasmanian Chapter, Australian College of Educators (2004). He has conducted research and published papers in curriculum development, educational leadership, teaching and the role of ICT in education and has had extensive experience in supervising students undertaking higher research degrees. He specialises in philosophic inquiry in education, with a particular emphasis on narrative studies.

Contents

Chapter 1

CLASSROOM ENVIRONMENT, STUDENTS' PERCEPTIONS OF ASSESSMENT, ACADEMIC EFFICACY AND ATTITUDE TO SCIENCE: A LISREL ANALYSIS

Jeffrey P. Dorman
Australian Catholic University
Australia

Darrell L. Fisher
Curtin University of Technology
Australia

Bruce G. Waldrip
University of Southern Queensland
Australia

This chapter reports a study linking students' perceptions of learning environments and assessment with academic efficacy and attitude to science in Australian secondary schools. Five scales of the What Is Happening In this Class questionnaire were used to assess the learning environment. A specially validated instrument, the Students' Perceptions of Assessment Questionnaire assessed five assessment characteristics: Congruence with Planned Learning, Authenticity, Student Consultation, Transparency and Diversity. Scales to assess attitude to science and one academic efficacy scale were employed as outcome measures. Multiple regression and structural equation modelling with LISREL 8.3 were used to study relationships among these variables and the extent to which a postulated model fitted the data. Results showed that classroom environment and student perceptions of assessment were significant positive predictors of academic efficacy and attitude to science.

1. Background

1.1 Classroom environment

The concept of environment, as applied to educational settings, refers to the atmosphere, ambience, tone, or climate that pervades the particular setting. Research on classroom environments has focussed historically on its psychosocial dimensions – those aspects of the environment that focus on human behaviour in origin or outcome (Boy & Pine, 1988). Reviews of classroom environment research by Fraser (1998a), Dorman (2002), Goh and Khine (2002) and Khine and Fisher (2003) have delineated at least 10 areas of classroom environment research. One of the strongest traditions of classroom environment research has been the study of links between classroom environment and student cognitive and affective outcomes. This chapter is situated within this tradition.

Results of studies conducted over the past 30 years have provided convincing evidence that the quality of the classroom environment in schools is a significant determinant of student learning (Fraser, 1994, 1998a). Studies conducted in Indonesia by Margianti, Fraser, and Aldridge (2001), Singapore (Fraser & Chionh, 2000; Goh & Fraser, 1998) and Brunei (Riah & Fraser, 1998) confirmed this general view. Research by Wong and Fraser (1996) in Singapore and Henderson, Fisher and Fraser (2000) focussed specifically on the relationship between science classroom environments and attitudinal outcomes.

A cross-national investigation of links among 10 classroom environment dimensions, student self-handicapping and student academic efficacy was reported by Dorman, Adams and Ferguson (2002). A sample of 3,602 students from 29 schools in Canada, England and Australia was surveyed. Simple and multiple correlation analyses between 10 classroom environment scales from the *What Is Happening In this Class* (WIHIC) and the *Constructivist Learning Environment Survey* (CLES) and self-handicapping were conducted with and without control for academic efficacy. Results showed that classroom environment scales accounted for appreciable proportions of variance in self-handicapping beyond that attributable to academic efficacy. Enhanced affective dimensions of the classroom environment were associated with reduced levels of self-handicapping. Commonality analyses revealed that the WIHIC scales accounted for a much greater proportion of variance in self-handicapping that did the CLES scales.

Other recent environment-outcomes studies have investigated school-level environments and student outcomes in mathematics (Webster & Fisher, 2004), the relationship between learning environments, family contexts, educational aspirations and attainment (Marjoribanks, 2004), the effect of classroom and home environments on student academic efficacy (Claiborne & Ellett, 2005) and the effect of technology on learning environments and student attitudes in secondary science classes (Temons, 2005).

The purpose of the present chapter is to report the use of classroom environment scales, perceptions of assessment scales and affective outcome measures in the one study. Most of the above studies reflect the strong tradition of investigating associations between environment and outcomes through simple, multiple and canonical correlation techniques. The research reported in this chapter uses structural equation modelling to study a postulated model in which classroom environment dimensions are linked to student perceptions of assessment, academic efficacy and attitude to science. This chapter also reports the use of confirmatory factor analysis to establish the structure of the 12 scales employed in this study.

1.2 Students' perceptions of assessment

Despite the growth in emancipatory conceptualisations of classrooms that embrace a constructivist epistemology, little contemporary evidence exists to support the view that students are genuinely involved in decision-making about their assessment tasks. That is, forms of assessment and specific assessment tasks employed in schools are overwhelmingly decided by teachers and administrators. Furthermore, even though reports like *The Status and Quality of Teaching and Learning in Australia* (Goodrum, Hackling, & Rennie, 2001) have asserted that assessment is a key component of the teaching and learning process, teachers tend to utilise a very narrow range of assessment strategies on which to base feedback to parents and students. In practice, there is little evidence that teachers actually use diagnostic or formative assessment strategies to inform planning and teaching (Radnor, 1996). This could be due to teachers feeling that they need to 'sacrifice learning with understanding for the goal of drilling students in the things for which they will be held accountable' (Hobden, 1998, p. 221).

Historically, teachers have received substantial levels of advice on assessment practices. Harlen (1998) advises teachers that both oral and written questions should be used in assessing student's learning. The inclusion of alternative assessment strategies, such as teacher observation, personal communication, and student performances, demonstrations, and portfolios, have been offered by experts as having greater usefulness for evaluating students and informing classroom instruction (Stiggins, 1994). Based on research with teachers, Barksdale-Ladd and Thomas (2000) identified five best practices in assessment:

- providing feedback to help students improve their learning;
- conceptualising assessment as part of a student's work, which can go into a working portfolio;
- providing flexibility so that assessment does not dominate the curriculum;
- ensuring that assessment informs instruction to help teachers improve their teaching, thereby ensuring student learning; and
- using more than one measuring stick to assess students' learning.

Reynolds, Doran, Allers, and Agruso (1995) argued that for effective learning to occur, congruence must exist between instruction, assessment and outcomes.

In the USA, assessment of student learning has become highly politicised with most states having standardised testing procedures in which even the teacher is, to some extent, marginalised from any professional judgment of whether a student is ready to move to the next year level. A similar trend is developing in Australia with benchmarking, testing and reporting to authorities assuming great importance in schools today. Paradoxically, while teachers have been bombarded with information from educators on what they should be doing regarding assessment, ideologically-driven state educational bureaucrats have become more prescriptive by deciding what teachers will do. Against this backdrop, the reality for students is one of almost complete exclusion from the assessment process. The overwhelming view is that, in form and design, assessment tasks should not involve students: bureaucrats have a role, teachers have a scaled-down role, students have no role.

Few textbooks on classroom teaching and assessment suggest a substantive role for students in developing assessment tasks. This position is historically and culturally based and is rooted in an outdated "assembly-line" view of learning in which recitation of facts is highly prized. In today's information age, jobs are increasingly demanding higher levels of literacy skill and critical thinking and these demands require students to actively engage and monitor their learning rather than passively receive knowledge. This requires a fundamental review of how teachers involve students in assessment tasks (Rogoff, 2001).

An effective assessment process should involve a two-way communication system between teachers and their students. Historically, teachers have used testing instruments to transmit to students and their parents what is really important for them to know and do. While this reporting tends to be in the form of a grade, the form and design of assessment can send subtle messages on what is important. There has been a substantial amount of research into types of assessment but very little research into students' perceptions of assessment (see e.g., Black & Wiliam, 1998; Crooks, 1998; Plake, 1993; Popham, 1997).

In one of the few studies conducted on students' perceptions of assessment, an American sample of 174 students in Years 4 to 12 responded to a specially-designed questionnaire (Schaffner, Bury, Stock, Cho, Boney, & Hamilton, 2000). This research, which also elicited teachers' self-reported perceptions of competence in the design and implementation of assessment tasks, found that teachers were not asking students about what should be included in assessment tasks. By including students in the teaching – testing – grading cycle, the validity of the assessment processes can be enhanced and invalid assessment instruments that result in very high failure rates can be avoided (see e.g., Steinberg, 2000).

1.3 Academic efficacy

The broad psychological concept of self-efficacy has been the subject of much theorising and research over the past two decades (see e.g., Bandura, 1997; Schunk, 1995). Within this field, one particularly strong area of interest is that of academic efficacy, which refers to personal judgements of one's capabilities to organise and execute courses of action to attain designated types of educational performances (Zimmerman, 1995). Consistent with self-efficacy theory, academic efficacy involves judgements on capabilities to perform tasks in specific academic domains. Accordingly, within a classroom learning environment, measures of academic efficacy must assess students' perceptions of their competence to do specific activities. It is therefore not surprising to find that much academic efficacy research has focused on specific areas of the formal school curriculum. For example, Pajares

(1996) investigated academic efficacy at mathematics-related tasks. Similarly, Schunk, and Rice (1993) studied self-efficacy among students receiving remedial educational services. Recently, Zeldin and Pajares (2000) explored the self-efficacy beliefs of women in mathematical, scientific and technological careers.

Research studies have provided consistent, convincing evidence that academic efficacy is positively related to academic motivation (e.g., Schunk & Hanson, 1985), persistence (Lyman, Prentice-Dunn, Wilson, & Bonfilio, 1984), memory performance (Berry, 1987), and academic performance (Schunk, 1989). Multon, Brown, and Lent (1991) performed a meta-analysis of research studies that related academic efficacy to the attainment of basic cognitive skills, coursework, and standardised achievement tests. This analysis revealed that academic efficacy is a consistent positive predictor of academic achievement. However, the influence of academic efficacy was not uniform. Whereas the strongest effect was for the influence of academic efficacy on basic cognitive skills, the weakest effect was for the influence of academic efficacy on standardised tests. According to Schunk (1996), the relationship between academic efficacy and both motivation and effort is reciprocal. That is, motivation and effort influence, and are influenced by, academic efficacy. This suggests a type of multiplier effect: as students perceive their progress in acquiring skills and gaining knowledge, their academic efficacy for further learning is enhanced. Schunk (1996) notes that academic efficacy influences persistence provided that the task is sufficiently difficult. In this situation, low academic efficacy students opt out whereas students with high academic efficacy persevere with the task.

According to Bandura (1997), there are four sources of self-efficacy: enactive mastery experiences, vicarious experiences, verbal persuasion and physiological and affective states. Analogously, Schunk (1996) believes that students appraise their academic efficacy through performance, vicarious (observational) experiences, forms of persuasion and physiological reactions. While not explicitly recognised by efficacy theorists, some of these sources can be attributed to the psychosocial learning environment that students experience in their schools and classrooms. For example, students in classrooms regularly observe their peers performing tasks successfully and unsuccessfully. Even a cursory review of the learning environment literature of the past three decades indicates that the learning environment is not an inert contributor to the sources of academic efficacy identified by Bandura and Schunk. Indeed it is striking that academic efficacy theory has not recognised the potential of psychosocial environment in explaining academic efficacy.

1.4 Attitude to science

Teachers have a profound effect on the learning environment in their classrooms. Given the national importance given to the teaching of science and inculcation of positive attitudes to science in students, it was both timely and opportune to examine classroom environment, students' perceptions of assessment tasks, academic efficacy and their associations with attitude to science. Successful implementation of teaching strategies to teach science is likely to result in the establishment and maintenance of positive students' attitudes to science and consequently, achievement. Previous research has shown that students' perceptions of classroom environment are related to attitudes to science (Fisher & Waldrip, 1999; Klopfer, 1992). This study built on these findings by including students' perceptions of assessment tasks as a construct in a hypothesised model that predicts student attitudes to science.

2. Design of Present Study

The aims of the study described in this chapter were to:

- validate the structures of five scales of the What Is Happening In this Class (WIHIC), the *Student Perceptions of Assessment Questionnaire* (SPAQ) and measures of academic efficacy and attitude to science using confirmatory factor analysis,

- identify classroom environment and perceptions of assessment dimensions that predict academic efficacy and attitude to science, and

- investigate whether a postulated model of relationships among the SPAQ scales and the five WIHIC scales and academic efficacy and attitude to science fits the data through the use of structural equation modelling.

2.1 Sample

The sample employed in this study consisted of 449 students in secondary schools in Queensland. Table 1.1 describes the sample which consisted of 203 year 8, 136 year 9 and 110 year 10 students.

Table 1.1 Description of Sample

Gender	Sample Size			
	Year 8		Year 8	
Male	95	Male	95	Male
Female	108	Female	108	Female
Total	203	Total	203	Total

2.2 Instrumentation

2.2.1 Assessment of classroom environment

To assess classroom environment, five scales from the What Is Happening In this Class? (WIHIC) instrument were selected. The WIHIC is a well-established and widely-used questionnaire in classroom environment research (see Aldridge & Fraser, 2000; Dorman, 2003). As this study involved data collection on four facets of classroom life for students (viz. classroom environment, perceptions of assessment, academic efficacy and attitude to science) it was decided in the interests of economy to use five of the seven WIHIC scales: Student Cohesiveness, Teacher Support, Involvement, Task Orientation, and Equity. A four-point Likert response format (viz. Almost Never, Sometimes, Often, and Almost Always) was used. Scale scores for each respondent were obtained by aggregating scores for the eight items for that scale.

The WIHIC's reliability and validity has been reported in many studies. Since its initial development, the WIHIC has been used successfully in studies to assess the learning environment in Singapore (Fraser & Chionh, 2000), Australia and Taiwan (Aldridge & Fraser, 2000), Brunei (Khine & Fisher, 2001), Canada (Zandvliet & Fraser, in press), Australia (Dorman, 2001), Indonesia (Adolphe, Fraser, & Aldridge, 2003), Korea (Kim, Fisher, & Fraser, 2000), the USA (Allen & Fraser, 2002), and Canada, England, and Australia (Dorman, 2003).

Table 1.2. Descriptive Information for Five Classroom Environment, Five SPAQ, and Two Outcome Scales

Scale	Scale Description	Sample Item
Classroom Environment		
Student Cohesiveness	The extent to which students know, help and are supportive of one another.	I am friendly to members of this class.
Teacher Support	The extent to which the teacher helps, befriends, trusts and is interested in students.	The teacher considers my feelings.
Involvement	The extent to which students have attentive interest, participate in discussions, do additional work and enjoy the class.	I explain my ideas to other students.
Task Orientation	The extent to which it is important to complete activities planned and to stay on the subject matter.	I know how much work I have to do.
Equity	The extent to which students are treated equally by the teacher.	I get the same opportunity to answer questions as other students.
SPAQ		
Congruence with Planned Learning	The extent to which assessment tasks align with the goals, objectives and activities of the learning program.	My assignments/tests are about what I have done in class.
Authenticity	The extent to which assessment tasks feature real life situations that are relevant to the learner.	I find science assessment tasks are relevant to what I do outside of school.
Student Consultation	The extent to which students are consulted and informed about the forms of assessment tasks being employed.	I have a say in how I will be assessed in science
Transparency	The extent to which the purposes and forms of assessment tasks are well-defined and clear to the learner.	I am clear about what my teacher wants in my assessment tasks.
Diversity	The extent to which all students have an equal chance at completing assessment tasks.	I have as much chance as any other student at completing assessment tasks.
Outcomes		
Academic Efficacy	Students' judgements of their capabilities to organise and execute courses of action to attain designated types of educational performances.	Even if science is hard, I can learn it.
Attitude to Science	The extent to which students are interested in, enjoy and look forward to lessons in that subject.	I enjoy the activities we do in science

2.2.2 Students' Perceptions of Assessment Questionnaire (SPAQ)

Students' perceptions of assessment were assessed with the 30-item SPAQ. These items are assigned to five internally consistent scales. Table 1.2 shows these scales, their descriptions and sample items. The SPAQ is the result of instrument development and validation procedures conducted in Essex, England (Dorman & Knightley, 2005) and Australia (Fisher, Waldrip, & Dorman, 2005). While discussion of this earlier work is outside the scope of the present chapter, validation statistics including the results of confirmatory factor analysis performed on data collected in the present study are presented later in this chapter. The present form of the SPAQ employs a four-point Likert response format for each item (Almost Never, Sometimes, Often, and Almost Always).

2.2.3 Outcome scales

Two outcome scales, Academic Efficacy and Attitude to Science, were employed in the present study. Perceived academic efficacy refers to students' judgements of their ability to master the academic tasks that they are given in their classrooms. A six-item scale using items developed by Midgley and Urdan (1995), Midgley et al. (1997), and Roeser, Midgley and Urdan (1996) was used to assess perceived academic competence at science class work. Each academic efficacy item was modified to elicit a response on academic efficacy at science. All items in the Academic Efficacy scale had a four-point response format with anchors of 1 (Disagree) and 4 (Agree). An 8-item scale assessed attitude to science. This scale was employed in Waldrip and Fisher's (2002) previous research on attitude to science. It is an adaptation of scales from the *Test of Science-Related Attitudes* (TOSRA: Fraser, 1981). All items in the Attitude to Science scale used a four-point response format with anchors of 1 (Disagree) and 4 (Agree).

2.3 Data collection procedures

Students were surveyed in science classrooms. This was particularly significant to the present study because classroom environment, perceptions of assessment, and the two outcomes measures (viz. academic efficacy and attitude to science) were subject specific. Students responded once to the questionnaire.

2.4 Data analysis and interpretation

There were three distinct components to the analyses conducted in the present study. First, confirmatory factor analysis (CFA) and scale reliability analysis were employed to substantiate the structures of the 12 scales. For each scale, a measurement model in which a *latent* variable was assessed by that scale's items was tested using CFA. Latent variables are not measured directly. Their values are indicated by observed variables.

Three indices for CFA models are reported in the present chapter: the Root Mean Square Error of Approximation (RMSEA), the Tucker-Lewis Index (TLI), and the Parsimony Normed Fit Index (PNFI). Whereas the RMSEA assesses model fit, the TLI and PNFI assess model comparison and model parsimony respectively. To interpret these indices, the following rules which are generally accepted in the SEM literature as reflecting good models were adopted: RMSEA should be below 0.08 with perfect fit indicated by an index of zero, TLI should be above 0.90 with perfect fit indicated when TLI = 1.00, and PFNI should be above 0.50 with indices above 0.70 unlikely even in a very sound fitting model. In addition to these fit indices, the Coefficient of Determination was computed. The Coefficient of Determination for measurement models indicates how much variance in the latent variable is accounted for by the observed variables. Accordingly, the Coefficient of Determination falls between 0.00 and 1.00 with good models having high values. Further discussion on indices and acceptable values is provided in Byrne (1998), Kelloway (1998) and Schumacker and Lomax (1998). The internal consistency reliability of all scales was explored.

Second, stepwise multiple regression analyses were used to identify those WIHIC and SPAQ scales which were significant predictors of the two outcome scales. Correlations among the WIHIC and SPAQ scales were used to identify significant relationships among these scales. This information was used subsequently to develop a baseline or *postulated* model for testing with structural equation modelling (SEM) using LISREL 8.3 (Jöreskog & Sörbom, 1989).

The third component of data analysis involved the testing of this postulated model which related salient WIHIC and SPAQ scales with academic efficacy and attitude to science. Structural equation modelling examined relationships among the latent variables. In this component of the analysis, each latent variable was indicated by one composite

observed variable. For example, in the present study, the latent variable
Involvement was indicated by a composite observed variable computed
from the involvement items of the questionnaire.

Holmes-Smith and Rowe (1994) used the theory of Munck (1979) to
show that loadings of paths (λ) which link composite observed variables
to latent variables and error variances (θ) for composite observed
variables can be fixed in structural equation modelling. Furthermore,
provided correlation matrices are analysed, these parameters are related
to scale reliability ® by the formulae

$$\lambda = \sqrt{r} \qquad \text{and} \qquad \theta = 1 - r.$$

This means that, provide scale reliabilities are known, paths from
composite observed variables to latent variables and error variances of
composite observed variables can be fixed. The advantage of this theory
is that the number of parameters to be estimated by LISREL is sharply
reduced with consequent improvement in model robustness.

As indicated earlier in this section, three fit indices are reported in
the present chapter: the Root Mean Square Error of Approximation
(RMSEA), the Tucker-Lewis Index (TLI), and the Parsimony Normed Fit
Index (PNFI). While the use of χ^2 tests to report goodness of fit of the
model to the data is acknowledged as problematic in SEM, it was used in
the present study to report improvements to the overall model fit as post-
hoc adjustments were made. The squared multiple correlation coefficient
(R^2) for each structural equation is also provided. The Total Coefficient
of Determination which is the amount of variance in the set of dependent
variables explained by the set of independent variables was also
computed. In addition to overall fit statistics, it is important to consider
the strength and statistical significance of individual parameters in the
model. Each path was tested using a t-test ($p < 0.05$).

3. Results

3.1 Confirmatory factor analysis – Measurement models for each scale

Measurement models for each of the 12 scales were tested using LISREL
8.3. Table 1.3 shows values for the RMSEA, TLI, PNFI and Coefficient
of Determination for each of these models. Apart from the SPAQ's
Diversity scale, all values for RMSEA are at or below the benchmark of

0.08. This indicates sound model fit to the data. Additionally, TLI values are very good for all scales with values at or above 0.95. Similarly PNFI values for all measurement models were generally sound. The Coefficient of Determination ranged from 0.74 (congruence with planned learning) to 0.93 (attitude to science), thus indicating good overall models for each scale.

Table 1.3. Results of CFA Measurement Models for 12 Scales

Scale	RMSEA	TLI	PNFI	Coefficient of Determination
Classroom Environment				
Student Cohesiveness	0.05	0.98	0.39	0.88
Teacher Support	0.08	0.98	0.49	0.91
Involvement	0.03	0.99	0.50	0.86
Task Orientation	0.07	0.97	0.39	0.87
Equity	0.08	0.98	0.40	0.92
SPAQ				
Congruence with Planned Learning	0.08	0.97	0.52	0.74
Authenticity	0.08	0.98	0.59	0.87
Student Consultation	0.06	0.97	0.52	0.85
Transparency	0.07	0.98	0.53	0.87
Diversity	0.09	0.95	0.45	0.79
Outcomes				
Academic Efficacy	0.07	0.98	0.52	0.91
Attitude to Science	0.07	0.98	0.52	0.93

3.2 Scale statistics

Reliability coefficients (Cronbach alpha coefficient) were computed for each scale (see Table 1.4). These results show that all scales had at least satisfactory internal consistency. Indices ranged from 0.66 for Congruence with Planned Learning to 0.90 for Attitude to Science. Table 1.4 also shows means, standard deviations and values for λ and θ for each scale according to the theory introduced in the previous section of this chapter.

3.3 Multiple regression analyses

To identify a set of predictor variables to be used in subsequent structural equation modelling, separate stepwise multiple regression analyses predicting academic efficacy and attitude to science were conducted. Separate analyses were performed with the five classroom environment scales and then with the set of five SPAQ scales as predictors of the two outcome variables. Results for the final step of these analyses are shown in Tables 1.5 and 1.6, respectively. The results in Table 1.5 show that Task Orientation was the strongest predictor of both Academic Efficacy and Attitude to Science (β = 0.53 and 0.38, respectively). Student Cohesiveness, Teacher Support, Task Orientation, and Equity were significant predictors of Attitude to Science. As shown in Table 1.6, the most potent SPAQ predictor of Academic Efficacy and Attitude to Science was Transparency (β = 0.35 and 0.28, respectively). A sizeable proportion of variance in these two outcome variables was accounted for by the predictor variables with R^2 = 0.32 for both models.

Table 1.4. Internal Consistency Reliability, Scale Statistics, Fixed Path Loadings and Error Variances for Five Classroom Environment, Five SPAQ, and Two Outcome Scales

Scale	Cronbach α (r)	Mean	Standard Deviation	$\lambda = \sqrt{r}$	$\theta = 1 - r$
Classroom Environment					
Student Cohesiveness	0.81	9.15	3.35	0.90	0.19
Teacher Support	0.87	11.75	4.24	0.93	0.13
Involvement	0.80	12.35	3.65	0.89	0.20
Task Orientation	0.84	9.81	3.62	0.92	0.16
Equity	0.88	10.03	4.19	0.94	0.12
SPAQ					
Congruence with Planned Learning	0.66	12.43	3.05	0.81	0.34
Authenticity	0.80	15.60	3.66	0.89	0.20
Student Consultation	0.73	16.69	3.69	0.85	0.27
Transparency	0.82	11.65	3.88	0.91	0.18
Diversity	0.64	14.87	3.33	0.80	0.36
Outcomes					
Academic Efficacy	0.87	12.56	4.13	0.93	0.13
Attitude to Science	0.90	18.70	5.77	0.95	0.10

Table 1.5. Results of Final Step Regression Analyses for Prediction of Two
Outcome Scales by Five Classroom Environment Scales

Outcome Scale	R^2	Predictor	B	SE B	β
Academic Efficacy	0.45	Teacher Support	0.10	0.04	0.11[*]
		Involvement	0.17	0.05	0.15[*]
		Task Orientation	0.61	0.05	0.53[*]
Attitude to Science	0.49	Student Cohesiveness	-0.14	0.07	-0.08[*]
		Teacher Support	0.41	0.06	0.31[*]
		Task Orientation	0.60	0.07	0.38[*]
		Equity	0.27	0.07	0.20[*]

*p<0.05

Table 1.6. Results of Final Step Regression Analyses for Prediction of Two
Outcome Scales by Five SPAQ Scales

Outcome Scale	R^2	Predictor	B	SE B	β
Academic Efficacy	0.32	Congruence with Planned Learning	0.16	0.07	0.11[*]
		Authenticity	0.13	0.06	0.12[*]
		Transparency	0.38	0.06	0.35[*]
		Diversity	0.13	0.07	0.10[*]
Attitude to Science	0.32	Congruence with Planned Learning	0.47	0.10	0.25[*]
		Authenticity	0.25	0.08	0.16[*]
		Transparency	0.41	0.07	0.28[*]

*p<0.05

3.4 LISREL analyses

Values for λ and θ for each scale were computed using Munck's (1979) theory described above (see Table 1.4). Apart from Student Consultation, all classroom environment and SPAQ scales were predictors of either Academic Efficacy or Attitude to Science. Correlations among the five classroom environment and five SPAQ scales revealed 14 statistically significant relationships (p<0.05). One key issue in constructing a postulated model is the identification of the predictor and mediating variables. Based on the view that perceptions of assessment results primarily from the classroom environment created by the teacher and students, it was decided to model SPAQ scales as mediating the influence of classroom environment on the outcome variables. Apart from its incorporation of these results, this model hypothesised that academic efficacy would predict attitude to science. The results of the multiple regression analyses and the 14 significant simple correlations suggested the postulated model shown in Figure 1.1. For example, because task orientation was significantly correlated with student consultation, an arrow links task orientation to student consultation.

A LISREL analysis of the postulated model shown in Figure 1.1 revealed only a mediocre fit to the data with an RMSEA of 0.10. The TLI of 0.96 and PNFI of 0.33 were very satisfactory (see Table 1.7). To improve model fit to the data through post-hoc adjustments, path coefficients were reviewed. Fourteen path coefficients were not statistically significant ($p<0.05$) and these paths were removed from the model. These paths and revised fit indices for the new model are listed under Model 2 in Table 1.7. This model achieved better fit with a sound RMSEA of 0.08 and an improved PNFI of 0.55.

Two final post-hoc adjustments resulted in the final model which is shown in Figure 1.2. As shown in Table 1.7, Model 3 is Model 2 with two additional paths added within the SPAQ latent variables. All path coefficients of this final model were significantly different from zero ($p<0.05$). Model fit, model comparison and model parsimony indices for this final model were sound (RMSEA = 0.06, TLI = 0.97, PNFI = 0.54). This model should be interpreted as having good fit to the data. The Total Coefficient of Determination for this final model was computed to be 0.96, indicating that the five classroom environment latent variables accounted for 96% of variance in the SPAQ and outcome latent variables. This indicates a very good overall model.

In general, the strength and direction of the statistically significant path coefficients are plausible. As shown in Figure 1.2, Involvement did not feature in the final model. Three SPAQ variables (viz. Congruence with Planned Learning, Transparency and Diversity) had direct, positive relationships with Academic Efficacy. It is particularly noteworthy that all path coefficients in the model were positive, indicating that increased levels of the classroom environment variables were associated with increased levels of respective SPAQ and outcome variables. For example, Teacher Support was a moderate, positive predictor of Attitude to Science ($\beta = 0.25$). Increased levels of Task Orientation had a strong positive effect on Academic Efficacy ($\beta = 1.88$) which was itself related positively to Attitude to Science ($\beta = 0.36$).

Table 1.7. Summary of Specifications and Fit Statistics for Two Structural Models

Model	Actions	χ^2	df	RMSEA	TLI	PNFI
1*	-	117.50	25	0.10	0.96	0.33
2	Path Task Orientation → Attitude to Science removed. Path Authenticity → Attitude to Science removed. Path Transparency → Attitude to Science removed. Path Authenticity → Academic Efficacy removed. Path Involvement → Academic Efficacy removed. Path Teacher Support → Academic Efficacy removed. Path Involvement → Congruence with Planned Learning removed. Path Involvement → Authenticity removed. Path Involvement → Student Consultation removed. Path Teacher Support → Student Consultation removed. Path Involvement → Transparency removed. Path Equity → Transparency removed. Path Equity → Diversity removed. Path Student Cohesiveness → Diversity removed.	138.99	39	0.08	0.96	0.55
3**	Path Student Consultation → Authenticity added. Path Authenticity → Congruence with Planned Learning added.	109.00	37	0.06	0.97	0.54

* (Postulated) See Figure 1.1
** (Final) See Figure 1.2

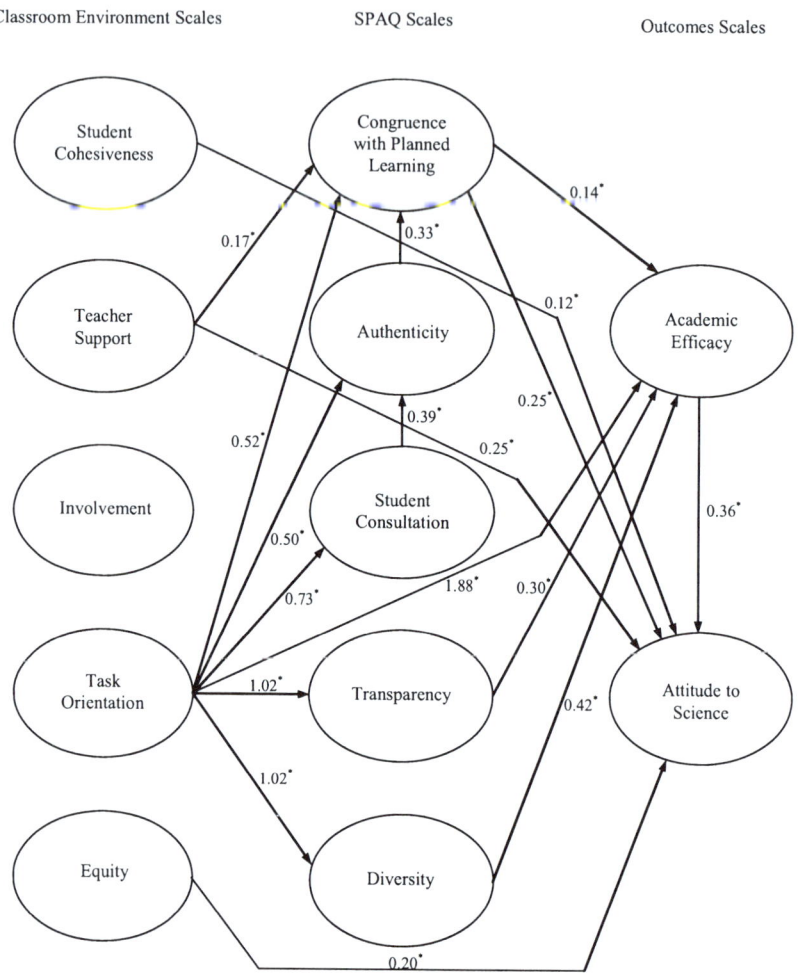

Figure 1.1. Postulated model.

*p<0.05
Note. Observed variables, fixed path loadings from observed
variables to latent variables and error variances for observed

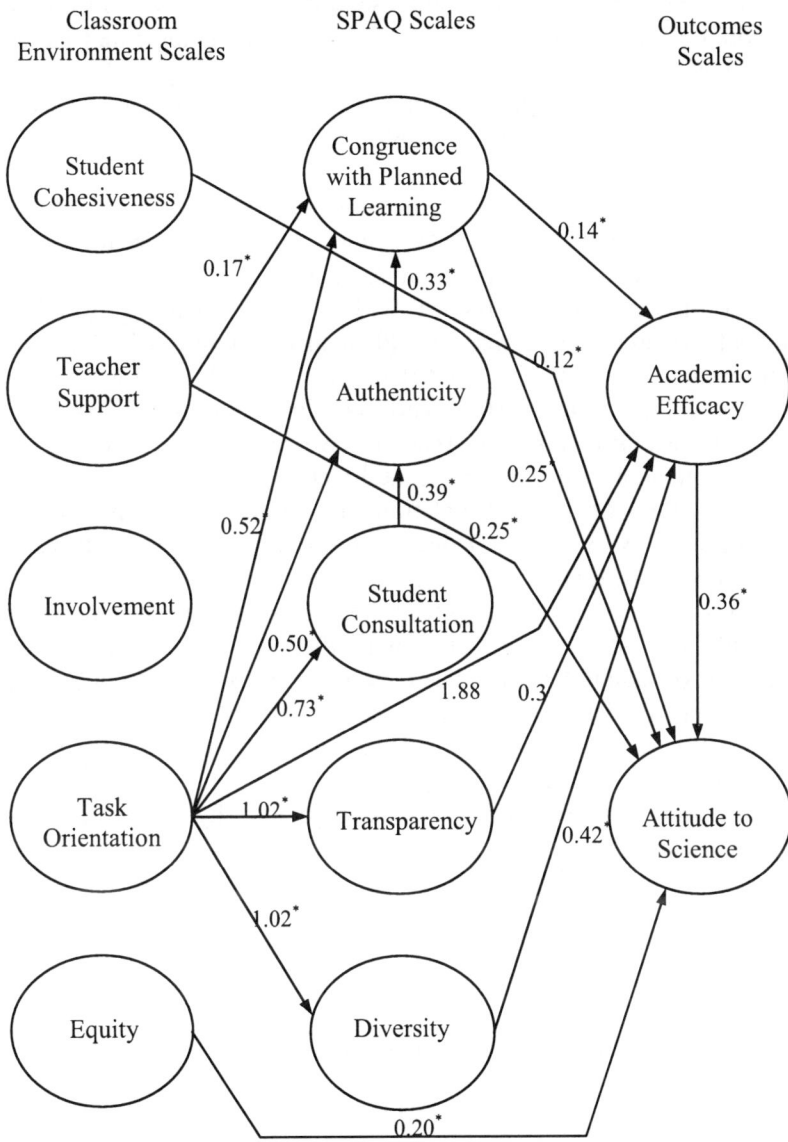

Figure 1.2. Final model.

* *p*<0.05

Note. Observed variables, fixed path loadings from observed variables to latent variables and error variances for observed variables have been omitted.

It is also useful to consider direct and indirect effects of the classroom environment scales. For example, the direct effect of Teacher Support on Attitude to Science ($\beta = 0.25$) is complemented by small indirect effect via Congruence with Planned Learning (0.17 x 0.25 = 0.043), and via Congruence with Planned Learning and Academic Efficacy (0.17 x 0.14 x 0.36 = 0.009) (see Figure 1.2) . That is, the total effect of Teacher Support on Attitude to Science is 0.30.

Task Orientation was by far the most potent classroom environment predictor of Academic Efficacy and Attitude to Science. Task Orientation had a direct effect on Academic Efficacy ($\beta = 1.88$) and indirect effects via Congruence with Planned Learning (0.07), via Authenticity and Congruence with Planned Learning (0.02), via Student Consultation, Authenticity, and Congruence with Planned Learning (0.01), via Transparency (0.31) and via Diversity (0.43). Thus the total effect of Task Orientation on Academic Efficacy is 2.72. Although Task Orientation did not have a significant direct effect on Attitude to Science, the total effect of Task Orientation on Attitude to Science was still sizeable (2.72 x .36 = 0.98) due to the multiple pathways from Task Orientation to Academic Efficacy.

With regard to students' perceptions of assessment, it is noteworthy that only one scale, Congruence with Planned Learning had a direct effect on Attitude to Science. The remaining four scales had only indirect effects via Academic Efficacy. Figure 1.2 also reveals that Student Consultation and Authenticity only had an effect on Academic Efficacy via Congruence with Planned Learning. That is, the effects of Student Consultation and Authenticity were mediated by Congruence with Planned Learning.

The squared multiple correlation coefficient for the prediction of Attitude to Science was computed to be 0.66 which indicates that 66% of variance in Attitude to Science could be explained by Student Cohesiveness, Teacher Support, Equity, Congruence with Planned Learning, and Academic Efficacy. Similarly, as the squared multiple correlation coefficient for the prediction of Academic Efficacy was computed to be 0.80, it can be asserted that over 80% of variance in Academic Efficacy was attributable to Task Orientation, Diversity, Congruence with Planned Learning and Transparency. Overall, Figure 1.2 provides a comprehensive structural model for these three outcome measures based on the data collected in the present study.

4. Discussion

Each of the findings illustrated in Figure 1.2 can be discussed in its own right. It is not surprising that all of the classroom environment scales and SPAQ scales that feature in the final model related positively with both academic efficacy and attitude to science. Previous research reported in Dorman (2002) and Fraser (1998b) has shown similar positive associations between classroom environment dimensions and attitudinal outcomes, especially attitude to science. Science teachers should consider these results as confirming long held anecdotal views. Teachers who provide support, demonstrate equity in the classroom, ensure that students complete learning activities and engender student cohesion in science classrooms are more likely to enhance their students' academic efficacy at science and attitude to science.

The present study extended previous environment – outcomes research by including perceptions of assessment as possible mediators. Findings relating specifically to perceptions of assessment indicated that all five SPAQ dimensions influence academic efficacy and attitude to science. Three scales, Congruence with Planned Learning, Transparency and Diversity have direct effects on academic efficacy. However, except for Congruence with Planned Learning, the effects of these scales on attitude to science are indirect.

These results provided evidence for science teachers who wish to enhance the outcomes of students. While classroom environment has been found to influence outcomes, the mediating effect of assessment tasks needs to be included in this discussion. Assessment is part of the fabric of classrooms and students are responsive to the characteristics of assessment. Students want assessment to be consistent with their learning. Assessment tasks that do not match with student learning have a detrimental effect on the confidence of students in successfully performing academic tasks. Similarly, authenticity and transparency are important assessment characteristics for students. They want tasks that are related to the real world and which are well-defined and clear. Little previous research has been conducted in this area and further research including replications of the current study is needed to substantiate these findings.

The relationship between academic efficacy and classroom environment has been the subject of recent research. Dorman (2001) found significant relationships between scales of the What Is Happening In this Class questionnaire (Aldridge & Fraser, 2000) and Academic Efficacy. He reported significant positive correlations between Academic Efficacy and Teacher Support, Involvement, Investigation, Task Orientation and Equity. The findings of the present study are consistent with Dorman's earlier findings.

5. Conclusion

This chapter has reported research linking secondary school students' perceptions of classroom environment, assessment, academic efficacy and attitude to science. A relatively new instrument, the Students' Perceptions of Assessment Questionnaire (SPAQ) was used in conjunction with established classroom environment, academic efficacy and attitude to science scales.

The research reported here is important to the study of learning environments because it demonstrates that classroom environment scales can be employed in complex studies in which relationships among several variables are examined simultaneously through structural equation modelling. Furthermore, structural equation modelling allows mediating variables to be included in models. This approach extends traditional regression techniques which involve a set of predictors and a set of dependent variables. However, one cautionary note to the use of these data techniques is that they analyse correlational data collected in ex post facto research designs. Because they do not have a true experimental design no causation can be implied. Further research in a variety of settings will improve our confidence in the specific findings of this study.

With regard to scale validation, this research is one of the few reported attempts to use measurement models within covariance structure modelling to validate scale structure in learning environment research. Typically, exploratory factor analysis has been used with classroom environment instruments to validate their structure. The WIHIC is a well-established, high-inference classroom environment instrument and this study has demonstrated the good structural characteristics of five of its scales. The SPAQ has also been shown to have sound characteristics. While the results of this study confirm the view that the quality of the science classroom environment is important to attitudinal outcomes in science (see Fraser 1998a), they also show that the quality of assessment tasks is linked positively to attitudinal outcomes.

References

Adolphe, F. S. G., Fraser, B. J., & Aldridge, J. M. (2003, January). A cross-national study of classroom environment and attitudes among junior secondary science students in Australia and Indonesia. In D. Fisher & T. Marsh (Eds.), *Science, mathematics and technology education for all: Proceedings of the Third International Conference on Science, Mathematics and Technology Education* (pp. 435-446). Perth, Australia: Curtin University of Technology.

Aldridge, J. M. & Fraser, B. J. (2000). A cross-cultural study of classroom learning environments in Australia and Taiwan. *Learning Environments Research, 3*, 101-134.

Allen, D. & Fraser, B. J. (2002). *Parent and student perceptions of the classroom learning environment and its influence on student outcomes.* Paper presented at the annual meeting of the American Educational Research Association, New Orleans, LA.

Bandura, A. (1997). *Self-efficacy: The exercise of control.* New York: Freeman.

Barksdale-Ladd, M. A. & Thomas, K. F. (2000). What's at stake in high-stakes testing: teachers and parents speak out. *Journal of Teacher Education, 51,* 384-397.

Berry, J. M. (1987). *A self-efficacy model of memory performance.* Paper presented at the annual meeting of the American Educational Research Association, New York.

Black, P. & Wiliam, D. (1998). Assessment and classroom learning. *Assessment in Education, 5*(1), 7-74.

Boy, A. V. & Pine, G. J. (1988). *Fostering psychosocial development in the classroom.* Springfield, IL: Charles C. Thomas.

Byrne, B. M. (1998). *Structural equation modeling with LISREL, PRELIS, and SIMPLIS: Basic concepts, applications and programming.* Mahwah, NJ: Erlbaum.

Claiborne, T. T. & Ellett, C. D. (2005, April). *Classroom and home learning environment contributions to eighth grade students' academic self-efficacy beliefs in mathematics.* Paper presented at the annual meeting of the American Educational Research Association, Montreal, Canada.

Crooks, T. J. (1988). The impact of classroom evaluation practices on students. *Review of Educational Research, 58,* 438-481.

Dorman, J. P. (2001). Associations between classroom environment and academic efficacy. *Learning Environments Research, 4,* 243-257.

Dorman, J. P. (2002). Classroom environment research: Progress and possibilities. *Queensland Journal of Educational Research, 18,* 112-140.

Dorman, J. P. (2003). Cross national validation of the What Is Happening In this Class questionnaire using confirmatory factor analysis. *Learning Environments Research., 6,* 231-245.

Dorman, J. P., Adams, J. E., & Ferguson, J. M. (2002). Psychosocial environment and student self-handicapping in secondary school mathematics classes: A cross-national study. *Educational Psychology, 22,* 499-511.

Dorman, J. P. & Knightley, W. M. (2005, September). *Development and validation of an instrument to assess students' perceptions of their assessment tasks.* Paper presented at the European Conference on Educational Research, Dublin.

Fisher, D. L. & Waldrip, B. G. (1999). Cultural factors of science classroom learning environments, teacher-student interactions and student outcomes, *Journal of Science Education and Technology, 17*(1), 83-96.

Fisher, D. L., Waldrip, B. G., & Dorman, J. P. (2005, April). *Student perceptions of assessment: Development and validation of a questionnaire.* Paper presented at the annual meeting of the American Educational Research Association, Montreal.

Fraser, B. J. (1981). *Test of Science-Related Attitudes handbook (TOSRA).* Melbourne, Australia: Australian Council for Educational Research.

Fraser, B. J. (1994). Research on classroom and school climate. In D. Gabel (Ed.), *Handbook of research on science teaching and learning* (pp. 493-541). New York: Macmillan.

Fraser, B. J. (1998a). Science learning environments: Assessments, Effects and determinants. In B. J. Fraser & K. G. Tobin (Eds.), *International handbook of science education* (pp. 527-564). Dordrecht, The Netherlands: Kluwer.

Fraser, B. J. (1998b). Classroom environment instruments: Development, validity, and applications. *Learning Environments Research, 1,* 7-33.

Fraser, B. J. & Chionh, Y. H. (2000, April). *Classroom environment, self-esteem, achievement, and attitudes in geography and mathematics in Singapore.* Paper presented at the annual meeting of the American Educational Research Association, New Orleans, LA.

Goh, S. C. & Fraser, B. J. (1998). Teacher interpersonal behaviour, Classroom environment and student outcomes in primary mathematics in Singapore. *Learning Environments Research, 1*, 199-229.

Goh, S. C. & Khine, M. S. (Eds.). (2002). *Studies in educational learning environments: An international perspective.* Singapore: World Scientific.

Goodrum, D., Hackling, M., & Rennie, L. (2001). *The status and quality of teaching and learning in Australian schools.* Department of Education, Training and Youth Affairs: Canberra.

Harlen, W. (1998). Teaching for understanding in pre-secondary science, In B. J. Fraser & K. G. Tobin (Eds.), *International handbook of science education* (pp. 183-198). Dordrecht, The Netherlands: Kluwer.

Henderson, D., Fisher, D. L., & Fraser, B. J. (2000). Interpersonal behaviour, laboratory learning environments and student outcomes in senior biology classes. *Journal of Research in Science Teaching, 37*, 26-43.

Hobden, P. (1998). The role of routine problems in science teaching. In B. J. Fraser & K. G. Tobin (Eds.), *International handbook of science education* (pp. 219-232). Dordrecht, The Netherlands: Kluwer.

Holmes-Smith, P. & Rowe, K. J. (1994, January). *The development and use of congeneric measurement models in school effectiveness research: Improving the reliability and validity of composite and latent variables for fitting multilevel and structural equation models.* Paper presented at the International Congress for School Effectiveness and Improvement, Melbourne.

Jöreskog, K. G. & Sörbom, D. (1993). *LISREL 8: User's reference guide.* Chicago, IL: Scientific Software International.

Kelloway, E. K. (1998). *Using LISREL for structural equation modeling: A researcher's guide.* Thousand Oaks, CA: Sage.

Khine, M. S. & Fisher, D. L. (2001, December). *Classroom environment and teachers' cultural background in secondary science classes in an Asian context.* Paper presented at the annual meeting of the Australian Association for Research in Education, Perth, Australia.

Khine, M. S. & Fisher, D. L. (Eds.). (2003). *Technology-rich learning environments: A future perspective.* Singapore: World Scientific.

Kim, H., Fisher, D. L, & Fraser, B. J. (2000). Classroom environment and teacher interpersonal behaviour in secondary science classes in Korea. *Evaluation and Research in Education, 14,* 3-22.

Klopfer, L. E. (Ed.) (1992). A summary of research in science education – 1990. *Science Education, 76*(3), 239-338.

Lyman, R. D., Prentice-Dunn, S. Wilson, D. R., & Bonfilio, S. A. (1984). The effect of success or failure on self-efficacy and task persistence of conduct-disordered children. *Psychology in the Schools, 21,* 516–519.

Margianti, E. S., Fraser, B. J., & Aldridge, J. M. (2001, April). *Classroom environment and students' outcomes among university computing students in Indonesia.* Paper presented at the annual meeting of the American Educational Research Association, Seattle, WA.

Marjoribanks, K. (2004). Learning environments, family contexts, educational aspirations and attainment: A moderation-mediation model extended. *Learning Environments Research, 6,* 247-265.

Midgley, C., Maehr, M., Hicks, L., Roeser, R., Urdan, T., Anderman, E. M., & Kaplan, A. (1997). *Manual for the patterns of adaptive learning survey.* Ann Arbor, MI: University of Michigan.

Midgley, C. & Urdan, T. (1995). Predictors of middle school students' use of self-handicapping strategies. *Journal of Early Adolescence, 15,* 389–411.

Multon, K. D., Brown, S. D., & Lent, R. W. (1991). Relation of self-efficacy beliefs to academic outcomes: A meta-analytic investigation. *Journal of Counselling Psychology, 18,* 30–38.

Munck, I. M. E. (1979). *Model building in comparative education: Applications of the LISREL method to cross-national survey data.* Stockholm: Almqvist & Wiksell.

Pajares, F. (1996). Self-efficacy beliefs and mathematical problem solving of gifted students. *Contemporary Educational Psychology, 21,* 325–344.

Plake, B. S. (1993). Teacher assessment literacy: Teachers' competencies in the educational assessment of students. *Mid-Western Educational Researcher, 6,* 21-27.

Popham, W. J. (1997). Consequential validity: Right concern-wrong concept. *Educational Measurement: Issues and Practice, 16*(2), 9-13.

Radnor, H. (1996). *Evaluation of key stage3 assessment in 1995 and 1996.* Exeter: University of Exeter.

Riah, H. & Fraser, B. J. (1998, April). *The learning environment of high school chemistry classes.* Paper presented at the annual meeting of the American Educational Research Association, San Diego, CA.

Reynolds, D. S., Doran, R. L., Allers, R. H., & Agruso, S. A. (1995). *Alternative assessment in science: A teacher's guide.* Buffalo, NY: University of Buffalo.

Roeser, R. W., Midgley, C., & Urdan, T. (1996). Perceptions of the school psychological environment and early adolescents' self-appraisals and academic engagement: The mediating role of goals and belonging. *Journal of Educational Psychology, 88,* 408–422.

Rogoff, B. (2001, September 14). Student assessment for the information age. *The Chronicle of Higher Education, 48*(3), p. B17.

Schaffner, M., Burry-Stock, J.A., Cho, G., Boney, T., & Hamilton, G. (2000, April). *What do kids think when their teachers grade?* Paper presented at the annual meeting of the American Educational Research Association, New Orleans, LA.

Schumacker, R. E. & Lomax, R. G. (1996). *A beginner's guide to structural equation modeling.* Mahwah, NJ: Erlbaum.

Schunk, D. H. (1989). Self-efficacy and cognitive skill learning. In C. Ames & R. Ames (Eds.), *Research on motivation in education. Vol. 3, Goals and cognitions* (pp. 13–44). San Diego, CA: Academic.

Schunk, D. H. (1995). Self-efficacy and education and instruction. In J. E. Maddux (Ed.), *Self-efficacy, adaptation, and adjustment: Theory, research, and application* (pp. 281–303). New York: Plenum.

Schunk, D. H. (1996, April). *Self efficacy for learning and performance.* Paper presented at the annual meeting of the American Educational Research Association, New York.

Schunk, D. H. & Hanson, A. R. (1985). Peer models: Influence on children's self-efficacy and achievement. *Journal of Educational Psychology, 77,* 313–322.

Schunk, D. H. & Rice, J. M. (1993). Strategy fading and progress feedback: Effects on self-efficacy and comprehension among students receiving remedial reading services. *Journal of Special Education, 27,* 257–276.

Steinberg, J. (2000, December 22). Student failure causes states to retool testing programs. *The New York Times,* p. A1.

Stiggins, R. (1994). Student-centered classroom assessment. Ontario: Macmillan College Publishing Co.

Temons, M. J. (2005, April). *Efficacy of using technology in secondary science in terms of learning environments and student attitudes.* Paper presented at the annual meeting of the American Educational Research Association, Montreal, Canada.

Waldrip, B. G. & Fisher, D. L. (2002). Student-teacher interactions and better science teachers. *Queensland Journal of Educational Research, 18,* 141-163.

Webster, B. J. & Fisher, D. L. (2004). School-level environment and student outcomes in mathematics. *Learning Environments Research, 6,* 309-326.

Wong, A. F. L. & Fraser, B. J. (1996). Environment-attitude associations in the chemistry laboratory classroom. *Research in Science and Technological Education, 14,* 91-102.

Zandvliet, D. B. & Fraser, B. J. (in press). Learning environments in IT classrooms. *Technology, Pedagogy and Education.*

Zeldin, A. L. & Pajares, F. (2000). Against the odds: Self-efficacy beliefs of women in mathematical, scientific and technological careers. *American Educational Research Journal, 37,* 215–246.

Zimmerman, B. J. (1995). Self-efficacy and educational development. In A. Bandura (Ed.), *Self-efficacy in changing societies* (pp. 202–231). Cambridge, UK: Cambridge University Press.

Chapter 2

REFLECTIVE ANALYSIS OF TEACHERS' BEHAVIOUR AND STUDENTS' PERCEPTION OF CLASSROOM INTERACTION

Myint Swe Khine
A. Lourdusamy
Nanyang Technological University
Republic of Singapore

This study addresses the issue of teachers' professional development in the area of interpersonal behaviour through reflective analysis of one's own behaviour and by getting feedback from students. By making comparisons of their own perception with that of their student teachers will be able to reflect on any marked differences in the perceptions and take remedial action to reduce the gap as creating a positive social learning environment is the key to enhancing learning. The Questionnaire on Teacher-Student Interaction (QTI), which was designed to assess the interpersonal behaviour of the teachers with the students in their classrooms, is used in this study. The study investigated differences between the teachers' reflective analysis of their own behaviour and students' perception of the classroom interaction in Singapore schools. The study involved 25 teachers and 994 students in science classrooms. Some significant differences were found in teachers' self-evaluation of their interpersonal behaviour and how students perceived them. This chapter reports the findings from the study, that is the perceived strengths and shortcomings of the trainee teachers, and discusses how the information may be utilized to assist in self-improvement of trainee teachers in classroom management as well as its implications for teacher education.

1. Introduction

Reflective analysis of one's own behaviour is one of the desirable characteristics in professional practice and it is particularly relevant in teaching profession. Reflective teachers are those who give a considerable amount of time and thought to self-evaluation teaching and learning experiences in order to improve their practices. While some teachers often analyze the effectiveness of their lessons after teaching, a systematic self-evaluation of interpersonal behaviour and classroom interaction are rarely conducted. It is important to make sensitive observations of classroom events, reflect on the meaning of those observations, and then decide to improve on practice (in a certain way). Some teachers think that they have displayed leadership qualities and given enough attention to the students. But do students feel the same way as do their teachers? A study to investigate differences between teachers' reflective analysis of their own behaviour and students' perception of the classroom interaction was carried out in Singapore schools. The *Questionnaire on Teacher-Student Interaction* (QTI), which was designed to assess the interpersonal behaviour of teachers and interactions with their students in the classroom, was used in this study. The study involved 25 teachers and 994 students in science classrooms. Some significant differences were found in teachers' self-evaluation of their interpersonal behaviour and how students perceived them. This chapter reports the findings from the study, that is the perceived strengths and shortcomings of the trainee teachers, and discusses how this information may be utilized to assist in the self-improvement of trainee teachers in classroom management as well as its implications for teacher education.

Effective teachers have good communication and interpersonal skills since classroom interaction demands a two-way process of exchange of information. Educators believe that good relationships between teachers and students are important in the learning process. There are numerous variables which determine, to differing degrees, the 'success' of any particular learning environment and one of the key variables is the nature of the student-teacher interaction. Studies investigating associations between interpersonal relationship and student outcomes have shown that particular teacher-student relationships are more effective for student achievement and attitudes than others. Arends (2004) is of the view that establishing authentic relationships with students is a prerequisite to everything else in teaching. Getzels and Thelen (1960) suggested that teacher-student interaction is a powerful force that can play a major role in influencing the cognitive and affective development of students. Furthermore, Walberg (1976) and Winne and Marx (1977) emphasized that students' perceptions of their teachers' behaviour should not be underestimated, rather it should be considered an important mediator between the instructional characteristics and academic achievement.

Wubbels and Levy (1993) reaffirmed the role and significance of teacher behaviour in the classroom environment and in particular how this can influence students' motivation and ultimately, achievement. From this, it follows that it is important for teachers to have a caring disposition towards their students, believe in their students' ability to learn, and establish a harmonious relationship with their students. Because it is from these relationships between the teacher and his/her students that student motivation to engage in learning can be realized.

Teacher behaviours in the classroom can also take on new significance when they are viewed as cues *for* certain student behaviour *by* the students. Effective teachers have a knowledge base that guides what they do as teachers in the classroom. With the use of this knowledge base they can provide leadership to a group of students in their charge. But at the same time it is important that this "teacher as leader" concept does not lead to excessive attention to control, orderliness and efficiency at the expense of giving responsibility to students for their own learning, and to be creative and spontaneous in behaviour. So there has to be a balance between control and freedom. The quality of interpersonal teacher behaviour and relationship with students is an indication of the quality of leadership in the classroom.

Though teachers often engage in a systematic reflection on a lesson delivered, seldom do teachers reflect on their interpersonal skills. Also, very few teachers ever venture to find out what the students think of their interpersonal behaviour in the class. Arends (2004, p. 21) stated that "effective teaching requires careful and reflective thought about what a teacher is doing and the effect of his or her action on students' social and academic learning".

Wubbels, Creton, and Hooymayers (1985) investigated teacher behaviour in the classroom and developed a model to map interpersonal teacher behaviour. Based on this model the Questionnaire on Teacher Interaction (QTI) was designed to gather students' and teachers' perceptions of teacher interpersonal behaviour.

2. Theoretical Framework for Interpersonal Behaviour

Leary (1957) believed that the way humans communicate is indicative of their personality. Along with other psychologists, he felt that the most important forces driving human behaviour are the reduction of fear and the corresponding maintenance of self-esteem. Therefore, when people communicate, they consciously or unconsciously choose behaviours which avoid anxiety and allow them to feel good about themselves. These may differ for each person and depend upon the personality of the communicating partner. One individual might choose an authoritarian style, whereas another prefers dependency to achieve the same end. Based on this conception Leary proposed a two dimensional model. He named these dimensions the Dominance-Submissive axis and the Hostility-Affection axis.

Wubbels, Creton, Levy, and Hooymayers (1983) adapted the Leary model to the context of education and developed the "Model for Interpersonal Teacher Behaviour" to describe the perception of students of the behaviours of their teachers. They investigated teachers' behaviour in classroom from a systems perspective, adapting a theory on communication processes developed by Watzwick, Beavin and Jackson (1967). Within the systems perspective on communication it is assumed that the behaviours of participants influence each other mutually. In line with the systems approach, they conceived classroom groups as ongoing systems with certain stability. After a few meetings with the teacher in the class, tentative ideas about the teacher will have stabilized and similarly the teacher's perceptions of the students. Henceforth, the behaviour of the teacher will be influenced by the behaviour of the students and in turn influences student behaviour.

Based on the work of Leary, they labeled the two dimensions of their model Proximity (Cooperation-Opposition) and Influence (Dominance-Submission). The Proximity dimension designates the degree of cooperation or closeness between those who are communicating. The Influence dimension indicates who is directing or controlling the communication and how often. Leary used the term Dominance-Submission to describe the continuum of behaviours in the Influence dimension. Figure 2.1 depicts the interpersonal teacher behaviour model and the coordinate system.

The sections in the model for interpersonal behaviour are labeled DC, CD, CS, SC, SO, OS, OD and DO according to their position in the coordinate system. For example, two sectors CS and SC are both considered to have elements of Cooperation and Submission. However, in the CS sector, the Cooperation aspect predominates over the Submission aspect.

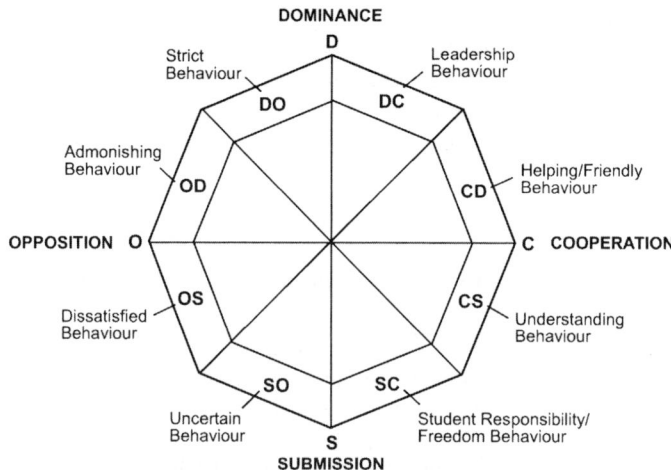

Figure 2.1. The Model of Interpersonal Behaviour.

3. Development of Questionnaire on Teacher Interaction (QTI)

Wubbels, Creton and Hooymayers (1985) tried to use Leary's *Interpersonal Adjective Checklist* (ICL) in education setting and found that not all its items were applicable to teachers. Based on this experience and their Model for Interpersonal Teacher Behaviour they initially developed the *Questionnaire for Interactional Teacher Behaviour* then later the Questionnaire on Teacher Interaction (QTI) (Wubbels & Levy, 1993). The original version of the QTI in the Dutch language consisted of 77 items and it was designed to measure secondary students' and teachers' perceptions of teacher interpersonal behaviour. After an extensive analysis, items found to be not correlated to the respective scales were deleted from the 77-item Dutch version and a 64-item version was developed and administered in the USA (Wubbels & Levy, 1991). After further experimenting an Australian version of the QTI containing 48 items came into being (Wubbels, 1993). This short economical version is now used extensively to examine the interpersonal behaviour in the classroom setting.

The response provision in the QTI is a five-point Likert-type scale which is scored from 0 (Never) to 4 (Always). In some questionnaire administrations, response sheets are sometimes given separately, but in the QTI, responses are given on the same questionnaire. This method of giving a response to each question facilitates a faster completion. In this way, the QTI can be administered easily and quickly in the class by the teacher. The items are arranged into eight scales corresponding to the eight interrelated sections of the model for interpersonal teacher behaviour. Table 2.1 provides the name of each scale, its description, and a sample item as it appears on the questionnaire.

Table 2.1. Description and Examples Items for Each Scale in the QTI

Scale	Description	Item
Leadership [DC]	Extent to which teacher provides leadership to class and holds student attention.	This teacher explains things clearly.
Helping/Friendly [CD]	Extent to which teacher is friendly and helpful towards students.	This teacher is friendly.
Understanding [CS]	Extent to which teacher shows understanding/concern/care to students.	If we don't agree with this teacher, we can talk about it.
Student Responsibility/Freedom [SC]	Extent to which students are given opportunities to assume responsibilities for their own activities.	We can influence this teacher.
Uncertain [SO]	Extent to which teacher exhibits her/his uncertainty.	It is easy to make a fool out of this teacher.
Dissatisfaction [OS]	Extent to which teacher shows unhappiness/dissatisfaction with student.	This teacher thinks that we don't know anything.
Admonishing [OD]	Extent to which teacher shows anger/temper/impatient in class.	The teacher is impatient.
Strict [DO]	Extent to which teacher is strict with and demanding of students.	We are afraid of this teacher.

Since its development, the QTI has been used in the Netherlands, the USA, Australia, and some Asian countries and cross validated in different contexts and cultures. All studies support the view that data obtained from the questionnaire provide useful information for teachers about their interpersonal behaviour in the learning environment.

4. Validity and Reliability of the QTI

The original 77-item version of the QTI has been shown to be a valid and reliable instrument when used in the Netherlands (Wubbels, Brekelmans & Hooymayers, 1991). Its cross-cultural validity and usefulness has been confirmed for the USA (Wubbels & Levy, 1991, 1993), for Australia (Wubbels, 1993), for Singapore (Khine & Lourdusamy, 2005; Lourdusamy & Khine, 2001,) and for Brunei Darussalam (Khine & Fisher, 2003). Table 2.2 indicates the alpha reliabilities for samples of students and teachers using the QTI. Table 2.2 also shows the size of each sample and indicates that each QTI scale displays satisfactory internal consistency.

Table 2.2. Internal Consistency (Alpha Reliability) of QTI Scales for Teacher and Student in Various Contexts

Scale	Teacher/ Student	The Netherlands*	USA*	Australia**	Singapore*	Brunei*
Leadership	Teachers	0.80	0.75	0.74	0.74	
	Students	0.83	0.80	0.83	0.80	0.76
Helping/ Friendly	Teachers	0.78	0.74	0.82	0.60	
	Students	0.90	0,88	0.85	0.84	0.83
Understanding	Teachers	0.83	0.76	0.78	0.74	
	Students	0.90	0.88	0.82	0.84	0.76
Student Responsibility/ Freedom	Teachers	0.72	0.82	0.60	0.61	
	Students	0.74	0.76	0.68	0.73	0.50
Uncertain	Teachers	0.83	0.79	0.78	0.71	
	Students	0.79	0.79	0.78	0.84	0.70
Dissatisfaction	Teachers	0.83	0.75	0.62	0.75	
	Students	0.86	0.83	0.78	0.87	0.77
Admonishing	Teachers	0.71	0.81	0.67	0.73	
	Students	0.81	0.84	0.80	0.81	0.88
Strict	Teachers	0.61	0.84	0.78	0.66	
	Students	0.78	0.80	0.72	0.71	0.49
Sample Size	Teachers	66	66	46	25	-
	Students	1105	1606	792	994	1188

* Original 77-item version of the QTI
** Economical 48-item version of the QTI

The reliability figures of the QTI scales in the various settings show that the QTI is quite robust for use in different contexts. The reliability of the economical 48-item version of the QTI is comparable to the original 77-item version.

The QTI can be used in a number of ways to obtain the perceptions of interpersonal behaviour of either teachers or students. Students can be asked for their perception of their actual teacher or their best teacher. Similarly, teachers can be asked for their perception of their interactions in their actual class or the behaviour they consider to be ideal. In this way, the ideal can be compared with the actual behaviour.

5. Past Use of the QTI

In 1991 Wubbels and Levy compared Dutch and American teachers and found very few differences in the way they interacted with their students in their class, although American teachers were perceived as stricter and Dutch teachers as giving students more responsibility and freedom. Wubbels (1993) used the QTI with a sample of 792 students and 46 teachers in Western Australia and Tasmania. The result showed that teachers do not reach their ideal and differ from the best teachers as perceived by students.

Wubbels, Brekelmans, Creton & Hooymayers (1990) and Berkelmans, Levy & Rodrigues (1993) used QTI to develop typologies of student perception of interpersonal behaviour in The Netherlands. Using cluster analysis, eight types was distinguished. The eight behavioural patterns were named: *directive, authoritative, tolerant/authoritative, tolerant, uncertain/tolerant, uncertain/aggressive, repressive, and drudging.* Figure 2.2 depicts the graphical representations using the eight sections of the Model of Interpersonal Teacher Behaviour. The proportion of the shaded part corresponds to the interpersonal relationship characterized by this sector.

The studies by Lourdusamy and Khine (2001) and by Khine and Lourdusamy (2005) supported the validity and reliability of the QTI in the Singapore context and they found that the perceptions of students differed from that of the trainee teachers of their interpersonal behaviour in the classroom. The results of these studies strongly support the validity and potential use of the QTI in different cultural contexts and suggest the possibility of its use in the professional development of teachers though reflective practice.

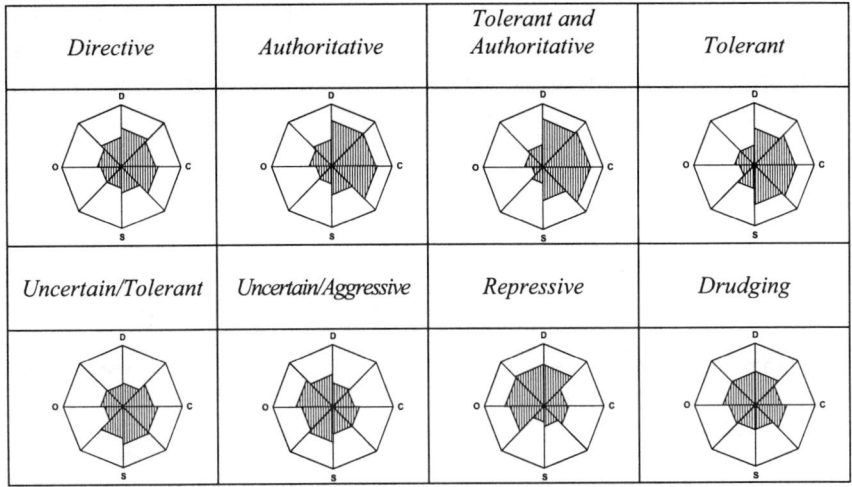

Figure 2.2. Graphical representations of the eight types of patterns of interpersonal relationship. (Brekelmans, Wubbels & den Brok, 2002) (Reproduced with permission)

6. Possible Use of QTI in Teacher Professional Development

Through the use of the QTI, teachers can become aware of how their students view them and how they view themselves from the profiles generated from the data collected. The provision of this type of information allows teachers or student teachers the opportunity to reflect on their own performance, particularly in relation to their relationships with their students. The knowledge that good teachers are perceived to score highly on the dimensions depicted on the right side of the model in Figure 2.1 can be used for considering possible changes in behaviour. For example, a teacher wanting to improve leadership behaviour could consider and implement strategies that will enhance this, or engage in professional development activities specifically designed to enhance classroom leadership behaviour.

Fisher, Fraser, and Cresswell (1995) used the QTI as the basis for professional development with six science teachers in an Australian school. These teachers were volunteers who embarked on a professional development exercise following their introduction to the QTI. Each teacher responded to the actual and ideal form of the instrument while the students of their classes gave their perceptions of the eight dimensions of the QTI for actual teacher behaviour. Scores were calculated for each of the eight dimensions, and the mean item score for each dimension on the three forms (teacher actual score, teacher ideal score, and the class mean of student actual scores) for each of the six teachers is shown in Table 2.3.

Table 2.3. Mean Item Scores for Six Teachers on Teacher Actual, Teacher Ideal and Student Actual Forms of QTI

Scale	Form	Mean item scores for teachers					
		A	B	C	B	E	F
Leadership	Teacher Actual	3.43	4.14	3.71	4.29	3.86	4.01
	Teacher Ideal	4.71	5.00	4.86	5.00	4.43	4.57
	Student Actual	3.01	3.27	4.29	3.86	2.32	3.03
Helping / Friendly	Teacher Actual	3.63	4.13	4.13	4.63	4.13	4.00
	Teacher Ideal	4.50	4.38	5.00	4.88	4.25	3.50
	Student Actual	3.97	3.63	4.50	3.79	2.18	2.77
Understanding	Teacher Actual	3.63	4.38	4.25	4.38	4.25	3.75
	Teacher Ideal	4.63	4.63	5.00	4.75	4.25	4.38
	Student Actual	3.81	3.82	4.35	3.69	2.38	3.16
Student Responsibility/ Freedom	Teacher Actual	2.13	1.88	2.88	1.75	2.00	2.13
	Teacher Ideal	2.88	2.38	3.13	2.63	2.50	2.63
	Student Actual	2.95	2.27	2.57	2.26	2.23	1.84
Uncertain	Teacher Actual	2.43	2.14	2.29	1.14	2.14	2.29
	Teacher Ideal	1.71	1.14	1.14	1.00	1.29	2.43
	Student Actual	2.29	2.80	1.40	1.52	3.07	1.96
Dissatisfaction	Teacher Actual	2.11	1.78	2.44	1.44	2.67	2.11
	Teacher Ideal	1.89	1.56	1.33	1.44	2.11	2.00
	Student Actual	1.70	1.97	1.58	1.96	3.16	3.27
Admonishing	Teacher Actual	2.13	1.50	1.75	1.88	2.50	1.63
	Teacher Ideal	1.00	1.13	1.00	1.25	1.75	1.63
	Student Actual	1.37	1.89	1.52	2.40	3.02	4.43
Strict	Teacher Actual	2.78	3.22	2.56	3.44	3.00	3.44
	Teacher Ideal	3.11	3.44	3.33	3.22	3.78	3.56
	Student Actual	2.38	2.99	2.65	3.35	2.98	3.40

(Source: Fisher, Fraser, & Cresswell, 1995, p. 12)

The results together with graphical profiles were shown to the teachers. The teachers were able to see how they saw themselves, their ideal teachers and how their students saw them. This proved to be a most useful format for self-reflection and for discussion with their colleagues. The teachers found the QTI to be a valuable source of information, particularly comparisons between their own and their students' perception for professional development purposes.

The teachers who participated in the study shared their results and discussed possible strategies they could implement to attempt to bring about a change in their own interpersonal relationships with their students. The value of the QTI was in its capacity to provide the teachers with a picture of their ideal teacher, how they see themselves and how their students see them. These pictures became the focus for the teachers' discussions on the interpersonal behaviour aspect of their teaching behaviours.

7. Singapore Case Studies

A similar study was carried out in the Singapore classroom context to investigate the differences between trainee teachers' reflective analysis of their own behaviour and students' perception of the classroom interaction. The study involved 25 teachers and their 994 students in science classrooms. The following are the results from the study that indicate the perceived strengths and shortcomings of the trainee teachers and discusses how the information may be utilized to assist in self-improvement of trainee teachers in classroom management as well as its implication for teacher education.

7.1 Objectives and methodology

According to Good and Brophy (2003), some personal qualities are basic to successful management of classrooms. There is evidence that teachers' interpersonal behaviour, communication style and personal qualities can affect the development of authentic human relationship with their students. However, in the process of analyzing themselves some teachers think that they are lenient in taking disciplinary action against students while some others think that they are already giving enough help to students in the class. There could be differing opinions of one's own assessment and the view of the others.

The objective of this study was to map the dispositions of the trainee teachers on the eight dimensions of interpersonal teacher behaviour and compare this with their students' perception on their interpersonal relationship with the class. The study made an attempt to find out whether there is a significant difference between the way teachers perceived themselves and the way they were viewed by their students. A small-scale study carried out by Wettasinghe and Lourdusamy (2002) showed that teachers' and pupils' perceptions of the classroom interaction were different in some aspects. This study aimed to investigate further into these differences and suggest how the findings may be used to help the trainee teachers to reflect and improve their own practice in their classrooms.

The QTI was administered to 25 trainee teachers (8 male and 17 female) to measure their self-perceptions of interpersonal behaviour while they were engaged in practicum in schools. The teachers involved in this study in turn administered the questionnaire to their classes to measure the students' perception of their teachers' interpersonal behaviour. The students' perceptions were measured in 25 classes taught by the trainee teachers in secondary schools. It involved a total of 994 students comprising 497 male and 497 female who are studying in secondary schools.

7.2 Results

7.2.1 Profile of individual teachers and the views of their class

The profile of the 25 teachers who participated in the study and the perception of the students about their teachers' interpersonal behaviours are shown in Table 2.4.

In general teachers perceive themselves exhibiting more of the positive behaviours like leadership, helping/friendly and understanding than the students perceive them to have. At the same time, the teachers also believe that they exhibit more of the negative behaviours like showing dissatisfaction, admonishing and being strict in their classroom compared with the views of their students.

7.2.2 Comparison of overall teachers' and students' perception on interpersonal relationship

An independent sample t-test was performed to determine whether there are significant differences in the perceptions of teachers and students on the different aspects of interpersonal relationships in the classroom environment. Levene's test for equality of variances showed a significant difference between the variances of teachers' scores on all the subscales and the scores of the students for the same scales.

Table 2.4. Group Statistics – Individual Teachers' Self Perceived and Respective Students' Perceptions of Their Teachers' Interpersonal Behaviour

	No	Lea	HFr	Und	Sre	Unc	Dis	Adm	Str
Teacher 1	34	16.00	18.00	21.00	8.000	9.000	10.00	8.000	15.00
Class mean		19.38	18.94	19.94	8.911	2.970	2.794	3.000	10.44
Teacher 2	37	13.00	17.00	15.00	10.00	13.00	8.000	11.00	12.00
Class mean		12.05	12.08	13.86	9.567	9.432	9.081	7.729	11.24
Teacher 3	40	18.00	20.00	21.00	11.00	8.000	10.00	11.00	14.00
Class mean		15.30	16.57	16.72	10.25	6.600	6.750	7.175	11.25
Teacher 4	36	16.00	17.00	14.00	12.00	13.00	12.00	11.00	13.00
Class mean		11.83	12.58	15.22	10.72	9.111	5.583	6.777	8.027
Teacher 5	62	16.00	18.00	20.00	11.00	14.00	7.000	9.000	7.000
Class mean		18.22	18.70	19.19	11.72	7.048	5.951	6.871	10.82
Teacher 6	38	10.00	16.00	19.00	12.00	11.00	14.00	13.00	10.00
Class mean		14.18	15.47	16.23	9.815	6.421	5.368	6.236	10.18
Teacher 7	34	17.00	21.00	20.00	10.00	5.000	11.00	12.00	14.00
Class mean		12.82	11.14	14.17	7.617	6.325	8.088	7.205	12.55
Teacher 8	44	20.00	18.00	22.00	6.000	4.000	6.000	6.000	14.00
Class mean		19.04	20.40	19.52	9.409	2.931	2.750	3.022	9.181
Teacher 9	40	16.00	17.00	20.00	11.00	8.000	8.000	10.00	7.000
Class mean		13.30	14.32	14.75	11.27	9.925	7.425	7.975	9.975
Teacher 10	39	18.00	22.00	21.00	8.000	2.000	3.000	9.000	13.00
Class mean		16.82	18.10	17.53	9.923	5.666	6.435	5.589	11.46
Teacher 11	34	17.00	19.00	20.00	11.00	3.000	5.000	7.000	10.00
Class mean		15.38	14.44	15.50	8.941	7.823	7.058	7.294	10.58
Teacher 12	34	18.00	21.00	22.00	8.000	6.000	2.000	4.000	16.00
Class mean		12.82	12.52	14.05	13.14	10.94	10.05	8.294	11.64
Teacher 13	28	12.00	15.00	23.00	11.00	8.000	6.000	8.000	13.00
Class mean		13.35	14.42	18.60	18.39	9.214	7.000	4.428	5.607
Teacher 14	30	10.00	20.00	21.00	17.00	13.00	3.000	5.000	6.000
Class mean		15.33	16.40	18.86	10.53	6.200	4.766	4.000	11.06
Teacher 15	40	14.00	17.00	16.00	9.000	7.000	10.00	12.00	14.00
Class mean		15.60	17.47	17.80	11.85	7.800	4.125	4.900	7.100
Teacher 16	38	14.00	23.00	22.00	13.00	8.000	8.000	6.000	12.00
Class mean		16.44	17.68	18.70	11.81	7.894	5.631	6.421	10.02
Teacher 17	41	16.00	17.00	22.00	11.00	7.000	5.000	6.000	11.00
Class mean		14.58	15.85	16.87	11.14	7.561	6.756	6.073	9.804
Teacher 18	31	13.00	17.00	21.00	15.00	8.000	7.000	7.000	10.00
Class mean		17.54	17.87	19.19	8.451	4.193	3.741	3.032	8.709
Teacher 19	37	15.00	21.00	18.00	8.000	7.000	8.000	9.000	11.00
Class mean		13.43	13.18	14.08	9.540	8.648	8.297	8.891	10.72
Teacher 20	90	17.00	14.00	19.00	10.00	6.000	13.00	9.000	16.00
Class mean		16.65	4.216	17.77	9.577	5.533	4.855	5.366	11.61
Teacher 21	28	13.00	18.00	16.00	10.00	10.00	12.00	14.00	10.00
Class mean		15.78	3.59	17.35	9.250	8.142	6.821	6.035	11.03
Teacher 22	39	15.00	19.00	22.00	9.000	4.000	5.000	3.000	11.00
Class mean		16.33	4.510	16.69	9.615	5.871	5.794	6.179	12.38
Teacher 23	42	13.00	18.00	18.00	9.000	7.000	6.000	6.000	10.00
Class mean		9.690	4.203	14.80	12.47	13.09	8.904	8.452	9.190
Teacher 24	38	17.00	17.00	17.00	10.00	8.000	12.00	8.000	11.00
Class mean		13.76	13.23	13.07	8.105	7.263	7.973	8.394	13.13
Teacher 25	40	20.00	19.00	19.00	7.000	4.000	8.000	11.00	18.00
Class mean		19.32	19.75	19.62	19.92	20.00	20.50	20.07	20.12

Thus, the authors assumed unequal variances. The data revealed significant difference between the mean scores of teachers and the mean scores of the students in four of the eight subscales. The difference was significant at the 0.05 level and less (see Table 2.5).

Table 2.5. Group Statistics – Teachers' Self Perceived and Students'
           Perceptions of Their Teachers' Interpersonal Behaviour

Teacher Behaviour Dimension	Group	Mean	Standard Deviation	t value
Leadership	Teacher	15.400	2.692	0.129
	Student	15.328	4.661	
Helping/Friendly	Teacher	18.360	2.157	5.021***
	Student	16.047	5.076	
Understanding	Teacher	19.600	2.449	5.288***
	Student	16.897	4.592	
Student Responsibility/Freedom	Teacher	10.280	2.406	-1.096
	Student	10.831	4.544	
Uncertain	Teacher	7.800	3.278	0.049
	Student	7.766	5.123	
Dissatisfaction	Teacher	7.880	3.295	1.570
	Student	6.810	5.391	
Admonishing	Teacher	8.600	2.857	3.044***
	Student	6.793	5.030	
Strict	Teacher	12.120	2.743	2.378*
	Student	10.772	4.462	

***$p<0.001$; *$p<0.05$

Teachers consider themselves to be friendlier and more helpful and understanding to their students than their students perceive to be so, i.e. students do not think their teachers are as friendly and helpful, and understanding as the teachers think they are. Teachers think that they admonish and are strict with their students more than their students perceive to be the case. Teachers seem to inflate both their negative and positive qualities compared with their students who are more moderate in their views of their teacher (see Figure 2.3). Looking at the standard deviations of the two sets of scores, i.e. teachers' scores and students' scores there is a greater variance in the views of the students compared with teachers' views of their interpersonal behaviour with students.

Figure 2.4 shows the general patterns of the interpersonal relationship in the classes as perceived by the teachers and as perceived by the students of these teachers. Comparing these patterns to the eight patterns derived by Brekelmans et al. (1993) the students, in general, seem to think that their teachers exhibit Authoritative behaviour whereas the teachers in general believe that they are Tolerant/Authoritative in their behaviour in the class.

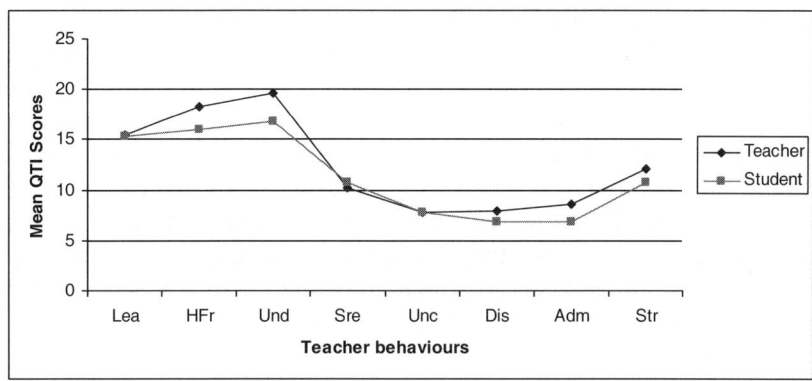

Figure 2.3. Profiles of mean QTI scores of teachers' self perceived and students' perceptions of QTI scores.

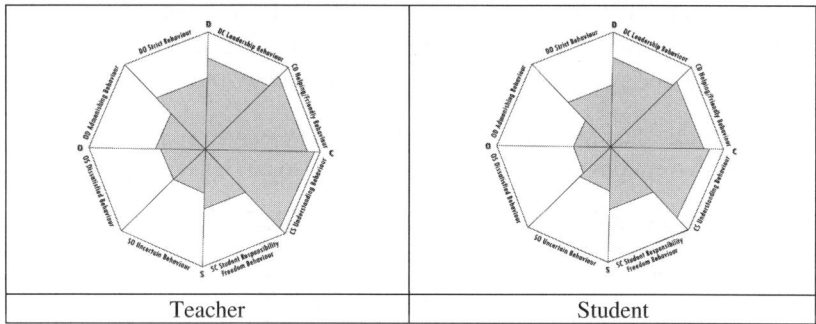

Figure 2.4. Graphical representation of teachers' and students' perceptions.

The Authoritative behaviour is more akin to the Lee Canter's Assertive Discipline Model of classroom management (Edwards, 2000). In the Authoritative atmosphere, the lesson is well planned, logically structured and task-oriented. Rules and procedures are clear and students don't need reminders. Students are attentive, and generally produce better work than their peers with a non-assertive teacher. The Authoritative teacher is enthusiastic and open to students' needs. He or she takes a personal interest in them. He or she is considered to be a good teacher by students.

The Tolerant/Authoritative pattern of teacher behaviour is assertive but also aware of students' needs. The Tolerant/Authoritative teacher develops close relationships with students. They enjoy the class and are highly involved in most lessons. Tolerant/Authoritative teachers maintain a structure which supports student responsibility and freedom. They use a variety of methods, to which students respond well. The results of this study suggest that either the teachers are exhibiting the caring behaviour and the students do not perceive it or the teachers are not exhibiting the behaviour as much as they believe. In general, two distinctive patterns have emerged from this study. Students in Singapore perceive their teacher to be in general authoritative while their teachers perceive themselves as more caring and understanding.

7.2.3. Analyses of two specific cases

Teacher A

Teacher A is a female teacher trainee and during her practice teaching she was assigned to teach a Secondary 3 chemistry class. The class had 44 students (24 were male and 20 female). Table 2.6 shows the teacher's and the students' perceptions of interpersonal behaviour in the class.

Table 2.6.   Individual Statistics – Teacher A' Self Perceived and Students' Perceptions of Their Teachers' Interpersonal Behaviour

Teacher Behaviour Dimension	Group	Mean	Standard Deviation
Leadership	Teacher	20.00	
	Student	19.04	4.822
Helping/Friendly	Teacher	18.00	
	Student	20.40	4.379
Understanding	Teacher	22.00	
	Student	19.52	4.910
Student Responsibility/Freedom	Teacher	6.000	
	Student	9.409	4.222
Uncertain	Teacher	4.000	
	Student	2.931	4.008
Dissatisfaction	Teacher	6.000	
	Student	2.750	3.531
Admonishing	Teacher	6.000	
	Student	3.022	4.217
Strict	Teacher	14.00	
	Student	9.181	4.970

n = 44 students

Figure 2.5 displays the self-perception of Teacher A together with the perception of her students. She scores highly on the Dominant sectors of the model and on the leadership behaviour, understanding behaviour and helping/friendly sectors. The teacher perceived only small amount of uncertainty, admonishing and student responsibility. This shows that Teacher A is similar to authoritative in nature. According to Brekelmans, Levy, and Rodriguez (1993), the authoritative environment is well-structured, pleasant and task-oriented. Rules and procedures are clear and students do not need reminders. The teacher is enthusiastic and open and takes personal interest in students. The lesson is well-planned and logically structured.

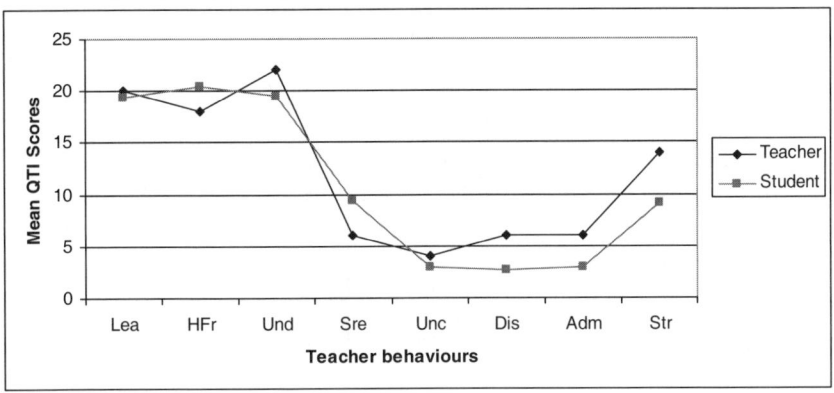

Figure 2.5. Profiles of mean QTI scores of Teacher A's self perceived and students' perceptions of QTI scores.

Student perceptions of Teacher A are slightly different from her own perception. Students see her being less understanding, more helpful/friendly and in providing opportunities for student to take responsibility. The students in her class also perceived her to be less uncertain, dissatisfied, admonishing and strict. This typology leads to consider her to be a tolerant/authoritative type. The students in this context feel that the teacher maintains a structure which supports student responsibility and freedom. They sometime organize their lessons or small group work and are highly involved in lessons. The teacher ignores minor disruptions and continues with the lesson. Students cooperate with the teacher to reach their goal.

Teacher B

Teacher B is a male teacher who taught CPA lessons during his practicum in Secondary 3 Normal Technical class. The class comprised 15 male and 25 female students. Table 2.7 shows the teacher's and his students' perception of the interpersonal behaviour in the class

Table 2.7. Individual Statistics – Teacher B' Self Perceived and Students' Perceptions of Their Teachers' Interpersonal Behaviour

Teacher Behaviour Dimension	Group	Mean	Standard Deviation
Leadership	Teacher	18.00	
	Student	15.30	3.666
Helping/Friendly	Teacher	20.00	
	Student	16.57	4.824
Understanding	Teacher	21.00	
	Student	16.72	4.260
Student Responsibility/Freedom	Teacher	11.00	
	Student	10.25	3.887
Uncertain	Teacher	8.000	
	Student	6.600	4.401
Dissatisfaction	Teacher	10.00	
	Student	6.750	4.705
Admonishing	Teacher	11.00	
	Student	7.175	4.717
Strict	Teacher	14.00	
	Student	11.22	3.951

n = 40 students

Teacher B felt that during his interaction with students he displayed more leadership, helping/friendly and understanding behaviours. While at the same time he perceived that he had displayed a certain amount of strict, admonishing and dissatisfaction behaviours. He also felt that he was giving a certain amount of responsibility to the students when he was teaching. These characteristics profile him to be a tolerant teacher. In this environment students appreciate the teacher's personal involvement and the ability to match the subject matter with their learning styles. Students work at their own pace and the classroom environment sometimes become confused. Often the teacher does not prepare the lesson well ahead and does not challenge the student (see Figure 2.6).

On the other hand, students in his class see him as a directive teacher. The students perceived that his interpersonal behaviours in leadership, helping/friendly and understanding are less than what he thought he had displayed. At the same time students perceived that he showed less uncertain, dissatisfied, admonishing and strict behaviours than his own perception of himself. This profile puts him into a Directive teacher. In a directive learning environment the class is well-structured and task-oriented. The teacher is efficiently organized and normally completes all lessons on time. The teacher dominates class discussion, but generally holds students' interest. The teacher is not very close to the students, but occasionally friendly and understanding.

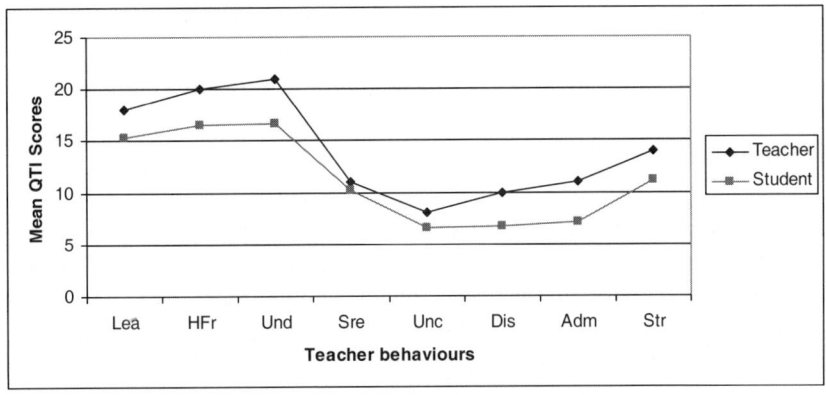

Figure 2.6. Profiles of mean QTI scores of Teacher B's self perceived and students' perceptions of QTI scores.

These profiles of the two teachers show the differences between what the teachers think of themselves and what the students see them as being in the class.

8. Follow up with the Trainee Teacher

At the end of the practicum the trainee teachers were debriefed. Each trainee teacher was given their own results together with the graphical profile in a form similar to that illustrated in Figure 2.4. The trainee teachers were able to see how they saw themselves and how their students saw them. Some of them expressed surprise at the gap between their perception and that of their students. As a group, they discussed the similarities and difference in their respective results. The trainee teachers also shared their experiences with each other and discussed some possible ways to bring about a change in their own interpersonal relationships with their students. At the end of the session they were asked to reflect on their interpersonal behaviours and encouraged to find ways with which they would be comfortable to minimize the gap between their own and their students' perception of them to create a conducive learning environment.

They were also tutored on how to score and use the QTI data for future use in their classrooms to determine their students' perceptions. The trainee teachers found the QTI to be a valuable source of information for their professional development in the area of classroom interaction. The trainee teachers also thought that such information would be helpful for them in creating a good learning environment.

9. Summary and Conclusion

This study described in this chapter aimed to map a profile of trainee teachers' perceived interpersonal behaviour from their self-reflection and their students' perceptions. The result shows that there are some significant differences in how the teachers see themselves and the way students viewed them. This was evident on the scales of Helpful/Friendly, Understanding, Admonishing and Strict. Trainee teachers considered themselves more favourably on the Helpful/Friendly and Understanding scales and less favourably on the Admonishing and Strict scales than did their students.

Self-evaluation of one's interpersonal behaviour is a potentially powerful exercise when a teacher attempts to create and maintain a favourable classroom learning environment. The effectiveness of this attempt can be further enhanced if teachers can also obtain feedback from their students with whom they are interacting to bring about the most desired learning climate through their interpersonal behaviour in the classroom. It is valuable to know whether students perceive the learning environment to be positive as the teacher himself or herself attempts to create. If there is any mismatch, based on the information collected from the class, the teacher can make a better decision on how to change his/her behaviour to create a more desirable learning environment.

The QTI is an easily administered instrument that teachers can readily use to reflect on their interpersonal behaviour in their classroom as well as to monitor their pupils' perceptions of their class learning environment. The information gained from such an exercise can provide a basis for guiding systematic attempts to improve classroom management when working with various teaching strategies such as whole-class and student-centred learning, and project work.

Teacher educators are likely to find the QTI to be a valuable instrument in providing data that allow teachers and student teachers to engage in self-reflection on their performance in their classrooms. The data can provide a valuable basis from which useful discussion on teaching strategies and learning climate can emerge. In teacher education programs, the use of the QTI during a practicum can be easily implemented assisting student teachers to determine their pupils' perception of their interpersonal behaviour. They can discuss the results with their cooperating teachers and/or university/college supervisors. In this manner, the trainee teachers can reflect on their practice and improve themselves in creating learning environments conducive to learning.

References

Arends, R. I. (2004). *Learning to teach* (6th ed.). Boston: McGraw-Hill.

Brekelman. M., Levy, J., & Rodriquez, R. (1993). A typology of teacher communication style. In T. Wubbels & J. Levy (Eds.), *Do you know what you look like?* (pp. 46-55). London: The Falmer Press.

Brekelmans, M., Wubbels, T., & den Brok, P. (2002). Teacher experience and the teacher-student relationship in the classroom environment. In S. C. Goh & M. S. Khine (Eds.), *Studies in learning environments: An international perspective* (pp. 73-99). Singapore: World Scientific.

Edwards, C. H. (2000). *Classroom discipline and management* (3rd ed.). New York: John Wiley & Sons.

Good, T. & Brophy, J. (2003). *Looking in classrooms.* (9th ed.). Boston: Allyn and Bacon.

Getzels, J. W. & Thelen, H. A. (1960). The classroom group as a unique social system. *National Society for Studies in Education Year Book, 59,* 53-82.

Khine, M. S. & Lourdusamy, A. (2005, May). *Self-perceived and students' perceptions of teacher interaction in the classroom.* Paper presented at Redesigning pedagogy: Research, Policy and Practice Conference. Singapore.

Leary, T. (1957). *An interpersonal diagnosis of personality.* New York: Ronald Press Company.

Lourdusamy, A. & Khine, M. S. (2001, December). *Self-evaluation of interpersonal behaviour and classroom interaction by teacher trainees.* A paper presented at the International Educational Research Conference, University of Notre Dame, Fremantle, Western Australia.

Rawnsley, D. & Fisher, D. L. (1998, December). *Learning environments in mathematics classrooms and their associations with students' attitudes and learning.* A paper presented at the Australian Association for Research in Education Conference, Adelaide, Australia.

Walberg, H. J. (1976) The psychology of learning environments: Behavioural, structural or perceptual? *Review of Research in Education, 4*, 142-178.

Watzlawick, P., Beavin, J., & Jackson, D. (1967). *The pragmatics of human communication.* New York: Norton.

Wettasinghe, C. M. & Lourdusamy, A. (2002, September). *Teachers' and students' perception of interpersonal relationship in the classroom.* A paper presented at the International Educational Research Conference, Singapore.

Winne, P. H. & Marx, R.W. (1997). Reconceptualizing research on teaching, *Journal of Educational Psychology, 69*, 668-678.

Wubbels, T., Brekelmans, M., & Hooymayers, H. (1991). Interpersonal teacher behaviour in the classroom. In B. J. Fraser & H. Walberg (Eds.), *Educational environments: Evaluation, antecedents and consequences* (pp. 141-160). Oxford: Pergamon Press.

Wubbels, T., Creton, H., & Hooymayers, H. (1985, March-April). *Discipline problems of beginning teachers: Interpersonal teacher behaviour mapped out.* Paper presented at the annual meeting of the American Educational Research Association, Chicago, Illinois, USA.

Wubbels, T., Creton, H., Levy, J., & Hooymayers, H. (1993). The model for interpersonal behaviour. In T. Wubbels & J. Levy (Eds.), *Do you know what you look like? Interpersonal relations in education.* (pp. 13-28) London: The Falmer Press.

Wubbels, T. & Levy, J. (1991). A comparison of interpersonal behaviour of Dutch and American teachers, *International Journal of Intercultural Relations, 15*, 1-18.

Wubbels, T. & Levy, J. (Ed.). (1993). *Do you know what you look like? Interpersonal relations in education.* London: The Falmer Press.

Chapter 3

FACTORS INFLUENCING STUDENTS' PERCEPTIONS OF THEIR TEACHERS' INTERPERSONAL BEHAVIOUR: A MULTILEVEL ANALYSIS

Darrell L. Fisher
Curtin University of Technology
Australia

Perry den Brok
Utrecht University
The Netherlands

Tony Rickards
Curtin University of Technology
Australia

This chapter describes a study in which student, teacher and class characteristics were associated with students' perceptions of their teachers' interpersonal behaviour. Using the Questionnaire on Teacher Interaction (QTI), two important dimensions of teacher interpersonal behaviour were investigated: influence (dominance vs. submission) and proximity (cooperation vs. opposition). Earlier work with the QTI in the USA and the Netherlands has shown that, in those countries, several factors affect students' perceptions of their teachers. These factors include student and teacher gender, student and teacher ethnic background, student age, teacher experience, class size, student achievement and subject. It has been found that each of these variables has a distinctive effect, but also that they interact with each other when determining students' perceptions. In this study, a meta-analysis was performed on a large Australian secondary student and teacher QTI data set. QTI dimension scores were examined against factors such as: gender, class size and subject. To investigate separate and combined effects of variables, a hierarchical analysis of variance (distinguishing between the school, class and student level) was conducted with ML3E software. This chapter discusses the effect sizes and variance explained by these variables.

1. Introduction

Much research has shown that students' perceptions of their teacher's interpersonal behaviour are an important factor in explaining their cognitive and affective outcomes (Brekelmans, Wubbels & den Brok, 2002; den Brok, 2001; Henderson, 1995; Rickards, 1998; Wubbels & Levy, 1993). Also, teacher-student interpersonal behaviour is seen as an important factor related to order in the classroom and is a major concern for both beginning and experienced teachers (Veenman, 1984). Researchers have mapped teacher-student interpersonal behaviour with the *Questionnaire on Teacher Interaction* (QTI) (Wubbels, Créton & Hooymayers, 1985; 1987; Fisher, Fraser, & Wubbels, 1993). In studies using the QTI, teacher-student communication style is usually reported in terms of two dimensions, influence (who controls communication, teacher or students?) and proximity (do teacher and students cooperate or are they opposites?), or in terms of eight sectors of behaviour (leadership, helpful/friendly, understanding, student freedom, uncertain, dissatisfied, admonishing and strict) (e.g., Leary, 1957; Wubbels, et al., 1985, 1987).

Additionally, research in the USA (den Brok, Levy, Rodriguez, & Wubbels, 2002; den Brok, Levy, Wubbels, & Rodriguez, 2003; Levy, den Brok, Wubbels, & Brekelmans, 2003; Levy, Wubbels & Brekelmans, 1992; Wubbels & Levy, 1993) and in Australia (Fisher, Fraser, & Rickards, 1997; Henderson, 1995; Rawnsley & Fisher, 1997; Rickards, 1998; Rickards & Fisher, 1997; Waldrip & Fisher, 1999) has shown that several student, class and teacher characteristics are related to students' perception of their teacher. Among these associated characteristics are student and teacher gender, student and teacher ethnic background, socio-economic status, attitude and achievement, age, teacher experience and subject taught.

While there has been a line of research (in Australia) investigating the relationship between student, teacher and class characteristics and students' perceptions of their teacher's interpersonal behaviour, this research has been subject to some limitations. Australian research has not used multilevel analysis to a great extent. This multilevel analysis adjusts for the fact that data have not been sampled randomly and allows the effects of multiple levels of the learning environment to exert an influence in the outcomes of any study.

It has been shown that non-randomly sampled data may lead to artificially increased associations, since respondents (in classes) share similar experiences, history and stimuli (Hox, 1995; Muthen, 1994). Using regular analysis of variance thus leads to an overestimation of possible effects (e.g., Hox, 1995). Also, only one variable at a time is often investigated in non-multilevel analyses, so effects that have not been corrected for the presence (and effects) of other, (partially) overlapping variables, may also lead to overestimation. In addition, no interactions between variables are investigated in "standard" uni-level data analysis. Finally, if variables are related to student perception scores, then sector or scale scores are used, rather than dimension scores (Levy, et al., 2003). While useful for feedback, sector scores have the disadvantage of being associated each other, whilst dimension scores are independent. Moreover, sector scores are not always reliable or valid (den Brok, Fisher, Brekelmans, Rickards, & Wubbels, in press).

This was the first time that multilevel analysis using QTI dimension scores had been conducted in Australia. Also, since the data set (Rickards, 1998; Fisher & Rickards, 2000) is rather large (nearly 4,000 students and 191 teachers), in some respect this study also represents a benchmark for Australian teacher-student interpersonal behaviour. It is hoped that this dataset will provide other researchers with a valuable source of comparative benchmarking and validation data.

2. Teacher-student Interpersonal Behaviour

To be able to describe the perceptions students have of the teacher-student interpersonal behaviour in their classrooms, Wubbels, Créton and Hooymayers (1985, see Wubbels & Levy, 1993) developed a model for interpersonal behaviour. They applied a general model for interpersonal relationships designed by Leary (1957) to the specific context of education. The Leary model, as it has become known, has been extensively investigated in clinical psychology and psychotherapeutic settings (Strack, 1996). It has proven to be a rather complete model to describe interpersonal relationships (see e.g., Foa, 1961; Lonner 1980). In the Leary model, two dimensions are important and Leary named them the Dominance-Submission axis and the Hostility-Affection axis. While the two dimensions have occasionally been given other names, - Brown (1965) used Status and Solidarity, Dunkin and Biddle (1974) Warmth and Directivity - they have generally been accepted as universal descriptors of human interaction. The two dimensions have also been easily transferred to education. Slater (1962) used them to describe pedagogical relationships, and Dunkin and Biddle (1974) demonstrated their importance in teachers' efforts to influence classroom events.

Adapting the Leary Model to the context of education, Wubbels, et al. (1985) used the two dimensions, which they named Influence (Dominance Submission) and Proximity (Opposition Cooperation) to structure the perception of eight behaviour segments: leadership, helpful/friendly behaviour, understanding behaviour, giving students freedom, uncertain, dissatisfied, admonishing and strict behaviour. Figure 3.1 presents a graphic representation of the Model for Interpersonal Teacher Behaviour developed by Wubbels, et al. (1985).

The model for interpersonal teacher behaviour (see Figure 3.1), as well as the Leary model, are special models because of their statistical properties and are theoretically linked to a particular branch of models named circumplex models (e.g., Blackburn & Renwick, 1996; Fabrigar, Visser, & Browne, 1997; Gaines, Panter, Lyde, Steers, Rusbult, Cox, & Wexler, 1997; Gurtman & Pincus, 2000). Circumplex models assume that the eight interpersonal sectors can be represented by two, independent dimensions (Influence and Proximity), are ordered with equal distances to each other in a circular structure and maintain equal distances to the middle of the circle.

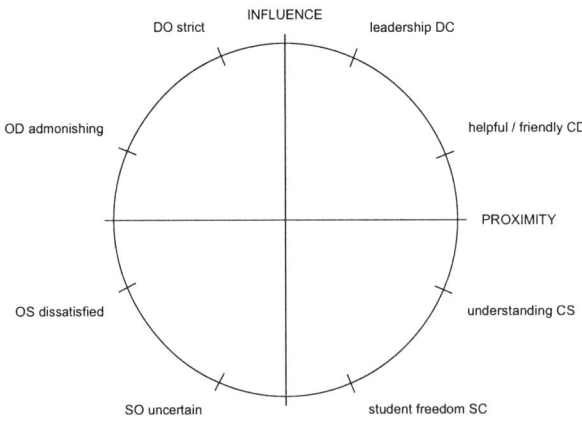

Figure 3.1. The Model for Interpersonal Teacher Behaviour.

The sections are labelled DC, CD, etc. according to their position in the coordinate system described in Figure 3.1. For example, the two sectors leadership and helpful/friendly are both characterised by Dominance and Cooperation. In the DC sector, the Dominance aspect prevails over the Cooperation aspect. A teacher displaying DC behaviour might be seen by students as enthusiastic, a good leader, and the like. The adjacent CD sector includes behaviours of a more cooperative and less dominant type; the teacher might be described as helpful, friendly.

3. Variables Affecting Students' Perceptions of Their Teacher's Communication Style.

Studies on differences in student ratings of teacher communication style suggest a number of variables that are important: student and teacher gender, student and teacher ethnic background, grade level, experience, subject taught, report card grade and class size.

Research on gender-related perceptions found that females at both the primary and secondary levels viewed their teachers as more dominant and more positive (e.g., teacher centered) and cooperative than do males (e.g., Goh & Fraser, 1995; Levy, et al., 1992; 2003; Rickards, 1998; Rickards & Fisher, 1997; Waldrip & Fisher, 1999; Wubbels & Levy, 1993). Despite these consistent patterns, gender-related differences with respect to other elements of classroom climate or learning environments research is less conclusive (e.g., Dart, Burnett, Boulton-Lewis, Campbell, Smith, & McCrindle, 1999; Ferguson & Fraser, 1998; Pianta & Nimetz, 1993; Waxman & Huang, 1998).

There is a clear relationship between student ethnicity and their perceptions of teacher communication patterns. Using self-designated ethnic group membership as an explanatory variable, investigators found that, in USA samples, Asian-American students perceived less dominance and proximity than students from African-American, Hispanic or Caucasian backgrounds (den Brok, et al., 2002; 2003; Levy, et al., 2003; Levy, Wubbels, & Brekelmans, 1996). In a similar vein, Hispanic students felt that their teachers were more dominant and cooperative than did other ethnic groups (den Brok, et al., 2002; 2003; Levy, et al., 1996). Interestingly, researchers in Australia found that Asian students perceived more influence and proximity and were described as perceiving their classes more positively than students originating from other cultural groups (Evans & Fisher, 2000; Rickards &

Fisher, 1997; Rickards, 1998). Of course, apart from differences in methodology (the Australian studies used regular analyses of variance, the American studies multilevel analysis) and sample distribution, the country of interest (USA vs. Australia) may help to explain these surprising differences. Primary home language was also found to be a significant variable in explaining the range of students' views. For example, it was found that those speaking English at home perceived less dominance than students speaking other languages (Levy, Wubbels, Brekelmans & Morganfield, 1997), while those speaking Spanish perceived the most cooperation (den Brok, et al., 2003).

In Australian studies, students speaking an Asian language at home were found to rate their teachers higher in terms of influence and proximity (Rickards & Fisher, 1997; Rickards, 1998). Finally, acculturation was found to be of importance: students who have lived longer in the country of interest noticed less dominance than those who had just arrived (Evans & Fisher, 2000, for Australia; den Brok, et al., 2003, for the USA).

Students' age occasionally has been found to significantly relate to their perceptions of teachers. Levy et al (1997) found that older students noted more teacher dominance than their younger peers, though no effect was found with respect to proximity. A similar effect was found in a later, comprehensive study (Levy, et al., 2003). In yet another study (Levy, et al., 1992) student age was found to be unrelated to either the influence or proximity dimensions. Students in higher grade-levels have reported greater influence and proximity than their younger peers (Ferguson & Fraser, 1998; Levy, et al., 1992).

Research investigating the associations between students' achievement and their perceptions of teacher behaviour are also inconclusive, showing significant but weak effects when report card grade is used as an indicator of achievement. Having a standardized set of items for the assessment of achievement has been shown to give more comparable within sample results when compared to inter-school reported class grades (Brekelmans, et al., 2002; Rickards, 1998). Levy, et al. (1992) found that report card grades were positively related to influence and proximity, but the same researchers were not able to replicate this finding in a later study (Levy, et al., 1997).

In a recent study, the effect was found to be reversed and was negatively related to influence and proximity (Levy, et al., 2003). Research using cognitive test scores and treating students' perceptions as the independent rather than the dependent variable did find consistent and positive relationships between achievement and influence and proximity (Brekelmans, et al., 2002; Rawnsley & Fisher, 1997; Rickards, 1998). Similar findings applied to affective variables, such as subject-related attitudes (Brekelmans, et al., 2002; den Brok, 2001; Rawnsley & Fisher, 1997; Rickards, 1998), although associations usually were investigated in terms of the effect of perceptions of interpersonal behaviour on student (affective) outcomes, but not vice versa (which is the case in the present study).

The more experience that a teacher had, the greater the perception of dominance, leadership and strictness (Levy, et al., 1992). While experience was found to positively relate to views on influence, those for proximity – including helpful/friendly or understanding behaviours – remained constant. In other words, students' did not perceive any increase in cooperative behaviour according to teacher experience (Brekelmans, Holvast & van Tartwijk, 1992; Brekelmans, et al., 2002; Somers, Brekelmans & Wubbels, 1997; Wubbels & Brekelmans, 1998; Wubbels & Levy, 1993).

In a number of investigations, teacher ethnic background related to students' views on teacher communication. Asian and Asian-American teachers were perceived as less dominant and cooperative than teachers from other ethnic groups (den Brok, et al., 2002; 2003; Levy, et al., 1996), while Hispanic teachers were perceived as more dominant and cooperative than their colleagues from other ethnicities (den Brok, et al., 2002; Levy, et al., 1996).

Class size, appeared to be negatively related to students' perceptions of teacher proximity, but was not related to their perceptions of teacher influence (Levy, et al., 2003).

Mixed results have been found for differences in subject taught. While a recent study indicated that students perceived physics, science and mathematics teachers as less understanding and displaying less leadership than teachers from other subjects (Levy, et al., 2003), other studies found them to be more cooperative and dominant (den Brok, 2001; Wubbels & Levy, 1993).

Waldrip and Fisher (1999) investigated differences between students from rural areas (mining students) and students living in the Perth metropolitan area. Mining area students had a distinctly different perception of teacher-student interpersonal behaviours. Some of these aspects could be due to the generally more transient nature of mining area students. Rural students were less likely to report the more positive aspects of student-teacher interpersonal behaviours and were more likely to report the negative aspects.

4. Research Questions

As mentioned in the Rationale section, the present study is the first of its kind to employ multilevel analyses on an Australian sample of secondary school teachers. Also, it is the first Australian study to use dimension scores, rather than scale or sector scores.

The following research questions were investigated:

1. To what extent do schools and classes contribute to differences in students' perceptions of their teachers' interpersonal behaviour?
2. Which student, class and school variables explain differences in students' perceptions of their teachers' interpersonal behaviour?
3. How are these variables related to students' perceptions and what is their relative strength?
4. How much variance in students' perceptions can be explained by all significant variables combined?

5. Method

5.1 Instrumentation

To assess interpersonal teacher behaviour, the QTI was designed according to the two-dimensional Leary model and the eight sectors. It was originally developed in the Netherlands and consisted of 77 items (Wubbels, et al., 1985), a 64-item American version was constructed in 1988 (Wubbels & Levy, 1991) and an Australian 48-item version in 1993 (Fisher, Fraser, & Wubbels, 1993). Items were formulated, based on large numbers of interviews with both teachers and students, and the construction process of the questionnaire included many rounds of careful testing (Wubbels & Levy, 1993).

The QTI has a five-point response scale, ranging from "Never/Not at all" to "Always/Very." It is scored on the basis of eight sectors or two summarising dimensions of Influence (or DS) and Proximity (or CO).

The Dominance/Submission (DS) dimension is primarily comprised of behaviours in the sectors closest to the DS axis - Strict, Leadership, Uncertainty and Student Freedom. The sectors that mostly make up the Co-operation/Opposition (CO) dimension are Helpful/Friendly, Understanding, Dissatisfied and Admonishing. In Table 3.1 typical items are provided for each of the eight sectors (scales) of the QTI.

Table 3.1. Typical Items of the English Version of the QTI

Scale (sector)	Typical item
DC – Leadership	This teacher acts confidently.
CD – Helpful/ Friendly	This teacher is friendly.
CS – Understanding	This teacher is patient.
SC – Student Freedom	We can influence this teacher
SO – Uncertain	This teacher is hesitant.
OS – Dissatisfied	This teacher is suspicious.
OD – Admonishing	This teacher gets angry quickly.
DO – Strict	This teacher is strict.

The QTI has acceptable reliability and validity when used in grades 7 to 12 (Wubbels & Levy, 1993, Rickards, 1998). A recent review on the validity and reliability of over 20 studies that have used the QTI during the last 17 years (den Brok, 2001) showed that reliability of the eight scales (sectors) is sufficient and consistent across classes. Moreover, the review showed that the theoretical structure of the Model for Interpersonal Teacher Behaviour was represented in the items and scales of the instrument.

While the QTI has been repeatedly judged to be an acceptable instrument for use in teacher research and professional development, it is nearly 20 years old. It was therefore important to re-examine whether the instrument still reflected acceptable reliability and validity. This study conducted reliability and discriminant validity analyses for the eight scales of the QTI. Table 3.2 provides reliability and percentages of variance at the class level for each of the scales of the QTI. As can be seen in Table 3.2, the instrument was found to be reliable and able to discriminate between classes.

Construct validity was investigated in a number of ways. First, an exploratory factor analysis was conducted on the (aggregated) scale scores in order to see if two dimensions were present in the data (see den Brok, Fisher, et al., in press; den Brok, Rickards, & Fisher, 2003). This analysis indicated that two factors with an eigenvalue larger than one could be extracted, explaining 79 percent of the variance. Inspection of the factor loadings suggested two dimensions that could be labelled in terms of influence and proximity.

Table 3.2. Reliability (Alpha) of QTI Scales at the Student and Class Level, and Variance at the Class Level (eta squared)

Scale	Alpha Student level	Alpha Class level	Eta
DC – Leadership	0.82	0.93	0.33
CD – Helpful/Friendly	0.88	0.96	0.35
CS – Understanding	0.85	0.95	0.32
SC – Student Freedom	0.66	0.82	0.26
SO – Uncertain	0.72	0.87	0.22
OS – Dissatisfied	0.80	0.93	0.23
OD – Admonishing	0.76	0.87	0.31
DO – Strict	0.63	0.78	0.23

Second, correlations were computed between scales at the class level. This correlation matrix was then investigated for its circular structure by computing a Correspondence Index (with the RANDALL-software; Tracey, 1994; Tracey & Schneider, 1995). The correspondence index indicates to what degree and with what probability a correlation matrix corresponds to a circumplex structure. If a circumplex model applies to the data, correlations should be highly positive for neighbouring scales, decreasing until they become highly negative with scales on the opposite end of the interpersonal circle (Gurtman & Pincus, 2000). CI for the correlation matrix was 0.72 (p=0.0008), indicating that a circular ordering applied to the scales of the QTI for the present sample. Third, a correlation between the two dimension scores was computed. For the current sample, the correlation was 0.24 (p=0.001), indicating some association between the two dimensions. Inspection of the plot of factor loadings, based on the factor analysis, suggested that the correlation could have been caused by two scales occupying different positions on the interpersonal circle than hypothesised: Understanding (CS), had moved counter-clockwise and changed places with the Helpful/Friendly (CD) sector, while Dissatisfied (OS) had moved clockwise and almost overlapped with Admonishing (OD). Despite these (minor) irregularities, given the high CI and outcomes of the factor analysis (and prior validity outcomes on an even larger Australian data set including the present one, (e.g., den Brok, Rickards & Fisher, 2003), the researchers conducting this study decided to use the QTI-based dimension scores.

Table 3.3. Variables used in Multilevel Analysis

Level	Variable	Description
Student	Gender	Dummy variable with boys indicated by a '1'.
	Attitude	Scale variable (recoded to a score between 0 and 1) indicating the motivation for class.
	Achievement	Scale variable indicating recent test score, ranging between 0 and 100 (percentage score).
	Language spoken at home	Students indicate which language is spoken at home most of the time. Recoded into dummy variable with '1' indicating English.
	Mother's country of birth	Students indicate where their mother was born. Recoded into a series of dummy variables (Europe, Asia, South-East Asia, Oceania, Africa, North America, South America), with a '1' indicating the specific country (Australia is baseline).
Class	Subject taught	Series of dummy variables indicating subject taught (Science, Math, Other subjects), with a '1' indicating a category hit.
	Grade level	Variable indicating the grade level, ranging between 8 to 12, recoded into a variable running from 1 to 6, with a higher score indicating a higher grade level.
	Class-size	The number of students in the class.
	Percentage boys	Variable indicating the ratio of boys in class (between 0 and 1).
Class	Percentage English	Variable indicating the ratio of students in class speaking English at home most of the time (between 0 and 1).

Table 3.3. Continued

Level	Variable	Description
Class	Percentage Australian	Variable indicating the ratio of students in class with their mother born in Australia (between 0 and 1).
	Class-achievement	Class average of achievement.
	Class-attitude	Class average of attitude
School	Type	Dummy variable indicating if a school is independent ('1') or not.
	State	Dummy variable indicating the state of location of the school (with a '1' indicating Tasmania).

In addition to students' perceptions of teacher interpersonal behaviour, several other students, class and school variables were investigated (see Table 3.3 for an overview of these variables). Students' ethnic background was measured in terms of a number of variables: language spoken at home most of the time (English or other), country of birth of the mother (Australia, Europe, Asia, South-East Asia, Oceania, Africa, Northern America and Southern America) and country of birth of the father (similar distinction). It was decided to only use country of origin for the mother. The language and ethnic membership data were recoded into sets of dummy variables for the multilevel analyses. The student ethnicity data were also used to create a number of class-related ethnicity variables.

For each class, the percentage of English-speaking students was determined, as well as the percentage of students with an Australian-born mother. Apart from ethnicity, students were asked to provide information regarding their gender, a recent achievement test and their attitude towards the teachers' lessons (using the *Test Of Science Related Attitudes* (TOSRA) (Fraser, 1981; Fisher, Henderson, & Fraser, 1995, Rickards, 1998). Class-mean equivalents for these variables were also calculated, as it was assumed that the level of the class might also affect students' perceptions.

At the class level, the following variables were created: class size (number of students in class), grade level, percentage of male students and subject taught. 'Subject taught' was divided into a number of dummy variables (indicating maths, science or other subjects). With respect to the school, information was gathered on the type of school (government or independent) and state (Tasmania or Western Australia).

5.2 Sample

The sample consisted of 3,994 students from 191 secondary school teachers in various subjects (Math, Science or combinations of these subjects). Teachers taught in 36 schools, located in two Australian states: Western Australia and Tasmania. Distribution of the sample was relatively equal in terms of state (2,204 students or 55.2 percent in Western Australia) and student gender (1,927 students or 48.7 percent). Most of the students reported perceptions of teachers in Science (3,227 students or 80.8 percent) and Math (554 students or 13.9 percent), leaving the remainder (5.3 percent) to subject combinations. The major part of the students indicated to speak English at home (3793 students or 95.8 percent). Three out of four students (72.8 percent) indicated that they had an Australian-born mother, leaving 1,072 students (27.1 percent) with mothers born outside Australia, for the major part in Asian, South-East Asian or African countries. Most of the surveyed students were in the eighth (32.7 percent), ninth (28.5 percent) or tenth (20.3 percent) grade. Two thirds of the students were in government schools (2,368 students or 59.3 percent).

In terms of class-composition variables, the sample was quite diverse. The average percentage of boys in the class was 50, but classes ranged from girls-only to boys-only. Most of the classes consisted of mainly English-speaking students, with a percentage range of English speaking students between 50 and 100. Class size ranged from 5 to 35, with an average class size of 24.

Achievement scores ranged between 3 and 97 percent (mean 62 percent, standard deviation 19.8 percent), attitude ranged between 0 and 1 (mean attitude was 0.60, standard deviation 0.20).

5.3 Analysis

Multilevel analyses were conducted on the dimension scores of the QTI (DS and CO). Models consisted of three levels: school, class and student. The models were tested in a number of steps. First, an empty model (with no independent variables) was tested in order to obtain raw percentages of variance in the sector scores at the student, class, and school level. Next, a model with all student variables from Table 3.3 was tested. Non-significant variables were deleted from the model until a model was achieved with significant student variables only. In the second step, class and school variables were added. Finally, interactions between variables, especially between the gender and ethnicity indicators, were tested, both within and across levels. Coefficients were estimated with the RIGLS method[1]. We also determined effect sizes, in order to compare the relative importance of variables, as well as percentages of variance explained by all the significant variables combined. To enhance interpretation, associations between the explanatory variables were established by means of correlational and cross-tabular analyses[2].

6. Results

6.1 Variance distribution in Influence (DS) and Proximity (CO)

Table 3.4 provides the sample mean scores for DS and CO, as well as the percentages of variance located at the school, class and student level. As can be seen, on average, Australian secondary school teachers were regarded as both dominant and cooperative (note that DS and CO scores can range between −3 and +3). Also, two thirds of the variance was located at the student level, with only minimal variance at the school level and the remainder of the variance was at the class (or teacher) level. These findings are in line with studies using multilevel analyses on American data (den Brok, et al., 2002; Levy, et al., 1997; 2003). They suggest that a school can hardly be recognised by its 'interpersonal' profile.

---

[1] Standard estimation procedures in multilevel analyses programs, such as Iterative Generalized Least Squares (IGLS), often produce biased estimates of coefficients and variance distribution, especially when small numbers of units are available at the higher levels (Luyten & De Jong, 1998). Because of the small number of schools and teachers involved in this study, it was decided to use the Restricted Iterative Generalized Least Squares (RIGLS) method, which is suitable for small numbers of units at the highest levels (Goldstein, 1995).

[2] No (significant) associations between explanatory variables were found.

Table 3.4.　Mean DS and CO Scores and Percentages of Variance at the
School, Class and Student Level (Empty Model)

	Influence (DS)	Proximity (CO)
Constant/mean (st. error)	0.48 (0.02)	0.71 (0.03)
Variance		
- School	0.0 %	1.5 %
- Class	30.1 %	28.3 %
- Student	69.9 %	70.2 %
-2*Loglikelihood	2778.46	6707.47

6.2 Variables explaining students' perceptions of their teachers'
interpersonal behaviour.

Table 3.5 provides an overview of the variables that had a significant impact on students' perceptions of their teachers' interpersonal behaviour. Table 3.5 lists both regular coefficients as well as effect sizes.

As can be seen in Table 3.5, the more positive the attitude of the student, the higher his or her perception of the teacher in terms of both influence and proximity. This finding resembles those of earlier studies (den Brok, 2001; Rickards & Fisher, 1997). For gender, a negative relationship was found with both influence and proximity. This means that boys perceived their teachers as less dominant and cooperative than girls, a finding that again is in keeping with most of the prior work (Levy, et al., 2003; Rickards & Fisher, 1997; Rickards, 1998).

Differences in perceptions were also reported with respect to ethnicity-related variables. Students speaking mainly English at home perceived their teachers as more dominant and more cooperative. As with gender and attitude, this finding supports earlier outcomes (den Brok, et al., 2003; Levy, et al., 1997; 2003). Also, students whose mother was born in South-East Asian countries reported higher perceptions of influence than students whose mother was born in Australia or any of the other countries.

For proximity, no differences were found with respect to country of origin of the mother. While earlier analyses on the same data set indicated similar findings for influence-related scales (Rickards & Fisher, 1997; Rickards, 1998), the absence of a relationship between ethnicity and proximity was different. It seems very likely that the analysis method used has contributed to this difference: apparently, when taking into account the fact that the data were not sampled randomly and when correcting the effect of ethnicity for other variables (in this case: gender, attitude and several class variables), the effect of ethnicity reduces and becomes non-significant.

Table 3.5. Variables Explaining Students' DS and CO Perceptions

	Influence (DS)		Proximity (CO)	
	Coefficients (st. error)	Effect size	Coefficients (st. error)	Effect size
Constant	-.69 (.28)	-	-1.24 (.11)	-
Student				
- attitude	.33 (.03)	.168	1.72 (.04)	.545
- gender	-.05 (.01)	-.058	-.10 (.01)	-.082
- language at	.06 (.02)	.033	.09 (.03)	.030
home	.06 (.5)	.030	-	-
- Mother born in				
SE-Asia	-	-	.10 (.05)	.056
Class	-	-	.22 (.06)	.077
- Math	-	-	-.17 (.08)	-.048
- Other subjects	.87 (.29)	.141	-	-
- Percentage	-.22 (.10)	-.108	-	-
boys	.31 (.16)	.073	1.59 (.17)	.230
- Percentage	.004 (.002)	.074	-	-
English-sp.				
- Percentage				
Australian				
- Class attitude				
- Class size				
School				
Variance				
- explained	6.5 %		52.7 %	
- school	0.0 %		1.5 %	
- class	26.5 %		6.5 %	
- student	67.0 %		39.3 %	
-2*Loglikelihood	2598.21		4766.93	

At the class level, it was found that teachers from other subjects than Science were perceived as more cooperative, but that no difference existed with respect to dominance. This adds to the mixed findings in earlier work, showing no consistent differences over studies. Class gender composition only had an effect on proximity: the more boys in the class, the less proximity was perceived. This finding supports that of an earlier study by Levy and colleagues (2003).

Ethnic make-up of the class also appeared to be relevant: the more English-speaking students in the class, the more dominant the teacher was perceived. This resembles outcomes at the student level. Also, the fewer students with Australian-born mothers, the more influence was perceived. Again, findings resembled those of the student level. Class attitude had a positive effect on both influence and proximity: students in highly motivated classes had a more favourable perception of their teacher.

Finally, class-size only had an effect on influence: the larger the class, the less dominant the teacher was perceived. Earlier studies only found an association between proximity and class size (e.g., Levy, et al., 1992; 2003). No school-level variables were found to be associated to students' perceptions. Similarly, no interaction effects were found.

Relative importance of single variables and all variables combined. Looking at the effect sizes reported in Table 3.5, it seemed that attitude was by far the most relevant variable in explaining variance in students' perceptions of their teachers' interpersonal behaviour. Its effect was two times stronger than that of most of the other variables. However, class composition variables such as percentage of students speaking English at home or having an Australian-born mother seemed also important. Gender, subject taught and class size was less relevant. However, in the case of class size, the picture may be misleading, since the coefficient provides the growth in influence per student: if a class, for example, contains five more students, this has an effect that is equal in size to that of (class) attitude.

Combined, the variables only explained a relatively small amount of variance (6.5 percent) in influence. This percentage is similar to that of earlier studies (e.g., Levy, et al., 2003) and suggests that other variables may be necessary in order to explain differences in perceptions between students and their classes. The model explained up to 11 percent of the variance at the class level, but only 7 percent of the variance at the student level.

A large amount of variance, more than half of it, was explained for proximity. This is a unique and surprising finding, as usually, similar amounts of variance are explained in influence and proximity. The model explained nearly all variance at the class level and about 30 percent of the variance at the class level. This is a very satisfying finding and adds value to this study as a source of validation for other studies.

7. Discussion

The study described in this chapter was the first of its kind to use multilevel analyses and dimension scores of the QTI to investigate differences in students' perceptions of teacher-student interpersonal behaviour. The study provides further support for many associations reported in earlier studies, such as those related to student gender, student and class ethnic background, and subject taught.

However, it should be noted that the study also differed from earlier work in a number of ways. Firstly, this study was amongst the first to investigate the effect of student and class attitude on students' perceptions. This variable proved to be of major influence and suggests researchers to include it in future investigations. The findings with respect to attitude also indicate the mutual effect that motivation and perception have on each other, which supports the system-oriented nature of communication in the classroom (Watzlawick, Beavin, & Jackson, 1967).

Secondly, the study found an effect of class size on the perception of influence, while earlier studies only reported effects on proximity. While the finding supports expectations - teachers need to be more strict and strong leaders to establish structure and order in a larger class - future research is needed to confirm its importance for influence.

Thirdly, this study managed to explaining large amounts of variance in ratings of proximity. On one hand, this might have been caused by the inclusion of subject-related attitude into the models. On the other hand, the finding is unique in studies using multilevel analyses on QTI scale or dimension scores, and might be related to sample characteristics or context. Future research is needed to also confirm the stability of this finding.

Unfortunately, the study was subject to some limitations. First, since most teachers participated with only one class (some participated with more classes), we were not able to distinguish between the teacher and class level. While expectations are that adding an extra level to the analyses would have altered the results only slightly, it might have showed some interesting findings with respect to stability of perceptions across classes of the same teacher. Secondly, in the models used in this study, no teacher variables such as experience, gender and ethnic background were included. Earlier research using the QTI has shown that these variables are also related to students' perceptions, and including them in the analyses may have provided even higher amounts of explained variance. Thirdly, there was a slight concern regarding validity of the QTI in this sample. While prior research showed the Australian QTI version to display adequate construct validity (den Brok, Fisher, et al., in press; Rickards, et al., 2003), in this study some association was found between the two dimensions, probably as a result of dislocation of the CS (understanding) and OD (admonishing) scales. It remains unknown to what extent these irregularities may exert an influence on the outcomes. Finally, the study only used quantitative (questionnaire) data. While such data enable researchers to describe and investigate more broad and comprehensive trends, it fails to explain in depth why these patterns are found, or how they may be caused. In the research from which this data set originated (e.g., Rickards & Fisher, 1997; Rickards, 1998) qualitative data were gathered by means of interviews with teachers and students. However, the interviewing was intended to support construct validity, rather than search for causal relationships with student or class characteristics.

The findings are significant for both researchers and teachers or policy makers. The results indicate that perceptions of the teacher may vary as a result of class size, ethnic composition and gender composition. Since students' perceptions of their teachers' interpersonal behaviour are strongly related to their achievement and motivation, the outcomes of this study suggest that, in order to obtain favourable perceptions (hence: student outcomes) of the classroom environment from all students, it is probably best to evenly distribute students in terms of characteristics such as gender and ethnicity. For teachers, it is important to realise that students from different backgrounds or gender perceive them differently. Knowledge of such differentiated perceptions may help teachers in establishing teaching methods that affirm all students (e.g., Nieto, 1996). For researchers, this study clearly shows the importance of student and class attitude in predicting students' perceptions of their learning environment and serves as a valuable comparative study for future research.

References

Blackburn, R. & Renwick, S. J. (1996). Rating scales for measuring the interpersonal circle in forensic psychiatric patients. *Psychological Assessment, 8* (1), 76-84.

Brekelmans, M., Holvast, A., & van Tartwijk, J. (1992). Changes in teacher communication styles during the professional career. *The Journal of Classroom Interaction, 27*, 13-22.

Brekelmans, M., Wubbels, T., & den Brok, P. (2002). Teacher experience and the teacher-student relationship in the classroom environment. In S. C. Goh & M. S. Khine (Eds.), *Studies in educational learning environments: An international perspective* (pp. 73-100). Singapore: New World Scientific.

den Brok, P. (2001). *Teaching and student outcomes.* Utrecht, the Netherlands: W. C. C.

den Brok, P., Fisher, D., Brekelmans, M., Rickards, T., Wubbels, T., & Levy, J. (2003, March). *Students' Perceptions of Secondary Science Teachers' Interpersonal Behavior in six countries: The cross national validity of the QTI.* Paper presented at the annual meeting of the National Association for Research in Science Teaching, Philadelphia.

den Brok, P., Levy, J., Rodriguez, R., & Wubbels, T. (2002). Perceptions of Asian-American and Hispanic-American teachers and their students on interpersonal communication style. *Teaching and Teacher Education, 18*, 447-467.

den Brok, P., Levy, J., Wubbels, T., & Rodriguez, M. (2003). Cultural influences on students' perceptions of videotaped lessons. *International Journal of Intercultural Relations, 27* (3), 355-374.

den Brok, P., Rickards, T., & Fisher, D. L. (2003, August). *What does the Australian teacher look like? An Australian typology for teacher-student interpersonal behaviour.* Paper presented at the annual meeting of the Western Australian Institute for Educational Research, Perth.

Brown, R. (1965). *Social psychology.* London: Collier-MacMillan.

Dart B., Burnett, P., Boulton-Lewis, G., Campbell, J., Smith, D., & McCrindle, A. (1999). Classroom environment and students' approaches to learning. *Learning Environments Research, 2*, 137-156.

Dunkin, M. J. & Biddle, B. J. (1974). *The study of teaching.* New York: Rhinehart & Winston.

Evans, H. & Fisher, D. L. (2000). Cultural differences in students' perceptions of science teachers' interpersonal behaviour. *Australian Science Teachers Journal, 46* (2), 9-18.

Fabrigar, L. R., Visser, P. S., & Browne, M. W. (1997). Conceptual and methodological issues in testing the circumplex structure of data in personality and social psychology. *Personality and Social Psychology Review, 1*, 184-203.

Ferguson, P. D. & Fraser, B. J. (1998). Changing in learning environment during the transition from primary to secondary school. *Learning Environments Research, 1*, 369-383.

Fisher, D. L., Fraser, B. J., & Rickards, T. W. (1997, April). *Gender and cultural differences in teacher-student interpersonal behaviour.* Paper presented at the annual meeting of the American Education Research Association, Chicago.

Fisher, D., Fraser, B., & Wubbels, T. (1993). Associations between school learning environment and teacher interpersonal behaviour in the classroom. In T. Wubbels & J. Levy (Eds.), *Do you know what you look like?* (pp.103-112). London: The Falmer Press.

Fisher, D., Henderson, D., & Fraser, B. (1995). Interpersonal behaviour in senior high school biology classes. *Research in Science Education, 25*, 125-133.

Fisher, D. L. & Rickards, T. (2000). Teacher-student interpersonal behaviour as perceived by Science teachers and their students. In D. Fisher & J. Yang (Eds.), *Improving classroom research through international cooperation* (pp. 391-398). Taipei: National Taiwan Normal University.

Foa, U. G. (1961). Convergence in the analysis of the structure of interpersonal behaviour. *Psychological Review, 68*, 341-353.

Fraser, B. J. (1981). *TOSRA: Test of Science-Related Attitudes Handbook.* Hawthorn: The Australian Council for Educational Research Limited.

Gaines, S. O., Panter, A. T., Lyde, M. D., Steers, W. N., Rusbult, C. E., Cox, C. L., & Wexler, M. O. (1997). Evaluating the circumplexity of interpersonal traits and the manifestation of interpersonal traits in interpersonal trust. *Journal of Personality and Social Psychology, 73*, 610-623.

Goh, S. C. & Fraser, B. J. (1995, April). *Learning environment and student outcomes in primary mathematics classrooms in Singapore.*

Paper presenting at the annual meeting of the American Education Research Association, San Francisco.

Goldstein, H. (1995). *Multilevel statistical models.* London: Edward Arnold.

Gurtman, M. B. & Pincus, A. L. (2000). Interpersonal adjective scales: confirmation of circumplex structure from multiple perspectives. *Personality and Social Psychology Bulletin, 26,* 374-384.

Henderson, D. G. (1995). *A study of the classroom and laboratory environments and student attitude and achievement in senior secondary Biology classes.* Unpublished doctoral dissertation, Curtin University, Perth, Australia.

Hox, J. J. (1995). *Applied multilevel analysis.* Amsterdam: TT Publicaties.

Leary, T. (1957). *An interpersonal diagnosis of personality.* New York: Ronald Press Company.

Levy, J., den Brok, P., Wubbels, T., & Brekelmans, M. (2003). Students' perceptions of interpersonal aspects of the learning environment. *Learning Environments Research, 6,* 5-36.

Levy, J., Wubbels, T., Brekelmans, M., & Morganfield, B. (1997). Language and cultural factors in students' perceptions of teacher communication style. International *Journal of Intercultural Relationships, 21,* 1, 29-56.

Levy, J., Wubbels, Th., & Brekelmans, M. (1996). *Cultural factors in students' and teachers' perceptions of the learning environment.* Paper presented at the annual meeting of the American Educational Research Association, San Francisco.

Levy, J., Wubbels, Th., & Brekelmans, M. (1992). Student and teacher characteristics and perceptions of teacher communication style. *Journal of Classroom Interaction, 27,* 23-29.

Lonner, W. J. (1980). The search for psychological universals. In H. C. Triandis & W. W. Lambert (Eds.), Handbook of cross cul tural psychology (vol.1) (pp. 143-204). Boston: Allyn and Bacon.

Luyten, H. & De Jong, R. (1998). Parallel classes: differences and similarities. Teacher effects and school effects in secondary schools. *School Effectiveness and School Improvement, 9,* (4), 437-473.

Muthén, B. (1994). Multilevel covariance structure analysis. *Sociological Methods & Research,* 22, 338-354.

Nieto, S. (1996). Affirming diversity: *The sociopolitical context of multicultural education.* New York: Longman.

Pianta, R. & Nimetz, S. L. (1993). *The student-teacher relationship scale: Results of a pilot study (research reports).* Harrison, VA: James Madison University. (ERIC Document reproduction Service No. Ed. 308961)

Rawnsley, D. & Fisher, D. L. (1997, January). *Using personal and class forms of a learning environment questionnaire in mathematics classrooms.* Paper presented at the International Conference on Science, Mathematics & Technology Education, Hanoi, Vietnam.

Rickards, T. (1998). *The relationship of teacher-student interpersonal behaviour with student sex, cultural background and student outcomes.* Unpublished doctoral dissertation, Curtin University, Perth, Australia.

Rickards, T. & Fisher, D. L. (1997, July). *A report of research into student attitude and teacher student interpersonal behaviour in a large sample of Australian secondary mathematics classrooms.* Paper presented at the annual meeting of the Mathematics Education Research Group of Australia, Rotorua, New Zealand.

Slater, P. E. (1962). Parental behaviour and the personality of the child. *Journal of Genetical* Psychology, *101*, 53-68.

Somers, T., Brekelmans, M., & Wubbels, Th. (1997, August). *Development of student teachers on the teacher-pupil relationship in the classroom.* Paper presented at the bi-annual meeting of the European Association of Research on Learning and Instruction, Athens, Greece.

Strack, S. (1996). Special series: Interpersonal theory and the interpersonal circumplex: Timothy Leary's Legacy, *Journal of Personality Assessment, 66*, 211-307.

Tracey, T. J. (1994). An examination of complementarity of interpersonal behaviour. *Journal of Personality and Social Psychology, 67*, 864-878.

Tracey, T. J. & Schneider, P. L. (1995). An evaluation of the circular structure of the checklist of interpersonal transactions and the checklist of psychotherapy transactions. *Journal of Counseling Psychology*, 42, 496-507.

Veenman, S. (1984). Problems of beginning teachers. *Review of Educational Research, 54*, 143-178.

Waldrip, B. G. & Fisher, D. L. (1999, November). *Differences in country and metropolitan students' perceptions of teacher-student interactions and classroom learning environments.* Paper presented at the annual meeting of the Australasian Association for Research in Education, Melbourne.

Watzlawick, P., Beavin, J. H., & Jackson, D. (1967). *The pragmatics of human communication.* New York: Norton.

Waxman, H. C. & Huang, S. L. (1998). Classroom learning environments in urban elementary, middle and high schools. *Learning Environments Research, 1,* 95-113.

Wubbels, T. T. & Brekelmans, M. (1998). The teacher factor in the social climate of the classroom. In B. J. Fraser & K. G. Tobin (Eds.), *International Handbook of Science Education* (pp. 565-580). London: Kluwer Academic Publishers.

Wubbels, T., Brekelmans, M., & Hermans, J. (1987). Teacher behaviour: an important aspect of the learning environment. In B. J. Fraser (Ed.), *The study of learning environments, Volume 3* (pp.10-25). Perth: Curtin University.

Wubbels, T., Créton, H. A., & Hooymayers, H. P. (1985). *Discipline problems of beginning teachers, interactional behaviour mapped out.* Paper presented at the American Educational Research Association annual meeting, Chicago. Abstracted in Resources in Education, 20, 12, p. 153, ERIC document 260040.

Wubbels, T., Créton, H. A., & Hooymayers, H. P. (1987). A school-based teacher induction programme. *European Journal of Teacher Education*, *10,* 81-94.

Wubbels, T. & Levy, J. (1991). A comparison of interpersonal behaviour of Dutch and American teachers. *International Journal of Intercultural Relations, 15*, 1-18.

Wubbels, T. & Levy, J. (1993). *Do you know what you look like?* London: The Falmer Press.

Chapter 4

IMPROVING THE CLASSROOM LABORATORY LEARNING ENVIRONMENT BY USING TEACHERS' AND STUDENTS' PERCEPTIONS

Avi Hofstein
The Weizmann Institute of Science
Israel

This chapter focuses on the science laboratory as a unique mode of instruction, and learning environment and is composed of five sections. The first section is an introduction that mainly reviews past and current research and literature regarding the science laboratory as a key feature in science teaching and learning. The second section describes the uniqueness of the laboratory in terms of teaching and learning. Also, in this section, I elaborate my belief that the laboratory is a unique learning environment. The third section briefly discusses the nature of long-term curriculum development (like the Israeli system) that allows for the use of results from one research study to be used in a new trial version i.e. improving the learning environment. The third section is divided into two subsections: the first is devoted to a review of the literature regarding the use of the SLEI in Australia and in Israel; the second part is a description of details the use of the measure over a period of about 10 years using both students' and teachers' perceptions to improve the chemistry laboratory learning environment and its educational effectiveness. Research findings are presented that helped us in an improvement of the pedagogy and educational effectiveness of the laboratory.

1. Introduction

Laboratory activities have long had a distinctive and central role in the science curriculum and science educators have suggested that many benefits accrue from engaging students in science laboratory activities (Lazarowitz & Tamir, 1994; Lunetta, 1998; Lunetta, Hofstein, & Clough, in press; Hofstein & Lunetta, 1982, 2004; Pickering, 1980; Tobin, 1990).

Since the end of the 19th century, when schools began to teach science systematically, the science laboratory has become a distinctive feature of science education. For more than a century, laboratory experiences were purported to promote central science education goals including the enhancement of students' understanding of concepts in science and its applications; scientific practical skills and problem solving abilities; scientific 'habits of mind'; understanding of how science and scientists work; and interest and motivation. Hofstein and Walberg (1995) suggested, for example, that inquiry-type science laboratories are central to learning science, since students are involved in the process of conceiving problems and scientific questions, formulating hypotheses, designing experiments, gathering and analyzing data, and drawing conclusions about scientific problems or phenomena.

Now, at the beginning of the twenty-first century, we are entering a new era of reform in science education. Both the content and pedagogy of science learning and teaching are being scrutinized, and new standards intended to shape and rejuvenate science education are emerging (National Research Council, 1996). The *National Science Education Standards* (NRC, 1996) reaffirm the conviction that inquiry is central to the achievement of scientific literacy. The *National Science Education Standards* used the term inquiry in two ways (Bybee 2000; Lunetta, 1998): (1) inquiry as *content understanding,* in which students have opportunities to construct concepts, patterns, and to create meaning about an idea in order to explain what they experience; and (2) inquiry in terms of *skills* and *abilities.* Under the category of abilities and skills, Bybee (2000) includes identifying and posing scientifically oriented questions, forming hypotheses, designing and conducting scientific investigations, formulating and revising scientific explanations, and communicating and defending scientific arguments. It is suggested that many of these abilities and skills are in alignment with those that characterize inquiry-type laboratory work, an activity that puts the student in the centre of the learning process. There is no doubt that the laboratory in general and the inquiry laboratory in particular are very challenging to both teachers and students (Kracjik, Mamlok, & Hug, 2001).

2. The Science Laboratory: A Unique Learning Environment

Kelly and Lister (1969), based on comprehensive research findings, suggested that the science laboratory is a unique mode of teaching and learning and that the abilities of students in the laboratory are only slightly correlated with their abilities in other non-practical learning experiences. Support for this was provided at a later stage by Tamir, (1972) and more recently by Yeany, Larusa and Hale (1989). A study on modes of learning and teaching in the context of chemistry was conducted by Ben-Zvi, Hofstein, Kempa, and Samuel (1977). The main goal of this study was to identify relationships between modes of learning in the chemistry laboratory and other modes of learning that prevail in high school chemistry.

Based on these studies it is fairly established that the laboratory is a unique environment regarding learning, teaching and assessing students in the natural sciences. In their 1982 review, Hofstein and Lunetta pointed out the importance of examining the uniqueness of the science laboratory-learning environment in research. They wrote:

> Since creating a healthy learning environment is an important goal for many contemporary science educators, there is a need for further research that will assess how time spent in laboratory activities and how the nature of students' activities in the laboratory affect the learning environment (p. 212).

The science laboratory is central in our attempt to vary the learning environment in which students develop their understanding of scientific concepts, science inquiry skills, and perceptions of science. The science laboratory, a unique learning environment, is a setting in which students can work cooperatively in small groups to investigate scientific phenomena. Hofstein and Lunetta (1982) and Lazarowitz and Tamir (1994) suggested that laboratory activities have the potential to enhance constructive social relationships as well as positive attitudes and cognitive growth. The social environment in a school laboratory is usually less formal than in a conventional classroom; thus, the laboratory offers opportunities for productive, cooperative interactions among students and with the teacher. These, it is suggested, have the potential to promote an especially positive learning environment. It should be noted, that the learning environment that exists in the science laboratory depends markedly on the nature of the activities conducted, the expectations of the teacher (and the students), and the nature of assessment. It is influenced, in part, by the materials, apparatus, resources and physical setting, but the learning environment that results is much more a function of the climate and expectations for learning, the collaboration and social interactions between students and teacher, and finally the nature of the inquiry that is pursued in the laboratory.

3. Opportunities for Long-term Developments and Implementation: The Israeli Case

More than 50 years ago, Tyler (1949) suggested that evaluation and curriculum development (curriculum research) must be closely integrated in the continuous cycle of curriculum planning, development, and implementation. According to Leithwood (1991) and Leithwood and Montgomery (1980), evaluation of implementation of curricula may assist in making accountability and management decisions. Accountability decisions are aided when information is provided about whether, or the extent to which, an innovation has been put into practice according to design; whether the outcomes were as planned whether what was delivered or paid for is being undertaken as planned. In addition, implementation evaluation may help specify the practices implied by the innovation; identify those conditions under which implementation is likely to succeed; explicate problems likely to be encountered and strategies available for their resolution; and determine the feasibility of innovation implementation.

Many of the curricular innovations developed during the 1960s tended to integrate small-scale evaluation (research) activities. These were mainly conducted following standard procedures. In general, the impact of these evaluation studies on further developments, decisions, and the enhancement of implementation initiatives were rather limited. Tamir (1985) suggested that one of the reasons for this was that, in general, the information resulting from assessment and evaluation was obtained only late in the curricular process. Whether the educational system is centralized or decentralized, it is clear that in order to foster innovation there is a need to provide for a systemic approach. This approach is characterized by longitudinal, dynamic, and progressive refinements of program development, school and classroom organization, teacher professional development, assessment, and cognitive research. All these aspects are considered and activated together under one integrated institutional roof (Ganiel, 1995). The settings that prevail in the Department of Science Teaching, The

Weizmann Institute of Science in Israel enabled us to implement a long-term systemic approach to the development and implementation of learning materials and pedagogical interventions in the sciences to be used in the Israeli educational system. This approach ensured that results of a certain research study could be used and implemented for the development of the next generation of curricular materials. Changes that were conducted in the approach to learning in the chemistry laboratory were highly based on opportunities that we had to use the results revealed from one study to make radical changes in another study conducted several years later.

4. Assessing the Classroom Laboratory Learning Environment: Students' Perceptions

4.1 The Science Laboratory Environment Inventory (SLEI):

In 1982 Hofstein and Lunetta wrote that:

> Because creating [a] healthy learning environment is an important goal for many contemporary educators, there is a need for more research that will assess how the time spent in laboratory work and how specific activities in the laboratory affect the learning environment. It will be desirable to study further the effects of different modes of practical work on the learning environment. (p. 212*).*

The need to assess the students' perceptions in the science laboratory was first approached seriously by a group of science educators in Australia (Fraser, McRobbie, & Giddings, 1993), who developed and validated the *Science Laboratory Environment Inventory* (SLEI) (for more details about the instrument see Table 4.1). This instrument, consisting of eight learning environment dimensions (scales); Student Cohesiveness, Open-Endedness, Integration, Rule Clarity, Material Environment, Teacher Supportiveness, Involvement, and Organization was found to be sensitive to different approaches to laboratory work, for example, high inquiry or low inquiry and in different science disciplines such as biology or chemistry laboratory learning environments (Fisher, Harrison, Henderson, & Hofstein, 1999; Hofstein, Lazarowitz, & Cohen, 1996).

Table 4.1. Descriptive Information of the Scales of the Science Laboratory Environment
Inventory (SLEI)

Sub-scale name	No. of items	Description (the extent to which)	Sample item
Teacher Supportiveness	9	Teacher/instructor is helpful and shows concern for all student	The teacher is concerned about students' safety during laboratory sessions (+)
Involvement	9	Students participate actively and attentively in laboratory activities and discussions	During laboratory group work students leave it to their partners to do all the work (-)
Student Cohesiveness	9	Students know, help and are supportive of one another	Students in this laboratory class get along well as a group.(-)
Open-Endedness	8	Laboratory activities emphasize an open-ended, divergent, individualized approach to experimentation	We know the results that we are supposed to get before we commence a laboratory activity (-)
Integration	9	Laboratory activities are integrated with non-laboratory and theory classes	We use the theory from our regular science class session during laboratory activities (+)
Organization	9	Laboratory activities are clearly defined and well organized	There is confusion during laboratory classes (-)
Rule Clarity	8	Behavior in formal rules	There is a recognized way of laboratory work (+)
Material Environment	9	Laboratory equipment and materials are adequate	The laboratory is too crowded when we are doing experiments (-)

The latter, confirmed the reliability and validity of the SLEI in an investigation of the association between students' perceptions of the biology laboratory learning environment and students' outcomes. Moreover, they suggested that differences between the perceptions of laboratories in of physics, chemistry, and biology resulted from the different experiences provided for the students in these laboratories. Fisher, Henderson, and Fraser (1997) have indicated significant correlations between students' perceptions of aspects of their learning environment and the students' attitudes and achievements.

The SLEI also has been used in several studies conducted in different parts of the world. One comparative study examined students' perceptions in six countries: UK, Nigeria, Australia, Israel, USA, and Canada (Fraser & McRobbie, 1995). Fraser, McRobbie, and Giddings (1993) in Australia, found that students' perceptions of the laboratory learning environment accounted for significant amounts of the variance of learning beyond that due to differences in their abilities.

4.2 Using students' and teachers' perceptions to improve the science laboratory learning environment

The SLEI has been used several times in Israel in the last 10 years in an attempt to probe into students' perceptions regarding the science (chemistry) laboratory learning environment and to improve instruction (and learning) in the science laboratory. Since the instrument was found to be sensitive to different laboratory settings and to different modes of instruction it was used in Israel in 1995 in order to assess the educational effectiveness of chemistry and biology laboratories used in the country (Hofstein, Lazarowitz, & Cohen, 1996). They used a Hebrew version of the SLEI for comparing students' perceptions of the *actual* (prevailing learning environment) and *preferred* (the learning environment students would like to have) of laboratory classes used in the context of chemistry and biology learning in upper secondary schools.

The biology curriculum that existed (at that time) in schools in Israel, was the Hebrew adaptation of the Biological Sciences Curriculum Study (BSCS) yellow version (BSCS, 1963). In this curriculum, biological concepts and principles related to major biological themes were taught and learned using an inquiry approach. The mode of instruction integrated students' reading with practical work and field exercises, discussions, analysis of research papers and individual projects (Tamir, 1976). More specifically, in regard to the laboratory, many of the concepts and biological principles were reached after performing experiments in the laboratory, and prior to the learning of the related subjects in the biology classroom.

The chemistry curriculum on the other hand used in the upper secondary schools was the *Chemistry a Challenge* (Ben-Zvi & Silberstein, 1986). This program was developed on the basis of an intensive and comprehensive study of students' learning difficulties and misconceptions in the context of their chemistry learning. Thus, the program was developed with the goal in mind of overcoming these difficulties. In regard to students' practical work, it was designed to:

(1) help in explaining concepts; (2) familiarize students with the properties of many substances and compounds; and (3) help students to understand the consecutive steps used to form a specific scientific theory. Generally speaking, these tasks in the chemistry laboratory are usually clear, 'close-ended' and are strictly related to the concept being taught at that time in the chemistry classroom.

In both the chemistry and biology groups, students expressed higher expectations for their preferred laboratory learning environment than for the actual environment experienced. More specifically, they claimed that they need more teacher support and that they want to be more involved in the learning process. Altogether it was found that students would like their classroom laboratory learning environment to be more open-ended, and be more integrated in the subject matter, activities to be more organized, rules to be clearer, and to obtain a better provision of learning materials (equipment and chemicals).

Similar information could be used effectively by both curriculum developers as well as teachers in attempting to improve the classroom laboratory learning environment. In other words, if the results of the actual classroom-laboratory-learning-environment are indeed outcomes of the instruction and procedures used by teachers in their laboratories, one may hypothesize that the preferred changes in the learning environment can only come about if the existing pedagogic procedures are altered. This, in fact, was a call for the various curriculum developers to re-structure the laboratory program in high school chemistry.

Five years later, partially based on the results that were obtained from the 1995 study and from studies conducted as part of development of leadership among chemistry teachers (Hofstein, Carmi & Ben-Zvi, 2003), the chemistry group in the Department of Science Teaching, developed a new laboratory program to be implemented in grades 11 and 12. This program was titled: *Inquiry in the Chemistry Laboratory*. (More details about this approach can be found in Hofstein, Shore, & Kipnis, 2004; Hofstein, Navon, Kipnis, & Mamlok-Namman, in press).

It is beyond the scope of this chapter to detail all the features and characteristics of the inquiry laboratory and its implementation in the chemistry laboratory but some information regarding its features is warranted. About 100 inquiry-type experiments were developed and implemented in 11th and 12th grade chemistry classes in Israel (for more details about the development procedure, assessment of students' achievement and progress, and the professional development of the chemistry teachers, see Hofstein, Shore, & Kipnis, 2004). Almost all the experiments were integrated into the framework of the key-concepts taught in high-school chemistry, namely, acids-bases, stoichiometry, oxidation-reduction, bonding, energy, chemical-equilibrium, and the rate of reactions. These experiments have been implemented in the school chemistry laboratory in Israel for the last five years. As previously mentioned (Hofstein, Shore, & Kipnis, 2004), under these conditions, such variables as the professional development of teachers, the continuous assessment of students' progress in terms of achievement in the laboratory, and the allocation of time and facilities (materials and equipment) for conducting inquiry-type experiments were controlled.

Typically, in the chemistry laboratory the students perform the experiments collaboratively in small groups (three to four), by following the instructions in the laboratory manual (see example in Table 4.2).

Table 4.2 presents the various stages that each of the groups undergo in order to accomplish the inquiry task. In the first phase (the pre-inquiry phase), the students are asked to conduct the experiment based on specific instructions. This phase is largely 'close-ended', in which the students are asked to conduct the experiment based on specific instructions given in the laboratory manual. Thus, this phase provides the students with very limited inquiry-type experiences. The 'inquiry phase' (the second phase) is where the students are involved in more 'open-ended-type' experiences such as; asking relevant questions, hypothesizing, choosing a question for further investigation, planning an experiment to find an answer to the question chosen for further investigation, conducting the experiment (including observations), and finally analyzing the findings and arriving at conclusions. It is thought that this phase allows the students to learn and experience science with greater understanding and to practise their metacognitive abilities. Moreover, it provides them with the opportunity to construct their knowledge by actually doing scientific work. In the process of conducting these experiments, the students are involved in:

- asking relevant questions concerning the phenomena that they have observed;
- formulating a hypothesis that is in alignment with the suggested questions;
- choosing an appropriate research question for further investigation; and

■   planning an experiment in order to investigate this question.

Table 4.2. A Detailed Description of a Typical Inquiry-type Laboratory

Phases in the experiment	Abilities and skills
Pre-inquiry	
■ Insert the two solids, A and B, into the plastic bag and mix them by shaking. ■ Pour 10 ml of water into the small glass. ■ Put the glass with the water inside the bag (be careful to avoid any contact between the water and the solids). ■ Put a thermometer inside the bag, to measure the temperature of the solids.	■ Conducting an experiment
■ Tie the bag carefully at its upper part (the thermometer is in the bag). ■ Turn over the glass and let the water completely wet the solids. ■ Record all your observations and answer the questionnaire that is enclosed.	■ Observing and recording observations ■ Asking questions and hypothesizing
The inquiry phase of the Experiment *1. Hypothesizing* ■ Ask relevant questions. Choose one question for further investigation. ■ Formulate a hypothesis that is aligned with your chosen question.	■ Planning an experiment ■ Conducting the planned experiment
2. Planning an experiment ■ Plan an experiment to investigate the question. ■ Present a plan to conduct an experiment. ■ Ask the teacher to provide you with equipment and materials to conduct the experiment. ■ Conduct the experiment that you proposed. ■ Observe and note clearly your observations. ■ Discuss with your group whether your hypothesis was accepted or you must reject it.	■ Analyzing the results, asking further questions, and presenting the results in a scientific manner

As an integrated part of the evaluation of the implementation of this program we conducted a comparative study during the academic years 2000 and 2001 focusing on the students' perception of the classroom laboratory learning environment (Hofstein, Levi Nahum, & Shore, 2001). In this study, the perceptions of two groups of students regarding the classroom laboratory learning environment were assessed and statistically compared. The first group consisted of students who were involved in the inquiry laboratory and the second group (control) consisted of students who were involved in laboratory activities that are clear, 'close-ended', and directly related to the concepts taught at that time in the regular classroom (i.e. non-inquiry laboratory experiences). The two groups were compared using both a quantitative method (using the SLEI) and a qualitative method, namely structured interviews. Students were given two versions of the SLEI questionnaire, namely, the *actual* version in which students were asked to present their perceptions regarding the existing learning environment and the preferred version in which they were asked to present their expected classroom learning environment.

Our analysis regarding the students' perceptions of their chemistry laboratory learning environment clearly demonstrated that students who were involved in inquiry-type investigation found the laboratory learning environment to be more open-ended, and more integrated with a conceptual framework than did students in a control group (a group of students who studied chemistry using the Chemistry a Challenge program described in Hofstein, Lazarowitz, & Cohen, 1996). Moreover, it was found that the gap between the actual and the preferred learning environment on the various scales of the SLEI was significantly smaller in the inquiry group than in the control group. Also, with regard to the actual and preferred learning environment in the chemistry laboratory, the most predominant and statistically significant differences were observed on the Open-Endedness and the Involvement scales, with the inquiry group having much more favorable perceptions than the control group. We observed that students perceived that they were more involved in the learning process and found the procedures more open-ended. These findings align with recent trends of enhancing the involvement of students in the learning process and in constructing their knowledge of scientific concepts and processes. A comparison of actual-preferred differences in a laboratory learning environment revealed that integration of the laboratory experiences with other pedagogical interventions and classroom instructional techniques was associated with a significant reduction in the magnitude of the differences. In other words, the inquiry group found the actual learning environment significantly more aligned with their preferred environment compared with the control group. The value of integration with the other experiences is well documented in the literature. In recent years there is a growing awareness that learning is conceptualized and that learners construct knowledge by solving genuine and meaningful problems (Brown, Collins, & Duguid, 1989). For a graphical presentation of the actual and preferred perceptions of the laboratory learning environment see Figure 4.1.

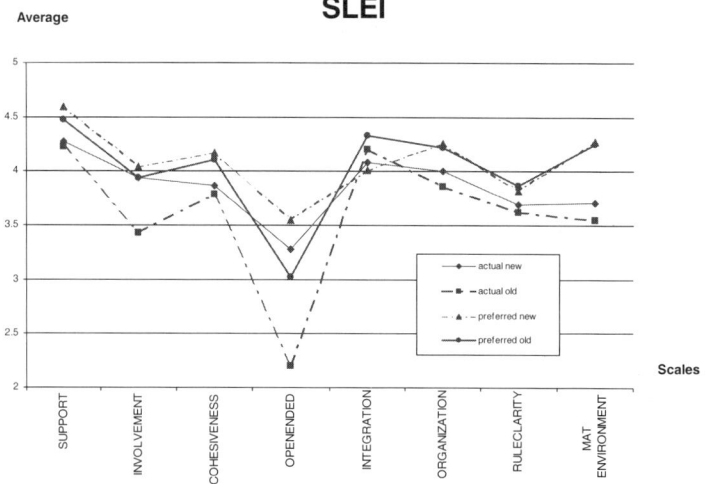

Figure 4.1. Comparison of the means of the SLEI scales (actual and preferred) regarding inquiry and traditional chemistry laboratories.

Similar results regarding students' perceptions were obtained from the interviews conducted among a small sample of students who participated in the program the following is a small sample of the comments that were made regarding their laboratory experiences:

- It gave me an opportunity to develop independent thinking.

- The experiments were connected to the topics and concepts that were discussed in the chemistry classroom; thus it helped me to better understand what is going on.
- I found out that the most difficult part of the inquiry exercise was the design of the experimental setting and the asking of relevant questions. However, it was challenging. I enjoyed sharing ideas and cooperating with my peers in the group.
- We got all the materials we needed.
- The teacher always around to provide help.

The inclusion of the results of the interviews with students in this study could be regarded as a method of validating the SLEI for its sensitivity to different instructional techniques used in the science laboratory classroom.

Similarly, interviews were conducted with teachers. An indication of satisfaction with the program and a feeling that introducing inquiry approaches to the chemistry laboratory had a positive impact on the learning environment were revealed from interviewing several participating chemistry teachers:

- It matches perfectly with my way of thinking regarding how I teach and how my students learn.
- I have flexibility in selecting inquiry experiments so that they will be tailored to my students' abilities and interests
- My students enjoy what they do. I believe that these experiences improve my students' attitude towards chemistry.
- The inquiry laboratory provided me with a new method to assess the progress of my students.
- It helped me in varying the instruction of high school chemistry.
- I feel that the inquiry laboratory increased my students' motivation to learn chemistry.

5. Discussion and Summary

Using students' perceptions as well as the teachers' perceptions gave us clear and profound evidence that the changes that were introduced to the chemistry curriculum resulted in an improvement in the classroom laboratory learning environment. Based on our study and on the literature, clearly, if students' positive perceptions of the science laboratory learning environment, i.e. cooperative learning, collaboration, and developing a community of inquiry are among the important intended outcomes of school laboratory experiences, then these outcomes should be assessed by teachers and researchers as a regular part of course evaluation. Also, the Science Laboratory Environment Inventory could be used by teachers as part of an action research study intended to examine the effects of a new laboratory teaching approach or strategy and as part of improving instruction.

Reforming the learning (and teaching) in the laboratory over a long period of time, could only take place in an academic establishment in which all the facets that construct the curricular framework (development, implementation, research, and evaluation) are conducted under the same roof. Very often, the knowledge accumulated within a given project does not contribute to future related developments. In particular, assessment results are not integrated into the continuous improvement of the innovation and implementation. Since they become available long after the termination of the developmental stage, they can contribute significantly to our scientific knowledge, but often do not have a practical impact. In addition, the various components of the curricular framework are often carried out by different educational agents. As a result, the coordination and integration of information and actions are severely impaired.

In this chapter, we have demonstrated that long-term curricular establishments (in the academia) can benefit from the fact that results obtained from one research study can be applied in another study (or educational reform) provided that the curricular process is conducted systematically and dynamically over a long period of time.

References

Ben-Zvi, R., Hofstein, A., Kempa, R. F., & Samuel, D. (1977). Modes of instruction in high school chemistry. *Journal of Research in Science Teaching, 14*, 433-439.

Ben -Zvi, R. & Silberstein, J. (1986). *Chemistry a challenge.* Rehovot: The Weizmann Institute of Science. (In Hebrew).

Biological Sciences Curriculum Study (BSCS) (1963). *Biological sciences: Inquiry into life.* New York: Harcourt, Brace & World.

Brown, J. S., Collins, A., & Duguid, P. (1989). Situated cognition and the culture of learning. *Educational Researcher, 18*, 32-41.

Bybee, R. (2000). Teaching science as inquiry, In J. Minstrel & E. H. Van Zee (Eds.), *Inquiring into inquiry learning and teaching in science* (pp. 20-46). Washington DC: American Association for the Advancement of Science (AAAS).

Fisher, D., Harrison, A., Henderson, D., & Hofstein, A. (1999). Laboratory learning environments and practical tasks in senior secondary science classes. *Research in Science Education, 28*, 353-363.

Fisher, D., Henderson, D., & Fraser, B. J. (1997). Laboratory environments and student outcomes in senior high school biology. *The American Biology Teacher, 59*, 214-219.

Fraser, B. & McRobbie, C. J. (1995). Science laboratory classroom environments at schools and universities: A cross-national study. *Educational Research and Evaluation, 1*, 289-317.

Fraser, B., McRobbie, C. J., & Giddings, G. J. (1993). Development and cross-national validation of a laboratory classroom instrument for senior high school students. *Science Education, 77*, 1-24.

Ganiel, U. (1995). Fostering change in science education: Creation, implementation, evaluation, and research-the Israeli experience. In A. Hofstein, B. Eylon, & G. J. Giddings (Eds.). *Science education: From theory to practice.* Rehovot: The Weizmann Institute of Science.

Hofstein, A., Lazarowitz, R., & Cohen, I. (1996). *Research in Science and Technological Education*, 14, 103-116.

Hofstein, A., Levi-Nahum, T., & Shore, R. (2001). Assessment of the learning environment of inquiry-type laboratories in high school chemistry. *Learning Environments Research*, 4, 193-207.

Hofstein, A. & Lunetta, V. N. (1982). The role of the laboratory in science teaching: Neglected aspects of research. *Review of Educational Research*, 52 (2), 201-217.

Hofstein, A. & Lunetta, V. N. (2004). The laboratory in science education: Foundation for the 21st century. *Science Education, 88*, 28-54.

Hoftsein, A., Navon, O., Kipnis, M., & Mamlok-Naaman, R. (2005). Developing students ability to ask more and better questions resulting from inquiry-type chemistry laboratories. *Journal of Research in Science Teaching, 42* (7), 791-806.

Hofstein, A., Shore, R., & Kipnis, M. (2004). Providing high school chemistry students with opportunities to develop learning skills in an inquiry-type laboratory-a case study. *International Journal of Science Education, 26,* 47-62.

Hofstein, A. & Walberg, H. (1995). Effective Instructional Strategies in Science. In: B. Fraser & H. Walberg (Eds.), *Improving science education*. The National Society for the Study of Education (NSSE) Yearbook.

Kelly, P. J. & Lister, R. E. (1969). Assessing practical abilities in Nuffield A-Level biology. In J. F. E. Eggleston & J. F. Kerr (Eds.), *Studies in assessment*. London: English Universities Press.

Krajcik, J., Mamlok, R., & Hug, B. (2001). Modern content and the enterprise of science: Science education in the twentieth century. In L. Corno. (Ed.), *Education across a century: The centennial volume* (pp. 205-238). NSSE: 100th Yearbook of the National Society for the Study of Education. Chicago: University of Chicago Press.

Lazarowitz, R. & Tamir, P. (1994). Research on using laboratory instruction in science, in D. L. Gabel (Ed.), *Handbook of research on science teaching and learning* (pp. 94-130). New-York: Macmillan.

Leithwood, K. A. (1991). Implementation evaluation. In A. Lewy (Ed.). *The international encyclopedia of curriculum,* (pp. 444-450), Oxford: Pergamon Press.

Leithwood, K. A. & Montgomery, D. J. (1980). Evaluating program implementation. *Evaluation Reviews, 4,* 193-214.

Lunetta, V. N. (1998). The school science laboratory: Historical perspectives and centers for contemporary teaching. In B. J. Fraser & K. G. Tobin (Eds.), *International handbook of science education.* (pp. 249-264). Dordrecht: Kluwer Academic Publishers.

Lunetta, V. N., Hofstein, A., & Clough, M, P. Learning and teaching in the school science laboratory: An analysis of research, theory, and practice. In N. Lederman & S. Abell (Eds.), *Handbook of Research on Science Education*, Lawrence Erlbaum, (in press).

National Research Council (1996). *National Science Education Standards*. National Academy Press: Washington, D.C.

Pickering, M. (1980). Are laboratory courses a waste of time? *Chronicle of Higher Education, 19,* 44-50.

Tamir, P. (1972). The practical mode a distinct mode of performance, *Journal of Biological Education, 6,* 175-182.

Tamir, P. (1976). The Israeli high school biology-a case curriculum adaptation, *Curriculum Theory Network*, *5*, 305-315.

Tamir, P. (1985). The potential and actual roles of evaluators. In P. Tamir (Ed.), *The role of evaluators in curriculum development.* London: Croom-Helm.

Tobin, K. G. (1990). Research on science laboratory activities; In pursuit of better questions and answers to improve learning. *School Science and Mathematics*, *90*, 403-418.

Tyler, R. W. (1949). *Basic principles of curriculum and instruction.* Chicago: University of Chicago Press.

Yeany, K. H., Larusa, A. A., & Hale, M. L. (1989, April). *A comparison of performance- based versus paper and pencil measures of science process and reasoning skills as influences by gender and reading ability.* Paper presented at the annual meeting of the: National Association for Research in Science Teaching (NARST), San Francisco.

Chapter 5

LEARNING ENVIRONMENT RESEARCH IN HIGHER EDUCATION: ASSESSING PATTERNS OF LEARNING AND TEACHING

Peter Van Petegem
Vincent Donche
University of Antwerp
Belgium

An important challenge for higher education in the new millennium is the implementation of constructivist learning environments to foster the development of students' learning skills in an effective way. In our view of understanding the complexities of these processes of educational change, it is important that future learning environment research focus on how students and teachers as main actors think about learning and teaching as well as which learning and teaching activities are undertaken. In this chapter, we want to draw attention to a research model which was used in several empirical studies to explore the intricate relationships between learning and teaching in higher education. In the first part of this chapter, a theoretical model of relationships between learning and teaching conceptions and learning strategies is discussed. In the second part, empirical outcomes of three research studies are reported which were directed to explore conceptions of learning and teaching as well as learning strategies and teaching strategies of students, student teachers and teachers. Results show that individual differences in learning and teaching are present. Different learning patterns are also associated with different preferences for learning environments. The studies also indicate that personal and contextual factors like learning orientations and types of education are associated with differences in learning patterns. In the final part of this chapter, an overview of possible research perspectives aimed to elaborate the present research model is described.

1. Introduction

An often heard plea in higher education concerns the implementation of new or powerful learning environments (De Corte, Verschaffel, Entwistle, & van Merriënboer, 2003). These constructivist learning environments are characterised by students who engage in more active and self-regulated learning and in which learning is viewed as a process of knowledge construction instead of knowledge reproduction (Vermunt, 2003). This also entails teachers engaging in more process-oriented teaching (Vermunt & Verschaffel, 2000).

It is remarkable that the implementation of new learning environments are often executed without an assessment of how students and teachers think about learning and teaching as well as how learning and teaching is actually being undertaken in learning environments. In the literature, it already has been indicated that not only attention should be given to how learning environments should be changed to become more powerful but also which conceptions students have about learning and teaching (Entwistle, McCune, & Hounsell, 2003). It appears that these conceptions have an effect on how learning is actually undertaken. In research it has been indicated that students have different preferences for learning environments (Entwistle & Tait 1990; Peltonen & Niemivirta, 1999; Roelofs & Visser, 2001; Wierstra & Beerends, 1996; Wierstra, Kanselaar, Van der Linden, Lodewijks, & Vermunt, 2003).

These preferences for learning environments are also related to the ways students learn. For instance, Entwistle & Tait (1990) found that reproduction-oriented learners prefer more learning environments in which surface learning strategies like memorising are central. According to Wierstra and Beerends (1996) meaning-oriented learning is related with a preference for learning environments in which learners are motivated to process learning content in a deep manner. In a cross-cultural meta-analysis Watkins (2001) stated that there are significant correlations between aspects of learning style and preferences for learning environments.

These studies underline how individual differences in learning may have an effect on how students perceive and react to new learning environments. In view of the aims of educational change in higher education and the pleas for more constructivist learning and teaching, it is therefore important to place research attention on how students and teachers think about learning and teaching and what kind of learning strategies and teaching strategies they employ. Assessment of the patterns of learning of students and patterns of teaching of teachers might in this respect give valuable answers to how learning and teaching has to be approached within learning environments. In the next part of the chapter, we focus attention on how patterns of learning of students and patterns of teaching of teachers can be described and to what extent these patterns are related to personal and contextual factors.

1.1 Patterns of learning

There is a vast body of knowledge regarding students' ways or styles of learning. This research domain has been developed in many ways. Studies have been undertaken dealing with cognitive aspects of learning (Kolb, 1984; Sadler-Smith, 1996), conceptions of learning and teaching and specific learning strategies (Rossum & Schenk, 1984; Säljö, 1979), aspects of self-regulation and metacognition (Boekaerts, 1997; Candy, 1991; Flavell, 1987; Weinstein, Zimmerman, & Palmer, 1988; Zimmerman, 2001) and motivational aspects of learning (Biggs, 1987, Entwistle, 1988, Pintrich, Smith, Garcia, & McKeachie, 1993). In many of these studies relationships were investigated between several of these aspects. This has led to multiple definitions of how learning styles should be conceived[1].

In the Netherlands, Vermunt (1998) has carried out research aimed at integrating many of the indicated aspects of learning within one learning style model. In Vermunt's model, learning styles are viewed as a coherent unity of learning activities which students use to develop the ways they regulate their learning processes, their conceptions of learning and teaching (mental learning models) and their study motives. Based on qualitative research Vermunt (1992) developed the *Inventory of Learning Styles* questionnaire (ILS) which enabled the analysis of four distinct learning styles among students in higher education: meaning oriented, reproduction oriented, application oriented and undirected. The characteristics of these learning styles are indicated in Table 5.1. This typology of learning styles can also be related to other approaches to learning[2]. In order to avoid the misunderstanding about learning styles as fixed 'traits', Vermunt (2005) recently used the term learning patterns. In this chapter, we apply the same terminology (see also section 1.3).

---

[1] For an overview: Jonassen & Grabowski (1993)
[2] For an overview: Vermunt (1998)

Table 5.1. Typology of Learning Patterns (based on Vermunt, 1998)

Learning Patterns	Cognitive learning strategies	Metacognitive learning strategies	Learning orientations	Learning conceptions
Meaning oriented	Relating and critical processing	Self-regulation	Personally interested	Construction of knowledge
Reproduction oriented	Memorizing and analysing	External regulation	Certificate and self-test-oriented	Intake of knowledge
Application oriented	Making concrete and applying	Self and externally regulated	Vocation oriented	Use of knowledge
Undirected	No specific cognitive learning activities	No regulation	Ambivalent	Stimulating education and cooperative learning

In several international studies, empirical evidence has been found that individual differences are found among learners using the ILS (Vermetten, Vermunt, & Lodewijks, 2002). In some of these studies it was found that learners could be clustered in groups of learners with common characteristics. This means that learners could combine some of the described learning patterns as a way to cope with learning in higher education (Boyle, Duffy, & Dunleavy, 2003; Vermetten, et al., 2002; Wierstra & Beerends, 1996). Investigating these aspects of learning of students could contribute to a better understanding of how students learn within learning environments.

1.2 Patterns of teaching

Research literature indicates that students' approaches to learning are influenced by the way teachers teach or the ways that learners are evaluated (Entwistle, et al., 2003; Entwistle & Ramsden, 1983; Kember & Gow, 1994; Prosser & Trigwell, 1999). Former findings have indicated that a surface approach to learning is more frequently used within learning environments which are characterised by heavy workload, little autonomy in learning and in which stepwise learning is supported regarding the use of assessment forms. A study by Kember and Gow (1994) has indicated that the way teachers think about learning and teaching and the way they approach teaching in their own practice are associated with students' approaches to learning. In this study it was found that departments in which a knowledge transmission model of learning and teaching dominates, students undertake to a lesser extent a deep approach to learning.

Departments in which learning processes of students are made more central, appeared to have more learners who apply in a lesser extent a surface approach to learning. If teachers' conceptions of learning and teaching and associated teaching strategies have an effect on the learning processes which students undertake, then it is not only important to assess the qualities of students' learning patterns but also to question which conceptions of teachers are dominating and how they relate with teaching strategies. Many studies have indicated that teachers can have different conceptions about learning and teaching. The distinction between knowledge transmission and a more student oriented model of learning and teaching has already been stated (Kember, 1997; Prosser & Trigwell, 1999; Samuelowicz & Bain, 2001).

Research dealing with the extent to which coherence appears between related teachers' conceptions about learning and teaching and teaching strategies is less undertaken (Fang, 1996). In literature, it is indicated that a clear relationship between conceptions about learning and teaching and teaching strategies is problematic (Entwistle, et.al., 2003; Prosser & Trigwell, 1999). Several studies show different results concerning these topics (Bolhuis, 2000; Kember & Gow, 1994; Kember & Kwan, 2000; Roelofs & Visser, 2001). For instance, Kember and Kwan (2000) found in a qualitative study similarities between teachers' learning content oriented conceptions of learning and teaching and teaching strategies which supported a knowledge transmission model.

A similar relationship was found among teachers who had process-oriented conceptions of learning and teaching strategies directed to support student learning. In survey-studies and observation-studies, it was found that less coherence appears between related conceptions and teaching strategies (Bolhuis, 2000; Roelofs & Visser, 2001). In order to extend the body of research, it is important to investigate whether teachers' conceptions and teaching strategies can be related to each other in terms of teaching patterns.

1.3 Personal and contextual factors

Many researchers indicate that students' learning is affected not only by factors in the learning environment but also personal factors. Learning patterns are in this respect not viewed as an invariant attribute of students but as the result of an interplay between personal and contextual variables (Vermunt, 2005). Personal influences (e.g., gender or personality traits) are understood to contribute to the consistency of learning patterns as learning environment related or contextual factors contribute to change of learning patterns. Many researchers have carried out research on these topics and underlined the relative changeability of learning patterns (e.g., Busato, Prins, Elshout, & Hamaker, 1999; Entwistle & Ramsden, 1983; Vermetten et al., 1999; Vermunt & Minnaert 2003; Wierstra & Beerends, 1996; Wierstra et al., 2003).

Also, teachers' conceptions and teaching strategies are understood to be affected by personal and contextual factors. Former research has indicated that (student) teachers' conceptions of educational practice are associated with the conceptions they have about learning and how they learn (Huibregtse et al., 1994; Powell, 1992; Stofflett & Stoddart, 1994). Studies have also indicated that teachers' own personal experiences with education, play an important role in how teachers undertake teaching strategies (Beijaard, et al., 2000; Prosser & Trigwell, 1999). Learning environment related or contextual factors are also associated with teachers' teaching. Entwistle, et al. (2003) described a broad model in which many influencing factors are situated in the learning environment like workload and contact hours, students' abilities and skills in learning, course design and organisation, assessment and feedback, and specific institutional and disciplinary contexts.

It seems clear from these studies that a thorough assessment of learning and teaching patterns within learning environments cannot ignore the impact of personal and contextual factors. In our view, a research model in which learning patterns and teaching patterns are placed centrally also has to integrate the interplay of a complex set of interacting factors. Figure 5.1 illustrates a way to theoretically synthesize the complex interactions between students' and teachers' learning or teaching patterns within a learning environment. In current learning environment research, we investigate students' and teachers' conceptions of learning and teaching and learning strategies as well as teaching strategies and take a dynamic look at how learning patterns and teaching patterns are associated with personal and contextual factors. Focussing on students' and teachers' conceptions about learning and teaching, learning strategies and teaching strategies, and personal and contextual factors, might add significant insight into how new learning environments or powerful learning environments could be designed or implemented in order to align with the learners' needs and teachers' competencies.

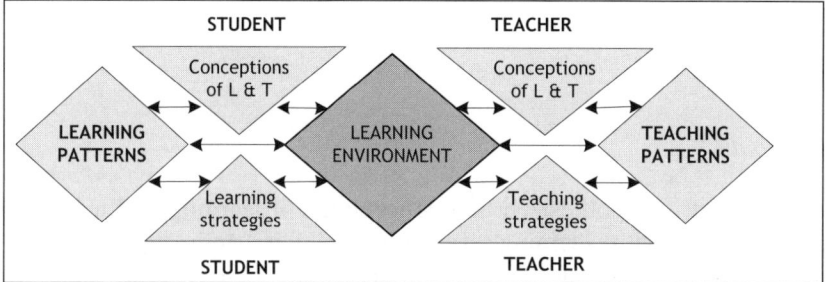

Figure 5.1. Research model.

In the following parts of the chapter, four studies conducted in Flanders (Belgium) are described that aim to test several expected relationships which are indicated in the model. We investigate whether students' conceptions of learning and teaching and learning strategies can be viewed as components of learning patterns and which personal and contextual factors are related with these learning patterns. We examine how teachers' conceptions of learning and teaching strategies are part of teaching patterns and which personal and contextual factors have an interplaying role. These studies also illustrate in what ways assessments of aspects of learning and teaching can take place according to the research model.

2. Present Study

In the first study, we explore the coherence between conceptions of learning and teaching and learning strategies in a sample of 858 first-year bachelor students. Study 2 examines at an institutional level the associations between personal and contextual variables and learning patterns of 1,340 student teachers. In Study 3 we apply an exploratory analysis using the same data as in Study 2 to investigate associations between learning patterns of student teachers and preferences for constructivist learning environments in their own teaching practice. Study 4 involves 119 teacher educators and examines associations between the conceptions of how students should learn to teach and their own teaching strategies. In the four studies, we expect associations between specific conceptions of learning and teaching and learning strategies and teaching strategies. In each study, we describe the goals, methods, results and conclusions[3].

2.1 Study 1

2.1.1 Goals

In literature it is hypothesized that conceptions of learning and teaching are associated with learning strategies. In this study we analysed individual differences in learning strategies of first-year students in relation to conceptions of learning and teaching.

2.1.2 Method

In this survey-study, 856 first-year bachelor students from a Flemish institution of higher education participated; among them are 390 male and 466 female students. Students from five different disciplines were involved: Business Management (232), Communication Management (244), Office Management (47), Information Management and Systems (169) and Tourism and Recreation Management (166).

Learning approaches of student teachers were measured by means of Vermunt's Inventory of Learning Styles (1992). This written questionnaire was slightly adapted for use in the local Flemish context of higher education. In this study, we focus on the results of scales measuring processing strategies, regulation strategies and learning conceptions. The items are responded to using a frequency scale ranging from (1) I seldom or never do this to (5) I (almost) always do this for the first 55 items, and using a Likert-scale ranging from (1) Completely Disagree to (5) Completely Agree for the rest of the items. An overview

---

[3] For a more comprehensive look on these studies we refer to Donche (2005).

of the 11 scales, Cronbach alpha coefficients from this study and sample items are described in Table 5.2.

Table 5.2. Overview of ILS-scales Measuring Processing Strategies, Regulation Strategies and Learning Conceptions

Scales	Sample item
Processing strategies	
• Deep processing (N = 11; α = 0.83)	I try to combine the subjects that are dealt with separately into a course into one whole.
• Stepwise processing (N = 11; α = 0.76)	I memorise lists of characteristics of a certain phenomenon.
• Concrete processing (N = 5; α = 0.65)	I pay particular attention to those parts of the course that have practical utility.
Regulation strategies	
• Self-regulation (N = 11; α = 0.73)	To test my learning progress. I try to answer questions about the subject matter which I make up myself.
• External regulation (N = 11; α = 0.64)	I study according to the instructions given in the course materials.
• Lack of regulation (N = 6; α = 0.68)	I notice that it is difficult for me to determine whether I have mastered the subject matter sufficiently.
Learning conceptions	
• Construction of knowledge (N = 9; α = 0.70)	If I have difficulty with understanding a particular topic, I should construct other books of my own accord.
• Intake of knowledge (N = 9; α = 0.73)	To me, learning means trying to remember the subject matter I am given.
• Use of knowledge (N = 6; α = 0.69)	The things I learn have to be useful for solving practical problems.
• Stimulating education (N = 8; α = 0.86)	The course team should encourage me to compare the various theories that are dealt with in a course.
• Co-operative learning (N = 8; α = 0.84)	I have a need to work with other students in my studies.

2.1.3 Results

In order to assess students' learning patterns, we carried out a cluster analysis on the 11 separated ILS-scales (Figure 5.2). Respondents were grouped together in clusters using the Ward method (1963). A three group clustering explained a mean variance of 19.0% of the 11 learning style scales; the lowest amount of variance was explained on the scale Use of knowledge (3.0%) and the highest amount on the scale Deep processing (40.0%). Three clusters can be related to the theoretical framework of Vermunt (1992) and results of former studies in which learning patterns were distinguished by means of cluster analysis on ILS-scales. The reproduction/undirected and meaning oriented learning pattern which were found among students is similar to what Vermetten, et al. (2002) labelled as *surface/undirected learners* and *deep learners*. Using cluster analysis Wierstra and Beerends (1996) also distinguished a flexible learning pattern among students.

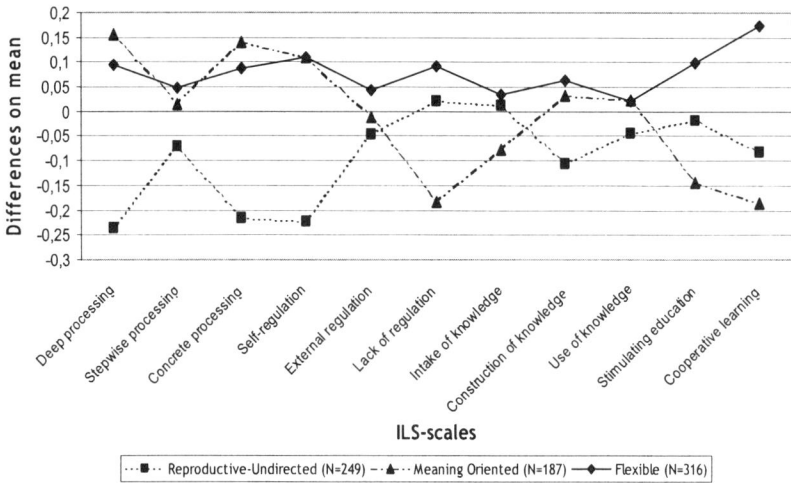

Figure 5.2. Cluster analysis on ILS-scales.

The three clusters can be described as follows.

Meaning Oriented Learning Pattern: 21.8% of the students stress that in education construction, the use of knowledge has to be centralised and not merely be the intake of knowledge. These students do not attach importance to education in which the stimulating role of teachers or peers is underlined. These students are self-regulated in their learning and prefer deep and concrete processing above stepwise processing during learning.

Reproductive Undirected Learning Pattern: 29.0% of the students attach a lot of importance to education in which the intake of knowledge is made central. Construction of knowledge is preferred far less. Learning is seen as a process in which they have to be stimulated by teachers and not by themselves. Compared with other students they are more externally regulated in their learning than self-regulated. Also lack of regulation is a typical feature. Concerning processing strategies they prefer stepwise processing above deep processing but are also more adrift in their cognitive processing.

Flexible Learning Pattern: 36.8% of the students attach a lot of importance to education in which the intake of knowledge is centralised, although it could not be stated that these students do not attach importance to the construction of knowledge in education. They stress the importance of education in which they are stimulated in their learning by others like teachers and peers. These students self-regulate their learning but are also depending on others to regulate their learning. Deep, stepwise and concrete processing are part of their cognitive learning strategies. Because these students have both meaning oriented as well as reproduction oriented features in common, these students are typified as having a flexible learning pattern.

2.1.4 Brief discussion

Study 1 made clear that students have different conceptions about directions of learning and teaching. Not all students seem to share the ideas of learning and teaching from a constructivist point of view. The study also shows that learners' conceptions of learning and teaching are interrelated with specific regulation strategies and processing strategies. The distinguished clusters in this study indicate that students' conceptions of learning and teaching are often in line with related learning strategies. This is the case with students having a meaning oriented or reproductive-undirected learning pattern. Flexible learners have dual conceptions of learning and teaching which is also reflected in their choice of regulation and processing activities. These findings seem to indicate that flexible learners can cope with different learning tasks aimed at undertaking all kinds of cognitive processes. The results of this study also seem to indicate that when learning environments are designed to capitalise on learners' self-regulation, not all students will be able to make this shift at once. Learners with reproductive-undirected learning patterns need different guidance in learning than meaning-oriented learners. These results also indicate that not all types of learning environments will be aligned with individual learner's needs. This raises also questions about what kind of learning environment related factors are correlated with these learning patterns.

2.2 Study 2

2.2.1 Goals

In the literature, it is claimed that personal and contextual variables are related to differences in learning patterns. This study was carried out in order to explore several personal and contextual variables in relationship with learning patterns.

2.2.2 Method

In this survey-study, 1,340 student teachers (293 male and 1,047 female) from a Flemish institution of higher education participated. Students followed different types of three-year teacher education: 314 students (kindergarten), 484 students (primary), 322 students (lower secondary A) and 220 students (lower secondary B). The distinction between lower secondary A and B was made because students of teacher education lower secondary B have a more specific sports-discipline related curriculum. There were 630 first-year, 379 second-year and 331 third-year students.

In this study learning approaches of student teachers were measured by means of Vermunt's ILS (1996, 1998). The alpha coefficients of the 11 scales measuring learning conceptions, regulation strategies and processing strategies were acceptable ranging from 0.65 to 0.88. In this study, we used the component of learning orientations which is also part of the ILS. With the additional use of this component, we aimed to explore whether more personal variables like motivation are related with learning patterns. The items are responded to by using a Likert-scale ranging from (1) Completely Disagree to (5) Completely Agree. An overview of the five scales, alpha coefficients and sample items are described in Table 5.3. The alpha coefficient of the scale 'personally oriented' is low and needs further careful interpretation.

Table 5.3. Overview of ILS-scales Measuring Learning Orientations

Scale	Sample item
Learning orientations	
• Personally interested (N = 5; α = 0.47)	I do these studies out of sheer interest in the topics that are dealt with.
• Certificate oriented (N = 5; α = 0.69)	I study above all to pass the exam.
• Self-test oriented (N = 5; α = 0.82)	I want to test myself to see whether I am capable of doing studies in higher education.
• Vocation oriented (N = 5; α = 0.60)	I have chosen this subject area, because I am highly interested in the type of work for which it prepares.
• Ambivalence (N = 5; α = 0.75)	I am afraid these studies are too demanding for me.

2.2.3 Results

As a first step, we analysed whether in this sample similar learning patterns could be found as in Study 1. We carried out a cluster analysis on the 11 ILS scales measuring conceptions of learning, regulation strategies and processing strategies. Results indicated that students could be similarly clustered as in Study 1. 39.7% of the students have a meaning oriented learning pattern, 35.8% of the students have a flexible learning pattern, and 24.4% of the students have a reproductive-undirected learning pattern.

In order to analyse the relationship between personal and contextual variables and learning patterns, a multinominal logistic regression was conducted. The benefits of this kind of analysis are that the effects of independent variables on clusters can be indicated within a total model. The independent variables in this study are: learning orientations, gender, type of teacher education, year of study. The dependent variables are the three groups of learners with different learning patterns. The reference group of this analysis are female student teachers who followed the third year lower secondary education B type of teacher education. The fit of the model is acceptable. The difference in Chi^2 with the intercept only model is 233.0 with 22 degrees of freedom (Table 5.4). The model is significant at the *p*<0.001 level.

Table 5.4. Multinominal Logistic Regression on Three Learning Patterns:
Results of a Likelihood Ratio Test

Effect	Chi^2	df	p
Certificate oriented	32.9	2	0.000
Vocation oriented	26.5	2	0.000
Self-test oriented	3.6	2	0.161
Personally interested	40.2	2	0.000
Ambivalent	34.8	2	0.000
Gender (1 dummy)	4.6	2	0.101
Type of teacher education (3 dummies)	20.2	6	0.002
Year of teacher education (2 dummies)	10.0	4	0.040

Table 5.5. Significant Parameter Estimates for the Model (MNLM), with Three
Learning Pattern Clusters as Dependent and 11 Independent Variables

Effect	Meaning oriented versus Flexible		Reproductive/ undirected versus Flexible	
	B	p	B	p
Intercept	4.65		4.21	
Gender	0.38	0.042		
Kindergarten			-0.54	0.041
Primary				
Lower secondary education A			-1.03	0.000
First-year teacher education	-0.48	0.005		
Second-year teacher education				
Certificate oriented	-0.52	0.000	-0.23	0.024
Vocation oriented	-0.64	0.000	-0.58	0.000
Self-test oriented				
Personally interested	0.38	0.001	-0.40	0.002
Ambivalence	-0.39	0.000	0.22	0.032

In Table 5.5, the parameter estimates for the multinominal logistic regression model (MNLM) are described. The reference category for the assessment of the four outcomes is the flexible learning pattern.

When the meaning-oriented learning pattern is compared with the flexible learning pattern, significant differences occur in regard to learning orientations. Flexible learners tend to be more certificate and vocation oriented in their studies as well as being more ambivalent compared with meaning-oriented learner who are more personally interested in their studies. We can also conclude that first-year students are more likely to have a flexible learning pattern than the reference group; the third-year students. A slight but significant effect also occurs concerning gender. Female students are more likely to have flexible learning patterns than the reference group; the male student teachers.

Comparison of the reproductive-undirected and flexible learning pattern shows that the type of teacher education and most of the learning orientations to be the best predictors. Student who are more ambivalent in their learning are more likely to have a reproductive-undirected learning pattern than a flexible learning pattern. Student teachers from kindergarten and lower secondary A are less likely to have a reproductive/undirected learning pattern than the reference group; the lower secondary B student teachers.

Based on the parameter estimates in Table 5.5, the learning patterns of student teachers has been predicted. The prediction of student teachers with a meaning-oriented learning pattern was in 62.9% of the cases correct. The flexible learning pattern could be positively predicted in 51.1% of the cases. The reproductive-undirected learning pattern was only positively predicted in 21.7% of the cases. The overall percentage of correct predictions was 48.6%. We can conclude that the background information of the student teachers to some extent predict how student teachers learn.

2.2.4 Brief discussion

The results of Study 2, indicate that personal and contextual variables, to some extent, are related to how student teachers think about learning and teaching and which learning strategies they undertake. The results indicate that within learning environments an interplay occurs between personal and contextual variables and students' learning patterns. However, it is unclear to what extent for instance didactic differences in the different teacher education types are also related with these differences in learning patterns. Motivational orientations were found to be relatively good predictors between learning patterns which seems to underline the importance of studying student characteristics in relationship with learning patterns. Results from this cross-sectional study suggest new hypotheses which in a longitudinal research study could be investigated. For instance, it remains unclear why first-year students have more flexible and less meaning oriented learning patterns than third-year students. It seems also that a maturing effect could play an intermediating role in the development of learning patterns which should be further investigated. The results of Study 2 also raises new questions about what kind of learning environments are needed to foster a further development of, for instance, meaning-oriented learning patterns.

2.3 Study 3

2.3.1 Goals

In the literature, it is claimed that there are associations between how student teachers think about educational practice in their own teaching practice and how they think about their own learning and how they learn. In this study, we aimed to investigate whether student teachers' learning patterns are sound predictors for constructivist preferences for learning environments in future teaching practice.

2.3.2 Method

In Study 3, we used the same sample and institution as presented in Study 2. In addition to the data we collected for Study 2, we used a second questionnaire in order to investigate student teachers' preferences for constructivist learning environments using items from an instrument of Roelofs and Visser (2001). After analysis, we used three scales that measure three different preferences for constructivist learning environments.

The first scale measures student teachers' preferences for a learning environment that takes pupils' interests and experiences into account. The scale is named Connectedness to Pupil's Interests and Experiences. The second scale is named Discovery Oriented Learning and measures the extent to which student teachers prefer a learning environment in which discovery-oriented learning takes place by pupils and in which pupils are self-regulated in their learning. The third scale named

Constructive and Cooperative Learning measures especially those activities that can be associated with a learning environment in which cooperation and construction of knowledge is fostered. The items are responded by using a Likert-scale of (1) This does not apply to me to (4) This does apply to me. The alpha coefficients of the scales were acceptable ranging from alpha 0.58 to 0.73. Sample items and scales of the questionnaire are presented in Table 5.6.

Table 5.6. Overview of Preferences for Learning Environment Scales

Scale	Sample item
• Connectedness to pupils' interests and experiences (N = 4; α = 0.58)	Learning content must be connected to the interests of pupils.
• Constructive and co-operative learning (N = 9; α = 0.66)	Pupils have to collect independently information about subjects dealt with during courses.
• Discovery oriented learning (N = 8; α = 0.73)	Pupils are able to determine where they want to work on.

2.3.3 Results

We first analysed student teachers' preferences for learning environment. We found that student teachers in general seem to mostly prefer a learning environment that takes into account pupils' interests and experiences (mean=3.28) and in which construction of knowledge and cooperative learning (mean=3.11) is central. A learning environment directed to discovery-oriented learning by the pupils and in which pupils have a lot of self-determination in their learning is less supported by student teachers (mean=2.78).

In order to examine the relationship between learning patterns and preferences for constructivist learning environments of student teachers, we conducted multiple regression analyses. The following predictors were included in the regression model: gender, year of teacher education, learning pattern, type of teacher education and learning orientations. We created dummy variables for all predictors. Male first-year student teachers from teacher education B2 with a flexible learning pattern were set as the reference group in order to avoid over-determination of the regression model. The results of the multiple regression analyses are shown in Table 5.7.

The analysis shows that reproductive-undirected student teachers prefer to a lesser extent learning environments in which constructive and co-operative learning takes place and in which pupils' interests and experiences are taken into account. Meaning-oriented learners prefer learning environments in which discovery oriented learning takes place. The other predictors indicate that the year of teacher training as well as type of teacher education are associated with different preferences for learning environments. For instance, third-year students have a greater preference for learning environments in which constructive and cooperative learning or discovery-oriented learning takes place.

Table 5.7. Predictability of References for Learning Environments

	Pupils' interests and experiences	Constructive and co-operative learning	Discovery oriented learning
Gender		0.07*	
First-year teacher education	-0.14***	-0.14***	
Third-year teacher education		0.07*	0.07*
Meaning oriented			0.08**
Reproductive-undirected	-0.07**	-0.12**	
Kindergarten	-0.12***	-0.24***	0.11***
Lower secondary A			-0.14***
Lower secondary B	-0.11***	-0.22***	
Personally interested			
Self-test oriented	0.09**	0.10**	0.09**
Certificate-oriented		-0.07*	
Vocation-oriented	0.19***	0.11***	0.06*
Ambivalence		-0.08**	
R^2	0.10	0.21	0.06

*$p<0.05$; ** $p<0.01$; *** $p<0.001$

Preferences for learning environments are also related to student teachers' orientations to learning. For example, student teachers who are more vocation oriented in their studies seem to have a greater preference for constructivist learning environments. The regression models explain a relative proportion of the variance of student teachers' preference for learning environments.

2.3.4 Brief discussion

In this study, we found the presence of relationships between student teachers' learning patterns and preferences for learning environments. Meaning-oriented learners prefer more constructivist learning environments compared with reproductive-undirected learners. These results are to some extent in line with former research in which a relationship was also found between meaning-oriented learning and a preference for a learning environment which supports more self-regulated and deep learning (Entwistle & Tait, 1990, 1993; Peltonen & Niemivirta, 1999).

However, the results are more specific in this study since it is indicated that personal and contextual variables have a unique effect on the preferences of student teachers for learning environments in future teaching practice. Relationships between students' patterns of learning and preferences for learning environments seem to indicate that in teacher education it is not only necessary to attach importance to how students think about their educational practice but also how learning actually takes places within learning environments, since these aspects are to some extent related. The results of this cross-sectional study also seem to indicate that preferences for learning environments are associated with the length of study as third-year student teachers have a greater preference for constructivist learning environments than first-year students. Perhaps experiences with more constructivist learning environments during the second and the third year of teacher education could play an important role as well as a growing expertise in teaching. However, these hypotheses should be further investigated in a longitudinal research design.

2.4 Study 4

2.4.1 Goals

In the literature, it is stated that conceptions of learning and teaching are associated with teaching strategies. We analysed how conceptions of learning to teach are related to teaching strategies of teacher educators.

2.4.2 Method

In this survey, 119 teacher educators from a Flemish institution of higher education participated. The teacher educators had 16 years of experience in teaching in general and 13 years of experience in teacher education specifically. Of the teacher educators, 18% are working in kindergartens, 42% in primary teacher education and 40% in lower secondary teacher education.

Two questionnaires were used. The first, developed for teachers, is based on the *Inventory Learning to Teach Questionnaire*, developed by Oosterheert for student teachers (2001). Seventeen items are related to conceptions of learning to teach and measure what teacher educators think that student teachers should think about learning to teach; 23 items are related to conceptions of cognitive and regulative activities and measure what teacher educators think about the kind of cognitive and regulation activities student teachers should undertake during teacher education; and nine items are related to emotion regulation and measure what teacher educators think about how students should cope with the regulation of emotions during teacher education. All items are answered on on a Likert-scale of (1) Completely Disagree to (5) Completely Agree. Sample items and scales of the questionnaire are described in Table 5.8.

A second questionnaire was based on items from a questionnaire of Roelofs and Visser (2001) but was adapted to measure the extent to which teacher educators are able to succeed in applying different teaching strategies. After analysis, seven scales could be found related to different teaching strategies. Six scales measure aspects of constructivist teaching strategies, while the seventh scale, Direct Instruction measures, the extent to which teacher educators apply a more controlling teaching strategy in classrooms. All items are responded to using a Likert scale ranging from (1) (almost) never to (4) (almost) always.

Table 5.8. Overview of Scales Measuring Learning-to-Teach Conceptions

Scale	Sample item
Conceptions about learning-to-teach	
• Practising and testing (N = 9; α = 0.77)	Teacher educators should focus on giving practical tips and suggestions.
• Strong self-determination in performance improvement (N = 3; α = 0.75	Students are best capable to determine which aspects of their teaching still need to be worked on.
• Raising consciousness under external control (N = 7; α = 0.69)	It is important that teacher educators and mentors stimulate students to think about their teaching behaviour.
Conceptions about learning activities and regulation	
• Proactive, broad use of the mentor (N = 6; α = 0.72)	Students have to ask to their mentor how (s)he would handle the situation.
• Independent search for conceptual information (N = 5; α = 0.69)	Students have to find answers to their questions about teaching by consulting the literature on their own.
• Actively relating theory to practice (N = 5; α = 0.68)	Students have to try to relate theory to their own teaching experiences.
• Developing views/ideas through discussion (N = 5; α = 0.77)	Students have to ask to experienced teachers in schools how they think about their opinions on teaching.
• Pupil-oriented evaluation criteria (N = 3; α = 0.60)	Students' satisfaction with a lesson has to be largely determined by the extent to which a good working climate occurs in the classroom.
Conceptions about emotion regulation	
• Avoidance (N = 5; α = 0.59)	Students have to search for the cause of a lesson which went awry.
• Preoccupation (N = 4; α = 0.69)	A lesson which went wrong should keep going through students' heads on at least the same day.

Table 5.9. Overview of Scales Measuring Teaching Strategies

Scale	Sample item
	In what extent do you succeed in …
• Connectedness to students' interests and experiences (N = 6; α = 0.66)	… giving students the possibility in lessons to present own experiences and information?
• Process-oriented instruction (N = 6; α = 0.75)	… stimulating students to solve a problem/ task on their own?
• Constructive learning environnent (N = 9; α = 0.78)	… letting students collect on their own information about subjects that are dealt with in lessons?
• Co-operative learning (N = 5; α = 0.69)	… letting students co-operate with other peers in groups?
• Discovery oriented learning (N = 7; α = 0.69)	… letting students decide where they will work on?
• Differentiation (N = 5; α = 0.77)	… giving different tasks to students with different achievement levels?
• Direct instruction (N = 8; α = 0.75)	… posing a lot of short questions during lessons in order to assess whether students comprehend the learning contents?

2.4.3 Results

In order to assess the teaching patterns a correlation study was used in which we investigated the correlations between the scales measuring conceptions of teacher educators about learning-to-teach and teaching strategies (see Table 5.10).

The correlations show that the extent to which teacher educators agree on the importance of self-regulation in the process of learning to teach and related cognitive and regulation strategies, positively correlates with realising aspects of process-oriented teaching in practice. An important addition to this result is that a positive correlation occurs between the conception that students should develop views and ideas through discussion with others and the realization of direct instruction in teaching practice of teacher educators. This result seems to indicate that a process-oriented conception of learning to teach is not always supported by a reduction in the use of direct instruction in teaching practice.

Table 5.10. Correlations between Conceptions of Learning-to-Teach (rows) and Teaching Strategies (columns)

	Strong self-determination in performance improvement	Independent search for conceptual information	Actively relating theory to practice	Developing views/ideas through discussion	Pupil-oriented evaluation criteria	Avoidance
Connectedness to students' interests and experiences	0.15	0.28**	0.11	0.38**	0.23*	-0.08
Process-oriented instruction	-0.06	0.08	0.19	0.21*	0.19	-0.26**
Constructive learning environment	-0.06	0.23*	0.03	0.42**	0.13	-0.10
Co-operative learning	0.12	0.23*	0.24*	0.30**	0.10	-0.04
Direct instruction	0.13	0.17	0.16	0.21*	0.12	-0.23*
Discovery oriented learning	0.23*	0.18	0.08	0.43**	0.04	-0.15
Differentiation	-0.12	0.08	0.02	0.25*	0.15	-0.02

*$p<0.05$; ** $p<0.01$

In order to examine the relationship between personal and contextual variables of teacher educators and their conceptions of learning to teach and teaching strategies, we conducted multiple regression analyses. The following predictors were included in the regression model: gender, type of teacher education, years of experiences in teaching and teacher education. We created dummy variables for the first two predictors. Male teacher educators who taught in primary teacher education were set as the reference group in order to avoid over-determination of the regression model. The results of the multiple regression analyses are shown in Table 5.11. Only the predicting scales are described in the table.

Table 5.11. Predictability of Conceptions of Learning-to-Teach and Teaching Strategies

	Kinder-garten	Experiences in teacher education	Experiences in teaching	R^2
Conceptions of learning-to-teach				
Independent search for conceptual Information			0.30**	0.09
Developing views/ideas through discussion		0.27**		0.07
Teaching strategies				
Process-oriented instruction	-0.31**			0.10

*$p<0.05$; ** $p<0.01$; *** $p<0.001$

The results indicate that differences in conceptions of teaching strategies in most of the cases cannot be explained by means of contextual predictors. However a single effect occurred concerning kindergarten teacher educators who seem to succeed to a lesser extent to realize process-oriented instruction. Differences in conceptions of learning to teach could in some extent be explained by personal predictors. Teacher educators who have more years of experience in teacher education or in teaching in general are likely to have more process-oriented conceptions about learning to teach. However the years of experience in teacher education or in teaching in general are not significantly related with the extent to which teachers succeed in realizing constructivist teaching strategies.

2.4.4 Brief discussion

Study 4 shows that teacher educators' conceptions about how student teachers should learn to teach are related to teaching strategies they undertake in practice. The correlations between these conceptions and strategies contribute to a better understanding of teaching patterns. However, more research is needed to further examine these relationships. The study made clear that process-oriented learning to teach conceptions can be related to the realization of more traditionally-oriented teaching strategies like direct instruction and realization of more process-oriented teaching strategies like discovery-oriented learning. The results of this study also indicate that teacher educators who have more years of experience in practice stress more the importance of aspects of process-oriented learning to teach, but do not put these principles in practice more than their younger colleagues. These results raise questions like what kind of other learning environment related or contextual factors are associated with the realisation of more process-oriented teaching strategies and to what extent do other personal factors play a mediating role. From this point of view it also important to look at how teachers' conceptions of learning and teaching and teaching strategies may develop throughout their professional careers and what kind of factors play an important role in this process.

3. General Discussion

3.1 Conclusions

On the basis of our theoretical research model (Figure 5.1) we expected that students' conceptions of learning and teaching are related with learning strategies within learning environments in terms of learning patterns. The results of Studies 1 and 2 provided substantial support for the presence of learning patterns among students and student teachers. Three distinct patterns of learning could be distinguished across two contexts, namely meaning-oriented, reproductive-undirected and flexible learning patterns. In previous studies, learning patterns were related to several personal and contextual variables. The results of Study 2 were consistent with this in that differences in learning were associated with personal variables like gender and motivation and contextual variables like type of teacher education and year of study. These results gave more evidence that learning patterns are the result of an interplay between factors in the learning environment and personal variables. In Study 3, we extended our research on preferences for learning environments by focussing on student teachers' preferences for learning environments in future teaching practice. An important finding of this study was that student teachers' conceptions of learning and teaching and learning strategies are related to preferences for learning environments in educational practice. The results seem to indicate that teachers' teaching strategies could also be related with their own conceptions of learning and their own teaching and learning strategies. However, this hypothesis should be further investigated. In Study 4 we empirically explored the teacher side in the theoretical model by investigating relationships between teacher educators' conceptions of learning to teach in teacher education and their own teaching strategies in terms of teaching patterns. Although correlations could be found more research should take place to examine the presence of teaching patterns across contexts. The results of Study 4 are also consistent with previous research in which it has been indicated that besides learning environment-related or contextual factors, personal factors like teachers' experiences with education have an effect on their conceptions of learning and teaching and teaching strategies.

3.2 Methodological concerns

The studies presented in this chapter all have a quantitative research approach in common. Conducting survey studies to look for patterns of learning and teaching has the benefit of producing more generalisable and comparable results. However, in carrying out several survey-studies we also came across limitations. One of these limitations was concerned with the use of self-report questionnaires. We do not know if the answers of students, student teachers and teacher educators also indicate how they really think or act in practice. Another limitation which has an effect on these results is the scope of questioning in the selected questionnaires. The items with which we tried to capture the richness of conceptions about learning and teaching, learning strategies and teaching strategies are restricted. Therefore, it seems to be appropriate in future research to use both qualitative and quantitative research methods in future learning environment research. A mixed research design (Tashakkori & Teddlie, 2003) could be useful for extending the present studies.

3.3 Future perspectives

In several actual research projects in Flanders, we are currently investigating how learning and teaching patterns within learning environments are affected by change and stability by taking a closer look on mediating personal and contextual variables (Donche, 2005; Van Petegem et al., 2005). In several contexts, confirmatory and exploratory studies are taking place to examine the variances in conceptions of learning and teaching, learning strategies and teaching strategies.

Headlines in our current and future learning environment research programme are:

1.   investigating patterns of learning and teaching in cross-sequential and mixed research designs in order to explore the development of learning and teaching within learning environments;
2.   integrating additional student related personal, learning environment related and contextual factors, e.g., socio-cultural capital, personality traits, motivational aspects like study interest, study choice and autonomous motivation goals;
3.   integrating additional teacher related personal, learning environment related and contextual factors, e.g., teachers' conceptions of own learning, attitudes towards assessment of learning outcomes, characteristics of course design, attitudes towards educational change and professionalism; and
4.   integrating additional institutional related factors like assessment culture, guidance and support for learning, infrastructure and material constraints.

Finally, we conclude by underlining the point that future learning environment research directed to better comprehend learning patterns should not avoid crossing the boundaries of research in higher education. Learning patterns are developed or sustained in primary and secondary education and are influenced by teaching patterns. Therefore, it also seems important to look for a better understanding of how individual learning patterns are developed and how teaching patterns can contribute to this development throughout a large longitudinal learning path. It is a challenging perspective for future learning environment research.

References

Beijaard, D., Verloop, N., Wubbels, T., & Feiman-Nemser, S. (2000). The professional development of teachers. In R. J. Simons, J., van der Linden & T. Duffy (Eds.), *New Learning* (pp. 261-274). Dordrecht/Boston/London: Kluwer Academic Publishers.
Biggs, J. B. (1987). *Student approaches to learning and studying.* Melbourne, Australia. Australian Council for Educational Research.

Boekaerts, M. (1997). Self-regulated learning: a new concept embraced by researchers, policy makers, educators, teachers and students. *Learning and Instruction, 7* (1), 133-149.

Bolhuis, S. (2000). *Naar zelfstandig leren: Wat doen en denken docenten?* [Towards autonomous learning: How do teachers think and act?] Leuven/Apeldoorn: Garant.

Boyle, E. A., Duffy, T., & Dunleavy, K. (2003). Learning styles and academic outcome: The validity and utility of Vermunt's inventory of learning styles in a British higher education setting. *British Journal of Educational Psychology, 73*, 263-290.

Busato, V. V., Prins, F.J., Elshout, J. J., & Hamaker, C. (1999). The relation between learning styles, the Big Five personality traits and achievement motivation in higher education. *Personality and Individual Differences, 26*, 129-140.

Candy, P. C. (1991). *Self-direction for lifelong learning.* San Francisco, CA: Jossey -Bass.

De Corte, E., Verschaffel, L., Entwistle, N., & van Merriënboer, J. (Eds.), (2003). *Powerful learning environments: Unravelling basic components and dimensions. Advances in learning and instruction series.* Amsterdam/Boston/London: Pergamom.

Donche, V. (2005). *Onderzoek naar kenmerken van leren en onderwijzen in het hoger onderwijs.* [Investigating aspects of learning and teaching in higher education]. Doctoral dissertation, University of Antwerp, Belgium.

Entwistle, N. (1988). Motivational factors in students' approaches to learning. In R.R. Schmeck (Ed.), *Learning strategies and learning styles* (pp. 21-51). New York: Plenum Press.

Entwistle, N., McCune, V. & Hounsell, J. (2003). Investigating ways of enhancing teaching-learning environments: Measuring students' approaches to studying and perceptions of teaching. In E. De Corte, L. Verschaffel, N. Entwistle, J. van Merriënboer (Eds.), *Powerful learning environments: unravelling basic components and dimensions, Advances in learning and instruction series* (pp. 89-107). Amsterdam/Boston/London: Pergamom.

Entwistle, N. & Ramsden, P. (1983). *Understanding student learning.* London: Croom Helm.

Entwistle, N. & Tait, H. (1990). Approaches to learning, evaluations of teaching and preferences for contrasting academic environments. *Higher Education, 19*, 169-194.

Fang, Z. (1996). A review of research on teacher beliefs and practices. *Educational Research, 38* (1), 47-65.

Flavell, J. H. (1987). Speculations about the nature and development of metacognition. In F. E. Weinert & R. H. Kluwe (Eds.), *Metacognition, motivation and understanding* (pp. 21-29), Hillsdale, New Jersey: Erlbaum.

Huibregtse, I., Korthagen, F. & Wubbels, T. (1994). Physics teachers' conceptions of learning, teaching and professional development. *International Journal of Science Education 16* (5), 539-561.

Jonassen, D. H. & Grabowski, B. L. (1993). *Handbook of individual differences in learning and instruction.* New Jersey/London: Lawrence Erlbaum Associates.

Kember, D. (1997). A reconceptualisation of research into university academics' conceptions of teaching. *Learning and Instruction, 7* (3), 255-275.

Kember, D. & Gow, L. (1994). Orientations to teaching and their effect on the quality of student learning. *Journal of Higher Education. 65* (1), 59-74.

Kember, D. & Kwan, K. P. (2000). Lecturers' approaches to teaching and their relationship to conceptions of good teaching. *Instructional Science, 28*, 469-490.

Kolb, D. A. (1984). *Experiential learning. Experience as a source of learning and development.* Englewood Cliffs, New Jersey: Prentice Hall Inc.

Oosterheert, I. (2001). *How student teachers learn – A psychological perspective on knowledge construction in learning to teach.* Doctoral dissertation Rijksuniversiteit Groningen: Shaker Publishing Maastricht.

Peltonen, A. & Niemivirta, M. (1999, August). *Motivation, self-regulation and perceptions of the learning environment.* Paper presented at the 8th European Conference for Research on Learning and Instruction, Gothenburg, Sweden.

Pintrich, P. R., Smith, D. A. F., Garcia, T., & McKeachie, W. J. (1993). Reliability and predictive validity of the Motivated Strategies for Learning Questionnaire (MSLQ). *Educational and Psychological Measurement, 53*, 801-813.

Powell, R. R. (1992). The influence of prior experiences on pedagogical constructs of traditional and non-traditional preservice teachers. *Teacher & Teacher Education, 8* (3), 225-238.

Prosser, M. & Trigwell, K. (1999). *Understanding learning and teaching: the experience of higher education.* Buckingham SRHE & Open University Press.

Roelofs, E. & Visser, J. (2001). Leeromgevingen volgens ouders en leraren: Voorkeuren en realisatie. [Parents and teachers about learning environments: Preferences and realization] *Pedagogische Studiën, 78,* 151-168.

Rossum, E. J. Van & Schenk, S. M. (1984). The relationship between learning conception, study strategy and learning outcome. *British Journal of Educational Psychology, 54,* 73-83.

Sadler-Smith, E. (1996). Approaches to studying: Age, gender and academic performance. *Educational Studies, 22* (3), 367-379.

Säljö, R. (1979). Learning about learning. *Higher Education, 8,* 443-451.

Samuelowicz, K. & Bain, J. (2001). Revisiting academics' beliefs about teaching and learning. *Higher Education, 41,* 299-325.

Stofflett, R. & Stoddart, T. (1994). The ability to understand and use conceptual change pedagogy as a function of prior content learning experience. *Journal of Research in Science Teaching, 31* (1), 31-51.

Tashakkori, A. & Teddlie, C. (2003). *Handbook of mixed methods in social & Behavioral research.* Thousand Oaks/London/New Delhi: Sage Publications.

Van Petegem, P., Donche, V. & Vanhoof, J. (in press). Relating preservice teachers' approaches to learning and preferences for constructivist learning environments. *Learning Environment Research, 8* (3).

Vermetten, Y. J., Lodewijks, H. G., & Vermunt, J. D. (1999). Consistency and variability of learning strategies in different university courses. *Higher Education, 37,* 1-21.

Vermetten, Y. J., Vermunt, J. D., & Lodewijks, H. G. (2002). Powerful learning environments? How do university students differ in their response to instructional measures. *Learning and Instruction, 12,* 263-284.

Vermunt, J. D. (1992). *Leerstijlen en sturen van leerprocessen in het hoger onderwijs – naar procesgerichte instructie in zelfstandig denken.* [Learning styles and regulation of learning in higher education – towards process-oriented instruction in autonomous thinking. Doctoral dissertation, Katholieke Universiteit Brabant, Tilburg. Amsterdam/Lisse: Swets & Zeitlinger.

Vermunt, J. D. (1998). The regulation of constructive learning processes. *British Journal of Educational Psychology, 68*, 149-171.

Vermunt, J. D. (2003). The power of learning environments and the quality of student learning. In E. De Corte, L. Verschaffel, N. Entwistle, & J. van Merriënboer (Eds.) (2003), *Powerful learning environments: unravelling basic components and dimensions, Advances in learning and instruction series* (pp. 109-124). Amsterdam/Boston/London: Pergamom.

Vermunt, J. D. (2005). Relations between student learning patterns and personal and contextual factors and academic performance. *Higher Education, 49,* 205-234.

Vermunt, J. D. & Minnaert, A. (2003). Dissonance in student learning patterns: when to revise theory? *Studies in Higher Education, 28* (1), 49-61.

Vermunt, J. D. & Verschaffel, L. (2000). Process-oriented teaching. In R.J. Simons, J. van der Linden, & T. Duffy (2000). *New learning* (pp. 209-225). Dordrecht/Boston/London: Kluwer Academic Publishers,.

Ward, J. H. (1963). Hierarchical grouping to optimise an objective function. *Journal of the American Statistical Association, 58*, 236-244.

Watkins, D. (2001). Correlates of approaches to learning: a cross-cultural meta-analysis. In R. J. Sternberg & L. Zhang. *Perspectives on thinking, learning, and cognitive styles* (165-195). Mahwah, New Jersey: Lawrence Erlbaum Associates.

Weinstein, C. E., Zimmerman, S. A., & Palmer, D. R. (1988). Assessing learning strategies: the design and development of the LASSI. In C. E. Weinstein, P. A. Alexander & E. T. Goetz (Eds.). *Learning and study strategies: Issues in assessment, instruction and evaluation* (pp.25-40). New York: Academic Press.

Wierstra, R. F. A. & Beerends, E. P. M. (1996). *Leeromgevingspercepties en leerstrategieën van eerstejaars studenten sociale wetenschappen* [Perceptions of learning environments and learning strategies of first-year students in social sciences]. Tijdschrift voor Onderwijsresearch, 21, 300-322.

Wierstra, R. F. A., Kanselaar, G., Van der Linden, J. L., Lodewijks, H. G., & Vermunt, J. D. (2003). The impact of the university context on European students' learning approaches and learning environment preferences. *Higher Education, 45* (4), 503-523.

Zimmerman, B. J. (2001). Theories of self-regulated learning and academic achievement: An overview and analysis. In B. J. Zimmerman & D. H. Schunk (Eds.), *Self-regulated learning and academic achievement. Theoretical perspectives* (pp. 1-37). Mahwah, NJ: Lawrence Erlbaum.

Chapter 6

CONVERGENCE AND DIVERGENCE BETWEEN STUDENTS' AND TEACHERS' PERCEPTIONS OF INSTRUCTIONAL BEHAVIOUR IN DUTCH SECONDARY EDUCATION

Perry den Brok
Utrecht University
The Netherlands

Theo Bergen
University of Nijmegen
The Netherlands

Mieke Brekelmans
Utrecht University
The Netherlands

This chapter discusses comparisons between students' and teachers' perceptions which are usable variables in investigating the teacher-learner process and the preparation and staff development of teachers. A review of over 30 learning environment studies that describe differences between teacher and student perceptions indicates that the majority of these studies have focused on teacher interpersonal behaviour, that differences often were not the main focus of these studies and that most studies focused on differences between groups of teachers and students, rather than individual teachers and their classes. It appeared that, on average, teachers have higher perception ratings than do their students, and that divergence seems to be related to teaching style (in terms of students' perceptions). The present study investigated divergence and convergence in the perceptions of 72 teachers (from various subjects) and their classes (1,604 students) with the Questionnaire of Instructional Behaviour (QIB) and pertained to teacher control of student learning (strong, shared or loose), clarity and classroom management. Results showed that almost half of the teachers had higher perception scores than did their students, that no relationship existed between teacher experience and the amount of divergence, and that teaching style was related to the amount of divergence found. It is argued that more research is needed in the domain of learning environments research that can explain convergence and divergence between student and teacher perceptions.

125

1. Introduction

Research over the last four decades has indicated that students' and teachers' perceptions are important elements in the psychological and social dimensions of classroom environments (Fraser, 1986, 1994, 1998). In the last 25 years, much attention has been given to the development and use of instruments to describe learning environments from the perspective of teachers and students (Fraser, 1998). Most of these instruments were questionnaires that mapped aspects of teaching and learning in the classroom. They are based on general theories assuming that human behaviour is shaped by the environment in interaction with the person (Lewin, 1936; Murray, 1938). Recently, learning environment researchers have used other data sources, such as observations or interviews, in association with questionnaires (Fraser, 1998).

In 1991, Brekelmans and Wubbels concluded that the majority of the studies in the domains of 'teacher thinking' and 'classroom environments research' either focused on teachers or students, but that studies incorporating both students' and teachers' views on the classroom and teachers' behaviour were scarce. Since their study, much has changed and many researchers have compared student and teacher perceptions of the classroom environment or teacher behaviour (for an overview, see den Brok, Levy, Rodriguez, & Wubbels, 2002; Fraser, 1998). Research investigating both teachers' and students' perceptions is regarded as important, because divergence and convergence between student and teacher perceptions have proven to be usable variables in investigating teaching-learning processes, or in the preparation of teachers and staff development (Brekelmans & Wubbels, 1991).

The present study[1] focuses on divergence and convergence between student and teacher perceptions of teachers' instructional behaviour in terms of control of student learning, classroom management and clarity. These elements of teachers' instructional behaviour were measured with the *Questionnaire on Instructional Behavior* (QIB, Lamberigts & Bergen, 2000). The study adds to the existing knowledge base in several ways.

---

[1] A preliminary version of this manuscript was presented as a paper at the annual meeting of the American Educational Research Association, Chicago, April 2003. The first author was supported with a grant of the Netherlands Organisation for Scientific Research (NWO, project no. 411-21-206).

First, most of the studies have focused on divergence with respect to teacher interpersonal behaviour (e.g., den Brok, et al., 2002). Studies investigating divergence focusing on control, classroom management and clarity have been less frequent (exceptions are studies by Beam & Horvat, 1975; Biemans, Jongmans, de Jong, & Bergen, 1999; Fisher & Fraser, 1983; Fraser, 1982). Second, in cases where teacher instructional behaviour was the object of interest, differences between the perceptions of teachers and students often were not the explicit focus of study (e.g., Bergen, Derksen & Lamberigts, 1997; Derksen, Engelen, Sleegers, Bergen, & Imants, 1999; Engelen, 2002; Engelen, Bergen, Derksen & Sleegers, 2000). As a result, differences or similarities between teachers' and students' perceptions were not statistically tested. Third, in most of the studies, statistical analyses, such as paired t-tests or analyses of variance (means analysis), were performed on normal difference scores. While such scores may be helpful in detecting and testing differences between teachers and students, they have a few limitations. One limitation is that positive and negative differences can balance each other out (Brekelmans & Wubbels, 1991). Another limitation is that the analyses performed were useful to detect differences between groups of teachers and students, but fall short in determining if a particular difference between one teacher and his or her class can be regarded as 'large' or 'significant' (Brekelmans & Wubbels, 1991).

This chapter begins with a discussion on earlier research focussing on differences between teacher and student perceptions of teacher behaviour. After this discussion, a number of hypotheses are presented and tested. Finally, the method and results of the study are presented.

2. Differences between Student and Teacher Perceptions

A literature review was conducted on studies that included both students' and teachers' perceptions of teacher behaviour (see Appendix A[2] for complete list in chronological order).

---

[2] We conducted an ERIC search using the following terms: 'student perceptions', 'student ratings', 'teacher perceptions', 'teacher ratings', 'teacher behaviour'. Documents were selected if they included one of the teacher and student search terms and if teacher behaviour was the topic of interest. Also, we reviewed all issues of the journals 'Learning Environments Research', 'Teaching and Teacher Education' and 'Journal of Research on Classroom Interaction' from 1990 to 2001. Articles including the above search terms

2.1 Studies on interpersonal behaviour

Quite a number of studies have focused on differences between teachers'
and students' perceptions with respect to *interpersonal teacher
behaviour* (den Brok, Levy, et. al., 2002). These studies investigated
teacher behaviour in terms of the two Leary (1957) based interpersonal
dimensions of teacher influence and teacher proximity, or in terms of
eight sectors of behaviour that make up these dimensions (leadership,
helpful/friendly, understanding, giving responsibility/freedom, uncertain,
dissatisfied, admonishing and strict behaviour) and used the
Questionnaire on Teacher Interaction (QTI, Wubbels, Créton, &
Hooymayers, 1985) to map students' and teachers' perceptions.

In most of these studies, considerable differences were reported
between teachers' and students' perceptions. On average, teachers
reported higher ratings of their own leadership, helpful/friendly and
understanding behaviour than did their students, while they reported
lower perceptions of their own uncertain, dissatisfied and admonishing
behaviour (e.g., den Brok, Levy, et al., 2002; Fisher & Rickards, 1999;
Harkin & Turner, 1997; Rickards & Fisher, 2000; Wubbels, Brekelmans,
& Hermans, 1987; Wubbels, Brekelmans, & Hooymayers, 1992; Yuen,
1999). Some studies also reported higher teacher than student
perceptions of strictness and lower teacher than student perceptions of
giving responsibility (Fisher & Rickards, 1999; Rickards & Fisher,
2000). Behaviours for which teachers reported higher perceptions than
their students – strictness, leadership, helpful/friendly and understanding
– have found to be positively related to student achievement and
motivation, while behaviours for which lower teacher than student
perceptions were reported were negatively associated with student
achievement and motivation (e.g., Brekelmans, Wubbels, & den Brok,
2002; den Brok, 2001). The differences between teacher and student
perceptions remained if the higher order interpersonal dimensions of
influence and proximity were used (Brekelmans & Wubbels, 1991;

combinations in their title or abstract and focusing on teacher behaviour were
included in the overview. Finally, conference papers and other documents sent
to us by colleagues were also included, as long as they were written in English.
In the Appendix, only those studies that were conducted in secondary
(vocational) education are included.

Brekelmans, et al., 2002; Fisher, Fraser, Wubbels, & Brekelmans, 1993; Levy, Wubbels & Brekelmans, 1993; Wubbels & Brekelmans, 1997).

Correlations between teachers' and students' perceptions seem to be moderate to low (Wubbels, et al., 1987). Looking at individual teacher-class combinations, Wubbels and colleagues (1992) found that 67 percent of the teachers had higher perceptions than their students on influence and proximity, while 33 percent had lower perceptions. Brekelmans and Wubbels (1991) reported that 92 percent of the teachers in their study showed divergence between their own perceptions and those of their students, and two thirds of these had higher perceptions than their students. A small number of studies reported non-significant differences between students' and teachers' perceptions (Ben-Chaim & Zoller, 2001; Wubbels & Levy, 1991).

It remains unclear to what extent differences in perceptions may be related to teacher experience. A study by Brekelmans and Wubbels (1991) on 1,156 teachers showed no significant relationships between teacher experience and divergence or convergence between students' and teachers' perceptions of influence and proximity. However, longitudinal studies involving 51 and 573 teachers indicate that differences with respect to proximity become larger during the teaching career, while they remain equal or become smaller for influence (Brekelmans, et al., 2002; Brekelmans, Holvast & van Tartwijk, 1993). Other evidence is provided by a small study involving six individual teachers and qualitative data in the form of classroom observations and teacher interviews (Fisher, Fraser & Creswell, 1995). In the latter study, however, experience seemed to influence differences in perceptions together with (initial) interpersonal teaching style.

Differences between students' and teachers' perceptions of interpersonal behaviour may also be related to ethnicity or cultural background of teachers and students. In one study, differences between Caucasian-American students and their Caucasian teachers were lower than between Asian-American or Hispanic-American students and their (Caucasian) teachers (Levy, Wubbels, Brekelmans, & Morganfield, 1997). A study comparing USA and Dutch teachers showed that, while statistically non-significant, differences between American students and their teachers were somewhat smaller than between Dutch students and teachers (Wubbels & Levy, 1991). In a third study, Hispanic-American teachers displayed larger divergence with their students than did Asian-American teachers (den Brok, Levy, et al., 2002), however, divergence between teacher and student perceptions is not related to both participants 'being of the same cultural background' or not.

Investigations of relationships between teaching style and divergence or convergence between teachers' and students' perceptions seemed to indicate that if student perceptions of influence and proximity were higher, divergence between student and teacher perceptions was smaller (Brekelmans & Wubbels, 1991; Wubbels, et al., 1987, 1992).

Thus, it can be concluded that most teachers have higher perceptions than their students for behaviours that are positively related to student outcomes, while they have lower perceptions for areas that are negatively associated with student outcomes. Moreover, divergence may be related to experience, ethnicity and interpersonal teaching style.

2.2 Studies on other classroom environment or teaching elements

Studies on differences between students' and teachers' perceptions outside the domain of interpersonal behaviour have investigated a variety of aspects with similar results. Statistically significant differences have been reported between students' and teachers' perceptions of teacher personal involvement, differentiation, stimulating student participation and promoting student independence (Fisher & Fraser, 1983; Fraser, 1982; Hofstein & Lazarowitz, 1986), task orientation, providing order and rule clarification (Fraser & Wubbels, 1995; Maor & Fraser, 1985), verbal and nonverbal teacher immediacy (Gorham & Zakahi, 1990), competition, democracy, goal direction, task difficulty, satisfaction, formality, involvement, rule clarity and cohesiveness (Moos, 1979), promoting student inquiry (Beam & Horvat, 1975), gender differentiation (Martin & Combs, 2000), and feedback (Voeller, 1982). Higher teacher than student perceptions have also been reported for primary education (Fraser & O'Brien, 1985) and higher education (Fraser, 1994). According to Moos (1979) and Fraser (1982) correlations between teachers' and students' perceptions are moderate to low. Moos and Fraser report average product-moment correlations of 0.50 and 0.51 and rank-order correlations of 0.37 and 0.77, respectively.

A study using the Questionnaire on Instructional Behaviour (Biemans, et al., 1999) in secondary vocational education reported significantly higher student than teacher perceptions on student-led control, teacher-led control, clarity and classroom management. The study also found that divergence between students' and teachers' perceptions was related to teachers' instructional style: highly controlling teachers showed more divergence than less controlling teachers.

A number of studies investigated student and teacher perceptions during a professional development program aimed at teachers' activating behaviour (Bergen, et al, 1997; Derksen, et al., 1999; Engelen, 2002; Engelen, et al., 2000). These studies showed that teacher perceptions, of activation, clarity and control, remained stable during the programs, and if they became higher, this was accompanied by a growth in student perceptions. Consequently, differences between students' and teachers' perceptions changed little, and in cases where they became smaller, this was merely achieved by students' perceptions becoming higher. In one study (Derksen, et al., 1997), differences between teachers' and students' perceptions even became larger as a consequence of the intervention program. However, none of these studies provided tests of significance for the differences found.

Thus, it seems that, regardless of the domain of teaching studied, teachers' on average have higher perceptions than their students with respect to the areas of interest. Moreover, divergences seem hard to change and may be related to teaching styles (in terms of student perceptions).

2.3 Issues with respect to divergence between students' and teachers' perceptions

The studies reviewed above generally used difference scores – e.g., teacher minus student ratings - to investigate discrepancies. While such scores are indicative for differences between teachers' and students' perceptions, an important disadvantage is that, if difference scores over groups of persons are the object of study, positive and negative difference scores may balance each other out. Therefore, Brekelmans and Wubbels (1991) advised the use of both *regular* difference scores as well as *absolute* difference scores. The latter can be use to determine overall magnitudes of divergence, the former can be used to distinguish teachers with positive divergence from teachers with negative divergence.

Another problem with most of the studies is that they use *groups* of teachers and their students to determine discrepancy, but provide no means of establishing whether an *individual* teacher should be regarded as convergent or divergent. Here, Brekelmans and Wubbels (1991) suggest that a difference score should be regarded as "divergence", if it becomes larger than the measurement error associated with it. If this is the case, it can be expected that, with at least a 67% chance, the difference is larger than zero (see note 3). The measurement error of the difference score is based on reliability and variance of both teachers' and students' perceptions (see note 2).

An important issue remains of how to *explain* divergence between perceptions. Some argue that student perceptions may be subject to "grading leniency" (Greenwald, 1997) and, as a consequence, may not be reliable. However, this view has been disputed because of the reciprocal nature between grading and perceptions, because many other elements determine students' perceptions, and because of the mixed evidence with respect to this assumption (Marsh & Roche, 1997). Moreover, research has shown that student perceptions are extremely reliable if elements are studied that do not relate to subject matter related (pedagogical) behaviour, and that students are well able to distinguish differences in teaching style between (their) teachers (d'Apollonia & Abrami, 1997). Others argue that attribution processes and teacher ideals may influence their perception of their own teaching (Brekelmans & Wubbels, 1991; Wubbels & Levy, 1993). In this line of reasoning, higher teacher than student perceptions may be the consequence of *wishful thinking*, while lower teacher than student perceptions may be the result of *protection against disappointment*. Evidence for the influence of such thought processes was found in teachers explanations of their own ratings (Wubbels & Levy, 1993). Psychologists have also argued that role differences between raters may contribute to divergence via attribution processes: *actors* (e.g., teachers) have been found to regard their own behaviour as more heavily influenced by environmental circumstances, while *observers* (e.g., students) have been found to focus on relatively stable traits or dispositions (Watson, 1982). As a consequence, both groups may focus on different elements or value elements in their observations differently, resulting in divergence. Some evidence for this view has been suggested by small-scale studies in which students and teachers were interviewed (e.g., Cothran & Ennis, 1997; Sheets, 2002).

3. Teachers' Instructional Behaviour

In this study, teacher behaviour is studied from an *instructional* perspective. This means that teaching is studied in terms of those behaviours that 'define' students' roles in the learning process. One important element in defining the students' role is the degree to which students have control over their own learning activities (den Brok, Bergen, Stahl, & Brekelmans, 2004). Another element is the degree to which teachers are explicit or clear about what students have to learn and how (e.g., Brekelmans, Sleegers, & Fraser, 2000; den Brok, 2001). The second element is often referred to as clarity (Cruickshank & Kennedy, 1986), the first is called teaching for active learning (Brekelmans, et al., 2000), activating instruction (Lamberigts & Bergen, 2000), control (den Brok, et al., 2004) or delegation (den Brok, 2001). Additionally, research on teacher effectiveness has shown that classroom management is an important prerequisite for student learning and student on-task behaviour (Creemers, 1994; den Brok, 2001).

Since at least the days of John Dewey, educators have disagreed with respect to the different forms and degrees of control that teachers can, do and should exhibit in facilitating students' completion of learning tasks. Most distinguish between three graduations of teacher control (Brekelmans, et al., 2000; den Brok, 2001; Simons & de Jong, 1992; Vermunt & Verloop, 1999): (a) *strong control*, or taking over or substituting the performance of students completion of learning-related tasks; (b) *shared control*, or activating and facilitating students to take a very active part in guiding and completing the target learning tasks; and (c) *loose control*, or stimulating and motivating students to complete learning activities by themselves with little if any teacher involvement in regulating their behaviours as they complete the needed tasks. For shared control, sometimes a further distinction is made between (a) *shared responsibility between student and teacher* and (b) *shared responsibility between student and student* (den Brok, et al., 2002). Others (Shuell, 1993, 1996) distinguish between two traditional forms of control: *student-control* (i.e., student-initiated control) and *teacher-control* (i.e., teacher-initiated control).

In the case of *strong teacher control*, the teacher takes over or substitutes for the major activities needed for completing targeted learning tasks from students. Examples of this are teacher behaviours such as presenting an outline, providing students with examples, and highlighting main points. In each instance, the teacher does what students could and presumably should be doing. In the case of *loose teacher control*, the teacher assumes that students on their own initiative will begin and complete all the needed cognitive, affective and regulative learning activities by themselves. In these instances, the teacher allows students to operate freely and independently during learning activities on the assumption that students know what they are to do, are doing and are expected to do and are in fact doing all that is needed to complete the activities in an acceptable way. Some might refer to this as a form of extreme 'laissez faire' overseeing of learning tasks by the teacher. With *shared control*, students are continually activated either implicitly or explicitly by their teacher to perform and complete targeted learning activities to some desired end. Examples of this construct of regulation are such teacher behaviours as asking questions, giving assignments or assigning tasks, and stimulating students to cooperate.

Although these constructs of control within the classroom include a range of meanings and conceptualisations, they all acknowledge that completing classroom tasks is not so much about the teacher presenting information and controlling the learning process, but about a shift of responsibilities for completing these tasks from the teacher to students. Within popular conceptions of 'teaching for active learning,' a distinction is made between *teacher-led*, *student-led* and *co-student-led* control. In instances of *teacher-led control*, teachers model learning activities for the students and try to elicit the prior knowledge that is necessary for performing the learning activities. According to Lamberigts and Bergen (2000), teacher-led control is theoretically linked to ideas that can be found in cognitive constructivism, or highly teacher-centred methods, such as Direct Instruction (Rosenshine, 1978, 1983; Stahl, 1992). In instances of *co-student-led control*, teachers stimulate students to cooperate while completing the learning activities. Presumably this type of control is consistent with the theoretical assumptions of optimal cooperative learning activities and activities aligned with the most social-oriented branches of constructivism (Stahl, 1999). In the situation of *student-led control*, teachers challenge, encourage and entice students to engage in learning activities by themselves as much as possible, while leaving students decisions like which activities to perform, in what order to complete the activities, and the time to take to complete each part of each activity. This type of control is theoretically linked to radical-individualistic constructivism and to popular notions associated with the concept of 'powerful learning environments' (Lamberigts & Bergen, 2000).

Table 6.1. Sample Items of the QIB

Scale	Sample item
Clarity	If s/he explains something, s/he is easy to understand.
Classroom Management	During his/her lesson, you can easily do something else.
Strong Control	S/he provides strategies for planning school work.
Shared Control	S/he stimulates us to help each other when working on a task.
Loose Control	S/he lets us determine our own pace in working on tasks.

To map teachers' instructional behaviour, Lamberigts and Bergen (2000) developed the Questionnaire on Instructional Behaviour (QIB). The QIB consists of 33 items in five scales. Using a five-point Likert scale, students indicate what they think of their teacher (as teachers do with respect to their own behaviour). Item values vary from "1" showing the indicated behaviour hardly ever, to "5" showing the indicated behaviour very often. The five scales (den Brok, Bergen, & Stahl, 2002) are: Clarity (7 items), Classroom Management (6 items), Strong Control (3 items), Shared Control (9 items) and Loose Control (3 items). Clarity refers to the degree to which it is clear to students what they have to do and how the lesson content is structured. Classroom Management deals with the extent to which students have to obey rules set by the teacher, or the degree to which inattentive behaviour is allowed. The Strong Control scale mainly consists of items on providing students with strategies to perform their learning activities, the Shared Control scale with items on sharing of responsibility between students and between student and teacher, while the Loose Control scale focuses on students' own decision making during the performance of learning activities. The shared teacher control factor includes items that refer to situations in which students are asked to work cooperatively and situations in which students can show initiative during whole class situations. Table 6.1 provides a sample item for each of the scales and Appendix B provides the complete instrument.

4. Hypotheses

This study investigated divergence and convergence between teachers' and students' perceptions of teachers' instructional behaviour focusing on clarity, classroom management, strong control, shared control and loose control. Based on the literature, the following hypotheses were formulated and put to the test:

H1: On average, teachers have higher perceptions than their students with respect to control, clarity and classroom management, and more teachers can be found displaying higher perceptions with respect to these behaviours than teachers displaying lower perceptions than their students.

H2: The more experience teachers have, the smaller divergence there is between their own perceptions of control, clarity and classroom management, and those of their students.

H3: Teachers with instructional styles (in terms of student perceptions) that are characterized by higher amounts of control, clarity and classroom management display smaller amounts of divergence than teachers with styles that are characterized by lower amounts of control, clarity and classroom management.

5. Method

To test our hypotheses, questionnaire data were gathered from 72 secondary education teachers - from seven schools - and their students (n=1,604). Fifty-one percent of the students were male. Students ranged in age between 13 and 17 years. Teacher experience varied between 1 and 29 years, 56 teachers had more than 10 years of experience, while 5 teachers had less than 5 years of experience. Teachers taught all school subjects, except physical education. The majority of the teachers either taught Math, Dutch Language, and English as a Secondary Language or Science. About half of the teachers were male.

Both teachers and students completed the Questionnaire on Instructional Behaviour (QIB). Quality of the scales of the QIB appeared to be satisfactory (see Tables 6.2 and 6.3). Reliability of the scales was sufficient: Cronbach's alpha ranged between 0.82 (Shared Control) and 0.92 (Classroom Management) for students' perceptions and between 0.64 (Loose Control) and 0.75 (Strong Control) for teachers perceptions. Intra class correlations of the scales ranged between 0.16 (Loose Control) and 0.67 (Strong Control), meaning that significant amounts of variance could be found at the teacher-class level as compared to the (individual) student level. Thus, the scales of the QIB differentiate between teachers. Also, mean inter-scale correlations ranged between 0.11 and 0.33 for students' perceptions and between -0.04 and 0.22

for teachers' perceptions, meaning that the scales measured distinct, though partially related elements of teachers' instructional behaviour.

Table 6.2. Reliability, Standard Errors, Intra Class Correlations (ICC) and Mean Correlation of QIB Scale with Other Scales for Student Perception Data

Scale	Alpha students	s.e. students	ICC	Mean correlation with other QIB scales
Clarity	0.85	0.18	0.21	0.33
Classroom M't	0.92	0.14	0.29	0.11
Strong Control	0.83	0.24	0.67	0.27
Shared Control	0.82	0.22	0.48	0.30
Loose Control	0.86	0.20	0.16	0.18

Note: s.e.=standard error

Table 6.3. Reliability, Standard Errors and Mean Correlation of QIB Scale with Other Scales for Teacher Perception Data

Scale	Alpha teachers	s.e. teachers	Mean correlation with QIB scales
Clarity	0.73	0.30	0.05
Classroom M't	0.70	0.28	0.08
Strong Control	0.75	0.40	-0.04
Shared Control	0.68	0.35	0.22
Loose Control	0.64	0.47	0.10

Note: s.e.=standard error

For each of the five scales, absolute and regular difference scores were computed, as well as the measurement error[3] of the regular difference scores. We considered a difference score larger than the measurement error as divergence, while scores smaller than the

---

[3] To calculate measurement error (m.e.) in the difference scores we used the equation: $m.e. = \sqrt{(se_t^2 \quad se_{st}^2)}$; se_t, se_{st} = standard error of measurement (se) in scale scores of the perceptions of teachers (t) and students (st). To calculate the standard error of measurement in the scale scores we used the equation: $se = st\sqrt{(1-r_{tt})}$; st = standard deviation of the scale score, r_{tt} = reliability of the scale scores, represented by Cronbach's alpha.

measurement error were considered as convergence (e.g., Brekelmans, et al., 1991)[4]. Next, absolute and regular difference scores were studied by means of correlations, t-tests, analyses of variance and cross tabular analyses to uncover the direction of the differences and establish relationships with teacher experience, which was measured as a categorical variable with the score 0 (1 - 5 years), 1 (6 – 10 years) or 2 (> 10 years). To test the last hypothesis, cluster analyses (squared Euclidian distances, Ward method) were performed to detect specific "styles" of instructional behaviour and determined if these styles displayed different amounts of divergence[5].

6. Results

The first step in the analyses consisted of computing absolute and regular difference scores, and measurement error of the difference scores. The results of these analyses are displayed in Table 6.4.

As can be seen in Table 6.4, mean absolute difference scores are larger than the measurement errors. This means that, on average, a divergence is found between teachers' and students' perceptions for all QIB scales. However, considerable differences can also be found in the absolute (and regular) difference scores, indicating that some teachers only marginally differ from their students in their perceptions, while others differ considerably. In the case of Clarity, Classroom Management

---

[4] When a difference score is larger than the measurement error we can expect, with at least 68% certainty, that this difference score is larger than zero. When a difference score is about twice as large as the measurement error, the expectation has a certainty of more than 95%.

[5] Student perceptions, rather than teacher perceptions or a combination of both, were used in these cluster analyses to determine instructional styles. One reason for this was the advantage student perceptions have over teacher perceptions (e.g. Fraser, 1982; den Brok, 2001): they are based on a series of lessons and comparison with other teachers, are less subject to mood swings or contextual influences due to the large number of students within a class and are usually very reliable. Another reason is the pragmatic importance of student perceptions: students' behaviour in class and their outcomes are determined by the effect teacher behaviour has on them (hence: their perception), rather than by how teachers perceive themselves. Other reasons are comparability to earlier research, the rather low number of teachers to obtain stable results when combining them with other variables and differences in conceptual structure of teacher perceptions (den Brok, et al., 2004).

and Loose Control, positive and negative divergence seem to balance each other out, since mean difference scores are close to zero, while in the case of Strong and Shared Control more negative divergence (higher teacher than student ratings) can be found.

Table 6.4. Measurement Errors (m.e.) of Difference Scores, Mean Absolute Difference Scores and Mean Difference Scores (scores represent student minus teacher perceptions) for QIB Scales

Scale	m.e. difference score	Mean absolute difference score (s.d.)	Mean difference score (s.d.)
Clarity	0.35	0.49 (0.38)	-0.04 (0.62)
Classroom Management	0.31	0.50 (0.35)	0.07 (0.61)
Strong Control	0.47	0.96 (0.71)	-0.75 (0.93)
Shared Control	0.41	0.51 (0.43)	-0.38 (0.55)
Loose Control	0.51	0.61 (0.47)	0.08 (0.77)

Note: m.e.=standard error; s.d.=standard deviation

Table 6.5 presents the numbers of teachers with divergence and convergence. As can be seen, about half of the teachers is divergent on the Shared and Loose Control scales, while about two-third of the teachers is divergent for Clarity, Classroom Management and Strong Control. The patterns of divergence are different from scale to scale: by far the majority of the teachers has higher ratings than their students on the Strong Control and Shared Control scales (as was already predicted from the results in Table 6.4); just over half of the teachers "overestimate" on the Clarity scale; less than half of the teachers to about one third has higher perceptions than their students on the Classroom Management and Loose Control scales.

To test the second hypothesis, we compared the experience of teachers with divergence and teachers with convergence. In this manner, two groups were formed: one with divergent teachers and one with convergent teachers. The mean experience of these groups per scale was compared with a t-test. The results of these analyses are reported in Table 6.6.

Table 6.5. Teachers with Convergence (Difference Score Smaller than
            Measurement Error), Overestimating (Teacher Rating Higher than
            Student Rating) and Underestimating (Teacher Rating Lower than
            Student Rating) on the Scales of the QIB

Scale	Convergence	Overestimating	Underestimating
Clarity	30	24	18
Classroom Management	29	18	23
Strong Control	22	43	7
Shared Control	36	31	5
Loose Control	34	14	24

Table 6.6. Average Experience of Teachers with Convergence and Divergence
            between Student and Teacher Perceptions

Scale	Convergence	Divergence	T-value	p (sig)
Clarity	0.53 (0.78)	0.76 (0.88)	-1.142	0.257
Classroom Management	0.55 (0.78)	0.74 (0.88)	-0.954	0.343
Strong Control	0.64 (0.79)	0.68 (0.87)	-0.202	0.841
Shared Control	0.75 (0.84)	0.58 (0.84)	-0.841	0.403
Loose Control	0.56 (0.79)	0.76 (0.88)	-1.032	0.306

Note: Experience can be scored as 0 (< 5 years), 1 (6 – 10 years) or 2 (> 10
years).

Table 6.7. ANOVA for Experience on Absolute Difference Scores in QIB
            Scales

Scale	< 5 years	6 – 10 years	> 10 years	F-value	p (sig)
Clarity	0.53 (.043)	0.48 (0.28)	0.43 (0.31)	0.407	0.667
Classroom Management	0.48 (.035)	0.44 (0.32)	0.59 0(.37)	0.872	0.423
Strong Control	0.94 (0.70)	1.01 (0.89)	0.97 (0.60)	0.042	0.958
Shared Control	0.60 (0.47)	0.35 (0.28)	0.44 (0.40)	2.113	0.129
Loose Control	0.62 (0.48)	0.55 (0.48)	0.63 (0.47)	0.141	0.869

It seems that the group of teachers with convergence is almost as
experienced as the group of teachers with divergence. Thus, results of
Table 6.6 show no statistically significant relationship between

experience and divergence. To investigate the relationship between experience and divergence more in detail, we compared the amount of divergence between the three experience groups. The difference scores are compared by means of an analysis of variance (ANOVA) and presented in Table 6.7.

According to Table 6.7, difference scores are not statistically different for the three experience groups. The largest, non-significant difference can be found for Shared Control: teachers with less than five years of experience have somewhat higher difference scores than teachers with more than five years of experience. Again, these outcomes indicate no relationship between experience and divergence or convergence. As a last check, we compared the amount of experience for teachers with higher perceptions than their students (over-estimation) and teachers with lower perceptions than their students (under-estimation) (see Table 6.8).

Table 6.8. Average Experience for Teachers with Over-estimation and Teachers with Under-estimation on QIB Scales

Scale	Underestimation	Overestimation	T-value	p (sig)
Clarity	1.22 (0.94)	0.42 (0.65)	3.108	0.004
Classroom Management	1.08 (0.91)	0.28 (0.57)	3.538	0.001
Strong Control	0.57 (0.79)	0.70 (0.89)	-0.354	0.725
Shared Control	0.60 (0.89)	0.58 (0.85)	0.047	0.963
Loose Control	0.96 (0.91)	0.76 (0.20)	1.840	0.074

Table 6.8 reports some significant results. It seems that the group with lower teacher than student perceptions on the Clarity scale is more experienced than the group with higher teacher than student perceptions. A similar pattern is found for the Classroom Management scale. The same pattern is also found for the Loose Control scale, although the difference is not significant. Thus, according to these last analyses, teachers that have higher perceptions than their students on a number of scales are less experienced than teachers that have lower perceptions than their students. It may be that inexperienced teachers are more idealistic than experienced teachers, as they are less shaped by everyday practice and influence of their teacher training may still be present. This

'idealism' may lead to wishful thinking, resulting in higher perceptions of their own behaviour as compared to perceptions of others (students).

To check whether teaching style was related to the amount of divergence or convergence, we first distinguished between different instructional styles. This was done by performing a cluster analysis (in SPSS). The cluster analysis was set up in such a manner, that it resulted in groups with maximally different styles. To check if differences between styles were significant with respect to the scale scores, analyses of variance (ANOVA) and Scheffé tests for post-hoc comparisons were performed. It seemed a distinction in four styles was optimal and yielded interpretable patterns and sufficiently large groups. These four styles were labelled as follows: 'teacher-centred' (24 teachers, scoring particularly high on Clarity, Classroom Management and Strong Control), 'laissez-faire' (9 teachers, scoring low on all scales, except for Loose Control), 'student-centred' (21 teachers, scoring particularly high on Shared and Loose Control and moderately high on the other scales), and 'ineffective' (18 teachers, scoring low on all variables). The mean scale scores for each of the four styles are graphically presented in Figure 6.1.

When comparing the four teaching styles (teacher-centred, laissez-faire, student-centred, ineffective) by means of a cross tabular analysis, we found no significantly different numbers of teachers showing divergence and convergence (see Table 6.9). Nevertheless, results were almost significant for Clarity: here, more teachers with convergence than divergence could be found for the Laissez-faire style, while for the other three styles more teachers with divergence than convergence could be found. Such patterns were recognizable also for the Strong and Shared Control scales, but, as was the case for Clarity, not statistically significant.

When teachers with teacher-centred and laissez-faire instructional styles showed smaller amounts of divergence for 'clarity' than teachers with other styles. Moreover, teachers with a teacher-centred instructional style displayed lower amounts of divergence on 'strong control' than teachers with other styles. For all other scales, amounts of divergence were not statistically different between instructional styles (see Table 6.10).

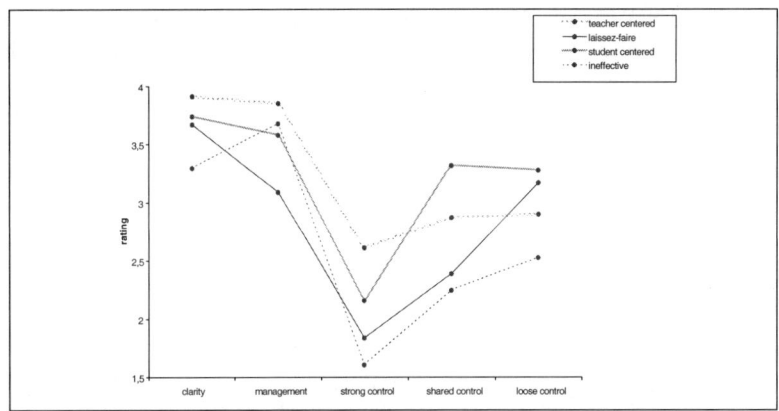

Figure 6.1. Profiles of instructional styles of teachers (N=72).

Table 6.9. Number of Teachers with Convergence and Divergence between Student and Teacher Perceptions on QIB Scales according to Teaching Profile

Scale	Profile	Convergence	Divergence	Chi-squared	*p* (sig)
Clarity	Teacher-cent	11	13	7.029	0.071
	Laissez-faire	7	2		
	Student-cent	7	14		
	Ineffective	5	13		
Classroom	Teacher-cent	11	13	0.775	0.855
Management	Laissez-faire	4	5		
	Student-cent	8	13		
	Ineffective	6	12		
Strong	Teacher-cent	11	13	4.610	0.203
Control	Laissez-faire	2	7		
	Student-cent	6	15		
	Ineffective	3	15		
Shared	Teacher-cent	10	14	1.937	0.586
Control	Laissez-faire	6	3		
	Student-cent	10	11		
	Ineffective	10	8		
Loose	Teacher-cent	9	15	2.810	0.422
Control	Laissez-faire	4	5		
	Student-cent	13	8		
	Ineffective	8	10		

Note: Teacher-cent=teacher-centred, student-cent=student centred.

Table 6.10. ANOVA of Absolute Difference Scores between Student and Teacher Perceptions on QIB Scales for Different Teaching Profiles.

Scale	Profile	Difference score	F-value	p (sig)
Clarity	Teacher-cent	0.39 (0.28)	3.036	0.035
	Laissez-faire	0.31 (0.39)		
	Student-cent	0.55 (0.39)		
	Ineffective	0.66 (0.40)		
Classroom management	Teacher-cent	0.47 (0.36)	0.272	0.845
	Laissez-faire	0.44 (0.35)		
	Student-cent	0.51 (0.34)		
	Ineffective	0.55 (0.38)		
Strong control	Teacher-cent	0.55 (0.37)	5.173	0.003
	Laissez-faire	1.18 (0.96)		
	Student-cent	1.07 (0.65)		
	Ineffective	1.27 (0.76)		
Shared control	Teacher-cent	0.49 (0.37)	0.581	0.629
	Laissez-faire	0.37 (0.32)		
	Student-cent	0.52 (0.40)		
	Ineffective	0.59 (0.56)		
Loose control	Teacher-cent	0.65 (0.48)	1.794	0.156
	Laissez-faire	0.53 (0.29)		
	Student-cent	0.44 (0.44)		
	Ineffective	0.77 (0.53)		

Note: Teacher-cent=teacher-centred, student-cent=student centred.

When checking for the direction of difference scores, statistical differences were found for Clarity and Loose Control (see Table 6.11). It appeared that for the ineffective style, more teachers could be found with higher perceptions than their students on these two scales, while most teachers in the other styles had lower perceptions than their students. No distinctive patterns could be found for the other variables.

As a last check, we computed correlations between student perceptions of the instructional variables and absolute difference scores (Table 6.12). It was found that the higher teachers were perceived on Classroom Management' by their students, the smaller their difference scores were (correlation was -0.31, $p=0.008$). A similar correlation was found for Shared Control (correlation of -0.41, $p=0.004$).

Table 6.11. Number of Teachers Under-estimating and Over-estimating on QIB
Scales for Each of the Teaching Profiles

Scale	Profile	Under-estimating	Over-estimating	Chi-squared	p (sig)
Clarity	Teacher-cent	7	6	9.872	0.02
	Laissez-faire	1	1		
	Student-cent	9	5		
	Ineffective	1	12		
Classroom	Teacher-cent	10	3	4.972	0.174
Management	Laissez-faire	1	4		
	Student-cent	7	6		
	Ineffective	7	5		
Strong Control	Teacher-cent	4	9	4.377	0.224
	Laissez-faire	1	6		
	Student-cent	1	14		
	Ineffective	1	14		
Shared Control	Teacher-cent	2	12	3.424	0.331
	Laissez-faire	-	3		
	Student-cent	3	8		
	Ineffective	-	8		
Loose Control	Teacher-cent	10	5	8.203	0.042
	Laissez-faire	5	-		
	Student-cent	6	2		
	Ineffective	3	7		

Table 6.12. Correlation between Absolute Difference Scores and Student
Perception Scores for QIB Scales

	Clarity	Classroom Management	Strong Control	Shared Control	Loose Control
Correlation	-0.25	-0.31*	-0.07	-0.41*	-0.22

Note: *=significant at .025
Negative values indicate that the lower the lower the students' perceptions on the scale,
the larger the absolute difference between student and teacher perceptions.

7. Discussion

In this study, three hypotheses with respect to differences between
teachers' and students' perceptions of teachers' instructional behaviour
were put to the test. According to the first hypothesis, most of the
teachers would have higher perceptions than their students on most of the

instructional behaviour scales of the QIB. This hypothesis was partially confirmed: about one-third to half of the teachers differed considerably – e.g., more than the measurement error of the difference – from their students, and of these divergent teachers, three quarters to less than half of the teachers had higher perceptions than their students. While these findings show patterns that are similar to those found in studies on interpersonal teacher behaviour (e g , Brekelmans & Wubbels, 1991) in many respects, there are also a number of striking differences. First of all, there is much variation between scales in the degree of divergence and amounts of teachers with divergent scores. More teachers seem to be divergent for the Shared and Loose Control scales than for the other scales. Also, there is variation between scales in the direction of divergence: while the majority of the teachers with divergence has a higher perception than their students for the Strong and Shared Control scales, the majority of the teachers with divergence has a lower perception than their students for the Classroom Management and Loose Control scales. It may be that some behaviours, such as clarity or strong control, are easier for teachers to (self) observe than some of the other behaviours. Also, recent, large-scale educational reforms in the Netherlands aiming at more student independence and self-directed learning may have led to wishful thinking on the part of the teachers. Of course, these interpretations are highly speculative, and more research is needed to provide empirical evidence. Such research should include teachers' explanations for their self-observations and interpretations of their own behaviour in the classroom, which could be extracted, for example, by means of interviews or classroom observations.

The second hypothesis stated that experienced teachers would show less divergence than relatively inexperienced teachers. This hypothesis could not be confirmed: no statistical relationship was found between teacher experience and divergence. Nevertheless, we did find that teachers with positive divergence (e.g., higher perceptions than their students) on Clarity and Classroom Management were relatively inexperienced, while teachers with negative divergence on these scales were more experienced. The weak or absent relationship between experience and divergence is in line with the results of the study by Brekelmans and Wubbels (1991) on interpersonal behaviour. However, given the mixed findings in earlier research as well as in the present study, more research on larger groups of teachers is needed to provide more convincing evidence for a possible relationship between experience and divergence. A valuable addition in this respect would be the use of longitudinal data.

The third and last hypothesis assumed that divergence would be related to instructional (teaching) style. Some evidence was found in favour of this hypothesis. It seemed that 'ineffective' teachers displayed more divergence for Clarity, while 'teacher-centred' teachers were less divergent on Clarity and Strong Control than teachers with other styles. Also, the amount of Clarity and Shared Control perceived by students was related to the amount of divergence: higher amounts related to lower divergence. These findings are in line with research in the interpersonal domain (Brekelmans & Wubbels, 1991; Wubbels, et al., 1987, 1992) and earlier research with the QIB (Biemans, et al., 1999).

An important issue that remains after this study is how to explain divergence. In a rational-cognitive-action view (e.g., Clark & Peterson, 1986) one would expect close resemblance between teachers' own perceptions and those of their students. In this view, it is assumed that teachers are rational actors who base their behaviour (in this case behaviour perceived by students) on their cognitions (of which self-perceptions and ideals can be regarded as elements) to a large degree. However, it seems very likely that teachers do not always act as rational professionals due to the nature of the classroom context (Doyle, 1986) and the unconscious nature of many cognitions (Fiske & Taylor, 1991; Korthagen & Lagerwerf, 1996). Moreover, personal theories of teachers (e.g., Groeben, 1981) may play an important role in the teaching process. Such theories often contain inconsistent elements and act as strong frameworks and filters that teachers use to interpret their environment. Of course, attribution processes and role differences between teachers and students (see section 2.3) may also be helpful in explaining divergence. More research is needed in this respect, particularly aimed at uncovering explanations provided by teachers and students (by means of interviews and observations) for divergence found. Also, interviews with teachers and students may help to uncover important variables or indicators that form the basis of observations, and consequently perceptions. For example, are perceptions of students and teachers based on the same observational cues? Are students' and teachers' definitions of clarity and control, among many other behaviours, similar? Then, studies could be conducted relating various class and teacher characteristics to difference scores (absolute and regular), not only investigating effects of these characteristics *separately* (as was done in the present study), but also *jointly* and/or *in interaction*.

The outcomes of the present study seem to suggest that the amount and direction of divergence may be related to the particular teacher behaviour of interest. It may very well be that teachers more easily can observe and interpret the effects of some behaviours, while it is hard for them to judge the effect of other behaviours. Future research, investigating other (combinations of) teacher behaviours can help in sorting out this issue.

Finally, the outcomes of this study stress the importance of using different sources when providing feedback to teachers or investigating the classroom environment. Using only the perceptions of teachers or students may lead to a one-sided and incomplete view, since considerable differences may occur between them. Conceptualizing and computing divergence may be a powerful tool in studying the relationship between teachers' thoughts and actions. Moreover, they can be used as a means of reflection, providing more insight on teachers' own beliefs and those of their students. They may form the starting point for changing particular behaviour, and as such act as points to seize upon in the preparation of teachers and in staff-development. Of course, an interesting question in this respect would be if such training and development can help to reduce differences, either through a change in self-perception or an alteration of behaviour.

References

Beam, K. J. & Horvat, R. E. (1975). Differences among teachers' and students' perceptions of science classroom behaviors, and actual classroom behaviors. *Science Education, 59*, 333-344.

Ben-Chaim, D. & Zoller, U. (2001). Self-perception versus students' perception of teacher personal style in college science and mathematics courses. *Research in Science Education, 31*, 437-454.

Bergen, T. C. M., Derksen, K. J. J., & Lamberigts, R. J. A. G. (1997). Peer coaching as a powerful approach to implement activating instruction in the classroom. In *The J.H.G.I. Giesbers, Reports on Education, number 2* (pp. 1-12). Department of Educational Sciences University of Nijmegen.

Biemans, H. A., Jongmans, C. T., de Jong, F. P. C. M., & Bergen, T. C. M. (1999). Perceptions of teachers' instructional behavior in secondary agricultural education. *Journal of Agricultural Education and Extension, 5,* 231-238.

Brekelmans, M., Holvast, A., & van Tartwijk, J. (1993). Changes in teacher communication styles during the professional career. *Journal of Classroom Interaction, 27,* 13-22.

Brekelmans, M., Sleegers, P., & Fraser, B. J. (2000). Teaching for active learning. In P. R. J. Simons, J. L. van der Linden, & T. Duffy (Eds.), New learning (pp.227-242). Dordrecht: Kluwer.

Brekelmans, M. & Wubbels, T. (1991). Student and teacher perceptions of interpersonal teacher behavior: A Dutch perspective. *The Study of Learning Environments, 5,* 19-30.

Brekelmans, M., Wubbels, T., & den Brok, P. (2002). Teacher experience and the teacher-student relationship in the classroom environment. In S. C. Goh & M. S. Khine (Eds.), *Studies in educational learning environments: an international perspective.* Singapore: World Scientific.

Clark, C. M. & Peterson, P. L. (1986). Teachers' thought processes. In M. C. Wittrock (Ed.), *Handbook of research on teaching* (3rd Ed.) (pp. 255-296). New York: MacMillan.

Creemers, B. P. M. (1994). *The effective classroom.* London: Cassell.

Cruickshank, D. R. & Kennedy, J. J. (1986). Teacher clarity. *Teaching and Teacher Education, 2,* 43-67.

Cothran, D. J. & Ennis, C. D. (1997). Students' and teachers' perceptions of conflict and power. *Teaching and Teacher Education, 13,* 541-553.

D'Apollonia, S. & Abrami, P. C. (1997). Navigating student ratings of instruction. *American Psychologist, 52,* 1198-1208.

den Brok, P. (2001). *Teaching and student outcomes.* Utrecht: W. C. C.

den Brok, P., Bergen, T., Stahl, R., & Brekelmans, M. (2004). Students' perceptions of teacher control behaviours. *Learning and Instruction, 14* (4), 425-443.

den Brok, P. Levy, J., Rodriguez, R., & Wubbels, T. (2002). Perceptions of Asian-American and Hispanic-American teachers and their students on teacher interpersonal communication style. *Teaching and Teacher Education, 18,* 447-467.

Derksen, K. J. J., Engelen, A. J. A., Sleegers, P. J. C., Bergen, T. C. M., & Imants, J. (1999, April). *The effects of a coaching programme to promote activating instruction.* Paper presented at the annual meeting of the American Educational Research Association, Montreal.

Doyle, W. (1986). Classroom organization and management. In M. C. Wittrock (Ed.), *Handbook of research on teaching* (3rd Ed.) (pp.255-296). New York: MacMillan.

Engelen, A. (2002). *Coaching inside-out.* [In Dutch.] Dissertation. Nijmegen: University Press

Engelen, A., Bergen, T., Derksen, K., & Sleegers, P. (2000, July). *Peer coaching as a means of activating instruction and teacher professional development.* Paper presented at the Association for Moral Education, (AME), Glasgow, Scotland.

Fisher, D. L. & Fraser, B. J. (1983). A comparison of actual and preferred classroom environment as perceived by teachers and students. *Journal of Research in Science Teaching, 20,* 55-61.

Fisher, D., Fraser, B., & Cresswell. J. (1995). Using the Questionnaire on Teacher Interaction in the professional development of teachers. *Australian Journal of Teacher Education, 20,* 8-18.

Fisher, D. L., Fraser, B. J., Wubbels, T., & Brekelmans, M. (1993). Associations between school learning environment and teacher interpersonal behavior in the classroom. *The Study of Learning Environments, 7,* 32-41.

Fisher, D. L. & Rickards, T. (1999, January). *Teacher-student interpersonal behavior as perceived by science teachers and their students.* Paper presented at the second international conference on Science, Mathematics and Technology Education, Taipei, Taiwan.

Fiske, S. T. & Taylor, S. E. (1991). *Social cognition.* New York: McGraw Hill.

Fraser, B. J. (1982). Differences between student and teacher perceptions of actual and preferred classroom learning environment. *Educational Evaluation and Policy Analysis, 4,* 511-519.

Fraser, B. J. (1986). *Classroom environment.* London : Croom Helm.

Fraser, B. J. (1994). Research on classroom and school climate. In D. Gabel (Ed.), *Handbook of research on science teaching and learning.* New York: MacMillan.

Fraser, B. J. (1998). Science learning environments: assessment, effects and determinants. In B. J. Fraser & K. G. Tobin (Eds.), *The international handbook of science education* (pp. 527-564). Dordrecht: Kluwer.

Fraser, B. J. & O'Brien, P. (1985). Student and teacher perceptions of elementary school classrooms. *Elementary School Journal, 85,* 567-580.

Fraser, B. J. & Wubbels, T. (1995). Classroom learning environments. In B. J. Fraser & H. J. Walberg (Eds.), *Improving science education* (pp. 117-144). Chicago: National Society for the Study of Education.

Gorham, J. & Millette, D. M. (1997). A comparative analysis of teacher and student perceptions of sources of motivation and demotivation in college classes. *Communication Education, 46,* 245-261.

Gorham, J. & Zakahi, W. R. (1990). A comparison of teacher and student perceptions of immediacy and learning: monitoring process and product. *Communication Education, 39,* 354-368.

Greenwald, A. G. (1997). Validity concerns and usefulness of student ratings of instruction. *American Psychologist, 52,* 1182-1186.

Groeben, N. (1981). Die Handlungsperspective als Theorierahmen für Forschung im pädogogischen Feld. In M. Hofer (Ed.), *Informationsverarbeitung und Entscheidungsverhalten von Lehrern* (pp. 110-158). München: Urban & Schwarzenberg.

Harkin, J. & Turner, G. (1997). Patterns of communication styles of teachers in English 16-19 education. *Research in Post-Compulsory Education, 2,* (3), 261-280.

Hofstein, A. & Lazarowitz, R. (1986). A comparison of the actual and preferred classroom in biology and chemistry as perceived by high-school students. *Journal of Research in Science Teaching, 23,* 189-199.

Korthagen, F. A. J. & Lagerwerf, B. (1996). Reframing the relationship between teacher thinking and teacher behavior: levels in learning about teaching. *Teachers and Teaching: Theory and Practice, 2,* 161-190.

Lamberigts, R. & Bergen, T. (2000, April). Teaching for active learning using a constructivist approach. Paper presented at the annual meeting of the American Educational Research Association, New Orleans.

Leary, T. (1957). *An interpersonal diagnosis of personality.* New York: Ronald Press Company.

Levy, J., Wubbels, T., & Brekelmans, M. (1993). Student and teacher characteristics and perceptions of teacher communication style. *Journal of Classroom Interaction, 27,* (1), 23-29.

Levy, J., Wubbels, T., Brekelmans, M., & Morganfield, B. (1997). Language and cultural factors in students' perceptions of teacher communication style. *International Journal of Intercultural Relations, 21,* 29-56..

Lewin, K. (1936). *Principals of topological psychology.* New York: Ronald Press Co.

Maor, D & Fraser, B. J. (1996). Use of classroom environment perceptions in evaluating inquiry based, computer assisted learning. *International Journal of Science Education, 18,* 401-421.

Marsh, H. W. & Roche, L. A. (1997). Making students' evaluations of teaching effectiveness effective. *American Psychologist, 52,* 1187-1197.

Martin, B. N. & Combs, C. (2000, October). Administrator, teacher and student perceptions of gender equity issues in elementary settings. Paper presented at the annual meeting of the Mid-Western Educational Research Association, Chicago.

Moos, R. H. (1979). *Evaluating educational environments.* San Francisco: Jossey-Bass Publishers.

Murray, H. A. (1938). *Explorations in personality.* New York: Oxford University Press.

Rickards, T. & Fisher, D. L. (2000, April). *Three perspectives on perceptions of teacher-student interaction: A seed for change in science teaching.* Paper presented at the annual meeting of the National Association for Research in Science Teaching, New Orleans.

Rosenshine, B. (1978). *Academic engaged time, content covered and direct instruction.* Campaign, IL: University of Illinois.

Rosenshine, B. (1983). Teaching functions in instructional programs. *Elementary School Journal, 83,* 335-352.

Sheets, R. H. (2002). "You're just a kid that is there": Chicano perception of disciplinairy events. *Journal of Latinos and Education, 1,* 105-122.

Shuell, T. J. (1993). Towards an integrated theory of teaching and learning. *Educational Psychologist, 28,* 291-311.

Shuell, T. J. (1996). Teaching and learning in a classroom context. In D. C. Berliner & R. C. Calfee (Eds.), *Handbook of educational psychology* (pp. 726-764). New York: Macmillan.

Simons, P. R. J. & de Jong, F. P. C. M. (1992). Self-regulation and computer-aided instruction. *Applied Psychology: An International Review, 41*, 36-346.

Stahl, R. J. (1992). *The direct instruction for application mastery model.* Unpublished paper. Tempe, AZ: Arizona State University.

Stahl, R. J. (1999, April). *The information-constructivist theoretical perspective as a psychological rather than an epistemological view of thinking and learning: Constructs, overview and rationale.* Paper presented at the annual meeting of the American Educational Research Association, Montreal.

Vermunt, J. D. & Verloop, N. (1999). Congruence and friction between learning and teaching. *Learning and Instruction, 9*, 257-280.

Voeller, D. (1982, April). *The relationship between students' and instructors' perceptions of feedback and the students' perceptions of the instructors' teaching effectiveness.* Paper presented at the annual meeting of the American Educational Research Association, ERICED 219383.

Watson, D. (1982). The actor and the observer: how are their perceptions of causality divergent? *Psychological Bulletin, 92*, 682-700.

Witty, J. P. & DeBarysch, B. D. (1994). Student and teacher perceptions of teachers' communication of performance expectations in the classroom. *Journal of Classroom Interaction, 29*, 1-8.

Wubbels, T. & Brekelmans, M. (1997). A comparison of student perceptions of Dutch Physics teachers' interpersonal behavior and their educational opinions in 1984 and 1993. *Journal of Research in Science Teaching, 34*, (5), 447-466.

Wubbels, T., Brekelmans, M., & Hermans, J. (1987). Teacher behavior: an important aspect of the learning environment? *The Study of Learning Environments, 3*, 10-25.

Wubbels, T., Brekelmans, M., & Hooymayers, H. P. (1992). Do teacher ideals distort the self-reports of their interpersonal behavior? *Teaching and Teacher Education, 8* (1), 47-58.

Wubbels, T. & Levy, J. (1991). A comparison of interpersonal behavior of Dutch and American teachers. *International Journal of Intercultural Relations, 15*, 1-18.

Wubbels, T. & Levy, J. E. (1993). *Do you know what you look like? Interpersonal relationships in education* (1st. ed.). London, England: The Falmer Press.

Wubbels, T., Créton, H. A., & Hooymayers, H. P. (1985, April). *Discipline problems of beginning teachers*. Paper presented at the annual meeting of the American Educational Research Association, Chicago, ERICED 260040.

Yuen, H. K. (1999). Communication styles of tertiary teachers. In J. James (Ed.), *Quality in teaching and learning in higher education* (pp. 3-8). Hong Kong: Hong Kong Polytechnic University.

Appendix A

Overview of studies investigating both students' and teachers' perceptions of teachers' behaviours in secondary (vocational) education. Studies appear in chronological order

Authors and year of publication	N	Teaching variables studied	Goal and method of study
Beam & Horvat, 1975	33	Inquiry	Alignment between observation and perception data. Divergence of direct interest. Divergence tested with t-tests.
Moos, 1979	295	Competition, formality, involvement, rule clarity, cohesiveness, satisfaction, task difficulty, goal direction, democracy	Exploratory study on student and teacher perceptions. Divergence of direct interest. Divergence tested with ANOVA, product-moment correlations and rank-order correlations
Fraser, 1982	34	Student participation, personal interaction, differentiation, inquiry, student independence	Study on differences between actual and preferred (ideal) perceptions. Divergence of direct interest. Divergence tested with ANOVA, product-moment correlations and rank-order correlations.
Fisher & Fraser, 1983	56	Student participation, personal interaction, differentiation, inquiry, student independence	Study on differences between actual and preferred (ideal) perceptions. Divergence of minor interest. Divergence tested with ANOVA.
Hofstein & Lazarowitz, 1986	52	Student participation, personal interaction, differentiation, inquiry, student independence	Study on differences between actual and preferred (ideal) perceptions in different subjects. Divergence of minor interest. Divergence tested with ANOVA.
Wubbels, Brekelmans & Hermans, 1987	66	Leadership, helpful/friendly, understanding, student responsibility, uncertain, dissatisfied, admonishing, strict	Study on instrument development and reliability of student perceptions. Divergence of direct interest. Divergence tested with product-moment correlations and t-tests.

Continued

Authors and year of publication	N	Teaching variables studied	Goal and method of study
Gorham & Zakahi, 1990	46	Verbal immediacy, nonverbal immediacy (22 indicators in total)	Study on instrument development. Divergence of direct interest. Divergence tested with t-tests.
Brekelmans & Wubbels, 1991	1156	Influence, proximity	Large-scale study on divergence between teacher and student perceptions. Divergence of direct interest. Divergence tested with t-tests, ANOVA and difference scores.
Wubbels & Levy, 1991	132	Leadership, helpful/friendly, understanding, student responsibility, uncertain, dissatisfied, admonishing, strict	Study on instrument development. Divergence of minor interest. Divergence tested with t-tests.
Wubbels, Brekelmans & Hooymayer, 1992	143	Interpersonal quality (average absolute difference on leadership, helpful/friendly, understanding, uncertain, dissatisfied and admonishing)	Study on differences between cognitions (ideals and teacher perceptions) and behaviour (student perceptions. Divergence of direct interest. Divergence tested with t-tests and difference scores.
Fisher, Fraser, Wubbels & Brekelmans, 1993	276	Influence, proximity	Study on relationship between instruments used to map teacher environment and school environment. Divergence of minor interest. Divergence not statistically tested.
Brekelmans, Holvast & van Tartwijk, 1993	573	Influence, proximity	Study on development of interpersonal behaviour during the teaching career. Divergence not of interest. Divergence not statistically tested.

Continued

Authors and year of publication	N	Teaching variables studied	Goal and method of study
Levy, Wubbels & Brekelmans, 1993	141	Influence, proximity	Study on factors influencing teacher or student perceptions. Divergence not of interest. Divergence not statistically tested.
Witty & DeBarysch, 1994	14	Encouragement of student involvement, avoidance of negative interaction, personal regard, individualized support	Study on teacher expectations. Divergence of direct interest. Divergence tested with t-tests.
Fisher, Fraser & Cresswell, 1995	6	Leadership, helpful/friendly, understanding, student responsibility, uncertain, dissatisfied, admonishing, strict	Descriptive study on teacher professional development. Divergence not of interest. Divergence not statistically tested.
Fraser & Wubbels, 1995	?	Task orientation, order, rule clarification	Study on teacher instructional behaviour. Divergence of minor interest. Divergence tested with ANOVA.
Maor & Fraser, 1996	10	Task orientation, order, rule clarification	Exploratory study on teacher behaviour in computer-assisted classrooms. Divergence of minor interest. Divergence tested with ANOVA.
Cothran & Ennis, 1997	4	Conflict, teacher power	Descriptive study on teacher professional development. Divergence not of interest. Divergence not statistically tested.
Levy, Wubbels, Brekelmans & Morganfiel, 1997	38	Influence, proximity	Study on culture/ethnicity and student perceptions of teacher behaviour. Divergence of minor interest. Divergence tested with ANOVA.

Continued

Authors and year of publication	N	Teaching variables studied	Goal and method of study
Wubbels & Brekelmans, 1997	45	Leadership, helpful/friendly, understanding, student responsibility, uncertain, dissatisfied, admonishing, strict	Study on differences in perceptions and beliefs over time. Divergence of minor interest. Divergence tested with t-tests.
Harkin & Turner, 1997	30	Leadership, helpful/friendly, understanding, student responsibility, uncertain, dissatisfied, admonishing, strict	Study on instrument development in higher education. Divergence of minor interest. Divergence tested with t-tests.
Gorham & Millette, 1997	?	Motivation enhancement	Study on factors influencing student and teacher behaviours. Divergence not of interest. Divergence not statistically tested.
Biemans, Jongmans, de Jong & Bergen, 1999	145	Student-led activation, teacher-led activation, clarity, control	Study on instructional behaviour in vocational education. Divergence of direct interest. Divergence tested with ANOVA and difference scores.
Derksen, Engelen, Sleegers, Bergen & Imants, 1999	22	Student-led activation, teacher-led activation, clarity, control	Study on the effects of a professional development programme. Divergence not of interest. Divergence not statistically tested.
Fisher & Rickards, 2000	173	Leadership, helpful/friendly, understanding, student responsibility, uncertain, dissatisfied, admonishing, strict	Study on value of student and teacher perceptions for professional development. Divergence of direct interest. Divergence tested with ANOVA.

Continued

Authors and year of publication	N	Teaching variables studied	Goal and method of study
Rickards & Fisher, 2000	164	Leadership, helpful/friendly, understanding, student responsibility, uncertain, dissatisfied, admonishing, strict	Study on value of student and teacher perceptions for professional development. Divergence of direct interest. Divergence tested with t-tests.
Ben-Chaim & Zoller, 2001	138	Leadership, helpful/friendly, understanding, student responsibility, uncertain, dissatisfied, admonishing, strict	Study on instrument development in higher education and professional development. Divergence of direct interest. Divergence tested with rank-order correlations.
Brekelmans, Wubbels & den Brok, 2002	51	Influence, proximity	Study on development of interpersonal behaviour during the teaching career. Divergence not of interest. Divergence not statistically tested.
Den Brok, Levy, Rodriguez & Wubbels, 2002	17	Influence, proximity Leadership, helpful/friendly, understanding, student responsibility, uncertain, dissatisfied, admonishing, strict	Study on ethnicity/culture and student or teacher perceptions. Divergence of minor interest. Divergence tested with t-tests.
Engelen, 2002	22	Teacher-led activation, student-led activation	Study on effects of professional development programme and coaching on student or teacher perceptions. Divergence not of interest. Divergence not statistically tested.
Sheets, 2002	4	Disciplinary behavior	Study on culture/ethnicity and perceptions of students or teachers. Divergence not of interest. Divergence not statistically tested.

Note: N=number of teachers involved

Appendix B

The Questionnaire on Instructional Behaviour
© 1991 Department of Educational Sciences, University of Nijmegen

1. When this teacher is explaining something, we have to listen.
2. During this teacher's lesson we can easily do other things.
3. This teacher stimulates us to help each other when working on a task.
4. At the beginning of the lesson, this teacher explains his/her plans for that lesson.
5. With the teacher, we check if our answer is correct.
6. If you do not exactly follow this teacher's directions, s/he will correct you.
7. This teacher provides us suggestions on how to learn for a test.
8. This teacher is willing to adjust his/her lesson plan.
9. This teacher provides suggestions on how to do homework.
10. This teacher explains clearly which content you have to study for a test.
11. This teacher lets us think in small groups on how to work on tasks.
12. At the end of the lesson, this teacher repeats important things.
13. During the lesson, this teacher provides suggestions on how to plan work for school.
14. This teacher tells you precisely, when your answer is correct.
15. This teacher repeats the content of prior lessons.
16. In this teacher's lesson, we can decide by ourselves how to do tasks.
17. If this teacher explains something, s/he is hard to understand.
18. In this teacher's lesson, you strictly have to follow the rules.
19. This teacher stimulates us to actively participate during the lesson.
20. If you pay attention, you can decide by yourself in this teacher's class.
21. When we work together, this teacher stimulates us to take responsibility for each other.
22. This teacher appreciates when we show initiative.
23. This teacher appreciates students' remarks.
24. When this teacher gives an assignment, we know exactly what is expected from us.
25. This teacher lets us decide by ourselves at what pace we work on an assignment.
26. This teacher stimulates us to discuss the results of our work with other students.
27. This teacher expresses himself/herself clearly.
28. If this teacher explains something, s/he stimulates us to think along with him/her.
29. This teacher explains clearly why an answer was wrong.
30. This teacher stimulates that we take responsibility for our work.
31. If this teacher gives a task, we have to follow his/her suggestions precisely.
32. When we are working on tasks, this teacher makes sure we are hard at work.
33. In this teacher's lesson, we can plan our work independently.

Chapter 7

STUDIES OF STUDENTS' PERCEPTIONS IN SCIENCE CLASSROOMS AT THE POST-COMPULSORY LEVEL

Craig R. Kerr
The Don College
Tasmania, Australia

Darrell L. Fisher
Curtin University of Technology
Australia

Bevis G. Yaxley
University of Tasmania
Australia

Barry J. Fraser
Curtin University of Technology
Australia

This chapter reports on two closely related learning environment studies undertaken in Tasmanian year 11 science classes over a five year period. The first study, undertaken in 1998, used the College Science Classroom Environment Survey (CSCES) to investigate science students' perceptions of their actual and preferred psychosocial learning environments. Learning environment data were correlated with student achievement and attitudinal data. Furthermore, why students selected a science subject and why they changed out of a science subject were also examined. Based upon results from this investigation, extensive science teacher professional development was implemented, and a second study was undertaken in 2003 to investigate changes in the context of new ICT-rich environments. This second study used the Technology-Rich, Outcomes-Focused, Learning Environment Inventory (TROFLEI) to assess ICT-rich psychosocial environments. Students' attitudes towards their subject, their usage of ICT, and academic efficacy were also measured. In addition, case studies of ICT-rich science learning environments were undertaken using a Computerised Classroom Ergonomic Worksheet (CCEW) and a Computerised Classroom Ergonomic Inventory (CCEI). Associations were examined between physical, psychosocial, and attitudinal data and comparison were made with results from the earlier study.

1. Background

1.1 Science education in Tasmanian colleges

Tasmania is unique in Australia because the State's eight secondary colleges are responsible for the providing education for all Years 11 and 12 students in government schools. While similar colleges exist in the Australian Capital Territory and to a lesser extent in Victoria and Western Australia, Tasmanian colleges provide a unique learning environment whose investigation is likely to provide insights for improving education in all Australian States.

Within the educational programs offered by the secondary colleges, there is a wide range of science courses, including pre-tertiary courses in the physical and life sciences, general science courses for those not planning to study science beyond this level, and science courses offered as an integral part of vocational training programs such as in rural or fisheries programs. Because these courses are optional, a number of students elect to study no science at all, thus resulting in a further loss of potential science students. Therefore, the identification and implementation of learning environments that lead to improved student participation, achievement and attitudes to science learning is of significance.

1.2 New technologies

The Commonwealth Department of Education, Science and Training (CDEST, 2001, p. 10), commented that "… it is increasingly evident that many forms of contemporary activity not only involve the incorporation of Information Communication Technologies (ICT) but, more importantly, are also premised on the expectation that ICT are integral to both life and work." Hence, in all Australian states, education departments are committed to students leaving their schools as proficient users of ICT (e.g., Tasmanian Department of Education, 2002a). Furthermore, Australian governments and school systems have invested billions of dollars in ICT over the past decade and it is estimated that half a billion dollars is now spent per year on ICT in public schools by all Australian Governments (Cappie-Wood, 2004).

Computers were introduced into schools about 25 years ago and early approaches to integrating computers into the school curriculum focussed on technology skills as an end in themselves (Newhouse, 1998). Early computers were stand-alone devices, often of varying design, operating system and brand. However, today most computers are a similar design to each other and are viewed as only a component in a grouping of classroom technologies or Information Communication Technologies (ICT). These include; the World Wide Web, email, networking, digital cameras, data projectors, scanners, colour printers and many other peripheral devices.

Early research into classroom use of computers focussed on student achievement outcomes (Khalili & Sashaani, 1994). However, more recently there has been a shift towards the quality of learning experiences (Godfrey, 2001), and researchers now describe ICT as a powerful teaching and learning tool supporting a variety of modes of learning and thinking skills (Newhouse, 1998). ICT are now considered not only as *an end in themselves* but as a tool applicable to learning in all subject areas and more broadly as an integral component of broader curricular reforms and as integral to the reform of education itself (DETYA, 2000).

1.3 Physical learning environments

The arrangement of the physical environment has long been recognised by professionals, in a range of fields, as significantly influencing those who occupy it (Loughlin & Suina, 1982). Furthermore, it is acknowledged that the physical design of a learning space can support or contradict a teacher's expectations, as well as impact upon the health of its users (Loughlin & Suina, 1982). This has led to the development of the science of *ergonomics*, the study of physical, physiological and psychosocial factors which can influence worker productivity and health (Woodson, Tillman, & Tillman, 1992). Significantly, Kroemer and Grandjean (2001), referred to the concept of *person-environment fit* (Fraser & Fisher, 1983; Hunt, 1975), and noted that the degree of fit between the characteristics of a person and the environment can determine their well-being and performance.

Hence, it is recognised that educators need to develop a conceptual framework of the physical learning environment if they are to produce predictable and desirable changes in learning and student behaviour (Marx, Fuhrer & Hartig, 2000). Educational research by Weinstein

(1979) concluded that indirectly student achievement could be increased with changes in the physical environment. However, Weinstein noted that there had been little research into the relationship between physical design and the educational program, and that much research was flawed in its methodology. Weinstein's report recommended correlation studies as a valid approach to physical environment research, and multidimensional methodology, as adopted by contemporary researchers such as Zandvliet (1999, 2003), has been adopted for this study.

1.4 Psychosocial learning environments

Classroom psychosocial learning environment research is founded upon the work of Lewin (1935, 1936) who recognised that both the environment and its interaction with personal characteristics of the individual are potent determinants of human behaviour. Seminal work by Moos (1976) suggested that the environment-behaviour link could only be understood if studied in a holistic way and proposed a 'social-ecological' approach. Moos, investigating human social environments, or "psychosocial" environments, recognised that three domains or dimensions existed, a *Relationship* dimension, *Personal Development* dimension, and a *System Maintenance and System Change* dimension. The foundation for the contemporary era of social environment studies was laid by the works of Moos (1973, 1974, 1976, 1979) and Walberg (1969, 1976, 1986) and many studies have built upon their work and applied it to educational settings (Fraser, 1994).

Research by Fraser and Tobin (1991) recognised the importance of combining quantitative and qualitative data, and their study indicated that combining both types of data gave greater richness and credibility to their findings. Studies have successfully combined qualitative and quantitative research methods in studying the classroom learning environment at different 'grain sizes' (Fraser, 1996). This can be used to show how individual students and the teacher can be investigated not only at the smallest grain size, but also at the class level, school level or system level to clarify whether particular teachers or students are typical of larger groups (Aldridge, Fraser, & Huang, 1999; Tobin & Fraser, 1998). In addition to multiple research methodologies, recent directions in psychosocial learning environment research include; changing the learning environment through the teacher acting as a learner and modeller (Guba & Lincoln, 1989), the paradigm shift from traditional learning environments to ICT-based environments (Chang & Fisher, 2003), metacognition and learning environments (Thomas, 2003), and the steady increase in cross-national learning environment studies (Fraser, 1998).

Several studies by Zandvliet (e.g., 1999, 2000, 2003) adopt a holistic and sometimes cross-national approach to the investigation of ICT-rich learning areas using a combined physical and psychosocial learning environments methodology. Zandvliet (2000) reported on an action-research investigation to apply information about effective physical and psychosocial learning environments to the re-tooling of a technology facility in Canada. His case study recognised that the careful design and manipulation of a learning space can effect meaningful change in student learning. Furthermore, Aldridge, Fraser, Fisher, and Wood (2002) reported upon the development and validation of a widely-applicable and distinctive questionnaire for assessing students' perceptions of their learning environments in outcomes-focused and technology-rich learning settings.

2. 1998 Study

2.1 Introduction

The aim of the first study described in this chapter was to identify and implement learning environments that lead to improved student participation, achievement and attitudes in science learning for Year 11 students in Tasmania. To achieve this, the *College Science Classroom Environment Survey* (CSCES) was constructed from already existing learning environment scales.

2.2 Methodology

The five objectives of this study were to:

(1) provide validation data for the CSCES;
(2) investigate differences between students' perceptions of their actual and preferred science classroom learning environments;

(3)   investigate associations between students' attitude to science and their perceptions of the classroom environment as assessed by the CSCES;

(4)   investigate students' reasons for their initial choice of a science subject in Year 11; and

(5)   develop some understanding why some students withdraw from their science studies while some other are very successful.

The CSCES was administered to all students in science classes in the eight secondary colleges in Tasmania. This provided a sample of 1,080 students. Each student responded to the Actual and Preferred Forms of the CSCES, an attitude scale, and from a provided list ranked their reasons for selecting science subjects in grade 11. Table 7.1 provides a description of each of the scales of the CSCES together with sample items. Items were scored by allocating 5, 4, 3, 2, 1, respectively, for the responses Almost Always, Often, Sometimes, Seldom, Almost Never.

The data were analysed to check the internal consistency and discriminant validity of the scales of the CSCES, together with an examination of its factor structure. The ability of the CSCES to differentiate between the perceptions of students in different classrooms was examined by performing a one-way ANOVA for each scale with class membership as the main effect.

Associations between students' attitudinal and cognitive outcomes and scales of the CSCES were investigated using simple and multiple correlation analyses.

Table 7.1. Description of Scales and a Sample Item for Each Scale of the CSCES

Scale Name	Description of Scale	Sample Item
Cooperation	Extent to which students cooperate rather than compete with one another on learning tasks.	I cooperate with other students when doing assignment work.
Teacher Support	Extent to which the teacher helps, befriends, trusts and is interested in students.	This teacher talks with me.
Involvement	Extent to which students have attentive interest, participate in discussions, do additional work and enjoy the class.	I discuss ideas in class.
Leadership	Extent to which the teacher leads, organises, gives orders, determines procedures and structures the classroom situation.	The teacher talks enthusiastically about his/her subject.
Relevance	Extent to which the learning is relevant to students' lives.	In this science class, I learn about the world outside of college.
Task Orientation	Extent to which it is important to complete activities planned and to stay on the subject matter.	I know what has to be done in this class.
Open Endedness	Extent to which the laboratory activities emphasise an open-ended, divergent approach to experimentation.	There is opportunity for me to pursue my own science interests in this class.
Integration	Extent to which laboratory activities are integrated with non- laboratory and theory classes.	My regular science class work is integrated with practical activities.
Independence	Extent to which students are allowed to make decisions and have control over their own learning and behaviour.	I have a say in deciding what activities I do.

2.3 Results

2.3.1 Validation of the CSCES

Table 7.2 reports validation information for the CSCES based on its use in Tasmania. The alpha reliability coefficient was used as the index of scale internal consistency and ranged from 0.72 to 0.86 for the Actual Form and 0.75 to 0.89 for the Preferred, suggesting that all scales of both versions of the CSCES possess satisfactory internal consistency. The mean correlations of one scale with the other scales ranged from 0.28 to 0.42 and 0.32 to 0.46 for the Actual and Preferred Forms, respectively. These values can be regarded as small enough to suggest that each scale of the CSCES has adequate discriminant validity, even though the scales assess slightly overlapping aspects of classroom environment.

Table 7.2. Internal Consistency (Cronbach Alpha Coefficient), Discriminant Validity (Mean Correlation with Other Scales) and Ability to Differentiate between Classrooms for the CSCES

Scale	Alpha Reliability		Mean Correlation with Other Scales		ANOVA Results (eta^2)
	Actual	Preferred	Actual	Preferred	Actual
Cooperation	0.81	0.83	0.28	0.38	0.15*
Teacher Support	0.82	0.81	0.42	0.42	0.25*
Involvement	0.84	0.85	0.36	0.32	0.15*
Leadership	0.85	0.80	0.38	0.40	0.32*
Relevance	0.83	0.85	0.40	0.46	0.25*
Task Orientation	0.84	0.89	0.40	0.43	0.14*
Open-Endedness	0.72	0.75	0.31	0.33	0.21*
Integration	0.86	0.87	0.38	0.43	0.19*
Independence	0.83	0.86	0.31	0.35	0.23*

*$p<0.01$ n= 1080

The eta^2 statistic was calculated to provide an indication of the degree to which each scale could differentiate between the perceptions of students in different classes. The eta^2 statistic, which is the ratio of 'between' to 'total' sums of squares and represents the proportion of variance in scale scores accounted for by class membership, ranged from 0.14 to 0.32 for the CSCES. This indicates that each scale of the CSCES is capable of differentiating significantly between classes ($p<0.01$).

Principal components factor analysis followed by varimax rotation resulted in the acceptance of both versions of the CSCES comprising 66 items in nine scales (Fisher, Fraser, & Yaxley, 2000). The *a priori* factor structure of the questionnaire was replicated with nearly all items loading on their *a priori* scale and no other scale.

2.3.2 Actual preferred differences and associations with attitude

Table 7.3 presents the observed differences between students' perceptions of their actual and preferred classroom learning environments. There is a consistent difference existing between actual and preferred mean scores for all nine scales. Preferred means were higher than actual means for all scales. In particular, this suggests that students would prefer to have their classes more task oriented, more personal relevance and to be given more opportunities for independent learning than was perceived to be present in the science classrooms. Overall, the learning environment dimensions measured by the scales of the CSCES could all be addressed in order to align the classroom environment more closely with that preferred by students which could result in an improvement in student attitudes and achievement.

2.3.3 Associations between students' attitudinal outcomes and scales of the CSCES

The students' attitudes to their science classes were assessed using a ten-item scale based on the *Test of Science Related Attitudes* (TOSRA) (Fraser, 1981). Table 7.4 reports associations of each scale of the CSCES with the students' attitudinal outcomes. Simple correlation coefficients were calculated between each scale of the CSCES and the attitude. Also a multiple regression analysis, involving the whole set of CSCES scales was conducted to provide a more conservative test of association of each scale of the CSCES with attitude when all other scales were controlled.

Table 7.3. Scale Means and Standard Deviations for the Actual and Preferred
Forms of the CSCES

Scale	Form	Scale Mean	SD	Mean Difference (P-A)
Cooperation	Actual	3.87	0.64	0.33*
	Preferred	4.20	0.59	
Teacher Support	Actual	3.59	0.79	0.35*
	Preferred	3.94	0.68	
Involvement	Actual	3.16	0.70	0.30*
	Preferred	3.46	0.70	
Leadership	Actual	3.92	0.72	0.38*
	Preferred	4.30	0.59	
Relevance	Actual	3.32	0.73	0.44**
	Preferred	3.76	0.72	
Task Orientation	Actual	3.96	0.62	0.57**
	Preferred	4.53	0.56	
Open Endedness	Actual	2.79	0.69	0.53**
	Preferred	3.32	0.74	
Integration	Actual	3.90	0.73	0.30**
	Preferred	4.20	0.69	
Independence	Actual	2.66	0.74	0.83**
	Preferred	3.49	0.75	

**$p<0.01$ *$p<0.05$ n=1080

Table 7.4. Significant Associations between CSCES Scales and Students'
Attitude in terms of Simple Correlations (r) and Standardised
Regression Coefficients (β)

Scale	r	β
Cooperation	0.17*	
Teacher Support	0.43*	
Involvement	0.35*	0.12*
Leadership	0.45*	0.14*
Relevance	0.39*	
Task Orientation	0.54*	0.32*
Open Ended	0.35*	
Integration	0.42*	
Independence	0.36*	0.12*

$R = 0.64*$ $R^2 = 0.41$

$p<0.01$ n = 1084   Cronbach Alpha for Attitude Scale = 0.82

An examination of the simple correlation coefficients in Table 7.4 indicates that there were statistically significant relationships ($p<0.001$) between students' perceptions of learning environment and students' attitudes toward the science class for all scales of the CSCES and that these associations were quite strong. Simple correlation coefficients were highest for the scales of Task Orientation, Leadership and Teacher Support. The multiple correlation, (R) was 0.64, which is statistically significant ($p<0.01$). An examination of the beta weights revealed that perceptions on Task Orientation, Leadership, Involvement and Independence were significantly and independently associated with attitude. The R^2 value of 0.41 indicates that 41% of the variance in students' attitudes to their classes can be attributed to their perceptions of their learning environment.

The data were then examined further and a three-level hierarchical model, partitioning the total variability in student attitude toward science was used. The three levels were college, class and student. When the outcome measure, student attitude toward science, was free to vary across the three levels, the proportion of variance accounted for at the college level was 7.3%, at the class level it was 32.1%, and at the individual student level was 60.5%. The proportion of variance of 32.1% at the class level is particularly noteworthy and reinforces the important role of the teacher. For students, it does matter to which class you are allocated.

2.3.4 Students' choice of science subject

Additional items were added to the questionnaire in order to obtain more information about why students elected to study science in Year 11. The students were asked to rate each of the following categories from 5 (a significant influence on your choice) to 1 (of little significance regarding your choice).

- your previous experiences of science at high school
- your interest in a career in science
- the influence of your friends at college
- the academic counselling you received
- other (please describe)

An interest in a career in science was the greatest influences on the students' original decision to study science in Year 11 (see Figure 7.1). The second most important factor was previous experience at the high school the students attended before they came to the secondary college. Interestingly, the influence of their friends was the least important. Similarly, the main reason for students not continuing with science in Year 12 was that they no longer needed science for their chosen career or university course. However, lack of interest and boredom with science were also important reasons.

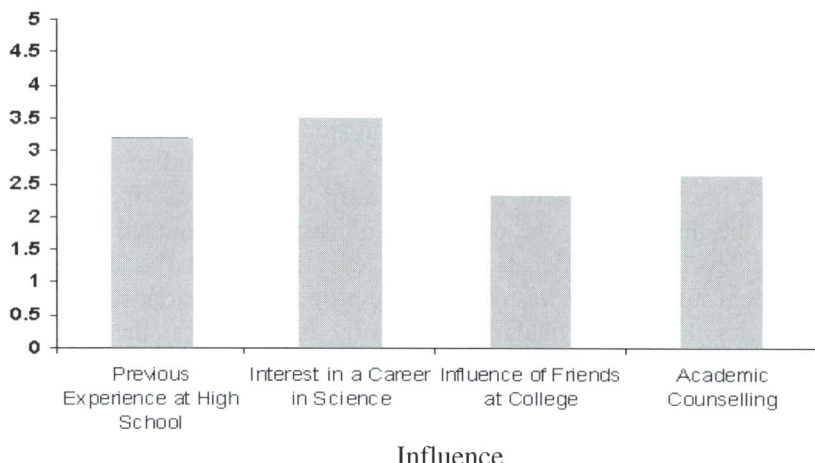

Figure 7.1. Significant influences on students' choice of science subject.

2.3.5 Continuing with science

The students were also asked whether they intended studying one or more science subjects at their college next year in Year 12. If they gave a negative response, they were then asked why they had decided not to study a science subject next year. The responses were then grouped into the 10 categories listed in Table 7.5. Again, the strong influence of career choice is apparent.

Table 7.5. Reasons For Not Studying Science Next Year

Reason	Responses
Not needed for career choice/university course	46
Not interested in any more science	34
Do not need any more science – have had enough	23
Do not like the work – boring	22
The work is too hard or there is too much work	11
Want to try different subjects	11
Going to a TAFE course next year	10
Do not want to	7
No time	7
Not enough prac work	2

2.4 Professional development using results of first study

During the study each college was provided with graphs of actual and preferred differences for that college and an indication of how their college compare with the average of the other seven colleges. The colleges also received a graph for each individual class that participated. The data provided to each college were a basis for further professional development for the teachers of science in these colleges. Teachers were able to consider the differences each of the nine scales of the learning environment. Where there was a significant difference for a particular scale, the teacher of the class was challenged to suggest why this might be so and what changes needed to be made to reduce the difference between the actual and preferred perceptions for that scale. Where there was, for example, a difference in the Teacher Support scale, why was this was the case and what changes needed to be made in the classroom to ameliorate this difference?

To support these activities, teachers from all colleges attended a one-day workshop in which the research findings were discussed and strategies considered for aligning the actual classroom climate with the preferred classroom climate. As a result of the workshop, each college undertook to implement strategies to enhance this alignment in their science classes.

Overall, the research findings of this project were an excellent empirical basis for developing teacher understanding of both the factors influencing effective classroom learning environments and the strategies needed to enhance these environments.

3. 2003 ICT-Rich Learning Environment Study

3.1 Introduction

Few educators would dispute the significant impact that technologies, and in particular ICT, have had upon their domain, and education departments in all developed countries spend significant components of their budget on supporting the information revolution (Twining, 2002). Government spending is supported by strategic policies and visionary statements, and Rickards (2003, p. 118) wrote that "Without development of an effective technology plan, governments risk widening the gap between globally competitive and non-competitive knowledge-based societies." ICTs are increasingly being recognised as fundamental to the reform of education (Muncey & MacQuillan, 1993), and the roles of students, teachers, curriculum frameworks, and assessment regimes are under review in many Australian states (e.g., Essential Learnings project, Tasmanian Department of Education, 2002b). However, education has a poor history of successfully integrating ICT into its curricula (Trinidad, 1998) and there has been little research into the benefits of ICT-rich learning environments (Trinidad, 2003). Furthermore, Zandvliet (1999) noted that this is particularly evident in the area of combined interactive and physical learning environment studies in the context of ICT-rich classrooms. This study examined the psychosocial and physical learning environments of over 800 year 11 science students in Tasmania and develops a model to support the productive delivery of teaching and learning in ICT-rich learning environments. Furthermore, comparisons are made with the learning environment as described by the first study, and the issue of teacher change is examined by research and teacher interviews.

3.2 Objectives

The objectives of this research were to check the reliability in a Tasmanian context of a widely-applicable questionnaire for monitoring outcomes-focussed and ICT-rich classroom learning environments, and to assess Tasmanian year 11 science students' psychosocial and physical ICT-rich learning environments. Questions following on from this research were:

(1)   How do year 11 science psychosocial learning environments in 2003 compare with those assessed in 1998, prior to the *Colleges' Online Project*?

(2)   Do ICT-rich learning environments promote Tasmanian science students' attitudes towards their subject, attitudes to their usage of ICT, and academic efficacy?

(3)   Are there associations between the psychosocial and physical ICT-rich learning environments of schools?

3.3 Conceptual model and methodology

The conceptual model adopted by this study is based upon Gardiner's global model which he called the Three Interfaces of Adam (Gardiner, 1989). Gardiner considered people as having to deal with the natural world, or ecosphere, other people, or sociosphere, and person-made things, or technosphere. He noted that the person is the only system within the universe that belongs to all three spheres, and hence exists, as described in Figure 7.2, at the centre of a triple overlap of these spheres.

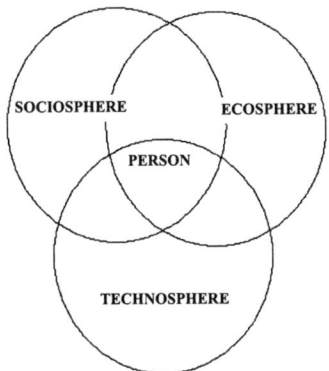

Figure 7.2. Gardiner's Three Interfaces of Adam.
Adapted from Gardiner (1989, p. 28)

While acknowledging arguments for one sphere, or an overlap of spheres to dominate our future direction, Gardiner supports the view that we are currently moving from an industrial society, based on energy, to a post-industrial society, based on information, and our current situation is therefore dominated by a *technosphere-as-cause* scenario. However,

Gardiner notes that this is not a sectorial shift of the *technosphere* but a structural shift with consequences for the entire model. Hence authors, such as Goumain (1989) favour a holistic approach to studies that examine technological, social, and environmental environments.

Based upon research by Zandvliet (1999, 2000, 2003) and Zandvliet and Buker (2002), Gardiner's global model has been adopted as the conceptual framework for this educational study. The *Person* at the centre of Gardiner's model is the *Student*, and their *Satisfaction*, and hence outcomes, can be considered dependent upon the classroom's *Sociosphere* or *Psychosocial* environment, *Ecosphere* or *Physical* environment, and *Technosphere* or *Use of ICT*. Figure 7.3 describes Gardiner's model in terms of this study.

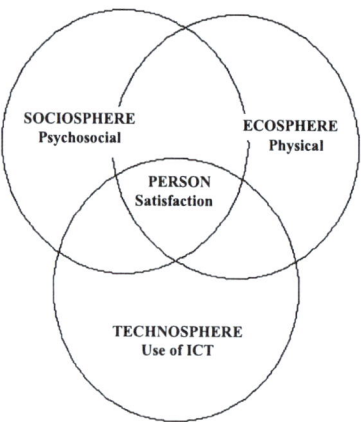

Figure 7.3. Gardiner's conceptual model related to this study.
Adapted from Zandvliet (1999)

In linking each model, the following diagram (Figure 7.4) describes potential factors influencing student satisfaction and links each to research methodologies adopted by this study.

As depicted in Figure 7.4, this study adopted a student questionnaire to assess classroom psychosocial learning environments. The instrument selected for this study was specifically designed for assessing students' perceptions of their actual and preferred classroom learning environments in technology-rich, outcomes-focused learning settings. The instrument, the *Technology-Rich, Outcomes-Focused Learning Environment Inventory* (TROFLEI) was developed by Aldridge, Fraser,

Fisher, and Wood (2002), and contains ten scales. These scales being Student Cohesiveness, Involvement, Investigation, Task Orientation, Cooperation, Teacher Support, Equity, Differentiation, Computer Usage and Young Adult Ethos.

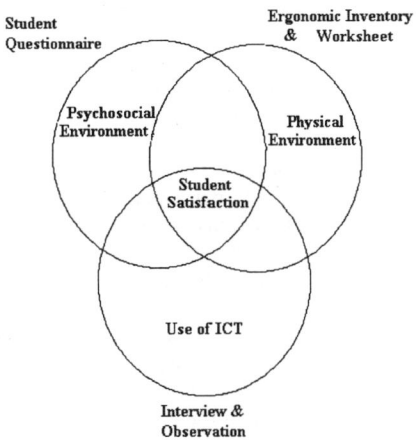

Figure 7.4. A conceptual model of potential factors influencing student satisfaction linked to methodologies used.
Adapted from Gardiner (1989) and Zandvliet (1999)

The ICT-rich physical environment of year 11 science students was assessed at each college using a case study approach. Case study methodology was based upon research by Zandvliet (1999), and included a map and photograph of each site and physical measurements using a worksheet (*Computerised Classroom Ergonomic Worksheet*, CCEW) and inventory (*Computerised Classroom Ergonomic Inventory*, CCEI). The CCEW and CCEI recorded and assessed factors such as workspace environment, computer environment, visual environment, and air quality.

While some TROFLEI questions asked students about their use of ICT, considerable detailed information and richness was gained by interviewing a sample of students that completed the learning environment instrument. Furthermore, to gain richer information on student and teacher use of ICT, and also teacher change, a sample of teachers (that taught interviewed students) was also interviewed. Table 7.6 describes each scale of the TROFLEI and Table 7.7 the Computerised Classroom Ergonomic Inventory (CCEI).

Table 7.6. Descriptive Information for Each Scale in the TROFLEI

Scale	Moos Category	Description	Sample Item
		The extent to which ...	
Student Cohesiveness	R	students know, help and are supportive of one another.	Students in this class like me.
Teacher Support	R	extent to which the teacher helps, befriends, trusts and is interested in students.	The teacher takes a personal interest in me.
Involvement	P	students have attentive interest, participate in discussions, do additional work and enjoy the class.	I explain my ideas to other students.
Investigation	P	emphasis is placed on the skills and processes of inquiry and their use in problem solving and investigation.	I find out answers to questions by doing investigations.
Task Orientation	S	it is important to complete activities planned and to stay on the subject matter.	I know the goals for this class.
Cooperation	R	students cooperate rather than compete with one another on learning tasks.	I work with other students on projects in this class.
Equity	R	students are treated equally by the teacher.	I am treated the same as other students in this class.
Differentiation	S	teachers cater for students differently on the basis of ability, rates of learning and interests.	I work at my own speed.
Computer Usage	S	students use their computers as a tool to communicate with others and to access information.	I use the computer to obtain information from the Internet.
Young Adult Ethos	P	teachers give students responsibility and treat them as young adults.	I am dealt with as a grown up.

R: Relationship Dimension; P: Personal Development Dimension; S: System Maintenance and Change Dimension
Adapted from Aldridge et al., 2002, p. 7

Table 7.7. Computerised Classroom Ergonomic Inventory (CCEI) Information

Scale	Item description
Workspace Environment	Workspace room, screen depth, chair quality, keyboard height above floor, screen height above floor
Computer Environment	Inclination of monitor, keyboard height above desk, monitor interface, colour monitor, software
Visual Environment	Glare, lighting, contrast, illumination, luminance
Spatial Environment	Adequate space, student number, resource areas, room finish, aisle width
Air Quality	Climate control, evenness of temperature, draughts, air volume, air flow rate

Finally, an instrument titled the Attitude and Efficacy Inventory (AEI) was used to investigate whether associations existed between psychosocial and physical classroom learning environments and student satisfaction, and hence student outcomes. The AEI, as adopted by Aldridge, Fraser, Fisher, and Wood (2002), assessed three affective outcomes, student attitude towards their subject, student attitude towards computer usage, and student academic efficacy. These three scales (18 questions) were included as part of the quantitative instrument.

3.4 Results

3.4.1 Case study results

Evaluation of case study data provided much quantitative and qualitative data about the physical learning environment of Tasmanian's year 11 science students. Case study data indicated that a wide range of ICT-rich facilities was in use, and these included; classroom computers, computers on trolleys, shared min-labs, computer clusters, and traditional computing laboratories. Most students and teachers indicated a preference for a range of facilities to suit multiple learning styles. Table 7.8 provides a summary of the layout of ICT-rich classrooms for the 12 case studies.

Environmental data indicated that many facilities were not purpose-built, and illumination levels were unsatisfactory, and this conclusion was supported by workspace environment ergonomic data. However, the balance of environmental and ergonomic issues such as; temperature, humidity, noise, computer environment, visual environment, spatial environment, and air quality were considered satisfactory or better.

Table 7.8. Summary of Room Layouts

Case Study	College	Number of Workstations	Room Layout	Where
1	1	14	Peripheral	Separate Room
2	2	5	Pod	Shared
3	3	17	Peripheral	Separate Room
4	3	4	Pod	Shared
5	3	3	Cluster	In Class (sep. door)
6	4	6	Peripheral	Separate Room
7	5	6	Peripheral	In Class
8	6	4	Peripheral	In Class & Shared
9	7	17	Peripheral	Separate Room
10	8	10	Pod	Shared
11	8	15	Peripheral	Separate Room
12	8	5	Peripheral	In Class (sep. door)

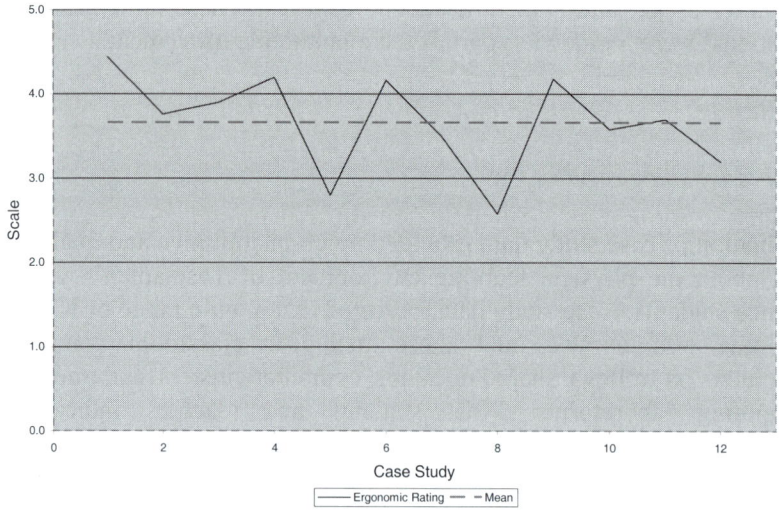

Figure 7.5. Overall ergonomic rating for each case study.

Of the twelve case study sites, only two received an overall below satisfactory rating. Figure 7.5 indicates mean ergonomic values and for each of the 12 case studies, and Figure 7.6 a mean rating for each of the five ergonomic issues.

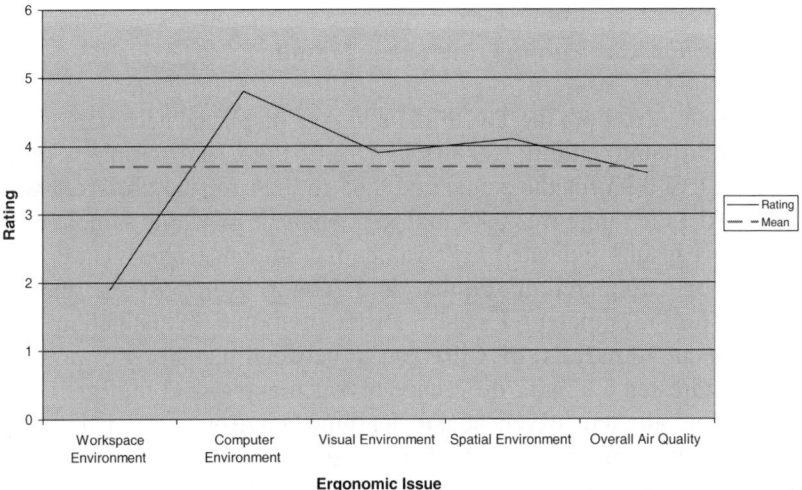

Figure 7.6. Overall ergonomic rating for each ergonomic issue.

A number of statistically significant correlations were found between ergonomic factors and the number of computer workstations. Positive correlations were found between the number of computers workstations and Visual Environment and Spatial Environment, and negative correlations between the number of workstations and Computer Environment and Overall Air Quality. The only statistically significant correlation found between physical variables was a positive correlation between Workspace Environment and Computer Environment.

Student and teacher interview data provided a rich source of information. Student and teacher interview data generally correlated with case study data as both often indicated dissatisfaction with workplace environment, and some hardware issues, but overall satisfaction with their physical learning environment. Both sets of interview data indicated substantial variation in teacher pedagogies. Students indicated there were many college science teachers still teaching in a traditional manner, and likewise many teachers indicated a reluctance to include ICT into their pedagogy. Furthermore, many students indicated their science class was the only one not using ICT. Many students, while indicating satisfaction with their physical ICT-rich environment, felt their previous high school science classes were often more ICT focussed. However, importantly, it should be noted that many student and teacher interviews indicated ICT-rich learning was taking place in college science classes.

3.4.2 Psychosocial learning environment results

It was found that both the TROFLEI and AEI displayed acceptable levels of reliability and validity (for the TROFLEI the Cronbach alpha ranges were 0.81 to 0.93 for the actual and 0.83 to 0.94 for the preferred while for the AEI the range was 0.79 to 0.89). Analysis of whole sample actual TROFLEI results indicated high values for Student Cohesiveness, Task Orientation, Cooperation, Equity, and Young Adult Ethos, and low values for Computer Usage, Differentiation, Investigation, and Involvement. Analysis of differences between actual and preferred results indicated a similar difference between actual and preferred mean scores for all ten psychosocial learning environment scales, with preferred environments the higher. Statistical analysis of differences between actual and preferred mean scores indicated that all differences were statistically significant.

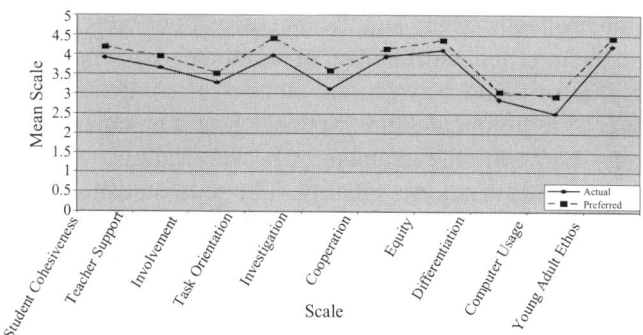

Figure 7.7. Whole sample scale means for the actual and preferred forms of the TROFLEI.

Results from the AEI indicated that students indicated an Academic Efficacy higher than their Attitude Towards Subject and Attitude Towards Computer Usage.

3.4.3 Analysis of results

It was found that the creation of outcomes-focussed and ICT-rich classroom learning environments are associated with more positive student attitudes and hence student satisfaction. The following table (Table 7.9) details statistical relationships between the TROFLEI scales and each of the three AEI scales.

Table 7.9. Associations Between Psychosocial Variables and Student Attitude Towards Subject, Attitude Towards Computer Usage, and Academic Efficacy, in Terms of Simple Correlations (*r*) and Standardised Regression Coefficients (*β*)

Psychosocial Scale	Attitude Towards Subject		Attitude Towards Computer Usage		Student Academic Efficacy	
	r	β	r	β	r	β
Student Cohesiveness	0.23**	-0.06	0.16**	0.02	0.16**	0.03
Teacher Support	0.51**	0.27**	0.10*	-0.11*	0.23*	0.05
Involvement	0.31**	0.04	0.08*	-0.02	0.20**	0.00
Task Orientation	0.48**	0.26**	0.27**	0.12**	0.29**	0.20**
Investigation	0.33**	0.09*	0.07	-0.06	0.24**	0.06
Cooperation	0.27**	-0.06	0.20**	0.05	0.15**	-0.05
Equity	0.48**	0.17**	0.20**	0.04	0.23**	0.07
Differentiation	0.04	-0.11**	-0.07*	-0.14**	0.12**	-0.06
Computer Usage	0.10**	- 0.01	0.03	0.08	0.24**	0.22**
Young Adult Ethos	0.40**	0.05	0.30**	0.19**	0.18**	- 0.03
Multiple Correlation (R)		0.61**		0.35**		0.36**
(R²)		0.36		0.11		0.12

*$p<0.05$ **$p<0.01$ n = 816

The multiple correlations (R) between students' perceptions of the set of ten TROFLEI scales and the Attitude Toward Subject, Attitude Towards Computer Usage, and Academic Efficacy scales were 0.61, 0.35, and 0.36 respectively, and each is statistically significant ($p<0.01$). The R^2 value indicated that 36 percent of the variance in students' attitude towards their subject, 11 percent of the variance in students' attitude towards computer usage, and 12 percent of the variance in students' academic efficacy can be attributed to their learning environment, and this result suggests that the learning environment is positively related to the students' attitudes towards their subject, attitude towards their subject, and academic efficacy.

Only a weak overall correlation was found between students' satisfaction and physical factors, and between psychosocial and physical factors. A total of 14 statistically significant simple correlations were found between psychosocial and physical variables but only seven of these were found to account for a significant amount of variance. These associations were between Differentiation and Workspace Environment and Spatial Environment, and between Overall Air Quality and Task Orientation, Investigation, Cooperation, Equity, and Young Adult Ethos. Table 7.10 details associations between physical variables and the three AEI attitudinal scales, and Table 7.11 details associations between physical variables and the TROFLEI psychosocial scales.

Table 7. 10.   Associations Between Physical Variables and Student Attitude Towards Subject, Attitude Towards Computer Usage, and Academic Efficacy, in Terms of Simple Correlations (r) and Standardised Regression Coefficients (β)

Physical Variable	Attitude Towards Subject		Attitude Towards Computer Usage		Academic Efficacy	
	r	β	r	β	r	β
Workspace Environment	-0.04	-0.04	0.02	-0.08	-0.06	-0.07
Computer Environment	-0.05	-0.06	0.03	0.03	0.02	0.08
Visual Environment	-0.06	0.06	0.05	-0.01	-0.02	-0.01
Spatial Environment	-0.04	-0.04	0.10**	0.14*	-0.08*	-0.10
Overall Air Quality	-0.05	-0.05	0.04	-0.01	0.06	0.07
Multiple Correl (R)		0.06		0.12		0.10
(R^2)		0.00		0.01		0.01

*$p<0.05$ **$p<0.01$ n=12 facilities

Few statistically significant associations were found between the number of computer workstations directly provided for science students, and physical, psychosocial, and attitudinal variables. Exceptions were, negative associations between the number of computers and Task Orientation, Computer Usage, Computer Environment and Overall Air

Quality, and positive correlations between the number of workstations and Visual Environment and Spatial Environment.

Table 7.11. Associations Between Physical Variables and Psychosocial Variables in Terms of Simple Correlations (r) and Standardised Regression Coefficients (β)

Psychosocial Variables	Physical Variables									
	Workspace Environment		Computer Environment		Visual Environment		Spatial Environment		Overall Air Quality	
	r	β	r	β	r	β	r	β	r	β
Student Cohesiveness	0.00	0.05	-0.01	0.00	-0.07*	-0.05	-0.05	-0.08	-0.01	0.04
Teacher Support	-0.05	-0.12*	0.00	0.03	0.06	0.04	0.03	0.06	0.02	0.00
Involvement	0.01	0.01	0.03	0.03	-0.01	-0.01	-0.01	-0.04	0.02	0.03
Task Orientation	0.00	-0.02	-0.02	0.05	0.04	0.04	0.07	-0.02	0.11**	0.14**
Investigation	0.08*	0.07	0.03	-0.06	0.07*	0.07	0.11**	-0.03	0.14**	0.13**
Cooperation	-0.03	-0.02	-0.01	-0.02	0.01	0.04	-0.01	-0.10	0.06	0.13**
Equity	0.05	-0.05	0.06	0.03	0.08*	0.03	0.13**	0.06	0.15**	0.12*
Differentiation	0.10**	0.19**	-0.09*	-0.01	-0.04	-0.09	0.04	0.19*	0.04	0.00
Computer Usage	-0.15**	-0.20**	-0.06	0.05	-0.04	-0.05	-0.06	0.05	-0.03	0.01
Young Adult Ethos	0.03	-0.03	0.02	-0.01	0.04	0.01	0.10**	0.02	0.15**	0.14*

**$p<0.01$ *$p<0.05$ n=12 facilities

3.4.4 Teacher interviews

Teacher interviews and research indicated several significant issues concerning ICT and teacher change. Teachers in Tasmania are an ageing population and many are thinking about their retirement and not considering taking on new teaching pedagogies. Many teachers prefer a teacher-centred pedagogy and are unwilling to accept change. The teachers felt threatened by forced change, access to and reliability of ICT, student skills and change itself. In not accepting change, many teachers indicated a lack of time for change to occur and indicated a preference for a block of professional learning time, usually later in the year.

Research has indicated that to accept change, teachers must be exposed to models of good practice, have on-going support and scaffolding in the form of collaborative networks, and be encouraged to take responsibility for their own learning. Hence, long-term professional development programs should be structured to address the issues of emotional support, technical assistance and instructional sharing and collaboration. Interestingly, interviewed teachers that indicated support for and acceptance of change and new pedagogies were not always recognised leaders within their school or young teachers.

3.4.5 A review of the conceptual model

While student interviews and observations indicated acceptable levels of student satisfaction with their learning, and significant associations were found between psychosocial factors and student satisfaction, only weak associations were found between students' physical environment and satisfaction, and physical and psychosocial environments. Furthermore, the conceptual model described in Figure 7.1 is very "broad" (Gardiner, 1989, p. 27), so the findings of this study have been used to propose a new model. The following diagram (Figure 7.8) presents a detailed re-working of the conceptual model, and effectively provides a summary of all statistically significant independent (positive and negative) associations, based upon regression analysis.

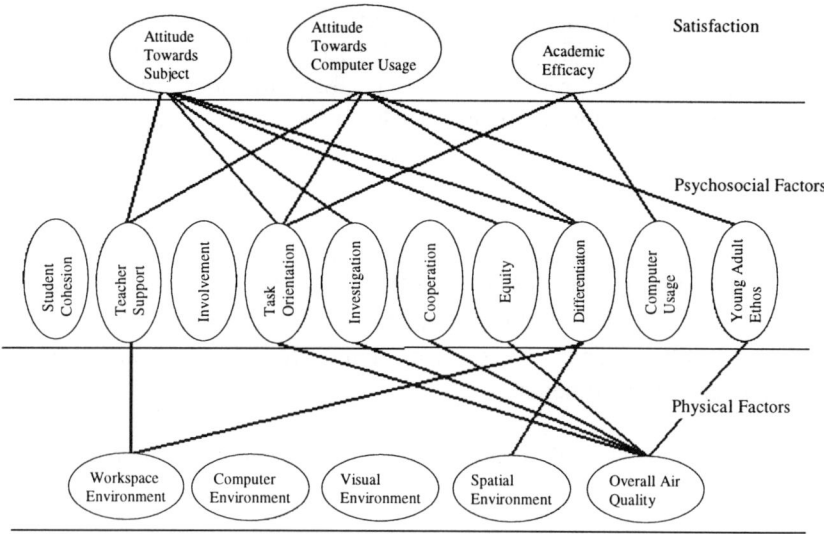

Figure 7.8. A model for educational productivity.

4. A Comparison Between the Two Studies

The 1998 SPIRT study used the College Science Classroom Environment Survey (CSCES) which has nine scales; Cooperation, Teacher Support, Involvement, Leadership, Relevance, Task Orientation, Open Endedness, Integration and Independence. Whereas, the 2003 study used the Technology-Rich Outcomes-Focussed Learning Environment Inventory (TROFLEI) which contains ten scales; Student Cohesiveness, Teacher Support, Involvement, Task Orientation, Investigation, Cooperation, Equity, Differentiation, Computer Usage, and Young Adult Ethos. While the scales are not identical, there are considerable similarities as each instrument has built upon the *What Is Happening In This Class?* instrument, and it is therefore considered valid to make a partial comparison between results. Four scales are the same for each instrument, and for the purposes of this comparison, the Open Endedness and Investigation scales are considered very similar. Table 7.12 displays actual and preferred CSCES and TROFLEI results for the five shared scales.

While differences between TROFLEI and CSCES results are not large, it is significant that TROFLEI results are for each scale higher than CSCES results. This therefore indicates an increase in Teacher Support, Involvement, Task Orientation, Cooperation, and Open Endedness/Investigation in colleges between 1999 and 2003 investigations.

Both studies found that students' preferred psychosocial learning environment was consistently higher than their perceived, and both studies also found statistically significant correlations between students' attitude towards their subject (satisfaction) and mutual psychosocial scales. Similar trends were also noted for gender variations in psychosocial environments.

Table 7.12. *Common Scale Means for the Actual Forms of the TROFLEI and CSCES*

Instrument /Scale		Form	Instrument/Scale Mean		Difference (T-C)
CSCES	TROFLEI		CSCES	TROFLEI	
Teacher	Teacher	Actual	3.59	3.65	0.06
Support	Support	Preferred	3.94	3.96	0.02
Involvement	Involvement	Actual	3.16	3.27	0.11
		Preferred	3.46	3.53	0.07
Task	Task	Actual	3.96	3.98	0.02
Orientation	Orientation	Preferred	4.53	4.42	-0.11
Cooperation	Cooperation	Actual	3.87	3.95	0.08
		Preferred	4.20	4.15	-0.05
Open	Investigation	Actual	2.79	3.12	0.33
Endedness		Preferred	3.32	3.60	0.28

$n_{CSCES} = 1080$ $n_{TROFLEI} = 816$

The following graph (Figure 7.9) compares actual CSCES and TROFLEI results.

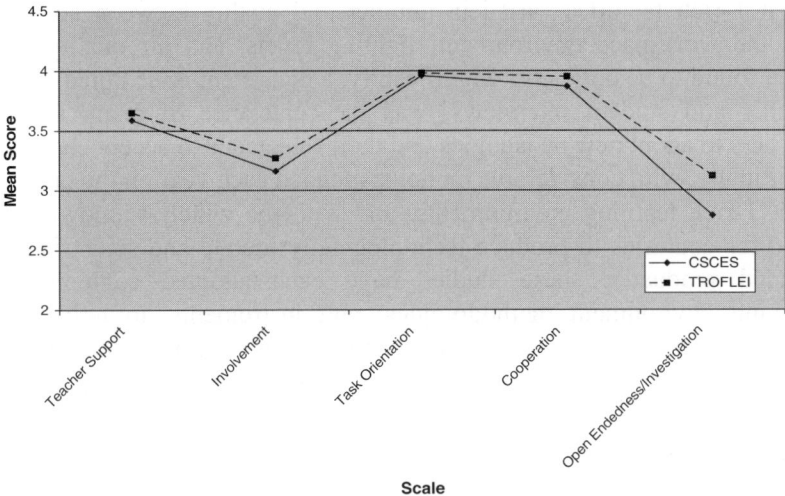

Figure 7.9. Common scale means for the actual forms of the TROFLEI and CSCES.

5. Conclusions

A particular value of both studies is that they have provided secondary college science teachers with important information that could help improve the quality of the teaching and learning process in senior science classrooms. Results from both studies have been reported to each college and the engagement of teachers in professional development is seen as an important achievement of these studies.

The holistic study examining the physical and psychosocial learning environment of over 800 year 11 science students in ICT-rich environments, using a range of research methodologies, has produced a model of productivity which can be used to guide educators and designers in the preparation and operation of such facilities. Furthermore, both studies have found strong associations between students' psychosocial learning environment and satisfaction, as measured by attitudes towards their subject and computer usage, and academic efficacy. Furthermore, while weak associations were found between student satisfaction and the physical environment, it has been noted that due to associations between students' physical and psychosocial learning environments, the physical environment can indirectly affect student satisfaction and hence outcomes.

ICT-rich facilities varied in number and quality between colleges, and the workspace environment, lighting levels, and air quality, was often found to be deficient. Significantly, a consistent issue noted during teacher and student interviews, was the reluctance of many science teachers to adopt new pedagogies and their reluctance to accept change.

Finally, with considerable money expended each year on the creation of ICT-rich learning environments, and with the widely-acknowledged need for countries to produce technologically literate and scientifically-minded graduates, these studies have each adopted contemporary learning environment methodologies, and instruments, to holistically combine data to gain a deeper understanding of student satisfaction and student outcomes, particularly in ICT-rich environments.

Acknowledgement

The first study was funded by the Australian Research Council for the period 1998 to 2000 under the SPIRT Program (Strategic Partnership with Industry for Research & Training).

References

Aldridge, J. M., Fraser, B. J., Fisher, D. L., & Wood, D. (2002). *Assessing students' perceptions of outcomes-focussed, technology-rich learning environments.* Paper presented at the annual meeting of the American Educational Research Association (AERA). New Orleans.

Aldridge, J. M., Fraser, B. J., & Huang, T.-C. I. (1999). Investigating classroom environments in Taiwan and Australia with multiple research methods. *Journal of Education Research, 93*, 48-57.

Cappie-Wood, A. (2004). Introductory address to National Seminar education.au titled *Transforming teaching and learning through ICT.* Retrieved May 30, 2005, from http://www.educationau.edu.au/ICT_seminar/300704.pdf

Chang, V. & Fisher, D. L. (2003). The validation and application of a new learning environment instrument for online learning in higher ceducation. In M. S. Khine & D. L. Fisher (Eds.), *Technology-rich learning environments: A future perspective* (pp. 1-20). Singapore: World Scientific.

Commonwealth Department of Education, Science and Training, (CDEST, 2001). *Making better connections: Models of teacher professional development for the integration of information and communication technology into classroom practice.* Retrieved May 16, 2004, from
http://www.dest.gov.au/schools/publications/2002/MBC.pdf

Department of Education, Training, and Youth Affairs (DETYA). (2000). *Good practice and leadership in the use of ICT in schools.* Retrieved May 16, 2004, from
http://www.edna.edu.au/sibling/leadingpractice .

Fisher, D., Fraser, B., & Yaxley, B. (2000, April). *Science learning environments at the post-compulsory level.* Paper presented at the annual meeting of the National Association for Research in Science Teaching, New Orleans.

Fraser, B. J. (1981). *Test of Science-Related Attitudes.* Melbourne: Australian Council for Educational Research.

Fraser, B. J. (1994) Research on classroom and school climate. In D. Gabel (Ed.), *Handbook of research on science teaching and learning* (pp. 493-541). New York: Macmillan.

Fraser, B. J. (1996). *'Grain Sizes' in educational research: Combining qualitative and quantitative methods.* Paper presented at the workshops/seminars on Research Methods in the Study of Science Classroom Environments, Taiwan.

Fraser, B. J. (1998). Science learning environments: Assessment, effects and determinants. In B. J. Fraser and K. G. Tobin (Eds.), *International Handbook of Science Education.* (pp. 527-564). Dordrecht, Netherlands: Kluwer Academic Publishers.

Fraser, B. J. & Fisher, D. L. (1983). Use of actual and preferred classroom environment scales in person-environment fit research. *Journal of Educational Psychology, 75,* 303-313.

Fraser, B. J. & Tobin, K. (1991). Combining qualitative and quantitative methods in classroom environment research. In B. J. Fraser & H. J. Walberg (Eds.), *Educational environments: Evaluation, antecedents and consequences* (pp. 271-292). Oxford, England: Pergamon Press.

Gardiner, W. L. (1989). Forecasting, planning, and the future of the information society. In P. Gourmain (Ed.), *High technology workplaces: Integrating technology, management, and design for productive work environments* (pp. 27-39). New York: Van Nostrand Reinhold.

Godfrey, C. (2001). Computers in schools: Changing pedagogies. *Journal of the Australian Council for Computers in Education, 16*(2), 14-17.

Goumain, P. (1989). Changing environments for high-technology workplaces. In P. Goumain (Ed.), *High technology workplaces: integrating technology, management, and design for productive work environments* (pp. 1-23). New York: Van Nostrand Reinhold.

Guba, E. G. & Lincoln, Y. S. (1989). *Fourth generation evaluation.* Beverly Hills: Sage Publications.

Hunt, D. E. (1975). Person environment interaction: A challenge found wanting before it was tried. *Review of Educational Research, 45,* 209-230.

Khalili, A. & Shashaani, L. (1994). The effectiveness of computer applications: A meta-analysis. *Journal of Research on Computing in Education, 27*(1).

Kroemer, K. & Grandjean, E. (2001*). Fitting the task to the man: A textbook of occupational ergonomics* (5th ed.). London: Taylor and Francis.

Lewin, K. (1935). *A dynamic theory of personality.* New York: McGraw.

Lewin, K. (1936). *Principles of topological psychology.* New York: McGraw.

Loughlin, C. E. & Suina, J. H. (1982). *The learning environment: An instructional strategy.* New York: Teachers College Press.

Marx, A., Fuhrer, U., & Hartig, T. (2000). Effects of classroom seating arrangements on children's question-asking. *Learning Environments Research, 2,* 249-263.

Moos, R. H. (1973). Conceptualizations of human environments. *American Psychologist, 28,* 652-665.

Moos, R. H. (1974). *Evaluating treatment environments: A social ecological approach.* New York: John Wiley and Sons.

Moos, R. H. (1976). *The human context: Environmental determinants of behaviour.* New York: John Wiley and Sons.

Moos, R. H. (1979). *Evaluating educational environments: Procedures, measures, findings and policy implications.* San Francisco, CA: Jossey-Bass.

Muncey, D.E. & McQuillan, P. (1993). Preliminary findings from a five-year study of the coalition of essential schools. *Phi Delta Kappan, 74*(6), 486-489.

Newhouse, P. (1998). The impact of portable computers on classroom learning environments. *Journal of the Australian Council for Educational Computing, 13*(1), 5-11.

Rickards, T. (2003). Technology-rich learning environments and the role of effective teaching. In M. S. Khine & D. L. Fisher (Eds.). *Technology-rich learning environments: A future perspective* (pp. 97–113). Singapore: World Scientific.

Tasmanian Department of Education. (2002a). *Learning in an Online World Goals.* Retrieved April 4, 2004, from http://connections.education.tas.gov.au/Nav/GoalSet.asp?ID=GS22.

Tasmanian Department of Education. (2002b). *Essential learnings framework 1. Tasmania, Australia.* Retrieved April 4, 2004, from http://www.education.tas.gov.au/ocll/currcons/publications/els1.pdf.

Thomas, G. P. (2003). Conceptualisation, development and validation of an instrument for investigating the metacognitive orientation of science classroom learning environments: The metacognitive orientation learning environment scale – Science (MOLES-S). *Learning Environments Research, 6*, 175-197.

Tobin, K. G. & Fraser, B. J. (1998). Qualitative and quantitative landscapes of classroom learning environments. In B. J. Fraser and K.G. Tobin (Eds.), *International Handbook of Science Education* (pp. 623-640). Dordrecht, The Netherlands: Kluwer Academic Publishers.

Trinidad, S. (1998). National overview: Table of state education department initiatives. *Australian Educational Computing, 13*(2), 4-5.

Trinidad, S. (2003). Working with technology-rich learning environments: Strategies for success. In M. S. Khine & D. L. Fisher (Eds.), *Technology-rich learning environments: A future perspective* (pp. 97-113). Singapore: World Scientific.

Twining, P. (2002). *ICT in schools: Estimating the level of investment.* Retrieved June 6, 2005, from http://www.med8.info/docs/meD8_02-01.pdf.

Walberg, H. J. (1969). Class size and the social environment of learning. *Human Relations, 22*, 465-475.

Walberg, H. J. (1976). The psychology of learning environments: Behavioural, structural, or perceptual? *Review of Research of Education, 4*, 142-178.

Walberg, H. J. (1986). Synthesis of research on teaching. In M. C. Wittrock (Ed.), *Handbook of research on teaching* (3rd ed.) New York: Macmillan.

Weinstein, C. S. (1979). The physical environment of the school: A review of the research. *Review of Educational Research, 49*(4), 577-610.

Woodson, W. E., Tillman, B., & Tillman, P. (1992). *Human factors handbook: Information guidelines for the design of systems, facilities, equipment, and products for human use* (2nd Ed.). New York: McGraw-Hill.

Zandvliet, D. B. (1999). *The physical and psychosocial environment associated with classrooms using new information technologies – A cross-national study.* PhD thesis, Curtin University of Technology. Retrieved March 21, 2004, from http://adt.curtin.edu.au/theses/available/adt-WCU20020502.121823/.

Zandvliet, D. B. (2000). *Designing productive learning environments for tomorrow's teachers.* In D. L. Fisher & Jong-Hsiang Yang (Eds.), *Proceedings of the Second International Conference on Science, Mathematics and Technology Education* (pp. 489-502). Perth: Curtin University of Technology.

Zandvliet, D. B. (2003). Learning environments in new contexts: Web-capable classrooms in Canada. In M. S. Khine & D. L. Fisher (Eds.), *Technology-rich learning environments: A future perspective* (pp. 133-156). Singapore: World Scientific.

Zandvliet, D. B. & Buker, L. (2002). *The internet in BC classrooms: Learning environments in new contexts.* Paper presented at the annual meeting of the American Educational Researchers' Association (AERA), April 2002, New Orleans, LA.

Chapter 8

MIXED METHOD APPROACHES FOR EXAMINING CLASSROOM LEARNING ENVIRONMENTS FOR RESILIENT AND NONRESILIENT STUDENTS IN URBAN ELEMENTARY SCHOOLS

Hersh C. Waxman
University of Houston
USA

Hui-Li Chang
National Louis University
USA

In recent years, the classroom learning environment paradigm has expanded its use of research methods from primarily using traditional surveys and questionnaires to incorporating more mixed methodology. The use of mixed method studies allows researchers to gain a more comprehensive picture of what is actually occurring in the classroom. This chapter summarizes recent research that incorporated the mixed methods of survey research (i.e., student questionnaires) and systematic classroom observation (i.e., low- and high-inference measures) to investigate various aspects of classroom environments for educationally resilient (i.e., academically successful) and nonresilient (i.e., academically unsuccessful) students in urban elementary schools located in the USA. In addition, we focus on how survey and observational data from individual teachers' classrooms can provide meaningful feedback to teachers that may help them improve their classroom instruction and learning environment. Finally, the chapter addresses some of the implications of our current mixed methods research on classroom learning environments for future research and teachers' professional development.

1. Classroom Learning Environments

The socio-psychological environment or classroom learning environment has been extensively researched in the past three decades. Although work in this area can be traced back over 70 years to the theoretical and conceptual work of Lewin (1935, 1936) and Murray (1938), it is only within the past three or four decades that this research has gained acceptance and credibility as a major educational research paradigm (Fraser, 1991, 1994). Contemporary classroom environment research begun by Walberg in the late 1960s and Fraser since the early 1980s has shown the importance of looking at students' perceptions of their learning environments. This line of research has generally emphasized: (a) the development, reliability, and validity of learning environment measures, (b) the impact of students' perceptions of such measures on cognitive, behavioural, and affective outcomes, (c) the extent to which teacher, school, or contextual factors affect learning environment measures, and (d) how these measures can be improved by changing classroom environments in desired directions.

From a theoretical perspective, classroom learning environment research emphasizes the student-mediating or student cognition paradigm which maintains that how students perceive and react to their learning tasks and classroom instruction may be more important in terms of influencing student outcomes than the observed quality of teaching behaviours (Knight & Waxman, 1991; Winne & Marx, 1982; Wittrock, 1986). This paradigm assumes that: (a) the classroom environment experienced by the student may be quite different from the observed or intended instruction (Waxman, 1991; Wittrock, 1986), and (b) teaching and learning can be improved by examining the ways that classroom instruction and the learning environment are viewed or interpreted by the students themselves since students ultimately respond to what they perceive is important (Chavez, 1984; Schultz, 1979). Students are considered to be the experts of their own views and experiences of school (Oldfather, 1995), and their perceptions of the learning environment are also essential for understanding the opportunities for learning that are provided to each student in class (Fraser, 1990).

Students' perceptions of their instructional and classroom learning environments have been found to explain a significant amount of variance for both students' cognitive and affective outcomes (Fraser, 1994; Fraser & Fisher, 1982; Haertel, Walberg, & Haertel, 1981). Generally, the results of these studies and reviews of research have found that the variables such as cohesiveness, task orientation, rule clarity, student satisfaction, and teacher support are positively related to students' gain in academic achievement. Furthermore, research has found that these outcomes can be improved by providing teachers with feedback from learning environment data (Burden & Fraser, 1993; Fraser & Deer, 1983; Fraser & Fisher, 1986; Fraser, Malone, & Neale, 1989).

In recent years, the classroom learning environment paradigm has expanded its use of research methods from primarily using traditional surveys and questionnaires to incorporating more mixed methods. The use of mixed method studies allows researchers to better understand what is actually occurring in the classroom. One complementary method that has been recently used with learning environment research is systematic classroom observation. By combining classroom observations with survey data, a more comprehensive assessment of the entire classroom environment can be made. In addition to understanding students' perceptions of their classroom learning environment, systematic classroom observations attempt to quantify specified behaviours and processes that occur during school while teachers are engaged in teaching (Waxman, 2003). The following section describes the use of systematic classroom observations.

2. Systematic Classroom Observation

Systematic classroom observation is a quantitative method of measuring classroom behaviours from direct observations that specifies both the events or behaviours that are to be observed and how they are to be recorded (Waxman, 2003). Generally, the data that are collected from this procedure focuses on the frequency with which specific behaviours or types of behaviour occurred in the classroom and the amount of time they occurred. There are several elements that are common to most observational systems: (a) a purpose for the observation, (b) the operational definitions of all the observed behaviours, (c) the training procedures for observers, (d) a specific observational focus, (e) a setting, (f) a unit of time, (g) an observation schedule, (h) a method to record the data, and (i) a method to process and analyze data (Stallings & Mohlman, 1988).

While there are several types of observational procedures or techniques that have been used to examine effective teaching (e.g., charts, rating scales, checklists, and narrative descriptions), the most widely used procedure or research method has been systematic classroom observation based on interactive coding systems. These interactive coding systems allow the observer to record nearly everything that students and teachers do during a given time interval (Stallings &

Mohlman, 1988). These interaction systems are very objective and typically do not require the observer to make any high inferences or judgments about the behaviours they observe in the classroom. In other words, these low-inference observational systems provide specific and easily identifiable behaviours that observers can easily code (Stodolsky, 1990).

Some of the major strengths of using classroom observation methods are that they: (a) permit researchers to study the processes of education in naturalistic settings, (b) provide more detailed and precise evidence than other data sources, and (c) can be used to stimulate change and verify that the change occurred (Anderson & Burns, 1989). The descriptions of instructional events that are provided by this method have also been found to lead to improved understanding and better models for improving teaching (Waxman, 2003; Waxman & Huang, 1999).

A final strength of this research method is that the findings from these observational studies have provided a coherent, well-substantiated knowledge base about effective instruction (Waxman, 1995; Waxman & Huang, 1999). Many of the reviews and summaries of the classroom observation research have consistently found that a number of classroom behaviours significantly relate to students' academic achievement (Brophy & Good, 1986; Rosenshine & Stevens, 1986; Walberg, 1995). In other words, research using classroom observation has provided us with a substantial knowledge base that has helped us understand effective teaching. These instructional behaviours have also been adopted and/or mandated as effective teaching practices by many states and school districts throughout the USA (Ornstein, 1991).

The next section describes how the use of learning environment measures and systematic classroom observation can be used to focus on resilient and nonresilient students.

3. Educational Resilience

There is a growing body of research trying to address the issues of why some students from at-risk home and school environments have been successful in school. The educational resiliency framework focuses on the predictors of academic success rather than on academic failure. It may help us identify those alterable factors that distinguish resilient and non-resilient students, as well as to design preventive measurements for average students who are at-risk of academic failure. To achieve academic equity and reduce achievement gaps, changes must be made within classrooms so that all learners, regardless of gender, ethnicity, socio-economic status, language, or disability will be successful in school. These issues of equity in academic achievement are directly related to the study of resiliency. The "at-risk" populations of students who are studied in terms of resilience often are the group of students who face the most severe barriers for becoming successful in schools.

Educational resilience should not be viewed as a fixed attribute of some students, but rather as alterable processes or mechanisms that can be developed and fostered in the classroom environment. Benard (1997), for example, maintains that there are four attributes or personal characteristics that can be altered or developed for children to become resilient: (a) social competence like responsiveness, (b) problem-solving skills, (c) autonomy, and (d) a sense of purpose. McMillan and Reed (1994) also describe four factors that appear to be related to resiliency: (a) individual attributes, (b) positive use of time, (c) family, and (d) school. These also are the psychological perceptions that students obtain from the environment; however, these perceptions can be altered so students may learn in the context of a school environment that is focused and perceived by students as a supportive environment for their development. Educators can create a classroom environment that facilitates educational success. They also can foster educational resilience through their classroom activities. Protective factors in the child, family, school, and community can be brought into the classroom as part of the contextual and connected classroom practices that make education meaningful for all students.

Teachers can play an important role in serving as an external support and protective mechanism that can help students cope with stress (Howard, Dryden, & Johnson, 1999). Supportive teachers can create a learning environment for students at-risk of academic failure to enhance learning outcomes (Gore, 2001). Pierce (1994), for example, found that when teachers provide a positive classroom environment, students respond in a meaningful way, enhancing motivation and increasing achievement outcomes as a natural by-product.

4. Summary of Recent Resiliency Research Focusing on Classroom Learning Environments

In a series of studies conducted by two USA Department of Education National Research Centers (Center for Education in the Inner Cities and Center for Research on Education, Diversity and Excellence), Waxman, Padrón, and their colleagues examined learning environment differences between resilient and nonresilient elementary school students from several urban school districts serving culturally and linguistically diverse students from low socioeconomic circumstances. These studies all incorporated learning environment questionnaires and systematic classroom observation methods. The following sections highlight some of these mixed methods studies.

4.1 Waxman, Huang, and Wang (1997)

Waxman, Huang, and Wang (1997) focused on resilient and nonresilient students from four elementary schools from a large urban school district located in a major metropolitan city in the south central region of the USA. Two fourth- and two fifth-grade classrooms were randomly selected from each of these four inner-city schools. Near the middle of the school year, teachers were asked to identify their population of students at risk (e.g., students from families of low socioeconomic status, living with a single parent, relative, or guardian). From this pool of at-risk students, teachers were told to select up to three "resilient" (i.e., high achieving on both standardized achievement tests and daily school work, very motivated, and excellent attendance) and three "non-resilient" students (i.e., low achieving on both standardized achievement tests and daily school work, not motivated, and poor attendance) in their class. Each of these resilient and non-resilient students: (a) completed learning environment and motivation surveys, and (b) was observed using a shadowing observation technique.

Shortened versions of three student self-report survey instruments were used in the study: (a) the *Multidimensional Motivation Instrument* (MMI) (Uguroglu & Walberg 1986), (b) the *Classroom Environment Scale* (CES) (Fisher & Fraser, 1983), and (c) the *Instructional Learning Environment Questionnaire* (ILEQ) (Knight & Waxman, 1990). All of the instruments were modified to a "personal form" of the instrument in the present study which elicits an individual students' responses to his/her role in the class rather than a student's perception of the class as a whole (Fraser, 1991). The instruments also were modified to specifically focus on students' perceptions of their content area classes (i.e., mathematics or reading) rather than on their general impressions of school as a whole. Shortened forms of all the instruments were used in this study because the school district only allowed us about 40 minutes to complete the three surveys. The alpha reliability coefficients of these scales aggregated by individual student ranged from 0.33 to 0.86, while the reliabilities aggregated by class ranged from 0.53 to 0.91. The reliability coefficients for the ILEQ are generally good, but the reliabilities for the MMI and CES scales aggregated by individual students were lower than expected. Overall, the reliability coefficients were somewhat satisfactory for scales that are composed of only a few items and they were similar to reliability coefficients found in studies conducted at the elementary school level. The mean correlations between the scales ranged from 0.08 to 0.24, indicating that the survey instrument has good discriminant validity.

The shadowing observations consisted of narrative descriptions of: (a) the physical environment of the classroom, (b) teachers' instructional approaches, behaviours, and attitudes toward students, and (c) students' observed attitudes, actions, mannerisms, and interactions. The shadowing observations were recorded on lap-top computers that were programmed to provide observers with specific time prompts that told them exactly when they were to record the information (i.e., narrative comments) about each student. A sample of "average" students from each classroom also was included in the study.

Overall, resilient students perceived their classrooms much more favorably than nonresilient students. Resilient students had higher academic self-concept and student aspirations than nonresilient students. They also perceived their teachers as having higher expectations for them and providing them with more feedback and appropriate pacing than nonresilient students. Furthermore, resilient students reported that they were more involved and satisfied in their classrooms than nonresilient students. They also perceived more task orientation and order and organization than nonresilient students. For the most part, average students' perceptions were generally similar to resilient students.

There were several prevalent themes and issues that emerged from the shadowing data. First, several important factors distinguished resilient from nonresilient students. Resilient students appeared to be persistent, attentive, demonstrated leadership skills, worked well with other students, frequently volunteered answers, and were often engaged in their school work. Resilient students were generally more enthusiastic, energetic, and better behaved than nonresilient students. Resilient students received more teacher attention and praise than nonresilient students did. On the other hand, nonresilient students often appeared to be shy or timid, frequently tired, not attentive to the teacher, or bored. They were not as engaged in the activities of the class as resilient students and appeared to get started on their work more slowly. Furthermore, many nonresilient students appeared anxious, restless, easily distracted, and sometimes resistant to doing their work. A few of the nonresilient students were disruptive in the classroom, either disturbing other classmates by talking to them or making a loud enough commotion at their desks that the teacher needed to reprimand them. It should be mentioned, however, that there was much more variation (i.e., less homogeneity) among the behaviours of nonresilient students than resilient students.

While the primary focus of the shadowing data was to focus on resilient and non-resilient students, the instructional contexts that were prevalent in these classrooms also were observed. The findings revealed that the overall instruction in these inner-city elementary schools was whole-class instruction with students working in teacher-assigned activities, generally in a passive manner (i.e., watching or listening). There was very little small group work observed in any of the classrooms, and when it did occur, it would typically be one student working with another student. Teachers were observed keeping students on task most of the time, focusing on the task, communicating the tasks procedures, and checking students' work. They also spent more time explaining than questioning, cueing, or prompting students. Teachers were not frequently observed encouraging extended student responses or encouraging students to help themselves or help each other. Generally, there was little engagement in the classroom and the intellectual level of the curriculum was low-level, with very few authentic activities occurring. Very little of the content was related to students' interests or the world outside school. The predominant culture of classrooms observed was related to "getting work done," rather than an emphasis on authentic learning situations.

Another important finding from this study was that in the few classrooms where a great deal of student-teacher interaction occurred, it was much more difficult to ascertain differences between resilient and nonresilient students. The direct instructional approach that predominated in both reading and mathematics classrooms appeared to be much more suited to resilient students, who were motivated, attentive, volunteered answers, and received more teacher attention and praise than nonresilient students, who appeared bored, reluctant to answer questions, and at times reluctant to work during the direct instructional approach. Overall, the qualitative findings indicated that resilient students were much more successful in classrooms employing direct instruction than nonresilient students were. Although there were great observable differences in the academic behaviours of these two groups of students, no remediation, adaptive, or enrichment activities were observed in any classrooms. For the most part, teachers did not treat individual students differently; they focused on the whole class and directed instructional activities toward everyone at the same time.

4.2 Padrón, Waxman, and Huang (1999)

Padrón, Waxman, and Huang (1999) compared the classroom instruction and learning environment of about 250 resilient, average, and nonresilient students in fourth- and fifth-grade classrooms from three elementary schools located in a major metropolitan area in the south central region of the USA. Students in the three schools were predominately Hispanic (>75%) and most of them (>90%) received free or reduced-cost lunches. Near the middle of the school year, teachers were asked to identify their population of students at risk (e.g., students from families of low socioeconomic status, living with a single parent, relative, or guardian). Students identified as "gifted or talented" or "special education" were excluded from the population in order to avoid potential effects related to ability differences. From this pool of at-risk students, teachers were then told to select up to three "resilient" (i.e., high achieving on both standardized achievement tests and daily school work, very motivated, and excellent attendance) and three "non-resilient" students (i.e., low achieving on both standardized achievement tests and daily school work, not motivated, and poor attendance) in their class.

The *My Class Inventory* (Dryden & Fraser, 1996; Fraser, Anderson, & Walberg, 1982; Fraser & O'Brien, 1985) was used to collect data on students' perceptions of their classroom learning environment near the end of the school year. The inventory is a 30-item questionnaire read to students in Spanish or English by researchers. Students circle either "Yes" or "No" in response to statements about their reading class. The questionnaire contains five scales that assess students' perceptions in the following areas: (a) Satisfaction, (b) Friction, (c) Competition, (d) Difficulty, and (e) Cohesion. The internal consistency reliability coefficients of the five scales ranged from 0.62 to 0.80, with an average of 0.72.

The observation instrument used in this study was the *Classroom Observation Schedule* (COS) (Waxman, Wang, Lindvall, & Anderson, 1988). It is designed to systematically obtain information on students' classroom behaviours. It documents observed student behaviours in the context of ongoing classroom instructional-learning processes. The COS has been modified to include a Language Used section for the present study since many of the students' primary language was Spanish. Individual students are observed with reference to (a) their interactions with the teacher or other students, (b) the selection of activity, (c) the type of activity they are working on, (d) the setting in which the observed behaviour occurs, (e) their classroom manner, and (f) the language used. Each student is observed for ten 30-second intervals during each class period. This observation schedule has been found to be valid and reliable in previous studies. In the present study, the inter-observers' agreements (Cohen's kappa) were found to be excellent, with a inter-observers' reliability coefficient of 0.96.

Near the end of the school year, all the fourth- and fifth-grade students completed the MCI and trained observers also used the COS to systematically observe the resilient and non-resilient students identified by teachers during regular reading and/or language classes.

The ANOVA results reveal that there were significant differences among resilient, average, and non-resilient students on two scales, Satisfaction and Difficulty. The Duncan post hoc results indicate that the resilient student group scored significantly higher on Satisfaction than the non-resilient group, and that there was no significant difference between resilient and average student groups or between average and non-resilient student groups on Satisfaction. Non-resilient students scored significantly higher on Difficulty than average and resilient students. Average students also scored significantly higher than resilient students on the Difficulty scale. There were no significant differences among the three student groups on the Friction, Competition, and Cohesion scales.

The results from the COS revealed that students spent over 65% of their time doing independent work (no interaction). They spent more time interacting with other students (14%) than with teachers (8%) for instructional purposes. Over 95% of the time, classroom activities were assigned by teachers. The most frequently observed activity types included working on written assignments, watching or listening, instructional discussion, and reading. Students were never observed working with technology, such as computers, calculators, or viewing video or slides. The predominant classroom setting is the whole class setting, which was observed over 75% of the time. The time-on-task varied greatly between resilient (85%) and non-resilient students (61%), as did the time being off task. Nearly 90% of the time, students were observed using English and they were observed using Spanish about 7% of time.

A *t-test for independent samples* was used to compare resilient and non-resilient students' classroom behaviours. The results reveal that resilient students were observed more frequently interacting with teachers for instructional purposes than non-resilient students, whereas non-resilient students were observed more frequently interacting with other students for social or personal purposes. Resilient students were observed watching or listening to teachers more frequently than non-resilient students, whereas non-resilient students were observed not attending to task significantly more often than resilient students. Resilient students were found to be on task significantly more often than non-resilient, whereas non-resilient students were found to be off task significantly more than resilient students. There was no significant difference in language used by resilient and non-resilient students.

4.3 Waxman, Rivera, and Powers (2006)

Waxman, Rivera, and Powers (2006) investigated the classroom learning environments of resilient, average, and non-resilient students in fourth- and fifth-grade reading classrooms consisting of predominantly 200 Hispanic students from one elementary school located in a major metropolitan area in the south central region of the USA. Most of the students come from socially- and economically-disadvantaged home environments and the academic achievement of students is lower than other students in the same school district and lower than the state average.

An adapted version of the My Class Inventory (Dryden & Fraser, 1996; Fraser, Anderson, & Walberg, 1982) was used to collect data on students' perceptions of their classroom learning environment near the beginning and near the end of the school year. The inventory is a 50-item questionnaire read to students in Spanish or English by researchers. Students circle either "Yes" or "No" in response to statements about their reading class. The questionnaire contains eight scales that assess students' perceptions in the following areas: (a) Satisfaction, (b) Friction, (c) Competition, (d) Difficulty, (e) Cohesion, (f) Self-Esteem in Reading, (g) Teacher Support, and (h) Equity. The instrument has been found to be reliable and valid in many different school settings and it is especially applicable for elementary school students (Padrón, Waxman, & Huang, 1999). The internal consistency reliability coefficients of the eight scales was found to range from 0.62 to 0.80, with an average of 0.70. In other words, the questionnaire has adequate internal consistency reliability. The discriminant validity for the sample (i.e., the mean correlation coefficient of a scale with each of the other scales) ranged from 0.01 to 0.59, with an average of 0.22, suggesting that there was adequate scale discriminant validity, although a few scales overlapped to a certain degree.

The observation instrument used in the study was again the Classroom Observation Schedule (COS) (Waxman & Padron, 2004). The inter-observer agreement for the present study was found to be excellent, with an inter-observer reliability of 0.96.

Near the beginning of the school year, teachers were asked to identify their population of students at risk (e.g., students from families of low socio-economic status, living with either, a single parent, relative, or guardian). Students identified as gifted, talented, or special education were excluded from the population to avoid potential effects related to ability differences. From this pool of at-risk students, teachers were then told to select up to three resilient (i.e., high-achieving students on both standardized achievement test and daily school work, very motivated, with excellent attendance) and three non-resilient students (i.e., low-achieving students on both standardized tests and daily school work, not motivated, with poor attendance) in their class.

Students were administered the MCI near the beginning of the school year and again near the end of the school year. Trained researchers read the survey to all students and told the students that the survey was not a test and their responses would not be seen by any school personnel.

Targeted students also were observed with the COS in their classrooms near the beginning of the school year and at the end of the school year. The COS was used to observe each student for ten 30 second intervals during each classroom period.

The ANOVA results for the beginning of the year revealed a significant main effect for Difficulty, and for the Reading Self-Esteem scale. Overall, non-resilient students reported having more difficulty in their class work than both average and resilient students. Meanwhile, resilient and average students reported higher levels of reading self-esteem than non-resilient students.

Near the end of the academic year, the ANOVA results for the MCI revealed that there were significant differences among resilient, average, and non-resilient students on two scales, Competition and Difficulty. The results indicated that the resilient and average student group scored significantly higher on Competition than the non-resilient group. Meanwhile, non-resilient students scored significantly higher in perceiving the classroom environment to be more difficult for them. Average students also scored significantly higher, than resilient students, on the Difficulty scale at the end of the year.

The ANOVA observation beginning of the year results revealed that non-resilient students were observed more frequently Not Attending to Task than resilient and average students. Non-resilient students were also observed more frequently distracted than resilient and average students. On the other hand, resilient student were observed on task more frequently than non-resilient students.

At the end of the year, the ANOVA results revealed that non-resilient students were observed more frequently Not Attending to Task than resilient and average students; non-resilient students were also observed more frequently Distracted than resilient and average students. On the other had, resilient student were observed On Task more frequently than non-resilient students.

The magnitude of these differences were both statistically and educationally significant. These findings also indicated that across time there are no significant changes in the classroom environment. In general, the classroom observations show that there was little interaction among peers or students and teacher. In other words, there were few teacher-student instructional interactions observed, and whole-class instruction predominated.

4.4 Chang and Waxman (2004)

Chang and Waxman (2004) identified the differences in perceptions of mathematics classroom learning environments among resilient, average, and nonresilient elementary students from three public elementary schools located in the vicinity of a major metropolitan city in the south central region of the USA participated in the present study. Teachers from the participating school were asked to identify approximately three resilient (i.e., high-achieving students on both standardized achievement tests and daily school work, very motivated, and excellent attendance) and approximately three nonresilient students (i.e., low-achieving students on both standardized achievement tests and daily school work, not motivated, with poor attendance) in their class. The remaining students were classified as average students.

The learning environment questionnaire contained 10 scales that assessed students' perceptions of their mathematics classrooms in the following areas: (a) cohesion, (b) competition, (c) difficulty, (d) satisfaction, (e) academic self-concept, (f) parent involvement, (g) student aspirations, (h) equity, (i) teacher support, and (j) academic efficacy. The questionnaire was adapted from the (a) My Class Inventory (MCI) (Dryden & Fraser, 1996), (b) Multidimensional Motivation Instrument (MMI) (Uguroglu & Walberg, 1986), (c) Instructional Learning Environment Questionnaire (ILEQ) (Knight & Waxman, 1990), (d) *What is Happening in This Class* (WIHIC) (Aldridge, Fraser, & Huang, 1998; Fraser, Fisher, & McRobbie, 1996), and (e) Classroom Environment Scale (CES) (Waxman & Huang, 1996; Waxman, Huang, & Padrón, 1997).

Two standardized observational instruments were used to carry out observational research: (a) the *Overall Classroom Observation Measure* (COM) (Ross & Smith, 1996), and (b) the Classroom Observation Schedule (COS) (Waxman, Wang, Lindvall, & Anderson, 1988). The COS instrument is a low-inference schedule whereas the COM instrument is a high-inference observation schedule. Overall observations, from the Classroom Observation Measure (COM) (Ross & Smith, 1996), were used to measure the extent to which instructional processes or strategies were used by teachers during instruction.

The learning environment results indicate that the nonresilient students scored significantly higher on the difficulty scale than the average and the resilient students, and the average students scored significantly higher than the resilient students on the same scale. Resilient students scored significantly higher on the cohesion scale than nonresilient students, and there was no significant difference between nonresilient and average student groups or between average and resilient students on the cohesion scale. In general, the resilient student group and the average group were significantly more satisfied with their class work and enjoyed their classroom environment more compared with the nonresilient student group.

The results from the COM instrument indicate that the only instructional practice used extensively in the classrooms was direct instruction. Many of the instructional practices and strategies, such as cooperative learning and technology-enhanced classrooms, that have been found to be especially effective for ELLs (English Language Learners) and other students at risk of failure (Waxman & Padrón, 2002), were not frequently observed in these classrooms.

Overall, descriptive statistics results from the COS revealed that students spent over 86% of their time doing independent work (no interaction). They spent more time interacting with other students (7%) than with teachers (4%) for instructional purposes. Students also were observed spending 3% of their time interacting with other students for personal or social reason. More than 98% of the time, classroom activities were designated by teachers. The most frequently observed activities included working on written assignments, watching or listening, instructional discussion, working with manipulative material or equipment, and not attending on task. The predominant classroom setting was the whole class setting, which was observed more than 96% of the time. Time on task varied greatly between resilient (85%) and nonresilient students (61%).

A one-way ANOVA was used to compare student classroom behaviours among resilient, average, and nonresilient students. Statistically significant differences were found on the Not Attending to Task scale. The Tukey Post Hoc results indicated that the nonresilient students were observed not attending to task more frequently than the resilient students. There were no other statistically significant differences between nonresilient and average students, or between average and resilient students during the observed periods. No statistically significant differences were found on any other item from COS.

5. Discussion

The combination of both survey and observational data used in these studies offers insight into the resilience phenomenon as well as our understanding of what distinguishes resilient and nonresilient students. The studies described in this chapter all focused on elementary school students who were predominantly from low income families and found that classroom learning environments and classroom behaviours significantly differed between resilient and non-resilient students. Despite coming from the same school environment and having similar home backgrounds and demographic characteristics, some students have done exceptionally well in their reading, language art, and mathematics classes, whereas others have done very poorly. The results from these studies indicate that resilient elementary school students generally perceive a more positive learning environment and they are more satisfied with their classrooms. These findings are similar to previous studies that reported that satisfaction differentiates resilient and non-resilient students (Alva, 1991; Reyes & Jason, 1993, Waxman, Huang, & Padrón, 1997). In addition, non-resilient students indicate that they have more difficulty in their class work than both average students and resilient students. The magnitude of these differences is both statistically and educationally significant. These findings provide a great challenge for classroom teachers who need to provide optimal learning environments for all their students.

The observational results from studies described in this chapter are extremely important given that the amount and quality of teacher and student academic interactions are two of the most influential variables that promote student outcomes (Wang, Haertel, & Walberg, 1993). The observational results summarized here indicate that there are several classroom behavioural differences between resilient and non-resilient elementary school students. One of the differences related to the amount and type of interaction that were found in the classroom processes. In some of the studies, resilient students spent significantly more time interacting with teachers for instructional purposes than nonresilient students. On the other hand, non-resilient students spent significantly more time interacting with other students for social or personal purposes than resilient students. These two student groups also significantly differed in classroom activity. Resilient students were observed more often watching or listening, whereas nonresilient students were observed more often not attending to task. The percentage of time resilient students were on task was much higher than that of nonresilient students in most of the studies. Resilient students were less often distracted or disruptive than nonresilient students.

In summary, the findings from the student observations support the learning environment data. Significant differences were found between resilient and non-resilient students on their classroom behaviours and learning environment. These findings have important educational implications because researchers have found that many of these variables are critical for the academic success of students. Besides these important differences in classroom behaviours between resilient and non-resilient students, a few common classroom processes deserve special attention. First, there was no verbal interaction between teacher and student or between students for both resilient and non-resilient student groups for over two-thirds of the time and students spent relatively little time interacting with teachers. Active learning is another critical instructional process that improves student outcomes, yet over 95% of the activities were assigned by teachers and students spent large proportions of time working on written assignments, watching, or listening to the teacher. Second, these students were observed in whole-class settings nearly all of the time. Such over reliance on whole-class instruction may be detrimental to student outcomes because teachers often have difficulty maintaining an appropriate pace that is suitable for all their students. In one of the studies (Waxman, Huang, & Wang, 1997), it was found to be especially harmful for nonresilient students.

Not surprisingly, the instructional and classroom learning environment differences found in this study may be consistent with teachers' expectations and attitudes toward resilient and non-resilient students. Thus, the use of teacher nomination to identify "resilient" and "non-resilient" students could be considered a limitation of all of the studies because there is the danger that having teachers identify or classify students as non-resilient could impact their treatment of students and ultimately impact students' success (Storer, Cychosz, & Licklider, 1995). On the other hand, the teacher nomination approach still appears to be a more valid identification procedure to identify resilient and non-resilient students than those exclusively based on grades and/or test scores which have been used in most other resiliency studies (e.g., Gonzales & Padilla, 1997; Waxman & Huang, 1996; Waxman, Huang, & Padrón, 1997). Our informal discussions with teachers about the nomination process revealed that they had no difficulty categorizing the students in their class. Several teachers, for example, shared specific examples with us of why certain students in their class were clearly resilient and non-resilient. The teachers also indicated that the resilience framework was a useful approach that helped them understand why certain students may be successful or unsuccessful.

The combination of both survey and observational data in these studies also provides rich insights to our understanding of the "resilience" phenomena as well as our interpretations of what distinguishes resilient and non-resilient students. The learning environment and classroom process differences found in these studies indicate that there are criteria other than academic achievement that distinguishes resilient and non-resilient students. Future research should examine if these learning environment and classroom process differences are stable or consistent across the entire school year, as well as investigate whether the differences persist beyond a given school year. Other studies should also examine if there are other important criteria that further distinguish resilient and non-resilient students.

Future research needs to explicitly test intervention models where teachers try to alter instructional patterns and the learning environment of classrooms that consist of large numbers of non-resilient students. One approach that has been found to be very effective is using feedback from classroom observation and learning environment measures to help teachers understand their current instructional strengths and weaknesses (Fraser, 1991; Fraser & Fisher, 1986; Stallings, & Mohlman, 1988; Waxman, 1995; Waxman, Huang, & Padrón, 1995). In several similar studies where we collected observation and survey data, for example, we provided individual teachers with an individual classroom profile. These profiles contained the teachers' individual data and a summary of the aggregated data across all the elementary schools. The class means for each of the indicators on both of the observation and survey instruments were presented along with the overall school district mean value. This allowed each teacher to compare their class means to the district's average. In some cases, school meetings were held where all the teachers and administrators received the profiles and discussed the implications. Feedback from these profiles was used to stimulate dialogue and discussion about instructional strengths and weaknesses in the school. The profiles also helped initiate discussion about specific instructional areas that needed to be improved in the school.

It should be pointed out again that these profiles provided some guidelines for practice, they were not attempts to tell teachers what to do. These profiles provide teachers with concepts and criteria that they can use to reflect about their own teaching (Nuthall & Alton-Lee, 1990). We did not view the feedback session as one where we would apply our research findings into specific rules or guidelines for teachers to follow. Rather, the observational and survey feedback was intended to be used as guides for teachers where they and their colleagues could reflect about their practices on their own and decide what action to take. Additional staff development programs would be appropriate if teachers wanted to build upon the strengths and weaknesses of their profile in order to help them improve their instruction and classroom learning environment. Quality staff development is one of the keys to successful school reform, and feedback from classroom observation and survey data can be the catalyst for this process.

Another approach to improving classroom instruction for non-resilient students centers on employing explicit teaching practices that have been found to be effective for lower-achieving students. Waxman and Padrón (2002), for example, describe five explicit practices that have been shown to improve the education of English language learners: (a) cognitively-guided instruction, (b) culturally responsive teaching, (c) technology-enriched instruction, (d) cooperative learning, and (e) instructional conversation. These research-based, instructional practices all stress a student-centered model of classroom instruction that emphasizes more active student learning and teachers becoming facilitators of learning. Other research may want to specifically investigate if the dramatic classroom process differences found in the present study diminish in more student-centered classrooms. This may be one of the more important lines of inquiry to highlight in the educational resilience field because it appears that reducing these tremendous gaps is essential if we are going to help non-resilient students become more successful.

While student success and failure in school is dependent upon a number of influential determinants, it is apparent that instructional practices and the classroom learning environment are contributing factors (Travis, 1995; Waxman, 1992; Waxman & Huang, 1997). The results of the present study are discouraging in that they paint a bleak picture of non-resilient, elementary school students who are not doing well in school. Many of the fourth- and fifth-grade students in this study appear to have already "given up" on school and several of the students that we talked to indicated that they don't even plan to finish high school. Furthermore, since the teachers in this study easily identified the resilient and non-resilient students in their classrooms, it is troublesome that we observed few remediation or corrective activities for the non-resilient students. In other words, teachers were aware that their non-resilient students were not doing well in their classrooms, but there was no apparent efforts to specifically help them or address their learning needs.

A final noteworthy concern related to promoting resiliency in schools is that teachers sometimes have difficulty discussing issues related to fostering students' resiliency because they do not know their students well. As Darling-Hammond (1997) puts it, the teacher's job is to get into the hearts and minds of their students. Many teachers know some basic demographic or background information about their students (e.g., number of siblings, employment status of parents), but many teachers do not know about the goals and aspirations of their students. During the past decade, we have conducted hundreds of classroom observations across the USA. Unfortunately, we seldom observed teachers discussing social or personal issues with students (Waxman, Huang, & Padrón, 1995; Waxman & Huang, 1998). Schools today are often very depersonalized and teachers appear to spend very little time learning about their students. This has to dramatically change in order to promote students' resiliency and reduce achievement gaps.

Schools need to provide continuous, quality professional learning experiences for all teachers. These learning experiences need to help teachers become optimistic, hopeful, and empowered so that they believe that they can help improve the education of all children. More meaningful, school-based projects are needed that focus on reculturing or changing the entire school climate so that teachers and administrators create more collaborative, supportive work cultures that enable them to be "out there" in ways that make a difference for all students (Hargreaves & Fullan, 1998). When teachers have a strong sense of their own efficacy, they can make a real difference in the lives of their students (Ashton & Webb, 1986). The educational failure of students is indicative of the failure of the school to teach and connect to students' lives in meaningful ways. Re-examining the classroom learning environment may assist educators in reorganizing the ecology of the classroom as an environment that can provide success for all students.

References

Aldridge, J. M., Fraser, B. J., & Huang, T. I. (1998, April). *A cross-national study of perceived classroom environments in Taiwan and Australia.* Paper presented at the annual meeting of the American Educational Research Association, San Diego, CA.

Alva, S. A. (1991). Academic invulnerability among Mexican-American students: The importance of protective resources and appraisals. *Hispanic Journal of Behavioural Sciences, 13*, 18-34.

Anderson, L. W. & Burns, R. B. (1989). *Research in classrooms: The study of teachers, teaching, and instruction.* Oxford, England: Pergamon.

Ashton, P. & Webb, R. (1986). *Making a difference: Teacher's sense of efficacy.* New York: Longman.

Benard, B. (1997). *Turning it around for all youth: From risk to resilience* (ERIC/CUE Digest No. 126). New York: ERIC Clearninghouse on Urban Education.

Brophy, J. E. & Good, T. L. (1986). Teacher behaviour and student achievement. In M. C. Wittrock (Ed.), *Handbook of research on teaching* (3rd ed., pp. 328-375). New York: Macmillan.

Burden, R. L. & Fraser, B. J. (1993). Use of classroom environment assessments in school psychology: A British perspective. *Psychology in the Schools, 30*, 232-240.

Chang, H.-L. & Waxman, H. C. (2004, April). *Classroom behaviour and mathematics learning environment differences among resilient, average, and nonresilient elementary school students.* Paper presented at the annual meeting of the American Educational Research Association, San Diego, CA.

Chavez, R. C. (1984). The use of high inference measures to study classroom climates: A review. *Review of Educational Research, 54*, 237-261.

Darling-Hammond, L. (1997). *The right to learn: A blueprint for creating schools that work.* San Francisco: Jossey-Bass.

Dryden, M. & Fraser, B. J. (1996, April). *Evaluating urban systematic reform using classroom learning environment instruments.* Paper presented at the American Educational Research Association, New York.

Fisher, D. L., & Fraser, B. J. (1983). Validity and use of Classroom Environment Scale. *Educational Evaluation and Policy Analysis, 5*, 261-271.

Fraser, B. J. (1990). Students' perceptions of their classroom environments. In K. Tobin, J. B. Kahle, & B. J. Fraser (Eds.), *Windows into science classrooms: Problems associated with higher-level cognitive learning* (pp. 199-221). Bristol, PA: Falmer.

Fraser, B. J. (1991). Two decades of classroom environment research. In B. J. Fraser & H. J. Walberg (Eds.), *Educational environments: Evaluation, antecedents and consequences* (pp. 3-27). Oxford, England: Pergamon.

Fraser, B. J. (1994). Research on classroom and school climate. In D. Gabel (Ed.), *Handbook of research on science teaching and learning* (pp. 493-541). New York: Macmillan.

Fraser, B. J., Anderson, G. J., & Walberg, H. J. (1982). *Assessment of learning environments: Manual for Learning Environment Inventory (LEI) and My Class Inventory (MCI)*. Perth, Australia: Western Australian Institute of Technology.

Fraser, B. J. & Deer, C. E. (1983). Improving classrooms through the use of information about learning environments. *Curriculum Perspectives, 3*(2), 41-46.

Fraser, B. J. & Fisher, D. L. (1982). Predicting students' outcomes from their perceptions of classroom psychosocial environment. *American Educational Research Journal, 19,* 498-518.

Fraser, B. J. & Fisher, D. L. (1986). Using short forms of classroom climate instruments to assess and improve classroom psychosocial environment. *Journal of Research in Science Teaching, 5,* 387-413.

Fraser, B. J., Fisher, D. L., & McRobbie, C. J. (1996). *Development, validation, and use of personal and class forms of a new classroom environment instrument.* Paper presented at the American Educational Research Association, New York.

Fraser, B. J., Malone, J. A., & Neale, J. M. (1989). Assessing and improving the psychosocial environment of mathematics classrooms. *Journal for Research in Mathematics Education, 20,* 191-201.

Fraser, B. J. & O'Brien, P. (1985). Student and teacher perceptions of the environment of elementary school classrooms. *The Elementary School Journal, 85,* 567-580.

Haertel, G. D., Walberg, H. J., & Haertel, E. H. (1981). Sociopsychological environments and learning: A quantitative synthesis. *British Educational Research Journal, 7*, 27-36.

Hargreaves, A. & Fullan, M. (1998). *What's worth fighting for out there.* New York: Teachers College.

Howard, S., Dryden, J., & Johnson, B. (1999). Childhood resilience: Review and critique of literature. *Oxford Review of Education, 25*, 307-323.

Gonzalez, R. & Padilla, A. M. (1997). The academia resilience of Mexican American high school students. Hispanic Journal of Behavioural Sciences, 19, 301-317.

Gore, J. M. (2001). Beyond our differences, a reassembling of what matters in teacher education. *Journal of Teacher Education, 52*, 124-135.

Knight, S. L. & Waxman, H. C. (1990). Investigating the effects of the classroom learning environment on students' motivation in social studies. *Journal of Social Studies Research, 14*, 1-12.

Knight, S. L. & Waxman, H. C. (1991). Students' cognition and classroom instruction. In H. C. Waxman & H. J. Walberg (Eds.), *Effective teaching: Current research* (pp. 239-255). Berkeley, CA: McCutchan.

Lewin, K. (1935). *A dynamic theory of personality.* New York: McGraw.

Lewin, K. (1936). *Principles of topological psychology.* New York: McGraw.

McMillan, J. H. & Reed, D. F. (1994). At risk students and resiliency: Factors contributing to academic success. *The Clearing House, 67*, 137-140.

Murray, H. A. (1938). *Explorations in personality.* New York: Oxford University Press.

Nuthall, G. & Alton-Lee, A. (1990). Research on teaching and learning: Thirty years of change. *The Elementary School Journal, 90*, 546-570.

Oldfather, P. (1995). Songs "come back to most of them": Students' experiences as researchers. *Theory into Practice, 34*, 131-137.

Ornstein, A. C. (1991). Teacher effectiveness research: Theoretical considerations. In H. C. Waxman & H. J. Walberg (Eds.), *Effective teaching: Current research* (pp. 63-80). Berkeley, CA: McCutchan.

Padrón, Y. N., Waxman, H. C., & Huang, S. L. (1999). Classroom and instructional learning environment differences between resilient and non-resilient elementary school students. *Journal of Education for Students Placed at Risk of Failure, 4*(1), 63-81.

Pierce, C. (1994). Importance of classroom climate for at-risk learners. *Journal of Educational Research, 88*, 37-42.

Reyes, O. & Jason, L. A. (1993). Pilot study examining factors associated with academic success for Hispanic high school students. *Journal of Youth and Adolescence, 22, 57 71.*

Rosenshine, B. & Stevens, R. (1986). Teaching functions. In M. C. Wittrock (Ed.), *Handbook of research on teaching* (3rd. ed., pp. 376-391). New York: Macmillan.

Ross, S. M. & Smith L. J. (1996). *Classroom observation measure observer's manual.* Memphis, TN: University of Memphis, Center for Research in Educational Policy.

Schultz, R. A. (1979). Student importance ratings as indicator of structure of actual and ideal sociopsychological climates. *Journal of Educational Psychology, 71*, 827-839.

Stallings, J. A. & Mohlman, G. G. (1988). Classroom observation techniques. In J. P. Keeves (Ed.), *Educational research, methodology, and measurement: An International handbook* (pp. 469-474). Oxford, England: Pergamon.

Stodolsky, S. S. (1990). Classroom observation. In J. Millman & L. Darling-Hammond (Eds.), *The new handbook of teacher evaluation: Assessing elementary and secondary school teachers* (pp. 175-190). Newbury Park, CA: Sage.

Storer, J. H., Cychosz, C. M., & Licklider, B. L. (1995). Rural school personnel's perception and categorization of children at risk: A multi-methodological account. *Equity and Excellence in Education, 28*(2), 36-45.

Travis, J. E. (1995). Alienation from learning: School effects on students. *Journal for a Just and Caring Education, 1*, 434-448.

Uguroglu, M. E. & Walberg, H. J. (1986). Predicting achievement and motivation. *Journal of Research and Development in Education, 19*(3), 1-12.

Walberg, H. J. (1995). Generic practices. In G. Cawelti (Ed.), *Handbook of research on improving student achievement* (pp. 7-19). Arlington, VA: Educational Research Services.

Wang, M. C., Haertel, G. D., & Walberg, H. J. (1993). Toward a knowledge base for school learning. *Review of Educational Research, 63*, 249-294.

Waxman, H. C. (1991). Investigating classroom and school learning environments: A review of recent research and developments in the field. *Journal of Classroom Interaction, 26*(2), 1-4.

Waxman, H. C. (1992). Reversing the cycle of educational failure for students in at-risk school environments. In H. C. Waxman, J. Walker de Felix, J. Anderson, & H. P. Baptiste (Eds.), *Students at risk in at-risk schools: Improving environments for learning* (pp. 1-9). Newbury Park, CA: Corwin.

Waxman, H. C. (1995). Classroom observations of effective teaching. In A. C. Ornstein (Ed.), *Teaching: Theory into practice* (pp. 76-93). Needham Heights, MA: Allyn & Bacon.

Waxman, H. C. (2003). Systematic classroom observation. In J. W. Guthrie (Ed.), *Encyclopedia of education* (2nd ed, pp. 303-310). New York: Macmillan.

Waxman, H. C. & Huang, S.-Y. L. (1996). Motivation and learning environment differences in inner-city middle school students. *The Journal of Educational Research, 90*, 93-102.

Waxman, H. C. & Huang, S.-Y. L. (1997). Classroom instruction and learning environment differences between effective and ineffective urban elementary schools for African American students. *Urban Education, 32*, 7-44.

Waxman, H. C. & Huang, S.-Y. L. (1998). Classroom learning environments in urban elementary, middle, and high schools. *Learning Environments Research, 1*, 95-113.

Waxman, H. C. & Huang, S. L. (1999). Classroom observation research and the improvement of teaching. In H. C. Waxman & H. J. Walberg (Eds.), *New directions for teaching practice and research* (pp. 107-129). Berkeley, CA: McCutchan.

Waxman, H. C., Huang, S. L., & Padrón, Y. N. (1995). Investigating the pedagogy of poverty in inner-city middle level schools. *Research in Middle Level Education, 18*(2), 1-22.

Waxman, H. C., Huang, S.-Y. L., & Padrón, Y. N. (1997). Motivation and learning environment differences between resilient and nonresilient Latino middle school students. *Hispanic Journal of Behavioural Sciences, 19*, 137-155.

Waxman, H. C., Huang, S. L., & Wang, M. C. (1997). Investigating the multilevel classroom learning environment of resilient and nonresilient students from inner-city elementary schools. *International Journal of Educational Research, 27*, 343-353.

Waxman, H. C. & Padrón, Y. N. (2002). Research-based teaching practices that improve the education of English language learners. In L. Minaya-Rowe (Ed.), *Teacher training and effective pedagogy in the context of student diversity* (pp. 3-38). Greenwich, CT: Information Age.

Waxman, H. C. & Padrón, Y. N. (2004). The uses of the Classroom Observation Schedule to improve classroom instruction. In H. C. Waxman, R. G. Tharp, & R. S. Hilberg (Eds.), *Observational research in U. S. classrooms: New approaches for understanding cultural and linguistic diversity* (pp. 72-96). Cambridge, United Kingdom: Cambridge University Press.

Waxman, H. C., Rivera, H. H., & Powers, R. A. (2006, April). *Classroom and instructional learning differences in reading between resilient, average, and nonresilient students.* Paper to be presented at the annual meeting of the American Educational Research Association, San Francisco.

Waxman, H. C., Wang, M. C., Lindvall, C. M., & Anderson, K. A. (1988). *Classroom observation schedule technical manual* (Rev. Ed.). Philadelphia: Temple University, Center for Research in Human Development and Education.

Winne, P. H. & Marx, R. W. (1982). Students' and teachers' views of thinking processes for classroom learning. *Elementary School Journal, 82*, 493-518.

Wittrock, M. (1986). Students' thought processes. In M. Wittrock (Ed.), *Handbook of research in teaching* (3rd ed., pp. 297-314). New York: Macmillan.

Chapter 9

SCIENCE EDUCATION IN INDONESIA: A CLASSROOM LEARNING ENVIRONMENT PERSPECTIVE

Wahyudi
Ahmad Dahlan University
Indonesia

David F. Treagust
Curtin University of Technology
Australia

This chapter discusses the status of science education in Indonesian lower secondary schools from a classroom learning environment perspective. The study investigated how science education was delivered in the classroom and how the students perceived their classroom-learning environment. The investigations were conducted in two stages and used both qualitative and quantitative research methods. A multi-site case study which was used to investigate science teaching and learning processes in the classroom included a questionnaire survey to explore students' perceptions of their classroom learning environment. A valid and reliable instrument, namely, the Indonesian version of the modified What Is Happening In this Class (WIHIC) questionnaire, was administered with a sample of 1,188 Year 9 students from 16 urban and rural schools. The findings showed that students tended to prefer a more favourable classroom learning environment than the one they actually experienced; female students generally held slightly more positive perceptions than did male students; and students in rural schools experienced a less positive learning environment than did their counterparts in urban areas. Findings from this multi-site case study that involved classroom observations in two urban and two rural schools supported the findings from the questionnaire survey. Classroom observations confirmed that science teaching in urban schools is better than that in rural schools, thus reflecting students' perceptions of their classroom environments.

1. Introduction

1.1 Overview of Indonesia

The Republic of Indonesia, located in South Eastern Asia, is the largest archipelago in the world covering an area of 1,919,444 square kilometres, being 5,150 kilometres from West to East and 1,930 kilometres from North to South. The country consists of approximetely13,700 islands of which 6,850 are inhabited and in 2002 it had more than 203 million inhabitants. The main islands are Sumatra (473,606 sq.km), Kalimantan (539,460 sq.km), Sulawesi (189,216 sq.km), Irian Jaya (421,981 sq.km), and Java (132,187 sq.km) (Indonesian Embassy in Prague, 2003). At the beginning of 1999, Indonesia still consisted of 24 provinces, two special regions (daerah-daerah istimewa, singular - daerah istimewa), and one special capital city district (daerah khusus ibukota) that included 246 districts (Kabupaten) and 55 municipalities (Kotamadia), 3,592 sub-districts (Kecamatan), and 66,594 villages (Desa or Kelurahan). One of the provinces, East Timor, was withdrawn from Indonesia in 1999 after a referendum. The government of the Republic of Indonesia has expanded the number of provinces and districts/municipals. Currently, there are 27 provinces, two special regions (daerah-daerah istimewa, singular - daerah istimewa), and one special capital city district (daerah khusus ibukota) that includes 269 districts (Kabupaten) and 85 municipalities (Kotamadia), 4,646 sub-districts (Kecamatan), and 69,255 villages (Desa or Kelurahan) (Ministry of Home Affairs, 2002).

1.2 Crisis in Indonesia

Indonesia has put high priority on educational development particularly with respect to universal basic education. Significant progress has been made over the past decades. However, the 1997-98 financial and economic crisis has interrupted this progress. Not only did the crisis force the Soeharto's regime to step down but also it has triggered other political and social crises.

The economic crisis has shaken the previous stability in Indonesia. The crisis affected the depreciation of the local currency, the rupiah; and led to the liquidation of many banks. It was estimated that five million people became unemployed during 1998; and the number of people living in poverty has increased significantly. Anticipating the effect of the crisis on education, namely, the increase of dropping out and the decrease of student enrolment, the Indonesian government, in collaboration with international bodies, such as UNICEF and UNESCO, launched the Social Safety Nets and Stay in School campaign programs. The programs have successfully alleviated parents and students from the impact of economical crisis. As a result, the number of students' dropping out was reduced and the rate of student enrolment was higher.

While the effects of the economic crisis on education can be anticipated, the effects of the social and political crisis in several provinces were obvious and remain unsolved. Hence, it can be said that Indonesia can be attributed to be one of the transitional societies of the world. Several provinces in Indonesia still experience the severe impact of social and maybe political conflict, or a combination of both. Nangroe Aceh Darussalam (NAD) and Molluca are among provinces that have suffered from both conflicts up to now. The conflicts have caused the death of a hundred thousand people, the displacement of a million people, and the paucity of educational processes for school pupils.

At the time this study was undertaken, the education system in Indonesia was still centralised meaning that each province conducted similar educational programs as planned from the office headquarters in Jakarta. Therefore, for safety and security reasons, this study was conducted in a relatively safe and secure province. Consequently, the study was carried out in Kalimantan Selatan province. While many research studies have focused mainly on the teacher, only a few have paid attention to the students' view of their education process. Therefore, this study tried to focus on both the work of teachers, particularly in science classrooms, and the perceptions of the students toward their classroom environments.

2. Theoretical Underpinnings

2.1 Classroom learning environment as a parameter of education quality

Research in science education that focuses on students' conceptual change asserts that effective teaching approaches which contribute to students' conceptual change requires a learning environment that is sensitive to learners' needs, feelings, and ideas (Scott, Asoko, & Driver, 1992). White (1989) also stated that the context in which learning takes place must be supportive and comfortable and free from any form of repression. Assertions from robust learning environment studies support those claims. For example, studies on classroom learning environments have found that there are four characteristics of the learning environment that promote cognitive and affective outcomes as a requirement of effective learning (Fraser, 1994; Fraser, Rennie, & Tobin, 1990; Fraser & Tobin, 1991). Those characteristics are high levels of personalisation, involvement, order and organisation, and task orientation. These findings reveal that teachers should give more opportunities for students to interact with each other and care about students' welfare and social growth (Personalisation); encourage students to participate in the learning process (Involvement); establish and maintain a well-organised class wherein students are behaving in an orderly manner (Order and Organisation); and provide students with clear tasks (Task Orientation). Moreover, these findings parallel the assertions of Haertel, Walberg, and Haertel's (1981) meta-analysis of 12 studies of learning environment-students' outcome relationships that involved 17,805 students in four nations. They argued that students' effective learning is positively related to the levels of cohesiveness, satisfaction, and task orientation in the classroom, and negatively related to levels of friction and disorganisation. Therefore, it is suggested, for the sake of students' effective learning, that a teacher must establish such a classroom learning environment within which students feel confident and able to express and discuss their opinions freely. Consequently, educational research like that described in this chapter also has the classroom learning environment as its focus.

One of the robust traditions in past learning environment studies is the investigation of association between students' cognitive and affective learning outcomes and their perceptions of the classroom psychosocial environments. Hattie (1987) found that in general students who perceived their learning environment positively outperformed those who perceived their classroom environment less positively. Furthermore, by using students' perceptions of their classroom psychosocial environment, it is possible to predict both affective and cognitive outcomes (Fisher & Fraser, 1982; Rentoul & Fraser, 1980). A study by Fisher and Fraser (1983), which employed both actual and preferred forms of questionnaires, indicated that actual-preferred congruence (person-environment fit) could be a determinant factor in predicting students' achievement. They suggested that changing the actual classroom environment in ways that bring it closer to that desired by the class might augment class achievement of certain outcomes.

With regard to Walberg's (1981) multi-factor psychological model of educational productivity, the classroom psychosocial environment plays a significant role in determining the learning process. This model states that learning is a function of student age, ability and motivation, quality and quantity of instruction and of the psychosocial environments of the home, the classroom, the peer group and the mass media. Empirical probes of this educational productivity model assert that among other factors, the classroom and school environment was a strong predictor of both achievement and attitude outcomes, even when a comprehensive set of other factors was held constant (Fraser, 1998a, 1998b). Therefore, it can be claimed that the status of classroom learning environment can be used as a parameter in measuring quality of education.

According to Walberg's (1981) model of educational productivity, efforts to improve student's learning will be more successful by raising factors that currently inhibit learning or are being ignored, rather than enhancing those that already are high (Fraser, 1998a, 1998b). Putting this argument into the Indonesian educational context, in which such efforts had been devoted mainly to instruction, improving other factors such as the psychosocial learning environment may improve students' learning. Thus, study in this area is needed to collect evidence to show all stakeholders that the educational learning environment should not be neglected.

2.2 Study of classroom learning environment in Indonesia

Despite the fact that learning environment research has been implemented since 1960 and become a salient research area in education around the world, few studies have been conducted in Indonesia. The development of research in the learning environment area in Indonesia during the last four decades displays an apparent lack of interest by Indonesian educators to conduct their research in this area. This claim is supported by the shortage of publications of learning environment research in Indonesia until 2000.

Over a period of nearly four decades, there have been a limited number of studies in Indonesian classrooms devoted to learning environment issues. Reviewing those studies (Fraser, Pearse, & Azmi, 1982; Irianto & Treagust, 2001; Mangindaan, Sembiring, & Livingstone,

1978; Margianti & Fraser, 2000; Margianti, Fraser, & Aldridge, 2001; Paige, 1978; Rideng & Schibeci, 1984; Schibeci, Rideng, & Fraser, 1987; Soeharto, 1998; Soerjaningsih, Fraser, & Aldridge, 2001), however, confirms that the classroom learning environment determines school achievement and should be taken into account. Furthermore, the discontinuity of the studies during four decades suggests that the status of learning environment studies in Indonesia is somewhat promising yet neglected, and that there is room for further study. Accordingly, this study was undertaken and focused on the students' perceptions of their classroom learning environment.

3. Aim of the Study

The aim of this study was to investigate the status of science teaching and learning processes in Indonesian lower secondary schools in Kalimantan Selatan, Indonesia. More specifically, this study was designed to answer the following research questions:

1. How do science teachers deliver their teaching in Indonesian lower secondary schools?
2. What are students' perceptions of their science classroom-learning environment?
3. Are there any significant differences between male and female students' perceptions of their science classroom-learning environment?
4. Are there any significant differences between rural and urban students' perceptions of their science classroom-learning environment?

4. Significance

Very few studies are concerned with rural schools in Indonesia, and only two studies had been conducted on Indonesian in rural primary schools (Iskandar, 1987; Mutiara, 1987). No study has been conducted in rural secondary schools. Hence, this study is significant because it (1) fills the absence of research on rural lower secondary schools in Indonesia; (2) informs the Ministry of National Education (MONE) of the Republic of Indonesia about the status of rural and urban schools' learning environments and educational practices, which can be used to formulate policy; (3) helps the principals and teachers particularly of rural schools to improve their practice in conducting science education; and (4) assists classroom teachers to enhance their classroom learning environment.

5. Research Methods

This study employed both qualitative and quantitative research methods. A quantitative research method, namely, a questionnaire survey was used to investigate students' perceptions of their science classroom learning environment. On the other hand, a qualitative research method that refers to a multi-site case study was utilised to explore science teaching and learning processes in the classroom. The following sections describe sampling procedures, instruments used, data collection and data analysis procedures.

5.1 Sampling

Purposive or purposeful sampling (Merriam, 1990, p. 48) as a non-probabilistic sampling method was used in selecting the sample for the study. This choice is based on the assumption that the researcher wants to discover, understand, and gain insight and that the researcher chooses the sample which will lead to the most understanding (Merriam, 1990, p. 48). Purposive sampling permits the researcher to decide prior the study who and what schools are to be included in the data collection. In so doing, a consultation with the Ministry of National Education of Kalimantan Selatan was sought. The samples involved in this main study included the willing and chosen participants of 1188 students of 72 classes and their science teachers in 16 lower secondary schools in urban, suburban and rural areas of Kalimantan Selatan, Indonesia.

5.2 Instrument used

The instruments, namely, the Indonesian version of the modified *What Is Happening In this Class* (WIHIC) questionnaire was used as the main tool to explore students' perceptions of their science classroom learning environments. This instrument has been validated and found as a good and reliable questionnaire to measure students' perceptions of classroom learning environment in an Indonesian lower secondary school context (Wahyudi & Treagust, 2003). No specific instrument was needed during classroom observation in this multi-site case study. However, to ensure that the data that emerged from classroom observation were well organised, a classroom observation schedule was developed. In so doing, Middleton's (1981) suggestions were taken into account, because 'It is better to record in detail rather more than is required' (Middleton, 1981, p. 23). Accordingly, the classroom observation schedule sheets contained any aspects of observations which focused on how the science teacher conducted the lesson in delivering the intended curriculum. This observation schedule should answer questions such as: (1) What is the topic of the lesson?, (2) Does the teacher have a lesson plan?, (3) Is there any specific activity suggested in the intended curriculum? (4) Does the teacher follow that suggestion? If not, why?, and (5) What do classroom transactions look like?

5.3 Data collection

Before conducting this study, formal permission from both the Ministry of National Education (MNE) of Kalimantan Selatan representative and the principals of the schools involved was sought and obtained. After a formal meeting with the principal, the first researcher was introduced to the science teachers whose classes were chosen in this study. After explaining the purpose of his visit, the first researcher together with the science teachers went to the assigned classes to administer the Indonesian version of WIHIC. An outline of the procedures undertaken by the first researcher in administering the Indonesian version of WIHIC is as follows:

1. The science teacher introduced the first researcher to the students and explained the purpose of his visit and his study.
2. Given the opportunity by the science teacher, the first researcher explained to the students the nature of the questionnaire and the instructions, and explained how it should be answered.
3. The first researcher encouraged students to ask him for explanation if they were unsure while answering the questionnaire.
4. The first researcher and the science teacher distributed the questionnaires and instructed students to begin answering it.
5. The first researcher collected the questionnaires from the students and the teacher at the end of the session.

These procedures were adhered to very closely for all 72 classes. On the whole, the administration of the questionnaire proceeded smoothly, all students had time to complete the questionnaire and very few students had any queries about the items.

Furthermore, using the classroom observation schedule, data regarding the science teaching and learning processes in the classroom were collected. Classroom observations were conducted during 12 weeks of the third term at each school where science was allocated three periods of 45 minutes. Therefore, a total of 36 class periods were spent by the first researcher in observing classroom interactions for each class in each school. At the first time of classroom observations, the teacher introduced the first researcher to the students and explained the purpose of his visit and his role. The teacher emphasized to the students that observations conducted by the first researcher were for research purposes and would not influence their grades and the teacher asked students to act normally. These explanations allowed the first researcher to gain a relatively real picture of the original settings of the teaching and learning practices in the classrooms being observed thus enhancing the credibility of the data.

Data regarding aspects of classroom transactions were recorded. Interviews, if needed, were conducted after the lessons to check or to confirm the phenomenon that occurred during observations or to pursue teacher explanations on how and why he or she did certain activities. Field-notes were also taken in anticipation of events that were relevant to the purpose of the study but not listed in the classroom observation sheet.

At the outset, the teachers were informed that during the observations the first researcher would only act as a non-participant and would not make any kind of personal value judgement about the quality of teaching. This effort was taken to ensure that classroom transactions occurred in a normal manner. The observations were simply recorded for further analysis what was happening in the classroom. Member checking was used as a way of ensuring validity of the data being collected. In so doing, after each observation, interviews with the teachers or students regarding events captured in the classroom observations were conducted to clarify the researcher's judgement. In addition, as a way of triangulating the qualitative data, interviews with the superintendent in charge of the participated school were also conducted.

5.4 Data analysis

To describe the classroom learning environment of science classes in Indonesian lower secondary schools, descriptive analyses were obtained based on students' responses to the Indonesian version of WIHIC. The average item mean, the scale mean divided by the number of items in a scale, was used as the basis of comparison between different scales of each instrument. A t-test using either paired samples or independent samples was conducted to investigate the differences between two groups' perceptions of each scale. In this study, comparisons were performed between students' perceptions of the actual and preferred science classroom learning environment, between male and female students' perception of the science classroom learning environment, and between students' perception of the actual science classroom learning environment based on the schools' locality.

With regard to qualitative data, after completing classroom observations, all the data gathered during these processes included records, field-notes, interview logs and photographs were organized to develop the case study database (Yin, 1984). This database was either chronologically or topically structured to enable the researchers to easily have access and analyse the data. From this database, categories or classifications and themes were developed. The data were then structured to explain those phenomena that contributed to the processes of teaching and learning science at the classroom level. The results are descriptively presented using a narrative account in the form of a vignette.

6. Findings and Discussion

6.1 The status of the science classroom learning environment

To explore the status of the science classroom learning environment, the average item mean (the scale mean divided by the number of items in that scale) and average item standard deviation of each scale for both actual and preferred forms of the questionnaire were calculated. A t-test for paired samples for students' responses to both actual and preferred forms was performed to check whether or not significant differences of students' perceptions of their learning environment take place. To provide a more detailed picture of the classroom learning environment, this study also sought the differences of students' perceptions of their science classroom learning environment based on gender and on the schools' locality. These differences were compared using t-tests with either paired or independent sample whichever was appropriate. The results related to the differences between students' perceptions of the actual and preferred science classroom learning environment, between male and female students' perception of the science classroom learning environment, and the differences between students' perception of the actual science classroom learning environment based on the schools' locality are presented in the following sections.

6.2 Differences between students' perception of the actual and preferred science classroom learning environment

Results from t-tests for paired samples showed that there are significant differences ($p<0.01$) between students' perceptions of their actual and preferred learning environment on all scales except the Involvement scale. A summary of the average item means and average standard deviation for the two versions of the questionnaire is reported in Table 9.1.

Table 9.1. Average Item Mean, Average Standard Deviation, and t Value from t-tests with Paired Samples for Differences Between the Actual and Preferred Perceptions (n=1,188)

Scale	Average Item Mean		Average Standard Deviation		t value
	A	P	A	P	
Student Cohesiveness	3.79	4.60	0.49	0.41	57.66**
Teacher Support	2.84	4.15	0.64	0.60	67.83**
Involvement	2.62	2.62	0.62	0.62	NA
Investigation	2.51	3.81	0.72	0.76	62.80**
Task Orientation	3.77	4.59	0.53	0.46	58.40**
Cooperation	3.25	4.03	0.61	0.65	43.93**
Equity	3.61	4.46	0.74	0.58	44.16**

**$p<0.01$*

The results, which are consistent with previous studies (Fisher & Fraser, 1983), suggest that most students would prefer a learning environment which is characterised by having more teacher support, enhancing student cohesiveness, providing clearer task orientation, doing more investigations, and ensuring greater cooperation as well as more equity during class sessions. These differences in both actual and preferred scales can be used by teachers or principals as a focus for improving the classroom learning environment in keeping with Fraser's (1989) five stages for learning environment enhancement.

Interestingly, students perceived the same level on the Involvement scale for both the Actual and Preferred Forms. This anomaly warrants further investigation. This scale's mean of 2.62 suggests that students have classroom experiences that constitute involvement that are in between 'seldom' and 'sometimes'. Therefore, it can be inferred that students were happy within the classroom atmosphere that allows them to be passive. This finding confirms Thair and Treagust's (1997) study, which asserted that the teacher in the Indonesian classroom has absolute authority and gives students little chance to participate.

6.3 Differences between male and female students' perceptions of the science classroom learning environment

Using the paired sample t-tests procedure, the average item mean for male and female students was used as the unit of analysis. Since the number of male and female students was not equal, therefore the data were organised into groups of males and females for each of the classes, resulting in 72 groups of males and 72 groups of females. These pairs of data were then matched for further analysis and the results are depicted in Table 9.2.

The results of this study maintains the assertions yielded from the previous studies (Goh & Fraser, 1995; Goh, Young, & Fraser, 1995; Riah, 1998; Riah & Fraser, 1998; Wong, 1994), in which females hold better perceptions of the classroom learning environment than do males. Table 9.2 suggests that generally females have perceptions slightly more favourable than the males on the actual science classroom-learning environment. While the magnitudes of the differences between male and female students' views of the classroom learning environment are small, statistically significant differences occur on two scales, namely, Teacher Support and Task Orientation. Only on the actual Teacher Support scale did males perceive more favourably than did females. On the other hand, males perceived task orientation set by their teachers less positively than did the females. Furthermore, females tended to have a higher preference on seven scales toward their ideal science classroom-learning environment than did the males do. In detail, significance differences ($p<0.05$) exist for four scales, namely, Student Cohesiveness, Investigation, Task Orientation, and Cooperation.

Table 9.2. Average Item Mean, Average Item Standard Deviation and t Value from t-tests with Paired Samples for Differences Between Male and Female Students' Perceptions of Science Classroom Learning Environment (n=72)

Scale	Form	Average Item Mean		Average Item Standard Deviation		t value
		Male	Female	Male	Female	
Student	Actual	3.76	3.76	0.27	0.25	-0.02
Cohesiveness	Pref	4.52	4.61	0.26	0.22	-2.50*
Teacher	Actual	2.89	2.78	0.41	0.34	2.15*
Support	Pref	4.11	4.14	0.34	0.33	-0.85
Involvement	Actual	2.59	2.64	0.39	0.31	-1.05
	Pref	2.59	2.64	0.39	0.31	-1.05
Investigation	Actual	2.54	2.51	0.49	0.38	0.48
	Pref	3.73	3.87	0.46	0.37	-2.49*
Task	Actual	3.69	3.81	0.31	0.30	-2.73**
Orientation	Pref	4.50	4.64	0.35	0.22	-3.38***
Cooperation	Actual	3.18	3.27	0.34	0.38	-1.13
	Pref	3.92	4.05	0.41	0.31	-2.45*
Equity	Actual	3.55	3.62	0.42	0.44	-1.24
	Pref	4.40	4.49	0.32	0.28	-1.86

*$p<0.05$; **$p<0.01$; ***$p<0.001$

6.4 *Differences between students' perceptions of the science classroom learning environment based on schools' locality*

To investigate the differences between students' perception of the science classroom learning environment based on schools locality, t-tests with independent samples procedure was carried out. All seven scales of both Actual and Preferred Forms of the Indonesian WIHIC were placed as the dependent variables, whereas schools locality variable was placed as the determinant variable. A summary of average item mean, average item standard deviation, effects size and t values from t-tests for independent samples for differences between rural and urban students' perceptions of their science classroom learning environment is provided in Table 9.3.

Table 9.3. Average Item Mean, Average Item Standard Deviation and t Values from t-test with Independent Samples for Differences Between Rural (n=544) and Urban (n=644) Students' Perceptions of Science Classroom-Learning Environment

Scale	Form	Average Item Mean		Average Item Standard Dev.		t value
		Rural	Urban	Rural	Urban	
Student	Actual	3.72	3.85	0.53	0.44	-4.40***
Cohesiveness	Pref	4.48	4.70	0.47	0.31	-9.91***
Teacher	Actual	2.78	2.90	0.67	0.62	-3.16***
Support	Pref	4.05	4.23	0.67	0.53	-5.22***
Involvement	Actual	2.54	2.69	0.65	0.58	-4.06***
	Pref	2.54	2.69	0.66	0.58	-4.02***
Investigation	Actual	2.42	2.59	0.73	0.70	-4.08***
	Pref	3.69	3.91	0.77	0.73	-5.11***
Task	Actual	3.68	3.84	0.56	0.50	-5.09***
Orientation	Pref	4.48	4.68	0.51	0.38	-7.83***
Cooperation	Actual	3.06	3.42	0.63	0.55	-10.63***
	Pref	3.89	4.15	0.67	0.60	-6.99***
Equity	Actual	3.46	3.74	0.78	0.69	-6.56***
	Pref	4.36	4.54	0.66	0.49	-5.43***

***$p<0.001$

Table 9.3 reveals that students in rural schools held less favourable perceptions than did students in urban schools for all seven scales. Statistically significantly differences ($p<0.001$) occurred for all seven scales between urban and rural students' perceptions for both actual and preferred classroom learning environment. This fact can be confirmed with findings from the classroom observations. In most cases, classroom transactions in rural schools were more dominated by teacher-centred methods, having less investigation or laboratory activities, and students were less sure of the teacher's expectation. Frequently, in rural schools students were told to copy notes from the blackboard before the teacher explained them (Classroom observations, Schools 2, 6, 8, 9). Consequently, students in rural schools did not have a chance to develop a better learning environment. Interviews with the superintendent also supported this assertion. One of superintendents informed the researcher that mostly rural schools are deprived due to their conditions, such as lack of resources and of teachers. It is common that a teacher should teach more than one or two subjects in which he or she is not competent, thus resulting in relatively poor teaching performance in these subjects (Interview, Superintendent A, 18.04.02).

7. Teaching and Learning Science Processes in the Classroom

In order to support or refute the findings from the questionnaire survey, a number of classroom observations during science lessons were conducted. A vignette of classroom transaction from urban and rural schools was deliberately selected so that the story in the vignette may best represent the classroom transaction in each school. The results are presented in the section below followed by the interpretive commentaries and discussion.

Vignette 1. Science teaching and learning in an urban school
Science in the last two periods (Classroom Observation, Teacher D, School 4, 24.01.02)

This was the first classroom observation that the researcher conducted in School 4. At quarter past twelve, the researcher arrived at the school office and met with Teacher D. We waited for the next period that started at 12.30 by having a discussion about the school's academic and socio-economic profiles. At 12.25, we went to the laboratory wherein the biology lessons were held. On the way to the laboratory, a couple of proverbs such as 'discipline is the key for success' and 'honesty, respect and tolerant are the attributes of excellent students' were nicely hung on the wall in the corridor. After the researcher was seated on the backbench in the laboratory, Teacher D went to the classroom and asked students to move to the laboratory with all their belongings. When all students were seated, Teacher D introduced the researcher, the purpose of his visit, and the duration of the classroom observations with the students. The students' responses were positive; some students waived their hands to the researcher while some of the others greeted him verbally. It took almost ten minutes before Teacher D began the lesson.

The lesson's opener

Teacher D used the first 15 minutes (12.40–12.55) as an introduction session. To start with, Teacher D reviewed materials being learned during previous biology lessons by passing the reviewed questions to the students. Almost 95% of this session was devoted to interactive questions and answers between teacher and students. It seems that Teacher D tried to use this method, in addition to the review questions on paper, to check students' understanding of the topic covered previously. Students' responses included their understanding of genetics terminologies and reproduction systems which were used as links to connect to the previous and the present lesson. Teacher D finished up the introduction session by emphasising the learning goals that students should achieve and the activity they would perform. Teacher D organised students into groups of four or five based on students' ability and gender (Interview, Teacher D, School 4, 24.01.02).

Main activities (12.55-13.40)

After each student was seated in a group, Teacher D distributed the students' worksheet and asked one student from each group to collect the genetic set kits. Teacher D asked students in each group to read the worksheet and to perform the suggested activities. The worksheet contained a summary of genetics and reproduction system terminologies, the goals, the procedures and questions that guided the learner to complete the topic. Two main topics were covered in two activities. The first activity was aimed at enabling students' understanding of the hybridisation process whereas the second activity was intended to allow students to comprehend the hybridisation products. Referring to the curriculum document, this activity can be classified as guided inquiry level 4 in which the teacher provides the problems, goals, and procedures, while students conduct the inquiry as prescribed in the worksheet.

The nature of learning activities as stipulated in the worksheet calls for students to work cooperatively. According to the worksheet, the activities required each group to have three main performers who are the executor, the reporter, and the recorder. As stated in the procedure, the activity asked each group to conduct repeated hybridisations from two boxes that contain gametes from male and female parents. It is the executor's duty to perform the activity. The reporter passed the results to the recorder for recording the evidence. To ensure that a group would perform as expected, a leader is appointed. Hence, the classroom became alive with students in each group negotiating among themselves about which role should be taken by each individual. Teacher D moved around the laboratory to check each group's abilities in facing and performing the tasks. During the first 15 minutes of this session, Teacher D accommodated and facilitated the students' and the group's needs.

It is impossible to capture all transactions that occurred in each group. Nevertheless, the spirit of teaching and learning processes can be brought to light. The activities facilitated students as both an individual and as a member of a group to be physically (hands-on) and mentally (minds-on) active. The evidence of hands-on activities can be confirmed with students actively performing their roles in each group, while those of minds-on activities can be verified from students' discussion in a group to determine the genotype and phenotype of offspring yielded from the hybridisation processes. The overall classroom observation supported this statement, although one student was observed to be off-task. The researcher captured a scene in which one student of a corner group was enjoying drumming his desk with a pencil while the fellow students in his group were busy with their tasks. Teacher D was not aware of this instance due to the large size of the classroom and the nature of learning activity. However, Teacher D was attentive to off-task students; it was observed that he always gently brought the inattentive students back on task, and encouraged the students to be focused on learning. 'I know guys that we are almost running out of energy. Yet, we are almost there. Please keep on that task' are the phrase or sentences that Teacher D often used to keep the students motivated.

At 13.40, Teacher D called for class discussion. Each group had finished both activities and had packed away the genetic kits. Teacher D led the discussion and asked two groups to voluntarily answer the first two questions. The first question asked students to determine and write down the genotype representation, whereas the second one called for students to determine the phenotype. Teacher D used the answers provided by the volunteer groups as a point for discussion. He did not only ask for agreement or disagreement of the answers by the rest of the group, instead he asked the other groups to provide explanations of their answers. Knowing that the lesson time was almost finished, Teacher D deliberately ended up the lesson by summarising the lesson and jogging students' memory about the discussion of the results from the second activity for the next lesson.

Finally, the lesson was wrapped up with a prayer and the students were dismissed after they had greeted their teacher. The students were lined up to the exit door where Teacher D stood up to shake his beloved students' hands

Interpretive commentary

It is unarguable that keeping the lesson alive during the last two periods of the day is a very challenging task. The students were already tired, sleepy and almost had no energy in a day that was characterised by high temperatures and very high humidity. Teacher D's efforts, however, to keep his class moving and cognitively and physically active was obvious. Using a group activity enabled Teacher D to involve all his students in learning activities. His effort in grouping students based on gender and ability allowed each group to make progress during the lesson. The use of fresh jokes and encouraging sentences lifted the classroom spirit and helped the students to stay on task.

With regard to the teaching structure, this classroom observation identified Teacher D's exertion to organise his teaching into a standardised structure that contained introduction, core activities and closure. These three elements were detected during the observation although the closure was performed abruptly due to the time constraint (Field note, Teacher D, School 4, 24.02.02). It was confirmed from further observations that Teacher D consistently used this kind of teaching structure.

Teacher D's utilization of questioning techniques was remarkable. Mostly, he used open-ended question to probe the students' understanding during discussion sessions, to anchor the previous topic with the present one being taught in the introductory lesson segment, and to guide students in achieving their learning goals at the closure.

Another aspect of the teaching practices of Teacher D that can be deemed as high quality were his classroom management skills. He moved around the classroom to ensure that each student was on task, to accommodate students' or the group's questions, and to gently return the disrupting or distracted students to the learning activity without humiliating them.

It was the researcher's responsibility to ask himself: 'Does the teacher perform as normal or does the teacher put in the best effort due to the observation?' This question helped the researcher to avoid bias during data interpretation and to support the assertion being made. Consequently, the interpretations of a single impression must be followed and confirmed with those of other observations. Similarly, the researcher gathered evidence from other classroom observations to confirm or reject the claims being made. It is indicated that the subsequent long-term classroom observations confirmed the evidence that Teacher D's teaching practices were consistent. The features attributed to Teacher D's teaching practices included providing clear learning expectations at the outset of each lesson, the use of appropriate teaching methods that allowed optimum students' involvement during the lesson, the use of good questioning techniques, and the utilization of effective classroom management skills.

Vignette 2. Science teaching and learning in a rural school
No textbooks, inadequate laboratory (Classroom Observation, Teacher B, School 2, 06.02.02)

This was the fifth classroom observation in Teacher B's classroom. As usual, the researcher arrived at 7.35 am, 25 minutes before the school began when it was still quiet and peaceful. The researcher waited for Teacher B at the teachers' office that was still unoccupied. Most teachers arrived on time or maybe later due to their locations; and only a few teachers did not arrive on time.

At 08.00, Teacher B rang the bell signalling the school had begun. All the students lined up in front of their classes and in an orderly manner, one by one, they went to their classrooms. When Teacher B came in, all the students stood up and greeted him and the class was started with a prayer. Teacher B told the students that they would have a class in the laboratory and asked students to pack their notebooks and physics textbooks, if any, and go down to the laboratory.

We went to the laboratory that was located 300 metres from the classroom. It was dusty, cobwebs were apparent at each corner of the walls and some posters with faded colours were worn out. The students were busy cleaning up their desks spreading the dust around the laboratory and this prevented Teacher B starting the lesson immediately. The lesson was not ready to begin until quarter past eight.

08.15: Teacher B open the lesson by asking questions related to last week's lesson, which was about electromagnetism induction. Students responded to the questions by opening their notebooks. Teacher B used this occasion to prepare the students for the next topic, namely, the generator, by repeating his explanation on the electromagnetism induction processes.

08.20: Teacher B wrote down the new topic being learned that day. Being aware that only very few students had the textbook, he wrote down the lesson material on the blackboard and asked students to copy it; the female students were more enthusiastic and active than the male students. When the students finished copying the notes, Teacher B explained the lesson and offered his students the opportunity to ask questions to clarify the details of the lesson.

08.40: Teacher B used the next five minutes to review the topic, before he moved to the new topic, namely, the generator. This time he asked question of the whole class rather than to individual students, with most questions requiring recall of facts and none requiring reasoning.

08.47: Teacher B wrote down the topic entitled 'Generator' on the blackboard. Again, he gave lesson notes on the blackboard, asked the students to copy them, and explained them later. He drew a simple electric generator and asked the students to copy it. When the students finished copying, he then explained how the generator works.

09.15: Teacher B used the next five minutes for questions and answers related to the 'generator' topic. Teacher B read the questions from the textbook and the students responded. The questions asked included the definition of electric generator, a recall question. Again, the researcher noticed that male students were not as enthusiastic as female students. Teacher B asked a student to clean up the blackboard before the class commenced another topic, namely, the transformer.

09.25: Teacher B continued the class with a new topic. He used a teaching aid, namely, trans-vision – a coloured printed transparency supplied by the government. However, he used it for a very short time due to the inadequate laboratory facilities that was not equipped with an overhead projector. As a result, Teacher B just showed the transparency for his students to glance at followed by a brief explanation. Although ten minutes later some students were not paying attention to the lesson, Teacher B kept going with the lesson and ignored these students.

09.45: Teacher B copied a table from the textbook that explained the correlation between input voltage, output voltage and the number of coils in a transformer. Based on the data presented, Teacher B asked the students to find the pattern and to draw a conclusion. However, the observation confirmed that the students had difficulty in doing so. Teacher B tried to explain and show the pattern, and finally drew a conclusion in the form of a formula that showed the correlation between the number of coils and voltages of a transformer. He wrote down the formula: $Vs/Vp = Ns/Np$; V and N referred to voltage and numbers of coils, while s and p indicated input and output, respectively. Based on this formula, Teacher B gave students an exercise to find the output voltage of a transformer if the input voltage and the number of both primary and secondary coils were given. However, even though Teacher B had assisted the students by writing down the formula, and filled in the information given as $(26 \text{ volt}) \times (400) = (240) \times Vs$, the students could not solve the problem. From the observations, it was apparent that to some extent the students had difficulty with this mathematics-related problem.

10.10: Teacher B gave more problems for homework and reminded the students about the next week's lesson before formally concluding the lesson.

Interpretive commentary and assertions

The teaching and learning activities being observed were about electromagnetic induction and the transformer. According to the lower secondary school science curriculum documents, ideally these topics should be taught using a process skills approach and an experiment as the teaching method. The observation confirmed that teaching practices performed by Teacher B were far from ideal because the scarcity of textbooks and the inadequacy of the laboratory prevented him from teaching science as expected in the curriculum documents. Most of the teaching time was devoted to note taking activity. Teacher B dictated or wrote down the lesson materials on the blackboard, and the students copied them to their notebooks. To some extent, science teaching in his classroom was a one-way communication. Another factor that inhibited the teaching and learning activity of Teacher B's classroom was the students' mathematics ability. As recorded during the observation, Teacher B needed to re-explain to the students about simple mathematics calculations.

Further classroom observations support this commentary in which most science teaching in Teacher B's classroom was dominated by traditional chalk-and-talk. Seldom did he employ recommended teaching methods, such as experiment and demonstration.

8. Discussion

Results from the questionnaire show differences between urban and rural students' perceptions of their classroom learning environments. Generally, students in rural schools had less favourable views of their classroom learning environment than did their counterparts in urban schools. This finding parallels the results from classroom observations. Obviously, classroom transactions in urban schools as represented by the teaching and learning practices of Teacher D in School 4, portray a conducive and positive learning environment. The results as described in vignette 1 suggest that Teacher D's classroom provides the students with a relatively conducive learning environment that is characterized by cohesiveness among students, good teacher support, establishment of students involvement in doing investigations, clear teaching expectation and task orientation. If Teacher D's classroom learning environment is able to represent those of other classrooms in urban schools, the findings from the questionnaire are supported.

In contrast, students in rural schools as represented by those in Teacher B's classroom may experienced a learning environment that is characterized by lack of student involvement, lack of investigation activity, unclear task orientation and teaching expectation, and less teacher support. Teaching and learning practices in Teacher B's classroom confirm this description. If Teacher B's classroom learning environment is typical of those of rural schools, the results from the questionnaire are supported. In other words, the data generated from the survey are validated by those that evolved from classroom observations. Consequently, the findings from this study may portray a reality of science education practices in Indonesia from a classroom learning environment perspective.

This study attempted to record the status of science education in Indonesian lower secondary school. The findings suggest that science education in Indonesia still can be improved. Based on the students' perceptions of their classroom learning environment, it is important to improve the quality of teaching and learning so that the students can experience a learning environment that they prefer. The study also documented that science education in rural school is under performed compared to that of the urban area. This study recommends that the Indonesian government should pay increased attention to this and assist rural schools so that the discrepancy of science and teaching practices between urban and rural schools can be minimized.

Being aware that this study was conducted in a relatively safe and secure province in Indonesia, we can assume that the quality of science teaching in school within conflict areas may be worse. As we reflected, within a normal situation we have faced lots of problems to conduct a good education, so what can we expect from education in provinces in upheaval, such as Aceh and Molluca?

References

Fisher, D. L. & Fraser, B. J. (1982). Use of classroom environment scale in investigating relationships between achievement and environment. *Journal of Science and Mathematics Education in Southeast Asia, 5* (2), 5-9.

Fisher, D. L. & Fraser, B. J. (1983). A comparison of actual and preferred classroom environment as perceived by science teachers and students. *Journal of Research in Science Teaching, 20*, 55-61.

Fraser, B. J. (1989). *Assessing and improving classroom environment (What Research Says, No. 2).* Perth: Curtin University of Technology.

Fraser, B. J. (1994). Research on classroom and school climate. In D. L. Gabel (Ed.), *Handbook of research on science teaching and learning* (pp. 493-541). New York: MacMillan.

Fraser, B. J. (1998a). Classroom environment instruments: Development, validity and applications. *Learning Environment Research: An International Journal, 1*, 7-33.

Fraser, B. J. (1998b). Classroom environment instruments: Development, validity and applications. *Learning Environment Research: An International Journal, 1*, 7-33.

Fraser, B. J., Pearse, R., & Azmi. (1982). A study of Indonesian students' perceptions of classroom psychosocial environment. *International Review of Education, 28*, 337-355.

Fraser, B. J., Rennie, L., & Tobin, K. G. (1990). The learning environment as a focus in a study of higher cognitive learning. *International Journal of Science Education, 12*, 531-548.

Fraser, B. J. & Tobin, K. (1989). Exemplary science and mathematics teachers. *What Research Says to the Science and Mathematics Teacher, 1*, 9.

Goh, S. C. & Fraser, B. J. (1995, April). *Learning environment and students outcomes in primary mathematics classroom in Singapore.* Paper presented at the Annual meeting of the American Educational Research Association, San Francisco, CA

Goh, S. C., Young, D. J., & Fraser, B. J. (1995). Psychosocial climate and student outcomes in elementary mathematics classrooms: A multilevel analysis. *The Journal of Experimental Education, 64* (1), 29-40.

Haertel, G. D., Walberg, H. J., & Haertel, E. H. (1981). Socio-psychological environments and learning: A quantitative synthesis. *British Educational Research Journal, 7*, 27-36.

Hattie, J. A. (1987). Identifying the salient facets of a model of student learning: A synthesis of meta-analyses. *International Journal of Educational Research, 11*, 187-212.

Indonesian Embassy in Prague. (2003). *The Republic of Indonesia.* Retrieved 09-02-2003, 2003, from www.indoneske-velvyslanectvi.cz/basic.htm.

Irianto, B. & Treagust, D. F. (2001, March). *Teachers' perceptions of the role of the laboratory in a National Professional Development Centre.* Paper presented at the annual conference of the National Association for Research in Science Teaching, St. Louis, Missouri.

Iskandar, R. (1987). *Pendidikan daerah terpencil di Kabupaten Tapin, propinsi Kalimantan Selatan: laporan penelitian (Education in remote area, Tapin district, Kalimantan Selatan province: research report).* Jakarta: Puslit Balitbang Dikbud (Ministry of Education and Culture of Republic of Indonesia).

Mangindaan, C. S., Sembiring, R. K., & Livingstone, I. D. (1978). *National assessment of the quality of Indonesian Education.* Jakarta: Ministry of Education and Culture of Indonesia in association with The New Zealand Council for Educational Research.

Margianti, E. S. & Fraser, B. J. (2000, January). *Learning environment, mathematical ability and students' outcomes in university computing courses in Indonesia.* Paper presented at the Second International Conference on Science, Mathematics and Technology Education, Taipei, Taiwan.

Margianti, E. S., Fraser, B. J., & Aldridge, J. M. (2001, April). *Learning environment, mathematical ability and student's outcomes in University computing courses in Indonesia.* Paper presented at the Annual Meeting of the American Educational Research Association (AERA), Seattle.

Merriam, S. B. (1990). *Case study research in education.* San Francisco: Jossey-Bass Inc.

Middleton, D. (1981). *Observing classroom processes.* Milton Keynes: The Open University Press.

Ministry of Home Affairs. (2002). *Keputusan Menteri Dalam Negeri Nomor 5 Tahun 2002 (The Decree of Ministry of Home Affair of the Republic of Indonesia Number 5 Year 2002).* Retrieved 09-02-2003, 2003, from www.depdagri.go.id/data/pdf/PP%20No5-2002.pdf.

Mutiara, A. G. (1987). *Pendidikan daerah terpencil desa Kolam Kiri dan Kolam Kanan, kecamatan Rantau Badauh, Kabupaten Barito Kuala, Propinsi Kalimantan Selatan (Education in remote area: Kolam Kiri and Kolam Kanan vilage, Rantau Badauh sub-district, Barito Kuala district, Kalimantan Selatan province).* Jakarta: Puslit Balitbang Dikbud (Ministry of Education and Culture of Republic of Indonesia).

Paige, R. M. (1978). *The Impact of the Classroom Learning Environment on Academic Achievement and Individual Modernity in East Java, Indonesia.* Unpublished Doctoral thesis, Stanford University.

Rentoul, A. J. & Fraser, B. J. (1980). Predicting learning from classroom individualization and actual-preferred congruence. *Studies in Educational Evaluation, 6,* 265-277.

Riah, H. B. (1998). *Learning environment and its association with student outcomes in chemistry in Brunei Darussalam's secondary schools.* Unpublished doctoral thesis, Curtin University of Technology, Perth, WA.

Riah, H. B. & Fraser, B. J. (1998, April). *The learning environment of high school chemistry classes.* Paper presented at the annual meeting of the American Educational Research Association, San Diego, CA.

Rideng, I. M. & Schibeci, R. A. (1984). The development and validation of a test of biology-related attitudes. *Research in Science and Technological Education, 2,* 21-29.

Schibechi, R. A., Rideng, I. M., & Fraser, B. J. (1987). Effects of classroom environments science attitudes: A cross-cultural replication in Indonesia. *International Journal of Science Education,* *9*, 169-186.

Scott, P. H., Asoko, H. M., & Driver, R. H. (1992). Teaching for conceptual change: A review of strategies. In H. Niedderer (Ed.), *Research in physics learning: Theoretical issues and empirical studies* (pp. 310-329). Kiel, Germany: Institute for Science Education, University of Kiel.

Soeharto, S. (1998). *The effects of a constructivist-learning environment on grade six student achievement and attitude toward mathematics in Indonesian Primary Schools.* Unpublished doctoral thesis, University of Houston, Houston.

Soerjaningsih, W., Fraser, B. J., & Aldridge, J. M. (2001, April). *Achievement, satisfaction and learning environment among Indonesian computing students at the university level.* Paper presented at the Annual meeting of the American Educational Research Association (AERA), Seattle, USA.

Thair, M. & Treagust, D. F. (1997). A review of teacher development reforms in Indonesian secondary science: The effectiveness of practical work in biology. *Research in Science Education, 27* (4), 581-597.

Wahyudi & Treagust, D. F. (2003). Science classroom learning environment and its associations with students' cognitive and attitude outcomes in Indonesian lower secondary schools. In S. P. Loo, A. Ayob, S. Yoong, A. T. S. Abdullah, L. W. Lee, & S. C. Toh (Eds.), *Proceeding of the ICASE 2003 World Conference on Science & Technology Education* (pp. 126-136). Penang, Malaysia: SEAMEO RECSAM.

Walberg, H. J. (1981). A psychological theory of educational productivity. In N. J. Gordon (Ed.), *Psychology and education: the state of the union* (pp. 81-108). Berkeley, CA: McCutchan.

White, R. T. (1989). *Learning science.* Oxford: Basil Blackwell.

Wong, F. L. A. (1994). *Determinants and effects of perceptions of chemistry laboratory environments in coeducational secondary schools in Singapore.* Unpublished doctoral thesis, Curtin University of Technology, Perth, WA.

Yin, R. K. (1984). *Case study research: Design and methods.* Newbury Park, CA: Sage.

Chapter 10

AN ACTION RESEARCH APPROACH WITH PRIMARY PRE-SERVICE TEACHERS TO IMPROVE UNIVERSITY AND PRIMARY SCHOOL CLASSROOM ENVIRONMENTS

Kathryn J. Saunders
University of Waikato
New Zealand

Darrell L. Fisher
Curtin University of Technology
Australia

In the study described in this chapter, pre-service science teachers were introduced to the field of learning environments by being involved in an action research process aimed at improving the learning environment of their university science education classes and concurrently to provide an opportunity for the student teachers to improve the learning environment of their primary school classrooms during their practicum teaching. The project focused on the use of CUCEI in a collaborative process that the lecturer and pre-service students used for examining and improving upon what was happening in their science education classes. This introduced the students to the current research base of the field of classroom environments and they were then provided with an opportunity to focus on the improvement of the environment of their primary school classrooms during their practicum teaching using WIHIC. The selection of these two instruments provided quantitative data results and the results from these questionnaires were enhanced by qualitative information collated from the pre-service students at the end of the science education course and at the end of their intensive seven week teaching practicum. The focus for the improvement were the scales of Personalisation and Individualisation from the CUCEI questionnaire. The project also provided the students with some strategies to examine, improve and reflect on the learning environment of their classrooms.

1. Context

Although the field of classroom learning environments has been valuable in assisting teachers to improve and reflect on their practice, there has been limited use for the assessment and improvement of university teacher education (pre-service education) in New Zealand.

With the recent increased emphasis on research and publication in the university environment in New Zealand, it is important that the quality of teaching remains high and that it is modeled, discussed and reflected on by both the lecturers and pre-service students. It is also valuable for pre-service teachers to be able to use their developing knowledge on classroom learning environments to examine the environment that they personally establish with their students. In the study described in this chapter, pre-service science teachers were introduced to the field of learning environments by being involved in action research which was aimed at:

- improving the environment of their university science education classes; and
- providing an opportunity to improve the environment of their primary school classrooms during their practicum teaching

2. Theoretical Framework

Foundations of early classroom environment research were laid more than 60 years ago when Lewin (1936) introduced the formula $B=f(P, E)$ to describe human behaviour (B) as a function of two independent influences, the person (P) and the environment (E). Murray (1938) developed this further in a needs press model which distinguished between the *alpha press* (the environment observed by a trained non-participant observer) and *beta press* (the environment perceived by "milieu inhabitants").

This distinction was then discussed further by Stern, Stein, and Bloom (1956) who put forward the view that each person has a view of the environment (*private* beta press) and that this may be different from a shared view of a group about the environment (*consensual* beta press). This had implications for researchers in that the design of their research needed to consider a level or unit of statistical analysis.

Over 30 years ago, Walberg developed the widely used *Learning Environment Inventory (LEI)* as part of the research of the Harvard Project Physics (Walberg & Anderson, 1968). Meanwhile, Moos (1974) began developing a scheme for classifying human environments. His scheme identified three basic dimensions that are still used to classify classroom environment instruments scales. These are: Relationship Dimensions which identify the nature and intensity of personal relationships within the environment and assess the extent to which people are involved in the environment and support and help each other; Personal Development Dimensions which assess basic dimensions along which personal growth and self enhancement; and System Maintenance and System Change Dimensions which involve the extent to which the environment is orderly, clear in expectations, maintains control and is responsive to change.

Moos' comprehensive program of research involving perceptual measures of a variety of human environments including psychiatric hospitals, prisons, university residences and work environments, ultimately resulted in the *Classroom Environment Scale* (CES) (Moos, 1979; Moos & Trickett, 1987).

Much attention has been given to the development and use of a variety of instruments to assess the science classroom learning environment from the perspective of the student (Fraser, 1986; Fraser & Walberg, 1991) as well as the association between the learning environment and student outcomes. The rationale for such an approach is that high quality learning takes place in a classroom environment where there is a congruence between student perceptions of actual and preferred environments (Fraser & Fisher, 1983a; Rentoul & Fraser, 1980).

Many of the classroom environment instruments, including the *College and University Classroom Environment Inventory* (CUCEI) and *What Is Happening In this Class* (WIHIC) used in this study have two versions, an actual and preferred. In the actual version, students provide information about the aspects of the classroom environment they are currently part of, whereas the ideal or preferred version involves students providing information about the classroom environment ideally preferred. Studies have shown consistently that there is an association between student perceptions of learning environment and student outcomes and that a closer link between students' actual and preferred environments could enhance student outcomes (Fraser, 1986, 1994; Fraser, Walberg, Welch & Hattie, 1987; Fraser & Fisher, 1983a, 1983b; Haertel, Walberg, & Haertel, 1981). Comparisons of the students' perceptions of their actual environment with their preferred environment give teachers the opportunity to reflect upon and modify the classroom environment to reduce the difference between the actual and preferred environments.

Fraser and Fisher (1986) have proposed a simple approach by which teachers can use information obtained from classroom environment questionnaires to guide attempts to improve their classroom environment. Other researchers have used this basic approach with a variety of instruments. (Fisher & Fraser, 1991; Fraser, Docker & Fisher, 1988; Wood & Fraser, 1995;). The approach incorporates five steps.

- *Assessment*: Students in the class respond to Preferred and Actual Forms of the instrument.
- *Feedback:* This provides profiles representing the class mean of students' actual and preferred environment scores. It enables identification of changes needed to reduce major differences between the actual and preferred environment as currently perceived by the students.
- *Reflection and discussion:* Private reflection and informal discussion about profiles to provide a basis for a decision on whether to attempt to change the environment in any of the dimensions.
- *Intervention:* Introduction of an intervention in an attempt to change the classroom environment.
- *Reassessment:* The student Actual Form is re-administered at the end on the intervention time to see if the students perceived the classroom environment differently from before.

Modifications of this process were used in this study and these are described in further detail in the section on research design and methodology.

Current directions in learning environment research show a combination of qualitative and quantitative methods to be a strong means in which the potential of research on learning environments can be maximized (Tobin & Fraser, 1998). Other directions include links between different environments; for example, home and school, and school level and classroom level; cultural and cross-national studies and in the area of teacher education.

3. Research Design and Methodology

The research design chosen for this project was an action research approach. The project focused on the use of the CUCEI in a collaborative process that the lecturer and pre-service students used for examining and improving upon what was happening in their science education classes. This introduced the students to the current research base of the field of classroom environments and they were then provided with an opportunity to focus on the improvement of the environment of their primary school classrooms during their practicum teaching using the WIHIC. The selection of these two instruments provided quantitative data results and the results from these questionnaires were enhanced by qualitative information collated from the pre-service students at the end of the science education course and at the end of their intensive seven week teaching practicum.

Introducing learning environment knowledge in teacher education through processes such as an action research approach would hopefully encourage, within the pre-service teachers, an awareness of value of the teacher as a reflective, action researcher in their own classroom. Grundy and Kemmis (1981) claim that action research has two principal aims. These are improvement (of practices, the situation, and understanding of both the practice and the situation) and involvement. They argue that it is a process of change, but not just for change's sake; that it is change specifically directed towards improvement and that it is a process directed **towards** and directed **by those** who are actually taking the journey. Grundy (1995) discusses the idea that action research is a powerful form of professional development and its power comes from the fact that the focus of inquiry and interest in action research is the participants' own practice. She also argues that it incorporates a commitment to collaborative inquiry and depends upon people acting together to bring about change. Grundy also goes on to describe the action research process as a journey in which reconnaissance is carried out first to provide the focus, followed by planning and carrying out the plans, collecting evidence along the way, and reflecting upon the evidence. She emphasises that it is cyclical rather than linear in nature and suggests that the elements of the process be called 'moments' rather than steps or stages.

One of the aims of action research, suggested by Alcorn (1986), was to "effect and monitor change in existing practice through an action phase aimed at bringing about a desired end" (p. 33). It is "research carried out by practitioners with a view to improving their own professional practice and understanding it better" (Cameron-Jones in Borg, Gall, & Gall, 1993, p. 390). Carr and Kemmis (1986) linked action research to curriculum development and school improvement programs, claiming that these activities had in common: "the identification of strategies of planned actions that are then implemented, and then systematically submitted to observation, reflection and changes" (p. 164).

As well as the collection of quantitative data from the CUCEI and WIHIC questionnaires this action research project also relied on a qualitative approach to research. Qualitative oriented research is a term first used in the social sciences in the late 1960s. It describes a number of research strategies that share certain characteristics representing a move away from the traditional scientific experimental approaches to strategies that assist in a deeper understanding of the research question. Qualitative research is holistic in its approach and begins with a search for understanding the larger meaning (Janesick, 1994). The data collected are usually "soft," meaning they are rich in description of people, places and events (Blaike, 1992). The findings of qualitative research have a quality of undeniability (Miles & Huberman, 1994). Miles and Hubernam argued that:

> Words, especially organised into incidents and stories, have a concrete, vivid, meaningful flavour that often proves more convincing to a reader than pages of summarised numbers.
> (p. 1)

Qualitative research design usually starts with a question that involves interaction with people so that the researcher can understand something of the meaning of the participants' lives in their own terms (Janesick, 1994). This means that qualitative research is usually carried out in a naturalistic setting, such as the participants' homes or workplaces with the researcher as the research instrument. If the researcher is to be the primary vehicle for collecting information, then the researcher's own personal skills and knowledge of the topic being researched are important factors in the research process. Miles and Huberman (1994) suggest that issues of validity and reliability ride largely on the skills of the researcher.

Furthermore, qualitative research has the advantage of being flexible in its approach. Bodgan & Bilken (1992) liken embarking on qualitative research to beginning a "journey" where the final destination is unknown:

We have a friend who, when asked where she is going on vacation, will tell you the direction she is traveling and then concludes with, 'I'll see what happens as I go along.' (p. 58)

4. Data Source

The study involved 26 pre-service teachers who are graduates from a variety of disciplines and have undertaken a one year program (two semesters) in primary education. The science education paper is a compulsory one and consists of three hours of campus-based lectures and workshops per week for twelve weeks. In addition, one morning for six of those weeks is spent teaching in a local primary school. At the end of Semester 2 the students then have a seven week fulltime teaching practicum in a local primary school.

5. Selection of Instruments

This study investigated student perceptions of two distinct aspects of learning environments using the CUCEI and WIHIC as instruments. The CUCEI is an instrument developed specifically for the higher education level (Fraser & Treagust,1986; Fraser, Treagust, & Dennis, 1986). There are seven scales that are assessed with this instrument and these are Personalization, Involvement, Cohesiveness, Satisfaction, Task Orientation, Innovation, and Individualisation. Each scale has seven items and the five response alternatives are Almost Never, Seldom, Sometimes, Often and Very Often. Table 10.1 presents descriptive information for each scale of the CUCEI as well as its classification according to Moos' scheme.

This instrument was used as a quantitative data-gathering tool. The two forms of the questionnaire (Actual and Preferred) were used at the beginning of the study and administered one day apart. The Actual Form of the questionnaire was used for reassessment after the intervention period to determine whether students perceived their classroom environment differently from before and to assess the success of the intervention strategies in improving the learning environment.

The other instrument used was the WIHIC. This instrument asks students for a personal perception of their role in the classroom environment rather than the perception of the whole class learning environment. It recognizes that learning is meaningful when it is a personal cognitive process that actively involves the learner in making sense of experiences in terms of their existing knowledge, and a social process in which this sense-making process involves consensus and negotiation with others (Tobin, 1993; von Glasersfield, 1989).

Table 10.1. Descriptive Information for Each Scale of the CUCEI

Scale name	Moos category	Description
Personalisation	Relationship	Emphasis on opportunities for individual students to interact with the instructor and on concern for students' personal welfare
Involvement	Relationship	Extent to which students participate actively and attentively in class discussions and activities
Student Cohesiveness	Relationship	Extent to which students know, help and are friendly to one another
Satisfaction	Relationship	Extent of enjoyment of classes
Task Orientation	Personal Development	Extent to which class activities are clear and well organised
Innovation	System Maintenance and System Change	Extent to which the instructor plans new, unusual class activities, teaching techniques and assignments
Individualisation	System Maintenance and System Change	Extent to which students are allowed to make decisions and are treated differently according to ability, interests and rate pf working

The use of a personal form enables the assessment of a student's perception of his or her role in the classroom environment, compared with the traditional class forms which ask the students to provide perceptions of the class as a whole. Fraser and Hoffman (1995) showed that personal forms of classroom environment scales enable the environment to be studied at "different grain sizes" so that individual students or groups of students can be investigated.

The instrument incorporates scales that had previously been shown to be significant predictors of learning outcomes (Fraser, 1994) along with additional scales to accommodate recent concerns in classroom learning such as equity issues. The instrument used in this study is a shortened and simplified version of that developed by Fraser, Fisher, and McRobbie (1996) so that the reading level is appropriate for the age level of the study. It assesses five scales which are Student Cohesiveness, Teacher Support, Involvement, Task Orientation and Equity. Each scale has five items and employs a four point Likert response scale (Almost Never, Sometimes, Often and Almost Always). Table 10.2 contains descriptive information for each scale of the shortened version of WIHIC as well as the classification of each scale according to Moos' scheme.

As with the CUCEI, two forms of the questionnaire (Actual and Preferred) were used at the beginning of the study and administered one day apart to the primary school children. The Actual Form of the questionnaire was also used for reassessment after the intervention period and this enabled the pre-service students to see whether the children perceived their classroom environment differently from before. It also enabled them to reflect on the success of the intervention strategies in improving the learning environment.

Table 10.2. Descriptive Information for Each Scale of WIHIC (shortened version)

Scale name	Moos category	Description
Student Cohesiveness	Relationship	Extent to which students know, help and are friendly with one another
Teacher support	Relationship	Extent to which the teacher helps, befriends, trusts and is interested in the students
Involvement	Relationship	Extent to which students participate in discussions and share their ideas
Task Orientation	System Maintenance and System Change	Extent in which it is important to be attentive, aware of and complete activities planned
Equity	System Maintenance and System Change	Extent to which the students are tested equally by the teacher

6. Method

As an action research spiral the method in this study involved a number of phases to bring about change in the learning environments of both university and primary classrooms.

6.1 College and University Classroom Environment Inventory

- **Week 4 (early)** - Initial workshop with pre-service teachers to introduce them to the basic concepts of learning environment studies, some of the basic research and the CUCEI and WIHIC instruments and how they are scored. One reading was supplied and this was *Assessing and improving classroom environment* (Fraser, 1989). This phase relates to the 'moment' of reconnaissance and planning in the action research spiral.
- **Week 4 (late)** - Assessment of student perceptions of both actual and preferred university classroom environments using CUCEI questionnaires. In terms of the action research spiral, this phase is one of acting and collecting evidence.
- **Week 5** - Presentation of the CUCEI results in the form of a profile and graph to the pre-service teachers. Discussion and reflection on the results with discrepancies between the actual and preferred environment used as the basis for selecting dimensions for change. Possible interventions were discussed.
- **Weeks 5-11** - Implementation of intervention strategies by lecturer and students to attempt to change the actual environment to reduce discrepancies in selected dimensions. This relates to another cycle of planning and acting in the research spiral.
- **Week 11** - Re-administer the CUCEI. This phase links in to another cycle of collecting evidence.
- **Week 12** - Presentation of the CUCEI results in the form of a profile and graph to the pre-service teachers. Discussion and reflection on the usefulness of results in attempting to improve the university learning environment. Students write short case paragraphs to show their reflections. This phase relates to the reflection phase of the spiral.

There were some limitations of this procedure. The timing constraints meant that the timing of some phases in the program was not ideal. The first phase was later than was considered ideal and the implementation phase could have been longer.

6.2 What is happening in this class? (shortened version)

The students followed a parallel method with their primary school students to that outlined above although the intervention time was shorter due to constraints of the program. Students were encouraged to take the opportunity to examine and look at improving their primary classroom environment on their practicum – it was not compulsory that they do so. It was also recommended that to simplify their individual projects, they could use a small group of students rather than the whole class.

- **Week 2 (early)** - Discussion with the associate teacher of their project with the emphasis on being an action researcher in the primary classroom. Assessment of primary children perceptions of both their personal actual and preferred classroom environments using the WIHIC questionnaires.
- **Week 2 (late)** - Discussion and reflection on the results with associate teacher and children. Discrepancies between the actual and preferred environment used as the basis for selecting dimensions for change. Possible interventions were discussed with both associate teacher and children.
- **Week 2-6** - Implementation of intervention strategies by pre-service students and primary children in an attempt to change the actual environment to reduce discrepancies in selected dimensions.
- **Week 6 (late)** - Re-administer the WIHIC
- **Week 7** - Reflect and discuss results with associate teacher and students. Write short case paragraphs on their attempts to improve the learning environment of their primary classrooms.

Both these questionnaires formed an important part of the reconnaissance notion in the action research spiral and provided quantitative data. The writing of the case paragraphs as part of the reflection and discussion phases of the spiral in the use of both instruments provided the qualitative data.

7. Reliability and Validity of the CUCEI and WIHIC

Table 10.3 provides a summary of the reported statistical information for the two instruments. This is information about each scale's internal consistency reliability (alpha coefficient) and discriminant validity (using the mean correlation of a scale with other scales in the same instrument).

Table 10.3. Reliability and Mean Correlation with Other Scales

Scale	Alpha Coefficient	Mean correlation with other scales
Personalisation	0.75	0.46
Involvement	0.70	0.47
Student Cohesiveness	0.90	0.45
Satisfaction	0.88	0.45
Task orientation	0.75	0.38
Innovation	0.81	0.46
Individualisation	0.78	0.34
Student Cohesiveness	0.80	0.35
Teacher Support	0.88	0.35
Involvement	0.86	0.48
Task Orientation	0.89	0.36
Equity	0.84	0.09

These values confirm the reliability and validity of these two instruments and are similar to earlier information about the reliability of the CUCEI reported by Fraser and Treagust (1986) for a sample of 372 university students and for the WIHIC by Fraser, Fisher, and McRobbie (1996) who reported on the reliability of this for 355 students.

8. Data Analysis and Interpretation

8.1 College and University Classroom Environment Inventory (CUCEI)

8.1.1 Quantitative

The findings are reported for both the Actual and Preferred Forms of the CUCEI for the class mean scores as a graphical profile. Differences between actual 1 and 2 and preferred on all scales are depicted in Figure 10.1.

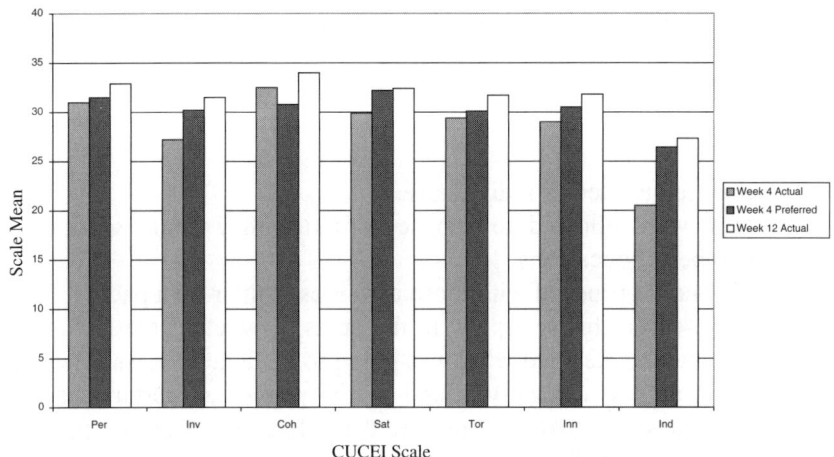

Figure 10.1. Scale means for actual and preferred versions of CUCEI.

The data depicted in Figure 10.1 indicate that there was a difference between senior pre-service students' perceptions of their actual and preferred classroom environment prior to implementation of intervention strategies. In comparison with the actual environment, students preferred an environment with higher levels of personalisation, involvement, satisfaction, innovation and individualisation. The greatest differences between preferred and actual perceptions were on the scales of Involvement and Individualisation. The differences were small between the actual and preferred in the scales of Personalization, Satisfaction, Innovation with little difference being shown on the scale of Task Orientation.

However, it is clear that the scale means for Involvement and Individualisation as well as showing the greatest discrepancies, were lower than for any of the other scales in both the preferred and actual perceptions of the students.

The Intervention strategies suggested by the students in the subsequent reflection and discussion session in Week 6 were recorded. To increase involvement, the strategies suggested were:

- more time to be spent on discussion and debate

- less time with lecturer talking
- more feedback or presentation of activities from workshops by students
- more discussion of individual teaching experiences following the six morning teaching episodes

Individualisation was discussed in great detail. The main points recorded were:

- they felt treated as individuals
- they were allowed to choose activities they could work on a number of occasions
- they could proceed with those activities at their own pace
- they scored this scale low in the areas of whether the lecturer or the students decided what was going to be done in class. They felt this was not a negative thing as the paper had certain learning outcomes and that they preferred the lecturer to plan a program towards achieving those outcomes
- they appreciated the use of an 'advance organiser' as they began each session so that they were aware of the learning intentions for the session
- they felt that this was what contributed to the high level of task orientation in the questionnaire results

As a result they decided that a worthwhile intervention strategy would be the carrying out of an investigative activity in which they chose a topic that interested them. This would be a focus for their teaching episodes and they would present this later to the rest of the group. It would provide an opportunity for them to pursue an area of interest to them, and the individual presentations would also link with some of the intervention strategies suggested for involvement.

After the intervention period of five weeks, during which the lecturer provided opportunities for the use of strategies discussed with the student group, the resurvey results indicate a strong improvement in the scales of Involvement and Individualisation in the actual perceptions of the students. In fact the resurvey results exceeded that of the initial preferred results. Although the strategies were designed to give students more opportunities for involvement in discussion, debate and presentation of activities as well as providing a choice in the topics presented from their teaching practice, such a way of working also produced a small improvement in the scales of Personalisation, Satisfaction, Task Orientation and Innovation in the resurvey results. These resurvey results also exceeded that of the initial preferred results.

The result for Student Cohesiveness was interesting. Initially, the actual mean scored higher than the preferred. The actual mean in the resurvey was higher still. After much discussion, the students were at a loss to explain this result, but generally consensus was that they were a cohesive group with strong working relationships continuing to be established over the semester.

8.1.2 Qualitative

A number of students wrote case paragraphs in which they reflected on the results and the process of reshaping the university classroom environment.

Chris:

> *We have a demanding program and so we are often keen to get classes over with so that we can get on with our lesson preparation or assignments. We tend not to get very involved in our classes so at first I was apprehensive about us thinking about our classroom environment as no one has asked us to do this before. Usually we only make evaluative comments at the end of a paper.*

> *I enjoyed our discussion of the initial results and thought that our strategies for changing were good. I liked the way that the feedback was taken and we were conscious of the efforts that X (lecturer) made. However I must say that we had already found this one of the more interesting and better organized classes. And it got better...... really better. I looked forward to coming to classes.*

> *I enjoyed the individual presentations – both giving mine and listening to the others. I got heaps of ideas for my teaching and learned heaps. I think it was inevitable that the involvement and individualization was improved at the end*

Anne:

> *It was interesting to go through the process and see whether the university environment could be improved. Also our university environment is not usually a personal one and it was interesting to see how having positive relationships between us and X made many of us start to enjoy science and feel excited about teaching it. The classes are always well organized and I enjoyed feeling more involved through the discussions and the sharing of our teaching episodes. X's feedback was also valuable and delivered constructively. The presentation of our investigations definitely increased the involvement and individualization. Modelling this process with us has made me keen to work this with my children in my next four weeks on practicum.*

Teresa:

> *The discussion about what was important in our university and classroom environment continued well out of class. We found ourselves wishing that other classes went through the same process. The first survey showed us that as a class we were scoring high on things such as satisfaction, innovation, personalization and cohesiveness (although it appeared at first we didn't want to be as cohesive as we were!). Individualization and involvement were the two that we decided to look at and the presenting of our investigations and discussing in more detail our teaching episodes were definitely things that increased the scoring in those areas. I would still want our lecturer to plan our program, but within the framework it is obvious we can still negotiate some things so that we still complete the requirements of the paper.*

8.2 What is happening in this class?

The data for this part of the study are also a mix of quantitative and qualitative information as recommended by Fraser and Tobin (1991). The findings below are reported from three pre-service students. The first student (Student A) was on practicum working in a Year 7 class in a suburban school in a low socioeconomic area.

Graphical profiles for Class 1 with Student A, showing differences between actual and preferred means on all scales are depicted in Figure 10.2.

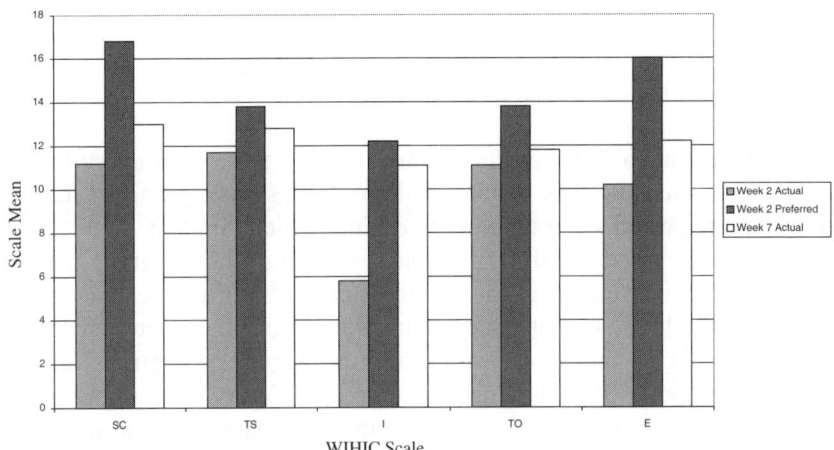

Figure 10.2. Scale means for actual and preferred versions of WIHIC Class 1.

The data depicted in Figure 10.2 indicate that there was a difference between the primary children's perception of actual and preferred environment. In comparison with the actual environment, students preferred an environment with higher levels of on all scales of the instrument. The greatest discrepancies between preferred and actual perceptions were in the scales of Student Cohesiveness, Involvement and Equity with the differences being smaller for Teacher Support and Task Orientation.

It is also clear that the scales for Involvement as well as showing a high discrepancy also scored at a lower level than any of other scales in the preferred perceptions of the students. It appeared that the students preferred to have an environment where there were lower levels of involvement in class discussions and the offering of their own ideas.

The intervention strategies that Student A discussed with her primary students in a class meeting in order to reduce the discrepancies between the actual and preferred perceptions were:

- Involvement: not putting people down when ideas are expressed; rules for discussion were set and put up on a poster; use of 'think, pair and share' strategy
- Teacher Support: spend more time with all students, not just those seeking support; survey of children to find out more about their interests and background and use of this information as appropriate
- Student Cohesiveness: more working together in groups both for inside as well as outside activities.

The students also asked for a class meeting to be held every Friday morning to discuss how each of these things was going. After an intervention period of four weeks, during which Student A used the strategies discussed at the first class meeting, the resurvey results indicate an improvement in the discrepancies of four of the five scales, especially the Involvement scale. There were also some improvements in the discrepancies between actual and preferred perceptions in the Teacher Support, Student Cohesiveness and Equity scales. Although addressing equity was not a specific focus, it appeared that the strategies employed to improve teacher support, also improved the children's perceptions of equity.

Student A:

> *The strategies that we discussed and used, worked reasonably well. It was good to have the discussion about what was going on in the classroom, as well as talking about it at the Friday class meeting. The time for trying to make changes was shorter than I would have liked but we did see some improvements in the Involvement scale. The setting of discussion rules together seemed to be helpful and I was able to refer to these as necessary so that a safe environment for discussions was created. Using 'think, pair and share' as a strategy also provided a safe environment for discussion because in smaller groups the children did not feel so 'exposed'.*

> *I was more careful about trying to give time to all children and found that I moved around the room more. I also thought carefully about the words that I used to encourage the students*

so that the encouragement was more meaningful in terms of the quality of their work or the way that they had gone about it. I feel that I got better at listening and responding to the children and considering their feelings more.

I found the professional discussions on the classroom environment with J. (associate teacher) to be valuable and I think she also found the process to be useful.

The second student (Student B) was on practicum working in a Year 8 class in a suburban school with a high socioeconomic rating. Graphical profiles for Class 2 with Student B showing differences between actual and preferred on all scales are depicted in Figure 10.3.

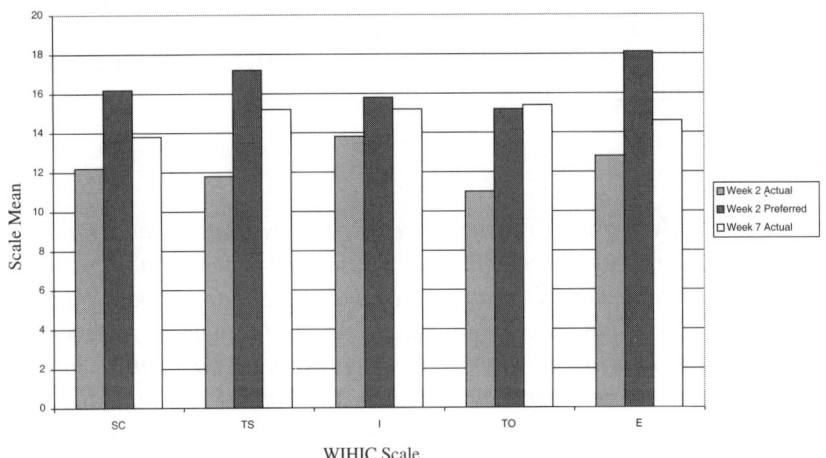

Figure 10.3. Scale means for actual and preferred versions of WIHIC Class 2.

The data depicted in Figure 10.3 indicate that there was a difference between the children's perception of actual and preferred environment and that the children preferred an environment with higher levels on all scales of the instrument. The greatest discrepancies between preferred and actual were on the Teacher Support, Task Orientation and Equity scales.

The intervention strategies used by Student B to reduce the discrepancies between actual and preferred perceptions in these three scales were:

- Teacher Support: Moving around the class more, encouraging and taking time to listen carefully and respond thoughtfully to their questions
- Task Orientation: Sharing learning intentions and success criteria on the whiteboard board at the beginning of each lesson and finishing the lesson by referring to these.
- Equity: Giving attention and encouragement to each child.

These intervention strategies were not decided with the children but agreed upon in consultation with the associate teacher. After the intervention period the resurvey results indicate an improvement in all three of the scales upon which the interventions were focused. In the scale of Task Orientation the discrepancy between actual and preferred was removed and the final actual perception by the children was slightly higher than the preferred.

Student B:

> *After analyzing the first survey result, P (associate teacher) and I decided on some strategies that I could try. I made an effort to move around the class more and talked to children about their work rather than their behaviour. I tried to let them know that I wanted to hear about when things were difficult for them so that together we could work out what needs to happen to enable them to learn. I used words such as "It's good you told me you were stuck - let's find out what you need so that you will be able to learn something new." I noticed that after a while some children started to speak more about their learning. I think that these conversations helped in reducing the discrepancies in the Teacher Support and Equity scales. It has certainly made a difference to my teaching because I used to focus more on getting the lesson done – now I am thinking more about what they are learning.*

Sharing learning intentions on the whiteboard with children at the beginning of each lesson I feel contributed to the large increase in the Task Orientation scale. I asked the children to come up with success criteria by asking them "How will we know if we have learned that?" I was surprised how well they were able to create success criteria. Many of the children seemed more focused on their learning and asked for learning intentions if I forgot! It was also very helpful for me as it also helped me to focus on the children's learning rather than the activity

The third student (Student C) was on practicum working in a Year 7 class in a suburban school with a mid socioeconomic rating. Graphical profiles for Class 3 with Student C showing differences between actual and preferred on all scales are depicted in Figure 10.4.

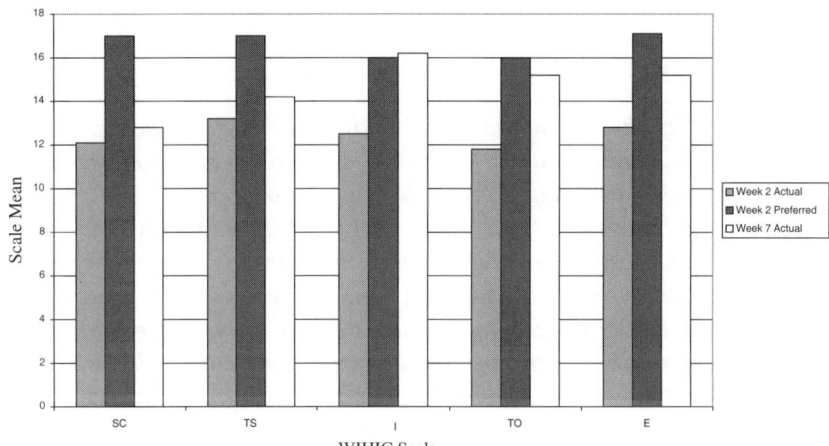

Figure 10.4. Scale means for actual and preferred versions of WIHIC Class 3.

The data depicted in Figure 10.4 indicate that like the other classes there was a difference between the children's perception of actual and preferred environment. The children preferred an environment with higher levels on all scales of the instrument with the discrepancies between preferred and actual on all scales being similar.

Student C chose two scales to implement intervention strategies to attempt to reduce the discrepancies between actual and preferred perceptions. These were:

- Involvement: Setting up with the children of classroom rules for discussion; use of concept cartoons in science lessons to allow children to represent their ideas through cartoon characters.
- Task Orientation: Writing learning intentions and success criteria on the whiteboard board and discussing these with the children at the beginning of the lesson.

Some of the intervention strategies were decided with the children, and others were decided by the student teacher.

After four weeks the resurvey results indicate a significant improvement in both the scales chosen as a focus. For the Involvement scale, the discrepancy between the actual and preferred was removed with the final actual perception being slightly higher than the preferred.

Student C

I began by discussing with the children the sorts of things that would be important if everyone was to feel good about participating in discussions and giving their opinions. We drew up a list together and displayed this prominently in the classroom. I also introduced them to concept cartoons in the science unit we were studying on sound. These gave the children opportunities to discuss their science ideas through the cartoon characters and then in some cases test their ideas by investigation. I believe that these, along with the creation and referral as necessary to the discussion rules, were helpful in improving the children's involvement in discussion of ideas, their confidence in giving opinions and explaining their ideas.

I also shared learning intentions with the children for each lesson. These were written on a flip chart and we finished each lesson by referring back to these. The learning intentions gave a clear focus for the lesson, not only for me but for the children as well.

9. Conclusion

This chapter describes a method for assessing the two aspects of classroom environments and using these assessments as a basis for improving the learning environments in both the university classroom and the primary classroom.

In this study, previous research was replicated in that overall the pre-service students and the primary students were found to prefer a more positive learning environment than they perceived to be present in the classrooms. This action research approach to improving the university classroom environment is based on information about student personal perceptions of their actual and preferred environments and then the use of this information to discuss and implement intervention strategies to try to improve the learning environment.

It has provided a means for examining what is going on in university classes and this in turn has provided a model for pre-service students to examine, using an appropriate instrument, the learning environment of a classroom they work in. The study was significant in that it combined both qualitative and quantitative methods to show that the intervention strategies for improving aspects of the learning environment were successful in bringing about some positive changes in the university teaching environment. The focus for the improvement was the scales for Personalisation and Individualisation from the CUCEI questionnaire. However, the interesting dimension that emerged was that as well as reducing the actual-preferred discrepancy in the Individualisation scale, the intervention strategies also reduced the Personalisation discrepancy.

The project also introduced pre-service teachers to current information about the field of learning environments by being involved in action research in their practicum classrooms. It has provided them with some strategies to examine, improve and reflect on the learning environment of their classrooms.

References

Alcorn, N. (1986). Action research: A tool for school development. *Delta, 37*, 33-44.

Blaike, N. (1992). *Approaches to social enquiry*. Cambridge: Polity Press.

Bodgan, R. & Bilken, S. (1992). *Qualitative research for education.* Massachusetts: Allyn & Bacon.

Borg, W., Gall, J., & Gall, M. (1993). *Applying educational research.* New York: Longman.

Carr, W. & Kemmis, S. *(1986). Becoming critical: Education knowledge and action research.* London: The Palmer Press.

Fisher, D. L. & Fraser, B. J. (1991). School climate and teacher professional development. *South Pacific Journal of Teacher Education 19*(1), 17-32.

Fraser, B. J. (1986). *Classroom environment.* London: Croom Helm.

Fraser, B. J. (1989). *Assessing and improving classroom environment.* (What Research Says, No 2). Perth: Curtin University of Technology.

Fraser, B. J. (1994). Research on classroom climate and school climate. In D. Gabel (Ed.), *Handbook of research on science teaching and learning* (pp. 493-541). New York: MacMillian

Fraser, B. J., Docker, J. G., & Fisher, D. L. (1988). Assessing and improving School Climate. *Evaluation and Research in Education, 2* (3), 109-122.

Fraser, B. J. & Fisher, D. L. (1983). Use of actual and preferred classroom environment scales in person-environment fit research. *Journal of Educational Psychology, 75*, 303-313.

Fraser, B. J. & Fisher, D. L. (1986). Using short forms of classroom climate instruments to assess and improve classroom psychosocial environment. *Journal of Research in Science Teaching, 5*, 387-413.

Fraser, B. J., Fisher, D. L. & McRobbie, C. J. (1996, April). *Development, validation and use of personal and class forms of a new classroom environment instrument.* Paper presented at the annual meeting of the American Educational Research Association, New York, USA.

Fraser, B. J. & Hoffman, H. (1995, April). *Combining qualitative and quantitative methods in a teacher-researcher study of determinants of classroom environment.* Paper presented at the annual meeting of the American Educational Research Association, San Francisco.

Fraser, B. & Tobin, K. (1991). Combining qualitative and quantitative methods in classroom environment research. In B. Fraser & H. Walberg (Eds.), *Educational environments: Evaluation, antecedents and consequences* (pp. 271-292). Oxford: Pergamon Press.

Fraser, B. & Treagust, D. (1986). Validity and use of an instrument for assessing classroom psychosocial environment in higher education. *Higher Education, 15*, 37-57.

Fraser, B., Treagust, D. & Dennis, B. (1986). Development of an instrument for assessing classroom psychosocial environment at universities and colleges. *Studies in Higher Education, 11*, 43-54.

Fraser, B. & Walberg, H.J. (Eds.). (1991). *Educational environments: Evaluation, antecedents and consequences.* Oxford: Pergamon Press.

Fraser, B. & Walberg, H. J., Welch, W. W., & Hattie, J. A. (1987). Synthesis of educational productivity research. *International Journal of Educational Research, 11*, 145-252.

Grundy, S. (1995). Action research as on-going professional development. *Affiliation of Arts Educators (WA).*

Grundy, S. & Kemmis, S. (1988). Educational action research in Australia: The state of the art. In S. Kemmis & R. McTaggart (Eds.), *The action research reader* (3rd ed.). Geelong: Deakin University Press.

Haertel, G. D., Walberg, H. J., & Haertel, E. H. (1981). Socio-psychological environments and learning: A quantitative synthesis. *British Educational Research Journal, 7*, 27-36.

Janesick, V. J. (1994). The dance of qualitative research design: Metaphor, methodolatry and meaning. In N. K. Denzin & Y. S. Lincoln (Eds.), *Handbook of qualitative research* (pp. 209-219). Sage: London.

Kemmis, S. & McTaggart, R. (1988). *The action research reader* (3rd ed). Geelong: Deakin University Press.

Lewin, K. (1936). *Principles of topological psychology.* New York: McGraw.

Miles, M. B. & Huberman, A. M. (1994). *Qualitative data analysis - an expanded source book.* (2nd ed.). Thousand Oaks, California: Sage.

Moos, R. H. (1974). *The social climate scales: An overview.* Palo Alto, CA: Consulting Psychologists Press.

Moos, R. H. (1979). *Evaluating educational environments: Procedures, measures, findings and policy implications.* San Francisco, CA: Jossey-Bass.

Moos, R. H. & Trickett, E. J. (1987). *Classroom Environment Scale manual* (2nd Ed.). Palo Alto, CA: Consulting Psychologists Press.

Murray, H. A. (1938). *Explorations in personality.* New York: Oxford University Press.

Rentoul, R. J. & Fraser, B. J. (1980). Predicting learning from classroom individualisation and actual-preferred congruence. *Studies in Educational Evaluation, 6*, 265-277.

Stern, G. G., Stein, M. I., & Bloom, B. S. (1956). *Methods in personality assessment.* Glencoe, IL: Free Press.

Tobin, K. (19930. *The practice of constructivism in science education.* Washington AAAS

Tobin, K. & Fraser, B. (1998). Qualitative and quantitative landscapes of classroom learning environments. In B. J. Fraser & K. G. Tobin (Eds.), *International handbook of science education* (pp. 623-640). Dordrecht, The Netherlands: Kluwer.

von Glasersfeld, E. (1989). Cognition, construction of knowledge, and teaching. *Synthese, 80*, 121-140.

Walberg, H. J. & Anderson, G. J. (1968). Classroom climate and individual learning. *Journal of Educational Psychology, 59*, 414-419.

Wood, J. & Fraser, B. J. (1995, April). *Utilising feedback data on students' perceptions of teaching style and preferred learning style to enhance teaching effectiveness.* Paper presented at the annual meeting of the National Association for Research in Science Teaching, San Francisco, CA.

Chapter 11

A CONTEMPORARY STUDY OF LEARNING ENVIRONMENTS IN JAMMU, INDIA

Rekha B. Koul
Darrell L. Fisher
Curtin University of Technology
Australia

One of the earliest learning environment studies reported from India was nearly three decades ago. Although since then lot of studies have been carried out in different parts of the world, little has been reported about Indian learning environments apart from some small-scale studies conducted by local students whose work was never published. The study described in this chapter is the first ever large-scale study conducted in Jammu (India) where multiple research methods were used to explore the nature of classroom environments and student-teacher interactions. A sample of 1,021 students from 32 science classes in seven co-educational private schools completed the questionnaires, What is Happening in This Class (WIHIC), Questionnaire on Teacher Interaction (QTI) and an attitude scale. The quantitative data provided a starting point from which other qualitative methods (interviews and observations) were used to gain a more in-depth understanding of the classroom environments. The findings from the quantitative data were supported by the findings of interviews and observations. It is hoped that the information in this chapter will give readers an understanding of the existing learning environments in Jammu, India.

1. Introduction and Background

According to Encarta (2000), formal education in India was well established as early as 1200 BC. Local priests ran the educational institutions and science was one of the major disciplines of instruction. During the British colonisation, the current system of education came into existence and at present this is the only officially recognised educational system. The primary aim of such a school was to select, filter out the bulk of the population and select a few who could help the rulers.

This also implied that those involved in the development and running of the school system were also its principal users and beneficiaries.

In the words of Mahatma Gandhi,

> I say without fear of my figures being challenged successfully, that today India is more illiterate than it was fifty or a hundred years ago, because British administrators, when they came to India, instead of taking hold of things as they were, began to root them out. They scratched the soil and began to look at the root, and left the root like that, and the beautiful tree perished. The village schools were not good enough for the British administrator, so he came out with his program. Every school must have so much paraphernalia, building, and so forth. Well, there were no such schools at all. There are statistics left by a British administrator which show that, in places where they have carried out a survey, ancient schools have gone by the board, because there was no recognition for these schools, and the schools established after the European pattern were too expensive for the people and therefore they could not possibly overtake the thing. (Mahatma Gandhi at Chatham House, London, October 20, 1931)

The above paragraph gives us a clear picture of the state of education in India in early to mid-twentieth century. Independence in 1947 led to the emergence of a strong political will to universalise education. Incentives were given to first generation learners. However, even though the profile of students entering schools has changed radically, the practices in the school have hardly been revised to take change into account. Teacher training continues to be traditional, concentrating on elementary communication skills (Kulkarni, 1988).

India became free from British colonisation in the year 1947 and in the year 1952, implemented her own constitution. By then, the British system of education had taken deep root and was the basis on which the existing educational policy was formulated.

2. India's National Policy on Education

India's commitment to the spread of knowledge and freedom of thought among its citizens is reflected in its constitution. The Directive Principle contained in Article 45 states, "The State shall endeavour to provide within a period of ten years from the commencement of this constitution, for free and compulsory education for all children until they complete the age of fourteen years".

Educational policy and progress have been reviewed in the light of the goals of national development and priorities set from time to time. In India's Resolution on the *National Policy on Education, 1968* there is an emphasis on quality improvement and a planned, more equitable expansion of educational facilities.

About a decade and a half later, in the year 1986, the *National Policy on Education* (NPE-1986) was formulated and was further updated in 1992. The NPE-1986 provides a comprehensive policy framework, for the development of education up to the end of the century and a *Plan of Action* (POA) 1992, assigning specific responsibilities for organising, implementing, and financing these proposals. In the years 2000-2001, a total expenditure on education in India was 4.11% of the total GNP (Source-Selected Educational Statistics). The following are among the distinguishing features and recommendations of this policy.

Since the inception of this present educational system, there have been changes from time to time. The National Council for Educational Research and Training (NCERT) implemented major changes in the early 1980s. Until that time, there was no uniformity in the educational systems in all the 32 states of the country. The NCERT gave a general guideline, which could be followed by the state boards. This system bought uniformity to the system and we can be confident that a sample taken from one state can be representative of the rest of the population.

The teaching of science as a part of general education up to year ten was re-emphasised in the *National Policy on Education-1986* (Malhotra, 1988). The task of developing curriculum and related instructional material in science was entrusted to the Department of Education in Science and Mathematics (DESM), National Council for Educational Research and Training (NCERT). Drafts of the guidelines for science education were developed keeping in view the spirit of the *National Policy on Education* and *Curriculum Framework*. Keeping these guidelines in view, books were written and efforts were made to provide more activities and facilitate learning (Balasubramanian, 1998).

Although NCERT has made a lot of effort to revise the curricula, there is no evidence of creating good learning environments in schools. Also, there has been no effort to investigate the Indian educational system and compare it with the rest of the world. Keeping the present global conditions in view it is very important for all countries to have compatible/comparable outcomes. Science education research, which crosses national boundaries, offers much insight for two reasons (Fraser, 1997). Firstly, there usually is greater variation in variables of interest (teaching methods, student attitudes) or the taken-for-granted familiar educational practices, beliefs and attitudes in one country can be exposed, made 'strange' and questioned in another country (Fraser & Tobin, 1998). In an effort to "provide a refreshing alternative to...research reports, which malign science education and highlight its major problems and shortcomings" (Fraser & Tobin, 1991), this study was undertaken. This is also in line with the research quoted by Fraser and Tobin (1991), which highlights educational accomplishments and paves the way for improvements in schooling.

An examination of past reviews of research (Aldridge, Fraser, & Haung, 1999; Anderson, 1982; Fraser, 1991; Fraser & Walberg, 1981; Templeton & Johnston, 1998; Wubbels, Creton, & Hooymayers, 1992) shows that international research efforts over the last three decades involving the conceptualisation, assessment and investigation of perceptions of various aspects of the classroom learning environment has been a thriving field of study. Furthermore, science education researchers have led the world in the field of classroom environment research, and this field has contributed much to understanding and improvement of science education (Aldridge, Fraser, & Haung, 1999; Anderson, 1982; Fraser, 1991; Fraser, 1998a; Rickards & Fisher, 1999). Classroom environment assessment provides a means of monitoring, evaluating and improving science curriculum planning and teaching.

The field of learning environment has undergone remarkable growth, diversification and internationalisation during the past 30 years (Fraser, 1998b). Although learning environment research originated in Western Countries, Asian researchers in the last decade have made many major and distinctive contributions (Fraser, 2002).

One of the earliest research studies establishing the validity of classroom environment instruments carried out in India (Walberg, Singh,

& Rasher, 1977). In this study, the classroom environment scale was translated into Hindi and validated. The research carried out in the Asian context has been a stimulating and guiding factor for the present study in India, where for the first time an effort has been made to study the existing student teacher interactions and science classroom learning environments.

3. Learning Environment Research

The notion that a learning environment exists which mediates aspects of educational development began as early as 1936 when Lewin (1936) recognised that the environment and the interaction of the individual were powerful determinants of behaviour and introduced the formula, B=f(P,E). Since Lewin's time, international research efforts involving the conceptualisation, assessment, and investigation of perceptions of aspects of the classroom environment have firmly established classroom environments as a thriving field of study (Fraser, 1986, 1994, 1998a; Fraser & Walberg, 1991). For example, recent classroom environment research has focused on constructivist classroom environments (Taylor, Fraser, & Fisher, 1997), cross-national constructivist classroom environments (Aldridge et al., 1999; Fisher, Rickards, Goh, & Wong, 1997), science laboratory classroom environments (McRobbie & Fraser, 1993), computer laboratory classroom environment (Newby, 1998) computer-assisted instruction classrooms (Stolarchuk, 1997) and classroom environment and teachers' cultural back grounds (Khine & Fisher, 2001).

Despite the fact that a great deal of classroom learning environment research has been carried out over the past 30 years, most of the initial work was conducted in western cultures (Fraser, 1986, 1994, 1998a; Fraser & Walberg, 1991). However, classroom environment research has gathered momentum in Asian countries in recent years (Aldridge et al., 1999; Khine & Fisher, 2001; Riah & Fraser, 1998). Evidence from these studies revealed that classroom learning environment dimensions are good indicators of teaching and learning process and their predictive power on a number of learning outcomes points towards the possibility of improving students' outcomes through changing classroom environments.

Around the world, in both developed and developing countries science education has become a very important area. In an era of science and technology we can face the challenges of science only by making necessary provision for science education. Ninety percent of eligible students in India do not have access to higher education. The Government spends a miniscule of 0.5 percent of GNP on this area. The Indian National Science Academy requested the government to take a fresh look at the country's science and technology system. (INSA, 2001). In this grim situation a positive teacher student relationship is very important.

The present interpretive study went beyond past research and involved a multi-method approach. The study explored factors associated with students' perceptions of learning environment. Furthermore, by drawing on a range of paradigms, a more in-depth understanding of socio-cultural and political influences on the classroom leaning environments in India was explored. The story ahead, as told by the first author, gives an insight into the existing educational culture in India.

4. A Science Theory Classroom

Deep in thought, watching the heavy traffic on the road, I was asked by para-military personnel to keep away. I became aware of my inattentiveness. I was waiting outside a school complex, where I had to conduct observations in a year nine science classroom on that day. Despite the fact that I had already obtained consent from the principal of the school to come and observe a nominated classroom, I was not allowed entry into the school. My driver was asked to park the car away from the school gate because of the safety regulations. I had to fill in a prescribed form stating the purpose of the visit and whom I intended to meet in the school. This form had to be sent in through the school orderly. Till then I was asked to wait on the road outside the school. After about 20 minutes an orderly came and let me inside the school. It was a solid concrete three-story building with a playground at the back. The entrance hall/foyer was well furnished and there was an eye-catching three by one metre poster which showed a burning candle and the words 'TEACHER IS LIKE A CANDLE, IT BURNS ITSELF TO GIVE LIGHT TO ITS STUDENTS'.

An orderly directed me to see the principal first. She was sitting in a comfortable chair in her office and an impressive collection of trophies could be seen behind her in large glass cabinet. The principal allocated a teacher to assist me who showed a lot of inquisitiveness about my study.

Other staff members first were conspicuously looking at me but later, when I was introduced to them, gave me friendly smiles. On the whole, every one was curious to know what I was doing. It was the first time that they wad witnessed such an activity being carried out in their institution. After the usual protocol, we headed towards the classroom, which was on the first floor. On my way to the classroom, I saw students returning quietly from a morning assembly in a neat straight queue. They were all wearing neatly-ironed school uniforms.

By the time I reached the class, which I was going to observe, the teacher had already arrived. On my entry into the class, the teacher paused and all the students got up as a mark of respect and welcomed me. I thanked them and requested them to sit down. The assistant teacher introduced me to the science teacher, who already was aware of my study. I tried not to disturb them and quietly went and sat on a chair at the back of the room. This was a well-ventilated classroom with nearly 50 students in it. The classroom was furnished with desks and benches, which were nearly 80 centimetres in length and three students shared each bench and desk. Big satchels hung at the back of their benches. Two fans were fixed to the ceiling but as it was a cold day they were not working; I was told that even in summer months they would face power failures/cuts from time to time. Male and female students sat on the opposite sides of the classroom. The walls of the classroom were decorated with educational charts, moral sayings and photographs of national leaders. There was an elevated dais for the teacher, which was furnished with a chair and a table. The teacher faced the students most of the time with a black chalkboard at her back, the only permanent visual aid, which she used. From time to time, the teacher used charts or specimens, which had to be specifically issued by the school library on request.

Although I tried not to disturb the class, students still started murmuring. I considered myself to be an intruder in the class and such condition was not only rare but also unthinkable for these students. The teacher gave a brief introduction about myself and the purpose of the visit. I could hear student hissing, "Researcher from Australia uh! Why?" There were quite a few short comments, which I could hear.

The teacher started that day's lesson and, indicated on the black board that she was going to teach 'Reflection by Spherical Mirrors'. The classroom had "pin-drop" silence but still I could hear the honking of the vehicles on the main road. The lesson started with an introduction to light, which the students must have studied in the previous year. There were quite a few questions and answers as previous knowledge of the topic was thoroughly reviewed.

The teacher started her lesson in a lively manner, and tried to include each student as she progressed in her lecture. Her eyes were wide open. The teacher then unfolded a chart showing the different positions and the nature of the images formed by a concave mirror. At the same time, the students had their textbooks opened and they were also referring to the book. While going through the lesson, the teacher also drew figures on the blackboard. Most of the students were listening to her intently and watching her, although I noticed two boys at the back quietly trying to snatch a piece of paper from each other. In this event, they happened to make a disturbing sound and the teacher, in a loud voice, asked them to refrain from doing so. I observed one more girl drawing in her notebook.

Later in the lesson, the teacher asked the students if they had any doubts about the content taught. The students raised their hands and the teacher answered each one of them in turn. While answering the queries of the students, the teacher also cross-examined them for their understanding by asking them further questions on the same topic. After this, the teacher wrote a few questions on the blackboard and the students were asked to answer them in their notebooks at home. Next day they would submit the homework to the teacher for correction. Only five minutes were left before the next class and two student representatives stood up. One started distributing the notebooks, which the teacher had corrected and brought with her, while the other one started collecting notebooks from the students where the homework given on the previous day was done. The assistant teacher told me that these students had class tests every Monday on the topics taught in the previous week. The weekend was said to be the right time to learn and then revise. The students had to get these answer books signed by their parents. Soon the school bell rang for the next lesson and all the students got up in respect for their teacher and farewelled her collectively. I also left the classroom at the same time. This account is of a typical year nine, science classroom in India.

Soon after the class teacher joined me outside on the verandah and explained that she encouraged students to use the library but they had to find their own time for study in the library; it was either during the recess period or if they had any free periods during the day, when the teacher concerned would be absent. She had assigned one science lesson a week for laboratory sessions, during which students in groups of four had the opportunity to research the topics taught. All the students were required to submit the reports of their practical work separately. The teacher perceived that practical sessions were less teacher-centered compared with the theory classes.

To further investigate student-teacher interactions and science classroom learning environments in India, a large-scale quantitative probe, using the *Questionnaire on Teacher Interaction* (QTI), the *What Is Happening In this Class?* (WIHIC) questionnaire and an attitude scale, was used to provide a view of students' perceptions of these science classrooms. The attitude scale provided a parsimonious view of the students' attitudes towards science lessons and teacher interactions.

5. The Instruments Used for Data Collection

The QTI was used to measure students' perception of their interactions with their teachers, the WIHIC was used to measure students' perceptions of their classroom environment, and an existing attitude scale was used to assess students' attitudes towards their science classes. All three instruments were given to students in the form of one questionnaire. The uniformity of the questionnaire was maintained to facilitate administration. As a result, for all the instruments, a five point frequency response scale was used. The questionnaires were worded in the personal manner to elicit the individual's perceptions of their role within the learning environment and to help the researchers to obtain a more accurate perceptions of gender and other subgroups within the class.

The QTI and WIHIC have been described elsewhere in this book. The Australian 48-item version of the QTI (Fisher, Henderson, & Fraser, 1995) was used in this study. The 56-item WIHIC version consisting of seven scales and 56 items (Fraser, Fisher, & McRobbie, 1996) was used. The seven scales are Student Cohesiveness, Teacher Support, Involvement, Investigation, Task Orientation, Cooperation and Equity. To measure students' attitudes towards their science classroom, an already existing attitude scale was used. The scale comprises eight items measuring the extent to which students enjoy, are interested in and look forward to science lessons.

6. Results

6.1 Validation of the QTI and WIHIC

The validity and reliability information for the QTI and WIHIC when used with the Indian sample is given in Table 11.1. To determine the degree to which items in the same scale measure the same aspect of teacher-student interpersonal behaviour, a measure of internal consistency, the Cronbach alpha reliability coefficient (Cronbach, 1951) was used. For the QTI the highest alpha reliability was obtained for the scales of Understanding and Dissatisfied and the lowest for Student Responsibility/ Freedom. The reliability results for the scales of the QTI were consistently above 0.50 which suggests that the QTI can be considered a reliable tool (De Vellis, 1991) for use with Indian students. However, results obtained for the Student Freedom scale should be interpreted with caution as the low alpha coefficient for this scale may be attributed to the nature of the Indian culture. The students may be reluctant to provide a frank opinion about this behaviour of their teachers.

The ability of a teacher-student interaction instrument to differentiate between classes is important. The instrument's ability to differentiate in this way was measured using one-way analysis of variance (ANOVA). The eta^2 statistic was calculated to provide an estimate of the strength of the association between class membership and the dependent variables as shown in Table 11.1. The eta^2 statistic for the QTI, indicates that the amount of variance in scores accounted for by class membership ranged from 0.13 to 0.25 and was statistically significant ($p<0.001$) for all scales. It appears that the instrument is able to differentiate clearly between the perceptions of students in different classrooms.

In the statistical analyses of the WIHIC the reliability coefficients for the different WIHIC scales ranged from 0.58 to 0.83. The highest alpha reliability (0.83) was obtained for the Equity scale and the lowest (0.58) for the scale Student Cohesiveness. The eta^2 statistic was again calculated and ranged from 0.09 to 0.14 and were statistically significant ($p<0.001$) for each scale. Thus, each scale of the WIHIC is capable of differentiating significantly between classes. Overall the reliability, and ANOVA results confirm that the WIHIC can be used with confidence for further research in India.

Table 11.1. Scale Internal Consistency (Cronbach Alpha Reliability) and Ability to Differentiate Between Classrooms (ANOVA results) for the QTI

Scales of QTI	Mean	Std. Dev.	Alpha Reliability	ANOVA (eta^2)
Leadership	3.15	0.5	0.71	0.13*
Helping/Friendly	2.28	0.53	0.65	0.14*
Understanding	3.06	0.55	0.72	0.20*
Student Freedom	2.32	0.48	0.50	0.13*
Uncertain	1.82	0.56	0.62	0.25*
Dissatisfied	1.84	0.64	0.72	0.18*
Admonishing	1.93	0.56	0.58	0.21*
Strict	2.65	0.51	0.53	0.16*
Scales of WIHIC	Mean	Std. Dev.	Alpha Reliability	ANOVA (eta^2)
Student Cohesiveness	4.77	0.54	0.58	0.10*
Teacher Support	4.00	0.87	0.78	0.14*
Involvement	3.89	0.79	0.76	0.14*
Investigation	3.89	0.83	0.77	0.10*
Task Orientation	4.84	0.63	0.70	0.12*
Cooperation	4.49	0.77	0.77	0.09*
Equity	4.57	0.89	0.83	0.14*

*$p<0.001$ Students n = 1,021; Classes n = 31

Item means and standard deviations were computed to determine the nature of science learning environment using the WIHIC. The very high mean scores shown in Table 11suggest a very positive classroom environment, with the mean scores ranging between 3.89 and 4.84. The students perceived Task Orientation, Student Cohesiveness and Cooperation most positively. The scores for these three scales are 4.84 for Task Orientation, 4.77 for Student Cohesiveness and 4.49 for Cooperation. The standard deviation for all the scales is less than 1, suggesting that there was not large diversity in the students' perceptions. Generally, the students perceive a very positive science classroom-learning environment.

6.2 Associations between learning environment and student attitudes

One of the aims of the study was to investigate whether the nature of the learning environment in Indian science classrooms affects students' attitudes. Associations between the perceptions of scales of QTI, WIHIC and students' attitudes were explored using simple and multiple correlation analyses. The results of the analyses are shown in Table 11.2.

For the QTI scales, Leadership, Helping/Friendly, Understanding and Student Freedom the associations are positive and statistically significant, where as for the Uncertain, Dissatisfied and Admonishing scales the associations are negative and statistically significant. The multiple correlation (R) between the set of QTI scales and attitude to science class was 0.39. The R^2 value, which indicates the proportion of variance in attitude to science class that can be attributed to students' perceptions of teacher-student interactions, was 15%. To determine which of the QTI scales contributed most to this association, the standardized regression coefficient (β) was examined for each scale. Only the scales of Leadership and Helping/Friendly retained their significance and were positively and significantly associated with attitude to science classes.

For the scales of the WIHIC the results of the simple correlation analysis revealed that all seven scales were significantly correlated with attitude to science class ($p<0.01$). It was found that these associations were positive and ranged from 0.17 to 0.38. The multiple correlation (R) was 0.43 and statistically significant ($p<0.01$). This strongly supports the conclusion that the nature of the classroom environment is strongly influencing students' attitudes towards science lessons. In order to further interpret this relationship, the standardised regression coefficient (β) was also examined. It was found that out of seven scales, three scales retained their significance ($p<0.01$). This means that the scales Investigation, Task Orientation and Equity are independent predictors of individual students' attitude towards science class. The R^2 value, which indicates the proportion of variance in attitude towards science class that can be attributed to students' perception of classroom environment, was 19%.

Table 11.2. Associations between QTI & WIHIC Scales and Attitude to Science
Class in terms of Simple Correlations *(r)*, Multiple Correlations and
Standardized Regression Coefficient *(β)*

Scales of the QTI	*r*	*β*
Leadership	0.31**	0.15*
Helping/Friendly	0.31**	0.16*
Understanding	0.28**	0.02
Student Responsibility/Freedom	0.07**	0.02
Uncertain	-0.21**	-0.07
Dissatisfied	-0.24**	-0.07
Admonishing	-0.25**	-0.09
Strict	-0.00	0.00
Scales of WIHIC	*r*	*β*
Student Cohesiveness	0.17*	-0.03
Teacher Support	0.23*	0.04
Involvement	0.24*	0.01
Investigation	0.27*	0.10*
Task Orientation	0.38*	0.27*
Cooperation	0.23*	0.00
Equity	0.32*	0.15
Multiple Correlations for the QTI $R = 0.39**$ for the WIHIC $R = 0.43**$ $R^2 = 0.15$		$R^2 = 0.19$

$*p<0.01, **p<0.001$ n = 1,021

6.3 Associations between learning environment and gender of the student

Gender differences in students' perceptions of classroom learning
environment were examined by splitting the total number of students
involved in the study into male (440) and female (581). To examine the
gender differences in students' perceptions of the learning environment
in science classes, the within-class gender subgroup mean was chosen as
the unit of analysis which aims to eliminate the effect of class differences
due to males and females being unevenly distributed in the sample. In the
data analysis, male and female students' mean scores for each class were
computed. Table 11.3 shows the scale item means, male and female
differences, standard deviations, and t-values. The purpose of this
analysis was to establish whether there are significant differences in
perceptions of students according to their gender.

Table 11.3. Item Mean and Standard Deviation for Gender Differences in
Students' Perceptions of Teacher-Student Interaction Measured by
the QTI Scales

Scales of the QTI	Gender	Item Mean	Mean Diff (M-F)	Std. Dev.	t
Leadership	Males	4.02	0.3	0.71	6.93**
	Females	4.32		0.59	
Helping/ Friendly	Males	3.66	-0.19	0.75	4.05**
	Females	3.85		0.67	
Understanding	Males	3.85	-0.41	0.78	8.69**
	Females	4.26		0.65	
Student Freedom	Males	3.16	0.12	0.64	2.91*
	Females	3.04		0.65	
Uncertain	Males	2.70	0.47	0.76	10.23**
	Females	2.23		0.68	
Dissatisfied	Males	2.73	0.49	0.88	9.18**
	Females	2.24		0.77	
Admonishing	Males	2.89	0.55	0.76	12.11**
	Females	2.34		0.64	
Strict	Males	3.53	-0.01	0.68	0.29
	Females	3.54		0.68	
Scales of WIHIC	Gender	Item Mean	Mean Diff (M-F)	Std. Dev.	t
Student Cohesiveness	Males	4.13	-0.07	0.45	2.38*
	Females	4.20		0.48	
Teacher Support	Males	3.52	0.04	0.75	0.83
	Females	3.48		0.77	
Involvement	Males	3.44	0.07	0.69	1.6
	Females	3.37		0.69	
Investigation	Males	3.47	0.09	0.66	1.98
	Females	3.38		0.77	
Task Orientation	Males	4.13	-0.16	0.59	5.00**
	Females	4.31		0.50	
Cooperation	Males	3.83	-0.17	0.69	3.92**
	Females	4.00		0.65	
Equity	Males	3.85	-0.26	0.68	5.25**
	Females	4.11		0.67	

*p<0.05, **p<0.001   males (n = 440); females (n = 581)

Out of eight scales of the QTI, differences in the perceptions of males and females were found to be statistically significantly different on seven scales. According to the results, female students perceived more positively the leadership displayed and the helping friendly and understanding behaviours of their teachers. On the other hand, male students perceived that their teachers displayed more uncertain, admonishing and dissatisfied behaviours and were giving more student freedom.

Out of seven scales of WIHIC, four scales were found to have significant differences in male and female student perceptions. These scales are Student Cohesiveness, Investigation, Cooperation and Equity. Female students perceived student cohesiveness more positively, showing their regard for their fellow students and helping and receiving help whenever needed. It was also found that female students perceived task orientation more favourably than did their male counterparts. The female students perceived that it is important to complete planned activities and stay on the subject matter more than did the male students who participated in the survey.

As for the Cooperation scale, female students perceived that more cooperation existed among the students. Also, female students perceived more equity in the classroom. From these analyses, it is apparent that female students perceived their learning environment more favourably than did male students, particularly in terms of Student Cohesiveness, Task Orientation, Co-operation and Equity.

6.4 Associations between learning environment and cultural group of the student

Differences in the perceptions of students, on the basis of the cultural group they come from, also were examined. The cultural group of the students was established by determining the language spoken at home. Jammu city is understood to be a melting pot of various cultures, because of the migration from neighbouring provinces into the city, due to various political situations occurring over the past five to six decades. Four groups containing sufficient numbers were identified, namely, Hindi, Kashmiri, Dogri and Punjabi. These four groups constituted 98% of the sample.

To examine the cultural differences in students' perception of students, in the science classes, the within-class cultural subgroup mean was chosen as the unit of analysis which aims to eliminate the effect of class differences due to the strength of various groups being unevenly distributed in the sample. In the data analysis, mean scores for each of the four cultural groups were computed. Table 11.4 shows the scale item means and F values of the scales of the QTI and WIHIC with the perceptions of students from the four main cultural groups.

Table 11.4. Item Mean for Cultural Differences (Language Spoken at Home) in Students' Perceptions Measured by the QTI and WIHIC Scales

Scales of the QTI	Language spoken at home				F value
	Hindi	Kashmiri	Dogri	Punjabi	
Leadership	4.22	4.16	4.12	4.16	1.01
Helping/ Friendly	3.78	3.86	3.64	3.71	3.48**
Understanding	4.14	4.12	3.86	4.08	6.82**
Student Freedom	3.07	3.12	3.10	3.12	0.33
Uncertain	2.41	2.34	2.64	2.36	6.11**
Dissatisfied	2.46	2.26	2.61	2.51	5.93**
Admonishing	2.59	2.45	2.71	2.60	3.94**
Strict	3.60	3.41	3.50	3.50	4.27**

Scales of WIHIC	Language spoken at home				F value
	Hindi	Kashmiri	Dogri	Punjabi	
Student Cohesiveness	4.23	4.15	4.08	4.06	6.77**
Teacher Support	3.52	3.51	3.43	3.41	0.93
Involvement	3.38	3.41	3.39	3.43	0.20
Investigation	3.42	3.47	3.36	3.40	0.76
Task Orientation	4.24	4.37	4.07	4.19	10.03**
Cooperation	3.95	3.98	3.81	3.83	2.91**
Equity	4.04	4.15	3.77	3.89	9.57**

$**p < 0.001$ $n = 522$ $n = 221$ $n = 175$ $n = 82$

The differences in the perceptions of students of their science teachers on six of the eight QTI scales are statistically significant. The scales in which there were significant differences were Helping/Friendly, Understanding, Uncertain, Dissatisfied, Admonishing and Strict. Tukey's post hoc test ($p<0.05$) revealed that for the Helping/Friendly scale the Kashmiri group of students was dominant and had statistically significant higher means while the Dogri group of students had the lowest mean for the scales of Understanding and higher means for the scales of Admonishing, Dissatisfied and Strict.

Statistical analysis indicated that student perceptions on four scales out of seven of the WIHIC had statistically significant differences according to the students' cultural group. These were the scales of Student Cohesiveness, Task Orientation, Cooperation and Equity. Tukey's post hoc test ($p<0.05$) revealed that, the students coming from the Kashmiri group had significantly higher means on the Student Cohesiveness, Task Orientation, Cooperation and Equity scales. The Dogri group of students perceived their classroom environment least on Involvement and Investigation than did the other three groups involved in the study.

6.5 Associations between learning environment and religion of the student

Next, associations between learning environment on the basis of the religious faith of the students were examined. The students in this present study came from five different religious faiths, namely, Hindu, Sikh, Muslim, Christian, and Jain.

While examining the religious differences in the students' perception of teacher-student interaction in the science classes, the within-class subgroup mean was chosen as the unit of analysis. Table 11.5 shows the scale item means and F values of the scales of the QTI. For the scales of the QTI there is no association between the perceptions of the students and their religious faith. Not one scale of the QTI showed a statistically significant difference.

Similarly differences in perceptions of students about their existing classroom-learning environment were investigated with WIHIC in the similar manner as for the QTI. Again, none of the scales of the WIHIC showed any statistically significant difference in the perceptions of the students on the basis of their religious faith.

After analysing the perceptions of students on teacher-student interactions and classroom-learning environments, it may be concluded by the results of this study that religion does not have any effect on these perceptions in India.

Table 11.5. Item Means for Religious Differences in Students' Perceptions of
            Teacher-Student Interactions Measured by the QTI and WIHIC
            Scales

Scale of the QTI	Religion					F value
	Hindu	Sikh	Muslim	Christian	Jain	
Leadership	4.19	4.14	4.28	4.42	4.02	0.82
Helping/friendly	3.76	3.74	3.87	3.97	3.45	0.90
Understanding	4.08	4.07	4.11	4.46	4.02	0.94
Student Freedom	3.10	2.98	3.15	3.32	2.69	1.70
Uncertain	2.45	2.35	2.23	2.19	1.97	2.25
Dissatisfied	2.46	2.43	2.42	2.17	2.14	0.63
Admonishing	2.59	2.59	2.51	2.26	3.45	1.26
Strict	3.54	3.57	3.54	3.45	3.50	0.10

Scale of WIHIC	Religion					F value
	Hindu	Sikh	Muslim	Christian	Jain	
Student Cohesiveness	4.18	4.16	4.04	4.11	4.44	1.63
Teacher Support	3.50	3.42	3.39	3.75	3.21	1.10
Involvement	3.40	3.48	3.24	3.38	3.23	1.00
Investigation	3.44	3.47	3.25	3.09	3.12	1.80
Task orientation	4.23	4.27	4.28	4.19	4.37	0.28
Cooperation	3.93	3.85	3.90	3.98	4.08	0.37
Equity	3.99	3.93	3.90	4.52	4.10	1.81
	$n = 883$	$n = 69$	$n = 48$	$n = 14$	$n = 7$	

6.6 Associations between learning environment and the cognitive achievement of the students

Table 11.6 reports the simple correlation *(r)* and the standardised regression weight *(β)* between cognitive achievement (students') and each individual QTI and WIHIC scale when all other dimensions are controlled.

Statistically significant associations were found between cognitive achievement and scales of the QTI. The simple correlation *(r)* figures in the Table 11.6 indicate that there were four significant relationships *(p<0.05, p<0.01)* out of eight scales of the QTI. These associations were positive for the scale of Understanding and negative for the scales of Uncertain, Dissatisfied and Admonishing. In summary, cognitive achievement was higher where the teachers demonstrated more understanding behaviours and less uncertain, dissatisfied and admonishing behaviours. An examination of beta weights reveals that three of the eight scales retained their significance. The Understanding and Student Freedom scales were positively associated, whereas the Dissatisfied scale was negatively associated with the cognitive achievement of the students. The R^2 figure in suggests that 5% of the variance in student cognitive achievement can be attributed to teacher-student interpersonal behaviour.

Table 11.6. Associations between QTI Scales and Students Cognitive
Achievement in terms of Simple Correlations (r) and Standardised
Regression Coefficients (β)

Scales of the QTI	r	β
Leadership	-0.00	-0.01
Helping/Friendly	0.04	-0.03
Understanding	0.08*	0.09*
Student Resp/Freedom	0.03	0.08*
Uncertain	-0.06*	0.05
Dissatisfied	-0.17**	-0.20**
Admonishing	-0.10**	-0.06
Strict	-0.02	0.04
Scales of WIHIC	r	β
Student Cohesiveness	0.05*	-0.02
Teacher Support	0.00	-0.10
Involvement	0.12**	0.17**
Investigation	0.04	-0.07
Task Orientation	0.14**	0.14**
Cooperation	0.05*	-0.03
Equity	0.09*	0.05*
Multiple Correlations for the QTI $R = 0.21**$ for the WIHIC $R = 0.19**$		
$R^2 = 0.05$		$R^2 = 0.04$

$*p<0.05, **p<0.01$ n = 1,021

Statistically significant associations were found with cognitive achievement and the scales of the WIHIC. The simple correlation (r) figures in Table 11.6 indicate that there were five significant positive relationships ($p<0.05$, $p<0.01$) on the scales of Student Cohesiveness, Involvement, Task Orientation, Cooperation and Equity. The simple correlation for the scales of the WIHIC varies from 0.05 for the scale of

Student Cohesiveness and Cooperation to 0.14 for the scale of Task Orientation. Cognitive achievement was higher where the classroom-learning environment was promoting cohesiveness, involvement, task orientation, cooperation and equity.

An examination of the beta weights reveals that three out of seven significant relationships, Involvement, Task Orientation and Equity retained their significance. The R^2 figure in Table 11.6 suggests that 4% of the variance in student cognitive achievement is attributable to students' perceptions of their classroom learning environment.

7. Chapter Summary

The quantitative data reported in this chapter report on the validation of the QTI and WIHIC. Associations between attitudes and cognitive achievement with teacher-student interactions and the classroom-learning environment in India, and differences in gender, cultural background, and religious faith are also reported. The results suggest that student attitudes to class were better when teachers exhibited more leadership, helping/friendly and understanding behaviours in their classrooms and were less uncertain, dissatisfied and admonishing. As for the classroom learning environment all the seven scales of the WIHIC had positive associations, but students perceived more positively teacher support, involvement and investigation. Gender differences generally indicated that female students perceived their teachers in a more positive way than did male students. For the cultural background indicator variables, students from Kashmiri backgrounds perceived their teachers in a significantly more positive way than did those from the other cultural groups. Religious faith of the students did not reveal any significant differences in the perceptions of students. Though the associations for cognitive achievements were consistently smaller than those values for attitude to class, they displayed significantly positive associations for the scale of Understanding and negative associations for the scales of Uncertain, Dissatisfied and Admonishing in the QTI. The Student Cohesiveness, Involvement, Task Orientation and Equity scales of the WIHIC demonstrated positive associations with the cognitive achievement of the students.

Through the qualitative data an effort has been made to describe researcher's experiences and observations about the teacher-student interactions and science classroom learning environments in Jammu,

India. The descriptions of school and classroom life presented in the form of narrative were intended to portray a cultural archetype so that it would be easier for the reader to relate to the context of the study. Life at school was identified as the main factor leading to a set pattern of beliefs, values, expectations and norms in the society. The main themes identified from the interviews, field notes, and observations were: status of teacher; examination-dominated curriculum and political unrest in the city. Critical reflexivity during the study enabled the first author to probe deeper into the overall culture created (influence of different factors), giving richer insights and understanding. It is clear that the social, cultural and political environment in Jammu, has led to the present perception of the learning environment which is probably the best learning environment possible at that place under present circumstances.

References

Aldridge, J. M., Fraser, B. J., & Haung, T. (1999). Investigating classroom environments in Taiwan and Australia with multiple research methods. *Journal of Educational Research, 93*, 48-57.

Anderson, G. J. (1982). The search for school climate: a review of the research. *Review of educational research, 52*, 368-420.

Balasubramanian, D. (1998). *National Curriculum for Primary and Secondary Education. NCERT.* New Delhi, India.

Cronbach, D. J. (1951). Coefficient alpha and internal structure of tests. *Psychometrika, 16* (3), 297-334.

De Vellis, R. F. (1991). *Scale development: Theory and application.* Newbury park: Sage Publications.

Fisher, D. L., Henderson, D., & Fraser, B. J. (1995). Interpersonal behaviour in senior high school biology classes. *Research in Science Education, 25* (2), 125-133.

Fisher, D. L., Rickards, T., Goh, S. C., & Wong, A. F. L. (1997). Perceptions of interpersonal teacher behaviour in secondary science classrooms in Singapore and Australia. *Journal of Applied Research in Education, 1* (2), 2-11.

Fraser, B. J. (1986). *Classroom environment.* London: Croom Helm.

Fraser, B. J. (1991). Two decades of classroom environment research. In B. J. Fraser & H. J. Walberg (Eds.), *Educational environments: Evaluation, antecedents and consequences* (pp. 3-27). Oxford, England: Pergamon press.

Fraser, B. J. (1994). Research on classroom and school climate. In D. Gabel (Ed.), *Handbook of research on science teaching and learning* (pp. 493-541). New York: Macmillan.

Fraser, B. J. (1997). NARST's expansion, internationalisation and cross-nationalisation. *NARST, News,* pp. 3-4.

Fraser, B. J. (1998a). science learning environments: assessment, effects and determinants. In B. J. Fraser & K. G. Tobin (Eds.), *The international handbook of science education* (pp. 527-564). Dordrecht, The Netherlands: Kulwer Academic Publishers.

Fraser, B. J. (1998b). Classroom environment instruments: development, validity and applications. *Learning Environment Research, 1,* 7-33.

Fraser, B. J. (2002). Learning Environment Research: Yesterday, today and tomorrow. In S. C. Goh & M. S. Khine (Eds.), *Studies in Educational learning Environments.* Singapore: World Scientific.

Fraser, B. J., Fisher, D. L., & McRobbie, C. J. (1996, April). *Development, validation and use of personal and class forms of a new classroom environment instrument.* Paper presented at the annual meeting of the American Education Research Association, Chicago.

Fraser, B. J. & Tobin, K. (1991). Combining qualitative and quantitative methods in classroom environment research. In B. J. Fraser & H. J. Walberg (Eds.), *Educational environments: Evaluation, antecedents and consequences* (pp. 271-292). Oxford, England: Pergamon Press.

Fraser, B. J. & Tobin, K. G. E. (1998). *International handbook of science education.* Dordrecht: Kulwer.

Fraser, B. J. & Walberg, H. J. (1981). Psychosocial learning environment in science classrooms: A review of research. *Studies in Science Education, 8,* 67-92.

Fraser, B. J. & Walberg, H. J. (1991). *Educational environments: Evaluation, antecedents and consequences.* Oxford, England: Pergamon Press.

(INSA), I. N. S. A. (2001, 23rd March). Higher Education in India. *Indian Express.*

Khine, M. S. & Fisher, D. L. (2001, December). *Classroom environment and teacher's cultural background in secondary science classes in Asian context.* Paper presented at the International Educational Research Conference of Australian Association of Research in Education, Perth.

Kulkarni, V. G. (1988). Role of language in science education. In P. Fensham (Ed.), *Development and dilemmas in science education* (pp. 150-168). The Falmer Press.

Lewin, K. (1936). *Principals of topological psychology.* New York: McGraw.

Malhotra, P. L. (1988). National Policy on Education.: Department of Education in Science and Mathematics, NCERT, India.

McRobbie, C. J. & Fraser, B. J. (1993). Associations between student outcomes and psychosocial science environment. Journal of Educational Research, *87*, 78-85.

Newby, M. (1998). *A study of the effectiveness of the computer laboratory classes as learning environment.* Unpublished PhD thesis, Curtin University of Technology, Perth.

Riah, H. & Fraser, B. J. (1998, April). *The learning environment of high school chemistry classes.* Paper presented at the annual meeting of the National Association for Research in Science Teaching, San Diego.

Rickards, T. (1999). *The relationship of teacher-student interpersonal behaviour with student sex, cultural background and student outcomes.* Unpublished PhD thesis, Curtin University of Technology, Perth.

Stolarchuk, E. (1997). *An evaluation of the effectiveness of laptop computers in science classrooms.* Unpublished PhD thesis, Curtin University of Technology, Perth.

Taylor, P. C., Fraser, B. J., & Fisher, D. (1997). Monitoring constructivist classroom learning environments. *International Journal of Educational Research, 27* (4), 293-302.

Templeton, R. A. & Johnston, C. E. (1998). Making the school environment safe: Red Rose's formula. *Learning Environments Research, 1* (1), 35-77.

Walberg, H. J., Singh, R., & Rasher, S. P. (1977). Predictive validity of students' perceptions: A cross-cultural replication. *American Educational Research Journal, 14*, 45-49.

Wubbels, T., Creton, H. A., & Hooymayers, H. P. (1992). Review of research on teacher communication styles with use of the Leary model. *Journal of Classroom Interaction, 27* (1), 1-12.

Wubbels, T. & Levy, J. (1991). A comparison of interpersonal behaviour of Dutch and American teachers. *International Journal of Intercultural Relations, 15*, 1-18.

Wubbels, T. & Levy, J. E. (1993). *Do you know what you look like? Interpersonal relationships in education* (1st. ed.). London, England: The Falmer Press.

Chapter 12

CREATING A COLLABORATIVE LEARNING ENVIRONMENT IN A COMPUTER CLASSROOM IN THAILAND USING THE CLES

Supatra Wanpen
Rajabhat University Udon Thani
Thailand

Darrell L. Fisher
Curtin University of Technology
Australia

This chapter describes a case study of a tertiary computer classroom in the northeast region of Thailand. The Constructivist Learning Environment Survey (CLES) was used with a large sample of students to determine its reliability for use in Thailand, and then administered to a class of students taking a computer course to find out their perceptions of their preferred learning environments in order to compare this with their perceptions of the actual situation. The data were used to plan improvements in learning environments through a classroom action research process by reshaping lessons and instructions, and encouraging changes in students' classroom behaviours. Students' reflective journals, discussions and small group work were used as tools to encourage students' expression of critical opinions, cooperation and shared control in their learning. After the intervention, the CLES was re-administered and showed that there had indeed been an improvement.

1. Introduction

The constructivist view of learning has become a prominent feature of science education during the past decade (Treagust, Duit, & Fraser,

1996). It represents a paradigm shift from education based on behaviourism to education based on cognitive theory (Collay & Gagnon, 2000). Constructivist epistemology assumes that students learn on the basis of their interaction with their environment. The emphasis here is how we can create a learning environment to support constructivist learning. It has been widely accepted that learning environment can influence students' attitudes and learning outcomes. If students are to make sense from what they learn, it is important for their ideas to be heard and critiqued during classroom transactions, for them to share control of the classroom, and for the teacher to provide support for learning (Tobin & Fraser, 1998).

Teaching and learning in computing courses often has followed the traditional pattern of lecture and practice. Some learners might find that they can complete the different tasks given with little understanding of the underlying concepts; moreover, they are often seated in a computer classroom that has a unique physical setting that provides a specific kind of learning environment. Since learning environment is one of the factors affecting learning outcomes, it may influence the learners' construction of knowledge. Furthermore, in studying a computer course, practising in a computer laboratory is necessary, and there is a specific physical setting which causes a unique climate of learning that might affect the overall learning outcomes. Therefore, it is interesting to know what the actual learning environment is like in a computer classroom, if it is constructivist, and how it associates with learning outcomes.

Computer education in Thailand began in 1959 when IBM donated the first computer to the faculty of Accounting and Commerce at Chulalongkorn University. The earliest purpose of its use was to teach statistics to graduate engineering students for assisting their thesis studies (Homhuan & Malaivongs, 1999; Preeyanont, 2003). Computing-related degree programs offered since that time in Thailand can be classified into Computer Science, Computer Engineering, Computer in Business, and Management Information System or Information Technology (Preeyanont, 2003).

Since the arrival of the first computer in Thai education, IBM 1620, several hundred models have been launched and used in education both as tools for studying other subjects and as learning materials for its own discipline. Changes have occurred rapidly in both hardware and software. To catch up with this rapid change in knowledge and innovation in the field of computing, students need to be constructive and should be place in a constructivist-oriented learning environment that can support their learning. Thus the overall aim of this paper is to report action research results on how the *Constructivist Learning Environment Survey* (CLES) was used to improve the learning environment in a computer classroom in Thailand.

2. Purposes of the Study

The purposes of this study were to:

- investigate constructivist learning environments in a computer classroom in Thailand
- improve the learning environment by making it more constructive as well as more collaborative.

3. Background and Theoretical Framework

Learning environments have received attention from educators and researchers for decades. Since Lewin (Lewin, 1936) presented the symbolic function for human behaviour: $B = f(P, E)$ or human behaviour (B) is a function (f) of person (P) and environment (E) together, there have been a lot of developments regarding the learning environment (Moos, 1974; Murray, 1938; Stern, 1970; Walberg, 1981).

One of the first questionnaires used to assess the learning environment was the *Learning Environment Inventory* (LEI) which was developed in the late 1960s (Fraser, Anderson, & Walberg, 1982; Walberg & Anderson, 1968). Following the LEI, there have been developments of many questionnaires for measuring different aspects of learning environments.

In particular, the questionnaire called the *Constructivist Learning Environment Survey* (CLES) (Taylor, Dawson, & Fraser, 1995; Taylor & Fraser, 1991; Taylor, Fraser, & White, 1994) was developed to assist educators and researchers to measure students' perceptions of the extent to which constructivist approaches are presented in the classrooms learning environment. This was an important development since teachers and educators expect the construction of meaning to take place in the classroom.

The first version of the CLES was introduced in 1991 (Taylor & Fraser, 1991) and was consistent with von Glasersfeld's (von

Glasersfeld, 1981, 1988) perspective of *radical constructivism*. The first version of the CLES was designed to measure students' perceptions of the extent to which the classroom learning environment enabled them to reflect on their prior knowledge, develop as autonomous learners, and negotiate their understandings with other students. Socio-cultural aspects were added to the instrument in the development of the revised versions.

Revised versions of the CLES (Taylor et al., 1997; Taylor, Fraser & Fisher, 1997) were developed based on its original version (Taylor & Fraser, 1991) and the perspective of *critical constructivism* (Taylor & Campbell-Williams, 1993). These versions of the CLES were designed to measure five key dimensions of a *critical constructivist learning environment* from the students' perception. The five key elements emphasised are: the degree of relevance the students find between their studies and the world outside of school; the degree of empowerment they gain to express their concern about the teaching and learning; the degree to which they are invited to share control of the design, management, and evaluation of their learning; the degree of their engagement and interaction with each other to improve their understanding; and the extent to which science is viewed as ever changing (Taylor et al., 1995; Taylor et al, 1997).

The new versions of the CLES are available in two forms: the Actual and Preferred (Taylor et al., 1995). In addition to the Actual Form that measures the learning environment as perceived by students, the Preferred Form is concerned with goals and value orientations and measures perceptions of the classroom environment ideally liked or preferred (Fraser, 1998). The item wording of the Preferred Form is slightly changed from the Actual version, for instance, the use of phrases like "I wish". Each form contains 30 items altogether, with six items in each of the five scales. The response alternatives for each item are Almost Always, Often, Sometimes, Seldom, and Almost Never.

Importantly, for the present study, learning environment research which has adopted a person-environment fit perspective (Hunt, 1975) revealed that the similarity between the actual environment and that preferred by students leads to improved student achievement and attitudes (Fisher & Fraser, 1983; Fraser & Fisher, 1983a, 1983b) The practical implication of these findings for the present study is that attempting to change the actual classroom environment in ways that make it more congruent with that preferred by the students could enhance student achievement. The scales of the CLES are listed as follows (Taylor et al., 1997):

- Personal Relevance: focuses on how school science and students' out-of-school experiences are connected, and how students make use of their everyday experiences as a meaningful context for the development of their scientific and mathematical knowledge.

- Uncertainty: assesses the extent to which opportunities are provided for students to experience the inherent uncertainty and limitations of scientific knowledge as arising from theory-dependent inquiry involving human experience and values, and as evolving, non-foundational, and culturally and socially determined.

- Critical Voice: examines the extent to which a social climate has been established in which students feel that it is legitimate and beneficial to question the teacher's pedagogical plans and methods, and to express concerns about any impediments to their learning.

- Shared Control: concerned with students being invited to share with the teacher control of the learning environment, including the articulation of learning goals, the design and management of learning activities, and the determination and application of assessment criteria.

- Student Negotiation: assesses the extent to which opportunities exist for students to explain and justify to other students their newly developing ideas, to listen attentively and reflect on the viability of other students' ideas and, subsequently, to reflect self-critically on the viability of their own ideas.

The new CLES has been used in studies of high school science and mathematics classrooms (Dryden & Fraser, 1998; Taylor et al., 1994, 1995) and validated and used in various studies in different countries (Churach & Fisher, 1999; Stolarchuk & Fisher, 2001). The CLES has also been translated and modified to suit each specific situation for use in both English and non-English speaking countries, for example, the online version or the *Constructivist On-Line Learning Environment Survey* (Taylor & Maor, 2000), the versions providing the Comparative Student

(CLES-CS), the Comparative Teacher (CLES-CT) and Adult (CLES-A) Forms in evaluating university/filed trip program (Nix, Ledbetter, & Fraser, 2001), the Chinese version in the cross-national study in Taiwan and Australia (Aldridge, Fraser, Taylor, & Chen, 2000), the Korean version (Kim, Fisher, & Fraser, 1999) and the 25-item Korean version (Lee & Fraser, 2000). However, it has never been used to measure the learning environment at the tertiary level in Thailand.

4. Methods

Prior to the main study, the Actual and Preferred Forms of the CLES were translated into Thai using the back-translation technique (Brislin, 1983). They had also been slightly modified after the pretest to make them more suitable for the use in a computer class and the sociocultural context. The Thai versions of the student Actual and Preferred Forms of the CLES were administered to 366 students undertaking computer courses in Thailand to determine the reliability of the CLES for use in Thailand.

Following this check on the reliability of the CLES, the main study followed the fundamental steps of: assessment, feedback, reflection and discussion, intervention and reassessment (Fisher, 1986; Fraser, 1999)

In the assessment stage, the Actual and Preferred Forms of the CLES were administered to a class of 29 students undertaking a computer course emphasising on the use of applications, for example, spreadsheets and an authoring program. The administration of the CLES was scheduled for the third week of the semester.

The instructor/researcher generated feedback information from the student responses to the questionnaires. Profiles were constructed from the class mean scores. The differences represented in both profiles between the actual or perceived and the preferred learning environments were used to consider which aspects of the constructivist classroom environment needed to be changed in order to align the actual environment more closely with that preferred by the students.

The profiles were considered in the reflection and discussion stage by the instructor/researcher with peer colleagues in order to clarify and interpret the profiles. A classroom environment improvement plan was developed after a decision was reached on which learning environment scales to attempt to change. The implementation of strategies to bring about changes formed the intervention stage. As statistically significant differences existed on all scales of the CLES, all five aspects of the constructivist learning environment, namely, Personal Relevance, Uncertainty, Critical Voice, Shared Control, and Student Negotiation, were selected for improvement.

The intervention was introduced to the class in order that all participants would be aware and agree on attempts to improve each aspect of the learning environment. The intervention started in the fifth week of the semester and lasted for 10 weeks. At the end of the intervention, the Actual Form of the CLES was re-administered to determine whether the students perceived their actual environment differently. These reassessment results were used to indicate whether changes in the learning environment had been achieved.

5. Results

The data gathered from the 366 students in 15 classes in a college in the northeast of Thailand studying tertiary computer courses, first were analysed to determine the internal consistency of the Thai version of the CLES. The results are presented in Table 12.1.

Table 12.1. Internal Consistency (Cronbach Alpha Coefficient) for the Thai Versions of Actual and Preferred Forms of the CLES

Scale	Unit of Analysis	Alpha coefficient	
		Actual	Preferred
Personal Relevance	Individual	0.81	0.88
	Class Mean	0.87	0.90
Uncertainty	Individual	0.76	0.82
	Class Mean	0.90	0.88
Critical Voice	Individual	0.84	0.90
	Class Mean	0.91	0.87
Shared Control	Individual	0.91	0.93
	Class Mean	0.96	0.94
Student Negotiation	Individual	0.80	0.89
	Class Mean	0.77	0.93

With the individual student as the unit of analysis, the alpha reliability ranged from 0.76 to 0.91 for the Actual Form and from 0.82 to 0.93 for the Preferred Form. When the class mean were used as the unit of analysis, the alpha reliability ranged from 0.77 to 0.96 for the Actual

Form and from 0.88 to 0.94 for the Preferred Form. This suggests that all scales of the Thai version of the CLES possess satisfactory internal consistency in both the Actual and Preferred Forms.

6. The Case Study

Students' responses to the CLES from the assessment stage were used to generate feedback information. Class mean scores were used to create profiles as shown in Figure 12.1. The comparisons of mean scores for the Actual and Preferred Forms of the CLES were checked for statistical significance using paired sample t-tests on differences between student perceptions of the actual learning environment and that preferred by the students. The actual and preferred differences were significant for all of the scales of the CLES as shown in Table 12.2. The instructor/researcher discussed the result with colleagues, who taught the same subject and this resulted in a decision to attempt to increase the level on each dimension of the CLES.

Table 12.2. Mean Scores for the Actual and Preferred Forms of the CLES

| Scale | Mean | | Std. Deviation | | Mean Differences | t |
	Actual (A)	Preferred (P)	Actual (A)	Preferred (P)	(P-A)	
Personal Relevance	3.29	4.16	0.644	0.652	0.87	5.01**
Uncertainty	3.39	3.89	0.546	0.744	0.50	2.61*
Critical Voice	3.34	4.00	0.603	0.692	0.66	4.25**
Shared Control	2.25	3.70	0.654	0.812	1.45	8.65**
Student Negotiation	3.28	3.99	0.819	0.589	0.71	3.84**

$*p < 0.05, **p < 0.01$ n = 29

In introducing the intervention to the class, a discussion was arranged in which students could reflect on how computers affected their real world experiences and the nature of rapid change in the field of computing. This contributed to the intervention strategies on the Personal Relevance and Uncertainty scales. After the discussion, the instructor/researcher and the students agreed on attempts to improve this class's learning environment. The use of small group work was applied in addition to the individual tasks assigned as an overall intervention, especially, for the Student Negotiation aspect.

The students were encouraged to write reflective journals on lessons they had learned as a part of improving the Critical Voice aspect. The reflective journals were explained to the class as a means of recording events, results, reactions and as a means of providing feedbacks to instructor. Students were also encouraged to speak up in the class and give their opinions on how the lessons were taught as well as their suggestions to improve learning. This was also an attempt to improve the Shared Control aspect.

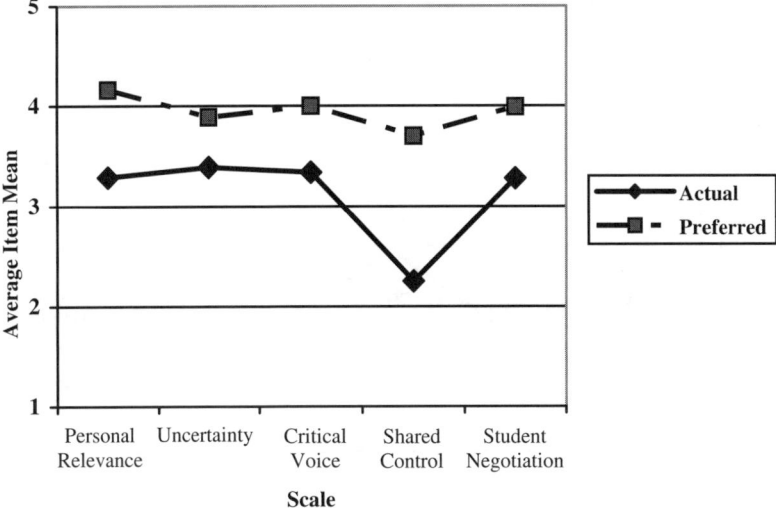

Figure 12.1. Differences between student perceptions of actual and preferred learning environment using the CLES.

Figures 12.2 illustrates the results of the reassessment at the end of the intervention stage while Table 12.3 confirms the changes of students' perceptions by using a t-test analysis for paired samples.

It was found out that students considered that their constructivist learning environment dramatically changed as they perceived their learning environment improved on all aspects (Table 12.3).

Table 12.3. Mean Scores for the Pretest and Posttest of the CLES

Scale	Mean		Std. Deviation		Mean Differences (Post-Pre)	t
	Actual (Pre)	Preferred (Post)	Actual (Pre)	Preferred (Post)		
Personal Relevance	3.29	3.91	0.644	0.366	0.62	4.38***
Uncertainty	3.39	3.92	0.546	0.487	0.53	3.43**
Critical Voice	3.34	3.74	0.603	0.594	0.40	2.71*
Shared Control	2.25	2.84	0.654	0.730	0.60	3.89***
Student Negotiation	3.28	3.89	0.819	0.601	0.60	3.07**

$*p < 0.05$, $**p < 0.01$, $***p < 0.001$ $n = 29$

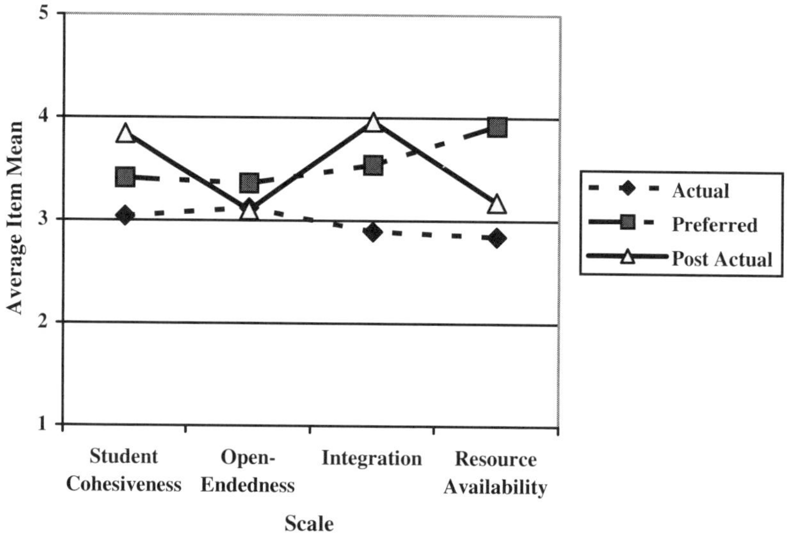

Figure 12.2. Pretest and posttest scores of student actual perceptions in comparison with their preferred learning environment using the CLES.

Qualitative results from student reflective journals added to the picture on how the students viewed their own learning and the learning environment on aspects that were not captured by using the questionnaires. It was interesting to note how students' journal comments reflected the quantitative results obtained from the CLES. Some interesting journal reflections were:

Some students keep repeating the same questions others have already asked. I don't understand why they do not pay attention when those questions were answered the first time. It's annoying. The instructor should be able to continue the lesson without wasting her time answering every question twice.

Everything has gone wrong today. I left my floppy disk in the laboratory last time and I saved those examples in that disk. It was gone and I can't remember anything. The instructor was captured by other classmates who always have problems. I asked a friend sitting next to me but she seemed to be too busy. I needed to wait for Tara* or Kattika*. I feel that only these two are not bored with me.

The instructor was speaking so fast that I couldn't take note on the part of using the motion function to move an object. I could take note of only half of the steps. If she weighs much on this part in the test, I will not be able get a high mark.

Sometimes when it comes to work within time limits, I could not make it. I know that I am quite slow and sometimes I do not understand the lecture and even the work sheet. I think it would help a lot if you slowed down your speed. If this annoys ones who are fast, what about saving all the demonstrations on the disks for me, or for others who might also need to repeat the lesson again and again?

The examples are reflections that could be related to the Student Negotiation and Critical Voice scales of the CLES. Apparently, the student reflective journals did assist in improving the critical voice aspect as there was a statistically significant improvement at the end of the intervention when the CLES was used to re-assess students' perceptions

---

* *Pseudonyms are used to substitute students' names to ensure confidentiality.*

of their actual learning environment. Comments and critiques on various aspects of teaching and learning were made in the journals although they were not obviously noticed during the classroom sessions. Student reflective journals are also good tools for the teacher to monitor how students learn and how they teach in order to improve their own teaching.

Additionally, the qualitative data also provided information on other aspects of learning environments that are not included in the CLES. For instance, some students complained about the condition of the mouse or the air-conditioning in the laboratory. Most of the complaints referred to the availability of the laboratory, in that it did not allow them to practice in their free time as often as they wished. However, all of them felt that they were encouraged to do the coursework with more effort than before, and although it was difficult, sometimes they found it was fun and useful to study this course.

7. Discussion and Conclusion

The results from this study suggest that the instructor was able to use the CLES to improve the learning environment of a computer class in Thailand. The students were involved in the intervention and they had more control of their own learning. Although small group work techniques were used, some reflections from the journals indicated that students were helpful to one another even when they were not involved in group work and this could be a good sign of the real cooperative situation in the classroom.

This study extended learning environment theories and instruments to a local context by paying emphasis on teaching and learning processes through a constructivist view in relation with learning environment in a computer classroom in Thailand. It provides implications for teaching practice in computer science area by focusing on computer classroom environments. The combination of qualitative and quantitative research methods led to a better understanding of a computer classroom and provides another alternative aiming to computer education studies in Thailand.

References

Aldridge, J. M., Fraser, B. J., Taylor, P. C., & Chen, C.-C. (2000). Constructivist learning environments in a cross-national study in Taiwan and Australia. *International Journal of Science Education, 22*, 37-55.

Brislin, R. W. (1983). Cross-cultural research in psychology. *Annual Review of Psychology, 34*, 363-400.

Churach, D. & Fisher, D. L. (1999). *Science kids surf the net: Effects on classroom environment.* Paper presented at the Western Australian Institute for Educational Research Forum 1999.

Collay, M. & Gagnon, G. W., Jr. *Constructivist learning design.* Retrieved 3 December, 2000, from http://www.prainbow.com/cld/cldp.html.

Dryden, M. & Fraser, B. J. (1998, April). *The impact of systemic reform efforts in promoting constructivist approaches in high school science.* Paper presented at the annual meeting of the American Educational Research Association, San Diego, C.A.

Fisher, D. L. (1986). *Changing the environment.* Retrieved 19 December, 2003, from http://www.scre.ac.uk/spotlight/spotlight2.html.

Fisher, D. L. & Fraser, B. J. (1983). A comparison of actual and preferred classroom environment as perceived by science teachers and students. *Journal of Research in Science Teaching, 20*, 55-61.

Fraser, B. J. (1998). Classroom environment instruments: Development, validity and applications. *Learning Environment Research: An International Journal, 1*, 7-33.

Fraser, B. J. (1999). Using learning environment assessments to improve classroom and school climates. In H. J. Freiberg (Ed.), *School climate: Measuring, improving and sustaining healthy learning environments* (pp. 65-83). London: Falmer Press.

Fraser, B. J., Anderson, G. J., & Walberg, H. J. (1982). *Assessment of learning environments: Manual for Learning Environment Inventory (LEI) and My Class Inventory (MCI).* Perth: Western Australian Institue of Technology.

Fraser, B. J. & Fisher, D. L. (1983a). Student achievement as a function of person-environment fit: A regression surface analysis. *British Journal of Educational Psychology, 53*, 89-99.

Fraser, B. J. & Fisher, D. L. (1983b). Development and validation of short forms of some instruments for measuring student perceptions of actual and preferred classroom environment. *Science Education, 67*, 115-131.

Homhuan, P. & Malaivongs, K. (1999). Survey on computer usage in educational institutes. *NECTEC Technical Journal, 1* (1), 2-10.

Hunt, D. E. (1975). Person-environment interaction: A challenge found wanting before it was tried. *Review of Educational Research, 45,* 209-230.

Kim, H., Fisher, D. L., & Fraser, B. J. (1999). Assessment and investigation of constructivist science learning environments in Korea. *Research in Science & Technological Education, 17* (2), 239-250.

Lee, S., & Fraser, B. J. (2000). *The constructivist learning environment of science classrooms in Korea.* Paper presented at the 31st Annual Conference of the Australasian Science Education Research Association, Fremantle.

Lewin, K. (1936). *Principles of topological psychology.* New York: McGraw-Hill.

Moos, R. H. (1974). Systems for the assessment and classification of human environments: An overview. In R. H. Moos & P. M. Insel (Eds.), *Issue in social ecology: Human milieus* (pp. 5-29). Palo Alto, CA: National Press Books.

Murray, H. A. (1938). *Explorations in personality.* New York: Oxford University Press.

Nix, R. K., Ledbetter, C. E., & Fraser, B. J. (2001). *A web (page) that works: What a concept (map)!* Paper presented at the annual meeting of the National Association for Research in Science Teaching, St. Louis, MO.

Preeyanont, S. (2003). *IT education in Thailand: Status, standard evaluation* (Internet). Bangkok: National Computer Software Training Center.

Stern, G. G. (1970). *People in context: Measuring person-environment congruence in education and industry.* New York: Wiley.

Stolarchuk, E. & Fisher, D. L. (2001). First years of laptops in science classrooms result in more learning about computers than science. *Issues In Educational Research, 11* (1), 25-39.

Taylor, P. C. & Campbell-Williams, M. (1993). Discourse towards balanced rationality in the high school mathematics classroom: Ideas from Habermas' critical theory. In J. Malone & P. C. Taylor (Eds.), *Proceedings of Topic Group 10 of the Seventh International*

Congress of Mathematics Educators (ICME-7): University of Quebec, Canada: Key Centre for School Science and Mathematics, Curtin University of Technology.

Taylor, P. C., Dawson, V., & Fraser, B. J. (1995, April). *A constructivist perspective on monitoring classroom learning environments under transformation.* Paper presented at the annual meeting of the American Educational Research Association, San Francisco, CA.

Taylor, P. C. & Fraser, B. J. (1991, April). *CLES: An instrument for assessing constructivist learning environment.* Paper presented at the Annual Meeting of the National Association for Research in Science Teaching (NARST), The Abbey, Fontane, Wisconsin.

Taylor, P., Fraser, B., & Fisher, D. (1997). Monitoring constructivist classroom learning environments, *International Journal of Educational Research, 27* (4), 293-302.

Taylor, P. C., Fraser, B. J., & White, L. R. (1994, April). *CLES:An instrument for monitoring the development of constructivist learning environments.* Paper presented at the annual meeting of the American Educational Research Association, New Orleans.

Taylor, P. C. & Maor, D. (2000, February). *Assessing the efficacy of online teaching with the Constructivist On-line Learning Environment Survey.* Paper presented at the 9th Annual Teaching Learning Forum, Perth: Curtin University of Technology.

Tobin, K. G. & Fraser, B. J. (1998). Qualitative and quantitative landscapes of classroom learning environments. In B. J. Fraser & K. G. Tobin (Eds.), *International handbook of science education* (pp. 623-640). Dordrecht, The Netherlands: Kluwer Academic Publishers.

Treagust, D. F., Duit, R., & Fraser, B. J. (1996). Overview: Research on students' preconceptual conceptions - The driving force for improving teaching and learning in science and mathematics. In D. F. Treagust, R. Duit, & B. J. Fraser (Eds.), *Improving teaching and learning in science and mathematics* (pp. 1-14). New York: Teacher College Press.

von Glasersfeld, E. (1981). The concepts of adaption and viability in a radical constructivist theory of knowledge. In I. E. Sigel, D. M. Brodinsky, & R. M. Golinkoff (Eds.), *New directions in Piagetian theory and practice.* New Jersey: Lawrence Erlbaum Associates.

von Glasersfeld, E. (1988). The reluctance to change a way of thinking. *The Irish Journal of Pyschology, 9* (1), 83-90.

Walberg, H. J. (1981). A psychological theory of educational productivity. In F. Farley & N. Gordon (Eds.), *Psychology and Education*. Berkeley, CA: McCutchan.

Walberg, H. J. & Anderson, G. J. (1968). Classroom climate and individual learning. *Journal of Educational Psychology, 59*, 414-419.

Chapter 13

BECOMING MORE EFFICIENT: ONE COLLEGE'S USE OF THE SLEQ

R. Anstine-Templeton
Marshall University
USA

Celia E. Johnson
Hwa Lee
Bradley University
USA

Guofang Wan
Ohio University
USA

Researchers conducting this study set out to investigate the factors that professional staff, faculty, and administrators in the College of Education and Human Services (COEHS) at Lake State University (LSU) described as conducive to an improved college (working, teaching and learning) environment. Participants completed the School-Level Environment Questionnaire (Fisher & Fraser, 1990). Results indicated that improvement was needed in the areas of Work Pressure, Professional Interest, and Resource Adequacy. Qualitative results pointed to the lack of personnel, increased student enrolment, and doing more with less, as the major cause of work pressure. Professional Interest and Resource Adequacy were interrelated in that individuals felt that the lack of human resources resulted in a situation where people did not have time to communicate with each other. A College Improvement Committee (CIC) was formed to examine the results, create and implement an action plan, and assess the progress.

1. Introduction

Higher education is definitely changing. Currently, high costs which lead to a flat or decreased enrolment, the movement for outcome-based assessment of student learning, and advanced technologies are influencing the calls from key sections of society for reform at the university level (Guskin & Marcy, 2002). In addition, post secondary institutions are under public and political pressure to demonstrate productivity and accountability (Garcia & Floyd, 2002). For now, individuals—faculty, professional staff, and administrators—are still creating effective models for teaching, learning, student engagement, integrating technologies, while at the same time, holding at bay the desperate financial circumstances (Guskin & Marcy, 2003). However, how much longer can this continue?

2. Purpose

Researchers conducting this pilot study set out to investigate the factors that professional staff, faculty, and administrators in the College of Education and Human Services (COEHS) at Lake State University (LSU) described as conducive to an improved college (working, teaching, and learning) environment. LSU, like many institutions of higher education, is plagued with diminished funding, a minimal increase in student enrollment, and a costly demand for technologically-infused, innovative programs. Therefore, the objective of this research project was to compare what COEHS personnel believed were important factors in developing a productive, positive, and innovative college environment with their actual school environment.

3. Perspectives

Many institutions believe the grave financial situation is short term and adopt a "let's tighten our belts" mode of operation—which involves keeping the status quo and not filling positions that become vacant. Guskin and Marcy (2003) label this approach to fiscal management as "muddling through" (p. 13) and warn that increasing faculty workloads, decreasing tenure-track positions, raising tuition, and increasing enrolment, will eventually mean that academic offerings will become less challenging and the quality of teaching and learning will be diminished.

To add to the present funding crisis, future projected demographics suggest that the student population in higher education (during the next decade) will decline further, become older, and be more diverse (Murdock & Hoque, 1999). Therefore, what is offered and how it is delivered will have to change to fit the needs of a different student population. Unless change is embraced, many colleges and universities, both public and private, will not be able to continue operating. However, this does not mean the demand for post-secondary, high skill education is decreasing. On the contrary, students completing degrees successfully will continue to be in demand for the current and future job markets (Gladieux & Swail, 2000). With the continued demand for degreed individuals and the need for organizational reform to survive, what might this structural change in higher education look like?

Current literature (Guskin & Marcy, 2003; Lovett, 2004; Schmidt, 1998; Schmitz, Baber, & John, 2003; Williams June, 2002; W.K. Kellogg Foundation, 2000) gives models for restructuring higher education to ensure its viable future. Along with some unique, model-specific characteristics, these change models have many similar components. These similarities include a focus on student learning rather than faculty teaching, transforming the delivery of learning and restructuring organizational systems.

First, to switch the focus from teaching to learning, institution-wide, common student learning outcomes must be established (Guskin & Marcy, 2003). With the focus on student learning, gone is the passive view of education, where students' traditional classroom responsibility is to sit, listen, and receive information from faculty members. "Students are expected to engage each other and their professors actively in a dynamic learning environment where discovery, the creation of meaning from new knowledge, and cooperative learning are valued" (W.K. Kellogg Foundation, 2000, p. 19). When students view themselves as both learner and teacher, they will contribute to the learning environment and understand the need to guide their own learning.

When teaching and learning become reciprocal and learning needs of students change, the traditional delivery of learning must be restructured. Faculty members need to become partners with not only students, but other campus and community professionals. Then, students will be able to participate in and contribute to a variety of instructional activities such as learning communities, experiential service learning, intensive residencies, accelerated learning formats, technology-infused study, and learning outside the classroom. With this experience, graduates will enter the work force fully prepared to be team players. With such a model, the focus is on learning productivity through the assessment of student learning outcomes, regardless of how or where learning occurs (Cox, 2001; Guskin & Marcy, 2003)

If learning and the delivery of instruction is reorganized to become more student-centred and vision-focused, then administrative leaders in institutions of higher education (IHE) must make changes in budgeting, services, and infrastructure or run the risk of spending more revenue than they generate. First, the budget allocation process must be examined. Guskin and Marcy (2003) recommend using a zero-based budgeting model, rather than the traditional incremental budgeting system, where administrators may have a tendency to keep account balances hidden and hoard resources. Second, student services and academic programs must be reviewed. To ensure a viable future, only those services and academic programs that promote the IHE's vision should be maintained (Diamond, 2002; Stetson Clarke, 2002). There is no room for duplication of services and across programs. Third, as the institution begins to transform, it will need an investment in infrastructures that support the change (Guskin & Marcy, 2003). For example, the most current technologies will be needed to support new types of students and instructional delivery systems (Hannum, 2002). Additionally, faculty will need new pedagogical skills and require professional development. Those institutions that invest in faculty and staff development will get a large return on their investment (Svinicki, 2002). Those who do not run the risk of losing students because of antiquated course work and dated program requirements.

As change begins to occur, administrators can play a key role by modeling "self-awareness, authenticity, empathy, commitment, competence, and professionalism in their daily interactions with [professional staff], students, [faculty], and colleagues" (W.K. Kellogg Foundation, 2000, p. 34). Student affairs and professional staff can play a vital role "in transforming the educational and organizational culture of their institutions" (W.K. Kellogg Foundation, 2000, p. 50) because they focus on both the students' curricular and co-curricular lives to develop a whole student perspective. With this comprehensive perception of students, professional staff can encourage students to make good choices and therefore increase their chances of completing a degree. Finally, in the promotion of change, the most vital role belongs to faculty members, who have the most in-depth interactions with students. Students have to believe that their teachers care about their success and will advise them to make appropriate career choices.

4. Methods

As advocated by Tobin and Fraser (1998) and others (Anstine Templeton & Jensen, 1993; Anstine Templeton & Johnson, 1998; Johnson & Anstine Templeton, 1999) researchers used both qualitative and quantitative methodologies to assess the learning environment.

4.1 Quantitative research

Individuals in the College of Education and Human Services completed the *School-Level Environment Questionnaire* (SLEQ) developed by Darrell Fisher and Barry Fraser (1990). Based partially on Rudolph H. Moos' work (1991) in various work environments, the SLEQ is designed to correspond to Moos's three psychosocial dimensions of Relationship, Personal Development, and System Maintenance/System Change by using eight subscales. The SLEQ has two scales (Student Support and Affiliation) that measure Relationship Dimensions, one scale (Professional Interest) that measures Personal Development, and five scales (Staff Freedom, Participatory Decision Making, Innovation, Resource Adequacy, and Work Pressure) that measure System Maintenance/System Change. The 56 items on each form (actual and preferred) have a five-point response format. Scoring for 29 of the 56 items is reversed. Responses range from Strongly Agree to Strongly Disagree. Reliability and validity have been established with three samples from Australian schools (Fisher & Fraser, 1990).

Questions in the SLEQ were updated and/or revised slightly to more appropriately fit higher education. For example, Questions 23, 39, and 55 where updated to reflect current availability of multimedia and technology. To illustrate further, from the Preferred Form, question 55, "Projectors and filmstrips, transparencies and films are usually available when needed" became "LCD projectors and computer equipment are usually available when needed." To highlight a slight revision, for professional staff, question three from the SLEQ Actual Form, "Teachers frequently discuss teaching methods and strategies with each other" became "Professional staff frequently discusses working methods and strategies with each other." Overall, the changes were minor and did not change the meaning of the questions. Table 13.1 clarifies the meaning of the eight scales by providing scale descriptions and sample items. Questionnaires were distributed to 55 COEHS professional staff, faculty, and administrators, with an 80% response rate. Once questionnaires were returned, aggregated scores were figured, averages were calculated, differences between actual and preferred scores were determined, and profiles were developed.

4.2 Qualitative research

To supplement the SLEQ data results and help answer questions that surfaced while analyzing the data, a qualitative research methodology similar to that employed by Erickson (1986, 1998) was also used in this study. Information was gathered by formal and informal interviews with professional staff, faculty and administrators; plus, an examination of curriculum materials, professional work and projects, photographs, portfolios, and newspaper articles, etc. was conducted. Data gathered were analyzed and used to form general themes. These broad themes were supported and/or refuted, as well as defined and redefined, through further collection of information.

4.3 Data source

Four university professors working at medium-sized comprehensive Midwestern universities conducted this study. Researchers teamed with individuals working in Lake State University's (LSU) College of Education and Human Services (COEHS), which had approximately 22 professional staff, 32 tenured or tenure-track faculty and six administrators. COEHS individuals completed the SLEQ, at the beginning of the 2003-2004 academic year.

LSU is located in a blue-collar community of approximately 14,000 people, whose incomes range from the lower to middle socioeconomic level. The University serves approximately 12,000 students on a main campus and four satellite campuses. The COEHS comprised of two offices: Student Academic Affairs Office (SAA), Dean's Office (DO) and four departments: School of Education (SOE), School of Criminal Justice (CJ), Television and Digital Media Production (TDMP), and Leisure Studies and Wellness (LSW). The College offers the majority of its programs on the main campus but also delivers curricula at five off-campus sites.

Table 13.1. Description of Scales in the SLEQ

Name of Scale	Description of Scales	Sample Item
Student Support	There is good rapport between faculty and students and students behave in a responsible self-disciplined manner.	Most students are helpful and cooperative. (+)
Affiliation	Faculty can obtain assistance, advice and encouragement and are made to feel accepted by colleagues.	I feel accepted by other faculty. (+)
Professional Interest	Faculty members discuss professional matters, show interest in their work and seek further professional development.	Faculty members avoid talking with each other about teaching and learning. (-)
Staff Freedom	Faculty are free of set rules, guidelines and procedures, and to supervise them to ensure rule compliance.	I am not expected to conform to a particular teaching style. (+)
Participatory Decision Making	Faculty members have the opportunity to participate in decision-making.	I have to refer even small matters to a senior member of administration for a final answer. (-)
Innovation	The school is in favor of planned change, experimentation, classroom openness, and individualization.	Faculty members are encouraged to be innovative in this college. (+)
Resource Adequacy	Support personnel, facilities, finance, equipment and resources are suitable and adequate.	The supply of equipment and resources is inadequate. (-)
Work Pressure	The extent to which work pressure dominates the school environment.	Faculty members have to work long hours to complete all their work. (+)

Items marked with a (+) are scored 5, 4, 3, 2, and 1, respectively for the responses Strongly Agree, Agree, Neither Agree nor Disagree, Disagree, and Strongly Disagree. Items designated (-) are scored in the reverse manner. Omitted or invalid responses are scored 3. Darrell Fisher & Barry Fraser developed the School-Level Environment Questionnaire.

5. Findings from Using Quantitative Methods

SLEQ results were analyzed and shared with stakeholders during a college-wide meeting. A discussion followed and individuals were encouraged to volunteer for interviews to help shed light on the questionnaires results. The total group decided to wait to see the results of the interviews, before forming a team or task force to create a plan of improvement to be implemented in the 2004-2005 academic year.

Table 13.2, shows the mean, standard deviation, and t-test results obtained for the actual and preferred form of each SLEQ scale. Results of t-tests show statistically significant differences between actual and preferred scores for all scales except for two areas (Staff Freedom and Innovation), where the significance is low even though the mean difference for "Innovation" was high. Composite mean scores are depicted graphically in Figure 13.1. These profiles highlight that there were sizable differences between actual and preferred forms for Work Pressure (inverted scale), Resource Adequacy, and Professional Interest. The scales with the smallest differences between the actual and preferred composite mean scores were Staff Freedom and Participatory Decision Making.

Table 13.2. Differences between Scores on Actual and Preferred Versions of SLEQ

Scale	Means		SD		t
	Actual	Preferred	Actual	Preferred	
Student Support	3.93	4.52	0.41	0.46	7.71*
Affiliation	3.66	4.37	0.66	0.55	-5.80*
Professional Interest	3.40	4.41	0.58	0.47	-8.55*
Staff Freedom	3.00	3.31	0.71	0.64	-2.52
Participatory Decision Making	3.20	4.03	0.92	0.72	-4.93*
Innovation	3.25	4.14	0.57	5.59	-8.20
Resource Adequacy	3.40	4.50	0.49	0.48	-9.60*
Work Pressure	3.67	2.50	0.76	0.46	9.07*

*$p<0.05$

As shown in Figure 13.1, there was a significant mean difference between the preferred and actual ratings of the Work Pressure subscale. This is an indication that COEHS personnel believed work pressure dominated their school environment. What was causing this work pressure? Was it institutional or self-pressure? Was the work pressure college specific or do most colleges experience these working conditions?

Resource Adequacy was another area of concern for COEHS personnel. This subscale which means personnel are not satisfied with existing support personnel, facilities, finance, equipment, and possibly other resources. However, exactly what did personnel feel they needed? Did the lack of resources interfere with their teaching, working, or administrative duties in the COEHS?

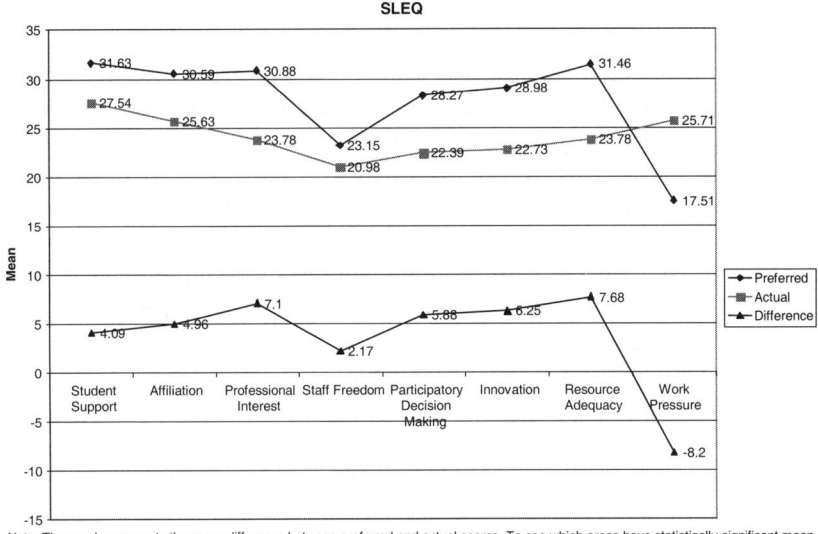

Note: The graph represents the mean difference between preferred and actual scores. To see which areas have statistically significant mean differences, T-Test analysis is needed.

Figure 13.1. Mean differences between preferred and actual scores.

Finally, Figure 13.1 shows a discrepancy between the actual and preferred subscale (composite mean score) of Professional Interest. So, the third area of significant concern for this group of individuals was their ability to discuss professional matters, show interest in their work, and seek further professional development. Did COEHS people want more time to discuss professional issues? Did they feel deprived of the opportunity for professional development? What circumstances were preventing them from remaining interested and motivated in their work?

To answer the above questions, individuals in the COEHS were asked to volunteer for formal and informal interviews. The results of these interviews are reported below in the qualitative section.

6. Findings from Using Qualitative Methods

Questions that surfaced from the SLEQ results were shared at a college-wide meeting (January 22, 2004) when the questionnaire results were discussed. Individuals were asked to volunteer for a face-to face interview, with one of the co-researchers outside their college and university. After this meeting, a college wide memo was emailed to individuals asking for interview volunteers. One week later, only three people (5%) had volunteered and most of those individuals were from the School of Education (SOE).

After discussing the situation with co-researchers, it was decided that telephone rather than face-to-face interviews should be offered to COEHS people, with a guarantee that all names would be removed from transcribed notes prior to sending them to LSU, for further analysis. A second college-wide email was sent detailing that interviews would be done by telephone, how confidentiality would be maintained, and asking for volunteers. Eleven more persons agreed to be interviewed, which brought the total to 14 or 34%. All areas (SOE, CJ, TDMP, LSW, SAA, and DO) were represented.

Interview questions (See Appendix 1) were developed using the results of the SLEQ questionnaire. To maintain consistency, interviewers were asked to define the subscales of Work Pressure, Resource Adequacy, and Professional Interest for interviewees. Also, having interviewers use similar language when asking identical questions preserved reliability.

Interview volunteers were asked to sign a form of consent to be interviewed. The form solicited interviewee consent to be interviewed using hand recorded notes and a tape recorder (See Appendix 2). If interviewees were not willing to have their responses recorded, then the interviewer would tell them their responses would be written only, checking for accuracy as the interview proceeded.

Themes that surfaced from the interviews are highlighted and discussed in Table 13.3, Barriers to Having a Positive College Environment and Table 13.5, Strategies to Improve the College Environment.

6.1 Barriers to having a positive college environment

Collectively, individuals in the COEHS believed they experienced excessive work pressure because of the lack of staff and faculty. One respondent notes: *"I think it [Work Pressure] comes from lack of resources, especially not having enough faculty members who can teach courses. Some people get overloaded with courses and others are not."* For faculty this meant that many had to teach more than the standard 12 hours to keep their programs running effectively and students graduating according to their academic plans or in a timely fashion.

Table 13.3. Barriers to Having a Positive College Environment

Categories	Themes	Sample Statements
Work Pressure (n=9/64%)	lack of staff and faculty, increasing enrollment, doing more with less, lack of communication	Work pressure comes from not having enough faculty to teach, so some get overloaded. Rapid growth, of course, which goes with the shortage of fulltime staffing. Another factor, major concern, is that fewer people now do more work.
Resource Adequacy (n=12/86%)	lack of faculty to teach, lack of support staff, lack of communication	I think we need definitely more support personnel. Someone to help with advisees and student teaching placement. I could use four-fulltime faculty to take care of my workload.
Career Interest & Professional Development	no problems in this area (n=7/50%) no time (n=4/29%) no funding (n=4/29%)	I don't find that a concern because my research has been well supported and conferences that I've wanted to attend have been well supported. The workload is such that it makes it difficult to get away to do those sorts of things. PD has been somewhat limited in terms of travel because of lack of funding

Table 13.4 shows the workload for faculty members in one department. Interestingly, for all five years listed below, some faculty members (2 to 9) had to teach an overload. The highest percentage (82%) of faculty members taught an overload in the Winter Semester 2004. According to projections for Fall Semester 2004, approximately another 60 hours of course work will have to be taught by adjunct instructors.

Teaching loads in the other departments within the College looked similar, if not more overloaded. The two smaller departments had all fulltime faculty members teaching workloads of 13 to 16 hours. This situation of additional teaching added to an already hectic schedule of teaching, service, and scholarly work and caused many faculty members to adopt survival strategies, such as not communicating with colleagues, students, staff, or administrators. Rapid growth or increase enrollment also added to personnel's work pressure because they had to continue to do more with similar or less resources. One individual highlights his or her concern: *"Another factor, a major concern, is that fewer people now do more work. When is it going to end?"*

Table 13.4. COEHS Faculty Workload for One Department

Semester	Number of Fulltime Faculty Members	Number of Faculty Members Teaching an Overload (>12 H)	Number of Hours Taught
Winter 2000	9	7 (78%)	13 to 15
Fall 2000	10	2 (20%)	13 to 17
Winter 2001	11	5 (45%)	13 to 15
Fall 2001	9	3 (33%)	13 to 15
Winter 2002	10	6 (60%)	13 to 15
Fall 2002	11	4 (36%)	15 to 16
Winter 2003	11	8 (73%)	15 to 16
Fall 2003	9 (1 Sabbatical)	7 (78%)	15 to 16
Winter 2004	11 (1 Sabbatical)	9 (82%)	13 to 16
Fall 2004 (Projected)	10 (1 Sabbatical) (1 full release)	7 (70%)	15 to 16

A second barrier to a positive COEHS environment and intimately connected to work pressure was adequacy of resources or more specifically, the lack of human resources. As some of the departments within the College experienced rapid student enrollment increases, no new support staff or faculty members were hired to handle the growth. Additionally, in the smaller departments, when faculty members retired, it was decided not to hire tenure-track replacements but to use part-time, adjunct instructors. Why?

One person explains his or her view:

It's coming from our growth and not enough staff—inadequate support staff for the growth of our college. I work with money and see everything, so I know where it comes from. It's not coming from somebody hiding money and not offering to get assistance or filling positions.

To further illustrate the grave situation developing in the COEHS, one respondent sums-up the situation succinctly: He or she states:

I could use four fulltime faculty [members] to take care of my workload here . . . . I would say, at this point, I don't expect those needs to be met right now. There is no time for planning, to look at where you are and where you want to be. There is definitely no time to talk with other departments or even students.

The third perceived hindrance to a positive college environment (according to the SLEQ results) was professional interest, which is defined as: individuals discuss professional matters, show interest in their work, and seek further professional development. Interview results for this area surprised researchers because 50% of those interviewed stated that they had no problems in this area. For example one interviewee stated:

And that one mystifies me. I find that very good here. Everything I've been interested with, I have been supported by administration. I have other faculty I could chat with. I don't see that as a concern from my experience base at all.

Others noted that professional development has been limited in recent years due to lack of funding for travel. Still others related the lack of professional interest and development to the lack of time. One person commented on time as a lacking resource. He or she said:

> *I don't see an attitude of openness and saying let's discuss this*
> *partly because of that work pressure and not having time. . .*
> *There needs to be time to have professional development*
> *seminars right in our College. Time to have lunch discussions*
> *right in our College. Time to have afternoon discussions or*
> *speakers in and things like that can work both college-wide and*
> *department-wide.*

Individuals freely discussed the impediments to having a positive College environment and were more than willing to make suggestions to improve the existing environment. Those improvement strategies will be discussed in the following section.

6.2 Strategies to improve the college environment

In the area of how to decrease work pressure, people (57% of those interviewed) stated that more personnel should be hired to teach and provide support services. Some individuals said that work pressure could further be reduced by collaborating more and taking time to communicate and build teams to work together.

Another improvement strategy that respondents (86% of those interviewed) felt was a primary resource need for their College was more faculty and support staff. One person highlighted the need for staff and faculty. He or she said:

> *"We do have an on-going need to keep our data up-to-date*
> *[support staff], but we also have the need to have sufficient*
> *number of faculty members to teach our students."*

A final improvement strategy that surfaced was a desire for more collaboration, cooperation, communication and team building. Illustrating this belief, one interviewee stated:

> *Well, we have to remember to all stick together as a team. And*
> *when there are struggles for personnel, struggles for resources, I*
> *see competition between units within our own College. So I think*
> *we need to be more team oriented and think about the good of*

*the College, instead of somebody's particular unit. We need to
inform each other.*

Table 13.5 Strategies to Improve the College Environment

Categories	Themes	Sample Statements
Decrease Work Pressure (n=8/57%)	hire more people to teach and do support service, collaborate and team building	Hire enough faculty to match the number of students. Lobbying for more support staff would help. We could set goals and change them with group decision.
Resources (n=12/86%)	hire more support people to help, more faculty to teach	I would see it as having more support staff. The biggest one that I would prioritize is faculty need.
Collaboration (n=5/38%)	decide together, more cooperation, collaboration, communication and team building, less micro-managing	We decide together what are goals are going to be and work toward it. We have to remember we have to stick together as a team. We have some embedded layers of micro-management that need to be examined.

7. Results of the Study

Results of the SLEQ indicated that professional staff, faculty and administrators believed improvement was needed in the areas of Work Pressure, Resource Adequacy, and Professional Interest. Using the SLEQ results as a guide, researchers developed a set of interview questions and asked for volunteers to do telephone interviews. Qualitative results point to the lack of personnel, increased student enrollment, and doing more with less, as the major cause of work pressure. Professional Interest and Resource Adequacy are interrelated in that some individuals felt that the lack of human resources, time and funding resulted in a situation where people did not talk to each other about career interests, do research and prepare presentations, or take time for professional development and conferences. Looking at the area of professional interest more closely, 50% of those interviewed stated that they had no concerns is this area. However, these same individuals willingly shared that professional interest might be an issue to others because of faculty overloads, advising, and lack of support services. One person gave his or her opinion on why 50% of faculty members are concerned about professional interest and the others are not. He or she said:

> *The only thing I could think of in terms of other colleagues is there is a chiasm between newer faculty and older faculty here. It is clear to me that a small number of older faculty [members] have no desire to be professionally interested. Anything that remotely smacks of more work; anything new is not what they are interested in, as they get one foot out the door on retirement. But for the newer faculty, I don't see anybody having any problem talking to other people generating interest or finding administrative support for it.*

The next steps for this research project in the 2004-2005 academic year involved having conversations, forming a committee, creating action plan, implementing those strategies, and assessing progress. The following section outlines the progress that was made in the College of Education of Human Services.

7.1 Becoming a more efficient college

The College Improvement Committee (CIC) was formed with 13 members representing professional staff, faculty, and administrators. The first three meetings were spent examining the results of study and determining in what ways the COEHS could improve its efficiency. The CIC determined it did not want to spend time focusing on issues (needing more tenure track faculty rather than adjuncts, fulltime staff rather than part time staff, or interim administrators rather than permanent leaders) that would be out of their authority to negotiate as the way to college improvement. Therefore, the question was, "What can we do here-and-now, based on our results, to improve our college from all levels?" After much discussion, improving communication at all levels to increase the college's effectiveness surfaced as the theme the committee would use to create an action plan.

Next, the committee spent time brainstorming ways to improve communication. It was determined that improved communication was needed between all departments, SAA, and the Dean's Office, faculty members and students, and students within the same college. The action plan that was created had several components. First, to improve communication between the Dean's Office and the departments, it was determined that the Dean of the COEHS should oversee the development of a monthly newsletter. The newsletter would contain updates from each of the departments, the Dean's Office, and inform individuals of important university issues, results of Dean's Council and department heads' meetings.

Students serving on the Dean's Student Advisory Committee (SAC) were asked to join the CIC members to determine how communication could be improved among students and faculty members and between students themselves. Students discovered that responsibilities they wanted to enforce upon faculty members were in violation of the faculty's union contract. So, instead of trying to impose more office hours, midterm grade reports, and more detailed syllabi, the SAC and CIC settled upon organizing "meet your professor night" each semester. To increase communication among students, the SAC decided to develop a COEHS student newsletter. Finally, the CIC and SAC determined that a year-end college-wide celebration held prior to graduation would bring individuals in the COEHS together and give them a sense of pride in their College. The event would be called the Annual COEHS Appreciation Day.

Each of these activities were implemented in the 2004-2005 academic year and deemed a great success through word-of-mouth, emails, and thank you notes. The Dean's newsletter continues, with the July issue being published shortly. The rest of the activities (student newsletter, meet your professor night, and annual appreciation day) will begin once the fall semester begins at the end of August. In September, the faculty, staff, and administration will assess the level of improvement in communication throughout the COEHS.

7.2 Discussion and educational importance of study

LSU needs to attend to what research notes and this study illuminates: that "muddling through" (Guskin and Marcy, 2003, p. 13) is a dangerous mode of behavior for an IHE who wants to ensure a strong and viable future. More specifically, the COEHS needs to look at the practices of raising enrollment, decreasing or maintaining existing tenure track positions, and increasing faculty workloads. These practices, as noted in the SLEQ results and highlighted in the interviews, caused personnel within the College to experience unnecessary work pressure, lack of time for communication or professional development and inadequate resources (mainly human resources).

Even though, the faculty, professional staff, and administration within the COEHS desire change and spent the academic year improving communication, it will require more—the entire University will have to be committed to launching extensive reform efforts. For example, LSU will have to examine ways to restructure its operations to be more regional rather than conducted at the college or department levels. Such things as figuring payroll, travel requests and reimbursements, distribution of grant money, student academic affairs tasks, etc. processed in a central location can save money and improve services (Leitzel, Corvey, & Hiley, 2004). Currently, many administrative and clerical personnel complete these tasks within each department or college at LSU.

Next, implementing a new budget model will revitalize the University's financial structure. Such a model may be zero-based but will definitely need to have built-in financial incentives for colleges and departments that generate revenues (increased enrollments), contain costs, encourage accountability, and promote the vision of the university. Putting more importance on fund raising is another effective reform strategy. LSU has new leadership (President and Vice President of Academic Affairs) and the timing is right for a major capital campaign or fund raising effort (Leitzel, Corvey, & Hiley, 2004).

Still another reform strategy involves examining learning: how it is designed, delivered, and assessed (Smith, 2004). The process of changing from a concentration on teaching to a focus on learning can begin at the top of the administrative structure. For example, instead of creating an institutional or Strategic Plan, LSU may want to consider creating an Academic Plan. An Academic Plan, as noted by Leitzel,

Corvey, and Hiley (2004), [will] "signal that the academic vision of the university—and its associated academic priorities—will drive all other university planning and decision-making" (p. 39). Such a plan will bind organizationally student affairs (whose goals are often not linked with academic priorities) and academic support services together in a reciprocal and dependent relationship (Leitzel, Corvey, & Hiley, 2004).

With all of the improvement strategies noted above, this is not to imply that all at LSU or in the COEHS is lost. Quite the contrary, throughout the COEHS, many reform efforts are taking place. The COEHS is changing the focus from faculty teaching to student learning. Major curricula revisions are taking place where the emphasis is on the creation of learning communities, experiential education, and outcomes based assessment. Also, this College is known for infusing service learning and civic engagement into its programs, long before they became the current trend.

Delivery of instruction that fits the new population of students is also promoted in the COEHS. Many faculty members design course work to be on line or provide a mixed format (part on line and part face-to-face). College educators are committed to providing educational opportunities to students in remote locations and travel long distances to fulfill this commitment. The department heads go to great lengths to create effective programs for off campus sights. Additionally, many College educators teach weekend and condensed (one week) courses to facilitate the learning needs of their students. Finally, people in the COEHS (especially students) believe that communication has definitely improved.

Not only is the COEHS moving forward, the University is involved in positive reform efforts. It has taken steps to consolidate its academic and student services. By way of example, rather than each college having its own technology assistance team, a university-wide Technology Assistance Center (TAC) has been created. Although a new unit (less than a year old), it appears that it has been effective in providing personnel with needed technology services. Presently, the academic affairs division at LSU is promoting a focus on learning, rather than teaching and has designed systems and incentives for faculty members to reorganize their course work. Another university-wide reform effort that will take place this summer is the delivery of four, eight, and twelve-week courses. As a new delivery model, many issues need to be resolved, so some people are nervous and have adopted a "wait-and-see" attitude. However, for those departments and colleges who forge ahead, they will be rewarded with financial incentives.

Reform efforts at LSU have definitely been set in motion and hopefully will pick-up speed and intensity as the new leadership begins to challenge and replace the traditional structures, for more viable and long-lasting options. None-the-less, if reform efforts stop and LSU cannot adapt to a complex world and graduate a qualified work force which is able to resolve the world's challenging problems (Schmitz, Baber, & John, 2000), it will become a disenfranchised victim of an antiquated, dying educational system. Definitely, times are ready for systemic school renewal in higher education. Rather than take a "wait-and-see" approach, LSU individuals are taking proactive steps to revitalize their institution. To end, more research is definitely needed to fully understand the role a College (professional staff, faculty and administration) plays in reinventing institutions of higher education to cost-effectively meet the learning needs of a changing student population in a global community.

The COEHS has chosen to proactively move forward in these reforms efforts and has demonstrated this commitment by taking part in this research project and using its results to improve communication at all levels. Finally, the COEHS wants University help in their change efforts, approximately 60% of those interviewed stated that the results of this project needed to be shared with upper administration, because they have the ability and authority to address the deeper rooted problems, such as replacing tenure track positions with part-time adjuncts, filling key positions with interims, or hiring part-time staff to avoid paying benefits.

References

Anstine-Templeton, R. & Johnson, C. E. (1998). Making the school environment safe: Red Rose's formula. *Learning Environments Research: An International Journal, 1* (1), 35-57.

Anstine-Templeton, R. & Jensen, R. A. (1993). How exemplary teachers perceive their school environments. In D. L. Fisher (Ed.), *The study of learning environments, 7*, 94-100.

Cox, M. (2001). Faculty learning communities: Change agents for transforming institutions into learning organizations. In D. Lieberman & C. Wehlburg (Eds.), *To improve the academy* (pp. 69-93).

Diamond, R. M. (2002). Curricula and courses: Administrative issues. In R. M. Diamond (Ed.), *Field guide to academic leadership* (pp. 135-156). San Francisco: Jossey-Bass.

Erickson, F. (1986). Qualitative methods in research on teaching. In M. C. Wittrock (Ed.), *Handbook of research on teaching* (3rd ed.; pp. 119-161). New York: Macmillan.

Erickson, F. (1998). Qualitative research methods for science education. In B. J. Fraser & K. G. Tobin (Eds.), *International handbook of science education* (pp. 1155-1173).

Fisher, D. & Fraser. B. J. (1990). *School-Level Environment Questionnaire.* Tasmanian State Institute of Technology: Launceston.

Garcia, J. A. & Floyd, C. E. (2002F). Addressing evaluative standards related to program assessment: How do we respond? *Journal of Social Work Education, 38*, 369-382.

Gladieux, L. E. & Swail, W. S. (2000). Beyond access improving the odds of college success. *Phi Delta Kappan, 81*, 688-692

Guskin, A. E. & Marcy, M. B. (2002). Pressures of fundamental reform: Creating a viable academic future. In R. M. Diamond (Ed.), *Field guide to academic leadership* (pp. 3-13). San Francisco: Jossey-Bass.

Guskin, A. E. & Marcy, M. B. (2003). Dealing with the future now: Principles for creating a vital campus in a climate of restricted resources. *Change, 35*, 10-21.

Hannum, W. (2002). Technology in the learning process. In R. M. Diamond (Ed.), *Field guide to academic leadership* (pp. 175-192). San Francisco: Jossey-Bass.

Johnson, C. E. & Anstine Templeton, R. (1999). Promoting peace in a place called school. *Learning Environments Research An International Journal, 2* (1), 65-77.

Leitzel, J., Corvey, C., & Hiley, D. (2004, January/February). Integrated planning and change management at a research university. *Change, 36* (1), 36-43.

Lovett, C. M. (2004, March). Letter from the president. *AAHE President Letter.* Retrieved March 22, 2004, from http://www.aahe.org

Moos, R. H. (1991). Connections between school, work, and family settings. In B. J. Fraser & H. J. Walberg (Eds.), *Educational environments: Evaluation, antecedents and consequences* (pp. 29-53). London: Pergamon.

Murdock, S. H. & Hoque, M. N. (1999). Demographic factors affecting higher education in the United States in the twenty-first century. In G. H. Gaither (Ed.), *Promising practices in recruitment, remediation, and retention* (pp. 5-13). San Francisco: Jossey-Bass.

Schmidt, K. (1998). Applying the four principles of total quality management to the classroom. *Tech Directions, 58* (1) 16-18.

Schmitz, C. D., Babor, S. J., & John, D. M. (2000). Creating the 21ˢᵗ-century school of education: Collaboration, community, and partnership in St. Louis. *Peabody Journal of Education, 75* (3), 64-84.

Smith, P. (2004, January/February). Curricular transformation: Why we need it: How to support it. *Change, 36* (1), 28-35.

Stetson Clarke, S. (2002) Supportive financial systems. In R. M. Diamond (Ed.), *Field guide to academic leadership* (pp. 295-309). San Francisco: Jossey-Bass.

Svinicki, M. (2002). Faculty development: An investment for the future. In R. M. Diamond (Ed.), *Field guide to academic leadership* (pp. 211-221). San Francisco: Jossey-Bass.

Tobin, K. & Fraser, B. J. (1998). *Qualitative and quantitative landscapes of classroom learning environments.* In B. J. Fraser & K. G. Tobin (Eds.), *International handbook of science education* (pp. 623-640). Dordrecht, The Netherlands: Kluwer.

Williams, J. A. (2002, December 6). 6 Creative ways colleges are cutting costs [Electronic version]. *The Chronicle of Higher Education. Retrieved August 2003, from http://chronicle.com.*

W. K. Kellogg Foundation (2000). *Leadership reconsidered: Engaging higher education is social change.* Battle Creek, MI: W. K. Kellogg Foundation.

COEHS
SLEQ Project
Interview Questions

Interviewers, please be sure to define each area for the interviewee.

Work Pressure: The extent to which work pressure dominates the school environment.

SAY: According to the School Level Environmental Questionnaire results, there appears to be a lot of work pressure in your environment.

1. Where do you think this work pressure comes from?

2. What suggestions do you have to decrease the work pressure in your department? In your college?

Resource Adequacy: Support personnel, facilities, finance, equipment and resources are suitable and adequate.

SAY: SLEQ results indicate that Resource Adequacy is another area of concern.

3. What do you see as the primary resource need within your area? Have you taken any steps to get those resource needs met? Explain.

Professional Interest: Individuals discuss professional matters, show interest in their work and seek further professional development.

SAY: Another area of concern was Professional Interest.

4. Why do you think individuals in your College feel concern in the area of Professional Interest? What could be done to alleviate this concern?

5. What do you think the College should do with the SLEQ results? What steps should be taken?

6. Finally, do you have any recommendations for improvement within your College that you would be willing to share?

Appendix 2

Interviewee Consent:

Date: ID Code or Name:

Thank you for volunteering to do this interview. For the purpose of recording accurate information, I would like to tape record our conversation. The recorded conversation will only be used to verify that we have accurate responses. Tapes will be transcribed with no names attached. Once the tapes have been transcribed, they will be erased.

Do I have your permission?

No _____   Yes _____

If I do not have your permission, I will just write down your responses and carefully verify what you have said.

Finally, I would like to ask if I may contact you by email or phone, if I have questions concerning your responses. For example, if I have forgotten to write down a complete sentence and cannot remember it; or if you have given permission to be recorded, and a part of the recording is not clear.

Thank you again for agreeing to be interviewed.

Chapter 14

"LEARNING DIGITALLY" — E-CLASSROOMS: COMPUTERS LOOKING FOR A PROBLEM TO SOLVE?

Garry Falloon
University of Auckland
New Zealand

The impact of recent moves by some schools in New Zealand towards the establishment of learning environments in which students have dedicated access to high numbers of computers with which to undertake curriculum tasks, has been little researched. In particular, no studies have been forthcoming relating to the manner in which students work within such environments, or the impact that they have on their social, affective and cognitive development. This chapter documents key findings of an eighteen-month doctoral case study into one such learning environment involving year 5 and 6 students at a suburban primary school. It examines the nature of teacher and student work practices in an environment where there was a ratio of one computer to approximately two students, and details the complexity of the interrelationship between teacher philosophy, curriculum design, and classroom organisational systems, that significantly impacted upon student work and social performance. It presents and discusses data captured using Camtasia video recording software, which enabled unique and unscripted 'insider views' to be gained of the manner in which students worked with the teacher, each other, and the software, as they undertook their learning tasks. The study revealed significant issues with regard to such aspects as teacher role, the limitations of software in being able to promote and extend student knowledge construction, and the impact of group organisational systems, within this digital classroom. It draws implications from this for student learning, and concludes by making a series of recommendations for schools wishing to embark on similar initiatives.

1. Introduction

While the inclusion of computers and other electronically-based communication technologies in learning environments in New Zealand is not a new phenomenon, recently schools have been experimenting with the use of these resources by establishing 'e' or digital classroom environments. These environments make available sufficient numbers of computers so that students are able to access and use them in pairs or small groups, for virtually all learning activities. By providing increased levels of access to computer equipment, these environments attempt to address one of the significant barriers identified by teachers regarding the use of computers in learning – namely the management and effective use of one or two computers in a class of thirty-plus students.

Proponents of such environments contend that by removing the 'numbers barrier' teachers would be in a better position to more fully utilise any learning potential inherent in the technology for all students, and in a way that made management by the teacher easier and the use of the resource more effective. Additionally, providing computers in large numbers within a single class would enable teachers to design curriculum which is significantly more individualised and student-centred – characteristics which have been identified by some authors as being desirable potential outcomes from computer use in schools (e.g., ACOT, 1998; Blackmore, Hardcastle, Bamblett, & Owens, 2003; Capper, 2001; Falloon, 1999; Heinecke, Blasi, Milman, & Washington, 1999; Iverson, 2001; Johnson & Johnson, 1996; McCombs & Whistler, 1997; Pittard, Bannister, & Dunn, 2004; Thornburg, 1999; Yelland, 1995).

Early views along this line perceived the computer as something of a 'surrogate teacher', capable of acting in a manner which would sustain student learning independent of teacher intervention, and help facilitate the development of simple knowledge constructs (Taylor, 1980). Furthermore, recent views have moved towards emphasising the potential for the computer to enhance cognitive elements such as higher-order thinking, problem solving, metacognitive and reflective thinking processes and so on – capabilities which are seen to be desirable in equipping students with the skill-set needed to function effectively in a rapidly changing, technologically saturated world (Heinecke, et al., 1999; McCombs, 2000; Page, 1999; Roschelle, Pea, Hoadley, Gordin, & Means, 2001; Thornburg, 1999).

While general research into the impact of computers on learning environments has yielded highly variable results (e.g., Bolstad, 2004; Cuban, 2002; Falloon, 1999; Fuchs & Woessmann, 2004), research into the impact of having ongoing access to high numbers of computers such as in an e-classroom, is practically non-existent (Falloon, 2005). While this could primarily be attributed to their relatively recent entry to the education scene, it could also be claimed that within such environments it is virtually impossible to isolate the impact of the technology from the multitude of other variables which influence the teaching and learning context. As with any learning environment – with or without computers, the manner in which it functions is the result of the interaction of a vast array of factors which include such things as social, personal, philosophical, organisational, resource and logistical elements, which are unique to each situation. While the respective influence of each of these factors is difficult if not impossible to quantify, what the following case study attempts to describe is how they blended to create a unique learning environment for students in an e-classroom, and how this, in turn, impacted upon their social, affective and cognitive development.

2. The E-classroom Environment

The context for this study was a year 1 to 6 suburban primary school in the northern region of New Zealand, specifically a year 5 and 6 composite class of 33 students. The school was located in a very low socio-economic area, and held the lowest possible ranking for schools on the Ministry of Education's decile rating system[1]. The students in the class were predominantly of Maori ethnicity, and like the school generally, it had a highly transient population. The e-classroom was an existing classroom which had been adapted rather than purpose-designed, although custom-made furniture had been installed which allowed the students to work together in pairs or small groups. Altogether there were twelve computer 'clients' which were networked using thin-client technology to a main server which housed all software, student files, and allowed school intranet and towards the end of the study, internet access. In addition to the twelve thin-client terminals, two 'stand alone' research machines were also available for student use during the research period. Although these two computers were incorporated into the school's network and as far as the students were concerned functioned in the same manner as the client machines, they had their own hard drives and were used to collected research data using a unique data collection tool known as Camtasia. A detailed explanation

---

[1] The decile rating is the indicator used to measure the extent to which schools draw from low socio-economic communities. Each state and state-integrated school is ranked into deciles (10% groupings) on the basis of the indicator. The indicator is based on Census data for households with school-aged children in each school's catchment area, together with ethnicity data from the school's roll returns. Decile ratings determine the allocation of Targeted Funding for Educational Achievement (TFEA), the Special Education Grant (SEG), the Careers Information Grant (CIG), and Decile Discretionary Funding

of the operation of Camtasia and how it was used in the study is provided later. However at this point it is important to note that Camtasia enabled data to be collected which provided unique insights into the manner in which students worked with each other and the computers as they undertook learning tasks, and was pivotal to the outcomes of this research.

Figure 14.1. The e-classroom setup showing the two 'stand alone' research computers in the background with a typical four computer pod in the foreground.

3. Research Questions and Researcher Role

As introduced in the opening section of this chapter, this study was prompted by the lack of research into the manner in which students learn in digitally-rich environments. More specifically, it centred on how such environments could influence student social, affective and cognitive activity, and on revealing the nature of their work practices as they interacted with computers for virtually all learning tasks. By way of placing this into context, the research also investigated the development rationale and establishment processes for the e-classroom, in an effort to identify how these contributed to and influenced the nature of the facility, and the learning programme which was delivered within it. In was expected that identifying such aspects would assist in the generation of recommendations that could be applied to this setting, in order to improve its performance in supporting the learning of its students. Although generalisation from these results was not the primary purpose of this study, examination of this learning environment in its entirety allowed for the development of a set of guiding principles which could be useful to other schools considering similar initiatives.

The overall goals of the research were defined as:

What is the nature of student work practices in an e-classroom environment, and what are the factors which influence this?

The research was guided by three primary research questions which contributed to the attainment of the overall goal. These questions were:

Upon what educational vision was the e-classroom environment at Parahaki School established, and what was the nature of the implementation processes associated with this?

How does the e-classroom environment impact upon the cognitive, affective and social development of its students?

In what areas might changes or improvements be made to optimise the learning potential of this e-classroom?

The study took place over a period of 18 months during which time I worked extensively in the e-classroom with the students and the teacher, and participated in the full array of learning experiences and other classroom activities. As with all case study research, the need to carefully balance my research priorities while as much as possible be 'naturalised' into the classroom environment, meant I adopted a number of different roles during the course of the study. These ranged from observer or participant-observer, to at times, acting in a role akin to a second teacher in the room, assisting students with their work and providing guidance when called upon. After consultation with the classroom teacher, it was decided that this would be a sound approach to adopt due to the nature of the students, and the length of time I was to be present in the room.

4. Research Methodology and Data Collection

This study utilised an intrinsic case study methodology and employed a variety of data collection tools during its 18-month duration. Case study methodology was particularly suited to this research, as the focus was not to develop a set of universals or 'rules' which could be applied to all or any situations of a like nature, but rather, as Erickson puts it, to determine the "particularisation" (1986, p. 130) of this example, and enable "the presentation, interpretation and investigation of detailed information on a single unit developing idiographic interpretations" (Burns, 1997, p. 383). As previously introduced, adopting such a methodology also allowed me to capitalise on what Erickson claims is one of the key strengths of case studies, that is, it "allows the immersion of oneself in the dynamics of a single social entity and enables the uncovering of events or processes that one might miss with more superficial methods" (Erickson, 1986, p. 238).

In addition to traditional data collection tools used by case study researchers, namely, researcher observations/case notes and participant (individual and pair) interviews, as mentioned earlier, this study utilised a unique data collection tool known as Camtasia. Briefly, this tool took the form of software which was installed and operated 'in the background' of the two stand-alone research computers which were included in the classroom network for the duration of the study. Camtasia was activated and deactivated by a single keystroke, and enabled the recording in movie format of all screen activity and associated oral discourse as the students worked individually and in groups on their learning tasks. These data were then saved onto the computer's hard drive and exported to DVD disks for later analysis.

Although the students were informed about the recording software on the two computers at the commencement of the study, they were not reminded of its presence and operation on each occasion it was used. The only visible external sign of its activation was a change in the colour of a small icon at the lower right-hand corner of the screen. Following discussion with the principal and the classroom teacher, we determined that this was the best option, as we considered that there was a strong likelihood that students would 'stage' performances if they knew they were being recorded, and therefore data would not be an accurate representation of their practice. In considering the ethical implications of this, we considered that the quality of data gathered through the use of this tool was critical to the accuracy and success of this study, and providing participant anonymity and researcher confidentiality was maintained, the advantages of using it outweighed any potential risk to participants.

It was interesting that in the 18 months of the study no student questioned the icon colour change triggered by the activation and deactivation of the software, or enquired as to when the software was being used. Whether or not they had forgotten that it was present or simply didn't care was unclear, but irrespective of this, data collected using Camtasia enabled unique, 'unscripted - insider' views of how the students worked together and interacted with the software as they undertook learning tasks. More information relating to Camtasia can be gained from www.techsmith.com.

Over the course of the research period, a total of over 80 hours of video activity was collected, analysed, and then coded using social, affective and cognitively-based categories derived from the second research question. Multiple work samples were collected and analysed from all students during the course of the study, to ensure that data as much as possible represented an accurate account of student practice in this room.

5. Significant Outcomes

5.1 The e-classroom establishment process

As indicated previously, although this study was primarily concerned with the impact of the e-classroom environment on students, in order to place this in context it was necessary to examine how the concept was conceived within the school, and what objectives were established for its presence. Such aspects in the final analysis proved to be highly relevant. Examining the wider environment in which the initiative was established enabled an overview to be developed which accounted, at least in some part, for the approaches adopted by the teacher in using the computers in the classroom, and the nature of the curriculum she developed for her students.

What became very apparent early on in the study in this respect was the influence of the school's principal in establishing the e-classroom, in particular, the extent to which his vision for the room was understood and shared by others in the school, and the wider education community. Much of the principal's vision for the e classroom centred on a perception that enabling student access to computers in this way would yield greater engagement in learning tasks, and promote superior student independence in learning. He also held firm beliefs in the importance for students from lower socio-economic areas to be exposed to technology in a way that would maximise any possible learning benefits. He considered such exposure would not be available in the homes of the majority of students at the school, and it was part of the school's responsibility to bridge this 'access divide'. Clearly, he viewed technology as being a 'hook' into learning for his students, and considered that it held powerful potential for enhancing students' attitudes to school and encouraging lifelong learning.

This philosophical perspective was also shared by the teacher who was approached to teach in the e-classroom. She had been at the school for a number of years and during that time, according to the principal, had displayed the philosophical characteristics, pedagogical strategies, and classroom practices he considered would be well-supported by having access to high levels of computer equipment. The implementation process also involved a network systems administrator, who worked in conjunction with the classroom teacher and the principal, in forming the implementation group. Technical support and advice for the classroom's development was gained from an external computer retailer.

In evaluating the impact the implementation process had on the overall development and performance of the e-classroom, there was little doubt that this initiative was poorly understood by other staff within the school, and that this factor contributed to a significant degree of isolation of the initiative from more 'mainstream' school programmes. Some teachers did not consider the level of expenditure on the facility to be justified, or felt it would have been better spent on other learning resources or more equitably distributed across all school programmes. This lack of support appeared to be linked to a generally limited understanding of the goals and objectives of the initiative held by other staff, and what was perceived by some as the 'closed' nature of decision-making processes associated with the room's development. In many ways what developed during this phase of implementation was a 'catch 22' situation, where project goals were never clearly defined or widely shared, leading to a lack of understanding or 'buy in' from other staff, which in turn fed a perception held by the implementation team that other staff had little to offer. The net impact of this was that the e-classroom was established within a wider school context which although not overtly 'anti' the innovation, was also not wholeheartedly supportive of it either. The principal justified such an approach by commenting on his desire to get the project underway, and that this could have been unnecessarily delayed if he had engaged in lengthy consultation and staff input processes.

In commenting on the apparent limitations of this process, it must be kept in mind that the e-classroom concept was pioneering new territory, and as for many initiatives of an experimental nature which break new ground, strong leadership is required to make things happen. The challenge in this respect was generating a workable balance between providing such leadership, whilst still creating an environment in which affected individuals considered their perspectives had been acknowledged, and where they had been given the opportunity to contribute to the overall goals of the initiative, where appropriate.

In many ways, limited support for the initiative within and external to the school appeared to act as additional motivation for the implementation group to make sure that it was successful, and, as the principal commented, to ensure that "it succeeded on its own merits" (Peter, interview, 2003). To this end, the students who were selected for the e-classroom were not 'hand-picked' in the sense that they were not the most capable students of that age level in the school. On the contrary and as will be illustrated later, it would be fair to state that the e-classroom had more than its fair share of difficult students – students who exhibited significant emotional or behavioural issues and presented management challenges to both the classroom teacher and school administration. This situation to a large extent was exacerbated by the internal reputation of the e-classroom teacher as being very capable in managing difficult students, which led to many such students 'migrating' to her class from other areas of the school on a regular basis.

Understanding the nature of the environment in which this initiative was developed is critical in gaining an insight into the context of this study. As will be illustrated later, to a considerable extent the rather uncertain nature of the implementation process had a 'flow on' influence to the nature of the programme which operated within it. The lack of clearly articulated or 'visible' goals or outcomes which were shared with and understood by all staff members, combined with the somewhat 'closed' nature of decision-making processes, contributed to creating an environment in which the e-classroom development and the teacher herself, were in many ways viewed in isolation from the rest of the school.

5.2 The e-classroom teacher and the e-classroom curriculum

The teacher selected to lead this innovation was an experienced practitioner already within the school. In the principal's view, she had fully extended the capabilities of the limited array of equipment she had previously had at her disposal, and was now in a position to explore the potentials of a dedicated room in which computers were available in sufficient numbers to allow all students continuous access.

It was very apparent that a high level of alignment existed between the principal and the e-classroom teacher, relating to philosophical views on the role of the teacher and the relevance and purpose of schooling. This alignment without doubt was the foundation of the high degree of trust which existed between the two, which in turn allowed the teacher considerable freedom to develop curriculum which she considered would best utilise the capabilities of the technology, and allow her to meet what she saw as the learning needs of her students. From the perspective of the teacher this relationship was pivotal to the success of her programme, as she realised the importance of gaining the professional respect and support of the principal, in enabling her to develop programmes which were viewed by many to be radically 'left-field' relative to others operating in the school.

In commenting on the impact that having access to large numbers of computers had on the nature of the learning programme in her room, the teacher stated that it had stimulated an 'evolution' in her practice towards a far more individualised and student-centred curriculum. She considered the computers were able to sustain learning activity for prolonged periods, independent of teacher supervision or input. According to her, this factor enabled the design and implementation of a curriculum within which groups of students were able to undertake different learning tasks involving a diversity of learning areas, at the same time. The transition to a more thematic approach in which units of learning tied together a range of knowledge areas, also allowed the teacher to reorganise the structure of the school day. This involved a movement away from the conventional timetabled subject 'blocks' in favour of a 'seamless' design which viewed work requirements more holistically, and allowed students a degree of freedom to organise their own programmes.

The perceived greater level of programme individualisation facilitated by having ongoing access to more computers, also assisted the teacher in making significant changes to her practice. She commented that the way in which she taught had changed considerably since commencing work in the e-classroom, with less time needing to be allocated to classroom behaviour management tasks, and more able to be spent on attending to individual learner needs. She also commented that she spent a lot less time on whole class teaching in favour of working with small groups or individuals, and that she found this personally more rewarding and enjoyable, and believed it to be more effective teaching. During the course of this study it was certainly noted that the level of learning task engagement by many students within this room was high, but as will be illustrated in the following section, upon closer examination the actual 'learning value' they were gaining from their use of the computer was, in many cases, marginal.

5.3 Student work processes in the e-classroom

The quality and effectiveness of student work in the e-classroom was the result of a complex interaction of primarily cognitive and social factors, which varied according to the individual or the composition of the workgroup. Analysis of the Camtasia videos revealed however, that the basic process of interaction with the computer was similar for most students, whether they were working individually, as a pair, or in a group of three. This simple process is detailed in Figure 14.2.

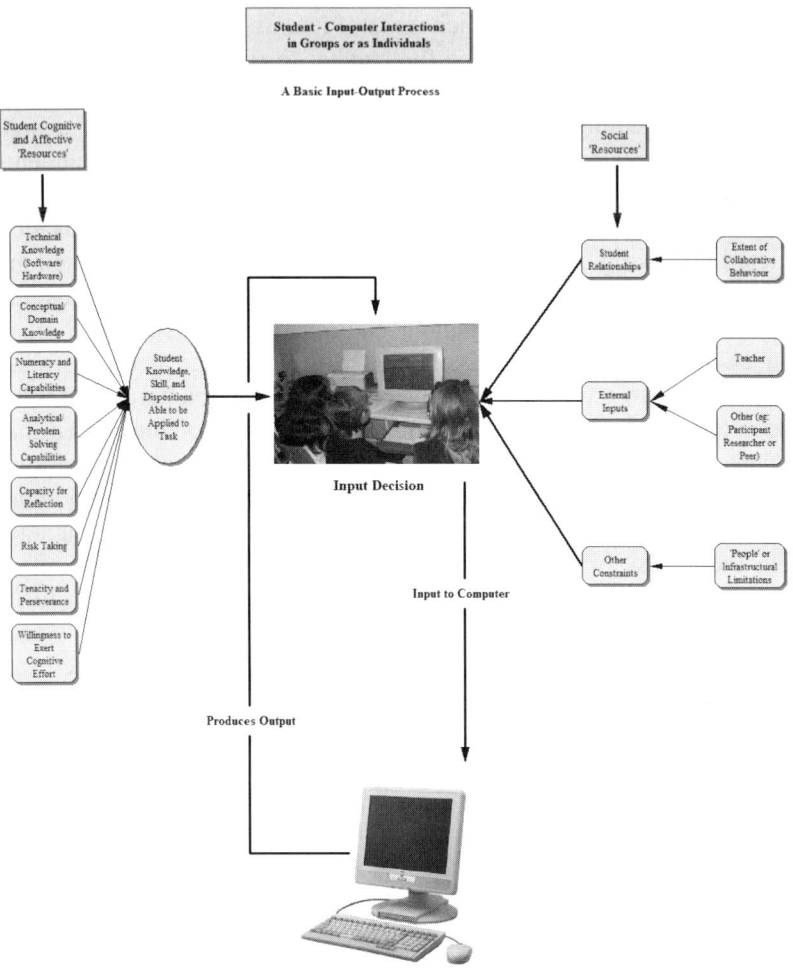

Figure 14.2. The simple input process used by most students when interacting with software.

The process resembles a basic input/output cycle, where input decisions were decided upon using a range of variously effective strategies, the output from which was then evaluated by the individual or group members before a new input was decided upon, enacted, evaluated, and so on. However, the 'learning value' students in this e-classroom were able to gain from this process was highly dependent upon the nature and quality of the learning 'resources' they were able to bring to the task. These 'resources' related to such things as knowledge possessed in relation to the context being studied (and/or their willingness/capabilities to access this), numeracy and literacy skills, analytical and problem-solving skills, and the work organisational structures they adopted. In this classroom, these factors integrated together in the formation of a working framework which was unique to each group, and depending upon the composition or 'blend' which was developed in each instance, the students were able to make variable progress with their learning tasks.

5.4 The impact of student workgroup organisation

The teacher in this classroom employed what was termed a 'self-select' organisational system in determining workgroup composition. Due to the numbers of computers that were available, it was necessary for students to work in groups of two or three. The 'self-select' system effectively meant that students were free to organise themselves into groups with whoever they liked, and to organise working roles within these groups to ensure set tasks were completed.

As revealed by the data, the organisational structures developed by students influenced significantly the 'learning value' they were able to extract from having access to the technology, and the greatest single element within this was the level of collaboration able to be generated between group members. Johnson and Johnson (1996) defined cooperative learning as "the instructional use of small groups so that students work together to maximise their own and each others learning" (p. 1018). However in this instance, collaborative learning is differentiated from cooperative learning in that in addition to being an organisational structure, the additional dimensions of equality and mutuality (Hooper, 1992) are present. Hooper defined mutuality as "the degree of engagement between group members" (1992, p. 23), and referred to equality as the extent to which members of the group, and their ideas and contributions, are viewed as being equal. The presence of these factors within cooperative group structures Hooper (1992) sees as essential in the establishment of a level of interdependence between group members, and in creating an environment in which students are able to freely experiment with, and challenge ideas.

Within this environment, the work practices of the students varied considerably. They were described as existing on a continuum, ranging from consistently non-collaborative at one end, to consistently collaborative at the other, with a large group oscillating between the two extremes, depending upon who it was they were working with or the nature of the task. The composition of these groups was closely aligned to the existing social organisation of the classroom, with those forming collaborative groupings being students who had strong existing friendships or social relationships which they carried over to their work. Collaborative groups changed little during the course of the study, and this characteristic was in many ways the cornerstone to their success.

The stability of this socially-based structure meant that these students were able to immediately 'slot into' a functional working arrangement, irrespective of the nature of the task, or other work variables. As they worked with the same person or persons each time, there was no need to re-establish 'working parameters' from one session to the next, meaning that they could very quickly get underway with their tasks and progress relatively independent of external organisational direction. It was apparent that students adopting collaborative practices were well aware of the benefits to their work of doing so. As one pair commented:

> **Simon**: ...we are best friends and think alike...
>
> **Zane:** We help each other out a lot when we get stuck...
>
> **Simon**: ...yeah, and we know what's happening and all that...see like if Zane's doing something on the one day, and I go to Dan and I say "Dan, what have you been doing?" and that usually takes up about a quarter of our time explaining what we have to do... so I would rather work with Zane.
> (Simon & Zane, interview 1, 2003)

Students working collaboratively displayed consistently high levels of mutuality and equality (Hooper, 1992), each recognising the strengths of the other in being able to contribute to the successful completion of tasks. Often there was a level of task specialisation between members of these groups, with individuals being offered and accepting responsibility for work in areas where they were best able to contribute. Decisions about specialisation was sometimes made on a technical basis – for example, the level of knowledge or skill possessed by a group member in relation to using hardware or software, while at other times it related to the input able to be made by a student to improving work outcomes. As recorded during a student interview:

> **Anton:** ...like Hemi, well he's good at writing stuff and reading and all that... and he has some cool ideas we can use...
>
> **Hemi:** ...and Anton, well he's really good at typing...
>
> ***Researcher:*** *So if Anton is working on the keyboard, what do you do then Hemi... only one person can get on the keyboard at a time, can't they?*
>
> **Hemi:** Well, I can control the mouse and can read some of it... so can Anton – we usually read a paragraph each. Sometimes we swap over as well, I get on the keyboard and Anton does the checking...
> (Anton & Hemi, interview 2, 2003)

Although many collaboratively functioning groups adopted a level of task specialisation at some point, there was also a strong sense of responsibility between members of the group to support and assist their workmates in strengthening areas of weakness. As revealed by the Camtasia videos, this support usually took the form of technical skill peer tutoring and high levels of verbal guidance and interaction, as members of the group supported each other in learning new skills, or developing the knowledge to enable successful task completion. As Simon stated:

> ...and I'm good at typing but I'm not good at spelling, so I type it up and he (Zane) tells me when I have made a mistake ...and if we have to do Maths like yesterday and he makes a mistake, then I tell him and try to explain where he went wrong...
> (Simon & Zane, case notes, 2003; interview, 2003)

Interestingly, students who adopted collaborative practices maintained these irrespective of the task which was set, or the nature of the expected output. For example, students were given an assignment to develop work portfolios for presentation at a parent information evening. Although the requirement was for an individual outcome, students working collaboratively generally worked together in completing both folios, with each contributing to the development of the others' by offering both content and technical input. This effectively kept both students engaged fully during each work session, and enabled higher quality outcomes to be produced more efficiently.

At the other end of the continuum a small group of students consistently displayed what were termed non-collaborative practices. They were students who were not part of a stable social structure as described above, but generally worked on their own. They tended to be highly transient in nature, often moving from group to group and applying a range of strategies in an effort to get time at a keyboard, while not really contributing in any positive way to a collaborative group effort. Because of their transient nature and the fact that they were unable to form any consistent working relationship, little progress was made on their work tasks. If they were able to secure access to a computer, they usually concerned themselves with peripheral activities such as engaging with drawing programs, or 'playing' with graphics or animation features of various software packages. Where a loose working arrangement was able to be forged with other students, this was generally of a temporary nature, as the terms of the relationship were usually dictated by the non-collaborative individual, and were generally unacceptable to other group members.

There also existed a large group of students whose practices at various times displayed a range of characteristics falling between these two extremes. While these students were able to organise themselves into working pairs or groups, these were seldom stable in nature, and would often change within and between tasks. Often these students could have up to three or four different 'workmates' within the same task (spanning a number of work sessions), which necessitated the continual re-establishment of understandings and working arrangements to accommodate the personnel changes. This proved to be a very inefficient way for these students to work, as usually what formed was a structure which resembled more of a 'resource sharing' arrangement than one based on the collaborative principles of mutuality and equality (Hooper, 1992). As students changed partners regularly, this often set up a situation in which they were effectively competing with each other for access to the keyboard in order to progress their own work. Unlike those working collaboratively, these students were more individualistic, and viewed the requirement to work with another person as a necessity imposed by the number of computers, rather than being an arrangement that could be advantageous.

Any collaboration which was witnessed between these students usually took the form of technical advice on how to use various software tools such as the spelling checker, or monitoring the accuracy of spelling or grammar as the other person typed. There was little active engagement in terms of the development of content, with each seeming to be happy to 'bide their time' while waiting for the other to complete their allotted time at the keyboard. Where joint tasks were set by the teacher, outcomes from students working in these groupings were usually disjointed and represented the sum of two or three individual efforts, rather than a coherent, coordinated effort such as those produced by students working collaboratively. The volume and quality of work produced by students working in these variably collaborative arrangements varied greatly. Most had issues with completing their work on time as they had fewer opportunities to engage with it, and some would regularly spend their intervals or lunchtimes working to 'catch up'.

Group organisation in this e-classroom had a significant impact upon student performance. Students who were members of stable collaborative structures held distinct advantages over those in non or variably collaborative arrangements, in that they were able to maximise the capacity of the computers to support their learning, relatively independent of teacher support. When they struck a problem, they were usually able to work it out between themselves, or call upon others within a known network of 'experts' working in similar arrangements within the class, to assist. These capabilities proved invaluable in enabling more rapid completion of tasks, and to a much higher standard, than was the case for others.

5.5 The e-classroom, curriculum design, and student knowledge

Although the collaborative social organisation for some students sustained their work with the computers, there appeared to be some limitations to this environment in supporting the independent development of hierarchical conceptual knowledge. This applied at some stage to all students, irrespective of their workgroup organisation, and was related to a combination of factors including the philosophical stance of the teacher, assumptions made which at times confused student *engagement* with student *learning,* and the individualised nature of the curriculum design.

It was apparent that the teacher in this classroom firmly believed in the capabilities of computers to support learning individualisation for her students, and actively sought to provide as many opportunities as possible for her students to plan and manage their own learning. While this was a worthy goal, the interpretation of this approach and a philosophical stance of minimal teacher intervention, resulted in the development of a curriculum which became increasingly fragmented over time.

One of the positive aspects of this environment identified by the classroom teacher was that it allowed her to evolve the learning curriculum from the conventional 'compartmentalised' model, to one in which groups of students were able to work on different units of learning simultaneously. In practice this meant that within any defined period, students could be working on up to four or five different thematic units, involving the integration of several curriculum areas. According to the teacher, the e-classroom environment was better able to sustain such a curriculum, as she considered the computers were able to provide engagement and support continuity, which allowed her students to independently complete work tasks with the minimum of 'down time'.

While to an extent this may have been true, the adoption of this approach posed significant challenges to the teacher, particularly regarding the monitoring and tracking of student work, and in student attainment of planned learning goals. While multiple independent activities were possible, there were significant issues in assessing student progress towards meeting any learning outcomes associated with these, and in physically managing the diversity of activity within the room. The demands on the teacher to respond to student requests which may range from creating spreadsheets, to developing concept maps or designing science animations all within a few moments, were acute.

Additionally, there needed to be developed a system by which student work over time could be easily accessed for both formative and summative assessment purposes. As all work was stored electronically in individual student folders on a central server, it was necessary for the teacher to individually search each folder if she wanted to access the work any student had completed, or was in the process of completing.

This was a time consuming process, and also one which, in many ways, did not give her an accurate indication of the progress the student was making. One of the issues that quickly became apparent was that completing and saving work electronically only allowed this teacher to make a single 'point-in-time' assessment of student progress. That is, unless students saved multiple copies of their work illustrating each stage of its development, the teacher only had access to what was essentially the end point of a learning process, with no explicit evidence of the 'working' or thinking that may have contributed to getting there. There was no 'paper trail' which could be used by the teacher to formatively track-back student progress, and little indication at which point errors, if any, were made. This limited the formative input of the teacher in guiding students' learning to informal interactions as she made her way around the classroom, and could also give a 'false reading' of student progress.

This latter phenomenon was captured on Camtasia video on several occasions, when students working on tasks appeared to hit a 'brick wall' imposed by limitations in the level of conceptual knowledge they possessed, and therefore could apply, to solving a problem. In the following example, two students had been assigned a Logo problem solving task to develop a pattern involving a series of rotated heptagons. After a short time 'doodling' drawing a range of unrelated square and circles, they managed to create two heptagons based on a formula supplied by the teacher (Figure 14.3).

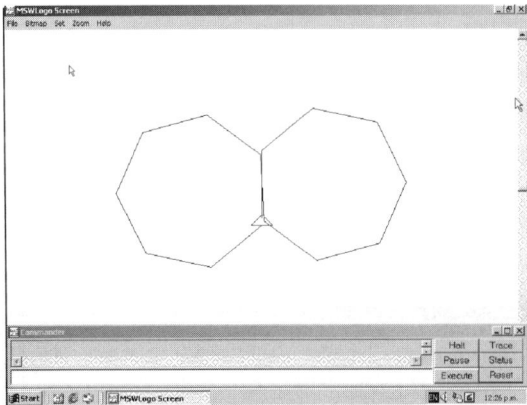

Figure 14.3. Two heptagons were created using a pre-determined formula.

At this point, there was considerable discussion between the students as to what the next step should be to enable the drafting of the third heptagon beneath the previous two. The following discourse was captured by Camtasia video:

> **Paul:** ...try lt50.
> Bondi enters lt50.
>
> **Paul:** Nah... you have to make it get in line with that *(indicating with mouse the base of second heptagon)* so you can get it down.
> *Bondi enters lt70 to bring turtle to base line* (Figure 14. 4).
>
> **Paul:** ...now go fd100... but put the pen up first.
>
> **Bondi:** What?
>
> **Paul:** PU – pen up!
> *Bondi enters PU followed by fd100. Turtle moves forward but goes off line* (Figure 14.5)

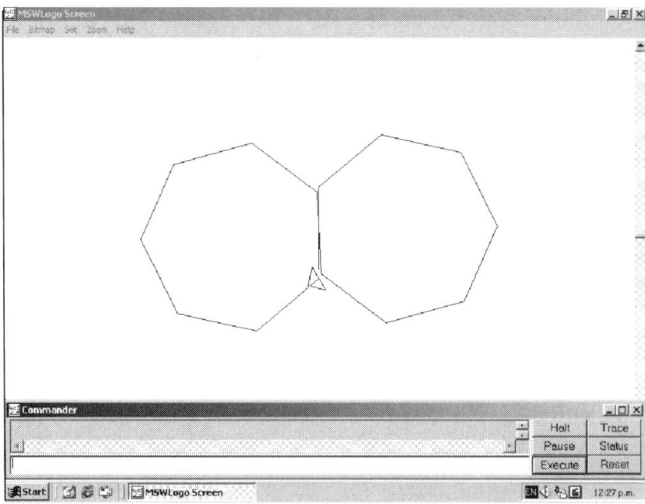

Figure 14.4. Bondi enters lt70 to bring turtle to baseline of second heptagon.

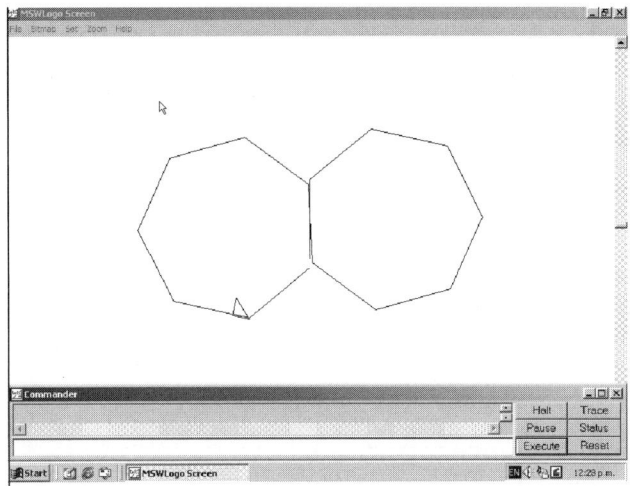

Figure 14.5. Turtle moves along and off base line.

Paul: It's gone off the line! *(pauses)*.

Bondi: Yeah, what d'ya think we should do about it?

Paul: Dunno… *(pauses)* too much hassle trying to fix it… use CS
Bondi enters CS in commander and screen clears (Figure 14.6)

Bondi: I know, let's make a hexagon!

Paul: Yeah, that'll be easier!
(Paul & Bondi, Camtasia clip, 2003)

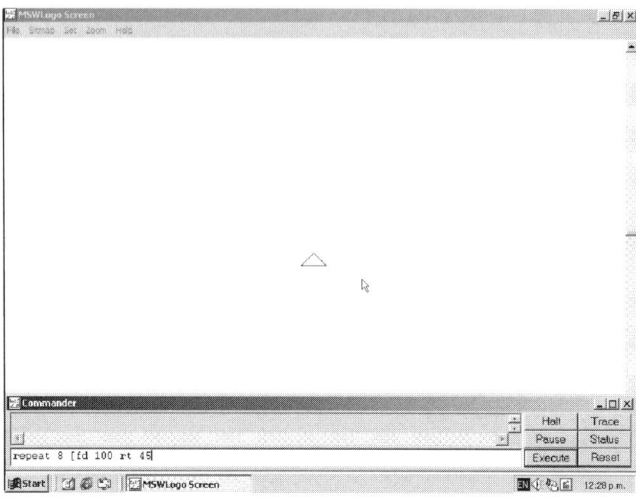

Figure 14.6. Bondi clears screen after error judged too difficult to rectify.

What is particularly relevant in this example, is that although these students were working collaboratively, they made no attempt to negotiate or debate a possible 'way out' of their problem. Nor did they seek advice from either the teacher or other students as to possible strategies they might adopt in solving it. The preference by many students to close the program or file, clear screens and start again, or 'adjust' the outcome to one which was within their existing capabilities (as in this case) held major implications for the rate at which many in this environment progressed their work. In some instances, it was possible for students to work for a complete session without actually achieving anything in terms of planned learning goals, having spent most of the time making multiple changes to an original, or restarting again from scratch. It was very difficult for the class teacher to monitor these performances, as there was no visible 'pathway' of preceding student activity upon which the teacher could base judgments about overall progress.

It was apparent in this environment that the computers, while able to sustain activity and engage students, were limited in their capacity to support hierarchical knowledge construction without the active engagement of the teacher or more capable peer. Due to the acute demands placed on the teacher in this environment as detailed earlier, teacher time was at a premium, and there appeared to be an assumption that the computers by themselves would be able to substitute. For many students this was not the case, and where support was unable to be gained, they tended to drift into peripheral activities or engage with tasks in ways which were termed 'diversionary'. These diversionary activities generally comprised exploring tangential features of the software being used, such as creating or experimenting with animation sequences, spending prolonged periods using drawing components, or selecting wordart, borders, or clipart, or changing font style, colour and so on. While these activities were undoubtedly engaging for the students, the engagement was with software, not the construction of knowledge or the attainment of learning goals. With the multiplicity of concurrent activities occurring in this environment, it was very difficult for the teacher to determine at any point in time whether students were in fact engaged in on-task or peripheral-diversionary activity.

6. Student Knowledge and the Use of Software Tools

In respect to the use of software, in particular tools such as the spelling or grammar checkers, it was interesting to note the level of implicit trust some students ascribed to the accuracy and appropriateness of the outcomes they produced. The appearance of a red or green line beneath a word was uncritically interpreted by many students as a mistake on their behalf, to be rectified by accessing the computer's correction tools. While this clearly is the purpose of such tools, the issue for some students was that they prioritised the accuracy and appropriateness of the computer's response over their own intuitive understanding of what they considered to be correct.

Several examples of this were recorded by Camtasia, with one rather amusing example being captured as a student, Julie, was developing a work portfolio for a parent information evening. She was creating a series of slides using the Powerpoint program highlighting what she considered to be her successes and challenges in relation to her work in the e-classroom. She was preparing a slide detailing her progress in Mathematics and was commenting on difficulties she had with her times tables tests, when she spelt the word *tests* incorrectly, entering it instead as *testes* (Figure 14.7). As the word *testes* was in the spelling checker database of the computer, a red line error indicator did not appear beneath the word. However, Julie seemed to be suspicious of whether or not the word was indeed correct, and carried out a manual spelling check of her own (Figure 14.8). When the 'check complete' notification came up she seemed surprised, and exclaimed "oh, it must be right then…" (Camtasia clip, 2003). She then continued on with her slide, accepting that 'testes' was spelt correctly, and was also the word she wanted.

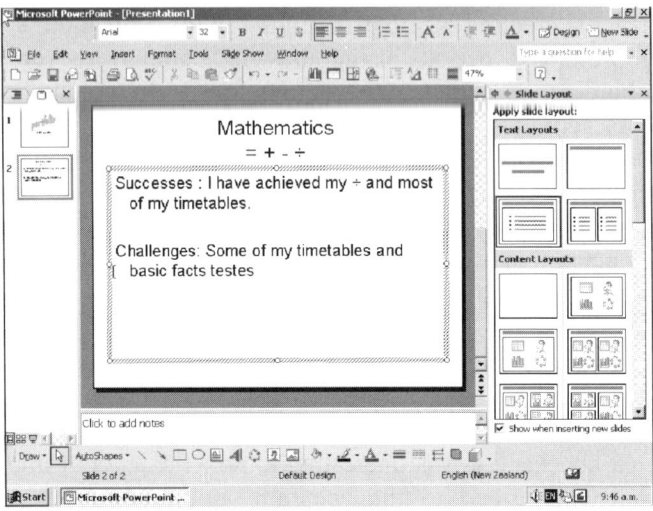

Figure 14.7. *'Tests'* is entered incorrectly as *'Testes'*.

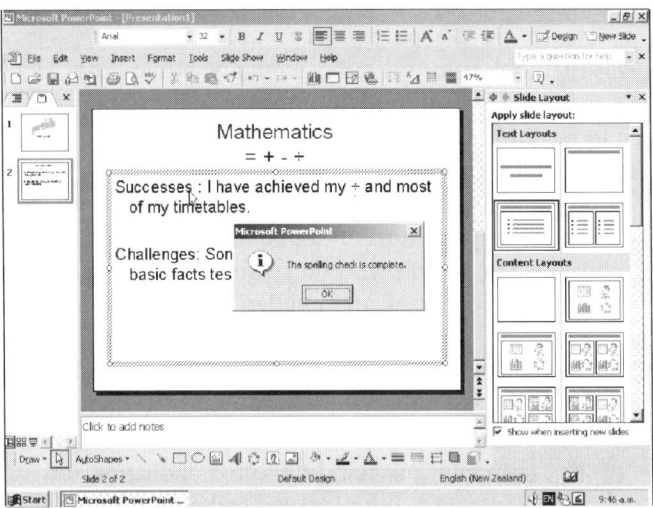

Figure 14.8. Julie carries out a manual spelling check.

When interviewed later about this event, Julie commented that even though there was no red line under the word she felt that it was not correctly spelt, and hence proceeded to carry out a manual spelling check. When this check indicated that there were no errors, she accepted this and carried on with the remainder of the slide. While the word was indeed correctly spelt, clearly it was the wrong word for this context, and neither the spelling nor the grammar checkers were able to provide any direction to indicate this. However, what is possibly more interesting was Julie's willingness to accept uncritically the result of the spelling check, and prioritise this over her own intuitive 'feeling' that the word was not correct. Had she cross-checked the word at this point using a dictionary, she would quickly have determined the inappropriateness of her selection. Several other examples of similar practices were recorded during this study, in particular when students were working on spreadsheets where formula had been incorrectly entered, or in the uncritical acceptance of discrepant and sometimes incorrect web-based information.

A critical issue revealed by this data was that without some foundational knowledge or skill within or supporting the domain being studied, students were in a weaker position to use the capacities and tools embedded in the software to progress their learning. For example, basic skills such as estimation and approximation were critical in being able to detect errors in spreadsheets, while well-developed literacy capabilities were needed to interact critically with web-based information, and to gain maximum advantage from built-in software tools. While computers used in this way provided these students with many opportunities to *exercise* and *refine* such knowledge and skills, they did not appear to be able to establish them if the foundations had not been firmly laid beforehand.

7. Student Attitudes to the E-Classroom Environment

With some exceptions, this e-classroom environment was seen by students as making a positive contribution to their perception of school. Much of this perception was based on the notion that the computers made work easier by taking away some of the more laborious physical aspects of classwork. Aspects such as handwriting, the need to make constant reference to paper-based materials such as dictionaries and encyclopaedias, and issues associated with difficulties in maintaining a consistent standard of accuracy and neatness, all featured prominently in student comments. As some commented:

> **Dan:** It's exciting …'cos there's heaps of computers and that…
>
> **Researcher:** *Why is that exciting?*
>
> **Dan:** …because you don't have to handwrite… it makes it easier.
>
> **Paul:** It's fun and it's easier because of all the computers. You don't have to work so hard…
>
> **Researcher:** *What do you mean?*
>
> **Paul:** …you don't get a sore hand from writing all the time. On the computer you just have to tap the key…
> (Dan, student interview 1, 2003; Paul, student interview 1, 2003)

Some students also appeared to view their work as being more akin to play than 'real work', with many of them commenting that they found using the computers 'fun and cool'. When asked to explain these comments, they stated that this was related to features of software they enjoyed using, such as the drawing tools or animation features.

> **Anton:** It's fun because of all the computers.
>
> **Nick:** Fun… it's fun to play on the computers.
>
> **Researcher:** *What do you mean, play?*
>
> **Nick:** You get to draw stuff and all that.
>
> **Abby:** I think it's cool… 'cos of all the computers… it's better than writing in your book!
> (Student interviews 1, 2003)

While most students at least initially agreed that the e-classroom environment enhanced their attitude to school this did not apply to all, and interestingly tended to diminish between the first and final interviews. Towards the end of the study, some students commented that they considered the use of software tools, in particular the grammar and spelling checkers, made them lazy, and encouraged them to take short-cuts which were not compatible with "real learning" (Sherilee & Susan, interview 2, 2003). Others commented that they felt they were unable to produce their best work using the computer, as they did not have the necessary levels of coordination or fine motor skills which enabled them to make best use of the keyboard or mouse, or found the manner in which software operated constrained what they were trying to achieve.

> **Simon:** I'm good at writing on the computer and not by hand, but I am better at drawing by hand than on the computer.
>
> **Zane:** I haven't got good mouse control… it's my hand!
>
> **Simon:** Yeah… I don't like to use the mouse when I draw. I like to do it by hand… it's not the same.
>
> **Zane:** And sometimes there is a grid or something and it won't go away.
>
> **Simon:** Like you can't get into properties and change it on Works like on some other programs, like Inspiration. (Simon & Zane, student interview 2, 2003)

While all students acknowledged the benefits of learning to use computers at a technical level, this was generally linked to mastery of hardware and software which was viewed as being important for future work opportunities, and also allowed them to produce work which was neat and attractive. In many ways, the technology 'leveled the playing field' for students who had difficulties in maintaining the neatness and legibility of their work, which undoubtedly added to their sense of self-efficacy. As Wendy commented:

> **Wendy:** …it looks better (her work) and it's tidier, much tidier… and I don't need to look at the keyboard either. I look at the screen. I don't have to work out what the letters are to write words on the screen, so I can concentrate more on what I am writing.
> (Wendy, interview 1, 2003)

A few students commented on the fact that they 'felt different' to other students in the school, and while they clearly considered their time in the e-classroom as a "good opportunity" (Simone & Hinemoa, interview 2, 2003), they suggested that it could be enhanced by lessening the emphasis on the use of computers in favour of a more balanced approach. They considered the use of computers for virtually all work tasks limited the range of activities they were able to do, and were in favour of a blended approach which involved the greater use of exercise books and a wider array of media and materials. This perspective was supported by an analysis of coverage of the mandatory curriculum during the course of the study, which revealed a significant imbalance in favour of learning activities of a language and mathematics nature – that is, those which could more easily be accommodated by the use of computer software. Some students also considered that using computers 'depersonalised' their work and did not allow them to produce an outcome they could easily share with others. As Melanie and Simone stated:

> **Melanie:** I think the computer is fun, but I think it would be better if only… say half the class was on books, and the other half could use the computers, and then we could swap over.
> (Melanie & Rose, interview 2, 2003)

> **Simone:** I think that if I had to choose between computers and writing in books, I would probably choose books, because it… it's actually your own work… you've got something to keep and show others what you've done.
> (Simone & Hinemoa, interview 2, 2003)

While students' attitudes to the e-classroom were generally very positive, data from this study indicated that it did not suit the learning preferences of all, and alerted to the dangers of making assumptions that this was the case. There was also a definite decrease in the motivational impact of the environment during the course of the study, as having full-time access to the computers appeared to 'normalise' over time, as the 'novelty value' eroded.

8. Summary and Conclusion

While it is not possible to adequately summarise in a short chapter all the complexities of this environment, overall the findings of this study indicate a 'mixed bag' of outcomes. While this environment was undoubtedly motivating for most, the 'learning value' students were able to extract from it was highly variable. This was largely dependent upon existing knowledge and skills, the way in which they organised themselves, who they worked with, and the extent to which they were prepared to engage cognitively with learning tasks. Students with sound foundational knowledge or skill who worked in collaborative arrangements were generally in the best position to use the computers for positive gain. Those in less collaborative working arrangements or who did not possess a solid grounding in key knowledge or skills relating to concepts being explored or topics studied, struggled to gain this from using the technology. These students tended to 'drift' in this environment, engaging in diversionary use of the software, producing less work, or adjusting outcomes to accommodate their limitations. Monitoring these activities was also problematic, with the highly individualised nature of the curriculum and the manner in which student work was stored, posing significant challenges to the teacher.

While acknowledging the pioneering nature of the initiative and the obvious limitations of this study, it does provide some useful insights and considerations which should be taken into account in the design of such environments. Clearly the rationale for establishing e-classroom environments needs to be soundly based, and as much as possible shared and understood by all those who will be affected by it. The nature of infrastructure must support, not drive the design, delivery, and monitoring of curriculum and student work, and where possible it appears to be advantageous to build on and utilise existing student social structures as the basis for workgroup organisation. Perhaps above all else, this study alerts to the dangers of making assumptions about the capability of computers to *teach* students critical knowledge. While there was undoubtedly high levels of *engagement* displayed by most students, data suggested that this was not necessarily converted into learning without significant, and at times direct, teacher intervention, to challenge misconceptions and *teach* students what they need to know to make progress. While computers are a powerful resource that can support learning, this study suggests that the role of a teacher in an e-classroom environment needs to be far more expert and active than the old cliché – "a guide on the side" would suggest.

References

Apple Computer (ACOT). (1998). *Summary from the Apple Classrooms of Tomorrow Project* (ACOT). Cupertino, CA: Apple Computer. Retrieved November 11, 2002, from http://www.apple.com/ education/k12/leadership/acot/library.html.

Blackmore, J., Hardcastle, L., Bamblett, E., & Owens, J. (2003). *Effective use of information and communication technology (ICT) to enhance learning for disadvantaged school students.* Geelong, Australia: Deakin Centre for Educational Change: Institute of Disability Studies, Deakin University.

Bolstad, R. (2004). *Evaluation report from the Notebook Valley Project* (unpublished). Wellington, New Zealand: Ministry of Education.

Burns, R. B. (1997). *Introduction to research methods* (3rd ed.). Melbourne: Addison Wesley Longman.

Capper, P. (2001). *Report on the implementation of ICT in New Zealand schools* (unpublished). Wellington, New Zealand: WEB Research.

Cuban, L. (2002). *Oversold and underused: Computers in the classroom.* Cambridge, MA: Harvard University Press.

Erickson, F. (1986). Qualitative methods in research on teaching. In M. C. Wittrock (Ed.), *Handbook of research on teaching* (3rd ed., pp. 119-161). New York: Macmillan.

Falloon, G. W. (1999). Developing exemplary practice: Why are some teachers better at IT than others? *Computers in New Zealand Schools, 11* (3), 19-23.

Falloon, G. W. (2005). *An analysis of the impact of an e-classroom environment on the social, cognitive and affective elements of student work practices.* Unpublished Doctor of Science Education Thesis. Curtin University of Technology: WA.

Fuchs, T. & Woessmann, L. (2004). *Computers and student learning: Bivariate and multivariate evidence on the availability and use of computers at home and at school.* CESifo Working Paper No. 1321. Ifo Institute for Economic Research, University of Munich. Retrieved April 22, 2005, from http://www.CESifo.de.

Heinecke, W., Blasi, L., Milman, N., & Washington, L. (1999). *New directions in the evaluation of the effectiveness of educational technologies.* Paper presented at the Secretary's Conference on Educational Technology. Retrieved October 18, 2002, from http://www/ed/gov/Technology/TechConf/1999/whitepapers/paper8. html.

Hooper, S. (1992). Cooperative learning and computer-based instruction. *Educational Technology Research and Development, 40* (3), 21-38.

Iverson, B. (2001). *Transformation of teaching and learning through technology: It's about the teaching, not the tools.* Chicago: Columbia College. Retrieved June 16, 2003, from http://nexus.colum.edu/ user/iverson/fipse/for%20printing/to_print.pdf.

Johnson, D. W. & Johnson, R. T. (1996). Cooperation and the use of technology. In D. H. Jonassen (Ed.), *Handbook of research for educational communications and technology* (pp. 1017-1044). New York: Macmillan.

McCombs, B. (2000). *Assessing the role of educational technology in the teaching and learning process: A learner-centered perspective.* Paper presented at The Secretary's Conference on Educational Technology: University of Denver Research Institute. Retrieved October 18, 2002, from http://www.ed.gov/Technology/techconf/ 2000/ccombs_paper.html.

McCombs, B. L. & Whisler, J. S. (1997). The learner-centered classroom and school: Strategies for increasing student motivation and achievement. San Francisco: Jossey-Bass.

Page, N. (1999). In search of a philosophy for ICT. *Computers in New Zealand Schools, 11* (3), 15-18.

Pittard, V., Bannister, P., & Dunn, J. (2004). *The big pICTure: The impact of ICT on attainment, motivation and learning.* A report to the Department for Education and Skills (DfES). Retrieved May 26, 2004, from www.dfes.gov.uk/ictinschools.

Roschelle, J. M., Pea, R. D., Hoadley, C. M., Gordin, D. N., & Means, B. M. (2001). Changing how and what children learn in school with computer-based technologies. *The Future of Children: Children and Computer Technology, 10* (2), 76-101.

Taylor, R. (1980). Introduction. In R. P. Taylor (Ed.), *The computer in the school: Tutor, tool, tutee.* New York: Teachers College Press.

Thornburg, D. D. (1999). *Technology in K-12 education: Envisioning a new future.* White paper commissioned for the Forum on Technology in Education – envisioning the future: Washington, D.C.

Yelland, N. (1995). Collaboration and learning with Logo: Does gender make a difference? *Proceedings of the Conference on Computer-Supported Cooperative Learning* (pp. 197-410). Bloomington, IN.

Chapter 15

MEASURING THE LEARNING ENVIRONMENT OF THE CLASSROOM AND ITS EFFECT ON COGNITIVE AND AFFECTIVE OUTCOMES OF SCHOOLING

Leonidas Kyriakides
University of Cyprus
Cyprus

The teacher effects research tradition was initially concerned with classroom climate factors defined as managerial techniques. Management is necessary to create conditions for learning and instruction, but management itself is not sufficient for student results. On the other hand, the psychological tradition of classroom environment research paid a lot of attention to instruments for measuring students' perceptions of climate. It is argued that researchers should take the first steps to integrate elements of these two research traditions. Specifically, this chapter presents results of a study attempting to show that teacher effectiveness research and research into teacher interpersonal behaviour can help us explain most of the student variance at classroom level. Thus, the main findings of both teacher effectiveness research and research into teacher interpersonal behaviour are presented. A stratified sample of 32 primary schools in Cyprus was selected and two questionnaires measuring student perceptions of teacher behaviour in the classroom according to each research tradition were administered to all year 6 students (N=1721) from each class (N=81) of the school sample. Evidence supporting the reliability, discriminate validity and construct validity of each questionnaire is provided. Moreover, data collected from most of the scales of both questionnaires were associated with student achievement gains in both cognitive (Mathematics and Greek Language) and affective outcomes of schooling. Implications of findings for the development of educational effectiveness research are drawn.

1. Introduction

Stringfield (1994) defines educational effectiveness research as the process of differentiating existing ideas and methods along dimensions deemed to be of value. Educational effectiveness research (EER) does not attempt to invent new ideas or programmes but to concentrate on understanding the lessons to be drawn from existing practices. In this

369

way, EER attempts to establish and test theories which explain why and how some schools and teachers are more effective than others. Using multi-level modelling techniques, studies on EER conducted in different countries revealed that the classroom level is more significant than the school and/or the system level (e.g., Kyriakides, Campbell, & Gagatsis, 2000; Yair, 1997). It has been also claimed that defining factors at the classroom level is a prerequisite for defining the school and the system level (Creemers, 1994). Thus, early research into educational effectiveness was mainly focused on investigating the effects of teacher behaviour in the classroom upon student achievement gains. This emphasis resulted in the development of a sub-domain within EER namely, instructional effectiveness research (Creemers & Reezigt, 1996).

However, EER has been criticized for the way it has conceptualised and measured teacher behaviour in the classroom. It was argued that EER was mainly focused on instructional variables and concepts, and in particular on direct instruction. Creemers and Reezigt (1996) claim that the popularity of direct instruction finds its roots in Carroll's model (Carroll, 1963), which is one of the most influential models that emerged from the educational psychological approach to educational effectiveness modelling. Carroll's model states that the degree of mastery is a function of the ratio of amount of time students actually spend on learning tasks to the total amount of time they need. Carroll (1963) argued that time actually spent on learning is defined as equal to the smallest of three variables: a) opportunity (time allowed for learning), b) perseverance (the amount of time students are willing to engage actively in learning), and c) aptitude (the amount of time needed to learn under optimal instructional conditions).

Numerous studies and meta-analyses have confirmed the validity of Carroll's model. It was also the basis for Bloom's concept of mastery learning (Bloom, 1968) and is also related to "direct instruction" as described by Rosenshine (1983). However, this focus of EER may have resulted in a relative neglect of other existing theories and concepts (e.g., Reynolds & Packer, 1994; Creemers & Scheerens, 1994; Scheerens, 1993).

This unique theoretical focus also had its effect on the way the learning environment of the classroom was measured. Most studies on effectiveness were concerned with climate factors defined as managerial techniques (e.g., Brophy & Good, 1986; Creemers, 1994; Lee, 1995). Management is necessary to create conditions for learning and instruction, but management itself is not sufficient for student results. This argument is supported by the fact that psychologically oriented research on classroom as a learning environment has shown that the impact of teachers upon students is determined by the students' psychological response to what the teacher does (Shulman, 1986). Shuell (1996) argues that the way in which learners perceive, interpret and process information in the instructional situation (including content and social processes) is crucial in determining what they will learn. Thus, the effect of teacher behaviour on student outcomes has also been studied within the domain of classroom environment research (e.g., Fraser, 1994), which found its origin in studies on the interaction between person and environment (Moos, 1979; Walberg, 1979).

Within the domain of learning environments research, a particular line of research has evolved around order and classroom atmosphere, studying teaching in terms of the teachers' interpersonal relationships with students (Wubbels & Brekelmans, 1998; Wubbels & Levy, 1991). This research tradition has managed to demonstrate relationships between teacher interpersonal behaviour and student outcomes (e.g., Brekelmans, Wubbels, & den Brok, 2002; den Brok, Brekelmans, & Wubbels, 2003).

In this context, it is argued that researchers should take the first steps to integrate elements of these two research traditions in order to study teacher contribution in creating a learning environment in his/her classroom and identify the effect of the learning environment of classroom on student achievement gains. Thus, the study reported here is an attempt to show that teacher effectiveness research and research into teacher interpersonal behaviour can help us: a) collect valid and reliable data about the teacher's role in creating a learning environment in his/her classroom, and b) explain most of the variance of student achievement at the classroom level.

For this reason, the next section provides a brief review of the literature on teacher effectiveness research which helps us justify the process which was followed in order to design a questionnaire measuring teacher behaviour in the classroom. The main findings of research into teacher interpersonal behaviour are presented in the third section of this chapter. The next two parts of the chapter present the methods and results of an effectiveness study which was conducted in order to identify the effect of variables associated with both research traditions of measuring teacher behaviour upon student achievement gains. Finally, implications of findings for the development of EER are drawn.

2. Research into Teacher Effectiveness: Factors Associated with Teacher Behaviours

Brophy & Good (1986) argue that research on effective teaching was slow to develop because of historical influences on the conceptualisation and measurement of teacher effectiveness. Early concern with teachers' personal traits led to presage-product studies and to an attempt to identify the psychological characteristics of an effective teacher: personality characteristics (e.g., permissiveness, dogmatism, directness), attitude (e.g., motivation to teach, empathy toward children, commitment), experience (e.g., years of teaching experience in grade level taught) and aptitude/achievement (e.g., professional recommendations, student teaching evaluations). Although this approach produced some consensus on virtues considered desirable in teachers, no information on the relations between these psychological factors and student performance was provided (Borich, 1992; Rosenshine & Furst 1973). The subsequent focus produced experimental studies attempting to investigate the impact of specific teaching methods upon student achievement.

However, the majority of these studies produced inconclusive results because the differences between teaching methods were not significant enough to produce meaningful differences in student achievement (Medley, 1979). Furthermore, the significant differences that did appear tended to contradict one another (Borich, 1992). The 1950s and 1960s brought concern about creating a good classroom climate and about the teaching competencies involved in producing student achievement. This led to an emphasis on measurement of teacher behaviour through systematic observation and by 1970 to a proliferation of classroom observation systems (Shavelson, 1973; Simon & Boyer, 1970). During the last three decades, researchers have turned to teacher behaviours as predictors of student achievement in order to build up a knowledge base on effective teaching. This research has led to the identification of a range of behaviours which are positively related to student achievement (Doyle, 1986; Borich, 1992; Brophy & Good, 1986; Everston, Anderson, Anderson, & Brophy, 1980; Galton, 1987). Many of these findings have been validated experimentally, but experimental findings are weaker and less consistent than correlational findings (e.g., Griffin & Barnes, 1986).

Thus, the main effectiveness factors associated with teacher behaviour in the classroom, which emerged from teacher effectiveness research, are presented below.

2.1 Quantity of academic activity

Brophy & Good (1986) argue that the most consistently replicated findings in American studies link student achievement to the quantity and pacing of instruction. Amount learnt is related to opportunity to learn and achievement is maximised when teachers prioritise academic instruction (Brophy & Everston, 1976). Opportunity to learn was also found to be a significant factor associated with both teacher and school effectiveness (Creemers, 1994; Kyriakides et al., 2000; Reynolds et al., 1994; Scheerens & Bosker, 1997). Consistent success is another significant factor associated with student achievement. To learn efficiently, students must be engaged in activities that are appropriate in difficulty level and suited to their current achievement levels and needs (Bennett et al., 1981; Stallings, 1985). This implies that there is a tension between the goal of maximising amount of curriculum covered by pacing the students through the curriculum as rapidly as possible and the need to move in small steps so that each new objective can be learnt readily and without frustration. Brophy & Good (1986) argue that the pace at which a class can move should depend on the students' abilities and developmental levels and the nature of the subject matter since students' errors should be held to a minimum.

2.2 Classroom management

Since opportunity to learn is related to student engagement and time on task and engagement has been used as a criterion variable in classroom management studies (Emmer & Everston, 1981), effective teachers are also expected to organize and manage the classroom environment as an efficient learning environment and thereby to maximise engagement rates (Creemers & Reezigt, 1996). Doyle (1986) points out that key indicators of effective classroom management include: good preparation of the classroom and installation of rules and procedures at the beginning of year, smoothness and momentum in lesson pacing, consistent accountability procedures and clarity about when and how can students get help and about what options are available when they finish. As far as the actual teaching process is concerned, research into classroom discourse reveals that although in the classes of effective teachers there is a great deal of teacher talk most of it is academic rather than managerial or procedural, and much of it involves asking questions and giving feedback rather than extended lecturing (Cazden, 1986).

2.3 Quality of teacher's organised lessons

The findings summarized above deal with factors associated with the quantity of academic activity. The variables presented below concern the form and quality of teacher's organised lessons and can be divided into those that involve giving information (structuring), asking questions (soliciting), providing feedback (reacting), and providing practice and application opportunities. As for structuring, Rosenshine & Stevens (1986) point out that achievement is maximised when teachers not only actively present materials but structure it by: a) beginning with overviews and/or review of objectives; b) outlining the content to be covered and signalling transitions between lesson parts; c) calling attention to main ideas; and d) reviewing main ideas at the end. Summary reviews are also important since they integrate and reinforce the learning of major points (Brophy & Good, 1986). These structuring elements not only facilitate memorising of the information but allow for its apprehension as an integrated whole with recognition of the relationships between parts (Creemers & Kyriakides, 2005).

Moreover, achievement is higher when information is presented with a degree of redundancy, particularly in the form of repeating and reviewing general views and key concepts. Clarity of presentation is also a consistent correlate of student achievement (Borich, 1992) and is seen as an important component of teacher's skills to give information to students. Specifically, effective teachers are able to communicate clearly and directly to their students without digression, speaking above students' levels of comprehension or using speech patterns that impair the clarity of what is being taught (Smith & Land, 1981; Walberg, 1986).

The focus on teacher actively presenting materials should not be seen as an indication that traditional lecturing and drill approach is an effective teaching approach. Effective teachers ask a lot of questions and attempt to involve students in class discussion (Creemers & Kyriakides, 2005). Although the data on cognitive level of question yield inconsistent results (Redfield & Rousseau, 1981), optimal question difficulty is expected to vary with context. There should also be a mix of product questions (i.e. expecting a single response from students) and process questions (i.e. expecting students to provide explanations) but effective teachers are also expected to ask more process questions (Everston et al, 1980; Askew & William, 1995). Length of pause following questions should also vary directly with their difficulty level. Brophy & Good (1986) point out that a question calling for application of abstract principles should require a longer pause than a factual question.

Once the teacher has asked a question and called on a student to answer, the teacher has to monitor the student's response and react to it. Correct responses should be acknowledged for other students' learning, while responses that are partly correct, require affirmation of the correct part, and rephrasing of the question (Brophy & Good, 1986; Rosenshine & Stevens, 1986). Following incorrect answers, teachers should begin by indicating that the response is not correct but avoid personal criticism (Rosenshine, 1971). In general, effective teachers are expected to answer relevant student questions or redirect them to the class and incorporate relevant student comments into the lesson (Brophy & Good, 1986; Borich, 1992; Flanders, 1970).

Effective teachers also use seatwork or small group tasks since they provide needed practice and application opportunities (Borich, 1992). The effectiveness of seatwork assignments are enhanced when the teacher explains the work that students are expected to do and once the students are released to work independently she/he circulates to monitor progress and provide help and feedback (Brophy & Good, 1986).

2.4 Classroom climate

Muijs & Reynolds (2000) point out that classroom climate is a factor that teacher effectiveness research has found to be significant. The classroom environment should not be only businesslike but also needs to be supportive for the students (Walberg, 1986). Effective teachers expect all students to be able to succeed and their positive expectations should be transmitted to students (Brophy & Good, 1986). Finally, teachers are expected to establish positive relationships with students (Scheerens & Bosker, 1997). It can, therefore, be claimed that effective teachers are able to create a positive, learning-centred environment with an atmosphere of mutual respect between students and between students and the teacher (Kyriakides, 2005a). As a consequence, the environment is both safe and caring and the students feel that they are treated fairly by their teachers.

2.5 Beyond classroom behaviour

Factors other than teacher behaviour in the classroom have been the focus of considerable research effort during the last two decades. Although these factors can be classified in a variety of ways, the category system adopted here follows that used by Wang, Haertel, and Walberg (1990) who evaluated 179 authoritative papers examining the factors associated with student learning. The papers encompassed 228 items organized into 30 scales within six categories. Four of the categories related to beyond classroom factors and are concerned with two types of professional knowledge (i.e., subject knowledge and teacher's general knowledge of pedagogy), teachers' beliefs, and teachers' sense of efficacy.

However, studies concerning variables associated with these four categories have not managed to demonstrate consistent relationships between any of these categories with student achievement gains. For example, although teacher knowledge is widely perceived as a factor affecting teacher effectiveness (Scriven, 1994), the evidence for the effect of subject and/or pedagogy knowledge on student achievement is problematic. Similar claims can be made about research on the beliefs of teachers (Askew, Rhodes, Brown, William, & Johnson, 1997) and on teacher efficacy beliefs. As a consequence, the questionnaire which emerged from teacher effectiveness research and used to generate explanatory variables for the effectiveness study presented here was only concerned with measuring student views of their teacher's behaviour in classroom.

3. Research into Interpersonal Teacher Behaviour

The previous section was concerned with the main findings of teacher effectiveness research. This section is concerned with research into interpersonal teacher behaviour in an attempt to identify factors associated with the learning environment of the classroom which did not emerge from the process-product model of teacher effectiveness research. As it has been argued above, a particular line of classroom environment research has evolved around order and classroom atmosphere, studying teaching in terms of the interpersonal relationship between teacher and students (Wubbels & Brekelmans, 1998; Wubbels & Levy, 1991).

Specifically, in line with the systems approach to communication (Watzlawick, Beavin, & Jackson, 1967) classroom groups are considered as ongoing systems. In the systems approach to communication the focus is on the effect of communication on the persons involved. Therefore, Wubbels, Creton and Hooymayers (1987) applied a general model for interpersonal relationships designed by Leary (1957) to describe the perceptions that students may have of the behaviour of their teachers. In the Leary model, two dimensions are important: the Dominance-Submission axis and the Hostility-Affection axis.

While the two dimensions have occasionally been given other names, they have generally been accepted as universal descriptors of human interaction. Adapting the Leary Model to the context of education, Wubbels et al. (1987) used the two dimensions, which they called Influence (describing who is in control in the teacher-student relationship) and Proximity (describing the degree of cooperation between teacher and students). The influence dimension is characterized by teacher dominance (D) on one end of the spectrum and teacher submission (S) on the other end. Similarly, the proximity dimension is characterized by teacher cooperation (C) on one end and by teacher opposition (O) on the other. The two dimensions can be depicted in a two-dimensional plane, that can further be subdivided into eight categories or sectors of behaviour: leadership (DC), helpful/friendly behaviour (CD), understanding behaviour (CS), giving responsibility/freedom (SC), uncertain behaviour (SO), dissatisfied behaviour (OS), admonishing behaviour (OD) and strictness (DO). The Model for Interpersonal Teacher Behaviour (MITB) also assumes that these eight categories of behaviour are ordered with equal distances to each other on a circular structure and maintain equal distances to the middle of the circle.

The *Questionnaire on Teacher Interaction* (QTI) was designed in order to map students' perceptions of his/her teacher interpersonal behaviour according to the MITB. Since its development, the QTI has been the focus of learning environment studies in many countries (den Brok, Brekelmans, Levy, & Wubbels, 2002) and has been translated into more than 15 languages (Wubbels, Brekelmans, van Tartwijk, & Admiraal, 1997). Some of these studies revealed positive relationships between student perceptions of Influence and Proximity or their related sub-sectors and cognitive student outcomes (e.g., Brekelmans, Wubbels, & Creton, 1990).

However, studies investigating the association of teacher-student relationship with affective outcomes revealed a much more consistent pattern than studies examining the effect of teacher-student relationships upon cognitive outcomes. Nevertheless, the effects of teacher student relationships upon student outcomes found in the learning environment studies were probably overestimated, because the nested structure of the data was not taken into account and multilevel analysis techniques were not used (Goldstein, 2003). In this context, this study attempts to identify the extent to which teacher effectiveness research and research into teacher interpersonal behaviour can help us: a) investigate the contribution of the teacher in creating a classroom-learning environment, and b) explain most of the variance of student achievement gains at the classroom level.

4. Research Design

The research reported in this chapter was conducted in three main stages. The first two stages were concerned with the construction of student questionnaires measuring teacher behaviour in the classroom. Each questionnaire was designed according to the main findings of the two research traditions dealing with the classroom-learning environment presented above. Then, an effectiveness study was conducted and both questionnaires were used to measure the effect of teacher behaviour on student achievement gains in both cognitive and affective outcomes of schooling. Each stage of the study is described in the following sections.

A) Stage 1: The design of a student questionnaire measuring quality of teaching

A questionnaire measuring students' views of teacher behaviour based on the main findings of the process-product model of teacher effectiveness research was constructed. Thus, the items of the questionnaire covered: a) the quantity of academic activity, b) the form and quality of teacher's organized lessons and c) classroom climate. Key indicators of the quantity of academic activity included: quantity of instruction and smoothness and momentum in lesson pacing, and classroom management.

More specifically, classroom management was measured by investigating the extent to which teachers managed to establish consistent accountability procedures for maintaining attention on lesson and appropriate classroom behaviour. Items concerning the form and quality of the teacher's organized lessons were divided into those that involve teacher's skills in giving information (structuring), asking questions (soliciting), providing feedback (reacting) and providing practice and application opportunities. As far as the measurement of classroom climate is concerned, students were asked to provide information regarding the extent to which: a) the classroom environment was businesslike and supportive for the students; b) their teacher managed to establish positive relationships with the students; and c) their teacher expect all students to be able to succeed.

Although it was not practical to include in the questionnaire items reflecting all the elements of quality of teaching as emerged from teacher effectiveness research (see Scheerens & Bosker, 1997, pp. 123-133), the nine indicators of the quality of teaching which were examined covered the most consistently replicated findings of teacher effectiveness research presented above.

The content validity of the questionnaire was examined by three researchers in the area of effectiveness, two senior lecturers in pedagogy, two post-graduate students in education and two primary inspectors, who were selected on the basis of their familiarity with the literature on teacher effectiveness. The "judges" of the content validity of the questionnaire were asked to examine whether each item contained: (1) a recognizable generic teaching skill which could be easily observed from year 6 students; and (2) one or more phrases that directly reflect a student's attitudes towards the way his/her teacher behaves in the classroom. In the light of their comments minor amendments were made, particularly where the structure used was not easily comprehensible or terms that had been used were seen as not familiar to primary students. The final version of the questionnaire met the two criteria to the satisfaction of each of the nine "judges".

B) Stage 2: The development of a Greek version of the QTI

The first step of the development of a Greek version of the American 64-item version of the QTI (Wubbels & Levy, 1991) was to check the relevance of each item of the QTI and the whole concept of each scale within the cultural context. With cross-cultural conceptual equivalence checked, items of the QTI were translated into Greek by an adult. The translator, fluent in both English and Greek, was a primary school teacher aware of many of the language difficulties that Cypriot primary students encounter. Many discussions between the researcher and the translator were held throughout this phase to ensure that the rewording of some items did not change their original meanings.

A panel of judges, consisting of three primary teachers and two teacher educators who were fluent speakers of both languages, checked the preliminary translated version of the QTI according to item clarity and face validity. The panel recommended further modification of some items. Back-translation procedures were then employed. (Smith, 1991). Specifically, two teacher educators who had not read the original English version of the QTI translated the final translation of the QTI from Greek back into English independently. The back-translation did not suggest that rewording was needed for any item.

C) Stage 3: Using the two student questionnaires in an effectiveness study in Cypriot primary schools to measure the effect of teacher behaviour in the classroom

An effectiveness study was conducted in Cyprus in order to test the validity of the comprehensive model of educational effectiveness (Creemers, 1994) in relation to different criteria of measuring effectiveness (both cognitive and affective) (Kyriakides, 2005a). Specifically, data on students' cognitive achievement in mathematics and Greek language were collected by using two forms of assessment (external assessment and teacher assessment). Affective outcomes of schooling were measured through asking students to answer a questionnaire concerning their attitudes towards peers, teachers, school and learning. The questionnaire and the two forms of assessment in mathematics and Greek language were administered to all year 6 students (N=1721) of 32 primary schools at the beginning and at the end of school year 2001-2002. The constructions of the tests and the questionnaire were subject to controls for reliability and validity (see Kyriakides, 2005a).

In order to test the main assumptions of Creemers' model, a selection was made of all possible variables of the model which were categorized as: context, time, opportunity and quality factors. Questionnaires to students of year 6, teachers and headteachers were administered in order to collect data about the variables used to test Creemers' model. In addition, observations were conducted in order to measure teacher behaviour in the classroom. Since this chapter is concerned with the measurement of teacher behaviour in the classroom, information about the internal reliability and the main forms of validity of two student questionnaires measuring teacher behaviour are provided in the next section.

It is also important to note that in March 2002, the students of our sample were asked to indicate the extent to which his/her teacher behaves in certain ways when he/she teaches mathematics and Greek language on a 5-point scale (never=1, and 5=always). In May 2002, the students were also asked to complete the Greek version of the QTI in order to identify their interpersonal relationships with their mathematics teacher and their Greek language teacher. The students were asked to complete the questionnaires when they were at the school (with permission given by the Ministry of Education) so that we had full data from 32 schools, 81 classes, and 1,721 students. Thus, the effects of the variables measuring teacher behaviour in the classroom on student achievement gains were examined by using multi-level modelling techniques.

As far as the participants of the study are concerned, stratified sampling (Cohen, Manion, & Morrison, 2000) was used to select 32 Cypriot primary schools. Specifically, the Cypriot primary schools were divided into groups according to the location of the school (rural or urban) and the choice of the school sample in each group was random. All the year 6 students (N=1,721) from each class (N=81) of the school sample were chosen. The chi-square test did not reveal any statistically significant difference between the research sample and the population in terms of students' sex (X^2=1.12, df=1, p<0.34). Moreover, the t-test did not reveal any statistically significant difference between the research sample and the population in terms of the age of students (t=0.27, df=18,722, p<0.79). Therefore, it may be claimed that a nationally representative sample of Cypriot year 6 students was drawn.

5. Results

Results concerning the internal reliability and the discriminant and construct validity of the questionnaire used to measure student views of the quality of teaching are presented in the first part of the results section. The second part refers to the reliability and validity of the Greek version of QTI. Finally, the last part of this section is an attempt to identify the extent to which data collected from the two student questionnaires are associated with achievement gains in cognitive and affective outcomes of schooling.

5.1 The questionnaire measuring student views about the quality of teaching

5.1.1 Reliability, consistency and variance at class level

Although data collected from student responses to the questionnaire on quality of teaching are aggregated at the teacher/classroom level, scale internal consistency was calculated at individual student level for each subject. As a consequence, to examine the reliability of the questionnaire, coefficient alpha values for the whole scale of the questionnaire and its sub-domains for each subject were calculated. For both subjects, the values of Cronbach Alpha for the scale of the questionnaire and for each sub-domain were higher than 0.78. It was also found that dropping any item from the overall scale of the questionnaire was not followed by a considerable increase in alpha value. This implies that we can be confident about the internal reliability of the data collected through the student questionnaire on the quality of teaching. Moreover, a Generalisability Study on the use of the student questionnaire revealed that the data collected could be used for measuring the quality of teaching of each teacher in each subject separately (see Kyriakides, 2001). Thus, for each subject, the score for each teacher in each questionnaire item was the mean score of the year 6 students of the class she/he taught.

5.1.2 Discriminant validity

The mean correlation of one scale with the other scales measuring a multidimensional construct indicates the degree of discriminant validity. The lower the scales correlate amongst each other, the less they measure the same dimension of the construct (Cronbach, 1990). Thus, the discriminant validity was calculated for the nine scales of the questionnaire (see Table 15.1).

We can observe that the scales correlated between 0.10 and 0.45. Moreover, in each analysis, only 9 out of 36 correlations were statistically significant and all of them refer to the relationships of indicators of the same major-dimension of the quality of teaching (i.e. the quantity of academic activity, the form and quality of teacher's organized lessons, and classroom climate). Furthermore, the correlation coefficients that refer to the relationships of indicators of the same dimension of quality of teaching were higher than those which refer to the relationships of indicators of two different dimensions of quality of teaching. Finally, the values of the mean correlation of a scale with the other scales were smaller than 0.30. This implies that the nine scales of the questionnaire, which refer to indicators of quality of teaching in each subject, differed sufficiently, although they partly measured the same general construct (i.e., the quality of teaching).

5.1.3 Construct validity

Using a unified approach to test validation (AERA, APA and NCME, 1999; Messick, 1989), this study provides construct related evidence of the questionnaire measuring student views of the quality of teaching. For the identification of the factor structure of the questionnaire, SEM analyses were conducted using EQS (Bentler, 1995). Each model was estimated by using normal theory maximum likelihood methods (ML). The ML estimation procedure was chosen because it does not require an excessively large sample size. More than one fit index was used to evaluate the extent to which the data fit the models tested. Specifically, the scaled chi-square, Bentler's (1990) Comparative Fit Index (CFI), and the Root Mean Square Error of Approximation (RMSEA) (Brown & Mels, 1990) were examined. Finally, the factor parameter estimates for the models with acceptable fit were examined to help interpret the models.

Table 15.1. Correlation Coefficients between the Student Scales and Average
Correlation between the Student Scales in Each Subject

Scale	Correlation coefficients								Average Correlation
	2	3	4	5	6	7	8	9	
A) Mathematics									
1	0.36**	0.21	0.27	0.25	0.14	0.26	0.12	0.19	0.225
2		0.11	0.19	0.24	0.17	0.20	0.10	0.13	0.195
3			0.42**	0.33**	0.38**	0.29	0.19	0.21	0.268
4				0.34**	0.24	0.21	0.16	0.20	0.254
5					0.32**	0.26	0.21	0.18	0.266
6						0.24	0.18	0.23	0.238
7							0.31**	0.44**	0.284
8								0.39**	0.208
9									0.246
B) Greek Language									
1	0.34**	0.20	0.25	0.28	0.16	0.22	0.10	0.17	0.215
2		0.12	0.18	0.14	0.22	0.25	0.11	0.15	0.189
3			0.44**	0.33**	0.32**	0.25	0.24	0.26	0.271
4				0.21	0.37**	0.18	0.19	0.22	0.255
5					0.33**	0.28	0.23	0.18	0.249
6						0.26	0.15	0.25	0.258
7							0.36**	0.40**	0.275
8								0.45**	0.229
9									0.260

Notes

Scales 1 up to 2 refer to the following indicators of quantity of academic activity:

1 = Quantity of instruction and smoothness and momentum in lesson pacing, and 2 = Classroom Management.

Scales 3 up to 6 refer to the following indicators of the form and quality of teacher's organised lessons:

3 = Giving information, 4 = Asking questions, 5 = Providing feedback, 6 = Providing practice and application opportunities

Scales 7 up to 9 refer to the following indicators of classroom climate:

7 = Creating a businesslike and supportive environment, 8 = Establishing positive relationships with pupils and 9 = Having Positive expectations from students

** $p < 0.001$

Having in mind that analyses of structural equation models based on multiple scales provide more stable parameter estimates than models based on individual items (Rigdon, 1998), exploratory factor analyses of students' responses to the 76 items of the questionnaire measuring the quality of teaching were conducted. For each subject, based on the results of the factor analysis (explaining 78% of the total variance in the case of Mathematics and 82% in the case of Greek Language), three mean scores representing students' views on each of the nine theoretically postulated sub-domains of the inventory were created. Thus, a first-order Confirmatory Factor Analysis model designed to test the multidimensionality of the questionnaire (Byrne, 1998) was used in order to examine the construct validity of the questionnaire.

Specifically, the model hypothesized that: (a) the 27 variables (i.e., mean scores) could be explained by nine factors concerning the nine sub-domains of the questionnaire used to measure quality of teaching; (b) each variable would have a nonzero loading on the factor it was designed to measure, and zero loadings on all other factors; (c) the nine factors would be correlated; and (d) measurement errors would be uncorrelated. The findings of the first order factor SEM analysis generally affirmed the theory upon which the questionnaire was developed. Although the scaled chi-square for the nine-factor structure in each subject (Mathematics: $X^2=508.8$, df=288, $p<0.001$; Greek Language: $X^2=495.3$, df=288, $p<0.001$) as expected was statistically significant, the values of RMSEA (Mathematics: 0.031 and Greek Language: 0.029) and CFI (Mathematics: 0.979 and Greek Language: 0.981) met the criteria for acceptable level of fit. Kline (1998, p. 212) argues that "even when the theory is precise about the number of factors of a first-order model, the researcher should determine whether the fit of a simpler, one-factor model is comparable".

Criteria fit for a one-factor model (Mathematics: $X^2=1549.4$, df=324, $p<0.001$; RMSEA=0.144 and CFI=0.455; Greek Language: $X^2=1364.8$, df=324, $p<0.001$; RMSEA=0.142 and CFI=0.435) provided values that fell outside generally accepted guidelines for model fit. Thus, a decision was made to consider the nine-factor structure as reasonable in both cases and the analysis proceeded and the parameter estimates were calculated. Figures 15.1 and 15.2 depict the nine-factor model and present the factor parameters estimates for each subject separately. All parameter estimates were statistically significant ($p<0.001$).

The following observations arise from Figures 15.1 and 15.2. First, the standardized factor loadings were all positive and moderately high. Their standardized values ranged from 0.59 to 0.78 and the great majority of them were higher than 0.65. Second, the correlations among the nine factors were positive and ranged between 0.27 and 0.42. Moreover, the majority of factor inter-correlations were higher than 0.30. It was therefore decided to examine whether the second-order factor model could explain the relatively high correlations among the nine first-order factors.

The relatively high values of the factor intercorrelations provided further support to our attempt to identify a higher order model which could explain the correlations among the nine first-order factors in each analysis. This model hypothesized that for each subject: (a) responses to the student questionnaire could be explained by nine first-order factors and one second-order factor (i.e. quality of teaching in general); (b) each item (i.e., scale score) would have a nonzero loading on the factor it was designed to measure, and zero loadings on all other factors; (c) error terms associated with each item would be uncorrelated, and (d) covariation among the nine first-order factors would be explained by their regression on the second order factor.

Figures 15.3 and 15.4 illustrate the models with one second-order factor for each subject. The fit statistics for both analyses (Mathematics: scaled $X^2=540.4$, df=315, $p<0.001$; RMSEA=0.028 and CFI=0.982; Greek Language: scaled $X^2=537.6$, df=315, $p<0.001$; RMSEA=0.027 and CFI=0.985) were acceptable. By comparing the second-order factor model that emerged from analysing the data of each subject with its theoretical first-order factor model, we could identify a minor decrease of the RMSEA (i.e. Mathematics: from 0.031 to 0.028 and Greek Language: from 0.029 to 0.027) and a very minor increase of the CFI (i.e. Mathematics: from 0.979 to 0.982 and Greek Language: from 0.981 to 0.985). Thus, the single second order model was considered as appropriate (Maruyama, 1998) and thereby the analysis proceeded and the parameter estimates were calculated.

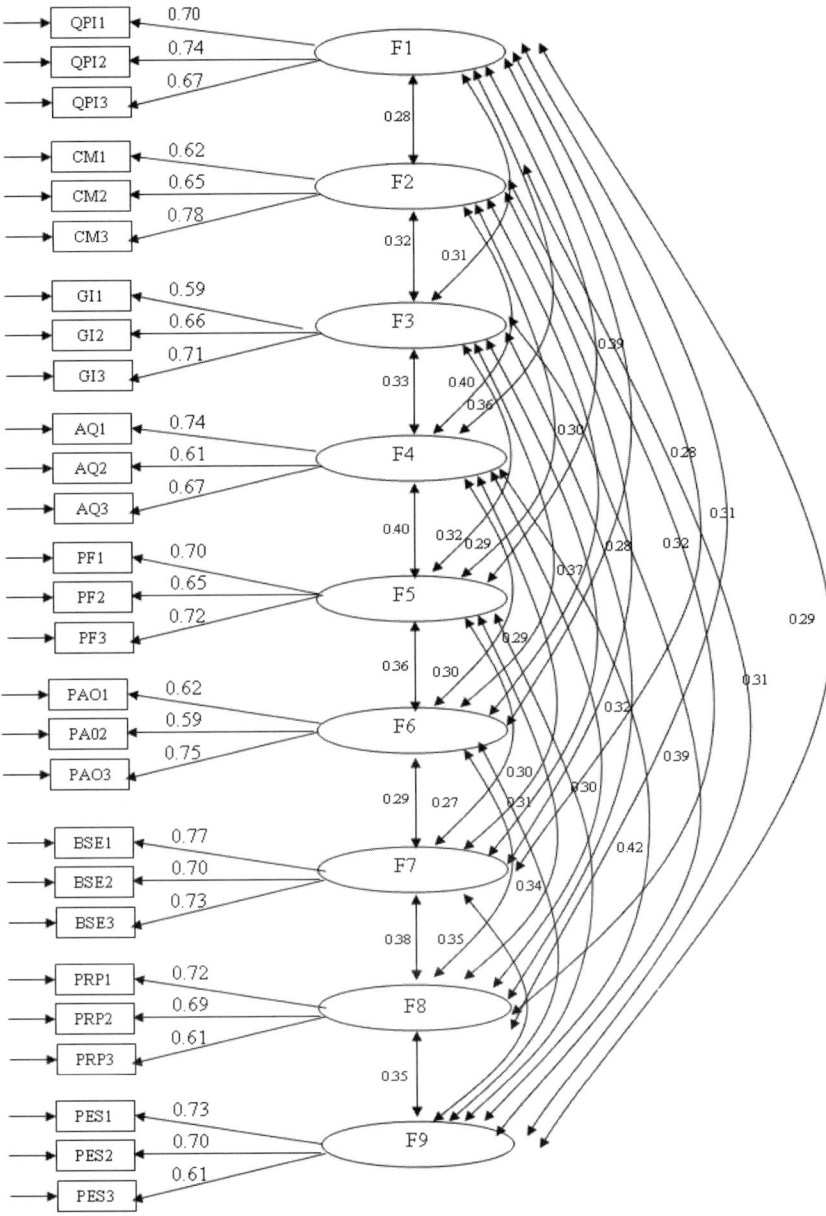

Figure 15.1. First-order factor model of the questionnaire measuring quality of teaching in Mathematics with factor parameter estimates.

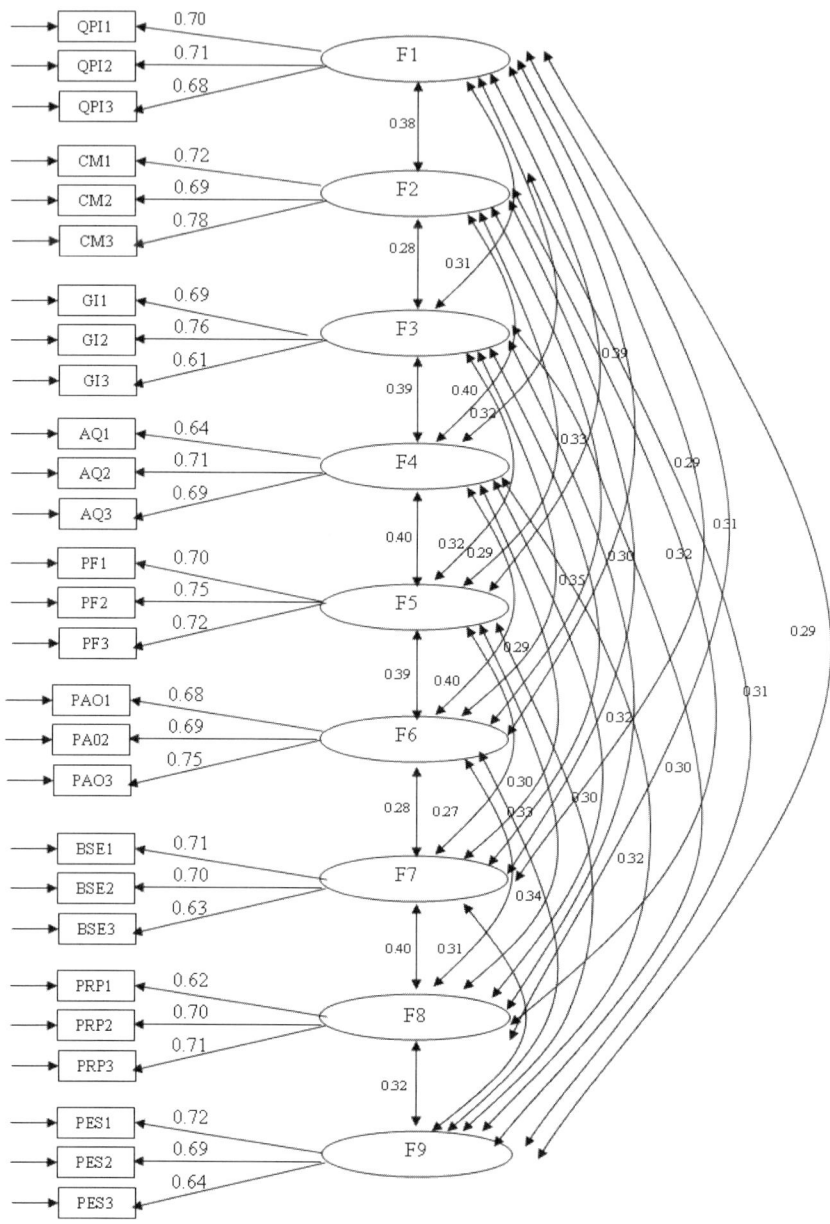

Figure 15.2. First-order factor model of the questionnaire measuring quality of teaching in Greek Language with factor parameter estimates.

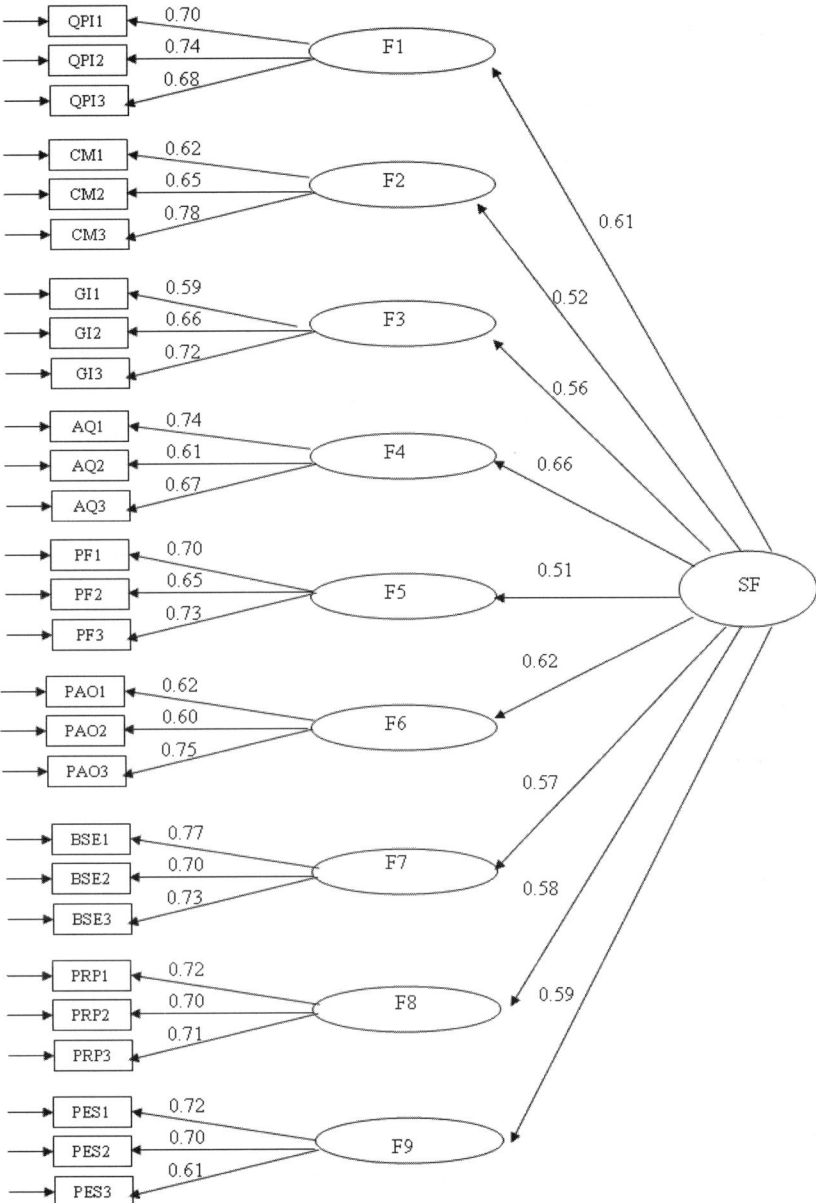

Figure 15.3. Second-order factor model of the questionnaire measuring quality of teaching in Mathematics with factor parameter estimates.

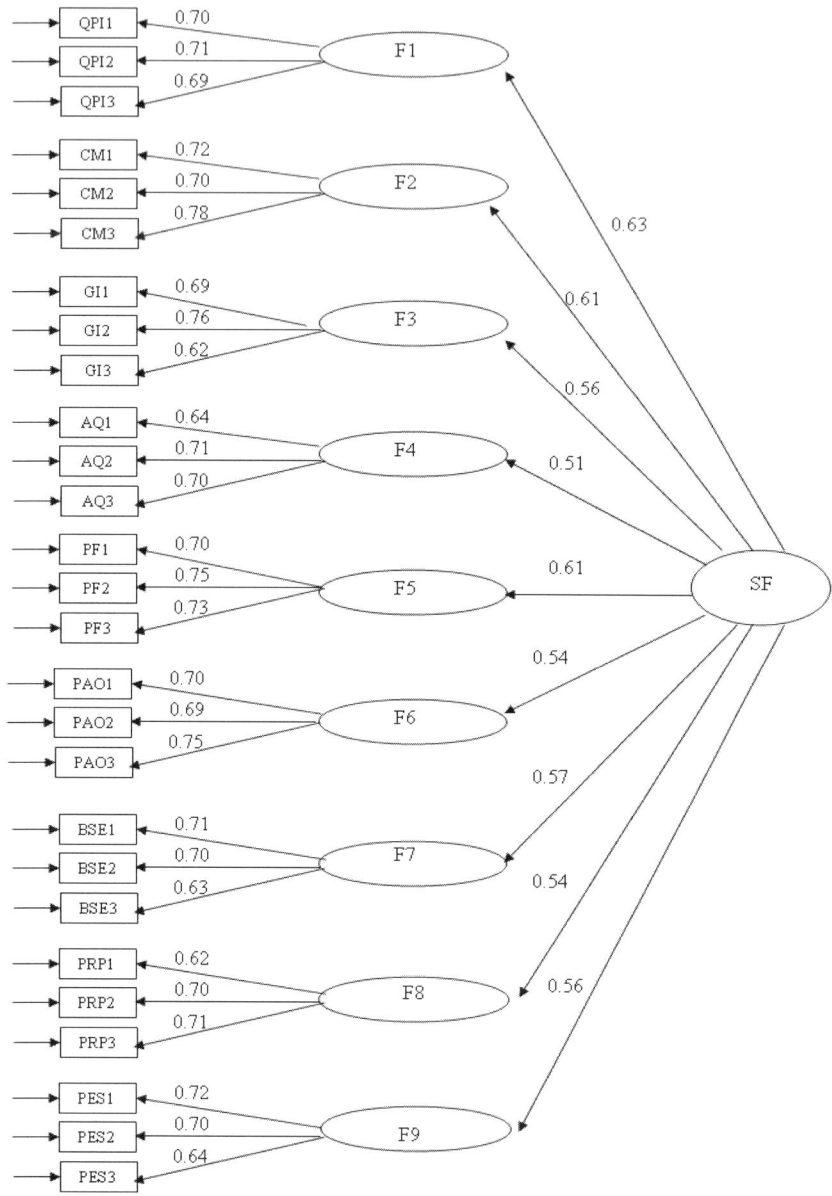

Figure 15.4. Second-order factor model of the questionnaire measuring quality of teaching in Greek Language with factor parameter estimates.

The following observations arise from Figures 15.3 and 15.4. In each model, the great majority of the standardized factor loadings were higher than 0.65. Moreover, the standardized factor loading revealed that the model explained more than 50% of variance of at least 15 items in each subject. Finally, the standardized path coefficients relating the first-order factors to the second-order factors were higher than 0.50. It is finally important to note that in terms of the theory upon which the questionnaire was based, the second-order factor, which has been identified through analysing data emerged from each subject separately, represents the quality of teaching in each subject.

5.2 The Greek version of the QTI

Taking into account the main assumptions of the theoretical framework upon which the design of the QTI was based, the reliability and validity of the Greek version of the QTI can be examined. As it was mentioned above, the QTI can be used to measure students' perceptions of teacher interpersonal behaviour according to the MITB, which is a special model because of its statistical properties. This model is theoretically linked to a particular branch of models called circumplex models. Thus, the design of QTI is based on four assumptions. First, the eight scales of the model are represented by two dimensions (or factors). Second, the two interpersonal dimensions that lay behind the sectors are uncorrelated. Third, the scales of the model can be ordered in a circular structure. Finally, the scales of the model are equally distributed over this circular structure. Thus, the investigation of the reliability and validity of the Greek version of QTI was based on an attempt to test these four assumptions.

5.2.1 Reliability, consistency and variance at class level

A learning environment instrument is expected to differentiate between perceptions of students in different classes. Students within a class usually view the learning environment similarly but differently from students in other classes. Thus, for each of the scales of the QTI we calculated the multilevel λ (Snijders & Bosker, 1999) and Cronbach alpha for data aggregated at the class level. We can observe from Table 15.2 that the reliability coefficients were very high (around .90). Moreover, the reliability of the scales "Giving Responsibility/Freedom"

(SC) and "Strict behaviour"(DO) were somewhat lower, while the reliability of the scale "Leadership" (DC) was the highest.

Using the Mplus (Muthén & Muthén, 1999) the intra-class correlations of the scales were computed. The intra-class correlations, which indicate what amount of variance of the QTI is located at the between level, are also illustrated in Table 15.2. We can observe that the percentages of variance at the between level (teacher-class level) were higher than 35 and can be considered satisfactory.

Table 15.2. Cronbach Alpha (Reliability), Multilevel Lambda (Consistency), and Intra-Class Correlations (ICC) of QTI Scales at the Teacher/Class Level in Each Subject

Scale	Mathematics			Greek language		
	Cronbach α	λ	ICC	Cronbach α	λ	ICC
DC	0.94	0.93	0.46	0.92	0.93	0.47
CD	0.91	0.91	0.41	0.90	0.92	0.40
CS	0.92	0.88	0.42	0.91	0.90	0.42
SC	0.84	0.85	0.36	0.85	0.88	0.36
SO	0.90	0.90	0.43	0.91	0.92	0.41
OS	0.91	0.89	0.41	0.93	0.89	0.39
OD	0.90	0.89	0.39	0.92	0.90	0.40
DO	0.88	0.87	0.39	0.87	0.86	0.36

Note
The scales of the QTI are as follows: Leadership (DC), Helpful/Friendly (CD), Understanding (CS), Giving Responsibility/Freedom (SC), Uncertain (SO), Dissatisfied (OS), Admonishing (OD) and Strictness (DO).

5.2.2 Construct validity

Construct validity of the QTI was investigated by subjecting the scale scores to a multilevel factor analysis using Mplus. From these analyses, it was found that an unequally-spaced circumplex model fitted the data well (Mathematics: $X^2=72.15$ df=13, $p<0.001$; CFI=0.988; RMSEA=0.041; and Greek Language: $X^2=50.59$, df=13, $p<0.001$, CFI=0.991; RMSEA=0.038). The factor loadings resulting from this model are presented in Table 15.3. This model is based on the assumption that the eight scale scores are ordered in a circle and represented by two independent dimensions. It is however not found that the eight sectors of teacher interpersonal behaviour are equally distributed over the circle or equally distanced to the circle centre. This implies that student responses to the Greek version of QTI helped us generate empirical evidence supporting the first three assumptions upon which the design of QTI was based. Therefore, the two dimension scores, rather than the eight sector scores, can be used to evaluate teacher interpersonal behaviour and to identify the effects of interpersonal teacher behaviour on student achievement gains in each subject.

Table 15.3. Factor Loadings for the Unequally Spaced Circumplex Model

Scale	Mathematics		Greek Language	
	Factor 1	Factor 2	Factor 1	Factor 2
DC	1.00	0.33	1.00	0.51
CD	0.29	0.96	0.35	1.05
CS	0.09	1.02	0.02	1.00
SC	-0.39	0.53	-0.44	0.59
SO	-0.99	0.14	-1.00	-0.16
OS	-0.18	-0.73	-0.08	-0.70
OD	-0.04	-0.88	0.04	-0.78
DO	0.34	-0.65	0.56	-0.52

Note: The meaning of each QTI scale is shown in Table 15.2.

5.3 The effect of teacher behaviour upon student achievement gains

This section is concerned with the extent to which data emerged from the two student questionnaires are associated with student achievement gains in cognitive and affective outcomes of schooling. In order to examine the extent to which variables measuring teacher behaviour show the expected effects upon student achievement in different outcomes of schooling, the analyses were performed separately for each dependent variable. Thus, the first step in each analysis was to determine the variance at individual, class and school level without explanatory variables (empty model).

In each of the three empty models, the variances at each level reached statistical significance ($p<0.001$). This implies that MLwiN can be used to identify the explanatory variables which are associated with student achievement in each outcome measure. Specifically, of the total variance in each outcome measure, the variance at school level was

11.5% in Mathematics, 9.7% in Greek Language and 14.3% in affective outcomes. The variance at classroom level was 15.2% in Mathematics, 16.8% in Greek Language and 17.8% in affective outcomes. This implies that in Cyprus the effect of both the school and the classroom was more pronounced on achievement in affective outcome measures rather than in cognitive measures in mathematics and Greek language (see Kyriakides, 2005a).

In subsequent steps explanatory variables at different levels were added, starting at the student level. Explanatory variables, except grouping variables, were centred as Z-scores with a mean of 0 and a standard deviation of 1. This is a way of centring around the grand mean (Bryk & Raudenbush, 1992) and yields effects that are comparable. Thus, each effect expresses how much the dependent variable increases (or decreases in case of a negative sign) by each additional deviation on the independent variable (Snijders & Bosker, 1999). Grouping variables were entered as dummies with one of the groups as baseline (e.g., boys=0). It is important to note that various explanatory variables, which can be categorized as context, time, opportunity and quality factors, were taken into account in order to test the main assumptions of Creemers' model (see Kyriakides, 2005a). However, this chapter is only concerned with the effects of student background factors and the effects of the various measures of teacher behaviour upon student achievement in Mathematics, Greek Language and affective outcomes of schooling. These effects are shown in Table 15.4.

In model 1 the context variables at student level (i.e., SES, prior knowledge, sex) were added to the empty model. Variables concerned with the context of each classroom, such as the average baseline score, the average SES score, and the percentage of girls were also added to the empty model. We can observe that all three contextual factors at student level (i.e., SES, prior knowledge, sex) had a significant effect upon achievement in each of the three outcome measures. Moreover, SES was correlated to a much higher degree with cognitive than affective achievement gains. Furthermore, the effect of gender background was not the same, since girls achieved lower scores than boys in mathematics and higher scores in Greek language and in affective aims of schooling. As far as the effect of the contextual factors at classroom level is concerned, only the average SES and the average baseline score were found to be associated with student achievement.

Finally, model 1 helped us explain almost half of the total-variance of student achievement in each outcome measure and most of which was at the student level.

In model 2, explanatory variables concerning the quality of teaching which emerged from the student questionnaire were entered. We can observe that eight out of the nine scales of the questionnaire were associated with student achievement gains in both Mathematics and Greek Language. On the other hand, the scale measuring teachers' positive expectations from their students did not have any statistically significant effect upon student achievement either in mathematics or Greek language. In order to measure the effect of these nine variables on the affective outcomes of schooling, we calculated the mean scores which emerged from student responses in relation to the behaviour of their mathematics teacher and their Greek language teacher.

The use of the mean scores can be attributed to the fact that the measure of the affective outcomes of schooling was based on the assumption that both mathematics and Greek language teachers are expected to help students develop positive attitudes towards peers, teachers, school and learning. Moreover, the Generalisability Study on the use of the student questionnaire revealed that the data collected could not be only used for measuring the quality of teaching of each teacher in each subject separately but also for measuring the behaviour of each teacher irrespective of whether he/she had to teach mathematics and/or Greek language (see Kyriakides, 2001).

Using this approach, it was found that the four scales which referred to the form and quality of teacher's organised lessons did not have any statistically significant effect. Moreover, the effect of each of the three scales measuring classroom climate on student achievement in affective outcomes was stronger than the effect of the scales measuring the quantity of academic activity. We can finally observe that model 2 helped us explain more than 5% of the total variance in each outcome measure and most of it was at the classroom level. However, in each analysis more than 6% of the total variance remained unexplained at the classroom level.

Table 15.4. Parameter Estimates and (Standard Errors) for the Models* used to Investigate Educational Effectiveness in Each Outcome of Schooling

	Mathematics			
Factors	Model 0	Model 1	Model 2	Model 3
Fixed part (Intercept)	37.4 (1.3)	37.2 (1.2)	39.4 (1.0)	40.4 (0.8)
Student Level				
Context				
Baseline score		2.18 (0.09)	2.10 (0.08)	2.03 (0.07)
Sex (Boys = 0, Girls = 1)		-0.81 (0.17)	-0.78 (0.07)	-0.76 (0.07)
Socio Economical Status (SES)		2.03 (0.12)	1.96 (0.10)	1.96 (0.10)
Classroom Level				
Context				
Average baseline score		2.30 (0.39)	2.31 (0.33)	2.30 (0.32)
Average SES		1.43 (0.44)	1.45 (0.42)	1.46 (0.42)
Percentage of girls		N.S.S.**	N.S.S.	N.S.S.
Quality of teaching				
Quantity and pacing of instruction			0.81 (0.09)	0.81 (0.09)
Classroom Management			0.90 (0.09)	0.92 (0.09)
Giving Information			0.96 (0.08)	0.97 (0.08)
Asking Questions			0.95 (0.10)	0.95 (0.09)
Providing Feedback			0.91 (0.10)	0.92 (0.10)
Practice and application			0.97 (0.09)	0.99 (0.09)
Classroom environment			0.84 (0.10)	0.84 (0.09)
Positive relationships with students			0.73 (0.09)	0.73 (0.09)
Positive expectations from students			N.S.S.	N.S.S.
Teacher Interpersonal Behavior				
DS (Influence)				0.81 (0.10)
CO (Proximity)				N.S.S.
Variance components				
School	11.5%	7.8%	7.6%	7.5%
Class	15.2%	10.4%	6.3%	5.0%
Student	73.3%	30.3%	28.3%	28.0%
Absolute	134.41	65.18	56.72	54.44
Explained		51.5%	57.8%	59.5%
Significance test				
X^2	1225.60	800.65	691.05	678.73
Reduction		424.95	109.60	12.32
Degrees of freedom		5	8	1
p-value		0.001	0.001	0.001

* The models were estimated without the variables that did not have a statistically significant effect. ** N.S.S. = No statistically significant effect (i.e. $p>0.05$)

Table 15.4 (Continued)

	Greek Language				Affective outcomes		
Model 0	Model 1	Model 2	Model 3	Model 0	Model 1	Model 2	Model 3
34.4 (1.3)	35.2 (1.0)	36.6 (0.72)	37.2 (0.61)	34.4 (1.3)	35.2 (1.0)	36.4 (0.81)	36.8 (0.71)
	2.08 (0.09)	2.07 (0.08)	2.07 (0.08)		2.38 (0.08)	2.39 (0.09)	2.39 (0.08)
	0.92 (0.15)	0.88 (0.15)	0.89 (0.15)		0.90 (0.18)	0.88 (0.18)	0.89 (0.18)
	2.06 (0.11)	2.06 (0.11)	2.07 (0.11)		1.26 (0.14)	1.27 (0.14)	1.27 (0.13)
	2.13 (0.35)	2.12 (0.34)	2.10 (0.33)		2.04 (0.33)	2.08 (0.33)	2.10 (0.33)
	1.64 (0.43)	1.63 (0.43)	1.63 (0.42)		1.05 (0.41)	1.13 (0.42)	1.43 (0.42)
	N.S.S.	N.S.S.	N.S.S.		N.S.S.	N.S.S.	N.S.S.
		0.80 (0.09)	0.81 (0.09)			0.70 (.012)	0.71 (0.12)
		0.94 (0.10)	0.92 (0.09)			0.73 (0.11)	0.72 (0.10)
		0.97 (0.08)	0.97 (0.08)			N.S.S.	N.S.S.
		1.01 (0.09)	1.07 (0.09)			N.S.S.	N.S.S.
		1.08 (0.10)	1.08 (0.09)			N.S.S.	N.S.S.
		0.93 (0.09)	0.93 (0.09)			N.S.S.	N.S.S.
		0.82 (0.09)	0.84 (0.09)			0.94 (0.09)	0.94 (0.09)
		0.69 (0.09)	0.69 (0.08)			0.97 (0.08)	0.99 (0.08)
		N.S.S.	N.S.S.			0.98 (0.08)	N.S.S.
			N.S.S.				0.77 (0.08)
			0.84 (0.09)				0.99 (0.08)
9.7%	8.9%	8.7%	8.7%	14.3%	13.1%	12.9%	12.9%
16.8%	12.5%	6.1%	5.0%	17.8%	14.6%	11.1%	8.9%
73.5%	27.6%	25.1%	24.3%	67.9%	24.0%	22.4%	21.2%
154.23	75.57	61.54	58.61	140.29	72.53	65.10	60.32
	51.0%	60.1%	62.0%		48.3%	53.6%	57.0%
1045.27	633.14	553.02	543.01	1124.25	812.12	721.00	710.68
	412.13	80.12	10.01		312.13	91.12	10.32
	5	8	1		5	5	1
	0.001	0.001	0.001		0.001	0.001	0.001

In model 3, the variables measuring teacher influence and proximity, which emerged from student responses to the Greek version of QTI, were entered. The mean scores that emerged from student views about their mathematics and Greek language teachers were taken into account in order to identify the impact of teacher interpersonal behaviour on affective outcomes of schooling.

Table 15.4 shows that teacher influence was associated with student achievement in mathematics and affective outcomes of schooling whereas proximity was associated with achievement in Greek language and affective outcomes of schooling. In the analysis of student achievement in affective outcomes of schooling, when "teacher proximity" was entered the effect of "positive expectations from students" was disappeared. We can also observe that the explanatory variables emerged from student responses to the QTI helped us explain 3.4% of the total variance in achievement of affective outcomes but less than 2% of the total variance in cognitive outcomes. However, in each analysis, the likelihood statistic reveals a statistically significant reduction ($p<0.001$) from model 2 to model 3, which justifies the selection of model 3.

6. Discussion

The evidence presented above is discussed in terms of its implications for the development of EER. First, this study has shown that data on teacher interpersonal behaviour emerged from student responses to the Greek version of QTI helped us explain variance on student achievement in both cognitive and affective outcomes of schooling. This implies that research into teacher interpersonal behaviour may help researchers in the area of EER to generate further variables associated with teacher effectiveness. However, further national and comparative studies should be conducted in order to identify the importance of treating variables associated with teacher interpersonal behaviour as educational effectiveness factors.

Research from cross-national studies and cross-cultural studies using the QTI indicate that the instrument and its theoretical model are cross-culturally valid (den Brok, Brekelmans, & Wubbels, 2003; Fisher, Henderson, & Fraser, 1995; Wubbels & Levy, 1991). Further support to this argument is provided by the results of this study concerning the psychometric properties of the Greek version of the QTI. Therefore, researchers can use the QTI in large-scale international effectiveness studies which may contribute in the establishment of the international dimension of EER. Such studies may also help us find out the extent to which teacher interpersonal behaviour explain effectiveness across countries and whether it should be included in generic and/or differentiated models of educational effectiveness (Kyriakides, 2005b).

Second, despite the fact that the study reported here generates data from only one country, it can be claimed that effects of interpersonal teacher behaviour are different for cognitive and for affective outcomes.

Specifically, variables associated with teacher interpersonal behaviour explained 3.4% of the total variance of student achievement in affective outcomes but less than 2% of cognitive achievement gains. Moreover, it was found that proximity has strong effects on affective achievement gains but has no effect on mathematics achievement gains.

On the other hand, influence has statistically significant effects on affective outcomes but has no effect on language achievement gains. Thus, differences in the effects of interpersonal teacher behaviour between cognitive achievement in different subjects were also identified. These findings seem to be similar to those emerged in studies conducted in other countries investigating the relationship of teacher interpersonal behaviour with student outcomes (e.g., Brekelmans, Wubbels, & den Brok, 2002; den Brok, Brekelmans, & Wubbels, 2003) but further national and/or international effectiveness studies are needed to examine their generalisability at the country-level. Moreover, studies attempting to provide explanations of the differential effect of these two variables on student cognitive achievement gains in different subjects are needed.

Third, this study has shown that variables emerged from the student questionnaire which was based on the major findings of teacher effectiveness research have similar effects on both mathematics and Greek language achievement gains. This finding seems to provide support to the argument that at least eight of the nine indicators of quality of teaching can be considered as generic skills that teachers of both Mathematics and Greek language should develop in order to become effective. However, the effects of these variables on affective achievement gains are not as strong as their effects on the cognitive achievement gains.

This implies that the variables measuring quality of direct teaching are more important for explaining variation on student achievement in cognitive outcomes whereas variables associated with teacher interpersonal behaviour are more important for explaining variation on student achievement in affective outcomes of schooling. It can, therefore, be claimed that there is a need to develop both generic and differentiated models of educational effectiveness by taking into account the two research domains concerning teacher behaviour in the classroom, which were examined by this study. This argument is also supported by the fact that the inclusion of both categories of variables associated with teacher behaviour helped us explain most of the variance on student achievement gains in both cognitive and affective outcomes of schooling.

Fifth, it is important to note that the great majority of the teachers of our sample (81.5%) had to teach both subjects to the same classroom. It was, therefore, possible to examine the extent to which there was consistency in their behaviour in teaching mathematics and Greek language. Calculating the Pearson correlation coefficient of each variable concerning teacher behaviour in teaching mathematics and in teaching Greek language, it was found that all of them were statistically significant ($p<0.001$) and that their values were higher than 0.54 but lower than 0.73. This finding implies that the teachers of our sample used to behave in a similar way in teaching the two core subjects of the Cyprus curriculum.

To examine further this assumption, it was decided to compare the effectiveness of teachers in teaching Mathematics and in teaching Greek language. Based on the results of the last model (i.e., model 3), the difference between the expected and the actual score in each subject for each teacher was plotted. The standard error of estimate for each teacher was also taken into account and was represented by the length of a vertical line. This line can be conceptualised as the range within which we are 95% confident that the "true" estimate of the teacher's residual lies (Goldstein, 2003).

Thus, where this vertical line did not cross the horizontal zero line and was also situated below the zero line we claimed that the teacher it represented was one of the least effective of our sample since the progress of his/her students was significantly lower than expected. On the other hand, where this line did not cross the horizontal zero line and was situated above the zero line, the teacher it represented was characterized as one of the most effective teachers. All the other teachers were characterized as typical. Based on the results of the classifications concerning each subject, it was found that the great majority of the teachers who taught both mathematics and Greek language (i.e., 59 out of 66) were equally effective in both subjects.

The fact that the teachers of our sample used to behave similarly in teaching the two subjects and their effectiveness did not vary provides further support to the argument that the skills measured through the student questionnaire on quality of teaching can be considered as generic teaching skills. It can also be claimed that the differentiated effect of proximity and influence on the two subjects can be attributed to differences in the nature of the two core subjects rather than on inconsistency in the behaviour of the teachers of our sample. Although further research is needed to examine the differentiated effect of teacher interpersonal behaviour on student achievement gains in different subjects, the fact that researchers in the area of EER should take into account teacher interpersonal behaviour in their attempt to build differentiated models of effectiveness seems to arise clearly from this study.

Further research on the effect of teacher interpersonal behaviour on different groups of students is also needed in order to help us test and expand the differentiated models of teacher effectiveness (see Campbell et al., 2004). Given that research on differentiated teacher effectiveness has shown that the effect of variables associated with the quality of direct teaching have different effect upon students of different background and personal characteristics (Campbell, Kyriakides, Muijs, & Robertson, 2004), it can also be assumed that the effect of influence and/or proximity on the achievement of students of different background and personal characteristics (e.g., SES, thinking style, personality type) may vary.

For example, researchers could examine whether proximity has stronger effects on achievement of low SES students due to the low self-esteem many of these students suffer from. Moreover, based on the theory of mental self-government (Sternberg, 1988), we could investigate the impact of teacher interpersonal behaviour upon the achievement of students with different thinking styles.

In this way, we could examine whether influence has stronger effect on achievement of students with executive style of thinking (i.e., students who prefer dealing with tasks that require implementation of preset rules) and/or whether its effect on achievement of students with legislative style (i.e., students who enjoy being engaged in tasks that require novel and creative ways of approaching the situation at hand) is much smaller or even not statistically significant. Such studies might help researchers in the area of EER to incorporate variables associated with teacher interpersonal behaviour into both generic and/or differentiated models of effectiveness.

Finally, it is important to note that this chapter provides support to the argument that research into teacher interpersonal behaviour could help us identify effectiveness factors at the classroom level and build a comprehensive model measuring teacher behaviour in the classroom. It could also be assumed that research into interpersonal behaviour may also help us identify effectiveness factors at the school level.

Specifically, further research could be conducted in order to examine whether variables associated with leaders' interpersonal behaviour (Fisher & Cresswell, 1998) explain variation on student achievement gains. In this context, an effectiveness study, which is currently conducted in Cyprus, investigates the effect of headteacher interpersonal behaviour and the effects of teacher interpersonal behaviour upon student achievement gains. It can be argued that by conducting such studies in various countries we could identify the extent to which it is possible to expand further the theoretical framework of EER by treating as effectiveness factors both the classroom and school level variables that emerged from research into interpersonal behaviour.

References

American Educational Research Association (AERA), American Psychological Association (APA), & National Council on Measurement in Education (NCME) (1999). *Standards for educational and psychological testing.* Washington, DC: American Psychological Association.

Askew, M. & William, D. (1995). *Recent research in mathematics education 5-16.* London: Office for Standards in Education.

Askew, M., Rhodes, V., Brown, M., William, D., & Johnson, D. (1997). *Effective teachers of numeracy: Report of a study carried out for the teacher training agency.* London: Kings College London School of Education.

Bennett, N., Desforges, C., Cockburn, A., & Wilkinson, B. (1981). *The quality of pupil learning experience: Interim Report.* Lancaster: University of Lancaster, Centre for Educational Research and Development.

Bentler, P. M. (1990). Comparative fit indexes in structural models. *Psychological Bulletin, 107*, 238-246.

Bentler, P. M. (1995). *EQS: Structural equations program manual.* California: Multivariate Software Inc.

Bloom, B. S. (1968). *Learning for mastery.* Washington, DC: ERIC.

Borich, G. D. (1992) (2nd Ed). *Effective teaching methods.* New York: Macmillan Publishing Company.

Brekelmans, M., Wubbels, T., & Créton, H. A. (1990). A study of student perceptions of physics teacher behavior. *Journal of Research in Science Teaching, 27*, 335-350.

Brekelmans, M., Wubbels, T., & Brok, P. den (2002). Teacher experience and the teacher-student relationship in the classroom environment. In S. C. Goh & M. S. Khine (Eds.), *Studies in educational learning environments: an international perspective* (pp. 73-100). Singapore: New World Scientific.

Brophy, J. & Everston, L. (1976). *Learning from teaching: A developmental perspective.* Boston: Allyn and Bacon.

Brophy, J. & Good, T. L. (1986). Teacher behavior and student achievement. In M. C. Wittrock (Ed.), *Handbook of research on teaching* (pp. 328-375). New York: MacMillan.

Brown, M. W. & Mels, G. (1990). *RAMONA PC: User Manual.* Pretoria: University of South Africa.

Bryk, A. S. & Raudenbush, S. W. (1992). *Hierarchical Linear Models.* Newbury Park: CL: SAGE.

Byrne, B. (1998). *Structural equation modeling with LISREL, PRELIS, and SIMPLIS: Basic concepts, applications and programming.* Mahwah, NJ: Lawrence Erlbaum Associates.

Campbell, R. J., Kyriakides, L., Muijs, R. D., & Robinson, W. (2004). *Assessing teacher effectiveness: A differentiated model.* London: Routledge Falmer.

Carroll, J. B. (1963). A model of school learning. *Teacher College Record, 64,* 723-733.

Cazden, C. B. (1986). Classroom discourse. In M. C. Wittrock (Ed.) *Handbook of research on teaching* (pp. 432-463). New York: MacMillan.

Cohen, D., Manion, L., & Morrison, K. (2000) (5th Ed). *Research methods in education.* London: Routledge/Falmer.

Creemers, B. P. M. (1994). *The effective classroom.* London: Cassell.

Creemers, B. P. M. & Kyriakides, L. (2005, April). *Establishing links between Educational Effectiveness Research and improvement practices through the development of a dynamic model of educational effectiveness.* Paper presented at the 86th annual meeting of the American Educational Research Association. Montreal, Canada.

Creemers, B. P. M. & Reezigt, G. J. (1996). School level conditions affecting the effectiveness of instruction. *School Effectiveness and School Improvement, 7,* 197-228.

Creemers, B. P. M., & Scheerens, J. (1994). Developments in the educational effectiveness research programme. *International Journal of Educational Research, 21* (2), 125-140.

Cronbach, L. J. (1990). *Essentials of psychological testing* (3rd ed.). New York: Harper and Row.

Dempo, M. & Gibson, S. (1985). Teachers' sense of efficacy: An important factor in school achievement. *The Elementary School Journal, 86*, 173-184.

Den Brok, P., Brekelmans, M., & Wubbels, T. (2003). Interpersonal teacher behaviour and student outcomes. *School Effectiveness and School Improvement, 15*, 407-466

Den Brok, P., Levy, J., Wubbels, T., & Rodriguez, M. (2003). Cultural influences on students' perceptions of videotaped lessons. *International Journal of Intercultural Relations, 27*, 268-288.

Den Brok, P., Brekelmans, M., Levy, J., & Wubbels, T. (2002). Diagnosing and improving the quality of teachers' interpersonal behavior. *The International Journal of Educational Management, 4*, 176-184.

Doyle, W. (1986). Classroom organization and management. In M. C. Wittrock (Ed.), *Handbook of research on teaching* (pp. 392-431). New York: MacMillan.

Emmer, E. T. & Everston, C. M. (1981). Synthesis of research on classroom management. *Educational Leadership, 38* (4), 342-347.

Everston, C. M., Anderson, C., Anderson, L., & Brophy, J. (1980). Relationships between classroom behaviour and student outcomes in junior high math and English classes. *American Educational Research Journal, 17*, 43-60.

Fisher, D. & Cresswell, J. (1998). Actual and ideal principal interpersonal behaviour. *Learning Environments Research, 1*, 231-247.

Fisher, D., Henderson, D., & Fraser, B. (1995). Interpersonal behavior in senior high school biology classes. *Research in Science Education, 25*, 125-133.

Flanders, N. (1970). *Analyzing teacher behavior.* Reading, MA: Addison-Wesley.

Fraser, B. J. (1994). Research on classroom and school climate. In D. Gabel (Ed.), *Handbook of research on science teaching and learning* (pp. 493-541). New York: Macmillan.

Galton, M. (1987). An ORACLE Chronicle: A decade of classroom research. *Teaching and Teacher Education, 3* (4), 299-313.

Goldstein, H. (2003) (3rd Ed.). *Multilevel statistical models.* London: Edward Arnold.

Griffin, G. A. & Barnes, S. (1986). Using research findings to change school and classroom practice: Results of an experimental study. *American Educational Research Journal, 23* (4), 572-586.

Kline, R. B. (1998). *Principles and practice of structural equation modeling.* New York: The Guilford Press.

Kyriakides, L. (2001). Measurement of teaching in Cyprus: Limitations of current practice. *Proceedings of the 4th Annual Conference of the Cyprus Educational Association.* Nicosia.

Kyriakides, L. (2005a). Extending the comprehensive Model of Educational Effectiveness by an empirical investigation. *School Effectiveness and School Improvement, 16* (2), 103-152.

Kyriakides, L. (2005b). *International comparative studies and educational effectiveness modelling: A secondary analysis of TIMSS 1999 data.* Paper presented at the MORE symposium of ICSEI 2005 conference. Barcelona: Spain.

Kyriakides, L., Campbell, R. J., & Gagatsis, A. (2000). The significance of the classroom effect in primary schools: An application of Creemers' comprehensive model of educational effectiveness. *School Effectiveness and School Improvement 11* (4), 501-529.

Leary, T. (1957). *An interpersonal diagnosis of personality.* New York: Ronald Press Company.

Lee, O. (1995). Subject matter knowledge, classroom management, and instructional practices in middle school science classrooms. *Research in Science Teaching, 32* (4), 423-440.

Maruyama, G. M. (1998). *Basics of structural equation modeling.* Thousand Oaks, California: SAGE.

Medley, D. (1979). The effectiveness of teachers. In P. Peterson & H. Walberg (Eds.), *Research on teaching: Concepts, findings and implications.* Berkeley, CA: McCutchan.

Messick, S. (1989). Validity. In R. Linn (Ed.), *Educational measurement* (3rd ed.) (pp. 13-103). New York: Macmillan Publishing Co.

Moos, R. H. (1979). *Evaluating educational environments: Procedures, measures, findings and policy implications.* San Francisco: Jossey-Bass.

Muijs, D. & Reynolds, D. (2000). School effectiveness and teacher effectiveness in mathematics: Some preliminary findings from the evaluation of the Mathematics Enhancement Programme (Primary). *School Effectiveness and School Improvement, 11* (3), 273-303.

Muthén, L. K. & Muthén, B. O. (1999). *Mplus user's guide*. Los Angeles, CA: Muthén & Muthén.

Redfield, D. & Rousseau, E. (1981). A meta-analysis of experimental research on teacher questioning behaviour. *Review of Educational Research, 51,* 237-245.

Reynolds, D., Creemers, B. P. M., Nesselrodt, P. S., Schaffer, E. C., Stringfield, S., & Teddlie, C. (1994). School effectiveness research: A review of the international literature. In D. Reynolds, B.P.M. Creemers, P. S. Nesselrodt, E. C. Schaffer; S. Stringfield, & C. Teddlie (Eds.) *Advances in school effectiveness research and practice* (pp. 25-51). Oxford: Pergamon.

Reynolds, D. & Packer, A. (1992). School effectiveness and school improvement in the 1990s. In D. Reynolds & P. Cuttance (Eds.), *School effectiveness: Research, policy and practice* (pp. 171-187). London: Cassell.

Rigdon, E. E. (1998). Structural equation modeling. In G.A. Marcoulides (Ed.), *Modern methods for business research* (pp. 251-294). Mahwah, NJ: Lawrence Erlbaum Associates.

Rosenshine, B. (1971). *Teaching behaviours and student achievement*. London: NFER.

Rosenshine, B. (1983). Teaching functions in instructional programs. *Elementary School Journal, 89*, 421-439.

Rosenshine, B. & Furst, N. (1973). The use of direct observation to study teaching. In R. M. W. Travers (Ed.), *Second handbook of research on teaching*. Chicago: Rand McNally.

Rosenshine, B. & Stevens, R. (1986). Teaching functions. In M. C. Wittrock (Ed.) *Handbook of research on teaching* (pp. 376-391). New York: MacMillan.

Scheerens, J. (1993). Basic school effectiveness research: items for a research agenda. *School Effectiveness and School Improvement, 4* (1), 17-36.

Scheerens, J. & Bosker, R. (1997). *The foundations of educational effectiveness*. Oxford: Pergamon.

Scriven, M. (1994). Duties of the teacher. *Journal of Personnel Evaluation in Education, 8*, 151-184.

Shavelson, R. J. (1973). What is "the" basic teaching skill? *Journal of Teacher Education, 14*, 144-151.

Shuell, T. J. (1996). Teaching and learning in a classroom context. In D. C. Berliner & R. C. Calfee (Eds.), *Handbook of educational psychology* (pp. 726-764). New York: Macmillan.

Shulman, L. (1986). Paradigms and research programs in the study of teaching: a contemporary perspective. In M. C. Wittrock (Ed.), *Handbook of research on teaching* (pp. 3-36). New York: MacMillan.

Simon, A. & Boyer, E. (1970). (Eds.). *Mirrors of behaviours: An anthology of observation instruments continued, 1970 supplement, Volumes A and B*. Philadelphia: Research for Better Schools.

Smith, N. L. (1991). Evaluation reflections: The context of investigations in cross-cultural evaluations. *Studies in Educational Evaluation, 17*, 3–21.

Smith, L. & Land, M. (1981). Low-inference verbal behaviors related to teacher clarity. *Journal of Classroom Interaction, 17*, 37-42.

Snijders, T. & Bosker, R. (1999). *Multilevel analysis: An introduction to basic and advanced multilevel modeling*. London: Sage.

Stallings, J. (1985). Effective elementary classroom practices. In M J Kyle (Ed.), *Reaching for excellence: An effective schools sourcebook*. Washington DC: US Governing Printing Office.

Sternberg, R. J. (1988). Mental self-government: A theory of intellectual styles and their development. *Human Development, 31,* 197-224.

Stringfield, S. (1994). The analysis of large data bases in school effectiveness research. In Reynolds, D., Creemers, B. P. M., Nesselrodt, P. S., Schaffer, E. C., Stringfield, S., & Teddlie, C. (1994). *Advances in school effectiveness research and practice* (pp. 55-72). Oxford: Pergamon.

Walberg, H. J. (1979). *Educational environments and effects: Evaluation, policy, and productivity*. Berkely: McCutchan.

Walberg, H. J. (1986). Syntheses of research on teaching. In M. C. Wittrock (Ed.), *Handbook of research on teaching* (pp. 214-229). New York: MacMillan.

Wang, M. C., Haertel, G. D. & Walberg, H. J. (1990). What influences learning? A content analysis of review literature. *Journal of Educational Research, 84* (1), 30-43.

Watzlawick, P., Beavin, J. H., & Jackson, D. (1967). *The pragmatics of human communication*. New York: Norton.

Wubbels, T. & Brekelmans, M. (1998). The teacher factor in the social climate of the classroom. In B. J. Fraser & K. G. Tobin (Eds.), *International handbook of science education* (pp. 565-580). London: Kluwer Academic Publishers.

Wubbels, T., Brekelmans, M., van Tartwijk, J., & Admiraal, W. (1997). Interpersonal relationships between teachers and students in the classroom. In H. C. Waxman & H. J. Walberg (Eds.), *New directions for teaching practice and research* (pp.151-170). Berkeley, CA: McCutchan Publishing Company.

Wubbels, T., Créton, H. A, & Hooymayers, H. P. (1987). A school-based teacher induction programme. *European Journal of Teacher Education, 10*, 81-94.

Wubbels, T. & Levy, J. (1991). A comparison of interpersonal behavior of Dutch and American teachers. *International Journal of Intercultural Relations, 15,* 1-18.

Yair, G. (1997). When classrooms matter: Implications of between-classroom variability for educational policy in Israel. *Assessment in Education, 4* (2), 225-248.

Chapter 16

THE USE OF THE CUCEI FOR MONITORING STUDENTS' CHARACTERISTICS IN JAPANESE HIGHER EDUCATION

Sonomi Hirata
Hakuoh University
Japan

Makoto Ishikawa
Joetsu University of Education
Japan

Darrell L. Fisher
Curtin University of Technology
Australia

This chapter reports three studies to describe associations between students' perceptions of their classroom environment and their individual characteristics in Japanese higher education. First, the CUCEI: College and University Classroom Environment Inventory and the Nowicki-Strickland Locus of Control Scale were administered to 406 students, and analysis of data revealed that students' academic achievement and internal locus of control were associated with satisfaction with learning. Secondly, analysis of data from 100 students clarified the relevance that existed between students' perceptions of actual and preferred satisfaction as well as innovation at learning. Thirdly, analysis of covariance structures, using structural equation modelling with data from 568 students, revealed that each preferred scale was a causal factor of the corresponding scale on the Actual Form. It was also shown that students' preferred personalization had a distinctive effect on all the other actual factors. These results suggest that student perceptions of their classes are clearly relevant to individual student characteristics and needs. This chapter concludes that it is useful to measure students' perceptions and needs for learning to better design and improve the curriculum and learning environments.

1. Introduction

Japan's higher education system is shifting towards universal access. The ratio of students who go on to higher education has risen to 50%, and it is predicted that students' academic levels and learning approaches will also become more diversified. Today the practice of students being asked to evaluate their university instruction is becoming common, and the Japanese Ministry of Education (2001) reported that 451 (69%) of universities actually did this. However, it is only recently in Japan that research in higher education classrooms began.

Meanwhile, numerous studies at elementary and secondary school levels have involved the effects of psychosocial classroom environments on students' cognitive and affective learning outcomes (Williamson, Tobin, & Fraser, 1986). According to Moos' (1974) schema, there are three basic types of dimensions for classifying psychosocial human environment, namely, Relationship Dimension, Personal Growth Dimension, and System Maintenance and System Change Dimension. Many instruments have been produced based on these three dimensions, and are commonly used to assess the nature of the psychosocial environment of elementary and secondary school classrooms. Similarly, Fraser, Treagust, and Dennis (1986) have developed the *College & University Classroom Environment Inventory* (CUCEI) for evaluating instructions at higher education. The CUCEI contains the seven scales of Personalization, Involvement, Cohesiveness, and Satisfaction in the Relationship Dimension, Task Orientation in the Personal Growth Dimension, and Innovation and Individualization in the System Maintenance and System Change Dimension.

Williamson, Tobin, and Fraser (1986) reported that adolescent and adult learners' satisfaction toward their classes had a significant association with all scales of the CUCEI, meaning that classroom satisfaction was higher in classes characterized by greater personalization, involvement, student cohesiveness, task orientation, innovation, and individualization. On the other hand, between locus of control and the environment variables significant univariate associations emerged only on the Student Cohesiveness and Task Orientation scales.

In regard to the locus of control, which assesses personal self efficacy among students, it has been shown that scores on this scale are not related to social desirability or intelligent test scores but are related to achievement (Nowicki & Strickland, 1973). Fraser, et al., (1986) pointed out that it is important to replicate considerable prior research at the elementary and secondary school levels at the higher education level. This chapter therefore describes associations between students' perceptions of their psychosocial environment at higher education, their achievement, and locus of control.

2. Students' Achievement, Personality, and the Learning Environment

2.1 Methods and procedures

2.1.1 Instrument

The present study initiated the development of a new instrument for the Japanese context, because research on the use of classroom environment assessments for improving teaching and learning at Japanese colleges and universities is in its infancy. Sako (2002) asked, in his preliminary investigation of the CUCEI, 10 professors and 38 students to evaluate all 49 CUCEI items on a five-point Likert scale ranging from Very Appropriate to Very Inappropriate for lectures in a large size classroom. Then he suggested, that some items in the Personalization, Innovation and Individualization sclaes, and all in the Cohesiveness scale were rated as inappropriate, and 37 items with an average over 3.00 on a five-point Likert scale were appropriate for lectures in a large size classroom. As the sample of classes in this study were all of large size (around 100 students), 35 items of the CUCEI suitable for lectures in large classrooms were chosen from Sako's previous study. Items are responded to on a five-point Likert scale ranging from Strongly Disagree to Strongly Agree, as 1 = Strongly Disagree, 2 = Disagree, 3 = neither agree nor disagree, 4 = Agree, and 5 = Strongly Agree.

All 40 items of the *Children's Nowicki-Strickland Internal-External Control Scale* (Nowicki & Strickland, 1973) were translated into Japanese by a bilingual translator and then translated back into English by a native speaking English translator. Adjustments were then made to obtain the most natural Japanese wordings and the instrument was pre-tested on Japanese subjects. Items were responded to on a two-point scale, as 1 = Agree or 2 = Disagree.

2.1.2 Sample

The sample consisted of a representative group of 406 college and university students in three kinds of psychology classes, namely, "Educational Psychology" in teacher-training courses, "Mental Health" in nursing courses, and "Environmental Psychology" in a landscape gardening course. There were 102 male and 304 female freshman and sophomore students from two universities and a college in the Tokyo metropolitan area involved. All of these classes were taught by the same instructor.

2.2 Findings and results

2.2.1 Scale construction

CUCEI: Factor analysis (principle components with varimax rotation) revealed five factors from the 35 items of CUCEI: (1) Satisfaction, (2) Innovation, (3) Individualization, (4) Personalization, and (5) Involvement, and the cumulative variance of these five factors was 37.6% (see Table 16.1). Satisfaction (Cronbach alpha coefficient = 0.89) consisted of ten items, for example, "Students enjoy going to this class", "The students look forward to coming to classes" and "After the class, the students have a sense of satisfaction". Innovation (alpha = 0.80) consists of four items, including "The instructor thinks up innovative activities for students to do", "The instructor often thinks of unusual class activities", and "Teaching approaches in this class are characterized by innovation and variety". Individualization (alpha = 0.48) consisted of two items, that is "Students are generally allowed to work at their own pace" and "Teaching approaches allow students to proceed at their own pace". Personalization (alpha = 0.62) consists of two items, that is "The instructor isn't interested in students' problem" and "The instructor is unfriendly and inconsiderate towards students". Involvement (alpha = 0.72) consists of two items, that is "Students have a say in how class time is spent" and "Students are allowed to choose activities and how they will work".

Table 16.1. Factor Structure of the College and University Classroom Environment Inventory

No.	Original Dimension	ITEM	I	II	III	IV	V
			Factor Loadings				
Factor I : Satisfaction							
Q 29	Satisfaction	Students enjoy going to this class	0.8212				
Q 3	Satisfaction	The students look forward to coming to classes	0.8066				
Q 24	Satisfaction	Classes are boring	-0.7881				
Q 13	Satisfaction	After the class, the students have a sense of satisfaction	0.7488				
Q 19	Satisfaction	Classes are a waste of time	-0.6793				
Q 4	Task Orientation	Students know exactly what has to be done in our class	0.5599				
Q 20	Task Orientation	This is a disorganized class	-0.5587				
Q 34	Satisfaction	Classes are interesting	0.5559				
Q 8	Satisfaction	Students are dissatisfied with what is done in the class	-0.5407				
Q 12	Involvement	Students "clockwatch" in this class	-0.5115				
Factor II : Innovation							
Q 15	Innovation	The instructor thinks up innovative activities for students to do		0.7879			
Q 31	Innovation	The instructor often thinks of unusual class activities		0.7482			
Q 21	Innovation	Teaching approaches in this class are characterized by innovation and variety		0.6678			
Q 5	Innovation	New ideas are seldom tried out in this class		-0.6038			
Factor III : Individualization							
Q 10	Individualization	Students are generally allowed to work at their own pace			0.8323		
Q 26	Individualization	Teaching approaches allow students to proceed at their own pace			0.5796		
Factor IV : Personalization							
Q 33	Personalization	The instructor is unfriendly and inconsiderate towards students				0.6487	
Q 27	Personalization	The instructor isn't interested in students' problem				0.5478	
Factor V : Individualization							
Q 16	Individualization	Students have a say in how class time is spent					0.5785
Q 22	Individualization	Students are allowed to choose activities and how they will work					0.5282
Eigenvalue			7.07	2.77	1.47	1.01	0.81
Variance (%)			20.20	7.90	4.20	2.90	2.30
Cumulative variance (%)			20.20	28.10	32.30	35.20	37.60
Cronbach's alpha coefficients (Actual)			0.89	0.80	0.48	0.62	0.72
Cronbach's alpha coefficients (Preferred)			0.90	0.83	0.72	0.77	0.59

* Factor loadings with absolute values of <.50 are not presented for the sake of clarity.

Locus of Control scale: The 40 items of the *Children's Nowicki-Strickland Internal-External Control Scale* were inter correlated and the items which had low correlation with the other items were deleted. In all, 33 items were chosen (alpha = 0.59), including "Do you believe that if somebody studies hard enough he or she can pass any subject?", "Do you often feel that whether you do your homework has much to do with what kind of grades you get?", and "Most of the time, do you feel that you can change what might happen tomorrow by what you do today?" The individual scores of all students on the Locus of Control scale were converted into z-scores. Students whose z-scores were greater than 1.0 were classified "external tendency group", while those with scores less than -1.0 were labeled "internal tendency group", and the others were the "middle group".

Achievement: As a measure of achievement, the individual scores of all students on an end-of-term examination at each class were similarly converted into z-scores, students whose z-score were greater than 1.0 were classified as the "high achieving group", those less than -1.0 as the "low achieving group", and the others were the "middle achieving group".

2.2.2 Students achievement, locus of control, and the CUCEI

The aim of the analysis was to consider associations between students' individual characteristics and the nature of the learning environment at higher education. The results were analyzed using a two-way analysis of variance with the CUCEI scores as dependent variables and achievement and Locus of Control scores for each student group as independent variables. Statistically significant differences were found for students' achievement and Locus of Control on Satisfaction (see Figure 16.1).

The interaction between the two variables was not statistically significant. It was shown that the high-achieving students felt more satisfaction toward their classes than the low-achievers (F [2, 131] = 18.89, $p<0.0001$), and that students with a more internal Locus of Control reported greater satisfaction in the classroom (F [2, 131] = 4.76, $p<0.01$). This is in agreement with major studies on the advantage of students' internal locus of control at school (e.g., Printrich & DeGroot, 1990; Rutter, 1983; Trice, 1990). Similarly these findings replicated and are in agreement with the numerous valuable research studies at the elementary and secondary school levels (e.g., Aldridge & Fraser, 2003) at higher education. The results here suggest that student perceptions of their classes are clearly relevant to their individual student characteristics.

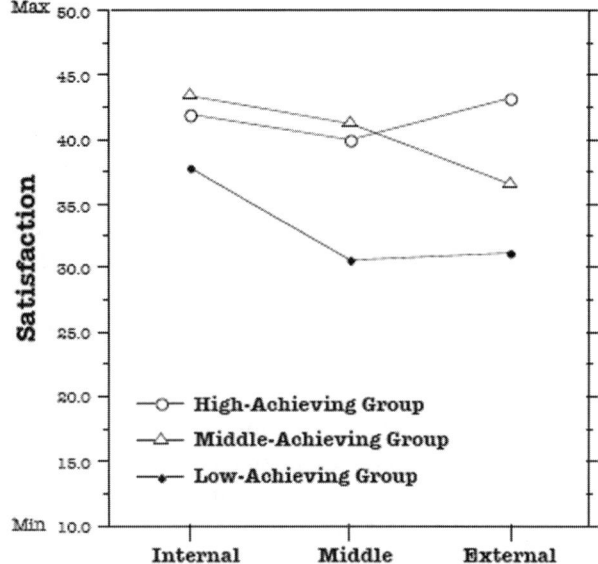

Figure 16.1. Student's achievement, Locus of control and the CUCEI score.

3. Students Needs, Achievements, and the Learning Environment

3.1 Methods and procedures

3.1.1 Instrument

As the sample of classes here were all of a large size (around 100 students), 35 items suitable for lectures in large classrooms were chosen from the CUCEI on Sako's (2002) previous study. Especially in this section, the Preferred Form of the CUCEI, as well as the Actual Form, were administered and both form of items were responded to on a five-point Likert scale ranging from Strongly Disagree to Strongly Agree, as 1 = Strongly Disagree, 2 = Disagree, 3 = neither agree nor disagree, 4 = Agree, and 5 = Strongly Agree.

3.1.2 Sample

We collected data from 100 members of the "Mental Health" class at a Nursing College in the Tokyo metropolitan area. Four male and 96 female freshmen comprised the class.

3.2 Findings and results

3.2.1 Scale construction

CUCEI: Factor analysis (principle components with varimax rotation) of the CUCEI revealed three factors: (1) Satisfaction, (2) Involvement, and (3) Innovation, and the cumulative variance of these three factors was 37.6% (Table 16.1). Satisfaction (Cronbach's alpha coefficients were: actual 0.89, preferred 0.90) consisted of ten items, for example, "The students look forward to coming to classes" and "Classes are interesting". Involvement (actual = 0.70, preferred = 0.79) consisted of ten items, for example, "Students are allowed to choose activities and how they will work" and "The instructor helps each student who is having trouble with the work".   Innovation (actual = 0.74, preferred = 0.77) consisted of ten items, for example, "The instructor thinks up innovative activities for students to do" and "New ideas are seldom tried out in this class".

Achievement: The individual scores of all students on their end-of-term examination were converted into z-scores. Students whose z-score over 1.0 were classified "high-achieving group", under -1.0 students were classified "low-achieving group", and the others were labeled "middle-achieving group".

Students' needs (preferred classroom environment): The individual score of all students on the preferred form of the CUCEI converted into z-scores and categorised as before into "high-needs", "low-needs", and "middle-needs" groups.

3.2.2 Students' needs and achievement

To begin with the mean scores of students' perceptions of their actual classroom environment were 4.28 (95% confidence interval: 4.18-4.38) on Satisfaction, 2.13 (2.00-2.26) on Involvement, and 3.51 (3.40-3.6 3) on Innovation. Meanwhile, students' mean scores of their preferred classroom environment were 4.64 (95% confidence interval: 4.57-4.72) on Satisfaction, 3.53 (3.38-3.69) on Involvement, and 3.76 (3.62-3.89) on Innovation. These showed that the 95% confidence interval of students' mean scores of their preferred learning environment were all more the each median (3.00) on each of the three factors. We can see that students have relatively high needs of satisfaction, involvement, and innovation in the class. Next, t-tests were utilized to compare the statistical significance of the differences between the scores on the Actual and Preferred Forms of the CUCEI. Statistically significant differences between mean scale scores were found for all factors. It was shown that students would prefer more Satisfaction (t=-8.30, p<0.0001), Involvement (t=-16.20, p<.0001), and Innovation (t=-3.63, p<0.0005) in their classroom.

Furthermore, the results were analyzed using one-way ANOVA with the actual scores as dependent variables, and students' needs (perceptions of their preferred learning environment) for each student group as independent variables. Statistically significant differences were found for students' needs on the Satisfaction and Innovation scales. Students who preferred more satisfaction at learning showed more satisfaction of their actual classroom than the students who need less satisfaction (F [2, 97] = 14.890, p<0.0001). Also, students who wished for a more innovative class perceived more innovation in their actual classroom environment (F [2, 97] = 11.283, p<0.0001). It follows, from these significant findings, that students' needs have relevance for their perceptions of their actual classroom.

Finally, the results were analyzed using two-way ANOVA with the CUCEI actual scores as dependent variables, and both students' needs and achievement for each student group as independent variables. Statistically significant differences were found for students' achievement on Satisfaction (Figure 16.2). It was shown that the high-achieving students felt more satisfaction of their classes than the low-achievers (F [2, 97] = 3.853, p<0.0245). As there were no high-achieving students at all who preferred less involvement and innovation in their class, this group could not be formed. Further analysis revealed that the scores of perceptions of the actual class by students related with the level of students needs. The interaction between forms and groups was not statistically significant. These results suggest that it is quite beneficial to measure students' needs of learning (preferred environment) not only for improving design of teaching and learning for various level of students, but also for analyzing the results of class assessment by students with precision.

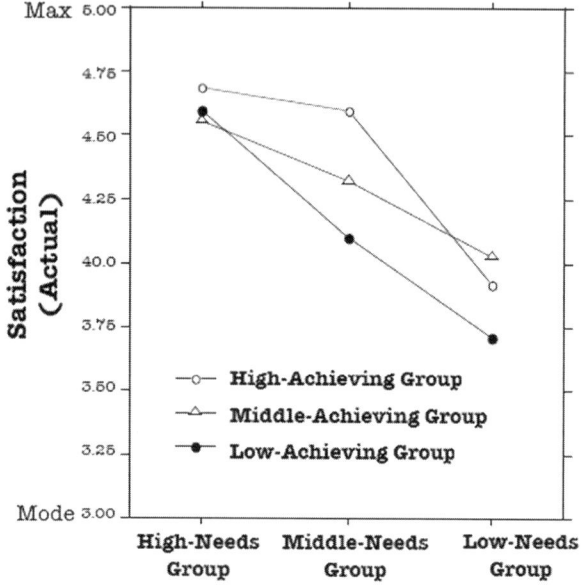

Figure 16.2. Students' needs toward a class, achievement, and the CUCEI score (actual satisfaction).

4. Causal Relationship between Actual and Preferred Learning Environment

In light of these above findings, Hirata and Ishikawa (2003) investigated the students' needs at higher education with the CUCEI. Results from the Actual and Preferred Forms of CUCEI were analyzed using ANOVA and chi-square. These results suggested that within the students' respective classes, statistically, their needs differ significantly, even for the same subject with the same teacher. In addition, it was clarified that there were various different groups with different needs in the same classroom. Further analysis found that the students' perceptions of the actual class related to the level of students needs. Hirata and Ishikawa (2003) have also reported that the structural equation modelling indicated that personalization and innovation are causal factors of satisfaction in an actual classroom (Figure 16.3). Personalization means interaction between teacher and students in class, and Innovation means the use of new technology in classrooms. It appears that students' perceptions of teacher involvement with students and the new use of educational methods at class apparently are linked to greater students' satisfaction.

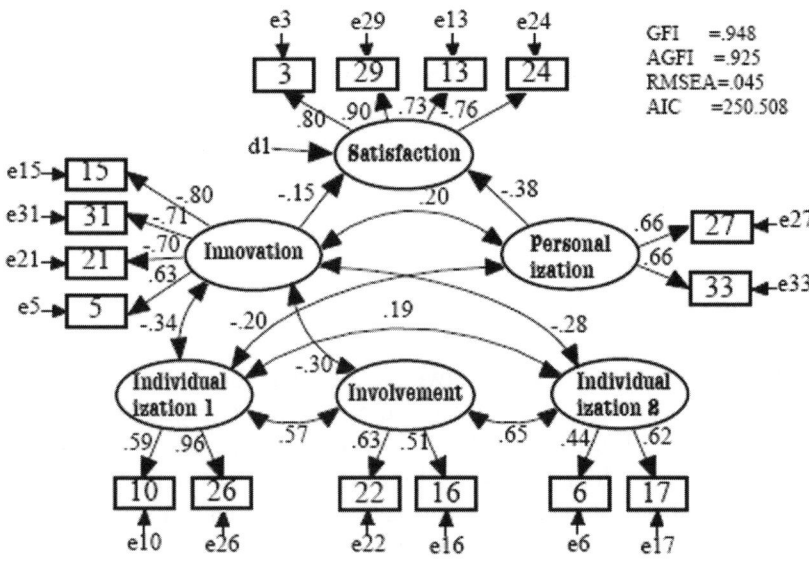

Figure 16.3. The causal relation model of the CUCEI factors
(Hirata & Ishikawa, 2003).

Next, we focused on causal relationships between the actual and preferred classroom environment. Most previous research in this field has been correlational, whereas this study focused on causal relationships between the actual and preferred classroom environment. If a causal relationship between preferred environment (students' needs) and their cognition toward actual classes could be identified, then teachers could put this information to various practical use, for example, in improving teaching and learning and planning new curriculum designs.

4.1 Methods and procedures

4.1.1 Instrument and sample

The Preferred and Actual Forms of the CUCEI were administered to a representative group of 568 college and university students in three kinds of psychology classes, namely, Educational Psychology and Mental Health in teacher-training and nursing courses, and Environmental Psychology in a landscape gardening course. All of these classes were taught by the same instructor. The 104 male and 464 female freshman and sophomore students from two universities and a college in the Tokyo metropolitan area were involved.

4.2 Findings and results

4.2.1 Scale construction

Exploratory factor analysis (unweighted least squares methods with oblique/promax rotation) revealed five common factors from the Actual and Preferred Forms of the CUCEI. The scales were named Dissatisfaction, Satisfaction, Innovation, Personalization, and Individualization. Using these five scales with 15 items, a causal relation model between actual and preferred classroom environment was investigated with SEM (structural equation modelling). In Dissatisfaction four items were chosen for SEM through their factor loadings. These were, "Classes are a waste of time", "This is a disorganized class", "Classes are boring", and "Students are dissatisfied with what is done in the class".

   Also four items in Satisfaction, "Students enjoy going to this class", "The students look forward to coming to classes", "After the class, the students have a sense of satisfaction", and "Classes are interesting", and three items in Innovation; "The instructor thinks up innovative activities for students to do", "The instructor often thinks of unusual class activities", and "Teaching approaches in this class are characterized by innovation and variety" were chosen.

   Then two items in Personalization; "The instructor helps each student who is having trouble with the work" and "The instructor talks individually with students", then as in Individualization the items;

"Students are generally allowed to work at their own pace" and "Teaching approaches allow students to proceed at their own pace" were selected. The results showed that GIF (goodness of fit index) and AGIF (adjusted goodness of fit index) values ranged from 0.93 to 0.96, and RMSEA (root mean square error of approximation) was under 0.45. These coefficients showed a certain degree of structural validity for these models.

4.2.2 Causal relationship between actual and preferred classroom environment

It was found that the Preferred Form of each of the five scales was a causal factor of the corresponding Actual Form of that scale. The causal coefficients were 0.89 for preferred Dissatisfaction to actual Dissatisfaction, 0.61 for preferred Satisfaction to actual Satisfaction, 0.56 for preferred Innovation to actual Innovation, 0.87 for preferred Personalization to actual Personalization, and 0.34 for preferred Individualization to actual Individualization. Students who need higher satisfaction felt more satisfaction toward their classes, similarly for Innovation, Personalization and Individualization. These findings suggested that students' higher needs and expectations for learning are indispensable to creating successful actual classroom environments.

4.2.3 Point in common with each five models

As stated above, it was suggested that there were causal associations between the preferred and the corresponding actual dimension of learning environments. It may be also helpful here to see the point in common with these five models of the causal relationship between actual and preferred classroom environment.

First, we considered the confidence interval and mean score of each of the five scales. With the Dissatisfaction scale for the actual class, the confidence interval was estimated from 1.982 to 2.163, there is a 95% level of confidence associated with this interval (a two-sided confidence interval). As the middle scale score is 3.00, then the population mean of Dissatisfaction could be judged statistically lower than that.

The mean score of Personalization was also lower, however, the mean scores for Satisfaction and Innovation were statistically higher. Thus we see the students were almost satisfied with their class except for the shortage of personal relationship to a instructor. The students rated all factors higher (but Dissatisfaction lower) than the middle score for their preferred classroom.

Having observed the outline of the subject classes, one can then return to the point in common with the five models.   Figure 16.4 shows that preferred Personalization is a causal factor of actual Satisfaction ($p<0.01$). Moreover, it was shown at five models that students' preferred Personalization was related statistically significantly to all the actual factors ($p<0.01$). As Personalization consisted of items like "The instructor helps each student who is having trouble with the work" and "The instructor talks individually with students", these results suggest that the extent of students' expectations for their personal relationship with their instructor or his/her help has an effect on students' perception of their actual classes.

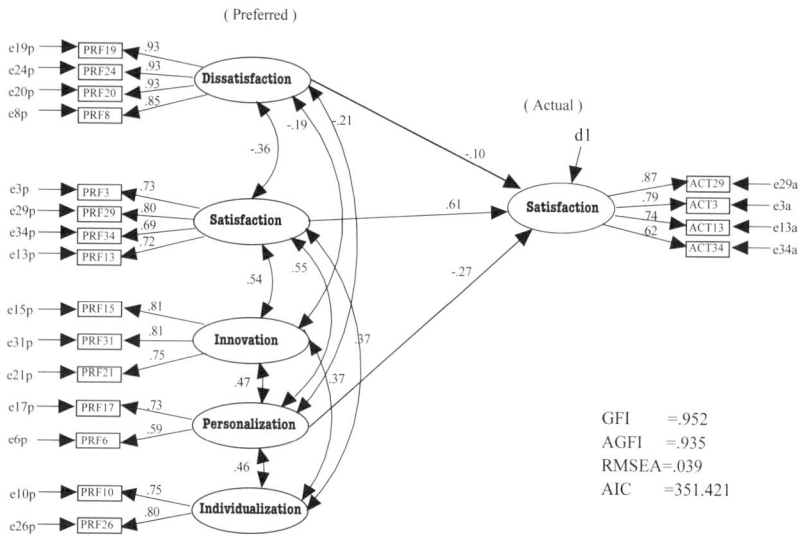

Figure 16.4. The casual relation model between "Satisfaction" in actual and five factors of preferred classroom. All coefficients are statistically significant ($p<0.001$), except for "Dissatisfaction" to actual "Satisfaction" ($p<0.05$).

5. Discussion and Conclusion

The main purpose of this study was to describe associations between the learning environment as perceived by college and university students, their achievement and locus of control, and then to replicate considerable prior research at the elementary and secondary school levels in higher education.

It was found that high-achieving students felt more satisfaction toward their classes than low-achievers, and that students with a more internal locus of control reported greater satisfaction in the classroom. These results are in agreement with numerous previous research at the elementary and secondary school levels. What is more, it was clarified that students who preferred more satisfaction of learning showed more satisfaction in their actual classroom than the students who needed less satisfaction, also students who wished for more innovation in class perceived more innovation in their actual environment. This means that students' needs affect their perception toward the actual classroom.

Finally, it was shown that the preferred score of each of five scales; Dissatisfaction, Satisfaction, Innovation, Personalization, and Individualization was a causal factor of the corresponding actual version of that scale. This means that high needs and expectations for learning are indispensable to creating successful actual classroom environments. Especially, it was shown that students' preferred personalization has a distinct effect on all the other actual factors. As personalization was an essential factor that related to students' satisfaction of classes, one may say that it is advisable for instructors to be more considerate toward students' personal needs even in large size classes.

The results of this study lead to the conclusion that it is quite beneficial to measure the students' individual needs, not only for designing and improving the curriculum, but also for interpreting the results of class evaluations accurately. Using these psychosocial measures, teachers can easily obtain valuable information about what is happening in their classroom. If instructors in colleges and universities can obtain information about their students' satisfaction with their class, they are in a position to improve particular causal factors of satisfaction reciprocally.

S. Hirata, M. Ishikawa & D. L. Fisher

References

Aldridge, J. M. & Fraser, B. J. (2003). Effectiveness of a technology-rich outcomes-focused learning environment. In M. S. Khine & D. L. Fisher (Eds.), *Technology-rich learning environments, A future perspective* (pp. 41-69). Singapore: World Scientific Publishing.

Fraser, B. J., Treagust, D. F. & Dennis, N. C. (1986). Development of an instrument for assessing classroom psycho social environment in universities and college. *Studies in Higher Education, 11*, 43-54.

Hirata, S. & Ishikawa, M. (2003). Analysis of classroom environment in college and university toward improvement of teaching and learning. *Japan Journal of Educational Technology, 27*, 129-132. (In Japanese).

Ishikawa, M. & Hirata, S. (2003). The use of class assessment scales with consideration toward students' needs on students at psychology classes in college and university. *Journal of the Liberal and General Education Society of Japan,* 57-63. (In Japanese).

Moos, R. H. (1974). *Correctional institution environment scale: Manual.* Palo Alto: Consulting Psychologists Press.

Nowicki, S. & Strickland, B. (1973). A locus of control scale for children. *Journal of Consulting and Clinical Psychology, 40* (1), 148-154.

Printrich, P. R. & De Groot, E. V. (1990). Motivation and self-regulated learning components of classroom academic performance. *Journal of Educational Psychology, 82*, 33-40.

Rutter, M. (1983). School effects on pupils progress: Research findings and policy implications. *Child Development, 54*, 1-29.

Sako, T. (2002). University students assess their classrooms: The construction of the Japanese version of CUCEI (The College and University Classroom Environment Inventory), *Human Science, 14* (2), 13-23. (In Japanese).

Trice, A. D. (1990). Adolescents' locus of control and compliance with contingency contracting and counseling interventions. *Psychological Reports. 67* (1), 233-234.

Williamson, J. C., Tobin, K. G., & Fraser, B. J. (1986, April). *Use of classroom and school environment scales in evaluating alternative high schools.* Paper presented at Annual Meeting of American Educational Research Association, San Francisco.

Chapter 17

USING STRUCTURAL EQUATION MODELLING TO INVESTIGATE ASSOCIATIONS BETWEEN ENVIRONMENT AND OUTCOMES IN TECHNOLOGY-RICH, OUTCOMES-FOCUSED CLASSROOMS IN AUSTRALIAN SECONDARY SCHOOLS

Jeffrey P. Dorman
Australian Catholic University
Australia

Jill M. Aldridge
Barry J. Fraser
Curtin University of Technology
Australia

This chapter describes the use of structural equation modelling to investigate associations between classroom environment and outcomes in Australian secondary schools. A new classroom environment instrument – the 80-item Technology-Rich Outcomes-Focused Learning Environment Inventory (TROFLEI) was used to assess 10 classroom environment dimensions. A sample of 2,178 high school students from Western Australia and Tasmania responded to the TROFLEI and three student outcome measures: attitude to the subject, attitude to computer use and academic efficacy. Confirmatory factor analysis using LISREL supported the 10 scale *a priori* structure of the instrument. Multiple regression identified particular classroom environment scales that were significant predictors of three outcome scales. Structural equation modelling using LISREL revealed that teacher support and equity predicted attitude to subject and that differentiation, task orientation, computer usage and young adult ethos predicted attitude to computer use. Academic efficacy mediated the effect of involvement and differentiation on attitude to subject. Task orientation had a direct effect and an indirect effect (via academic efficacy) on attitude to subject. Overall, the modelling indicated that improving classroom environment has the potential to improve student outcomes.

1. Background

During the past 35 years, the study of classroom environments has received increased attention by researchers, teachers, school administrators and administrators of school systems. The concept of environment, as applied to educational settings, refers to the atmosphere, ambience, tone, or climate that pervades the particular setting. Research on classroom environments has focussed historically on its psychosocial dimensions – those aspects of the environment that focus on human behaviour in origin or outcome (Boy & Pine, 1988). Reviews of classroom environment research by Fraser (1998a), Dorman (2002), Goh and Khine (2002) and Khine and Fisher (2003) have delineated at least 10 areas of classroom environment research. One of the strongest areas of classroom environment research has been the study of links between classroom environment and student cognitive and affective outcomes.

Because of the ethical dilemma of deliberately manipulating environments in a true experimental design, almost all environment – outcomes research has used *ex post facto* designs and correlational data techniques. Results of studies conducted over the past 30 years have provided convincing evidence that the quality of the classroom environment in schools is a significant determinant of student learning (Fraser, 1994, 1998a). That is, students learn better when they perceive the classroom environment more positively. Importantly, many of these studies have controlled for background variables with students' perceptions of the classroom environment accounting for appreciable amounts of variance in learning outcomes, often beyond that attributable to background student characteristics. Goh and Fraser (1998) used the *Questionnaire on Teacher Interaction* (QTI) and a modified version of the *My Class Inventory* (MCI) to establish associations between student cognitive and affective outcomes and perceived patterns of teacher-student interaction in 39 primary school mathematics classes in Singapore. In particular, higher cognitive outcomes were associated with better classroom teacher leadership, more helping/friendly classroom environments and teacher behaviours that demonstrate understanding and empathy towards students. Additionally, the affective outcome measure, student liking and interest in mathematics, was related positively with improved levels of student cohesion and reduced levels of classroom friction.

Dorman, McRobbie, and Foster's (2002) study involving 1,317 secondary students in 17 Sydney Catholic secondary schools found statistically significant positive associations between the environment in religious education classes as assessed by the seven-scale *Catholic School Classroom Environment Questionnaire* (CSCEQ) and four dimensions of students' attitudes to Christianity. A total of 21 of the 28 simple Pearson correlation coefficients were statistically significant ($p<0.05$), a result which is about fifteen times that which could be expected by chance alone.

A cross-national investigation of links among 10 classroom environment dimensions and student self-handicapping was reported by Dorman and Ferguson (2004). A sample of 2,006 students from 13 schools in Canada and Australia was surveyed. Simple and multiple correlation analyses between 10 classroom environment scales from the *What Is Happening In this Class* (WIHIC) and the *Constructivist Learning Environment Survey* (CLES) and self-handicapping were conducted. Results showed that classroom environment scales accounted for appreciable proportions of variance in self-handicapping. Enhanced affective dimensions of the classroom environment were associated with reduced levels of self-handicapping. Commonality analyses revealed that the WIHIC scales accounted for a much greater proportion of variance in self-handicapping that did the CLES scales.

In a recent environment-outcomes study conducted with 661 middle school students in the USA, Ogbuehi and Fraser (2005) reported associations between dimensions of the classroom environment and students' attitudes to mathematics. Scales of the WIHIC and CLES were correlated moderately with two scales, normality of mathematicians and enjoyment of mathematics. Positive classroom attitudes were linked positively with involvement, task orientation, personal relevance and shared control.

During the last decade, significant research on the use of computers in classrooms has been conducted. Much of this research has focussed on the effect of computer usage on student attitude, social outcomes, motivation and interest (see Bain, McNaught, Mills, & Lueckenhausen, 1998; Goh & Tobin, 1999; Lajoie, 1993; Schofield, Eurich-Fulcer, & Britt, 1994). However, few studies have investigated psychosocial dimensions of computer classroom environments. In one study that did involve classroom environment, Mucherah (2003) investigated the environment in social science classrooms using technology. This study raised important issues concerning the inadequacy of training and support of teachers who attempt to integrate the use of computers in the curriculum.

All of the above classroom environment studies reflect the strong tradition of investigating associations between classroom environment and outcomes through simple, multiple and canonical correlational techniques. The purpose of the present chapter is to report the use of a relatively new classroom environment instrument, the *Technology-Rich Outcomes-Focused Learning Environment Inventory* (TROFLEI) which has ten internally consistent scales: Student Cohesiveness, Teacher Support, Involvement, Investigation, Task Orientation, Cooperation, Equity, Differentiation, Computer Usage and Young Adult Ethos. Details of the development and validation of actual and preferred forms of the TROFLEI using multitrait-multimethod (MTMM) modelling within a confirmatory factor analysis framework have been reported by Aldridge, Dorman, and Fraser (2004). The research reported in this chapter uses structural equation modelling to study a postulated model in which classroom environment dimensions are linked holistically with outcome measures in a structural model. This chapter also reports the use of confirmatory factor analysis to establish the structure of the TROFLEI compared to the traditional reliance on exploratory factory analysis.

2. Design of Present Study

The aims of the present study were to:

- validate the structure of the Technology Rich Outcomes Focussed Learning Environment Inventory (TROFLEI) using confirmatory factor analysis,

- identify classroom environment dimensions that predict three outcomes scales, and

- investigate whether a postulated model of relationships among the classroom environment scales and the three outcomes scales fits the data through the use of structural equation modelling.

2.1 Sample

The sample employed in this study consisted of 2,178 students in secondary schools in Tasmania and Western Australia. Table 17.1 describes the sample which consisted of 1,533 year 11 students and 645 year 12 students. The largest sub-sample was Year 11 students in Western Australia who constituted 48.2% of the full sample.

Table 17.1. Description of Sample

Gender	Sample Size				Total
	Western Australia		Tasmania		
	Year 11	Year 12	Year 11	Year 12	
Male	577	190	237	113	1,117
Female	474	222	245	120	1,061
Total	1051	412	482	233	2,178

2.2 Instrumentation

2.2.1 Assessment of classroom environment

The TROFLEI consists of 80 items assigned to 10 underlying scales (8 items per scale). Table 17.2 shows scale descriptions and a sample item for each TROFLEI scale. Seven of the 10 TROFLEI scales are from the What Is Happening In this Class? (WIHIC) instrument which is a well-established and widely-used questionnaire in classroom environment research (see Aldridge & Fraser, 2000; Dorman, 2003). The WIHIC scales are: Student Cohesiveness, Teacher Support, Involvement, Investigation, Task Orientation, Cooperation, and Equity.

The robust nature of the WIHIC's reliability and validity has been widely reported in studies that have used the instrument in different subject areas, at different age levels and in nine different countries. Since the initial development of the WIHIC, the questionnaire has been used successfully in studies to assess the learning environment in Singapore (Fraser & Chionh, 2000), Australia and Taiwan (Aldridge & Fraser, 2000), Brunei (Khine & Fisher, 2001), Canada (Zandvliet & Fraser, in press), Australia (Dorman, 2001), Indonesia (Adolphe, Fraser & Aldridge, 2003), Korea (Kim, Fisher, & Fraser, 2000), the USA (Allen & Fraser, 2002), and Canada, England and Australia (Dorman, 2003).

Table 17.2. Descriptive Information for the Ten TROFLEI Scales

Environment Scale	Scale Description	Sample Item	Moos's Schema
Student Cohesiveness	The extent to which students know, help and are supportive of one another.	I am friendly to members of this class.	R
Teacher Support	The extent to which the teacher helps, befriends, trusts and is interested in students.	The teacher considers my feelings.	R
Involvement	The extent to which students have attentive interest, participate in discussions, do additional work and enjoy the class.	I explain my ideas to other students.	R
Investigation	The extent to which skills and processes of inquiry and their use in problem solving and investigation are emphasised.	I carry out investigations to test my ideas.	P
Task Orientation	The extent to which it is important to complete activities planned and to stay on the subject matter.	I know how much work I have to do.	P
Cooperation	The extent to which students cooperate rather than compete with one another on learning tasks.	I share my books and resources with other students when doing assignments.	P
Equity	The extent to which students are treated equally by the teacher.	I get the same opportunity to answer questions as other students.	S
Differentiation	The extent to which teachers cater for students differently on the basis of ability, rates of learning and interests.	I do work that is different from other students' work.	S
Computer Usage	The extent to which students use their computers as a tool to communicate with others and to access information.	I use the computer to take part in on-line discussions with other students.	S
Young Adult Ethos	The extent to which teachers give students responsibility and treat them as young adults.	I am encouraged to take control of my own learning.	P
Student Cohesiveness	The extent to which students know, help and are supportive of one another.	I am friendly to members of this class.	R

Note: R: Relationship P: Personal Development S: System Maintenance and System Change

Within these countries, the WIHIC has assessed the environment in a range of curriculum areas including high school science (Aldridge & Fraser, 2000), mathematics (Margianti, Fraser, & Aldridge, 2001), mathematics and science (Raaflaub & Fraser, 2002) and mathematics and geography (Fraser & Chionh, 2000).

Three new scales of educational importance were developed for the purpose of this study. To capture the individualised nature of an outcomes-based program, a Differentiation scale was adapted from the *Individualised Classroom Environment Questionnaire* (ICEQ; Fraser, 1990). This scale assesses the extent to which the teacher provides opportunities for students to choose the topics on which they would like to work and to work at their own pace. Because technology-rich learning environments require students to use computers in a range of ways, the Computer Usage scale was developed to provide information about the extent to which students used computers in various ways (e.g. email, accessing the internet, discussion forums). Finally, a Young Adult Ethos scale was developed to assess the extent to which teachers give their students responsibility for their own learning.

Historically, negatively-worded items have been used in classroom environment instruments to guard against passive responses. However, Barnette (2000) questions the utility of such items, as they cannot be considered direct opposites of their positively-worded counterparts. In addition, studies reveal that positively-worded items improve response accuracy and internal consistency (Chamberlain & Cummings, 1984; Schreisheim, Eisenbach, & Hill, 1991; Schriesheim & Hill, 1981). It was considered appropriate, therefore, to use only items with a positive scoring direction in our study.

Students respond to items using a five-point Likert format (viz. Almost Never, Seldom, Sometimes, Often, Almost Always). To provide contextual cues and to minimise confusion to students, it was considered appropriate to group together those items that belong to the same scale instead of arranging them randomly or cyclically (Aldridge, Fraser, Taylor, & Chen, 2000). Scale scores for each respondent are obtained by aggregating scores for the eight items for that scale.

One important consideration that has been part of classroom environment theory since the early 1970s has been Moos' (1979) conceptual framework for human environments which categorizes environment as having relationship, personal growth and system maintenance and system change dimensions. Whereas relationship dimensions are concerned with the nature and intensity of personal relationships, personal growth dimensions focus on opportunities for personal development and self-enhancement. System maintenance and system change dimensions assess the extent to which the environment is orderly, clear in expectations, maintains control and is responsive to change. Table 17.2 shows the classification of each TROFLEI scale according to Moos' conceptual framework

2.2.2 Outcome scales

Three outcome scales were employed in the present study. These 7-item scales were: Attitude to Subject (which assesses the extent to which students are interested in, enjoy and look forward to lessons in that subject); Attitude to Computer Use (the extent to which students are comfortable with and enjoy using computers) and Academic Efficacy (which refers to personal judgements of one's capabilities to organise and execute courses of action to attain designated types of educational performances in a subject area).

   The first scale, Attitude to Subject, is based on the enjoyment of science lessons scale from the *Test of Science-Related Attitudes* (TOSRA: Fraser, 1981). It was modified to suit a range of school subjects used in the present study. A typical item is "I look forward to lessons in this subject". The second scale, Attitude to Computer Use, is adapted from the Computer Attitude Scale developed by Newhouse (2001). This scale was adopted because technology-rich learning environments require students to spend a considerable amount of their time using computers. One item on this scale is "I am comfortable trying new software on the computer". The third scale, Academic Efficacy, is based on a scale from the *Morgan-Jinks Student Efficacy Scale* (MJSES: Jinks & Morgan, 1999). A typical item from this scale is "I am good at this subject."

2.3 Data collection procedures

As this study attempted to link classroom environment with outcomes, students were surveyed in the classrooms of particular subjects. This was particularly significant to the present study because two of the outcomes measures (viz. attitude to subject and academic efficacy) were subject specific. Students responded once to the questionnaire.

2.4 Data analysis and interpretation

There were three distinct components to the analyses conducted in the present study. First, confirmatory factor analysis (CFA) and scale reliability analysis were employed to substantiate the structure of the TROFLEI. A second-order CFA model was hypothesised. Figure 17.1 illustrates this model in which classroom environment (as assessed by the TROFLEI) was the second-order variable which was indicated or assessed by 10 first-order variables (the 10 TROFLEI scales). In turn each of these 10 scales were indicated by eight observed variables (the eight items for each TROFLEI scale). The internal consistency of each of the three outcome scales was explored.

Second, computed composite variables were used in stepwise multiple regression analyses. The purpose of these analyses was to identify those TROFLEI scales which were significant predictors of the three outcome scales. This information was used subsequently to develop a baseline or *postulated* model for testing using structural equation modelling (SEM) using LISREL 8.3.

Accordingly, the third component of data analysis involved the testing of the postulated model relating salient TROFLEI scales composite variables based on the results of the above regression analyses. Structural equation modelling examines relationships among *latent* variables. Such variables are not measured directly. Their values are indicated by observed variables. For example, in the present study, the latent variable student cohesiveness was indicated by an observed variable computed from eight student cohesiveness items.

Munck (1979) showed that loadings of paths (λ) which link observed variables to latent variables and error variances (θ) for observed variables can be fixed in structural equation modelling and that, provided correlation matrices are analysed, they are related to reliability (r) by the formulae

$$\lambda = \sqrt{r} \qquad \text{and} \qquad \theta = 1 - r.$$

These formulae allow for paths from observed composite variables to latent variables and error variances of observed composite variables to be fixed. The advantage of this theory is that the number of parameters to be estimated by LISREL is sharply reduced with consequent improvement in model robustness.

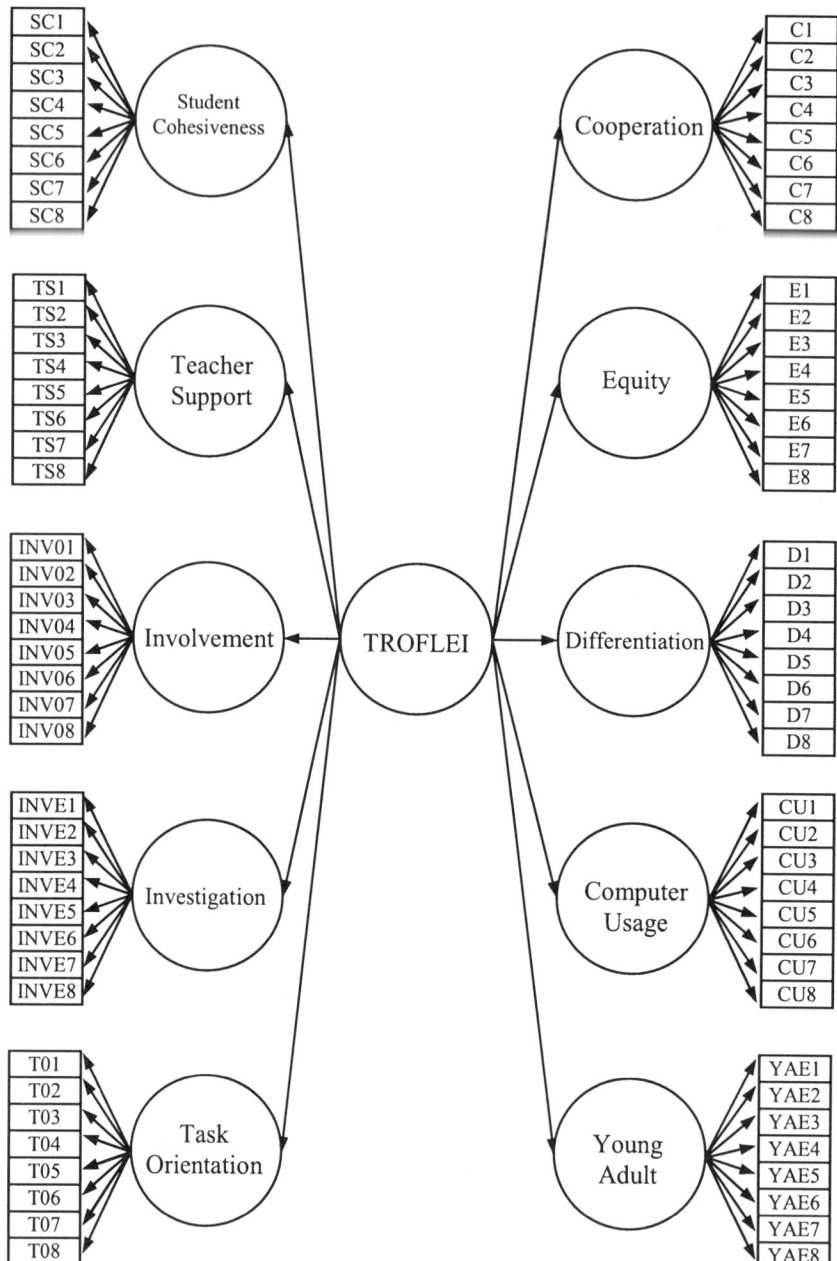

Figure 17.1. Second order CFA model for TROFLEI.

Note. Error variances for each observed variable have been omitted.

Of the many indices available to report model fit, model comparison and model parsimony in structural equation modelling, three indices are reported in the present article: the Root Mean Square Error of Approximation (RMSEA), the Tucker-Lewis Index (TLI) and the Parsimony Normed Fit Index (PNFI). Whereas the RMSEA assess model fit, the TLI and PNFI assess model comparison and model parsimony respectively. To interpret these indices, the following rules which are generally accepted in the SEM literature as reflecting good models were adopted: RMSEA should be below 0.08 with perfect fit indicated by an index of zero, TLI should be above 0.90 with perfect fit indicated when TLI = 1.00, and PFNI should be above 0.50 with indices above 0.70 unlikely even in a very sound fitting model. Further discussion on indices and acceptable values is provided in Byrne (1998), Kelloway (1998) and Schumacker and Lomax (1998). While the use of χ^2 tests to report goodness of fit of the model to the data is acknowledged as problematic in SEM, it was used in the present study to report improvements to the overall model fit as posthoc adjustments were made.

Statistics reported in the present study include the squared multiple correlation coefficient (R^2) for each structural equation and a total coefficient of determination (Jöreskog & Sörbom, 1989). While R^2 is a measure of the strength of a linear relationship, the total coefficient of determination is the amount of variance in the set of dependent variables explained by the set of independent variables. In addition to overall fit statistics, it is important to consider the strength and statistical significance of individual parameters in the model. Each path was tested using a t-test ($p<0.05$).

3. Results

3.1. Confirmatory factor analysis

As indicated above, confirmatory factor analysis (CFA) was performed on the data to substantiate the structure of the 80-item Technology Rich Outcomes Focussed Learning Environment Inventory (TROFLEI). Classroom environment (as assessed by the TROFLEI) was the second-order latent variable which was indicated or assessed by ten first-order latent variables (the ten TROFLEI scales). In turn each of these ten scales were indicated by eight observed variables (the eight items for each TROFLEI scale). Fit statistics for this model were: RMSEA = 0.05, TLI = 0.93 and PNFI = 0.79. These statistics indicate good model fit to the data and confirm the 10-scale structure of the TROFLEI. Loadings for the 80 paths from observed variables to the ten TROFLEI scales ranged from 0.41 to 0.92 (M = 0.77, SD = 0.12). For the paths between the 10 TROFLEI scales and the TROFLEI, loadings ranged from 0.56 to 0.73 (M = 0.67, SD = 0.06).

3.2. Scale statistics

Reliability coefficients (Cronbach coefficient alpha) were computed for each scale (see Table 17.3).

Table 17.3. Internal Consistency Reliability, Scale Statistics, Fixed Path Loadings and Error Variances for 10 TROFLEI and 3 Outcome Scales

Scale	Cronbach α (r)	Mean	Standard Deviation	$\lambda = \sqrt{r}$	$\theta = 1 - r.$
Classroom Environment					
Student Cohesiveness	0.87	31.18	5.39	Not in Structural Model	
Teacher Support	0.92	28.68	6.71	0.96	0.08
Involvement	0.90	25.79	6.22	0.95	0.10
Task Orientation	0.88	31.37	5.55	0.94	0.12
Investigation	0.92	23.79	6.88	0.96	0.08
Cooperation	0.91	30.14	6.41	Not in Structural Model	
Equity	0.94	32.56	6.80	0.97	0.06
Differentiation	0.77	24.15	6.24	0.88	0.23
Computer Usage	0.88	24.68	7.91	0.94	0.12
Young Adult Ethos	0.93	32.81	6.20	0.96	0.07
Outcomes					
Attitude to Subject	0.86	23.67	5.78	0.93	0.14
Attitude to Computer Use	0.82	27.00	5.36	0.91	0.18
Academic Efficacy	0.88	21.60	5.65	0.94	0.12

These results show that all scales had very satisfactory internal consistency. Indices ranged from 0.77 for Task Orientation to 0.94 for Equity and compared favourably with those reported in previous learning environment research (e.g., Dorman, Adams, & Ferguson, 2002; Dorman & Ferguson, 2004). Table 17.3 also shows means and standard deviations for each scale.

3.3. Multiple regression analyses

To identify a set of predictor variables to be used in subsequent structural equation modelling, separate stepwise multiple regression analyses for each of the three outcome measures with the set of 10 environment scales as predictors were conducted. Results for the final step of these analyses are shown in Table 17.4.

Table 17.4. Results of Final Step Regression Analyses for TROFLEI Scales Predicting Three Outcome Scales

Outcome Scale	R^2	TROFLEI Scale	B	$SE\ B$	β
Attitude to Subject	0.31	Teacher Support	0.31	0.02	0.31^*
		Task Orientation	0.30	0.03	0.25^*
		Equity	0.11	0.02	0.11^*
Attitude to Computer Use	0.11	Computer Usage	0.20	0.02	0.26^*
		Differentiation	-0.15	0.02	-0.19^*
		Task Orientation	0.14	0.03	0.12^*
		Young Adult Ethos	0.10	0.02	0.10^*
Academic Efficacy	0.26	Involvement	0.27	0.02	0.26^*
		Task Orientation	0.27	0.02	0.23^*
		Differentiation	0.12	0.02	0.15^*
		Investigation	0.08	0.02	0.09^*

$^*p<0.05$

Attitude to Subject had three significant predictors: Teacher Support, Task Orientation and Equity. Attitude to Computer Use had four significant predictors: Computer Usage, Differentiation, Task Orientation, and Young Adult Ethos. Academic Efficacy had four significant predictors: Involvement, Task Orientation, Differentiation, and Investigation. The square of the multiple regression coefficients for these models (R^2) were: 0.31 (Attitude to Subject), 0.11 (Attitude to Computer Use), and 0.26 (Academic Efficacy).

3.4 LISREL Analyses

Values for λ and θ for each scale were computed using Munck's (1979) theory described above (see Table 17.3). As shown in Table 17.4, two scales (Student Cohesiveness and Cooperation) were not identified as predictors of any of the three outcome variables. Accordingly, these two scales were not included in the postulated model shown in Figure 17.2. Apart from its incorporation of the regression analyses results, this model hypothesised relationships among the three outcome variables. Based on the definitions of these scales, it was hypothesised that Academic Efficacy would predict Attitude to Subject and that, because the subjects were technologically-based, Attitude to Computer Use would predict Attitude to Subject. The LISREL analysis of the postulated model shown in Figure 17.2 revealed a very good fit to the data with an RMSEA of 0.03 (see Table 17.5).

Table 17.5. Summary of Specifications and Fit Statistics for Two Structural Models

Model	Actions	χ^2	df	RMSEA	TLI	PNFI
1 (Postulated) (see Figure 17.2)	-	42.31	14	0.03	0.99	0.25
2 (Final) (see Figure 17.3)	Path Investigation→ Academic Efficacy removed. Path Attitude to Computer Use → Attitude to Subject removed.	47.82	16	0.03	1.00	0.29

However, a review of path coefficients revealed two paths for which the coefficients were not statistically significant (viz. Investigation → Academic Efficacy and Attitude to Computer Use to Attitude to Subject). These two paths were removed from the model and revised fit indices are shown in Table 17.5.

Figure 17.3 shows this final model with path coefficients, all of which were significantly different from zero ($p<.05$). While model fit and model comparison indices for this final model were very good (RMSEA of 0.03 and a TLI of 0.99), the model parsimony was not above the benchmark value of 0.50 indicating mediocre parsimony in the model (see Table 17.5). Nevertheless, this model should be interpreted as having good fit to the data.

In general, the strength and direction of the statistically significant path coefficients are plausible. For example, Teacher Support was a moderate, positive predictor of Attitude to Subject ($\beta = 0.33$). Increased levels of Involvement were positively related to Academic Efficacy ($\beta = 0.32$) which was itself related positively to Attitude to Subject ($\beta = 0.16$). Task Orientation was a significant, positive predictor of Academic Efficacy ($\beta = 0.27$) and Attitude to Computer Use ($\beta = 0.15$). It is noteworthy that, apart from the effect of Differentiation on Attitude to Computer Use ($\beta = -0.28$), all classroom environment dimensions had positive effects on outcomes. Task Orientation had a direct effect on Attitude to Subject ($\beta = 0.23$) and a small indirect effect on Attitude to Subject ($0.27\text{x}0.16 = .04$) due to the path via Academic Efficacy.

The squared multiple correlation coefficient for the prediction of Attitude to Subject was computed to be 0.41 which indicates that 41% of variance in Attitude to Subject could be explained by its contributing variables (viz. Teacher Support, Task Orientation, Equity, and Academic Efficacy). Over 32% of variance in Academic Efficacy was Attributable to Involvement, Task Orientation and Differentiation. Similarly, Task Orientation, Differentiation, Computer Usage and Young Adult Ethos accounted for nearly 17% of variance in students' Attitude to Computer Use. The total coefficient of determination was calculated to be 0.61 indicating that 61% of variance in Attitude to Subject, Attitude to Computer Use and Academic Efficacy was explained by Teacher Support, Equity, Involvement, Differentiation, Task Orientation, Computer Usage and Young Adult Ethos. Overall, Figure 17.3 provides a comprehensive structural model for these three outcome measures based on the classroom environment data collected in the present study.

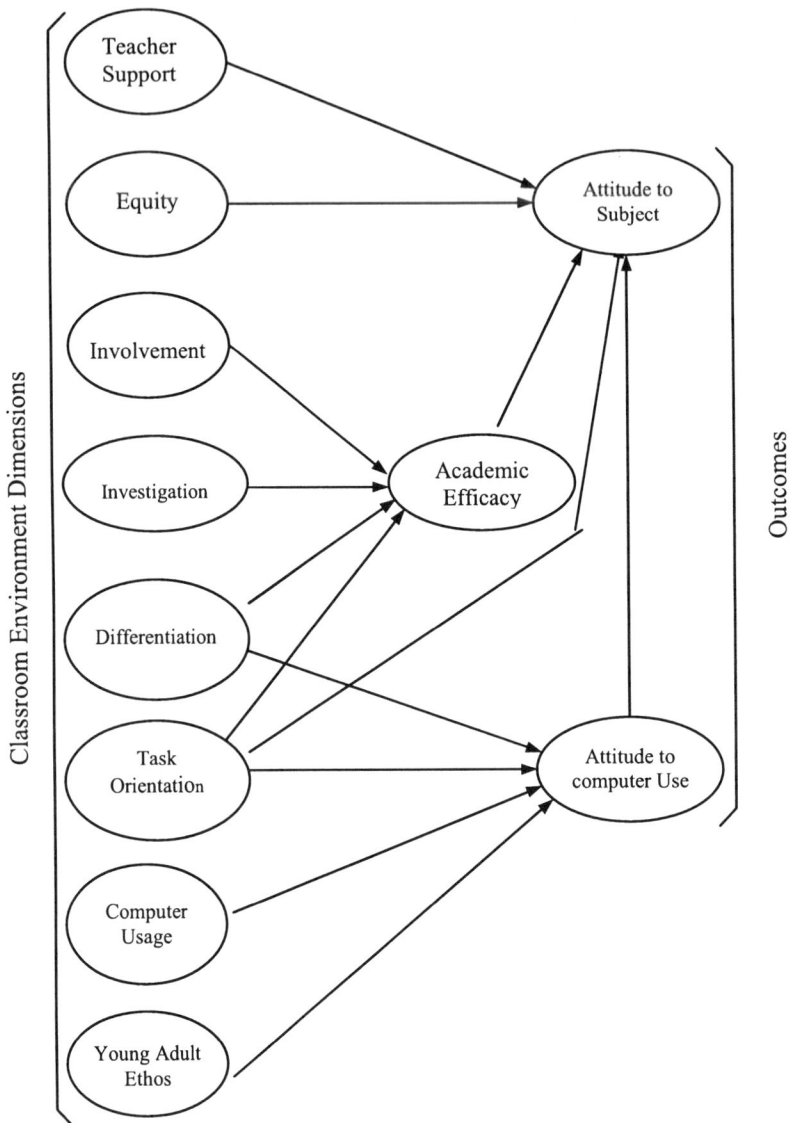

Figure 17.2. Postulated model for three outcome variables.

Note. Observed variables, fixed paths from observed variables to latent
variables and error variances for observed variables have been omitted.

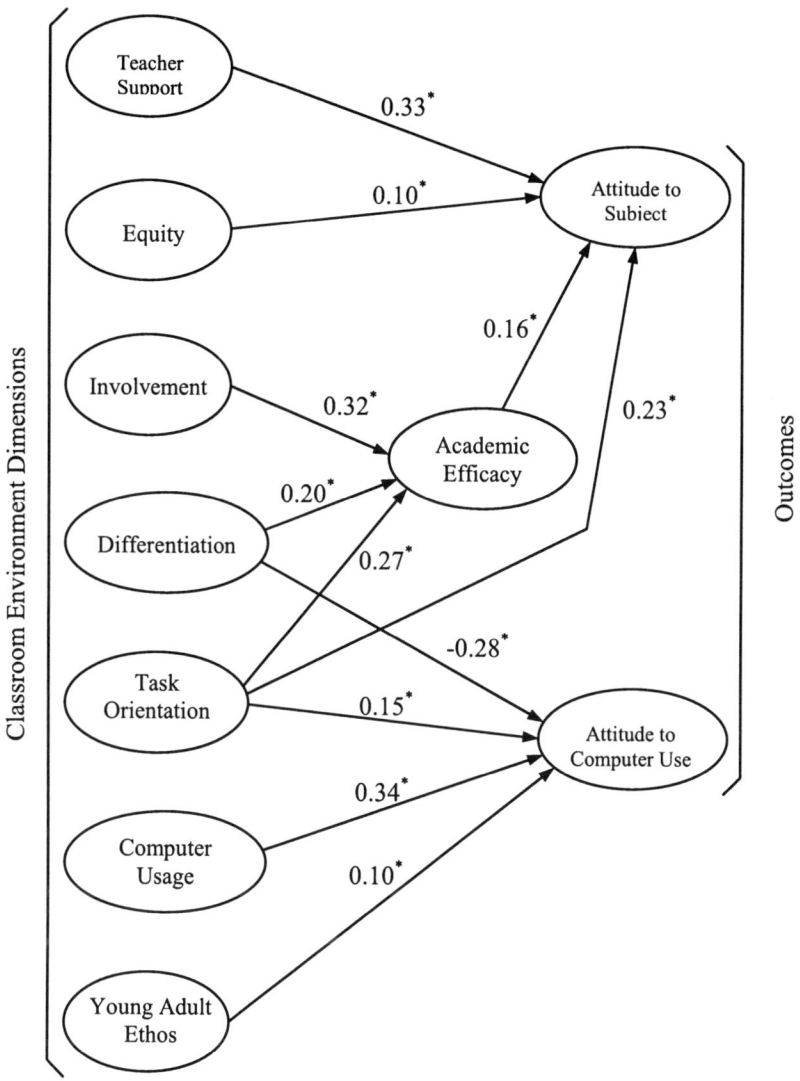

Figure 17.3. Final structural model for three outcome variables.

Note. Observed variables, fixed path loadings from observed variables to latent variables and error variances for observed variables have been omitted. *$p<0.05$

4. Discussion

Each of the findings of the previous section can be discussed in its own right. It is not surprising that Attitude to Subject was predicted positively by Teacher Support, Equity, Task Orientation and Academic Efficacy. Furthermore, Differentiation and Involvement had small positive indirect effects on Attitude to Subject via Academic Efficacy. That is, five of the ten TROFLEI scales were related to Attitude to Subject. Previous research reported in Dorman (2002) and Fraser (1998b) has shown similar positive associations between classroom environment dimensions and attitudinal outcomes, especially attitude to science. Teachers should consider these results as confirming long held anecdotal views. Teachers who provide support, demonstrate equity in the classroom, ensure that students complete learning activities, involve students in classwork and cater for diverse students' needs are more likely to enhance student attitudes to their subject.

A particularly noteworthy finding of this study was that, although computers were used widely in classes, there was no significant link between attitude to computer use and attitude to subject. There was neither a significant positive nor significant negative relationship between attitude to computer use and attitude to subject. As noted above, the postulated model set a path from attitude to computer use to attitude to subject but this path was removed in the final model. This suggests that students differentiate between subjects and the use of computers in those subjects. They do not view computers as integrally linked to a subject. On the basis of this study, much more work needs to be done on integrating computers in the formal school curriculum.

While it is plausible that task orientation, computer usage and young adult ethos would be positively linked to attitude to computer use (see Figure 17.2), it is unclear why differentiation was negatively related to attitude to computer use. The results of this study indicate that the more students perceive the teacher to be catering for individual needs, the more uncomfortable students are with computer use. While this relationship is not easily explained, it does provide a rationale for attitude to computer use not being linked to attitude to subject.

The relationship between academic efficacy and classroom environment has been the subject of recent research. Dorman (2001) found significant relationships between scales of the What Is Happening In this Class questionnaire (Aldridge & Fraser, 2000) and academic efficacy. He reported significant positive correlations between academic efficacy and teacher support, involvement, investigation, task orientation and equity. The findings of the present study and Dorman's earlier findings do not match exactly. Nevertheless there is a small but growing body of evidence supporting positive links between environment and academic efficacy.

5. Conclusion

This chapter has reported the use of a new classroom environment instrument, the Technology-Rich Outcomes-Focused Learning Environment Inventory (TROFLEI).

The research reported here is important to the study of learning environment for three reasons. First, these analyses have shown the TROFLEI to have very sound structural characteristics. The TROFLEI is an important addition to the suite of high-inference classroom environment instruments developed over the past 35 years. Second, this research is one of the few reported attempts to employ confirmatory factor analysis in validating the structure of learning environment instruments. Various reviews of learning environment research and instruments (e.g., Fraser, 1994, 1998b) and validation studies of specific instruments (e.g., Fisher & Waldrip, 2002; Thomas, 2003) have typically used exploratory factor analysis to establish factor structure. Third, the results of the study support the view that the quality of the classroom environment is associated with improved attitudinal outcomes.

As teachers, administrators, and learning environment researchers fulfill important professional roles, they need valid instruments to assess contemporary classroom environments. While the research reported in this chapter has provided substantive validation of the TROFLEI in Australia, further validation work with the TROFLEI should be conducted in other countries.

References

Adolphe, F. S. G., Fraser, B. J., & Aldridge, J. M. (2003, January). A cross-national study of classroom environment and attitudes among junior secondary science students in Australia and Indonesia. In D. Fisher & T. Marsh (Eds.), *Science, mathematics and technology education for all: Proceedings of the Third International Conference on Science, Mathematics and Technology Education* (pp. 435-446). Perth, Australia: Curtin University of Technology.

Aldridge, J. M. & Fraser, B. J. (2000). A cross-cultural study of classroom learning environments in Australia and Taiwan. *Learning Environments Research, 3,* 101-134.

Aldridge, J. M., Dorman, J. P., & Fraser, B. J. (2004). Use of multitrait-multimethod modelling to validate actual and preferred forms of the Technology-Rich Outcomes-Focused Learning Environment Inventory (TROFLEI). *Australian Journal of Educational and Developmental Psychology, 4,* 110-125.

Aldridge, J. M., Fraser, B. J., Taylor, P. C., & Chen, C.-C. (2000). Constructivist learning environments in a cross-national study in Taiwan and Australia. *International Journal of Science Education, 22,* 37-55.

Allen, D. & Fraser, B. J. (2002). *Parent and student perceptions of the classroom learning environment and its influence on student outcomes.* Paper presented at the annual meeting of the American Educational Research Association, New Orleans, LA.

Bain, J. D., McNaught, C., Mills, C., & Lueckenhausen, G. (1998). Describing computer-facilitated learning environments in higher education. *Learning Environments Research, 1,* 163-180.

Barnette, J. J. (2000). Effects of stem and Likert response option reversals on survey internal consistency: If you feel the need, there is a better alternative to using those negatively worded stems. *Educational and Psychological Measurement, 60,* 361-70.

Boy, A. V. & Pine, G. J. (1988). *Fostering psychosocial development in the classroom.* Springfield, IL: Charles C. Thomas.

Byrne, B. M. (1998). *Structural equation modeling with LISREL, PRELIS, and SIMPLIS: Basic concepts, applications and programming.* Mahwah, NJ: Erlbaum.

Chamberlain, V. M. & Cummings, M. N. (1984). Development of an instructor/course evaluation instrument. *College Student Journal, 18,* 246-250.

Dorman, J. P. (2001). Associations between classroom environment and academic efficacy. *Learning Environments Research, 4,* 243-257.

Dorman, J. P. (2002). Classroom environment research: Progress and possibilities. *Queensland Journal of Educational Research, 18,* 112-140.

Dorman, J. P. (2003). Cross national validation of the What is Happening in This Class questionnaire using confirmatory factor analysis. *Learning Environments Research., 6*, 231-245.

Dorman, J. P., Adams, J. E., & Ferguson, J. M. (2002). Psychosocial environment and student self-handicapping in secondary school mathematics classes: A cross-national study. *Educational Psychology, 22,* 499-511.

Dorman, J. P. & Ferguson, J. M. (2004). Associations between students' perceptions of mathematics classroom environment and self-handicapping in Australian and Canadian high schools. *McGill Journal of Education, 39, 68-86.*

Dorman, J. P., McRobbie, C. J., & Foster, W. J. (2002). Associations between psychosocial environment in religious education classes and students' attitude to Christianity. *Religious Education, 97*, 23-42.

Fisher, D. L & Waldrip, B. G. (2002). Measuring culturally sensitive factors of classroom learning environments with the CLEQ. In S. C. Goh & M. S. Khine (Eds.), *Studies in educational learning environments: An international perspective* (pp. 27-48). Singapore: World Scientific.

Fraser, B. J. (1981). *Test of Science-Related Attitudes handbook (TOSRA).* Melbourne, Australia: Australian Council for Educational Research.

Fraser, B. J. (1990). *Individualised Classroom Environment Questionnaire.* Melbourne: Australian Council for Educational Research.

Fraser, B. J. (1994). Research on classroom and school climate. In D. Gabel (Ed.), *Handbook of research on science teaching and learning* (pp. 493-541). New York: Macmillan.

Fraser, B. J. (1998a). Science learning environments: Assessments, effects and determinants. In B. J. Fraser & K. G. Tobin (Eds.), *International handbook of science education* (pp. 527-564). Dordrecht, The Netherlands: Kluwer.

Fraser, B. J. (1998b). Classroom environment instruments: Development, validity, and applications. *Learning Environments Research, 1*, 7-33.

Fraser, B. J. & Chionh, Y. H. (2000, April). *Classroom environment, self-esteem, achievement, and attitudes in geography and mathematics in Singapore.* Paper presented at the annual meeting of the American Educational Research Association, New Orleans, LA.

Goh, S. C. & Fraser, B. J. (1998). Teacher interpersonal behaviour, classroom environment and student outcomes in primary mathematics in Singapore. *Learning Environments Research, 1*, 199-229.

Goh, S. C. & Khine, M. S. (Eds.). (2002). *Studies in educational learning environments: An international perspective.* Singapore: World Scientific.

Goh, S. C. & Tobin, K. (1999). Student and teacher perspectives in computer-mediated learning environments in teacher education. *Learning Environments Research, 2,* 169-190.

Jinks, J. L. & Morgan, V. (1999). Children's perceived academic self-efficacy: An inventory scale. *Clearing House, 72,* 224-230.

Jöreskog, K. G. & Sörbom, D. (1993). *LISREL 8: User's reference guide.* Chicago, IL: Scientific Software International.

Kelloway, E. K. (1998). *Using LISREL for structural equation modeling: A researcher's guide.* Thousand Oaks, CA: Sage.

Khine, M. S. & Fisher, D. L. (2001, December). *Classroom environment and teachers' cultural background in secondary science classes in an Asian context.* Paper presented at the annual meeting of the Australian Association for Research in Education, Perth, Australia.

Khine, M. S. & Fisher, D. L. (Eds.). (2003). *Technology-rich learning environments: A future perspective.* Singapore: World Scientific.

Kim, H., Fisher, D., & Fraser, B. (2000). Classroom environment and teacherinterpersonal behaviour in secondary science classes in Korea. *Evaluation and Research in Education, 14,* 3-22.

Lajoie, S. P. (1993). Computer environments as cognitive tools for enhancing learning. In S. P. Lajoie & R. Derry (Eds.), *Computers as cognitive tools* (pp. 261-288). Hillsdale, NJ: Erlbaum.

Margianti, E. S., Fraser, B. J., & Aldridge, J. M. (2001, April). *Classroom environment and students' outcomes among university computing students in Indonesia.* Paper presented at the annual meeting of the American Educational Research Association, Seattle, WA.

Moos, R. H. (1979). *Evaluating educational environments: Procedures, measures, findings and policy implications.* San Francisco: Jossey Bass.

Mucherah, W. M. (2003). The influence of technology on the classroom climate of social studies classrooms: A multidimensional approach. *Learning Environment Research, 6,* 37-57.

Munck, I. M. E. (1979). *Model building in comparative education: Applications of the LISREL method to cross-national survey data.* Stockholm: Almqvist & Wiksell.

Newhouse, C. P. (2001). Development and use of an instrument for computer-supported learning environments. *Learning Environment Research, 4,* 115-138.

Ogbuehi, P. I. & Fraser, B. J. (2005, April). *Evaluation of an innovative strategy for teaching and learning systems of linear equations in terms of classroom environment, attitudes and conceptual development.* Paper presented the annual meeting of the American Educational Research Association, Montreal.

Raaflaub, C. A. & Fraser, B. J. (2002, April). *Investigating the learning environment in Canadian mathematics and science classes in which computers are used.* Paper presented at the annual meeting of the American Educational Research Association, New Orleans, LA.

Schofield, J. W., Eurich-Fulcer, R., & Britt, C. L. (1994). Teachers, computer tutors, and teaching: The artificially intelligent tutor as an agent for classroom change. *American Educational Research Journal, 3,* 579-607.

Schumacker, R. E. & Lomax, R. G. (1996). *A beginner's guide to structural equation modeling.* Mahwah, NJ: Erlbaum.

Schriesheim, C. A., Eisenbach, R. J., & Hill, K. D. (1991). The effect of negation and polar opposite item reversals on questionnaire reliability and validity: An experimental investigation. *Educational and Psychological Measurement, 51,* 67-78.

Schriesheim, C. A. & Hill, K. D. (1981). Controlling acquiescence response bias by item reversals: The effect on questionnaire validity. *Educational and Psychological Measurement, 41,* 1101-1114.

Thomas, G. P. (2003). Conceptualisation, Development and validation of an instrument for investigating the metacognitive orientation of science classroom learning environments: The Metacognitive Orientation Learning Environment Scale - Science (MOLES-S). *Learning Environments Research, 6,* 175-197.

Zandvliet, D. B. & Fraser, B. J. (in press). Learning environments in IT classrooms. *Technology, Pedagogy and Education.*

Chapter 18

DESIGNING INFRASTRUCTURES FOR LEARNING WITH TECHNOLOGY

Lasse Lipponen
Jiri Lallimo
Minna Lakkala
University of Helsinki
Finland

Classical infrastructures such as transport (for instance railroads, highways), utilities (for instance electricity, water systems, telecommunication networks), and municipal services (postal system, police protection), are essential for the functionality of the modern society. By exploiting the idea of infrastructures, we argue that the functionality, the implementation and use of technology in schools and in workplaces, is based on, and requires the creation of a set of interconnected structural elements. Our argument is that these interconnected structural elements, such as social practices, and educational use of technology, form infrastructures that can be designed in similar way as, for instance, technical infrastructures are designed. We call these infrastructures learning oriented infrastructures. Learning oriented infrastructures provide a framework for designing the entire structure of teaching and learning with technology. In this chapter, we analyze the characteristics of these infrastructures in complex learning environments and demonstrate how they are related, and support working with technology.

1. Introduction

Nobody wants to apply new technology in schools to reproduce old practices of teaching and learning. However, recent research (Cuban, 2001; Salomon, 2002) implies that new technology has been slowly adopted by teachers, and how teachers teach or how students learn has not dramatically changed. Teachers and students use new technology to do a little better what they were already doing without technology. Technology is very easily and very often assimilated into existing instructional practices.

Adapting and applying new technology in schools is not easy. When educators implement new technology, they face a complex challenge of meshing new ideas with well-established beliefs and practices (Bruce,

1993; Salomon, 2002). In the past, it was common to attach the failures of adapting and applying new technology to teachers' knowledge and skills. Cuban (2001), who may be considered as one of the more prominent researchers taking a critical stance towards new technology in schools, argues that the slow adoption of technology and new practices of teaching and learning is not the fault of teachers. They are not technophobic by nature nor do not resist change anymore than any other profession.

The fact is that technology will not go away, but the complex world of technology artifacts that mediates teachers' and students' actions is here to stay, and changing all the time. In the long run, teachers and students have to adapt and apply a variety of new technological solutions, whether they want to or not. Thus, there is an increasing need for a better practical understanding of the challenges teachers and students face whilst adapting and applying new technology.

In this chapter, we offer a practical perspective on the adaptation and application of new technology in schools. Our perspective could be characterized as an infrastructural approach. We argue that the prevailing trend is that technology in schools, is implemented as a top-down process. This leads to a situation, where technologies to be introduced, as well as existing technologies and practices in schools, are seen as separate and independent rather than as parts of complex overlapping infrastructures. In this chapter, we analyze the characteristics of infrastructures in complex learning environments, and demonstrate how they are related, and support learning with technology.

2. Technology-Oriented and Practice-Oriented Views of Implementing Technology

In the beginning of the nineties, Bruce (1993) proposed two approaches to implementing technological innovation in an educational context, namely, technology-oriented and practice-oriented. According to Bruce, in the conventional (and we would say, still prevailing) technology-oriented view, the technological innovation is implemented as a well-defined plan of action, often accompanied by associated objects, such as teachers' guides, and student texts. This approach represents the idea of reproduction of the idealization of the technology, and the tendency to conceive technology independent of its context and use (Bruce, 1993).

Technologies to be introduced are seen as separate and independent of existing technologies and practices, not as intertwined. From this point of view, the expectation has been that new technology, all on its own, will bring about a change in education.

In the alternative view, those who implement and apply technology in education understand that technology is much more than its design and functionality (Lin & Hatano, 2001). Even if it exits with an implicit model of use, the construction and use of technology requires construction of meaning that evolves in everyday use (understanding that technology is invented in everyday practice does not mean that the design of technology, and in a large sense, designing technology would not have any effect on how it is used, and how it is possible to use in schools). The technology is re-created, re-appropriated, reinterpreted, and invested with new significance by the teachers and students who actually use it (Brown & Duguid, 1994; Bruce, 1993). In this case of reinterpretation, the technology and its meaning frequently drift away from the original design and implementation purpose (this is, how designers are considering the activities technology should support) (Ciborra, 2004). From this practice-oriented point of view, technology exists as technology-in-use, and can be considered as social practice (Suchman, Blomberg, Orr, & Trigg, 1999; Tuomi, 2002). This means that technology is understood only within the sites and in relation to its everyday use: it is the community of users where it is possible to explore and understand the social use of artifacts (Brown & Duguid, 1994). The idea that use of technology and social practices are closely intertwined gives us a good starting point to think about them as infrastructures.

3. Characteristics of Infrastructures

What then are infrastructures, and how are they related to the implementation and adaptation of technology in an educational context? While speaking about infrastructures, one typically refers to things such as transport (railroads, highways), utilities (electricity, water systems, telecommunication networks), and municipal services (postal system, police protection). These are essential for the functioning of modern society.

To understand infrastructures, you can do a thinking experiment. Think about the house you live in; you will discover that most of the important stuff is invisible. The foundation, framing, wiring and plumbing do not arrest your attention, but you would notice if they were not there. These interconnected, mostly invisible elements, are fundamental for the functioning of your house. In a similar way, learning environments have invisible elements, vital for the practices of teaching and learning. Briefly, infrastructure is not just a thing, but refers to a network of relationships and facilities that are developed to support a wide range of human activities. In the following paragraphs, we concentrate more closely on the characteristics of infrastructures.

A characteristic of infrastructure is that different elements are linked together so that every element is based on, and links to the existence of other elements (Hanseth, 2004). In other words, in infrastructures new technical artifacts and practices need to be integrated into ongoing technologies and practices; each task needs to fit with most other tasks, social arrangements, and technologies (Brown & Duguid, 1994). For instance, in an educational context, the collection of artifacts such as books, pencils, blackboards, and computers should fit with the practices of teaching and learning, and vice versa. Paper and pencil work, and work to be done with computers should fit smoothly with each other (this, in our observation, is seldom the case).

The second feature of infrastructure is that once invented and created by a community, it does not have to be reinvented for each task (Bowker & Star, 1999; Hanseth & Lundberg, 2001). Practices and technology are taken for granted, and nobody questions this 'routinised' and scripted quality of knowledge and action. This makes communities relatively stable. For instance, in an educational context, the division of labour between teacher and students is a deeply rooted taken-for-granted practice that is very resistant to change (Lipponen & Lallimo, 2004a).

The fact that social arrangements are largely based on conventions, and that technology does not have to be implemented everyday, make infrastructures 'invisible' and 'transparent'. While everything is working well one does not notice the existence of infrastructures. In this sense, infrastructures are invisible and transparent for the actors, existing as a part of the background of their activities (Starr, 1999). However, imagine a community that is starting to use new technology to support its everyday working practices. This new technology has to be integrated into the existing technologies and in established practices. This is what happens when, for instance, the traditional paper pencil work in classroom is transformed to be done with computers, and students' writings are made public with shared databases. This transition entails infrastructural changes: what one is going to do with paper and pencil; what should be done with computers; what is made public and what is not; and so on. In many cases, this type of change is not a painless process but causes disturbances in everyday practices. These moments of transition are vulnerable to breakdown, and the normally invisible and transparent quality of infrastructure becomes visible expressing itself in the form of disturbances (Hall, Stevens, & Torralba, 2002). Good, usable, and stable practices disappear almost by definition. The easier the old technology is to use, and the older the practices are, the harder they are to see and to change (Bowker & Star, 1999).

According to Star (1999), infrastructures are learned as part of a membership of a community of practice. The taken-for-granted nature of artifacts and social arrangements are fundamental prerequisites for membership in a community of practice. Outsiders and newcomers face infrastructures as target objects to be learned about. For instance, the newcomers of a community have to learn the conventions of meetings and writing reports. In the case of technical resources, they have to learn the conventions of using email and shared documents. Children entering school have to learn 'to play school'; how to behave in lessons, what is the division of labour between students and teachers, what is one permitted to do with different artifacts such as computers, and so on. Becoming a member of a community means familiarity with its technology and practices.

As stated earlier, infrastructures are invisible, taken for granted, co-evolve over a long period of time and individual pieces of knowledge are dependent on each other. For this reason, infrastructures are stable and hard to change and one cannot change the overall infrastructure at once. However, sometimes infrastructures need to be willfully designed.

4. Designing Social Infrastructure

We acknowledge that because technical and social resources are intertwined, they should be designed or changed simultaneously (or while one is changed it will affect the other as well). Although they are intertwined, one could make, for analytic purposes, a conceptual difference between these two. Technical resources (physical artifacts such as books, pencils, blackboards, and computers) could be considered forming a *technical infrastructure*, and, in the case of education, teaching and learning practices a *social infrastructure*. Technical and social infrastructures are parts of complex overlapping system that we name *learning oriented infrastructure*. To illustrate better the challenge the design of infrastructures brings, we separate these two in our following analysis.

Whilst designing infrastructures that support learning with technology in schools one should, instead of focusing extensively only on the technology, turn also towards thinking about the relation of technical and social infrastructure from the very beginning. This way of thinking reflects an important transformation from a technology-oriented, to a practice-oriented approach in implementing and adopting new technology.

Infrastructures have been mainly studied in working life contexts, and labeled as *working infrastructures* or *work-oriented infrastructures* (Bowker & Star, 1999; Ciborra, 2002; Hanseth & Lundberg, 2001). The idea is not totally new in education. In an educational context, designing infrastructure refers to the supporting social structure that enables the desired interaction between collaborators using collaborative technology, and has been named *social infrastructure* (Bielaczyc, 2001). According to Bielaczyc (2001), one of the key factors in successful implementation of technology in educational settings is to build an appropriate social infrastructure around the technical infrastructure. Bielaczyc proposed three levels of social infrastructure important for successful implementation and use of technology: these three include the cultural level (the philosophy and norms established among educators and students); activity level (practices); and tool level (technology).

Bielaczyc's idea concerning social infrastructure is definitely useful. However, whilst arguing that the social infrastructure should be build around the technical tools, she implicitly considers the technology infrastructure as primary to the social infrastructure. Thus, in this sense, it still represents the conventional, technology-oriented implementation and takes in use of technology.

We think that in designing social infrastructure, the central questions are, how routine, taken-for-granted practices (and philosophy and norms) can be challenged, reconsidered, and reformulated. *Disclosing New Worlds*, a book written by Spinosa, Flores, and Dreyfus (1997), offers a good starting point for thinking about designing social infrastructure. They present three ways of changing the taken-for-granted, everyday practices in some domains of human culture: articulation, cross-appropriation, and re-configuration.

Let us imagine that teachers (of some particular school) have agreed to promote students' participation in a research-like process of collaborative inquiry as one of the core learning activities. But for some reason, this way of working even though it still exists, has become peripheral in this community. When some teachers are starting to think about fostering again the inquiry way of learning, and in making their attempt and the lost practices visible, they engage in articulation. *Articulation*, say Spinosa, et al. (1997) is a process of making explicit what is already implicit within an ongoing practice, and not noticed by every member of a community. Articulation does not only concern practices, but disclosing the existing ideas and tools as well. Thus, articulation does not produce a whole new way of seeing and dealing with things and people.

According to Spinosa, et al. (1997), *cross-appropriation* occurs when practices used successfully by a community in one area are appropriated by another for use elsewhere. In other words, ideas, tools, and practices are adopted from other social worlds. An example would be collaborative technology. Educational applications for collaboration, such as networked learning environments, knowledge spaces and discussion forums have been developed and applied following the idea of research conducted in the field of Computer-Supported Cooperative Work (CSCW). This research has revealed issues about the collaborative nature of work supported by groupware. These ideas generated in the field of working life research have been found useful, and cross-appropriated to the field of education (Lipponen & Lallimo, 2004b).

A third way of designing social infrastructure is re-configuration. *Re-configuration* is the act of recognizing anomalies and disturbances in everyday practices of a community. Disturbances may emerge, for instance, when teachers and students are trying to coordinate learning activities to be done with different tools such as paper and pencil or with computers, or when they are trying to share the individual knowing and competence for the good of the whole class. Re-configuring means recognizing and making the emerging disturbances visible. From a pedagogical point of view, anomalies and disturbances offer a trail to the zone of proximal development of the particular community (Engeström, 1999). Solving anomalies and disturbances always require the creation of new forms of activities. We do not maintain that these three ways of designing social infrastructure are easy to conduct. Instead, it is learning process for a whole community to be able to apply them.

5. Designing Technical Infrastructure

According to Hanseth and Lundberg (2001), designing technical infrastructures means defining standards, this is, setting agreed rules for the production of textual or material objects (Bowker & Star, 1999). Thus, whilst designing technical infrastructure, new technology needs to be integrated and linked into ongoing technologies, (and of course, into practices and stable conventions).

Hanseth (2004) offers three suggestions for designing technical infrastructure: extension, moderation, and radical change. Adding something to the existing technical infrastructure means *extension* of it. Extension takes place, for instance, when new computers are added to the existing computer network at school. *Moderation* is replacing one standard with another, for example, replacing old computer applications with new versions. *Radical* change of infrastructure means replacing an old standard with a radically new one. In an educational context, replacing paper and pencil work with computers represents a radical change. In the radical case, infrastructure grows to solve a specific problem or needs. In a radical change, the community needs technology to do something it cannot do without it.

In the following paragraphs, we present an example of the extension of a technical infrastructure and the effects it had on practices. In addition, to our observations, we illustrate the difference between technology-oriented and practice-oriented views in designing technical infrastructure. These observations are, in our experience, rather typical in schools adopting new technology.

Building a technical infrastructure can at its simplest mean the location of computers in schools. However, our observations show that this seemingly trivial issue has significant implications for practitioners' options to organize their activities. There are two basic solutions of placing computers in school. A technology-oriented solution is not interested in teachers' and students' opinions, and as a consequence, computers are typically placed in one or two computer rooms. Another way of building technical infrastructure is to create several activity centres (with desktop computers and laptops) all over the school (and in classrooms) in which students can work. This solution presupposes that there is a larger number of computers than in the first case (of course the solutions are not mutually exclusive).

In the case of our Finnish ICT experiments (Lipponen, Hakkarainen, Muukkonen, & Rahikainen, 1999) these two solutions of building technical infrastructure had clear impacts on the everyday practices of teaching and learning. Teacher A had seven computers in his own classroom for teaching and learning. However, Teacher B had to take her students to a computer room located on another floor in order to use computers. In the computer room, however there were not, enough computers for all students to work with them simultaneously, or even in pairs. As a consequence, Teacher B had to arrange the students in two groups, one working in a computer room and one in the classroom. The problem was that she was not able to be at these two places simultaneously, and she found herself running up and down stairs trying to get both of the groups to work effectively.

In the case we describe, the school staff did not question the location of computers, but it was taken for granted, and the building of the infrastructure was left for the engineers. The problem was that the engineers did not understand how the technical infrastructure was utilized by the practitioners, and how the location of computers and plugs affected the daily practices of teaching and learning. One main reason for the lack of practical understanding of the everyday use of computers in schools is that very few software developers and researchers actually go to the classroom to see what teachers and students do (and what they don't do) with technology. To understand that technological systems are themselves embedded in a set of social and cultural practices that give them meaning, and at the same time being constrained and transformed by them, implies that we should understand the systemic nature of implementation and use of technology (Dourish, 2001).

6. Conclusions: The Present and the Future

In this chapter, we argue that the implementation and adaptation of technology in schools (and in workplaces), is based on, and requires the creation of a set of interconnected structural social and technical elements. In summary, technical and social infrastructures are parts of complex overlapping system of what we call learning oriented infrastructure.The characteristics of a learning infrastructure is that it is a shared technical and social resource, developed to support specific work tasks and practices as part of human organization (Hanseth & Lundberg, 2001; Star, 1999). Infrastructures constitute the foundation on which collaboration and division of labour in a community rest, supporting, coordinating and mediating human activities.

Although we have examined the design of social and technical infrastructure separately, our future goal is to develop the idea of co-evolution and co-design of these infrastructures and to understand more deeply how they form learning oriented infrastructure. Whilst designing infrastructure one thing is certain: improvements and changes in technical and social infrastructure require a close relationship between practitioners and engineers. Only practitioners knowing the area can discover potential improvements and the limits of existing technical infrastructure; improvements will be found only in the work (Hanseth & Lundberg, 2001).

To advance this line of thought, a promising idea of co-configuration is offered by Victor & Boynton (1998) and further developed by Engeström (2004). Supporting consciously this co-evolution and co-design of infrastructures could be called *co-configuration*. According to Engeström (2004), *co-configuration* refers to a dialogue in which the parties rely on real-time feedback information on their activity. The interpretation, negotiation, and synthesizing of such information between the parties requires new, dialogical and reflective knowledge tools as well as collaboratively constructed functional rules and infrastructures. In the context of education, this means that teachers and students should be, at least co-designers of the technical infrastructure of a school.

References

Bielaczyc, K. (2001). Designing social infrastructure: the challenge of building computer-supported learning communities. In Dillenbourg P, Eurelings, A., & K. Hakkarainen (Eds.), *European perspectives on computer-supported collaborative learning. The proceedings of the First European Conference on Computer-Supported Collaborative Learning* (pp. 106–114). Maastricht: University of Maastrich.

Bowker, G. C. & Star, S. L. (1999). *Sorting things out. Classification and its consequences*. Cambridge, Mass: The MIT Press.

Brown, J. S. & Duguid, P. (1994). Boderline issues: Social and material aspects of design. *Human-Computer Interaction*, *9*, 3-36.

Bruce, B. (1993). Innovation and social change. In B. Bruce, J. Peyton, & T. Batson (Eds.), *Networked-based classrooms: Promises and realities* (pp. 33-49). New York: Cambridge University Press.

Ciborra, C. (2002). *The labyrinths of information. Challenging the wisdom of systems*. Oxford: University Press.

Ciborra, C. (2004). Encountering information systems as a phenomenon. In C. Avgerou, C. Ciborra, & F. Land (Eds.), *The social study of information and communication technology* (pp. 17-37). Oxford: University Press.

Cuban, L. (2001). *Oversold and underused: Computers in the classroom*. Cambridge, Mass: Harvard University Press.

Dourish, P. (2001). *Where the action is. The foundation of embodied interaction*. Cambridge, Mass: The MIT Press.

Engeström, Y. (1999). Activity theory and individual and social transformation. In Y. Engeström, R. Miettinen, & R.-L. Punamäki (Eds.), *Perspectives on activity theory*, (pp. 19-38). Cambridge: Cambridge University Press.

Engeström, Y. (2004) New forms of learning in co-configuration work. Available: http://is.lse.ac.uk/events/ESRCseminars/engestrom.pdf. Retrieved 02.09.2005.

Hall, R., Stevens, R., & Torralba, T. (2002). Disrupting representational infrastructure in conversations across disciplines. *Mind, Culture & Activity, 9*, 179-210.

Hanseth, O. (2004). Knowledge as infrastructure. In C. Avgerou, C. Ciborra, & F. Land (Eds.), *The social study of information and communication technology,* (pp. 103-118). Oxford: University Press.

Hanseth, O. & Lundberg, N. (2001). Designing work oriented infrastructures. *Computer Supported Cooperative Work, 10*, 347-372.

Lin, X. & Hatano, G. (2001). Cross-cultural adaptation of educational technology. In T. Koschmann & N. Miyake (Eds.), *CSCL2: Carrying forward the conversation*. Mahwah, NJ: Lawrence Erlbaum Associates.

Lipponen, L., Hakkarainen, K., Muukkonen, H., & Rahikainen, M. (1999) (in Finnish). *Ala-asteen oppilaiden käsityksiä energiasta. CSILE–ympäristö osana tutkivan oppimisen projektia. Helsingin kaupungin opetusviraston julkaisusarja* A3:1999.

Lipponen, L. & Lallimo, J. (2004a). From collaborative technology to collaborative use of technology: Designing learning oriented infrastructures. *Educational Media International, 41,* 111-116.

Lipponen, L. & Lallimo, J. (2004b). Assessing applications for collaboration: From collaboratively usable applications to collaborative technology. *British Journal of Educational Technology, 35,* 433-442.

Salomon, G. (2002). Technology and pedagogy: Why don't we see the promised revolution? *Educational Technology, 42,* 71-75.

Spinosa, C., Flores, F., & Dreyfus, H. L. (1997). *Disclosing new worlds: Entrepreneurship, democratic action, and the cultivation of solidarity.* Cambridge: The MIT Press.

Star, S. L. (1999). The ethnography of infrastructure. *American Behavioral Scientist, 43,* 377-391.

Suchman, L., Blomberg, J., Orr., J. E., & Trigg, R. (1999). Reconstructing technologies as social practice. *American Behavioral Scientist, 43,* 392-408.

Tuomi, I. (2002). *Networks of innovation: Change and meaning in the age of the Internet.* New York: Oxford University Press.

Victor, B. & Boynton, A. C. (1998). *Invented here: Maximizing your organization's internal growth and profitability.* Boston: Harvard Business School Press.

Chapter 19

ASSESSING THE EFFECTIVENESS OF A BLENDED WEB-BASED LEARNING ENVIRONMENT IN AN AUSTRALIAN HIGH SCHOOL

Vinesh Chandra
Darrell L. Fisher
Curtin University of Technology
Australia

The enhanced accessibility, affordability and capability of the Internet has created enormous possibilities in terms of designing, developing and implementing innovative teaching methods in the classroom. As existing pedagogies are revamped and new ones are added, there is a need to assess the effectiveness of these approaches from students' perspective. For more than 30 years, proven qualitative and quantitative research methods associated with learning environments research have yielded productive results for educators. While much of the research has focussed on characterising the learning environment, fewer investigations have used the results as a tool to refine the learning environment. This chapter presents the findings of a study in which *Getsmart*, a teacher designed website, was blended into science and physics lessons at an Australian high school. It shows how the results of learning environments research were used in assessing the effectiveness of the approach from the students' perspective. The investigation also gave an indication of how effective *Getsmart* was as a teaching model in such environments.

1. Introduction

Goodrum, Hackling and Rennie's (2001) report titled *The status and quality of teaching and learning of science in Australian schools* pointed out that on average, the actual picture of science was "disappointing" and the quality of teaching ranged from "brilliant to appalling" (p. 85). As a result of this grim picture, enrolments in science have probably

461

diminished significantly and according to Harrison (as cited in Roberts, 2002, p. 13) science "was in danger of becoming an optional snack in a smorgasbord of subjects".

The report *Australia's teachers: Australia's future* (2003) argued for an immediate need to improve "scientific and mathematical education and technological capability" (p. 1). It also emphasised the need for ongoing innovation as a prerequisite for "future growth and prosperity in a competitive global economy" (p. 1). Apart from giving science, technology and mathematics a high national priority in education, the report also suggested the need for high levels of research and development. The report also highlighted the decline in the number of students who completed year 12 physics, chemistry and biology as a national concern.

In order to reinvigorate student interest, is blending technologies in science a feasible option? Cooke (2005) pointed out that all innovative approaches, no matter how simple or complex should be designed with the students in mind. Students' perspective on such innovations was a critical issue. For many high school students, systematic integration of web-based applications into teaching routines is still in its infancy. New initiatives can be sustained provided there are appropriate research and development mechanisms in place to evaluate them. By applying some of the research techniques associated with learning environments, the success of such innovative practises can be adequately ascertained.

2. Learning Environments

Research has shown that the learning environment is an alterable educational variable which can directly influence cognitive and affective outcomes (Wang, Haertel, & Walberg, 1993; Waxman & Huang, 1998). It is not the only variable which affects learning outcomes; nonetheless, it is a very important one. By using various reliable instruments and a variety of qualitative methods, researchers have been able to assess the perceptions of educators and learners of their learning environments. This has enabled them to "theorise teaching and learning from different vantage points" (Tobin, 1998, p. 223).

A learner is constantly interacting with his or her learning environment. In 1935, Lewin proposed the Lewinian formula, $B = f(P,E)$. This formula hypothesizes that human behaviour (B) is a function of the personal characteristics of an individual (P) and his or her environment (E) (Fraser, 1998). This hypothesis has since generated considerable interest and formed the basis for further research in various situations where human behaviour is demonstrated. Since an individual is always interacting with his or her environment, observed behaviour is a result of the combined effect of the interaction between variables P and E.

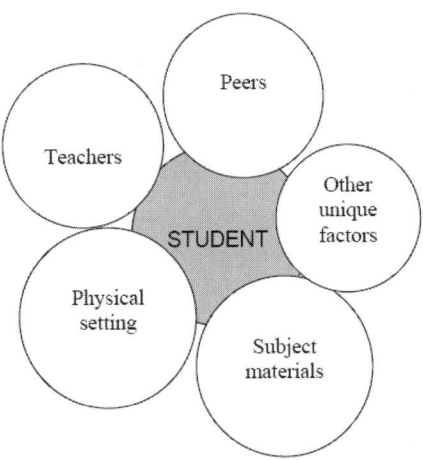

Figure 19.1. Variables in a student's learning environment.

In an educational setting, a learner is constantly interacting with an array of variables, such as teachers, peers, physical settings, subject materials and a cluster of factors unique to different learners (Figure 19.1). For this reason, there was a need to develop suitable learning environment instruments that had the capability of quantitatively measuring the impact of the learning environment on a learner in different settings. These economical, reliable and valid learning environment instruments enabled researchers to assess classroom environments from a student's perspective (Henderson & Fisher, 1998).

The foundations for this now flourishing field of learning environments was initially laid by two psychologists who were working independently of each other. The work of Walberg (1976) and Moos (1974) led to the development of a variety of learning environment instruments. Despite the development of several learning environment instruments over the years, the design is essentially the same. Learning environment instruments have scales and within each scale is a series of items, which help formulate student perceptions for that scale. The construct validity of each scale is determined by gathering qualitative data from the respondents.

3. The Web based Learning Environment Instrument (WEBLEI)

The *Web-based Learning Environment Instrument* (WEBLEI) (Chang & Fisher, 1998, 2003) was used to gather data quantitatively on students' perceptions of their web-based learning environment in a tertiary environment. In the design of the WEBLEI, Chang and Fisher (1998) created four scales and the first three were adapted from Tobin's (1998) work on *Connecting Communities of Learning* (CCL). The CCL was developed by Tobin to study the perceptions of maths and science education students enrolled in an asynchronous mode.

The WEBLEI measures students' perceptions across four scales – Access, Interaction, Response, and Results. According to Chang and Fisher (1998), for students to use this medium, they have to successfully access the Internet. Consequently, the Access scale establishes the extent to which variables associated with accessing this medium meet students' expectations. Once the students have logged in successfully, they should be able to interact productively with their peers and their teachers. Hence, the Interaction scale explores the extent to which this is achieved from students' point of view. The Response scale gives an indication of how they felt about using a web-based medium and the Results scale gives an idea of whether they accomplished any of the learning objectives by using the learning resources accessed through this medium.

The purpose of the research described in this chapter was to assess the effectiveness of an innovative website as a teaching model in a blended learning environment by using the WEBLEI and other qualitative methods. These results would then be used in the further refinement of *Getsmart* and the teaching approach used in the study.

4. The Modified Version of the WEBLEI

In this study, the WEBLEI was modified and used for quantitative measurements. The initial version of the WEBLEI was designed by Chang and Fisher (1998, 2003) to quantify students' perceptions of their learning environment in a higher-learning institution where the entire course was offered online. In this research, the course was offered in a blended environment to students in a high school. While in a university environment, courses are generally delivered through sophisticated software (e.g., *WebCT*), in this instance, the course was delivered by *Getsmart*. In this teacher-developed website, the learning activities were different. Therefore, most of the items in the WEBLEI were either amended or changed to suit this study. The modified version had a total of 32 items with eight items in each scale (Chandra, 2004). The total number of items and the number of items per scale were similar to those in the original version of the WEBLEI.

5. Design and Development of *Getsmart*

Liber (2005) argued that the design of e-learning environments should not be left to the technicians and programmers. There is a need for teachers to become more proactive in driving the technology. Through such an approach, teachers have a far greater control in terms of how the learning activities are designed, developed and sequenced.

In this study, *Getsmart* was designed on the electronic cognitive apprenticeship teaching model (Collins, Brown, & Newman, 1989; Wang & Bonk, 2001) by a teacher with no formal training in the field of ICT's. Within this framework a variety of learning opportunities such as modelling, coaching, scaffolding, articulation, reflection, exploration, and questioning were created through web-based lessons, tests, online chats, and interactive activities (Chandra, 2004; Chandra & Fisher, 2004).

Brooks, Nolan, and Gallagher (2001) proposed numerous features that websites should have in order to improve learning outcomes. A high degree of interaction was one of their suggestions. Features which promoted interaction included provisions for asynchronous discussion (emails and bulletin boards) and synchronous discussion (chat rooms). They suggested that websites should use hypertext links to enable readers to make decisions about their reading, web-based assessment tools such as quizzes and tests, visual media such as still images and images in motion and a "neat" domain address to identify the website.

Janicki and Liegle (2001) developed WebTAS (*Web-Based Tutoring Authoring System*) which blended parts of instructional design theories and ideas proposed by web researchers. WebTAS incorporated features such as multiple examples and exercises, consistent layout design, feedback management, and tracking process capability.

CONTENT'S PAGE : CHOOSE YOUR TOPIC

CHECK MY RESULTS NEW
CHECK MY LOGIN HISTORY NEW

SUBJECTS AND TOPICS

PHYSICS

MOTION Scalars & Vectors; Speed & Velocity, Acceleration, Equations of Motion; Motion graphs(1); Motion graphs(2), Application of motion concepts; Free falling objects, Projectile motion, Circular motion, Non-uniform circular motion, Review Questions(1), Review Question(2)

ENERGY & MOMENTUM Momentum; Conservation of momentum; Momentum Problems (1); Momentum Problems (2); Kinetic Energy; Potential Energy; Kinetic and Potential Energy combined ;Work and Energy; Forces(1), Forces(2), Review Questions

ELECTRONICS Semi conductors, More on doping, Common electronic components; Capacitors, Diodes, Light Dependent Resistors in action, Capacitors in action, NPN & PNP Transistors, Logic Gates, Electronics Revision

ATOMIC PHYSICS History of the atom, The hydrogen atom, Frank-Hertz Experiment, Radioactivity, Radioactivity data analysis, Binding Energy, Atomic Physics Revision

ELECTRICITY AND MAGNETISM Electric charges (Chapter Summary), , Review questions , Electricity formula review

OPTICS Plane mirrors, Reflection in a curved mirror, Ray diagrams (concave mirrors), Ray diagrams (convex mirrors), Mirror formula, Practice ray diagrams (mirrors), Mirrors chapter summary, Refraction, Convex Lens, Concave Lens, Practice ray diagrams (lens), Lens formula, Optics revision

Figure 19.2. Part of the content's page of Getsmart.

The educational value of the website has to blend in with good web design principles. Issues such as the process, interface and site designs, page design, typography, editorial style, graphics, and multimedia were recognized as essential ingredients of a good website (www.webstyleguide.com). While all these ideas were acknowledged in the design of *Getsmart,* one of the key aspects which steered its development was the feedback gathered from the WEBLEI and qualitative data gathered through emails and written surveys.

The website had a neat domain address (u2cangetsmart.com). Students accessed the website via the *Splash Page*. Once their user name and password was validated, students were then able to access the *Contents Page*. A part of this page is shown in Figure 19.3.

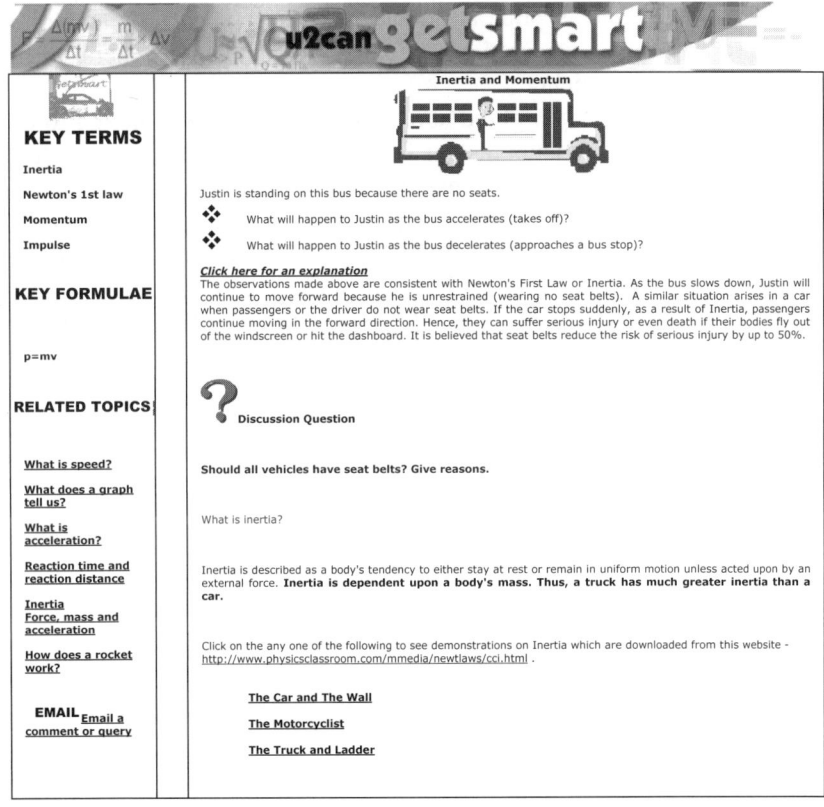

Figure 19.3. Part of the lesson page on Inertia and Momentum.

The *Lesson Pages* were designed on single topics that focussed on a handful of concepts. Each page highlighted the key terms and formulae. Links were also provided to WebPages that that were either embedded in *Getsmart* or on other websites. Discussion questions and solutions to worked examples were also provided on most pages. Students also had the option to email queries. A part of the *Lesson Page* on Inertia and Momentum which was designed for year 10 science students is shown in Figure 19.3.

According to a recent report (Goodrum, Hackling, & Rennie, 2001), in Australian schools, the quality of formative assessment and teacher feedback on student progress varied. Only 7% of high school students were given a quiz to see how they were going in every lesson and 16% participated in formative tasks once a week It was also interesting to note that 23% of the student population had never seen such tests and almost one third had never received any feedback from their teachers on how they were going in science.

For the reasons highlighted above, an online test was linked to each lesson which gave students instant feedback. The results were written to a database against the user's name. Each test consisted of either ten multiple-choice or short answer questions. The feedback indicated the percentage correct but did not indicate the specific questions that were correct or incorrect. This was done on purpose to ensure that students revisited the questions and compared their answers with their colleagues and teachers. This created discussion opportunities. A part of the *Test Page* linked to the Reaction Time and Distance lesson (designed for year 10 science students) is shown in Figure 19.4.

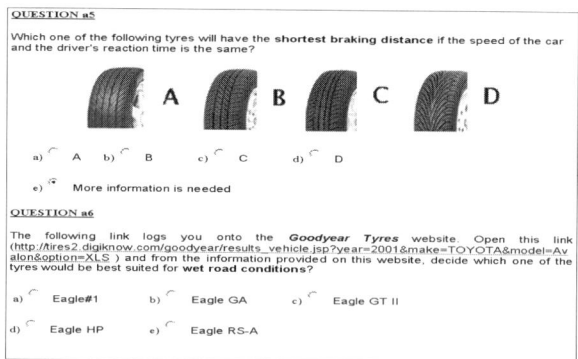

Figure 19.4. Part of the *Test Page* on Reaction Time and Distance.

6. Implementation of *Getsmart*

The website was aimed at students in years 10, 11, and 12 (ages 15-17 yrs.) studying junior science and physics. For this reason, ease of use was central to its development. The lessons were designed so that they would keep students on task and could be completed within a normal school period. Students accessed the website for one period each week and web-based lessons were designed for units of work that lasted for a term. Each school period lasted for a maximum of 31 minutes (it generally required three to five minutes for students to login into the school computers). Students could also access the website outside class times including their homes. A total of 261 students from 11 classes participated in the study.

7. Data Collection and Analysis

Once students had completed their unit of work in the blended mode, the WEBLEI and a written survey were administered. Data from the WEBLEI survey were coded and entered as 1 (Strongly Disagree), 2 (Disagree), 3 (Neither Agree nor Disagree), 4 (Agree), and 5 (Strongly Agree). Emails were received throughout the course. Not all students responded via emails or to written surveys.

Statistical measurements such as mean, median, standard deviation, alpha reliability, and discriminant validity were determined. All emails and answers to written questions were read and the key points were identified in each instance.

8. Results

8.1 Reliability and validity of the modified version of the WEBLEI

The reliability analysis gives an idea of the extent to which items in the same scale of a learning environment instrument are related to each other. The Cronbach alpha reliability coefficient measures the internal consistency and is based on the average inter-item correlation. All values above 0.60 obtained through this calculation are considered to be acceptable (Nunnally, 1967). In this study, the alpha reliability coefficient of the four scales of the WEBLEI ranged from 0.78 to 0.86 (Chandra, 2004). The discriminant validity determines the extent to which a scale measures an unique dimension not covered by other scales in the instrument. In this study, the discriminant validity (the mean correlation of one scale with each of the other scales) of the modified version of WEBLEI obtained ranged from 0.52 to 0.59 for the four scales (Chandra, 2004) indicating that each of the four scales measures distinct, though partly overlapping elements of the web-based environment.

8.2 WEBLEI results

The mean obtained for each scale was very close to four for all scales (except for the Interaction scale where it was 3.53). For the Response and Results scales, the means were slightly higher than those reported by Chang and Fisher (2003). They reported means of 3.96 for the Access scale, 3.55 for the Interaction scale, 3.37 for the Response scale and 3.72 for Results scale. In this research, means of 3.94, 3.51, 3.74, and 3.88 were obtained for the Access, Interaction, Response, and Results scales respectively (see Table 19.1).

Table 19.1. Mean and Standard Deviations for the Four scales of the WEBLEI (Phase 1)

WEBLEI Scales	Descriptive Statistics		
	Mean	Standard Deviation	Valid Cases
Access	3.94	0.66	214
Interaction	3.51	0.77	213
Response	3.74	0.72	213
Results	3.88	0.68	214

A mean of 3.94 (SD = 0.66) for the Access scale suggested that students agreed that their learning environment was convenient and easily accessible at locations suitable to them. It enabled them to work at their own pace. A web-based environment also gave them greater autonomy in achieving their learning objectives. A further analysis of each of each items in this scale suggested relatively high agreement in each instance (Table 19.2).

Table 19.2. Means and Standard Deviations of Students Responses to the Items of the Access Scale

Item No.	Statement	Mean	Standard Deviation
1	I can access lessons on the Internet at times convenient to me.	4.08	0.94
2	Lessons on the Internet are available at locations suitable for me.	4.14	0.80
3	I can access lessons on the Internet on days when I am not in class or absent from school.	3.90	1.20
4	Lessons on the Internet allow me to work at my own pace to achieve learning objectives.	4.07	0.99
5	Lessons on the internet enable me to decide how much I want to learn in a given period.	3.83	1.07
6	Lessons on the Internet enable me to decide when I want to learn.	3.78	1.08
7	The flexibility of lessons on the Internet allows me to meet my learning goals.	3.79	0.96
8	The flexibility of the lessons on the Internet allows me to explore my own areas of interest.	3.93	1.01

N = 214

The Interaction scale produced a mean of 3.58 (SD = 0.71) (see Table 19.1), the lowest of all three scales. An average of three implied that students neither agreed nor disagreed with all the items in the scale. A mean of four suggested that they agreed with the statements. A mean of 3.58 suggests that there was agreement to a certain degree to the items of the Interaction scale. The means and standard deviations for each item of this scale also were analysed and are presented in Table 19.3.

From the means shown in Table 19.3, it is obvious that Items14 and 15 which were connected with enhanced verbal interactions with peers during Internet lessons received the highest rating. However, items (9, 11, 12, and 13) that were related to emails were the ones in which the students expressed the greatest uncertainty (Neither Agreed nor Disagreed). The results to these items could be interpreted as follows. Students had the option of asking teachers questions by sending an email (Item 11), however, they were not sure if they felt comfortable sending teachers emails (Item 12). For this reason, not all students sent emails (Item 9) and consequently, they did not receive a reply from their teachers (Item 13). However, of the 171 emails, received in the study, very few had specific questions that needed to be addressed. Most of them highlighted positive aspects of the blended approach to learning science and while all emails were acknowledged and responded to, it was the researcher who replied to them and not the teachers. This provides another explanation for the low mean obtained for Item 13.

Table 19.3. Means and Standard Deviations of Students Responses to the Items of the Interaction Scale

Item No.	Statement	Mean	Standard Deviation
9	I communicate with my teacher in this subject electronically via email.	3.41	1.29
10	In this learning environment, I have to be self-disciplined in order to learn.	3.40	1.20
11	I have the option to ask my teacher what I do not understand by sending an email.	3.61	1.27
12	I feel comfortable asking my teacher questions via an email.	3.31	1.34
13	The teacher responds to my emails.	3.10	1.23
14	I can ask other students what I do not understand during Internet lessons.	3.98	1.08
15	Other students respond positively to questions in relation to Internet lessons.	3.76	0.93
16	I was encouraged by the positive attitude of my friends towards the Internet lessons.	3.55	0.98

N = 213

A mean score of 3.74 (SD = 0.72) was obtained for the Response scale (see Table 19.1) which implied that students generally agreed web-based learning was satisfying and it enabled them to interact with other students and their teachers. They also enjoyed learning in this environment and they believed that this approach held their interest in the subject for the whole term. While the lowest rating item for the Response scale was Item 24 (I felt a sense of boredom in this subject towards end of this term.) with a mean of 3.05 (SD = 1.27), I enjoy learning in this environment rated the highest with a mean of 4.15 (SD = 0.92). All other items generally demonstrated agreement to the items with means greater than 3.6 (Table 19.4).

Table 19.4. Means and Standard Deviations of Students Responses to the Items of the Response Scale

Item No.	Statement	Mean	Standard Deviation
17	This mode of learning enables me to interact with other students and my teacher.	3.60	1.11
18	I felt a sense of satisfaction and achievement about this learning environment.	3.62	1.03
19	I enjoy learning in this environment.	4.15	0.92
20	I could learn more in this environment.	3.93	1.08
21	I can easily get students to work with me on the Internet.	3.89	0.98
22	It is easy to work with other students and discuss the content of the lessons.	3.96	0.91
23	The web-based learning environment held my interest in this subject throughout this term.	3.74	1.13
24	I felt a sense of boredom in this subject towards end of this term.	3.05	1.29

N = 213

For the Results scale, Chang and Fisher (1998) reported a mean of 3.75. In this research, the mean score of 3.88 (SD = 0.68) (see Table 19.1) for this scale suggested that students agreed they could establish the purpose of web-based lessons. It was also easy to follow, well sequenced, and clear. The structure kept them focussed and it helped them learn better the work that was done in class. The content was presented well and it was appropriate for delivery in a web-based learning environment. The tests at the end of the lessons, improved their understanding in the subject. In the Results scale, individual items had means that ranged from 3.62 to 4.12. It was interesting to note that items 25, 26, 30, 31, and 32 had means greater than 3.88 (Table 19.5).

Table 19.5. Means and Standard Deviations of Students Responses to the Items of the Results Scale

Item No.	Statement	Mean	Standard Deviation
25	I can work out exactly what each lesson on the Internet is about.	3.88	0.92
26	The organisation of each lesson on the Internet is easy to follow.	4.13	0.83
27	The structure of the lessons on the Internet keeps me focused on what is to be learned	3.62	1.05
28	Internet lessons helped me better understand the work that was taught in class.	3.68	1.04
29	Lessons on the Internet are well sequenced.	3.78	0.92
30	The subject content is appropriate for delivery on the Internet.	3.90	0.91
31	The presentation of the subject content is clear.	4.01	0.84
32	The multiple choice test at the end of each lesson on the Internet improves my learning in this subject.	4.01	1.04

N = 214

9. Discussion and Conclusions

The data generated through the WEBLEI suggested that students had positive perceptions of their web-based learning environment. This was also confirmed by qualitative data gathered through student surveys and emails (see Chandra, 2004).

Results gathered across the four scales suggested that the integration web-based learning in science and physics lessons was convenient and accessible, promoted autonomy of learning and enabled students to work at their pace. It also promoted positive interactions between peers during Internet lessons, enhanced enjoyment and learning opportunities in the subject, and sustained interest in the subject. Lessons on *Getsmart* were clear, easy to follow and understand, and well sequenced. Online tests provided valuable feedback.

While the WEBLEI painted a positive picture of *Getsmart* as a teaching model in a blended environment, it also showed that emails as a vehicle for electronic interaction were not preferred to the extent to which they were initially intended. Students' qualitative responses provided additional evidence on this issue.

I agree that I can communicate via email but prefer to have my questions answered face to face.

I didn't communicate via email because there might be a pause of one day before a response, in which case I would have already forgotten my problem.

I don't like the email all that much and if I don't understand something, I'd rather talk to someone face to face.

The WEBLEI was initially designed for students at universities in off-campus environments where the interaction between learners and educators via the Internet was essential. In a blended learning, high school environment, learners are probably looking for an interactive learning environment with technology. They are looking for an opportunity to be away from the classroom momentarily and from human beings. While emails are productive for the ideal student who reviews his or her work on a daily basis, identifies problems, and forwards queries electronically to his or her teacher, very few students probably fall in this category. High schools are probably still a few years away from producing a learning culture where learners have the confidence to conduct their learning in this manner. For many, asking the teacher questions face to face in class is probably viewed as a more feasible and preferred option.

The findings of this research also suggested that the items on the Interaction scale of the WEBLEI were inadequate in measuring the interaction between learners and technology. Students appear to have achieved more through their interaction with the technology itself by using applets, simulations, online tests, and online experiments. Qualitative data and teacher observations supported this view (Chandra, 2004). In the initial design of the WEBLEI, Chang and Fisher (1998) proposed the following connection between the scales:

Scale 1 (Access) → Scale 2 (Interaction) → Scale 3 (Response) → Scale 4 (Results)

In this study, it appears that the Interaction scale was not as significantly interconnected as the other three. When Chang and Fisher (2003) administered the WEBLEI to university students, they reported values of 3.96, 3.55, 3.37, and 3.72 for Access, Interaction, Response and Result scales, respectively. In their study, the Response scale was rated the lowest. In this study, the Interaction scale was rated the lowest. While the characteristics of the items in the Interaction scale are important qualities of online learning, in this case it appears that there was significant interaction between students and technology. It is probably this interaction (rather than interaction between learners and educators) which led to a significantly higher mean for the Results scale. Otherwise, given the rationale of the design of the WEBLEI, these results may not have been obtained. For this reason, another scale should most probably be added to the existing WEBLEI design with items that specifically measure the interaction of learners with technology in an online learning environment.

The learning environments research undertaken in this study has demonstrated the usefulness of *Getsmart* as a model for teaching science and physics in a blended environment. Additionally, the findings of the research have also produced areas within the model that need further development and refinement.

Acknowledgments

We thank the teachers of the high school in Queensland, Australia where this research was conducted. The first author of this paper is also grateful to Education Queensland for the award of the Premier's Smart State Teacher's Excellence Scholarship.

References

Brooks, D. W., Nolan, D. E., & Gallagher, S. M. (2001). *Web-Teaching* (Second ed.). New York: Kluwer Academic/Plenum Publishers.
Chang, V. & Fisher, D. L. (1998). *The validation and application of a new learning environment instrument to evaluate online learning in higher education.* Retrieved 31 July, 2003, from http://www.aare.edu.au/01pap/cha01098.htm.
Chang, V. & Fisher, D. L. (2003). The validation and application of a new learning environment instrument for online learning in higher

education. In M. S. Khine & D. L. Fisher (Eds.), *Technology-rich learning environments A future perspective* (pp. 1-20). Singapore: World Scientific.

Chandra, V. (2004). *The impact of a blended web-based learning environment on the perceptions, attitudes and performance of boys and girls in junior science and senior physics.* Unpublished thesis, Curtin University of Technology, Perth.

Chandra, V. & Fisher, D. L. (2004, July). *Developing and implementing a blended web-based learning environment.* Paper presented at the Australian Computers in Education Conference, Adelaide.

Collins, A., Brown, J. S., & Newman, S. E. (1989). Cognitive apprenticeship: Teaching the craft of reading, writing and mathematics. In L. B. Resnick (Ed.), *Knowing, learning and instruction: Essays in honor of Robert Glaser.* (pp. 453-494). Hillsdale: NJ: Erlbaum.

Cooke, S. (2005). *Theme Speaker - Implementation.* Paper presented at the Association of Learning Technology Conference, Manchester, England.

Department of Education, Science and Training (2003). *Australia's teachers: Australia's future. Advancing innovation, science, technology and mathematics. Agenda for action* Canberra. Retrieved 23 October, 2005 from http://www.dest.gov.au/sectors/school_education/policy_initiatives_r eviews/reviews/teaching_teacher_education/default.htm.

Fraser, B. J. (1998). Science learning environments: Assessment, effects and determinants. In B. J. Fraser & K. G. Tobin (Eds.), *International handbook of science education* (pp. 527-564). Dordrecht: The Netherlands Academic Publishers.

Goodrum, M., Hackling, M., & Rennie, L. (2001). *The status and quality of teaching and learning of science in Australian schools.* Canberra: Department of Education, Training and Youth Affairs.

Henderson, D. & Fisher, D. (1998). Assessing learning environments in senior science laboratories. *Australian Science Teachers Journal, 44,* 57-61.

Janicki, T. & Liegle, J. O. (2001). Development and evaluation of a framework for creating web-based learning modules: A pedagogical and systems perspective. *Journal of Asynchronous Learning Networks, 5* (1), 58-82. Retrieved June 2, 2003, from http://www.sloanc.org/publications/jaln/v5n1/pdf/v5n1_janicki.pdf.

Lewin, K. (1935). *A dynamic theory of personality*. New York: McGraw.

Liber, O. (2005). *Theme Speaker - Architectures and Infrastructures.* Paper presented at the Association of Learning Technology Conference, Manchester, England.

Moos, R. H. (1974). *The social climate scales: An overview*. Palo Alto, CA: Consulting Psychologists Press.

Nunnally, J. (1967). *Psychometric theory*. New York: Mc-Graw Hill.

Roberts, J. (phase 1 , April 20). High school teachers 'letting science down'. *The Australian,* p. C13.

Tobin, K. G. (1998). Qualitative perceptions of learning environments on the world wide web. *Learning Environments Research, 1*, 139-162.

Walberg, H. J. (1976). Psychology of learning environments: Behavioral, structural, or perceptual? *Review of Research in Education. 4*, 142-178.

Wang, F.-K. & Bonk, C. J. (2001). A design framework for electronic cognitive apprenticeship. *Journal of Asynchronous Learning Networks, 5* (2), 131-150. Retrieved February 10, 2003, from http://www.sloan-c.org/publications/jaln/v5n2/pdf/v5n2_wang.pdf.

Wang, M. C., Haertel, G. D., & Walberg, H. J. (1993). Toward a knowledge base for school learning. *Review of Educational Research, 63*, 249-294.

Waxman, H. C. & Huang, S. (1998). Classroom learning environments in urban elementary, middle and high schools. *Learning Environments Research, 1* (1), 95-113.

Chapter 20

VALIDATION OF AN INSTRUMENT FOR ASSESSING PSYCHOSOCIAL ENVIRONMENTS AT COLLEGES AND UNIVERSITIES IN TAIWAN

Shwu-yong L. Huang
National Taiwan University
Taiwan

Little research on psychosocial environments at the higher education level has been reported in recent years, despite an increasing awareness of the important role of environment on student performance. This chapter describes the validation of the College and University Environment Inventory - Students (CUEI-S) and an initial assessment of psychosocial environments as perceived by college and university students. The data source is the recently established Taiwan Higher Education Databank. A randomly selected sample of 5,626 juniors from 35 public colleges and universities and 9,776 juniors from 34 independent colleges and universities in Taiwan were examined. Exploratory factor analysis resulted in the seven dimensions of the CUEI-S: Student Cohesiveness, Faculty-Student Relations, Administrative Services, Language Ability, Emotional Development, Library Resources, and Student Affairs. Each scale has adequate internal consistency reliability and discriminant validity with either group of students. The CUEI-S confirms the diversity of university environments. The results of an application of the CUEI-S reveal that, in Taiwan, most juniors had favourable relations with other students and with administrative staff, and perceived positively their library resources and emotional development. Student-faculty relations, university system support to student affairs, and language learning, however, may need to be improved. Implications of the findings are discussed.

1. Introduction

Prior research on learning environments has focused on elementary and secondary schools and has contributed remarkably to their subsequent improvement (Fraser, 1999). Little research on the psychosocial aspects of learning environments at the higher education level, however, has been reported in recent years, despite an increasing awareness of the important role of environment on student performance. In order to bridge the gap and to provide a better understanding at the tertiary level, this chapter describes the development and validation of the instrument, *College and University Environment Inventory - Students* (CUEI-S), and an initial assessment of psychosocial environments as perceived by college and university students in Taiwan.

Most educational evaluation research has relied heavily on assessments of student academic achievement and other learning outcomes. For post-secondary education, measuring academic achievement and other learning outcomes is much more complex than at the elementary or secondary levels, since students major in various subjects or disciplines, and their campus interactions are generally more varied. In other words, cognitive measures alone cannot give a comprehensive picture of academic learning processes and outcomes, because the psychosocial aspect is equally important; as Reigeluth (1999) argued, the affective domain could actually dominate the cognitive domain.

Aspects of psychosocial environments on campus are significantly correlated with outcomes of university students (Astin, 1993a, 1993b). College students who rated their campus environment positively reported making more progress in personal and social development as well as in general education than less satisfied students (Glover, 1996). Transfer students' perceptions of the university over time, and particularly of its academic environment, were important predictors of their graduation and persistence (Kearney & Kearney, 1994). Furthermore, students with higher levels of academic development, faculty interaction, and peer group interaction indicated higher levels of professional commitment (Fjortoft & Lee, 1994). To create a campus environment that supports academic excellence requires an understanding of the present conditions of the psychosocial environment on campus, and a clear mandate from top administrators to build a supportive and enabling environment.

Investigating college students' perceptions of their psychosocial environments is particularly meaningful for the recent reform movement in Taiwan. Due to the significant changes in educational policies of the Taiwanese government, restrictions on the establishment of independent (private) colleges and universities have been removed. As a result, the number of higher education institutions in Taiwan has grown dramatically from around 50 to over 150 in the past decade. According to the Taiwanese Ministry of Education in 2004, the student body has also tripled. Because the total education budget has not likewise increased, the financial resources of each institution have been seriously diluted. Public universities that are funded mainly by the government have suffered the most. Student services and staff have had to be cut. Furthermore, the new educational system provides alternative ways of gaining admission to colleges and universities, superseding the single decisive college entrance examination creating an additional workload for faculty and administrative staff. These new educational developments may have a profound impact on the higher education environment.

In order to obtain a comprehensive picture of the current status of higher education, a team of educators and researchers proposed the establishment of the *Taiwan Higher Education Data System*, a longitudinal project sponsored by the Ministry of Education and the National Science Council in 2003. The design of the system is to collect freshman, junior, graduate, faculty and institutional data with systematic follow-ups. The data source of the present study is from the recently completed databank for college juniors. This study concentrates on college students' perceptions of their psychosocial environment on campus. It consults relevant literature to determine the dimensions to be included in the instrument, and then takes multiple approaches including exploratory factor analysis, internal consistency reliability, discriminant validity, and univariate analysis of variance to develop and validate an instrument for assessing the psychosocial environments of colleges and universities.

2. Assessment of College and University Environments

The important role of educational environments is recognized in ancient Chinese literature. The story that the mother of the great Chinese philosopher, Mencius, moved three times in order to find an environment conducive to young Mencius' intellectual development is well known to most Chinese; however, investigation of higher education environments has been lacking among Chinese educational researchers.

In the West, modern research on educational environments has theoretical foundations in Lewin's (1936) field theory that the interactions of personal characteristics and environments are determinants of human behavior, $B = f(P, E)$. Murray (1938) followed Lewin's ideas and proposed a needs-press model, in which personal needs refer to motivational personality characteristics representing tendencies to move in the direction of certain goals, whereas environmental press provides an external situation counterpart that supports or frustrates the expression of internalized personality needs (Fraser, 1994). In the 1950's, Pace and Stern adopted Murray's model and developed the *College Characteristics Index*, specially focused on higher education institutions (Pace & Stern, 1958; Stern, 1970). Later, Moos' *Work Environment Scale* (1979, 1981), originally designed for used in a work milieu, was adapted to describe educational environments. It includes 10 scales to measure three dimensions of psychosocial environment: The Relationship Dimension, the Personal Development Dimension, and the System Maintenance and System Change Dimension. The Relationship Dimension measures the extent to which people involved in the environment support and help each other. The Personal Development Dimension measures the extent to which personal growth and self-enhancement tend to occur. The System Maintenance and System Change Dimension measures the extent to which the environment is orderly, clear in expectation, controlled, and responsive to change (Fraser, Docker, & Fisher, 1988).

Fraser, Treagust, and Dennis (1986) identified concepts and ideas relevant to higher education settings and developed the *College and University Classroom Environment Inventory* (CUCEI). It is an instrument for assessing students' and instructors' perceptions of seven dimensions of the actual and preferred classroom environment of university or college seminars or tutorials, but not for lectures or laboratory classes. It contains seven scales: Personalization, Involvement, Student Cohesiveness, Satisfaction, Task Orientation, Innovation and Individualization. Each has seven items measured on a four-point scale: strongly agree, agree, disagree, and strongly disagree. It was validated with both Australian and American samples. The alpha reliability coefficients of scales ranged from 0.61 to 0.92 for students and from 0.53 to 0.83 for faculty members.

Assessing both students' and faculty members' perceptions of the psychosocial environment with the same instrument is advantageous for providing a sound base for comparative study. Nevertheless, this is more appropriate for investigating classroom environments than for overall college and university environments because faculty and students in the same classroom tend to participate in the same activities and share the same climate, whereas their out-of-classroom experiences and perspectives could be very different. Hence, an instrument specifically for students named the College and University Environment Inventory for Students (CUEI-S) is the focus of this study; another instrument for faculty, yet to be developed, might be called the College and University Environment Inventory for Faculty (CUEI-F).

In the present study, the scope of the psychosocial environments of colleges and universities is broadly defined as the psychological, social and academic contexts that help learning and influence student achievement and attitudes. This study emphasizes a mediating paradigm, with college students actively processing information and interpreting their academic experiences. Students' perceptions of the psychosocial environments of their colleges or universities are essential for understanding the quality of higher education. What students perceive and react to, in their educational environments -- subjective as it may be -- affects their overall growth more than what is observed by outsiders.

The purpose of this study is to determine what aspects ought to be included in a parsimonious instrument for assessing the psychosocial environments at colleges and universities, to attest the validity and reliability of the instrument, and to initiate an assessment of the psychosocial environments as perceived by college students in Taiwan. It thus establishes a starting point for recommending strategies for fostering better learning environments.

3. Initial Development of the Instrument

The data source of the study is the recently established Taiwan Higher Education Databank. In the databank, a stratified random sample of student data were collected, representing 23% of the junior student body from both public and private colleges and universities all over Taiwan. It used a self-response questionnaire that includes seven sections such as demographic background, financial resources, courses and learning, campus living, student views of the university and of self, and future plan. In each section, an initial pool of items was developed and then modified several times by the research team with item analysis and tests of validity and reliability (Peng & Wang, 2005). Junior student data were used instead of freshman because juniors have generally completed two years of study at their universities and thus have more insightful perceptions of the psychosocial environment on campus than freshmen. The present study used items selected from the sections on student background and general views of college or university. In order to develop the construct of the College and University Environment Inventory for Students (CUEI-S), relevant literature was consulted and a few guidelines were set.

1. The study adapted Moos' three categories of environment dimensions for the conceptualization of psychosocial environments of colleges and universities.
2. The instrument selected only items salient to higher education settings from the student databank.
3. Parsimony was a priority. A limited number of items and scales are included in the CUEI-S while keeping satisfactory psychometric properties of the instrument.

According to the above criteria, three categories of items were selected from the questionnaire: A) How is your personal relationship with others at this college or university? B) Do you feel that your college or university is helpful in developing a diversity of ability? C) Are you satisfied with various aspects of the college or university? A total of 38 items from the three categories was chosen for further examination. Each item was scored on a four-point Likert-type scale with 1 indicating strongly disagree or not helpful and 4 indicating strongly agree or extremely helpful.

In the initial development of the instrument, data from 5,626 juniors from 35 public colleges and universities were used, excluding those from four-year professional colleges. Among these juniors, the gender distribution is fairly equal. About 63% of these students come from middle class backgrounds. Nearly 23% of them used the library frequently. Eighty percent of them planned to pursue advanced degrees.

To estimate the construct validity of the CUEI-S, exploratory factor analysis was performed. Factor loadings, scree plot, and eigenvalues were used as criteria for item and factor selection. Factor loadings are the correlation coefficients between the item variables and factors. "Scree" is a word used to describe loose stones or rocky debris at the base of a hill; in factor analysis, a scree plot graphically groups factors, which makes it easy to separate the retainable constructs from those that are not useful (Santos & Clegg, 1999). It shows the sorted eigenvalues from large to small, and is a determinant of the number of factors to retain. The eigenvalue for a given factor estimates the variance in all the variables which is accounted for by that factor. If a factor has a low eigenvalue, then it is contributing little to the explanation of variances in the variables and may be ignored.

Because of the very large dataset and possibility of correlations between factors, promax (non-orthogonal) rotation was chosen instead of varimax (orthogonal) rotation in the exploratory factor analysis (Fabrigar, Wegener, MacCallum, & Strahan, 1999). The rotated promax pattern produced seven factors (scales): Student Cohesiveness, Faculty-Student Relations, Administrative Services (Relationship Dimension), Language Ability, Emotional Development (Personal Development Dimensions), Library Resources, and Student Affairs (System Maintenance and System Change Dimension). The scree plot showing a flat slope after the seventh factor attests to the results. Items with factor loadings lower than 0.45 were omitted, resulting in 25 useful items. Eigenvalues of all seven factors were larger than 2.0, and the percentage of total variance explained was 67%. The construct validity of the CUEI-S was thus confirmed.

Each item was also tested, using individual students as the unit of analysis, in order to ensure that items in the same scale measure the same dimension. Internal consistency reliability coefficients (correlations between one item and the rest of the scale items) ranged from 0.76 for Student Cohesiveness to 0.85 for Administrative Services, with a mean value of 0.80, indicating that the instrument has acceptable reliability in measuring attitudes or perceptions. When the college or university was used as the unit of analysis, the alpha reliability coefficients of the seven scales ranged more widely, from 0.70 to 0.94, with a higher mean value of 0.87. Altogether, the results suggest that the CUEI-S is reliable in measuring student perceptions of psychosocial environments in colleges and universities, with either the individual student or the college/university mean as the unit of analysis.

Discriminant validity coefficients which estimate the mean correlations of one scale with the other six scales ranged from 0.21 to 0.32, with an overall mean value of 0.27, indicating that these scales are weakly related; each scale measures an independent aspect of the psychosocial environment. When the college or university was used as the unit of analysis, the interscale correlation coefficients of the seven scales ranged more widely, from 0.14 to 0.51, with a slightly higher mean value of 0.35, suggesting that although a few environmental scales correlated moderately with others, the CUEI-S generally has adequate discriminant validity at both levels of analysis.

This instrument is also capable of differentiating psychosocial environments among colleges or universities. One-way analysis of variance (ANOVA) with college/university membership as the independent variable showed that these college and universities vary significantly ($p<0.001$) in six of the seven environmental aspects, except student cohesiveness. The probability level was set at $p<0.001$ because of the large sample size. Table 20.1 reports the internal consistency reliability, discriminant validity, and ANOVA results.

Table 20.1. Alpha Reliability, Discriminant Validity, and ANOVA Results of the CUEI-S Scales for Public Colleges and Universities

Scale	No of items	Alpha Reliability		Discriminant Validity		ANOVA by college
		Student	College	Student	College	
Student Cohesiveness	3	0.76	0.70	0.21	0.14	1.97
Faculty-Student Relations	4	0.82	0.94	0.25	0.15	6.18*
Administrative Services	3	0.85	0.91	0.25	0.36	9.69*
Language Abilities	4	0.80	0.80	0.32	0.51	6.68*
Emotional Development	4	0.83	0.93	0.32	0.46	4.17*
Library Resources	3	0.79	0.91	0.24	0.35	71.78*
Student Affairs	4	0.77	0.90	0.33	0.48	10.61*

Note. N = 5,626. *$p<0.001$

4. Description of the CUEI-S

The newly developed CUEI-S contains 25 items in seven scales, with three to four items in each scale. A brief description of the scales and a sample item from each follows:

Student Cohesiveness – The extent to which students get along well and get help from one another (e.g., "I make good friends at this college/university.")

Faculty-Student Relations – The extent to which professors and students interact positively with each other (e.g., "I seek advice from professors regarding course work and other problems.")

Administrative Services – The extent to which administrative staff is cordial in providing services to students (e.g., "In general, staff at the Academic Office is friendly in providing service.")

Language Ability – The extent to which the college/university is helpful in enhancing student abilities in writing, reading, and speaking Chinese and/or foreign languages (e.g., "My college/university is helpful in strengthening my speech and presentation ability.")

Emotional Development – The extent to which the college/university is helpful in fostering student self-discipline, problem-solving capabilities, spiritual growth, and emotional maturity (e.g., "My college/university is helpful in fostering my self-discipline.")

Library Resources – The extent to which the library has adequate resources and good services, and is quiet and comfortable (e.g., "The library has adequate collections and resources.")

Student Affairs – The extent to which the college/university provides satisfactory counseling and special services to students (e.g., "The counseling services provides by the university are satisfactory.")

In the present study, all items elicit individual students' general perceptions of the college/university as a whole rather than their role in a certain class. In addition, all items were designed to be generic so that students infer their responses across all subjects and classes. The underlying rationale is that the study intends to validate an instrument that assesses how students perceived their overall institutional-level environment, while taking into consideration individual students' diverse experiences on campus.

5. Validation of the CUEI-S

5.1 Sample subjects

To cross-validate the CUEI-S, students in a different type of college/university were used as sample subjects. A total of 9,776 juniors from 34 independent (private) colleges and universities from the same databank were examined. Likewise, student data from professional four-year independent colleges were omitted. The present study classifies colleges and universities into two types: public and independent, because they differ considerably in governance, funding, tuition and fees, research orientation, and student background and academic aspirations. On the other hand, each type has great homogeneity in its regulations and financial resources. In addition, differences in psychosocial work environments in different types of schools were reported in previous research (Docker, Fraser, & Fisher, 1989.)

Among juniors in the independent colleges and universities, gender distribution is less equal than that among their public counterparts; 43% of them were male and 57% were female. About 65% of these students came from middle-class backgrounds. About 18% of them used the library frequently. Furthermore, only 66% of these juniors planned to pursue advanced degrees.

5.2 Construct validity

The factor structure using independent college student data confirms that the CUEI-S has good construct validity. All the factor loadings were above 0.45 and each item had its highest loading within its scale. Item factor loadings in each scale were higher than those found in public colleges and universities, except the Library Resources scale. Eigenvalues of all seven factors ranged from 2.66 to 4.72, and were larger than those found in public colleges and universities. The percentage of total variance explained was also slightly higher at 68%. The scree test proposed to retain seven factors. Table 20.2 displays the factor analysis results in parallel for both public and independent colleges and universities.

Table 20.2. Factor Loadings of the Seven Scales of the CUEI-S with Two Student Groups

Item	Student Cohesiveness		Faculty-Stu Relations		Admin Services		Library Resources		Students Affairs		Language Ability		Emotional Development	
type	Pub.	Ind.	Pub. Ind.		Pub.	Ind.	Pub.	Ind.	Pub.	Ind.	Pub.	Ind.	Pub.	Ind.
1	0.74	0.75												
2	0.73	0.74												
3	0.68	0.72												
4			0.79	0.81										
5			0.74	0.71										
6			0.69	0.71										
7			0.68	0.68										
8					0.93	0.96								
9					0.92	0.93								
10					0.58	0.64								
11							0.81	0.79						
12							0.74	0.73						
13							0.68	0.66						
14									0.75	0.82				
15									0.69	0.76				
16									0.66	0.67				
17									0.57	0.57				
18											0.88	0.91		
19											0.72	0.73		
20											0.64	0.67		
21											0.54	0.58		
22													0.85	0.81
23													0.77	0.79
24													0.57	0.54
25													0.55	0.48
Eigen value	2.53 2.66		3.29 3.63		3.20	3.93	2.99	3.31	3.98	4.72	4.24	4.63	4.09	4.46

Note. Items with factor loadings lower than .45 were omitted

5.3 Internal consistency reliability

Two units of analysis were also employed to estimate internal consistency reliability and discriminant validity (inter-scale correlations) for independent colleges and universities. The results reveal that with individual students in independent colleges and universities as the unit of analysis, the average internal consistency reliability coefficients of the seven scales ranged from 0.78 to 0.88, with a mean value of 0.82. When the independent college or university was used as the unit for analysis, the average internal consistency reliability coefficients of the seven scales ranged more widely, from 0.82 to 0.97, with a higher mean value of 0.91. All seven scales have satisfactory internal consistency reliability with either unit of analysis. Similarly, both sets of internal consistency reliability coefficients were greater than those estimated with students in public colleges and universities.

Table 20.3. Alpha Reliability, Discriminant Validity, and ANOVA Results of the CUEI-S Scales for Independent Colleges and Universities

Scale	No of items	Alpha Reliability		Discriminant Validity		ANOVA by college
		Student	College	Student	College	
Student Cohesiveness	3	0.78	0.82	0.21	0.34	1.86
Faculty-Student Relations	4	0.82	0.95	0.28	0.22	6.80*
Administrative Services	3	0.88	0.96	0.31	0.53	8.82*
Language Abilities	4	0.81	0.82	0.33	0.54	5.52*
Emotional Development	4	0.84	0.93	0.36	0.58	6.80*
Library resources	3	0.78	0.92	0.27	0.53	82.36*
Student Affairs	4	0.82	0.97	0.37	0.62	29.56*

Note. N = 9,776. $*p<0.001$

5.4 Discriminant validity

Using the individual student in the independent colleges and universities as the unit of analysis, discriminant validity coefficients (inter-correlations between scales) of the seven scales ranged from 0.21 to 0.37 with a mean value of 0.30, indicating that these scales are weakly related; each scale measures a unique aspect of the psychosocial environment. When the college or university was used as the unit of analysis, the interscale correlation coefficients of the seven scales ranged more widely, from 0.23 to 0.58, with a higher mean value of 0.48, revealing that a few environmental scales correlated moderately with others; however, the conceptual distinctions among scales as shown by the factor loadings, scree plot and eigenvalues are crucial in determining whether to retain the seven scales in the CUEI-S. Table 20.3 reports the internal consistency reliability, discriminant validity, and the ANOVA results of the psychosocial environment scales among independent colleges and universities with both units of analysis.

5.5 Ability to differentiate colleges and universities

The CUEI-S confirms the disparities of psychosocial environments in independent colleges and universities. A series of ANOVA tests comparing the seven environment scales by colleges and universities reveals that the instrument is capable of differentiating environments among colleges and universities. There were significant differences ($p<0.001$) in all seven scales but one: Student Cohesiveness. Like the results in public colleges and universities, the greatest difference among independent colleges and universities was found in the adequacy of library resources, and it was followed by the university system support of various services provided to students.

Altogether, alpha reliability, construct and discriminant validity, and ANOVA results indicate that although the CUEI-S was originally developed to assess the psychosocial environment at public colleges and universities, it is also a feasible tool for assessing the psychosocial environment at independent colleges and universities.

6. The Results of an Application of the CUEI-S

Since the CUEI-S is a valid and reliable instrument for measuring the psychosocial environments at both public and independent colleges and universities, an initial assessment using individual students in all 69 colleges and universities was performed. The descriptive statistical results reveal that most of the junior students had favourable relations with other students and were satisfied with services provided by administrative staff. They thought that their library had adequate resources and that the college or university environment was helpful to their emotional development. Relations between faculty and students, university system support to student affairs, and language learning, however, may need to be improved. The standard deviations for the Administrative Services, Emotional Development, and Library Resources scales were relatively higher than other scales, suggesting that there was a greater variance among students' perceptions. Table 20.4 displays the means and standard deviations of the seven environmental aspects.

Table 20.4. Means and Standard Deviations of the Psychosocial Environment Perceived by College and University Students

Scale	N	M	SD
Student Cohesiveness	15402	3.00	0.58
Faculty-Student Relations	15402	2.38	0.61
Administrative Services	15402	2.54	0.69
Language Abilities	15306	2.23	0.64
Emotional Development	15307	2.50	0.68
Library Resources	15402	2.66	0.68
Student Affairs	15402	2.38	0.60

7. Discussion and Conclusion

The study demonstrates an initial attempt to use the Taiwan Higher Education Databank to construct an instrument for assessing current higher education environments as perceived by college and university students. It developed a parsimonious instrument – the CUEI-S, containing a limited but essential 25 items -- and identified seven environment aspects in three dimensions according to Moos' conceptual framework (Moos, 1979, 1981). Exploratory factor analyses, internal consistency reliability, and discriminant validity, with both the individual students and the college/university as the unit of analysis, completed the validation of the instrument. Furthermore, the study has shown that the CUEI-S is valid and reliable in assessing psychosocial environments in not only public but also independent colleges and universities.

The results based on the application of the CUEI-S indicate that, in general, junior students perceived fairly positively the psychosocial environments of their colleges or universities. A majority of students had good friends on campus and helped each other. They felt that the service attitudes of administrative staff in the Academic Office, Student Services Office, and Departmental Offices were friendly. Most of them were satisfied with the collections, the services, and physical comfort in the academic library. About half of them thought that the college/university was helpful in enhancing their ability to solve diverse problems, in fostering their self-discipline, and in advancing self-understanding as well as spiritual growth. Here, spiritual growth implies cultivating the ability to observe one's own mind in action and the inner development of values, beliefs, and morality (Astin, 2004a, 2004b).

A less promising result was students' relations with faculty members. Interactions between faculty members and students were limited. Students seldom sought advice from their professors regarding their course work or personal problems. Only a few students felt that their professors cared very much of them and provided them timely help. A large number of students were not satisfied with the university system support for student affairs, such as counseling services, computer and information resources, summer courses, handling of student grievances, and execution of university regulations. The most discouraging finding was students' low rating of the development of their language abilities. Apparently, a majority of students did not perceive that their institutional environment was conducive to enhancing their competency in reading, writing, or speaking either Chinese or foreign languages. This is especially troublesome, given the importance of language ability in an era of globalization and the emphasis of the Ministry of Education on proficiency in English and other foreign languages. One plausible explanation is that, without an equivalent rise in national education budget, the rapid expansion of higher education institutions and the dramatic increase in student enrollments may have had a negative influence on the resources, facilities, and services shared by these students, as shown in the decrease of annual provisions for each student from about US$5,700 to US$4,500 per capita (Ministry of Education).

The preliminary findings suggest that colleges and universities in Taiwan could improve some key aspects of their educational environments. Since the students perceived weak faculty-student relations, faculty members may need to be more actively involved with students through mentoring and advising programs, involving students in research and special projects, and representing the concerns and needs of students to university committees. Faculty do matter. Previous research has noted that students report higher levels of learning and engagement at institutions where faculty members use active and collaborative learning techniques, engage students in experiences, emphasize higher-order cognitive activities in the classroom, interact with students, challenge students academically, and value enriching educational experiences (Umbach & Wawrzynski, 2005). In addition, the cognitive demands set by professors and the social supports provided by both professors and other students affect students' perceived academic control and coping strategies. In turn, the pedagogical environment and the psychological dispositions affect students' academic achievement (Clifton, Perry, Stubbs, & Roberts, 2004).

Colleges and universities may also need to design strategies for enhancing the effectiveness and efficiency in their supportive services to students.

The CUEI-S has expanded learning environment research from elementary and secondary schools to colleges and universities. It is distinctive from the CUCEI developed two decades earlier by Fraser, Treagust, and Dennis (1986) because it focuses on the institutional-level rather than classroom-level environments. It includes, in particular, two essential aspects of higher education outcomes: emotional development and language ability. With the validation of the CUEI-S, it has become possible to stimulate and facilitate future research and applications involving psychosocial environment in colleges and universities in Taiwan and abroad. One approaches would be to further calibrate the CUEI-S with focus groups, expert advice, and in-depth interviews to cross-validate the student questionnaire (Ouimet, Bunnage, Carini, Kuh, & Kennedy, 2004), and to try it out with other samples and in other countries for cross-cultural comparisons. Feedback from these studies can be used as a basis for reflecting upon, discussing, and working systematically to improve the psychosocial environments in colleges and universities. Another approach would be to explore variables influencing students' perceptions as well as the relation of their perceptions to intellectual growth. Furthermore, when the CUEI-F is developed and validated, investigation of both faculty and student perceptions may offer new insights into academic environments at the tertiary level.

Acknowledgements

The author would like to acknowledge the educational researchers who have contributed to the establishment of the Taiwan Higher Education Data System. This project was supported by a research grant from the National Science Council, Taiwan (NSC 92-2413-H-007-006). The opinions expressed in this paper may not necessarily reflect the position, policy, or endorsement of the granting agency. The instrument CUEI-S can be obtained upon request from the author.

References

Astin, A. W. (1993a). An empirical typology of college students. *Journal of College Student Development, 34*, 36-46.
Astin, A. W. (1993b). *What matters in college: Four critical years revisited.* San Francisco: Jossey-Bass Publishers.

Astin, A. W. (2004a). *Spirituality in college students: Preliminary findings from a national study.* Los Angeles, CA: Higher Education Research institute.

Astin, A. W. (2004b). Why spirituality deserves a central place in liberal education. *Liberal Education, 90* (2) 34-41.

Clifton, R. A., Perry, R. P., Stubbs, C. A., & Roberts, L. W. (2004). Faculty environments, psychosocial dispositions and the academic achievement of college students. *Research in Higher Education, 45,* 801-828.

Docker, J, G, Fraser, B. J., & Fisher, D. L. (1989). Differences in psychosocial work environment of different types of schools. *Journal of Research in Childhood Education, 4,* 5-7.

Fabrigar, I. R., Wegener, D. T., MacCallum, R. C., & Strahan, E. J. (1999). Evaluating the use of exploratory factor analysis in psychological research. *Psychological Methods, 4,* 272-229.

Fjortoft, N. F. & Lee, M. W. L. (1994). *Professional commitment: An analysis of students and alumni.* Paper presented at the annual meeting of the American Educational Research Association, New Orleans.

Fraser, B. J. (1994). Research on classroom and school climate. In D. Gabel (Ed.), *Handbook of research on science teaching and learning* (pp. 483-541). New York: Macmillan.

Fraser, B. J. (1999). Using learning environment assessment to improve classroom and school climate. In H. J. Freiberg (Ed.), *School climate: Measuring, improving, and sustaining healthy learning environment* (pp. 65-83). London: Falmer Press.

Fraser, B. J., Docker, J. D., & Fisher, D. L. (1988). Assessing and improving school climate. *Evaluation and Research in Education, 2,* 109-122.

Fraser, B. J., Treagust, D. F., & Dennis, N. C. (1986). Development of an instrument for assessing classroom psychological environment at universities and colleges. *Studies in Higher Education, 11* (1), 43-54.

Glover, J. W. (1996). *Campus environment and student involvement as predictors of outcomes of the community college experience.* Paper presented at the Annual Meeting of the Association for the Study of Higher Education, Memphis.

Kearney, G. W. & Kearney, T. J. (1994). *Transfer students' expectations and satisfaction: Predictors for academic performance and persistence.* Paper presented at the Annual Meeting of the Association for the Study of Higher Education, Tucson, AZ.

Lewin, K. (1936). *Principles of topological psychology*. New York: McGraw.

Moos, R. H. (1979). *Evaluating educational environment: Procedures, measures, findings, and policy implications*. San Francisco: Jossey-Bass.

Moos, R. H. (1981). *Manual for Work Environment Scale*. Palo Alto, CA: Consulting Psychology Press.

Murray, H. A. (1938). *Explorations in personality*. New York: Oxford University Express.

Ouimet, J. A., Bunnage, J. C., Carini, R. M., Kuh, G. D., & Kennedy, J. (2004). Using focus group, expert advice and cognitive interviews to establish the validity of a college student survey. *Research in Higher Education, 45*, 233-250.

Pace, C. R. & Stern, G. G. (1958). An approach to the measurement of psychological characteristics of college environments. *Journal of Educational Psychology, 49*, 269-277.

Peng, S. & Wang, S. Y. (2005). *An introduction to the Taiwan Higher Education Data System*. A report presented at the Conference of Taiwan Higher Education Databank and Related Issues, Taipei.

Reigeluth, C. M. (1999). Visioning public education in America. *Educational Technology, 39* (5), 50-55.

Santos, J. R. A. & Clegg, M. D. (1999). Factor analysis adds new dimension to extension survey. *Journal of Extension, 37* (5), 1-7.

Stern, G. G. (1970). *People in context: Measuring person-environment congruence in education and industry*. New York: Wiley.

Umbach, P. D. & Wawrzynski, M. R. (2004). Faculty do matter: The role of college faculty in student learning and engagement. *Research in Higher Education, 46* (2), 153-184.

Chapter 21

SCHOOL CLIMATE IN INDONESIAN JUNIOR SECONDARY SCHOOLS

Wahyudi
Ahmad Dahlan University
Indonesia

Darrell L. Fisher
Curtin University of Technology
Australia

This chapter describes the working environments in an Indonesian junior secondary school context. Using the Indonesian version of the School Level Environment Questionnaire (SLEQ), the study found that teachers view their school environments positively on all scales, except that of Staff Freedom. A comparison between actual and preferred perceptions showed statistically significant differences on all scales, except Staff Freedom and Work Pressure. Teachers prefer a working environment that provides more student support, better affiliation among teachers and other staff, strengthens their professional interest, provides teachers with greater opportunity to participate in decision making, has better resources, places more emphasis on accomplishing tasks, and offers more innovation. It was also found that urban school teachers viewed their school environment less favourably than did their counterparts in rural and suburban schools. Statistically significant differences were found on the Participatory Decision Making and Work Pressure scales. Urban and suburban school teachers participated more in their schools' decision making, and perceived greater work pressure in their working place than did teachers at urban schools. Finally, based on subject taught the study indicated that generally non-science teachers held a more positive view of their working environment on all scales, except Staff Freedom, than did biology and physics teachers. Biology teachers shared similar views to Physics teachers on four scales, namely, Students Support, Affiliation, Professional Interest, and Innovation. On the other hand, biology teachers perceived more Staff Freedom and Work Pressure, but less Participatory Decision Making and Resource Adequacy than did physics teachers. This study suggests that these findings should be used as a starting point for improving working environments in rural, suburban, and urban schools in Indonesia.

1. Introduction

> *Much like the air we breathe, school climate is ignored until it becomes foul* (Freiberg, 1998).

The working environment or school climate may influence teachers in conducting their teaching processes and thus determine student learning and student outcomes. The notion that learning environment plays an important role can be found in the science curriculum documents of Indonesian lower secondary schools. Explicitly, it is stated that along with teacher, teaching methods, curriculum, and resources, the learning environment (natural, social and cultural) determines teaching and learning processes and thus in turn influences students' outcomes (Kurikulum sekolah lanjutan tingpat pertama: Petunjuk pelaksanaan proses belajar mengajar [Curriculum for lower secondary school: Guide for conducting teaching and learning process], 1994). This notion parallels the findings of research emphasising that a good school environment is linked with student achievement. The simple assumption is that if teachers have a good working environment, then better student achievement will result. For example, Brookover, Schweitzer, Schneider, Beady, Flood, and Weisenbaker (1978) suggested that the quality of school climate could influence the behaviour of all participants and particularly students' academic achievement. Purkey and Smith (1985) noted that research is persuasive that student academic performance is strongly affected by school culture. Furthermore, Hughes (1991) emphasized that every school has a pervasive climate, which influences the successful outcomes of behaviour of teachers and students in teaching and learning.

Freiberg's (1998) notion of the marginalisation of school climate as a factor that determines learning process is rendered in the practice of an Indonesian educational context. Despite acceptance of the notion that school environment is vital for enhancing teaching and learning processes, only a few studies of school environment have been done in Indonesia. Therefore, more research in this area is needed in the Indonesian educational context. Accordingly, this study was done to fill this gap and to provide evidence of the importance of school environment upon teaching and learning processes in schools.

2. Theoretical and Historical Background

2.1 The importance of school environment

School environment is defined as a set of factors that give each school a personality, a spirit, a milieu, a culture and an atmosphere (Fisher & Fraser, 1990; Tye, 1974). Over the last three decades, school environment has consistently been identified as one of the main factors that affect the effectiveness of a school (Creemers, Peters, & Reynolds, 1989). In conjunction with curriculum, resources, and leadership, the school environment plays a significant role in creating a school's effectiveness. The better the school environment, the more effective is the school. This notion is confirmed by the findings of various studies. For example, Fisher and Fraser (1990) believed that the improvement of school environment could enhance school effectiveness, and in turn provide students with better learning.

Freiberg (1998) claimed that a healthy school climate contributes to effective teaching and learning. Establishment of a conducive school working environment enables all members of the school community to teach and learn at optimum levels. Van de Grift, Houtveen, and Vermeulen, (1997) measured instructional climate in 121 Dutch senior secondary schools and showed that student achievement in mathematics is positively influenced by students' enjoyment of maths, attitude toward high grades, appreciation of teachers' efforts, and an orderly instructional climate. Atwool (1999) suggested that a school climate, wherein children have the opportunity to establish meaningful connections within the school environment, is pivotal to enhance student ability to learn, to facilitate appropriate behavior and has the potential to counteract the impact of difficulties at home. Moreover, Samdal, Wold, and Bronis, (1999) have also identified three aspects of psychosocial school setting as predictors of students' perception of their academic achievement. These are students' satisfaction with school, students' feeling of appropriate teacher expectation, and a good relationship with their fellow students. They suggested that interventions that enhance the students' satisfaction with school are likely to improve their achievement as well. Hoy and Hannum (1997) claimed that school environment with better teacher affiliation, resource support, academic expectation, and institutional integrity promoted better student achievement. Furthermore, Sweetland and Hoy (2000) indicated that school climate which has strong teacher empowerment is crucial for school effectiveness thus affecting student achievement.

Past research has also provided evidence of the association between school environment and student satisfaction and achievement. Generally, student achievement and satisfaction are greater in the schools that have better student support. It is asserted that more effective and satisfying student learning is significantly linked to teachers' friendliness and supportiveness (Griffith, 2000; Hoy, Tarter, & Bliss, 1990; Moos, 1979; Stockard and Mayberry, 1992). In turn, student satisfaction leads to positive attitudes toward subject matter. Papanastasious (2002) found that school climate has a direct and indirect effect on student attitude toward science.

2.2 Instruments for assessing school environment

The development of instruments to describe organisational working environments can be traced back to the late 1950s when Pace and Stern (1958) developed the *College Characteristics Index* (CCI) to measure students' or teachers' perceptions of 30 environmental characteristics. Based on this instrument, Stern (1970) constructed the *High School Characteristics Index* (HSCI) to measure high school climate. Among the existing instruments, perhaps the most widely used instruments for measuring an organisational working environment were the *Organizational Climate Description Questionnaire* (OCDQ; Halpin & Croft, 1963) and the Work Environment Scale (WES; Moos, 1974). Later, these two instruments were used as a basis for the development of new instruments, namely, *School Level Environment Questionnaire* (SLEQ; Rentoul & Fraser, 1983) and *School Organisational Climate Questionnaire* (SCOQ; Giddings & Dellar, 1990) that are more suitable to a secondary school environment.

2.3 The descriptions of the original SLEQ

When they developed the School Level Environment Questionnaire (SLEQ), Rentoul and Fraser (1983) recognised and considered the potential strength and problems associated with the existing school environment instruments. Therefore, they explored the SLEQ's validity through intensive interviews with teachers, to ensure that dimensions and individual items covered what teachers saw as salient, and that only material which was specifically relevant to the school was included.

They also attempted to achieve questionnaire economy by keeping to a relatively small number of reliable scales, each containing seven items. In order to capture all aspects of school environment, the SLEQ also covers Moos' three general categories of dimensions, namely, relationship, personal development and system maintenance and system change. A description of the scales of the SLEQ is provided in Table 21.1 together with sample items.

Table 21.1. Description of Scales in SLEQ

Scale	Description of Scale	Sample Item
Student Support	There is good rapport between teachers and students, and students behave in a responsible self-disciplined manner.	There are many disruptive, difficult students in the school. (-)
Affiliation	Teachers can obtain assistance, advice and encouragement and are made to feel accepted by colleagues.	I feel that I could rely on my colleagues for assistance if I should need it. (+)
Professional Interest	Teachers discuss professional matters, show interest in their work and seek further professional development.	Teachers frequently discuss teaching methods and strategies with each other. (+)
Staff Freedom	Teachers are free of set rules, guidelines and procedures, and of supervision to ensure rule compliance.	I am often supervised to ensure that I follow directions correctly. (-)
Participatory Decision Making	Teachers have the opportunity to participate in decision-making.	Teachers are frequently asked to participate in decisions concerning administrative policies and procedures. (+)

Table 21.1. (Continued)

Scale	Description of Scale	Sample Item
Innovation	The school is in favour of planned change and experimentation, and fosters classroom openness and individualisation.	Teachers are encouraged to be innovative in this school. (+)
Resource Adequacy	Support personnel, facilities, finance, equipment and resources are suitable and adequate.	The supply of equipment and resources is inadequate. (-)
Work Pressure	The extent to which work pressure dominates the school environment.	Teachers have to work long hours to keep up with the workload. (+)

Items designated (+) are scored by allocating 5, 4, 3, 2, 1, respectively, for the responses Strongly Agree, Agree, Not Sure, Disagree, and Strongly Disagree. Items designated (-) are scored in reverse manner. Omitted or invalid responses are given a score of 3.

2.4 Study using the SLEQ

Many studies employing the School Level Environment Questionnaire (SLEQ) have been conducted and the questionnaire is seen to have maintained its validity and reliability. For example, Fisher and Fraser (1991a) investigated 109 primary and high schools teachers' perceptions of their school environments. They found that primary teachers held more favourable perceptions of their school environment than did high school teachers. Previously, Fisher and Fraser (1990b) presented the validity and reliability of each of the SLEQ scales, and offered a case study that used the SLEQ to improve school environment. They indicated that school environment could be improved by harmonizing the level of teachers' actual and ideal perceptions of their school environments. Furthermore, Dorman and Fraser (1996) used a modified SLEQ to investigate the differences between Catholic and government school environments. With a considerably large sample of 208 science and religion teachers from 32 schools, they maintained that Catholic school teachers viewed their schools as more empowering and higher on

Mission Consensus than government school teachers did. More recently, Templeton and Johnson (1998) have employed the SLEQ to assess school environment of an urban school in the USA to clarify factors that play roles in developing a safer school environment. They indicated that teachers desired more student support, more resources and less work pressure as conditions of a "safer" school environment. In the Indonesian educational context, Irianto (2002) has used the Indonesian version of the modified SLEQ to measure working environment at The Centre for Development and In-service for Science Teachers in Indonesia. He documented that trainers in this institution perceived positively their working environments on five scales, namely, Affiliation, Professional Interest, Mission Consensus, Empowerment, and Innovation and viewed less favourable Resource Adequacy and Work-Pressure scales.

2.5 The objectives of the study

The objectives of this study were to develop and use a questionnaire for assessing school environments in an Indonesian educational context. More specifically, the objectives were formulated in the following research questions:

1. Is it possible to validate and use the Indonesian version of modified SLEQ for measuring school environments in Indonesian lower secondary schools?
2. What are teachers' perceptions of their school environment in Indonesia?
3. In Indonesia, are there any significant differences between rural, suburban and urban school teachers' perceptions of their school environments?
4. Are there any significant differences between science and non-science teachers' perceptions of their school environments in Indonesia?

3. Significance of the Study

This study is distinctive in that it will bring teachers', principals', and school administrators' attention to the importance of working environment to enhance educational practice in their schools.

Hence, the significance of this study is that it will:

1. fill the absence of research particularly in working environment area at urban and rural lower secondary schools in Indonesia;
2. provide information to the Ministry of National Education (MONE) of the Republic Indonesia about the status of rural and urban school working environments, which can be used to formulate further policy;
3. help principals and teachers to improve their practice in conducting science education; and
4. assist principals and teachers to enhance their school working environment.

4. Research Methods

4.1 The development of the Indonesian SLEQ

After conducting an intensive literature review, the SLEQ was chosen as the main instrument for two reasons. First, it has been validated and proven as a robust instrument to measure secondary school environment (Fisher & Fraser, 1990). Secondly, it is relatively simple and easy to administer. The original SLEQ contains 56 items, which disperse equally into eight scales namely, Students support, Affiliation, Professional Interest, Staff Freedom, Participatory Decision Making, Innovation, Resource Adequacy, and Work Pressure.

The teacher needs to spend approximately 30 to 45 minutes to complete the questionnaire. In addition, all statements on the SLEQ are non-threatening so that this feature may enhance a teacher's willingness and honesty in answering the questionnaire.

Modifications were made in order to ensure the instrument's suitability for measuring school level environment in an Indonesian educational context. Those modifications included combining both Actual and Preferred Forms in one package of questionnaire, and a contextual rather than textual translation and back translation of the original version of SLEQ. The integration of both forms of the questionnaire was made to reduce the bias of teachers answering the questionnaire repetitively. It is assumed that when respondents are given similar questionnaires in different times, the later feedback is commonly inconsistent with the previous. Therefore, integration of both forms was considered in this instrument development.

To ensure that the original meaning of the SLEQ is captured in the Indonesian version, Brislin's (1980) suggestion is observed. First, the first author translated the English version of the SLEQ into the Indonesian language. Second, this translation was given to an independent person who is fluent in both English and Indonesian to be back translated into English. This back translation was compared with the original version of the SLEQ, to check whether or not the Indonesian version of the SLEQ had captured the original one.

4.2 Sampling

A combination of purposive and stratified sampling methods was employed in this study. A stratified sampling method was used to ensure that the sample used in this study was representative of all types of schools. Purposive or purposeful sampling (Merriam, 1990) as a non-probabilistic sampling method was used, with the assumption that the researcher wanted to discover, understand, gain insight and choose the sample which will lead to the most understanding (Merriam, 1990). Consequently, purposive sampling permits the researcher to decide prior to the study who and what schools are to be included in the data collection. In so doing, a consultation with the Ministry of National Education of Kalimantan Selatan was sought. As a result, the samples involved in this study were composed of willing and chosen participants. There were 25 non-science teachers and 106 science teachers of urban and rural junior secondary schools from Kalimantan Selatan, Indonesia.

4.3 Data collection

A questionnaire survey was used as the main data collection method. However, teachers' interviews regarding their work environment were also conducted. The interviews were semi-structured, and were aimed to scrutinize teachers' expressions of their working environment. To increase the validity of the data, the interview transcript was given to the teacher as a method of checking and re-checking.

4.4 Data analysis

Data from the questionnaire survey were analysed using the SPSS 10.0 program. This study also aimed to cross validate the Indonesian version of the SLEQ. Therefore, internal consistency reliability or Cronbach alpha coefficient and mean correlation of each scale were calculated. In addition, an analysis of variance or ANOVA test was also conducted to check whether or not the Indonesian version of SLEQ is able to differentiate different groups of teachers' perceptions. To explore the nature of the working environment of the schools, the mean of the standard deviation of each scale was calculated. Furthermore, the differences between science and non-science teachers', and between rural, suburban and urban school teachers' perceptions of their working environment were also investigated. To increase the robustness of the findings, data from teacher interviews were analysed using interpretive methods.

5. Findings and Discussions

5.1 Validation of the Indonesian version of SLEQ

The final version of the Indonesian SLEQ comprised eight scales in which each scale has seven items. The results for the Indonesian version of the SLEQ are presented in Table 21.2. The final version of the Indonesian SLEQ comprised eight scales in which each scale has seven items. The Cronbach alpha coefficients for all scales ranged from 0.64 to 0.82, except Staff Freedom, Participatory Decision Making, and Work Pressure where the range was from 0.41 to 0.54. These relatively low reliabilities imply that teachers perceived most items in each scale of these three scales inconsistently. While most items in the original SLEQ measure aspects of school environment which are appropriate for western school culture, yet these items may not perfectly fit into Indonesian school culture. For example, the responses to the items in Participatory Decision Making scale are most contradictory of each other. This is probably due to cultural bias which may be held by teachers when they interpreted the item. While teachers in Western countries can provide 'yes' or 'no' answers towards such items or questions that ask about their role in determining their school program, seldom are teachers in Indonesia able to do this. The following interview transcripts support this interpretation.

I: When the school conducts a program, such as additional lessons after school hours, especially for Year nine students, are you and other teachers involved in determining that program?

T: There were many stages to determine a program. First, the school calls for inputs from all teachers about the proposed program. Second, the school invited BP3 (Parent Association) representative to discusses the proposed program. Finally, the school [the principal and his or her staff] organised the program.

Table 21.2. Cronbach Alpha Coefficient (Internal Consistency Reliability), Discriminant Validity, and ANOVA Results of the Actual Form of the Indonesian Version of SLEQ (n = 131)

Scale	Number of Items	Alpha Coefficient	Mean correlation with other scales	Eta^2
Student Support	7	0.64	0.31	0.11***
Affiliation	7	0.67	0.35	0.04**
Professional Interest	7	0.65	0.39	0.09***
Staff Freedom	5	0.54	0.20	0.00
Participatory Decision Making	5	0.48	0.33	0.12***
Innovation	7	0.72	0.45	0.15***
Resources Adequacy	7	0.82	0.37	0.08**
Work Pressure	7	0.54	0.18	0.19***

** $p<0.01$ and *** $p<0.001$

Teacher responses as illustrated in the transcript reveal a 'diplomatic response' rather than a direct yes or no answer. If teachers respond to the questionnaire in this way, no doubt their responses in such scales as Innovation, Staff Freedom and Participatory Decision Making were somewhat variable which resulted in a relatively low scale reliability. Consequently, changes in items are needed, particularly on these three scales for which the reliabilities are less than 0.60, in order to improve their reliabilities. Nevertheless, these values are considered acceptable because of the considerably small sample (Stevens, 1992). Therefore, all 56 items in both actual and preferred versions of the Indonesian SLEQ were maintained for further analysis to explore the nature of school level learning environment.

The mean correlations of all scales ranged from 0.18 to 0.37, with the exception of Innovation which had the highest mean correlation (0.45). These values are comparable to those of previous studies (Irianto, 2002) and show that each scale of the Indonesian SLEQ measures a distinct aspect of the school environment, although overlapping still exists to a degree. Furthermore, the analysis of variance (ANOVA) results show that all scales in the Indonesian SLEQ, except Staff Freedom, are capable of differentiating between perceptions of teachers from different groups. The eta^2 values ranged from 0.04 (Affiliation, $p<0.01$) to 0.19 (Work Pressure, $p<0.001$). These features support the reliability and validity of the Indonesian SLEQ, allowing the claim that the Indonesian SLEQ is a reasonably robust instrument to measure Indonesian secondary schools' environments can be made with confidence, however, it could be improved even more before a future use.

5.2. Teachers perceptions of schools' environment

To describe Indonesian teacher perceptions of their learning environments, the average item means and the average item standard deviations of each scale for both the actual and preferred versions were calculated. A t-test for paired samples was conducted to investigate whether or not the teacher perceptions of their actual and preferred school environment were significantly different. A summary of the average item means and average standard deviation for the two versions of the questionnaire is reported in Table 21.3 and the same data graphed in Figure 21.1.

Results from the t tests for paired samples show that there are statistically significant differences ($p<0.001$) between teachers' perceptions of their actual and preferred working environment on all scales except Staff Freedom and Work Pressure scales. Furthermore, we can draw tentative assertions from Figure 21.1. First, teachers hold their views of their school environment positively, except on Staff Freedom. Interestingly, teachers indicate they prefer school environments that have less staff freedom than they perceive to be actually present. An explanation of this is that teachers might be accustomed to work under certain orders and procedures provided by the principal or school administrator.

Table 21.3. Average Item Mean, Average Item Standard Deviation, Different
Effect Size and *t* Test for Paired Samples for Differences Between
Actual and Preferred Forms of The Indonesian School Level
Learning Environment (n=131)

Scale	Average item mean		Average Standard Deviation		t
	A	P	A	P	
Student Support	3.94	4.42	0.46	0.43	-9.17*
Affiliation	3.87	4.18	0.40	0.49	-7.08*
Professional Interest	3.81	4.17	0.42	0.45	-8.36*
Staff Freedom	2.73	2.65	0.54	0.71	1.57
Participatory Decision Making	3.22	3.52	0.56	0.59	-4.23*
Innovation	3.53	4.16	0.53	0.46	-12.78*
Resources Adequacy	3.22	4.49	0.76	0.48	-16.60*
Work Pressure	3.15	3.20	0.52	0.57	-1.09

*$p<0.001$

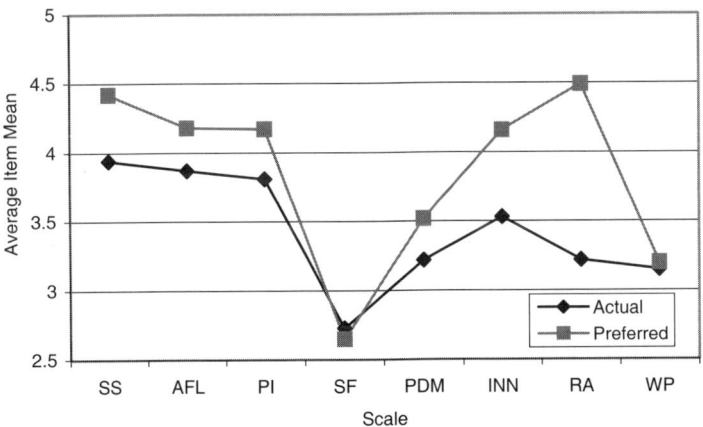

Figure 21.1. Comparison between teachers' perceptions of the actual and
preferred school level learning environments.

Alternatively, teachers tend to work constantly in order to cover all material for final examination purposes. Therefore, they are content to work in an environment that has certain procedures set down rather than in a completely unstructured free atmosphere. Secondly, the greatest difference between actual and preferred perception, which is more than twice the standard deviation occurs on the Resource Adequacy scale. This means that teachers want their schools to have more resources, such as more textbooks and laboratory equipment, to support them in conducting teaching and learning practices. Thirdly, teachers also tend to have desired school environments in which more innovations occur. This may contradict with teachers' perceptions on Staff Freedom scale, since innovation calls for staff freedom. However, it can be explained that teachers' preference for more innovation in their school environments has a collective meaning. Fourth, teachers have similar degrees of preference for their schools environments to have more affiliation and student support, and provide them with more professional development and more teacher involvement in school decision making. Fifth, teachers are content with the extent to which schools emphasise work pressure as no significant difference is found on this scale. A better explanation for this is that teachers tend to be happy with the degree of work pressure set by their school at slightly above 'sometimes'. They did not want their schools to exert higher work pressure since it will require them to stay longer at school and to do extra jobs. In fact, most teachers in Indonesia have a second or even third job teaching at other schools to make additional income. Therefore, being happy with their perception of work pressure scale at 'sometimes' level is reasonable.

5.3 Comparison of teachers' perception of their school environments based on locality and subject matter

In order to answer the third and fourth research questions, an investigation of the differences in teacher perceptions of their school environment based upon school locality and subject matter taught by the teachers was conducted. In doing so, a one-way between groups ANOVA with post-hoc comparisons was carried out. All eight scales of the Indonesian SLEQ were placed as the dependent variables, whereas school locality and subject matter variables were placed as the determinant variables, respectively. The Tukey's honesty significant difference (HSD) multiple comparison test was used to confirm statistically significant differences that exist between groups. When school locality was used as an independent variable, the statistically significant differences only existed on the Participatory Decision Making, and Work Pressure scales. In contrast, while using subject matter as an independent variable, significant differences were found on all scales, except Affiliation and Staff Freedom. Figures 21.2 and 21.3 provide comparisons of the average item means for eight scales of the Indonesian SLEQ based on school locality and teachers' subject matter, respectively.

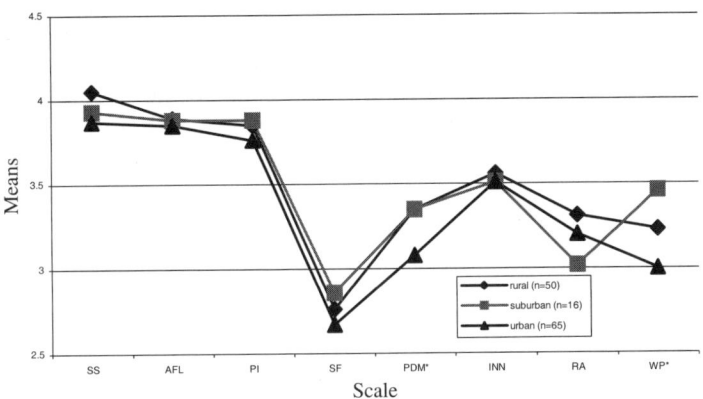

Figure 21.2. Comparison of teacher perceptions of the actual school environments based on school locality.

Generally teachers in rural (n=50) and suburban (n=16) schools experienced a more favourable working environment than do teachers at urban schools (n=65). When all teachers share relatively similar perceptions on three scales, namely, Affiliation, Professional Interest, and Innovation, their perceptions were slightly different on Student Support, Staff Freedom, and Resource Adequacy. Only the Work Pressure scale is perceived significantly different by all groups, while Participatory Decision Making is viewed similarly by rural and suburban teachers, but significantly differently between them and teachers at urban schools.

   Figure 21.2 shows that teacher perceptions on the Student Support scale are greater at rural schools and decrease at urban schools. This means that teachers at rural school faced fewer problems with their students' behaviour than did urban and suburban teachers. This finding is parallel with the data that emerged from school and classroom observations followed by teacher interview. Teachers at urban and suburban schools admitted that schools were sometimes disturbed by students' disruptive behaviour such as fighting, leaving school without permission, and "off tasking" during the lessons. In contrast, rural teachers found their students as polite and good members of the class or school community. Tentatively, these differences can be explained as a result of societal differences between rural and urban settings. Dynamic rhythm of urban living affects, either positively or negatively, the value and culture held by the community members. It was reported that students' crime and misbehaving increased both quantitatively and qualitatively in urban areas and schools during the late 1990s (Kompas, 1999). On the other hand, stable rural living enabled the people to hold firm their values and culture. Consequently, students from this area are humble; respect their elder, and are cooperative with their peers.

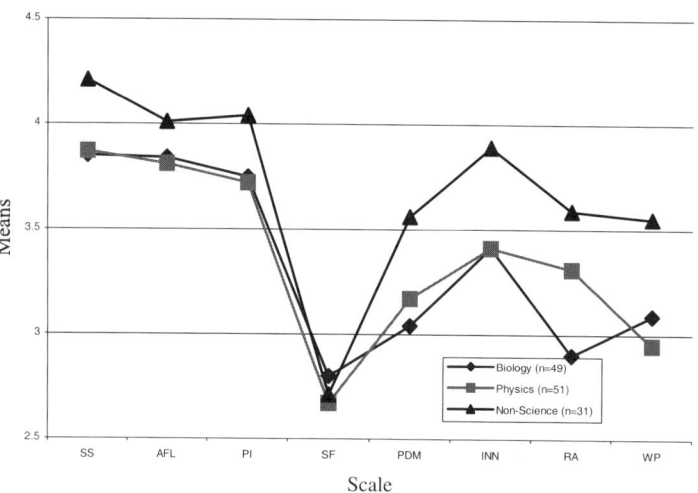

Figure 21.3. Comparison of teacher perceptions of the actual school environments based on school locality.

In general, non-science teachers (n=31) hold a more favourable view of their school working environments on all scales, except Staff Freedom, than do science teachers. Biology (n=49) and physics (n=51) teachers perceived their school environments similarly; but small differences between their perceptions were found on three scales, namely Staff Freedom, Participatory Decision Making, and Work Pressure. Statistically significant difference between their perceptions was found on Resource Adequacy scale. Biology teachers hold a more positive view of their working environment on Staff Freedom and Work Pressure, but less favourable on Participatory Decision Making and Resource Adequacy than physics teachers did. With regard to Resource Adequacy, this finding implies that most schools have more equipment for physics than for biology. This condition may be due to the expensiveness of biology laboratory equipment. While most biology lessons require expensive consumable material, physics lessons can use materials that are readily available and much cheaper. Therefore, most schools tend to have better and more adequate physics resources than biology ones.

5.4 Concluding comments and future research direction

This study found that the Indonesian version of the SLEQ is a valid and reliable instrument for assessing the working environment at junior high school. Therefore, in conjunction with the importance of school environment for enhancing school effectiveness and the scarcity of research in this area of Indonesian schools, this study recommends use of the developed instrument for further research.

The differences between perceptions of school environments of biology and physics teachers and among rural, suburban and urban schools teachers, particularly on adequacy of resources, warrant further investigation. It is necessary to identify why their perceptions are different in order to provide an appropriate intervention.

This study indicates that the differences between teachers' views of actual and preferred school environments are not only statistically but also practically significant. Most scales, except Staff Freedom and Work Pressure, have differences between actual and preferred versions which ranged from 0.52 to 2.05. It is suggested that research for improving school environments, by matching teachers' actual and preferred perceptions, is noteworthy and needs further investigation.

References

Atwool, N. (1999). Attachment in the school setting. New Zealand *Journal of Educational Studies, 34* (2), 309-322.

Brislin, R. (1980). Translation and content analysis of oral and written material. In H. Triandis & J. Berry (Eds.), *Handbook of cross-cultural psychology: Methodology* (Vol. 2, pp. 389-444). London: Allyn & Bacon.

Brookover, W. B., Schweitzer, J. H., Schneider, J. M., Beady, C. H., Flood, P. K., & Weisenbaker, J. M. (1978). Elementary school social climate and school achievement. *American Educational Research Journal, 15*, 301-318.

Creemers, B., Peters, T., & Reynolds, D. (1989). *School effectiveness and school improvement.* Lisse, The Netherland: Swets & Zeitlinger.

Dorman, J. P. & Fraser, B. J. (1996). Teachers perceptions of school environment in Australian catholic and government secondary schools. *International Studies in Educational Administration, 24* (1), 78-87.

Fisher, D. L. & Fraser, B. J. (1990). School Climate, (*SET Research information for teachers No. 2*). Melbourne: Australian Council for Educational Research.

Fisher, D. F. & Fraser, B. J. (1991a). Validity and use of school environment instruments. *Journal of Classroom Interaction, 26* (2), 13-18.

Fisher, D. L. & Fraser, B. J. (1991b). School climate and teacher professional development. *South Pacific Journal of Teacher Education, 19* (1), 17-32.

Freiberg, H. J. (1998). Measuring school climate: Let me count the ways. *Educational Leadership, 56* (1), 22-26.

Giddings, G. & Dellar, G. (1990, April). *The development and use of instrument for assessing the organisational climate of schools.* Paper presented at the Annual Metting of the American Educational Research Association, Boston, MA.

Griffith, J. (2000). School climate as group evaluation and group consensus: Student and parent perceptions of the elementary school environment. *The Elementary School Journal, 101* (1), 35-61.

Halpin, A. W. & Croft, D. B. (1963). *Organizational climate of school.* Chicago, IL: Midwest Administration Centre, University of Chicago.

Hoy, W. K., & Hannum, J. W. (1997). Middle school climate: An empirical assessment of organisational health and student achievement. *Educational Administration Quarterly, 33* (3), 290-311.

Hoy, W. K., Tarter, C. J., & Bliss, J. R. (1990). Organizational climate, school health, and effectiveness: A comparative analysis. *Educational Administration Quarterly, 26* (3), 260-279.

Hughes, P. W. (1991). Teachers' professional development. Melbourne, Victoria: Australian Council for Educational Research.

Irianto, B. (2002). *An investigation of current problems facing the science teachers' development and training centre in Indonesia.* Unpublished PhD Thesis, Curtin University of Technology, Perth, Western Australia.

Kompas. (1999, March 29). Kepemimpinan kepala sekolah paling pengaruhi tawuran pelajar (*Principal's leaderships influence on students fighting*). Available:
www.kompas.com/kompas%2Dcetak/9903/29/DIKBUD/kepe26.htm
[2003, 4 February].

Kurikulum sekolah lanjutan tingkat pertama: Petunjuk pelaksanaan proses belajar mengajar (*Curriculum for lower secondary school: Guidance for conducting teaching and learning process*) (1994). Jakarta: Ministry of Educational and Culture of the Republic of Indonesia.

Merriam, S. B. (1990). *Case study research in education.* San Fransisco: Jossey-Bass Inc.

Moos, R. H. (1974). *The social climate scales: An overview.* Palo Alto, CA: Consulting Psychologist Press.

Moos, R. H. (1979). *Evaluating educational environment.* San Francisco: Jossey-Bass.

Pace, C. R. & Stern, G. G. (1958). An approach to the measurement of psychological characteristic of college environment. *Journal of Educational Psychology, 49,* 269-277.

Papanastasiou, C. (2002). School, teaching and family influence on student attitudes toward science: Based on TIMSS data for Cyprus. *Studies in Educational Evaluation, 28* (1), 71-86.

Purkey, S. C. & Smith, M. S. (1985). Too soon to cheer? Synthesis of research on effective schools. *Educational Leadership, 40,* 64-69.

Rentoul, A. J. & Fraser, B. J. (1983). Development of a school-level environment questionnaire. *Journal of Educational Administration, 21,* 21-39.

Samdal, O., Wold, B., & Bronis, M. (1999). Relationship between students' perceptions of school environment, their satisfaction with school and perceived academic achievement: An international study. *School Effectiveness and School Improvement, 10* (3), 296-320.

Stern, G. G. (1970). *People in context: Measuring person-environment congruence in education and industry.* New York, NY: Wiley.

Stevens, J. (1992). *Applied multivariate statistics for the social sciences.* Hillsdale, NJ: Lawrence Erlbaum Associates.

Stockard, J. & Mayberry, M. (1992). *Effective educational environment.* Newbury Park, CA: Corwin.

Sweetland, S. R. & Hoy, W. R. (2000). School characteristic and educational outcomes: Toward organisational model of student achievment in middle schools. *Educational Administration Quarterly, 36* (6), 703-729.

Templeton, R. A. & Johnson, C. E. (1998). Making the school environmnet safe: Red Rose's formula. *Learning Environment Research: An International Journal, 1,* 35-57.

Tye, K. A. (1974). The culture of school. In J. I. Goodlad & M. F. Klein & J. M. Novotney & K. A. Tye (Eds.), *Toward a mankind school: An adventure in humanistic education* (pp. 123-138). New York, NY: McGraw-Hill.

Van de Grift, W., Houtveen, T., & Vermeulen, C. (1997). Instructional climate in Dutch secondary education. *School Effectiveness and School Improvement, 8* (4), 449-462.

Chapter 22

TURKISH SECONDARY EDUCATION STUDENTS' PERCEPTIONS OF THEIR CLASSROOM LEARNING ENVIRONMENT AND THEIR ATTITUDE TOWARDS BIOLOGY

Sibel Telli
Jale Cakiroglu
Middle East Technical University
Turkey

Perry den Brok
Utrecht University
The Netherlands

The domain of learning environments research has produced many promising findings, leading to an enhancement of the teaching and learning process in many countries. However, there have been a limited number of studies in this field in Turkey. For that reason, the purpose of the present study was to examine Turkish high school students' perceptions of their classroom environment in biology and to investigate relationships between these perceptions and students' attitudes toward biology. Secondly, the study aimed to investigate differences in students' attitudes toward biology by gender, grade level, and parental education. Perception data were gathered with 1,983 ninth and tenth grade students from 57 biology classes at schools in two major Turkish cities. Data were collected with an adapted and translated version of the What is Happening in This Classroom (WIHIC) instrument and the Test of Science Related Attitudes (TOSRA). Correlation and regression analyses revealed that students' perceptions of their learning environment in biology were significantly associated with their attitudes. In addition, results of the study revealed that there were significant differences in gender and grade level. This chapter discusses these findings and compares them with prior learning environment studies.

1. Introduction

According to Fraser (2000), students have spent approximately 20.000 hours in classrooms by the time they finish their university education. This time devoted to schooling is focused mainly on the academic achievement of students. Teachers, students and schools face a variety of problems when realizing a productive learning environment for all these hours, such as lack of choice and opportunity in educational programs, lack of funding, dissatisfied and burnt-out teachers, problems in teacher quality, low grades, etc. Another problem, often mentioned by both experienced and beginning teachers, is low attitudes of students toward school and school subjects (e.g., Veenman, 1984). Because student attitudes are such a point of concern, in particular in the science subjects, because they are the focus of many governments due to shortage of teachers and students in these subjects, and due to the fact that there is a strong relationship between students' attitudes and their academic and cognitive achievement (e.g., Creemers, 1994), the present study focuses on student attitudes and the way these are affected by the classroom environment.

Fraser (1986) argues that perceptions of students and teachers are crucial if one is to investigate the learning environment (see also Wubbels & Brekelmans, 1998). The role of teachers' and students' perceptions of the classroom environment in influencing cognitive and affective outcomes has been addressed in many learning environment studies and a strong link between student outcomes and their perceptions of learning environments have been shown by many researchers (den Brok, Brekelmans, & Wubbels, 2004; Fraser & Fisher, 1982; Wubbels, & Brekelmans, 1998). In his review of past studies, Fraser (1998) stated that associations between outcome measures and classroom environment perceptions have been replicated for a variety of cognitive and affective outcomes, with a variety of instruments, across numerous countries and grade levels. Learning environment research has studied these associations in different types of classroom environments (Fraser, 2002), such as science laboratory classroom environments, computer-assisted instruction classrooms, constructivist classroom environments, cross-national studies of science classroom environments and computer laboratory classroom environments.

Researchers studying classroom environments have used various instruments for collecting data over the years (Fraser, 1998)[1]. Based on these instruments and the links shown with student outcomes, Fraser, Fisher, and McRobbie (1996) developed a learning environment instrument called the *What Is Happening In This Class?* (WIHIC) questionnaire. This questionnaire has been used by many researchers from different countries to collect data about the classroom environment. It has been validated in Australia (Rawnsley & Fisher, 1998), Taiwan (Aldridge, Fraser, & Huang, 1999), Singapore (Chionh & Fraser, 1998), Korea (Kim, Fisher, & Fraser, 2000), Indonesia (Margianti, Fraser, & Aldridge, 2002) and the USA (see den Brok, Fisher, Rickards, & Bull (in press) for an overview) and validated cross-nationally (Dorman, 2003). Because of its cross-cultural validity, the WIHIC was selected as one of the questionnaires for this study in Turkey.

Strong associations between students' perceptions and students' outcomes have been reported for almost all scales of the WIHIC (Chionh & Fisher, 1998; Rawnsley & Fisher, 1998; Riah & Fraser, 1997; Wahyudi, 2004). Although most classroom environment research involved students in Western countries, a number of important studies have been carried out in non-Western countries (Fraser, 1998, 2002). While a growing body of research is based on the subject of learning environment in Western and non-Western countries, such research is scarce in Turkey. The domain of learning environments research is a new born research field in Turkey, although a few related works are available (Rakıcı, 2004; Şimşeker, 2005). This study is the first of its kind to connect the WIHIC to student attitudes in Turkey and thereby adds significantly to this field in the region. Moreover, the study adds to the existing knowledge base on WIHIC-related studies by investigating effects on student attitudes conjointly with other possible relevant background variables, something that has not been attempted before. The outcomes of this study might be a basis for improvement and evaluation of teaching and classrooms in Turkey. Finally, this study may add to the cross-national validity of the learning environment instruments used, thereby providing more insight in the cultural variation that may exist in

---

[1] Early instruments used in the educational learning environment include the Learning Environment Inventory (LEI), The My Class Inventory (MCI) and Questionnaire on Teacher Interaction (QTI), Individualized Classroom Environment Questionnaire (ICEQ), College and University Classroom Environment Inventory (CUCEI), the My Class Inventory (MCI), Questionnaire on Interaction (QTI), Science Laboratory Inventory (SLEI), and Constructivist Learning Environment Survey (CLES).

learning environments across the world, an area of current and future interest to the learning environments domain (e.g., Fraser, 2002).

In this chapter, we discuss some of the previous research (in other countries) that has investigated the link between student attitudes and the learning environment. Before doing so, we will shortly elaborate on the topic of students' subject-related attitudes. We will also elaborate on the context of our study, the Turkish educational system. After a presentation of the research questions and methodology of our study, we provide the results and compare these with prior research. Ultimately, we present some implications, in particular with respect to possible future research.

2. Education in Turkey: The Context of the Study

This section introduces a brief overview of Turkey, its geographical location, as well as background information about the Turkish educational system.

Turkey, officially named as The Republic of Turkey, is located on the two continents of Europe and Asia and had a population of 67.8 million in 2000. The Ministry of National Education is responsible for all educational services in the country excluding higher education. Furthermore, the government provides scholarships and other means to support the education of successful students coming from materially deprived families.

The Turkish education system consists of two main divisions: formal and non-formal education. Formal Education is divided into four levels: (1) pre-school education, (2) primary education, (3) secondary education, and (4) higher education. Pre-school education is the broad term applied to non-compulsory programs for children from birth to the age of six years. Primary education is compulsory for every Turkish citizen from the age of six to the age of fourteen and is free-of-charge in state schools. The students who graduate from eight years primary education may take the Secondary Education Selection and Placement Examination (SESPE) to enrol in selective high schools or can continue their studies at a general high school, depending on the graduate's grades of primary education. Secondary education includes two main sectors, which are general high schools and vocational-technical high schools education. Students who graduate from both types of schools have the right to complete a University Selection and Placement Examination (USPE).

3. Conceptual framework

In this section, we first provide a definition and means of operationalising science-related attitudes. Next, we briefly discuss the structural framework behind the elements of the learning environment studied in this contribution and measured with the WIHIC. Finally, we summarize prior research that has linked student's perceptions on the WIHIC to their (science-related) attitudes.

3.1 Defining and measuring students subject-related attitudes

One of the purposes of the present study is to investigate whether associations exist between the classroom environment and students' attitudes. To find a clear term to define students' affective outcomes has been a difficult task and debated by researchers in the past. In 1979, Peterson and Carlson used the "attitude" term without any clarification with "interest". Evaluative quality is the central attribute of the attitude concept—like or dislike (Shrigley, Koballa, & Simpson, 1988), including terms such as interest, enjoyment, and satisfaction (Gardner & Gauld, 1990) and even curiosity, confidence, and perseverance (Shulman & Tamir, 1972). Shrigley (1983) stated that it is generally agreed that attitude is not innate, but learned as part of culture. Klopfer (1976) alleviated the semantic problems caused by the multiple meanings attached to the term *'attitude toward science'* by developing six categories of conceptually different attitudinal aims. These categories were: manifestation of favourable attitudes to science and scientists; acceptance of scientific enquiry as a way of thought; adoption of scientific attitudes; enjoyment of science learning experiences; development of interest in science and science-related activities; and development of interest in pursuing a career in science (Shulman & Tamir, 1972).

Scientists have developed instruments and a variety of different techniques to assess students' attitudes towards a subject (Laforgia, 1988; Wubbels, Créton, & Hooymayers, 1985). For the present study to evaluate students' attitudes towards their biology classes the *Test of Science Related Attitudes* (TOSRA), developed by Fraser (1981) was selected, due to its wide implementation in previous studies in Western and non-Western countries and its high degree of reliability (Goh, 1994). We discuss the TOSRA in more in detail in the Method section.

3.2 Defining and measuring students' perceptions of their learning environment

Developed by Fraser, Fisher, and McRobbie (1996), the WIHIC measures high school students' perceptions of their classroom environment. The WIHIC measures a wide range of dimensions that are important to the current situation in classrooms. The WIHIC includes relevant dimensions from past questionnaires and combines these with dimensions that measure particular aspects of constructivism and other relevant factors operating in contemporary classrooms. It was designed to bring parsimony in the field of learning environments research (Dorman, 2003). A description of each scale in the WIHIC is presented in Table 22.1.

One important consideration that has been part of classroom environment theory since the early 1970s has been Moos' (1979) conceptual framework for human environments that characterises environments as having relationship, personal growth and system maintenance and change dimensions. Whereas relationship dimensions are concerned with the nature and intensity of personal relationships, personal growth dimensions focus on opportunities for personal development and self-enhancement. System maintenance and system change dimensions assess the extent to which the environment is orderly, clear in expectations, maintains control and is responsive to change. Table 22.1 additionally shows the classification of each WIHIC scale according to Moos' scheme. The instrument itself and its qualities are discussed in more detail in the Method section.

3.3 Prior research linking the WIHIC to student outcomes

There are not many studies that have investigated the link between students' subject-related attitudes (in terms of the TOSRA) and their perceptions of the learning environment (in terms of the WIHIC), as is the case in the present study. A study by Rawnsley and Fisher (1998) investigated associations between learning environments in mathematics classrooms and students' attitudes towards that subject in Australia using the WIHIC questionnaire. It was found that students developed more positive attitudes towards their mathematics in classes where the teacher was perceived to be highly supportive, equitable, and in which the teacher involved them in investigations.

Table 22.1. Scale Descriptions for Each Scale in the WIHIC Questionnaire

WIHIC scale	The extent to which...	Moos dimension
Student Cohesiveness	...students are friendly and supportive of each other.	Relationship
Teacher Support	... the teacher helps, befriends, and is interested in students.	Relationship
Involvement	... students have attentive interest, participate in class and are involved with other students in assessing the viability of new ideas.	Relationship
Investigation	..there is emphasis on the skills and of inquiry and their use in problem-solving and investigation.	Personal growth
Task Orientation	... it is important to complete planned activities and stay on the subject matter.	Personal growth
Cooperation	... students cooperate with each other during activities.	Personal growth
Equity	... the teacher treats students equally, including distributing praise, question distribution and opportunities to be included in discussions.	System maintenance and System change

Chionh and Fraser (1998) used the Actual and Preferred Forms of the WIHIC to further validate the instrument and to investigate associations between actual classroom environment and outcomes. The associations between five different outcome measures namely, examination results, self-esteem, and three attitude scales and the seven actual classroom environment scales were investigated in geography and mathematics classrooms in Singapore and Australia. The study revealed that better examination scores were found in geography and mathematics classrooms where students perceived the environment as more cohesive. It was also found that self-esteem and attitudes were more favourable in classrooms perceived as having more teacher support, task orientation and equity.

Riah and Fraser (1997) used a modified version of the WIHIC in Brunei, and reported on the associations between perceptions of learning environment and attitudinal outcomes. Simple and multiple correlations showed that there was a significant relationship between the set of environment scales and students' attitudes towards chemistry theory classes. The Student Cohesiveness, Teacher Support, Involvement, and Task Orientation scales were positively associated with the students' attitudes.

A study by Wahyudi (2004) found associations between students' outcomes and the status of classroom learning environments. Both simple analysis and multiple regression analysis procedures showed that all scales of the Indonesian WIHIC were statistically significantly positively associated with two scales of the Indonesian adapted TOSRA and students' cognitive scores.

Hoffner-Moss and Fraser (2002) reported that attitudes are particularly favourable in investigative, task oriented and equitable classes in their study with 364 biology students in 18 classes. They also revealed that all students in the study perceived relatively high level of Task orientation.

Allen (2003) reported the results of A simple correlation analysis between scales of the WIHIC and TOSRA. In his study, the scale of Investigation was significantly correlated with Inquiry. Additionally, Involvement, Task Orientation and Investigation were significantly correlated with Enjoyment. All correlations found were positive.

In a cross-cultural study conducted with Indonesian and Australian students, Adolphe, Fraser and Aldridge (2003) remarked on a reasonably strong and positive association between all the WIHIC scales and the TOSRA scales.

Overall, these findings show that many or all of the WIHIC scales are positively related to student attitudes. High associations have particularly been found for the scales Teacher Support, Equity and Investigation. However, previous studies cannot easily be compared with the present study for a number of reasons. First, many were focused at primary education, while the present study is focused at secondary education. Second, the previous studies were conducted in several subject domains, but few (e.g., Hoffner-Moss & Fraser, 2002) have been undertaken in the Biology classroom. Third, as mentioned previously, none of the studies has been undertaken in Turkey. Fourth, although the studies were careful in their analyses procedure, they may have overestimated the effects of scales, because they consistently investigated associations between a single WIHIC scale and student attitudes, thus not taking into account the (partially) joint effect of possible other (WIHIC) elements of the learning environment or taking into account the effect of background characteristics of students, teachers or classes that may have affected attitudes and student perceptions as well. The present study hoped to address some of these limitations by including background variables, by investigating the joint effects of all scales, and by doing this on a secondary education biology sample in Turkey.

4. Research Questions

In order to obtain a comprehensive image of science classroom environments in Turkish high schools, this study was designed to achieve the following objectives:

- to describe students' general perceptions of their biology learning environments;
- to explore the demographic and academic background variables that may be related to these students' attitudes toward biology; and
- to investigate associations between students' perception of their learning environment and their attitudes toward biology

Specifically, the research questions that this study attempted to answer were:

1. Can the *What Is Happening in this Class* (WIHIC) questionnaire be used in a valid and reliable manner with grade 9 and 10 biology students in Bursa and Ankara, Turkey?
2. Are there relationships between biology students' perceptions of their learning environment and their attitudes toward biology?
3. Are there differences in students' attitudes toward biology by gender, grade levels, and parental educational level?

5. Method

5.1 Sample

The participants of this study were 1,983 ninth grade and tenth grade students from nine high schools. Data for the study were collected from 57 biology classes[2]. Class size in these schools varied from 30 to 40 students. Schools were selected conveniently from two city centres, Bursa and Ankara, two of the major cities in Turkey. All types of Turkish secondary education (Anatolian high schools, vocational high schools and general high schools) were represented in the sample. The sample (see Table 22.2) consisted of grade 9 (59.5 %) and grade 10 students (31, 9 %), a slight majority of which were boys (50.1 %).

Table 22.2. Number of Students by Gender and Grade Level

	Number of Student in Grade 9	Number of Student in Grade 10	Total
Girls	608	254	862
Boys	663	424	1087
Total	1271	678	1749
Unknown	-	-	134

The education level of parents showed a wide distribution from primary school to graduate level in our sample, which is indicated in Table 22.3.

Since the sample comprised the majority of the secondary education schools in the two cities involved, the sample can be considered representative for these two locations. However, no information is available on how these cities compare to Turkey as a whole.

---

[2] Unfortunately, due to a computer problem during the data collection phase of the study, no individual data was recorded for student class and school identification. This means we could only investigate the effect of individual student characteristics and only some effects of class or school background characteristics (for example grade level). Of course, we realise this is a limitation to our study.

Table 22.3. Students' Parental Education Level

Educational Level	Mother Education Level	Percentage (%)	Father Education Level	Percentage (%)
Primary School	714	32.9	422	19.4
Junior High School	322	14.8	321	14.8
High School	553	25.5	589	27.1
Bachelor Degree	299	13.8	507	23.4
Graduate degree	26	1.2	77	3.5
Total	1914	88.2	1916	88.3
Unknown	257	11.8	255	11.7

5.2 Instrumentation

All students responded to two questionnaires: the What is Happening in This Classroom (WIHIC) and the Test of Science Related Attitudes (TOSRA).

The original version of the WIHIC contained 90 items and nine scales, but was refined by statistical analysis of the data from 355 high school science students, and extensive interviewing of students about their views of their classroom environments in general, the wording and salience of individual items and their questionnaire responses (Fraser, Fisher, & McRobbie 1996). Only 56 items in seven scales survived these procedures, although this set of items was expanded to 80 items in eight scales for the field-testing of the second version of the WIHIC, which involved high school science classes in Australia and Taiwan. The Australian sample consisted of 1,081 students in 50 classes who responded to the original English version. The Taiwanese sample of 1,879 students in 50 classes responded to a Chinese version that had undergone careful procedures of translation and back translation (Aldridge, Fraser, & Huang, 1999). This led to a final form of the WIHIC containing the seven eight-item scales.

Most of the studies using the WIHIC have provided information with respect to both validity and reliability. Research seems to indicate that the reliability of the scales (Cronbach's Alpha) of the instrument is usually above 0.70 at the student level and above 0.85 at the class level. Exploratory and confirmatory factor analyses (e.g., Dorman, 2003) indicate that the items of the WIHIC usually have factor loadings above 0.40 on their *a-priori* scales and lower loadings on other scales. Moreover, the factor structure has been shown to be invariant across grade levels, countries, cultures and gender (Dorman, 2003), which suggests its usefulness in studying multicultural and heterogeneous school populations (as is the case in the present study). Average correlations between the scales of the WIHIC – a convenient measure of discriminant validity (Fraser, 1998) – have been reported between approximately 0.20 and 0.50, indicating that each of the seven scales measures distinct, though partly overlapping elements of the classroom environment.

For the present study, the questionnaire was first translated and adapted into Turkish by the first two authors. The next step involved an independent back translation of the Turkish version into English by two qualified, bilingual Turkish graduate students who were not involved in the original translation. Then the Turkish authors of this study checked the back translations and, for some items, necessary modifications in the Turkish translation were carried out. A pilot study was conducted with 399 eleventh grade high school students. Based on the pilot study results, modifications were made. After this, the instrument was distributed among the classes and students involved in the present study.

The final modified form of instrument was constructed with a five-point Likert-type response scale with the following alternatives: (1) Never, (2) Seldom, (3) Often, (4) Usually, (5) Always. Scale reliability (Cronbach's alpha) for different WIHIC scales ranged from 0.75 to 0.88 (see Table 22.4) in this Turkish sample.

In Table 22.5, WIHIC scale intercorrelations are displayed. As can be seen, all scales are positively related, meaning that if students have higher perceptions of one element of their learning environment, they also tend to see more of the other elements of the learning environment. Nevertheless, correlations rarely exceed 0.50, and the average scale correlation between one WIHIC scale and the other scales ranges between 0.34 (Student Cohesiveness) and 0.44 (Involvement). These are indications that the scales of the instrument measure distinct elements of the learning environment and only display partial overlap.

Table 22.4. WIHIC Scales, Sample Item, and Reliability (Cronbach's Alpha)

Scale	Typical item	N items	Alpha (student)
Student Cohesiveness	Students in this class like me.	8	0.75
Teacher Support	The teacher talks with me.	8	0.86
Involvement	I discuss the ideas in class.	8	0.80
Investigation	I carry out investigation to test my ideas.	8	0.86
Task Orientation	I do as much as I set out to do.	8	0.81
Cooperation	I learn from other students in this class.	8	0.83
Equity	My work receives as much praise as other student's work.	8	0.88

N=1,983 students

Table 22.5. WIHIC Scales Correlations and Average Correlation

	Cohes	Supp	Involv	Invest	Taskor	Coop	Average correlation
Cohes							0.34
Supp	0.23						0.36
Involv	0.43	0.43					0.44
Invest	0.25	0.39	0.49				0.40
Taskor	0.28	0.34	0.35	0.51			0.39
Coop	0.54	0.32	0.47	0.40	0.38		0.42
Equit	0.29	0.47	0.44	0.38	0.50	0.42	0.42

Note: all correlations were significant at $p=0.01$.

The second questionnaire used in this study is the *Test of Science Related Attitudes* (TOSRA). It is originally consisted of seven scales and 70 items and was developed by Fraser (1981). The seven original scales were: Social Implications of Science, Normality of Scientists, Attitude to Scientific Inquiry, Adaptation of Scientific Attitudes, Enjoyment of Science Lessons, Leisure Interest in Science, Career Interest in Science.

Each of the seven scales included 10 items. The TOSRA-items are scored on a 5-point scale, ranging from strongly agree (5) to strongly disagree (1).

Since we were mainly interested in subject-related attitudes, rather than in the more general concept of science-related attitudes, four scales from the original form of the TOSRA were selected: Attitude to Scientific Inquiry, Enjoyment of Science Lessons, Leisure Interest in Science, and Career Interest in Science. These four scales of the questionnaire were translated and adapted, similar to the procedure for adaptation of the WIHIC questionnaire. After the before-mentioned pilot study, a factor analysis was run and necessary modifications, such as deleting some of the items, were made. The final modified version of the TOSRA for the Turkish context in the present study (T-TOSRA) included 32 items (see Table 22.6).

Table 22.6. Scales and Short Scale Description for the T-TOSRA Questionnaire

Scale	Scale description
Attitude to Scientific Inquiry	Acceptance of scientific inquiry as a way of thought
Enjoyment of Science Lessons	Enjoyment of science learning experiences
Leisure Interest in Science	Development of interest in science and science related activities
Career Interest in Science	Development of interest in pursing a career in science

Similar to the WIHIC questionnaire, we conducted some analyses on the TOSRA scales to check for their reliability and construct validity. In Table 22.7, a sample item is presented for each TOSRA scale. Moreover, we have investigated scale reliability by computing Cronbach's Alpha. As can be seen, all of the TOSRA scales were sufficiently reliable (e.g., above 0.70).

Table 22.7. TOSRA Scales, Sample Item and Reliability

Scale	Sample item	N items	Alpha (student)	Mean	St. dev.
Inquiry	I would prefer to do experiments than to read about them.	8	0.71	0.61	0.17
Enjoyment	Science lessons are fun.	10	0.89	0.61	0.21
Leisure	I would like to belong to a science club.	8	0.80	0.55	0.20
Career	Working in a science laboratory would be an interesting way to earn a living.	5	0.75	0.50	0.21

N=1,983 students
Note: 5-points scales were transformed into a score between 0 and 1.

To check whether the TOSRA scales measured sufficiently different concepts, we computed scale intercorrelations (see Table 22.8). It seemed that three out of four scales displayed some overlap (average correlations ranged between 0.49 and 0.54), while the Inquiry scale was least connected to the other scales (average correlation was 0.16).

Table 22.8. T-TOSRA Scales and Intercorrelations

	Inquiry	Enjoyment	Leisure	Average correlation
Inquiry				0.16
Enjoyment	0.09			0.49
Leisure	0.19	0.73		0.54
Career	0.19	0.64	0.69	0.51

Note: all correlations were significant at $p=.01$.

5.3 Analyses

To investigate how individual students' attitudes were related to their personal perceptions of the learning environment, we first computed simple correlations between the TOSRA scales and the WIHIC scales. As a second step, we performed regression analyses on the TOSRA scales, using WIHIC scales as independent variables. To correct the effect of the learning environment for other covariates, we also entered some background variables into these regression analyses. These variables were: student gender, grade level, and socio-economic background. The latter variable was measured in terms of education level of the father and education level of the mother. Grade level was recorded into a binary variable, with a 1 indicating grade 9 (and a 0 grade 10). Gender was recoded into a binary variable, with boys represented by a 1 and girls by a 0. Education level (of both parents) was measured in terms of five categories, with a 5 representing the University level and a 1 indicating no education at all. To test overall fit of the regression models we computed an F-value (and its significance) as well as the percentage of variance explained by the model. We used the 'enter' method, meaning that the computer entered variables into the model in order of their effect size up to the point that variables added no significant amounts of variance to the model.

6. Results

As can be seen in Table 22.9, on average, Turkish students perceive their classes as highly task oriented, moderately cohesive, cooperative and equitable, but less teacher supportive, leading to involvement or stimulating investigation. The average class profile is similar to the profile displayed in Australia and the USA, where also high ratings are reported for Student Cohesiveness, Task Orientation and Equity. Nevertheless, it seems the students are slightly more moderate in their responses, as differences between scale means are smaller than in the USA.

Looking at the standard deviations, it seems that Turkish students disagree mostly on Teacher Support, Investigation and Equity.

According to Table 22.7, Turkish high school students have moderate science attitudes (e.g., their scores are just above the scale medium score of 0.50 or 50 percent). They are most favourable about Enjoyment and Inquiry in Biology, and least favourable about the prospect Biology has for their career. Also, looking at the standard deviations, it appears there is quite some variation in students' attitudes with respect to the Inquiry, Leisure and Career scales.

Table 22.9. Turkish Students' Mean Perceptions on the WIHIC Scales (Standard Deviation), Mean Perception Scores in the USA and Australia

WIHIC scale	Mean perception (standard deviation) Turkey (N=1983)	Mean perception USA (source: den Brok, et al., in press) (N=655)	Mean perception Australia (source: Rawnsley & Fisher, 1998) (N=490)
Student Cohesiveness	0.69 (0.16)	0.74	0.58
Teacher Support	0.46 (0.22)	0.43	0.58
Involvement	0.55 (0.18)	0.46	0.50
Investigation	0.54 (0.20)	0.41	0.40
Task Orientation	0.75 (0.17)	0.78	0.68
Cooperation	0.59 (0.19)	0.68	0.63
Equity	0.66 (0.21)	0.64	0.68

Note: the original studies reported their scale means as a score between 1 and 5, for the present study these scores were linearly transformed to a score between 0 and 1.

Table 22.10 provides simple correlations between the attitude scales and the learning environment scales in this study. In all instances, the raw correlations are positive, suggesting a positive effect of perceptions of the learning environment on subject-related attitudes. Highest correlations can be found for Involvement (around 0.20), Investigation (between 0.26 and 0.42) and the lowest correlations can be found for Student Cohesiveness (around 0.10). Students' perceptions of the learning environment seem least related to Inquiry and most to Leisure. Perceptions of Teacher Support, Task Orientation and Equity are variably related to students' attitudes: low associations are found with Inquiry, but much higher associations are found with Enjoyment, Leisure and Career.

Table 22.10 Simple Correlations between TOSRA and WIHIC Scales

	Inquiry	Enjoyment	Leisure	Career
Cohesiveness	0.14	0.13	0.13	0.10
Teacher Support	0.05*	0.33	0.30	0.22
Involvement	0.21	0.21	0.22	0.18
Investigation	0.26	0.36	0.42	0.32
Task Orient	0.09	0.39	0.40	0.32
Cooperation	0.16	0.16	0.19	0.14
Equity	0.07	0.32	0.28	0.19

N=1,983   Note: *=non-significant at p=.025 (two-sided).

Interestingly, the pattern of associations changes somewhat if covariates are included in the analyses and if associations are studied taking into account the effect of the other learning environment scales of the WIHIC (see Table 22.11). It seems that Investigation remains positively and significantly associated with each of the four attitude scales. However, the association of Involvement with students' attitudes diminishes or even disappears. Negative relationships are even found between Teacher Support and Inquiry – which seems logical: the more teachers play a role in the learning process, the less chance there is for the students to do so –between Cooperation and Enjoyment, and between Cooperation and Career prospect. Task Orientation also seems positively related to three out of four attitude scales (an exception is Inquiry).

Table 22.11 also shows that younger students (grade 9) have more positive attitudes than older students (grade 10). Girls seem to have less positive attitudes in terms of Career than boys. Education level of the mother is negatively associated with three out of four attitude scales, education level of the father positively related to Enjoyment. The models explain 13 to 25 percent of the variance, which is quite impressive.

Table 22.11. Regression Analyses on TOSRA Scales

Variables	Enquiry	Enjoyment	Leisure	Career
WIHIC scales:				
- cohesiveness	0.08	-	-	-
- teacher support	-0.08	0.19	0.10	0.09
- involvement	0.10	-	-	-
- investigation	0.27	0.16	0.26	0.21
- task orientation	-	0.23	0.24	0.16
- cooperation	-	-0.11	-	-0.09
- equity	0.08	0.08	-	-
Background variables:				
- grade level	0.08	0.12	-	0.10
- gender	-	-	-	-0.09
- educ level mother	-0.10	-	-0.07	-0.09
- educ level father	-	0.12	-	-
Total model fit:				
- F-value	26.05	58.57	97.15	35.12
- Significance	0.00	0.00	0.00	0.00
- % explained	13.3	25.4	24.4	16.8
-				

N=1,983   Note: coefficients are standardized (beta-weights). Only significant coefficients (at $p=.01$) are displayed.

7. Discussion

This study provided insights into biology classroom environment in high schools in Bursa and Ankara, two of the major cities in Turkey. This chapter has described a pioneering study for Turkey in the domain of learning environments research in some respect. It has shown that the WIHIC is a valid and reliable instrument for use in the Turkish secondary education context.

The results of the study indicated that participating high school students had moderately favourable attitudes of their learning environment in biology, with higher ratings for Inquiry and Enjoyment than for Career. The somewhat higher ratings found for Inquiry and Enjoyment could be the result of the presence of students from Anatolian (e.g. more cognitively oriented) high schools, who have a high(er) tendency to follow science courses and usually have higher examination scores. Their high achievement may also lead to relative higher enjoyment. The lowest ratings on the Career scale could be the result of many things. A possible explanation might lie in the fact that in Turkey, occupations related with this subject usually require longer and more concentrated education with a heavy curriculum involving many other subjects, resulting in a relative downplay of Biology itself, and causing many students not to go for such occupations.

It was also found that some elements of the learning environment (e.g., Student Cohesiveness, Task Orientation and Equity) were perceived as more visible than others. Although the average perceptions did not differ from those reported in other countries (e.g., den Brok, et al., in press; Rawnsley & Fisher, 1998), we try to interpret them with the Turkish educational context in mind. In Turkey, generally teachers have limited time to pay personal attention to their students due to large (average) class sizes. This may be a cause for the relatively low score on Teacher Support. In a similar fashion, it can be argued that due to the large class size, the time for each student to participate in the lesson is limited. Besides this, the main concern of many Turkish teachers is to cover the curriculum on time. Therefore, to some degree, the relatively low rating for Involvement is not very surprising. Since Turkish students are very much inclined to pass their exams, and because there is high pressure from society and parents on students to be successful, this may explain why students are inclined to be highly task oriented and may perceive their environment as such.

Additionally, it was found that younger students, boys and higher socio-economic background of the father (but lower background of the mother) were more positively associated with student's subject-related attitudes in Biology. Usually, in (Turkish) society science is approached from a masculine perspective and many science-related occupations are dominated by males. In this respect, Turkey is no exception. This general trend may affect girls' career preference negatively and reduce their motivation for subjects such as Biology. Furthermore, gender has been found to be a significant factor that differentiates students' perceptions of biology learning environments. For example, according to Mok (2002), female students had both higher developmental expectations of their schools and more positive perceptions of the classroom atmosphere. Outcomes of grade level point out that younger students (grade nine) have more positive attitudes than older students (grade ten). Biology curriculum at grade nine in Turkey is lighter than grade ten and students generally spend less effort on following the lessons. The topics in grade ten are more concentrated and students have to reserve many hours additional to class hours to follow lessons. It is usually boring and exhausting for students to have so many hours of science per week with such an intensive curriculum. Additionally, they feel more pressure for the University Selection and Placement Examination (USPE) at this grade since the time is closer than in the previous year.

Finally, when all variables are included in the analyses, it seemed perceptions of Investigation were most strongly and positively related to students' attitudes, followed by Task Orientation. The teacher's limited time for students on an individual base may stimulate the development of students' investigation skills and perceptions of the learning environment stimulating this. As long as students are finding out by themselves, it seems their interest and attitudes may develop positively toward the subject. Interestingly, when all other elements are considered, Cooperation contributes negatively, as does Teacher Support on Inquiry.

More generally, this study also replicated the finding that there is a strong link between student outcomes and their perceptions of the learning environment (Fraser & Fisher, 1982; den Brok, Brekelmans, & Wubbels, 2004; Wubbels & Brekelmans, 1998). More specifically, the findings are similar to those of other studies using the WIHIC and TOSRA (e.g., Adolphe, Fraser, & Aldridge, 2003; Allen, 2003; Chionh & Fraser, 1998; Hoffner-Moss & Fraser, 2002; Rawnsley & Fisher, 1998; Riah & Fraser, 1997; Wahyudi, 2004). In particular, previous findings were replicated with respect to the positive associations with the Investigation and Task Orientation scales. However, the study also showed that including background variables of students and taking into account the effect of other environment variables may downplay the additional or separate effect of scales, due to their overlap with these variables. As such, it is important for learning environments researchers to take these factors into account.

The first limitation of the study is the fact that multilevel analysis could not be performed. This could have helped to report and explain some of the educational processes at the class level, which have not come into view at this point. These processes include effects of such variables as class size and teacher on the average attitudes of the students within one class. The study at this point only attempted to explain individual student attitudes from a personal point of view. Because class level variables were not included, the effect of learning environment perceptions has only been adjusted for some background characteristics.

Moreover, other elements of the learning environment, such as teacher interpersonal behaviour, for example, have not been included. Moreover, there is no clue as to what amount of the differences between students is actually to be found at the class, teacher, school or even region level. Consequently, some of the effects reported in this study may have been overestimated. Second, the sample is relatively small and only covered a small part of Turkey. Therefore, results cannot be easily generalized to the country as a whole, and future research with larger samples from different cities will be necessary to shed light on this point. Such research could also confirm (or reject) some of the associations found in the present study. Last, although the focus on affective outcomes is considered relevant and important, of course this study cannot suggest anything about the associations between the learning environment and other outcome measures (e.g., achievement). This might be another avenue for future research in Turkish learning environments research.

The classroom is the basic unit of organization of the Turkish educational system. By continuing to increase our knowledge of the interactions that occur within the classroom, we shall be able to enhance our understanding of this important educational unit. As we increase our understanding of how students, teachers and science come together within the classroom environment, we should be able to improve the quality of science education in Turkey.

It has been assumed that having a positive classroom environment is an educationally desirable end in its own right. This study provides biology teachers with information about aspects of the learning environment that, if altered, could lead to increases in students' attitudinal and achievement gains. The practical implication of this research is that student outcomes might be improved by creating classroom environments found empirically to be conducive to learning. Understanding students' perceptions of their classroom learning environments and the factors associated with their perceptions may help us to find out some alternative ways that enhance the student's learning. Findings of this study identified gender, grade levels, and parental educational level variables as factors that predict learning environment perceptions. For that reason, educational researchers in Turkey should focus on the disparities between boys and girls and find strategies that may create positive and productive learning environment for boys. Furthermore, educators should recognize the importance of creating supportive, stimulating, enjoyable and productive learning environment by considering the types of schools. In addition to this, the effect of parental-education level on student's attitudes and perceptions could be the subject of further studies.

References

Adoplhe, F. S. G., Fraser, B. J., & Aldridge, J. M. (2003, January). *A cross national study of learning environment and attitudes among junior secondary science students in Australia and Indonesia.* Paper presented at the Third International Science, Mathematics and Technology Education Conference, East London, South Africa.

Aldridge, J. M., Fraser, B. J., & Haung, T. (1999). Investigating classroom environments in Taiwan and Australia with multiple research methods. *Journal of Educational Research, 93*, 48-57.

Allen, D. (2003). *Parent and student perceptions of science learning environment and its influence on students outcomes.* Unpublished doctoral dissertation. Perth: Curtin University of Technology.

Chionh, Y. H. & Fraser, B. J. (1998, April). *Validation and use of the 'What is Happening in this class?' (WIHIC) questionnaire in Singapore.* Paper presented at the Annual Meeting of the American Educational Research Association, San Diego, CA.

Creemers, B. P. M. (1994). *The effective classroom.* London: Cassell.

den Brok, P., Brekelmans, M., & Wubbels, T. (2004). Interpersonal teacher behaviour and student outcomes. *School Effectiveness and School Improvement, 15* (3/4), 407-442.

den Brok, P., Fisher, D. L., Rickards, T., & Bull, E (in press). Californian science students' perceptions of their classroom learning environments. Paper accepted for publication in *Educational Research and Evaluation.*

Dorman, J. P. (2003). Cross-national validation of the What is Happening in This Class ? questionnaire using confirmatory factor analysis. *Learning Environments Research, 6*, 231-245.

Fraser, B. J. (1981). *The Test of Science–Related Attitudes(TOSRA).* Melbourne: Australian Council for Educational Research.

Fraser, B. J. (1986). *Classroom environment.* London: Croom Helm.

Fraser, B. J. (1998). Classroom environment instruments: Development, validity and applications. *Learning Environment Research, 1*, 7-33.

Fraser, B. J. (2000). Twenty thousand hours: Editor's introduction. *Learning Environments Research, 4, 1–5.*

Fraser, B. J. (2002). Learning environments research: yesterday, today and tomorrow. In S. C. Goh & M. S. Khine (Eds.), *Studies in educational learning environments: an international perspective* (pp.1-27). Singapore: World Scientific Publishers.

Fraser, B. J. & Fisher, D. L. (1982). Predicting students' outcomes from their perception of classroom psychosocial environment. *American Education Research Journal, 19*, 468-518.

Fraser, B. J., Fisher, D. L., & McRobbie, C. J. (1996, April). *Development, validation and use of personal and class forms of a new classroom environment instrument.* Paper presented at the annual meeting of the American Educational Research Association, New York, USA.

Gardner, P. (1975). *Attitudes to science: A Review.* Studies in Science Education, 2, 1 – 41. Gardner, P. & Gauld, C. (1990). Labwork and students' attitudes. In E. Hegarty-Hazel (Ed.), *The student laboratory and the science curriculum* (pp. 132-156). London: Routledge.

Goh, S. C. (1994). *Interpersonal teacher behavior, classroom climate and student outcomes in primary Mathematics classes in Singapore.* Doctoral dissertation. Perth: Curtin University of Technology, Science and Mathematics Education Centre.

Hoffner, M. C. & Fraser, B. J. (2002, April). *Using environment assessments in improving teaching and learning in high school biology classrooms.* Paper presented at the annual meeting of the National Association for Research in Science Teaching, New Orleans.

Kim, H., Fisher, D., & Fraser, B. (2000). Classroom environment and teacher interpersonal behaviour in secondary science classes in Korea. *Evaluation and Research in Education, 14*, 3-22.

Klopfer, L. E. (1976). A structure for the affective domain in relation to science education. *Science Education, 60*, 299-312.

Laforgia, J. (1988). The affective domain related to science education and its evaluation. *Science Education, 72* (4), 407-421.

Margianti, E. S., Fraser, B. J., & Aldridge, J. M. (2002, April). *Learning environment, attitudes and achivement: Assesing the perceptions of Indonesian university students.* Paper presented at the Annual Meeting of the American Educational Research Association, New Orleans, LA.

Mok, M. C. (2002). Determinants of students' quality of school life: a path model. *Learning Environments Research, 5*, 275-300.

Moos, R. H. (1979). *Evaluating educational environments: procedures, measures, findings and policy implications*. San Francisco: Jossey Bass.

Peterson, R. W. & Carlson, G. R. (1979). A summary of research in science education. *Science Education, 59*, 207-210.

Rakıcı, N. (2004). *Eight grade students' perceptions of their science learning environment and teacher interpersonal behaviour*. Unpublished master thesis. Ankara: Middle East Technical University.

Rawnsley, D. & Fisher, D. L. (1998, December). *Learning environments in mathematics classrooms and their associations with students' attitudes and learning*. Paper presented at the Australian Association for Research in Education Conference, Adelaide, Australia.

Riah, H. & Fraser, B. J. (1997). Chemistry learning Environment in Brunei Darussalam's secondary Schools. In D. L. Fisher & T. Rickards (Eds.), *Science, Mathematics and Technology Education and National Development: Proceedings of the Vietnam conference* (pp.108-120). Hanoi; Vietnam.

Shrigley, R. L. (1983). The attitude concept and science teaching. *Science Education, 67*, 425-442.

Shrigley, R. L., Koballa, T. R., & Simpson, R. D. (1988). Defining attitude for science educators. *Journal of Research in Science Teaching, 25*, 659-678.

Shulman, L. S. & Tamir, P. (1972). Research on teaching in the natural sciences. In R. M. W. Travers, (Ed.), *Second handbook of research on teaching* (pp. 1098-1148). Chicago, IL: Rand McNally.

Şimşeker, M. (2005). *Eight grade students' perceptions of their mathematics teachers' interpersonal behaviors*. Unpublished master thesis. Ankara: Middle East Technical University.

Veenman, S. (1984). Problems of beginning teachers. *Review of Educational Research, 54*, 143-178.

Wahyudi, D. (2004). *Educational practices and learning environments in rural and urban lower secondary science classrooms in Kalimantan Selatan Indonesia*. Unpublished doctoral dissertation. Perth: Curtin University of Technology.

Wubbels, T., Créton, H., & Hooymayers, H. (1985, March). *Discipline problems of beginning teachers, interactional teacher behavior mapped out*. Paper presented at the annual meeting of the American Educational Research Association, Chicago, IL.

Wubbels, T. & Brekelmans, M. (1998). The teacher factor in the social climate of the classroom. In B. J. Fraser & K. G. Tobin (Eds.). *International handbook of Science education, part one* (pp.565-580). London: Kluwer Academic Publishers.

Chapter 23

A BRIEF CRITIQUE ON THE FUTURE OF LEARNING:
ASSESSING THE POTENTIAL FOR RESEARCH

Stephen Quinton
Curtin University of Technology
Australia

Recent advances in computer and communications technologies are opening up new opportunities for learning design requiring a thorough (perhaps revolutionary) reappraisal of the goals and purpose of education. The potential of the Internet and the technologies it inspires makes it feasible to not only access and manage information in productive and efficient ways, but also to deliver dynamically interactive, personalised solutions tailored to the needs and preferences of all learners. Therefore, it is important to extend our understanding of how computer technologies can enhance student learning whilst providing some insight into the future of learning. If we accept for the moment that graduates are not adequately equipped to cope with current skill requirements, and combine this view with the complexity of devising suitable electronic delivery methods, there is cause for concern as to the capacity of current learning design models to cater for the diverse skill demands of a technologically driven world. Such concern for the future is not new, but certain emerging factors suggest there is merit in constructing advanced learning models that take advantage of the growing sophistication of computer technologies. The challenge will be to harness technological innovations in ways that will assist to deliver high quality learning outcomes relevant to the changing needs of learners.

1. Introduction

Computers and communications technologies have influenced almost every facet of our lives, including the way we view the world around us. Over the past ten years or so, we have witnessed the widespread integration of information technology systems into classrooms, libraries, homes, businesses and communities. In turn, the use of educational technologies has led to unprecedented access to vast repositories of information paralleled by a pronounced transformation in the type, production, and ease of access to high quality teaching and learning resources. The problem however, is that for the most part, the current debate on the use of educational technologies is directed toward deriving a plausible purpose rather than determining how the same technologies may assist to enhance learning. Instead of posing the question "how can this technology be used?" a more appropriate question should be along the lines of: "what is it about the learning process that needs to be improved?" The question that naturally follows is "in what ways might the technology enable such improvements?" Taking this line of thought further, we must also reflect on the implications these questions hold for the future of education. Analysing such potential changes gives rise to the question of "how is it possible to derive knowledge from a vast storehouse of disorganised data and information that is expanding at rates impossible for any individual to process?" As will be emphasised, in answering the latter question it becomes apparent there is an uneasy tension between what is possible, and what is actually needed (McLean & Lynch, 2004, p. 2).

In many instances, learning is viewed as a one-way, 'distribute-then-learn' system. Teaching is not about delivering content as though it is water channelled down a pipe nor can the process of learning be compared to filling an empty bucket with water. Such a model cannot embrace all the complexities of learning. We have reached a point where information and the knowledge that can be derived from it have become far too prodigious and unmanageable for it to be absorbed in the minds of individuals. As information and knowledge increases in size and in complexity, it will, out of necessity, become the shared property of networked individuals and communities. That is, for the individual to cope with increasing complexity, the production of knowledge must be viewed as a communal activity.

The growing recognition of the untapped power of educational technologies is an area that researchers are only just beginning to explore. Consider for example, the potential of technology inspired delivery techniques and strategies for creating learning environments designed to manage and facilitate an unfettered exploration of the countless relationships that thread throughout globally distributed networked repositories of knowledge and information. Given this potential, consider also that the capacity to extend the learning experience beyond accepted epistemological distinctions as delineated by established disciplines and specialist subject areas is now technically feasible. Using advanced technologies such as the Internet and learning objects, traditionally separate nodes of data and information can be dynamically interlinked in highly imaginative and novel ways. It is also feasible for example, to enhance the learner's capacity to generate new knowledge by designing learning environments that assist to connect prior insights and understandings to multiple, at times incongruent contexts.

If we reflect on the implications these musings present, it is conceivable that education as we have known it over the past century is poised on the verge of entering into new realms of possibilities that will revolutionise the long held views on the purpose of learning. The emergent power of the web and related technologies makes it both desirable and viable to not only access and manage far more information than previously thought possible, but also to deliver learning environments anytime and anywhere convenient to the learner. Regardless of the obvious appeal of such prospects, we must not lose sight of the fact that ready access to information does not always equate to being educated, in particular where asynchronous and computer-mediated 'distance' communication modes are concerned. As indicated, it is not enough to simply deliver information and assume learning will ensue. In practice, the issues and strategies for designing effective learning environments are highly complex and diverse.

It is not just bridging the transition from 'traditional' learning to electronically mediated learning that is fraught with difficulties. The speed of change in the socio-economic and education environments necessitates a continuous search for radically different and innovative teaching strategies and learning models to address the learning requirements of future graduates. For example, any attempt to accommodate the skill needs and preferences of current generation, computer 'literate' students will inevitably compel educational designers to think entirely "outside the box" and consider design strategies that are more in line with student's expectations and demands. In order to satisfy the needs of the new Internet 'literate', it will be necessary to provide content interactive features that permit users to search by preferred keyword, annotate at will, dynamically hyperlink to alternative materials relative to the current context, and generate customised interactive assessment and feedback responses tailored to their immediate learning needs.

Unless we think about learning as a flexible process that takes into account place, time, and context, then it is likely that the new technologies will not enhance the learning experience. On the contrary, the absence of these factors may act as an impediment to the resultant depth and quality of learning. New models of learning are required that connect people to people and people to technology. With these goals in mind, this chapter will explore the issues related to current and future trends with a view to gaining an insight into the role and purpose of learning as derived from an understanding how the delivery of education may be shaped and refined by technology in the next decade. To this end, several research studies will be proposed that share a central aim of devising innovative teaching strategies and design techniques for delivering advanced learning solutions in a technologically driven future. A common thread underpinning the discussions to follow will be the potential for emerging technologies to improving the quality and effectiveness of learning.

2. Technology is Redefining Traditional Boundaries

The characteristics of the emerging technologies are such that they play a significant role in breaking down the mental barriers imposed by industrial centric thinking, which if sustained, will prove inadequate for resolving the demands that will be placed on education over the next decade. While some countries are experiencing a transitional stage of actively re-examining their education system, others are resisting change and react only to the pressures imposed by the demands made at the local level. It is significant that education in general is still described using the language and metaphors of the industrial era while school organisations continue to reflect the practices and beliefs of the industrial model. A failure to integrate information technology into the school curricula is often the result of a mismatch between the values of the school organisation and the values ascribed to the new technologies. However, change is inevitable, and a reluctance to accommodate the effects brought about by change could result in a formal education system that is out of step with the goals and needs of an information society. Only those educational institutions willing to take advantage of the opportunity to overcome and lead the processes of change will be prepared for the challenges of the future (McCune, 1991). However, there are signs that not all educational institutions are resisting change as indicated by their growing recognition of several worldwide phenomena: an information explosion of unprecedented magnitude; the rapid proliferation of new advanced technologies; significant changes in work practices; an increasingly fragile environment; the expanding interdependence of societies; and concerns about changes in established values and institutional practices.

As the restrictions of time and space become less problematic, new connections are being electronically forged from which the concepts of 'global villages' and 'networked communities' have gradually assumed prominence in learning design. Universities must acknowledge the realities of an electronically connected world otherwise they risk losing a unique opportunity to become the main drivers of a new dynamic vision for the future of learning. Just as the origins of the modern university arose out of the decisive changes that ultimately defined the existing boundaries of knowledge and learning, the new reality is that the old traditions are fast becoming obsolete due to the pressures information and communications technologies (ICT) are exerting on the role and purpose of learning.

Redefining the boundaries both within and outside the university sector will be the key to ensuring its relevance in the coming decade. At each of the local, national, and international levels, networked groups and organisations will assume greater prominence through inter-institutional cooperation and the interconnection of knowledge disciplines that will result from the convergence of highly advanced learning environments and 'just-in-time' access to vast repositories of networked resources. Collectively, these factors will lead to a radical rethink on the value of the relationships that are conducive to achieving genuine 'collaboration' as opposed to the longstanding industrial notion of 'competition'. In time, the traditional classroom may be replaced by 'virtual' communities of learning as new forms of delivery are devised and the purpose of learning is tested against the demands of the digital age. A number of significant trends support these claims (Siemens, 2004, p. 1):

- many learners will move into a variety of unrelated careers over the course of their lifetime
- informal learning is now recognised as a significant aspect of the learning experience. Learning now occurs in a variety of ways – through communities of interest, personal networks, and work-related activities. Formal education is no longer the primary source of learning.

- learning is a continual process lasting a lifetime, so that learning and work related activities are no longer separate. For many individuals, they are the same.
- technology is altering (rewiring) our brains. The tools we use define and reshape our thinking.
- both organisations and the individual are now viewed as learning organisms. Increased attention to information/knowledge management highlights the need for a theoretical base on which to explain the link between individual and organised learning.
- many of the processes previously structured by learning theories (especially cognitive information processing and constructivism) are now supported by technology
- 'know-how' and 'know-what' are being supplemented with 'know-where' (an understanding of where to locate the knowledge needed to complete a task).

If the implications of technology-directed change are ignored, most notably in relation to learning, then the task of managing an exploding information and knowledge base will soon become insurmountable. As Hill and Hannafin (2001, p. 1) observe, while the potential of technology for enhancing teaching and learning may be substantial, it may also be the case that accepted educational practices will not prepare graduates for the demands of an information driven society. Thus, it would seem prudent that in order to manage change, education must first identify the changes to teaching and learning that are now occurring in response to the rising influence of the digital world. Otherwise, it is likely that within the coming decade, the skills and thinking abilities currently taught to students will not support their career needs once they graduate. Some understanding of the issues and preferences that need to be addressed in relation to current and future graduates is provided in a report recently released by the Greater Expectations National Panel (2005, pp. 1 - 3). One of the key recommendations calls for a dramatic reorganisation of undergraduate education to ensure that all college aspirants gain not just entry into college, but access to an education of lasting value. A new vision points to the kind of learning students will need to manage the challenges of a changing workplace in a complex, interconnected world.

Other current research literature reveals that within the Australian context, technology is changing at such an accelerated rate it is difficult to comprehend the full extent of the possibilities that will emerge as a result. The consensus is that the student of the future must develop a broad knowledge base and prepare to be flexible in all their endeavours.

Students will need to absorb new concepts and technologies quickly and understand that without the skills to learn they will not be equipped to compete in a complex digital world. The graduate of the future cannot afford to focus only on one discipline without a good understanding of at least one other discipline. Thus, part of the new flexibility will be to undertake cross-discipline research and studies. Preferably, future graduates will need to acquire a balanced mix of several disciplines all of which require a technological mindset. Teaching must therefore move away from core disciplines and faculties, and embrace an interdisciplinary model. As a start, the most optimal strategy is for educators to encourage students to apply a lifelong approach to all their learning and research activities. Increasingly, Australian tertiary institutions permit students to undertake hybrid degrees as research expands into cross-disciplinary research and studies. In summary, as they progress through grades K-12 and then onto the undergraduate years, and at successively more challenging levels, students should learn to:

- effectively communicate orally, visually, in writing, and in a second language
- understand and employ quantitative and qualitative analysis to solve problems
- interpret and evaluate information from a variety of sources
- understand and work within complex systems and with diverse groups
- demonstrate intellectual agility and the ability to manage change
- transform information into knowledge and knowledge into judgment and action.

3. Technology is Transforming the Role and Purpose of Learning

The rapid acceptance of the Internet, combined with the inexorable World Wide Web led revolution in information distribution has given rise to new, previously unknown dimensions in human communications and expression that directly challenge accepted cultural and institutional boundaries. Moreover, the convergence between computers and communications has created 'virtual' communities and organisations in all fields of endeavour made possible due to the removal of the age-old barriers of time and distance. In the past, these barriers precluded collaboration on a wide range of tasks and activities. Because these restrictions are no longer a factor, it has become feasible for students and teachers from all over the world to 'meet', collaborate, and exchange views. However, the impact of the recent developments on the way humans interact, construct and apply knowledge using ICT is at present unknown, particularly in relation to education. What is known is that students can be taught to be competent in the use nonlinear forms of digitised text and images that encourage the application of visual literacy skills and permit interactive authoring. Static print formats and passive absorption of knowledge can be replaced with the provision of multiple connections to electronic information augmented by active participation in the construction of knowledge. To date, educators have acquired little more than a brief insight into the enormous potential of technology as an aid to learning.

Even though 15 years have passed, Healy (1991) proposed that if students are to experience the type of meaningful learning that will enable them to manage the challenges of the information age, then three convergent elements are necessary. That is, meaningful learning occurs at the point where developmental readiness, curiosity, and new subject matter combine to create previously unrecognised learning experiences. However, the task of bringing all three elements together to produce quality learning is not always a straightforward process. This is because the culture of many organisations and homes are characterised by fast-paced lifestyles combined with an increasing desire for instant, visual gratification, which to some extent is attributable to a growing need to cope with rapid technological change. Healy further warned that these new cultural 'norms' may in effect impede meaningful learning as indicated by shorter attention spans, an inability to express ideas verbally, a reduced capacity to reason analytically, and an absence of transferable problem solving skills.

If no attempt is made to address the potential barriers to learning noted above it will become increasingly difficult, if not impossible, to equip students with the skills required for managing the demands of the digital age. The successful transition from formal education to coping with the demands of a fast changing future remains largely contingent upon ensuring students are equipped with the 'traditional' skills of higher order thinking, critical analysis, problem-solving, research, communication and writing. Equally important, is the need for skills that are best developed through teamwork: group presentation, negotiation and conflict resolution, the provision and acceptance of feedback, active listening, cross-cultural communication, and last but not least, time and project management. What I am alluding to here is the educational significance and value of collaborative learning environments. The acquisition of thinking skills and the conversion of information into knowledge are not isolated processes. Many factors must contribute to the creation of learning environments in which the requisite skills of an information age may be cultivated. Often the outcome is the result of group dynamics forming an interactive synergy in which the whole becomes more than the sum of the parts. Given the complexity of the task, how can educators begin to teach students the skills that are relevant to a digital world? The short answer is that the level of competency and complexity required is such that learners must also acquire information processing and knowledge creation skills.

4. Managing an Expanding Body of Knowledge

As the new computer and communications technologies become more sophisticated and enhance the processes by which information can be manipulated and distributed, our understanding of knowledge is constantly being transformed and redescribed. The problems and possibilities that emerge whenever information is applied to divergent knowledge domains are highly varied and unpredictable. The inevitable outcome of these complex processes is increasing quantities of information and knowledge produced at rates that are impossible for the human mind to comprehend. In the face of rapidly expanding networks of readily accessible information, the implications for sustaining productive management and critical inquiry should not be ignored.

Then there is also the blurring of boundaries between discipline areas to consider. As the quantum of available information expands, newer, more diverse fields of knowledge are being defined and redefined, making it difficult to preserve existing boundaries and avoid further diversification and division. An increase in the number of speciality disciplines reduces the learner's capacity to grasp the broader conceptual underpinnings that thread throughout all areas of knowledge. The effective and creative management of an exponentially expanding knowledge base requires the strategic application of higher order thinking skills combined with a need to remember that each area of knowledge is in fact an integral part of a broader epistemological whole.

If university graduates are to cope with future skill demands and work practices, they must understand knowledge is constantly subject to change. The only constant is change itself. It is also vital that teachers encourage students to develop advanced levels of proficiency in problem-solving and critical analysis skills. Otherwise, their ability to derive new or useful knowledge from information (knowledge construction) is adversely limited. Any increase in the volume of available information diminishes the capacity to discern fact from fiction, useful information from useless information, and to convert quality information into meaningful knowledge. To have any chance of success in achieving complex levels of critical awareness, not only must learners apply higher order cognitive skills to enable the collection, management and analysis of data and information (information processing), but systems thinking and metacognition skills must also be mastered in ways that enhance the effective management of information. Thus, it is increasingly essential learners develop a heightened awareness of the many complex and multi-faceted issues that will be encountered during the course of their life. As a useful starting point, Schuur (2003, pp. 3 & 7) outlines the design of learning environments for the future and provides a vision of ICT based learning by raising a series of discussion points aimed at promoting greater awareness of the issues involved:

- eLearning should offer possibilities for ordering and classifying the most important information and knowledge and make it accessible both technically and through the use of mental schemas
- in the age of networking, community networks are crucial. Given that a network consists of nodes and connections, eLearning should focus on strengthening the competencies of the individual and on developing connections between individuals (communication).
- although learning is important in terms of content, the focus of design should also be on the development of processes in learning delivery and on managing the complexities of the system
- new learning paradigms should be defined and adopted where learning systems are not restricted to existing learning philosophies and become relevant to a networked society
- eLearning environments should fulfil the needs of the user. Often a simple resource can be more effective than a well-composed, complete and complex learning environment, and

- evaluation of eLearning environments must be a continuous iterative process, and should focus more on the criteria of the user, than on design, functionality, or cost benefit.

5. Accommodating the Needs of Learners

The increasing presence of ubiquitous, flexible technologies has led to new complex interactions between the technology-based classroom activities of today's youth and their out of school, post school experiences. Where young people are concerned, the new technologies constitute a natural part of the environment. As they grow into adulthood, they will naturally strive to extend the boundaries of the available digital innovations and associated activities, which could for example extend to self-directed learning. In the process, it is likely that innovations in information and communication technologies will continue to be adapted and refined to support the complex, learning activities of diverse and widely distributed networks of online users (Candy, 2004). Thus, designers of learning environments must distinguish between the information-age mindset that has become more common amongst students growing up in a globally connected, digitally defined information culture, and the more prevalent industrial mode of thinking.

In his examination of current generational uses of information and communication technologies, Candy (2004) concludes that an unexpected yet fundamental reconceptualisation of the purpose of learning has emerged over recent years. The extent of this shift is such that it represents a marked transformation in the learning expectations of young people, which is partly attributable to the fact that they are viewed as the most innovative exploiters of the new mediums, and partly because they will become the next generation of self-directed adult learners. The Millennials (approximate birth years 1976 to 2000) for example, have grown up in a world where computers, cell phones, and cable television are a normal part of everyday life. They are inundated with information from a multitude of sources, and are capable of using a wide variety of media and devices to communicate, learn, and to be entertained. The most favoured methods are those that permit instantaneous, concurrent communication with multiple people regardless of geographic boundaries. Millennials are also a genuinely interactive generation (Mask, 2002) in that virtual chat is used to communicate directly with their peers. Chat archives attest to the frequent and topical use of the Internet in late night, peer-to-peer conversations that are conducted within the boundaries of their own unique cultural framework (Carmean & Haefner, 2002). Today's students not only regularly engage in interactive communications, they expect it. As a result, they are exposed to an unprecedented flow of customs and ideas that is so unique it may represent a significant step in the development of human cognitive processing.

Success in meeting the needs of future learners requires radically new design methods and learning strategies. Such strategies may include the provision of content interactive features that offer for example: 'intelligent' search tools capable of meaningfully interpreting learner input; the ability to input and record ideas online that automatically trigger dedicated 'intelligent agents' designed to seek out and display supporting information; user (manual) and dynamically (automatic) generated supplementary materials relative to students' progress, learning styles, and visual preferences; and the 'intelligent' display of customised content such as interactive assessments and constructive feedback tailored to students' immediate learning needs. For such interventions and strategies to be effective, university libraries must become a key source of learning materials in a vast, complex network of digitised information and resources. In effect, the fundamental nature of the online learning environment must undergo dramatic transformation, in particular the use of ICT, educational design, online learning strategies, and universal access to high quality learning resources irrespective of device, location and time.

If resolving the diverse needs and expectations outlined above seem difficult enough, then consider that the Internet may be cultivating a new type of user who is developing hitherto unexpected proficiencies in navigating electronic environments. Students of today display a remarkable adeptness in juggling text, popup-windows, and hyperlinks simultaneously – strong indicators of a transition in culture and cognition. Current generation students are developing the ability to operate in complex digital environments and no longer prefer to use the printed page. What at first may appear to be an inability to focus might in fact be a preference for working in digital environments. As alluded to earlier, we may be witnessing the emergence of new cognitive capabilities.

A thorough understanding of how students cope in complex information environments will inevitably trigger a major rethink on human computer interfaces (HCI), web layout design, and navigation strategies. The development of delivery systems and interfaces to support the changing needs of learners raises a number of fundamental research issues around the use of flexible, adaptive HCI based on natural forms of interaction and intelligent response mechanisms tailored to the expectations of both current and future generations. In practice, these preferences may compel educational designers to rethink their approach to learning design. We have known for some time that it is no longer adequate to convert printed materials into a digital format without further adjustment. Many users do not respond to the screen in the same way as they do to the printed page. Hence, particular emphasis is placed on screen layout, image position, animation, video, audio, colours, textures, font type, size and style. Page sequencing, navigation and hyperlink options are designed first to attract the learner's attention and second, as a prompt for locating and accessing information.

As an indication of what may be in store for learners, consider the work of the Columbia Centre for New Media, Teaching and Learning (CCNMTL) at Columbia University in New York. The CCNMTL is working closely with the university library to create electronic multimedia study environments (MSEs) on topics ranging from history to literature to sociology. Access to texts is enabled in digital form through MSEs and the Web. At present, searchable text for more than 10,000 books is available online. Faculty and students are able to access fully-digitised encyclopaedia entries, dictionaries and other reference sources. These developments permit a 'search inside the book' approach to research and information gathering. For students of the future, search engines and hyperlinks will replace indexes and bibliographies while a 'search inside the book' technology will replace concordances. These transmutations from print-based to digital-based methods are clearly one step removed from delivering 'just-in-time', 'on-the-fly', and incremental learning environments. The notion of a 'borderless learning environment' is becoming a reality.

6. The Effects of Technological Change

The computer should no longer be viewed just as an analytical device: it is also a gateway to a vast global storehouse of information and teaching resources. The strength of the web is that it is both desirable and feasible to access information and deliver engaging learning environments anywhere, anytime. Using the right technology, traditionally separate nodes of information can be interlinked in highly imaginative and creative ways. For example, learning objects (to be described later) hold the potential to extend the learning experience beyond accepted epistemological boundaries as delineated by established disciplines and specialist subject areas. By designing learning environments that assist learners to connect and reconnect new insights to multiple contexts, it may be possible to enhance their capacity to learn. The vision of a distributed network system of learning resources can be extended to include the delivery of exactly the right content, at the right time, in the right amount of detail, and via the right device to match the specific needs of individual learners. The possibilities are endless.

The assumption (some would say the problem) that has prevailed whenever a new technology is introduced whether it be television, hypertext, hypermedia, multi-media, presentation slides, interactive video or even the web, has been the continual reliance on a transmissionist pedagogy. Still today, we are witnessing the unconscious transference of the same approach to the often-misunderstood terms 'eLearning' and 'flexible learning'. Compounding the confusion even further, are the many attempts to introduce collaborative learning environments intended to emphasise constructivist principles using online discussion boards and chat lines. What is overlooked in many instances is that the transmissionist model prevails while the transference model fails to be fully realised. The irony of a lack of comprehension of what the new technologies afford is that for many decades a well-known example of transference learning has been readily available. It is generally referred to as the 'OxBridge' (Oxford/Cambridge) tutorial model.

While 'technically' students may be ready to engage in the digital world, can we be sure they are adequately prepared for learning in the electronic environment? Using the Internet as a mode for delivering teaching does not necessarily translate to quality learning outcomes (let alone improve learning outcomes). As Taylor (2002, p. 11) reminds us, there are many factors to consider:

> In efforts to determine an appropriate approach to online teaching and learning, there is a need to acknowledge the importance of the complex interplay of different epistemologies, modes of thinking and associated types of subject matter in different academic disciplines, different educational objectives

for a course of study, and not least, the extant levels of expertise of the student target audience.

With any form of information or knowledge, providing students with access to meaningful content does not guarantee learning, a factor frequently overlooked by developers of WWW based learning materials. What is also important to learning are the levels of learner engagement (Oliver, Omari & Herrington (1998, p 121).

The key to implementing the type of changes necessary for success in delivering quality learning during the coming decade is the need to undo the thinking of the past. A good start is a planned holistic approach to curriculum design that:

- recognises a larger scale of commitment is required to ensuring the overall quality of teaching resources and learning outcomes are not compromised
- reappraises the nature of 'what is taught' and 'why it is taught'. Teaching materials continue to be delivered using traditional design approaches without recognising that the new technologies have opened up new insights into learning design.
- questions the goals of education and what students are expected to learn by the time they graduate. There is a clear need to prepare graduates for a highly complex, more dynamic future than many of us have experienced. This can be achieved by placing greater emphasis on information and knowledge management, problem solving and analysis skills, and cultivating a lifelong approach to learning.

The challenge for lecturers and content developers is to construct environments that are concurrently learning centred, content centred, community centred, and assessment centred. There is no single, correct medium for delivering eLearning, nor is there a set of formulaic specifications that dictates the kind of interaction most conducive to learning in all domains for all learners. Rather, lecturers must develop their eLearning skills so that they can respond to student and curriculum needs by developing a wide range of activities that are adaptable to the diverse variety of student needs. Table 23.1 illustrates how the affordances of these emerging technologies can be directed to create environments that support "how people learn" (Anderson, 2004, p. 54).

Table 23.1. Affordances of the Network Environment and the Attributes of "How people learn"

"How people learn" framework (Bransford et al.)	Affordances of the current Web	Affordances of the Emerging Semantic Web
Learner centred	Capacity to support individualised and community centred learning activities.	Content that changes in response to individualised and group learner models
Knowledge centred	Direct access to vast libraries of content and learning activities organised from a variety of discipline perspectives	Agents for selecting, personalising, and reusing content
Community centred	Asynchronous and synchronous; collaborative and individual interactions in many formats	Agents for translating, reformatting, time shifting, monitoring, and summarising community interactions
Assessment centred	Shifted multiple time and place opportunities for formative and summative assessment by self, peers, and teachers	Agents for assessing, critiquing, and providing "just in time feedback"

High on the list of priorities for any educational institution aspiring to promote innovative teaching practices should be a comprehensive research plan for realising the potential advantages of seamlessly blending the known modes of learning with information and communications technologies (ICT) to deliver flexible learning solutions. To this end, the essential focus of all ICT related research is to identify and explore the educational benefits that can be derived by applying advanced learning techniques, methodologies and pedagogical innovations to the complex task of delivering personalised learning environments tailored to the specific needs of all individuals. The development of online delivery systems that support flexible learning options inevitably raises a number of crucial research issues. The first (noted beforehand) applies to the design, development and use of flexible, adaptive human computer interfaces (HCI). To be effective, such interfaces must not only interact with and respond directly to learners' needs, but also intuitively and cost effectively align with the diverse preferences and requirements of lecturers, students, and institutions alike. Then there are the recent innovations aimed at enabling ubiquitous access to learning through the use of portable devices such as laptops and personal digital assistants (PDAs) that further engender issues arising from: the educational value of synchronous and asynchronous interactions; the efficient storage and appropriate display of learning resources to suit all screen sizes; and, the complexities of interface design and performance efficiency. Alongside these complex issues are the broader questions of accepted standards and specifications to permit automatic transference and interoperability of solutions across all delivery platforms regardless of the learner's location and preferred method of access. Most important however, is the need to ensure that the inherent design structures supporting advanced delivery systems at best align with, but preferably exceed proven best practices in ICT supported learning.

Another major challenge for educationalists is to design and deliver innovative solutions that represent and facilitate navigation of complex knowledge structures. In addition, advanced learning design methodologies must be devised that employ emerging technologies to support the refinement of the higher order cognitive skills of analysis, problem-solving, conceptual thinking, and metacognition (which is dependent on tacit, experiential knowledge). Such skills will be highly valued by individuals, organisations, and society in general. However, proficiency in the application of higher order cognitive competencies to the creative construction of knowledge extends well beyond the transmission of prescribed knowledge and related prerequisite skills. This in turn raises the many latent and complex problems of how to model and structure knowledge and how to predetermine the relationships that connect knowledge structures to selected teaching content while taking into account their contextual relevance and innate cultural biases. Resolving such issues requires an unreserved commitment to: identifying the key properties and relationships that serve to model the structure of targeted knowledge domains to provide effective navigational strategies; devising 'intelligent' methods for managing and transferring knowledge skills; and, the strategic deployment of teaching resources through the dynamic generation and contextualisation of the content to be displayed within a given learning environment. With these goals in mind, the ideal learning environment should also assist learners to derive answers to the broad level 'meta-questions' of: how do I know what I need to learn?; how do I get there?; how am I progressing?; are my goals still relevant?; what are the best learning models for me?; and, what are the effects of social change, culture, and market needs on my personal learning goals?

The social element of collaborative learning also poses significant challenges to ICT supported systems, in particular environments in which the relationship between collaboration and learning is crucial. As many educators would agree, there are many instances where learning is a collaborative activity, involving active interchange of ideas and views between individuals within a community and between communities, or amongst individuals and other communities. Some communities may confine their focus to the knowledge and skills of a specific profession or others may span several disciplines united by a common purpose (operating for example, as a multi-disciplinary networked partnership). Alternatively, a networked community may be structured as a single organisation or span many organisations. Given the complexities and issues raised thus far, delivery systems designed for ICT supported collaborative learning must also:

- enable productive social interactions in a virtual world
- identify and provide for the needs of communities of interest established within broader networks of learners
- define learners' roles and accommodate both individual and group preferences and behaviours
- manage the creation and transfer of knowledge within virtual learning communities, and,
- establish the ownership of knowledge generated by individual learners and groups participating within and across networked communities.

Regardless of what the future holds, we must not lose sight of the fact that ready access to information is not the same as learning, more specifically the depth of learning that takes advantage of the immediacy of face-to-face and ICT mediated communications. In a similar way, the design of most web-based learning solutions has amounted to little more than a digitised replication of traditional publishing formats that rely on fixed modes of delivery. As a result, the learning effectiveness has been open to question and criticism. In a climate where is generally recognised that learning design is shifting towards learner-centric, responsive, and highly flexible modes of delivery, the current use of the web as a learning tool is no longer suited to meeting students' needs. What is required for a technology driven future are delivery platforms that permit content developers to create environments designed to work the way a learner thinks. This model of online learning demands a radically different approach to web design, navigation and interaction that in turn requires a comprehensive reappraisal of content delivery platform functionality. Underpinning this same model is the notion of applying an 'all sizes possible' approach to replace the current pedagogically restrictive 'one size fits all' delivery platforms.

7. Strategies for Designing Advanced Learning Environments

As touched on several times, the new technologies are changing not only what students learn, but also how they learn. That is, curricula must eventually align with the demands of the digital age by focusing less on 'knowing facts' and more on 'strategies for learning that which is not known' (in the sense that learning must be given greater priority over the skill of memorising facts). Success in acquiring such skills requires that learners are provided the freedom and the resources that will motivate them to be active and independent. In this model, the teacher serves as a facilitator or consultant, not as the sole provider of information. Furthermore, access to education should not be confined to schools, technical colleges, and universities. Learning opportunities reside not just within these institutions, but also in homes, community centres, art galleries, museums, and workplaces. Perhaps the direction that needs to be considered is less about choice between institutions, and more about choice in what students learn, and how they prefer to learn. Already there are many educational institutions that advocate a 'learning to learn' agenda that encourages students to be more involved in making decisions about the way they learn (Leadbeater, 2004). Such shifts in thinking naturally introduce the notion of advanced learning environments in which students are enabled to learn in a way that best matches their individual characteristics and needs.

No longer is it enough to offer information online. Ultimately, researchers will need to devise new learning technologies attuned to the needs of current and future generations of learners. Over the coming decade, new methods for the design and delivery of challenging, highly interactive learning environments are crucial to the success of learning. As made evident thus far, already today's youth show signs of a readiness to be much more creative with computers than many educators recognise. Therefore, it is argued that new learning design models are required that demonstrate how personal needs and preferences can be taken into account within a framework of universal relevance and benefit to divergent generational groups. Leadbeater (2004) suggests it may be useful to think about learning from another perspective. He points out that today's youth are far more avid and aware than previous generations. They have developed an entrenched sub-culture that is bound to exert an effect on how they perceive learning and education should be provided. Many secondary school age youth now possess mobile phones, which provide instant access to services twenty-four hours, seven days a week, thus creating an expectation that all services should be made available in a similar manner. They have also become accustomed to a world in which they can search for, download and share digital music on the Internet. Their inventiveness and desire for innovative thinking is evidenced in the way they have developed uses for new technologies that were not anticipated by the original designers. A simple but notable example is the pervasive use of SMS messaging, which has led to the invention of a shorthand language for quickly conveying large amounts of information. Hence, the common use of the term 'thumb people' that refers primarily to SMS messages and more generally, to those using the new technologies (Candy, 2004). What is now needed are the hardware and software solutions that will permit learners to be fully immersed in seeking out and creating new knowledge.

One of the strongest arguments for promoting advanced learning environments lies in the potential to improve and even revolutionise teaching and learning. However, the evidence to date does not support this view as effective forward thinking methods for delivering teaching and learning using ICT have not yet materialised. As a result, a great deal of scepticism surrounds the promises of a revolutionary effect of the new technologies on learning. Of the many approaches available today, learning object technology offers the most potential (OECD, 2005, pp 109 & 221).

Learning objects are the 'technology-in-waiting' that could 'enable' the models described (later) in this chapter to be put into practice. The inherent attributes of learning objects are such that they permit notions of 'systems-based' design models comprised of multiple nested levels, all interrelated through complex networks of connections that provide the means for all participants to contribute to the learning process (for each of the individual, group, and the institutional levels). In this model, it is the 'negotiation of new meanings' rather than 'decision-making' that leads to the emergence of new knowledge. Thus, 'vertical' hierarchies of knowledge transference can be complemented by 'horizontal', knowledge-sharing communities of interest and practice (Wenger, 2005, p. 31) where all 'constituent components' (learners, academics, administrators) benefit. Weblogs for example, illustrate this model of learning interactivity. Communities of practice are in effect 'networked learning systems' representing a systemic approach to learning design and delivery that 'connects' all participants and learning system components across multiple levels of practice and inquiry. In brief, the key principles that apply to systems theory include:

- all systems are nested within other systems that interact in a network fashion, or more simply, networks within networks that have no hierarchical structure, only larger or smaller systems networked with other systems.
- nature does not reveal the existence of independent components, but instead appears as a complex web of relationships between the various parts of a unified whole
- all systems are integrated wholes whose properties cannot be reduced to those of the smaller parts. Systemic properties are destroyed when a system is reduced to its component parts.
- the essential or 'systemic' properties of the whole arise from the 'organising relations' of the parts (Sheldrake, 1988, p. 314)
- the simple laws that govern the various elements of a system also act to generate behaviour that extends far beyond their individual capacities (Holland, 1998, p. 5)
- all system levels represent differing levels of complexity where each level exhibits unique phenomena known as 'emergent' properties
- properties of emergence displayed at one level, do not exist at lower system levels (Capra, 1996, p. 37).

The use of digitised learning objects has the capacity to enable learners to explore information and knowledge in ways that until now have not been feasible. Rather than divide the curriculum into bounded disciplines and subject areas, the focus of learning could be directed toward identifying and exploring the rich connections that thread throughout different knowledge domains utilising key concepts, themes, and issues. In this model, concepts that are not introduced until university level could be accessed and made available to learners of all age groups (Resnick, 2002). As indicated earlier, it should not be assumed that learning takes place within set age groups and confined to timetabled schedules. The new digital technologies permit convenient access to learning from all locations and throughout all stages of life. Thus, the traditional classroom as we know it needs to be fundamentally reorganised. Students should not be grouped according to age, but instead all age groups could be encouraged to work together on team projects thus empowering them to learn from one another and to teach each other. Learners could also be given opportunities to collaborate over extended periods thereby enabling them to explore ideas in more meaningful ways that are relevant to their personal experiences and needs. As the full potential of the new technologies are gradually realised by greater numbers of individuals and institutions, new learning opportunities will surface, prompting the emergence of virtual networked communities or "knowledge building communities" in which individuals located anywhere in the world collaborate and learn.

In practice, learning objects foreshadow the phasing out of the traditional design model where the individual academic is responsible for the majority of the work (and where courses are generally created new rather than complied from existing resources). Instead, the lecturer and content designer can work in partnership to assemble a course largely or entirely from third-party materials, or even adopt a complete third party course (OECD, 2005). This brief introduction into learning objects underpins all of proposed learning models to be described in the next section. Note also, that the flexible delivery approach applies to all the models described thereafter.

8. Exploring the Possibilities - Future Trends

With careful planning, it is feasible to structure learning environments that address many of the issues outlined to this point. Future learning models that potentially support research studies aimed at devising advanced learning environments include applications such as: Flexible Learning; Intelligent Learning Support Systems; Individualisation / Personalisation of Learning; Networked Learning Communities;

Contextualised Learning; and, Systems Design; each of which could inspire the development of new learning technologies. The models described in the following pages provide some indication of the research to naturally arise from the preceding discussions. Note however, the models as outlined are not exclusively independent. Elements of each may be extracted and recombined in a number of potentially useful ways to form new models more suited to addressing the required learning needs.

8.1 Flexible delivery

The key to visualising a model of learning suited to the needs of learners now and in the future is to examine the implications and benefits of a flexible delivery approach to learning. In general terms, most definitions of flexible delivery encompass dimensions of time (learning opportunities are available anytime) and space (access to learning is provided anywhere from the main campus to many locations around the world). Some definitions may incorporate various mixes of information and communications technologies combined with one or more modes of learning (face-to-face, audio and video resources, print-based material, CD-ROM and other computer-based resources, and online). In essence, most descriptions infer a delivery approach that provides for all possible choices of all available modes, across all courses, for all students. In determining the implications of establishing an effective flexible delivery programme, a useful starting point is to consider the key elements of a working definition of flexible delivery. Two broad descriptions of flexible teaching and learning provide useful directions:

> Flexibility in learning is not an end in itself but a means of achieving core educational objectives, and ultimately producing more skilled and satisfied students and teachers. It should never be simply equated with on-line learning (Reid, 2002, p. 9).

> Quality teaching is about finding the right balance between face-to-face communications, interaction via other media and individual work so that each learning experience is maximised. Flexible delivery of teaching is not intended to cut costs but to improve access and the quality of the learning experience for students (DEST, 2002, p. 7).

From a teaching and learning perspective, a personal definition of flexible delivery that aspires to accommodate the individual needs of learners is expressed as follows:

> The capacity to deliver any mode of learning, at any time, to any place, in any combination, and permit learners to seamlessly move from any mode to another. All modes must include provision for multiple learning style preferences and permit lecturers to design and deliver teaching solutions using the full spectrum of learning theory principles ranging from behaviourist through to individual constructivist.

Three interdependent aspects are alluded to in the above: flexible delivery, flexible teaching and flexible learning. As a way of highlighting the need to examine what each aspect means in actual practice, it is useful to unpack their essential distinguishing features:

Flexible delivery is relatively easy to explain. The term 'relative' is used to highlight the fact that once we enter into an explanation of the remaining two terms it will become evident that not only are all three interrelated, but the level of complexity and the costs required to facilitate flexible teaching and flexible learning escalate considerably as we delve further into what is potentially feasible. An institution's ability to provide flexible delivery options is dependent on its administrative and technical infrastructure and its preferred modes of delivery. In general, the flexible delivery options provided will encompass face-to-face, paper-based and online distance education, open learning, all electronic modes including CDROM, videoconference, digitised library resources, discussion boards, whiteboards, personal digital assistants (PDAs) and wireless mobile devices.

Flexible teaching requires lecturers and tutors to be proficient in the design, provision, assessment and evaluation of learning materials for all available modes (or combinations thereof) of teaching as described above. The task of the online course designer and the lecturer is to choose, adapt, and perfect (through feedback, assessment, and reflection) educational activities that maximize the affordances of the chosen technologies. In doing so, they create learning-, knowledge-, assessment- and community-centred educational experiences aimed at delivering quality learning to all students.

Flexible learning is highly dependent on the available flexible delivery and flexible teaching provisions. As learner's demands for customisation and personalisation increases so too does the requirement to configure a more sophisticated technical infrastructure and either equip or enable lecturing staff to access increasingly higher levels of technical expertise and support. The level of complexity is further compounded by the learner's need for multi-modal delivery options that suit their changing circumstances, individual preferences, skill levels, work and social demands, and access opportunities all of which define their personal learning environment. For learning to be effective, students will need to plan and manage their time and possess the skills required to adapt to any mode of delivery and teaching without difficulty. In this model, students may choose to learn for many reasons: degree course; skills training/competency; professional development; research; collaborative networks (communities of practice / interest); just-in-time learning; on-the-fly learning; and incremental learning.

The ideal flexible delivery system will be based on a plan that flows from a full understanding of two fundamentals. That is, all teaching and learning systems should be built on the needs of students, and the learning outcomes of the course or programme (the knowledge, skills, and attributes that students need). In addition, it should not be assumed that flexible delivery is the same as 'distance education' or even online learning. Flexible learning subsumes all other delivery modes and should enable students to make choices as to how and when to learn in accordance with their unique circumstances and needs.

In devising an educationally sound flexible delivery model, teaching will involve facilitating learning rather than transmitting content. Learning environments will need to be designed so that they are highly customised and interactive, and challenge students to research, evaluate and apply information to solve complex problems. This means in effect, that academics involved in a flexible delivery programme need to be proficient in the use and application of a range of ICT skills including productivity tools, university delivery systems and the use of design tools for developing and delivering teaching units online. For this to occur, staff also need to work as members of a team to facilitate and support student learning. Thus, for learning to be effective, lecturing staff must share a common understanding of what flexible delivery entails and possess the skills, knowledge, and attitudes needed to support the agreed vision.

8.2 Intelligent learning support systems

The higher order thinking skills of problem solving and critical analysis require the ability to: see parts/wholes in relationship to each other; balance the processes of both analysis and synthesis; abstract and manage complex issues; adapt to real world change; and, command multiple strategies for solving problems. A learning model designed to cultivate such skills must first take into account a range of factors that include: the difficulty of interpreting interconnectedness or interdependency in complex systems; the problems of deriving meaning or managing the loss of meaning from a surfeit of information; tracking patterns of connection across divergent systems; and recognising properties of emergence in complex systems that are often difficult to interpret using simple trend analysis and future projection techniques (National Board of Employment, Education and Training, 1996).

The strategic use of digital technologies has enhanced our capacity to explore the inner workings of natural and human phenomena in ways that until now have not been possible. As a result, not only has there been a noticeable shift in what students learn, but also how they learn. To keep pace with these changes, the task of devising advanced models of learning must embody the development of highly innovative learning techniques, design methodologies and pedagogical strategies that are supported by 'intelligent' software agents. Other strategies that might provide new insights into educational design include the adaptation of games theory principles to enhance student interaction and motivation to engage in teaching content that place less emphasis on memorising facts and more on utilising cognitive strategies for discovering knowledge; and extending the support structures for teaching and learning to utilise digital libraries that deliver more than just content and instead assist the learner to organise, reflect, analyse and synthesise new knowledge. Learning models designed to teach abstract thinking and conceptual understanding could also be supported by 'intelligent' response mechanisms or agents, interfaces and portals that are designed to accommodate the diverse mental models or cognitive maps that learners draw on in their search for understanding in the construction of knowledge; and, rather than segment the curriculum into bounded disciplines and subject areas, the focus should be directed towards 'intelligently' enabling identification and exploration of the rich connections that thread throughout all knowledge domains.

8.3 Individualisation/personalisation of learning

Many educators now recognise that the current use of the web is no longer adequate for meeting the individual needs of all learners. In response, electronically mediated learning is moving towards learner-centric, 'intelligently' responsive, highly flexible modes of delivery. The design and development of online delivery solutions that assist learners to cultivate knowledge creation and thinking skills requires several interrelated areas of research: an analysis of the properties, modelling structures and representation of knowledge domains to facilitate strategic navigation using multiple learning pathways; methods for managing and transferring tacit and cognitive knowledge; and the contextualisation of information and knowledge to prompt user identification of the interrelationships that elicit metacognitive thinking. Just as important, the tacit knowledge skills of predictive analysis, creative thinking, entrepreneurial acumen, and the ability to move from problem solving to opportunity identification and acquisition, have not as yet, been comprehensively studied.

A parallel area of research applies to students' learning styles and their emerging cognitive skills. That is, to have any noticeable effect on learning outcomes, attention should be directed toward identifying and profiling learner behaviours to provide a useful benchmark for continuously monitoring, and refining the dynamic display of content based on individual attitudes to learning, technology and display preferences, communication skills, prior knowledge, and personal values. The tools and techniques that may assist to facilitate these goals include: the automation generation and updating of a learner profile utilising a software agent that monitors learner's progress and stores individual learning preferences; the individuation of learning styles and methodologies taking into account the cultural and generational aspects of learner preferences; and, the use of "intelligent' agents designed to provide feedback and interactive responses through the automatic selection and dynamic assembly of contextually relevant learning resources (as informed by the learner profile agent).

The advent of technically sophisticated delivery platforms such as content management systems offer the promise of accessing the myriad sources of digitised teaching resources located throughout the world, thus raising the possibility of 'borderless' learning environments. A networked system of learning resources could be configured to deliver content that extends the learning pathways to subject areas and disciplines that under normal circumstances may never be explored. Add to this vision the capacity for emerging technologies such as learning objects to deliver teaching materials directly matched to individual learning style preferences and the significance of undertaking research in this area is manifestly evident.

8.4 Networked learning communities

Learning is a collaborative activity involving active dialogue both within and between communities. The rapid acceptance of the Internet combined with the current revolution in information distribution spawned by the convergence of computers and communications technologies has given rise to the concept of 'virtual', networked communities. Composed of modular, interchangeable components, ICT supports the construction of flexible, networked, dynamic solutions for engaging human discourse and interaction. That is, ICT technologically empowers individuals and communities by facilitating the efficient distribution of information and knowledge to geographically dispersed audiences whilst enabling widespread contribution to decision-making activities. ICT also emulates how people function: integrating information, text, voice, images, and video in all their various formats, while providing a cost effective and efficient means of engaging in anywhere, anytime dialogue and collaboration. Students and teachers located around the world can now form communities of interest to discuss and exchange views. These same principles can also be applied to the design of electronic learning environments.

A networked learning environment can assist learners (individuals and groups) to seek greater value from their learning experiences. The fundamental components are people, places and ideas connected through a combination of design and random chance to inspire creative thinking and innovation. In turn, such interactions motivate learners to understand that a networked learning environment has the capacity to cultivate a climate in which new processes and systems may evolve or even spontaneously surface on occasion. Learning ensues when people interact with new ideas and concepts. Nonetheless, enhanced learning will not be the only outcome. Learning networks may also provide the catalyst to redefine what schools, colleges, and ultimately, what universities will do in the future. Economic and technological factors aside, signs of the complex issues to arise out of the changes described above are becoming evident, much of which will impact on the role of education and how learning will be delivered in the future.

8.5 Contextualised learning

As individuals encounter information from different perspectives and backgrounds, and for different purposes, so too does meaning change. The initial meaning of a picture, report, or graph is continually redefined according to pre-existing actions and events as well as the unique intentions and perceptions of different individuals. Once contextualised meaning has been established, information becomes organised as knowledge operating in a larger context of meaning encompassing many related patterns, biases, and interpretations. These ambiguities raise the perplexing question of how learning can be supported in complex information systems given that the meaning of the available information can change from user to user and in relation to the goals of individual learners.

The design of online environments using learning object technology provides much more than just a new way of organising content and the information it contains. It also has the potential to influence the meaning of the information provided. However, for learning to be effective, teaching resources must be contextualised in a way that governs the intended relevance and meaning and assists to fulfil the expected learning outcomes. An effective pedagogical strategy for influencing learner understanding is to apply selected teaching resources to varying contexts. Although a resource may be inherently meaningless, it is the act of embedding that same resource in alternative contexts that reveals new insights and meanings. As new data and information are presented to the learner, the relationships formed through past experiences are challenged and subsequently realigned, revealing new insights and unknown aspects that previously were not apparent. In this sense, context and content are interdependent. This notion raises deeper questions about knowledge for the act of knowing depends upon the meaningful organisation of data and information. Thus, new methods of organisation imply existing forms of knowledge must change in the process.

By manipulating context, it is not difficult to imagine learning activities where the right technology could assist students to be critical users of information. Learning objects afford the capacity to impose patterns of organisation on existing information and to facilitate the learner's ability to imagine new patterns of organisation through the formation of meaningful relationships. That is, whenever information is processed in some way, and reordered, reorganised, or re-categorised, new relationships and new meanings are formed. Learning objects could also be used to teach students multiple strategies for problem solving and information retrieval. Alternatively, learning objects may be programmed to assemble dynamically in ways that assist lecturers and students alike to focus on the critical processes of interpreting and organising information as opposed to the traditional tasks of acquiring and memorising facts. Lecturers therefore, can encourage learners to explore the interconnections between theory, content, and context. Thus, regardless of the learning activity, there will always remain a crucial role for the lecturer or tutor to provide continual guidance and support.

8.6 A systems design model

An alternative understanding of how information is organised or structured to infer meaning can be derived by determining the existing associations and/or interrelationships between collections and patterns of information (using principles of systems theory as applied to systems, sub-systems, and networked interrelationships). The application of systems principles to learning design provides the means to identify and define conceptual relationships, which in turn has the effect of fostering deeper insights into the information presented to the learner. These principles present a plausible theoretical foundation upon which a new, technologically driven model of learning may be established. Each principle holds the key to devising a range of strategies for manipulating learning objects that may assist learners to develop a broader, more holistic perspective as they work on the given course content. Whether applied separately or integrated as appropriate, a systems approach offers new opportunities to design online teaching environments that connect with other subject areas and even knowledge disciplines in ways that learners may otherwise not have considered. The benefit of course, is to provide the student increased exposure to new knowledge relationships and in so doing, gradually expand their conceptual schema into wider, more diverse cognitive perspectives. Thus, the significance of learning object technology is again underscored by the fact that it affords considerable flexibility in the design of electronic learning environments.

Given the potential for applying a more inclusive, systems design model, the educational implications of interconnected learning objects are profound. Beyond permitting students to proceed through electronic materials using prescribed pathways, they can focus their investigations on the questions that are informed by their own unique interests and experiences. Students are also able to organise and progress through the learning materials in ways that make sense to them while developing and comprehending their own heuristics. As new understandings emerge, they discuss their findings with their lecturer/tutor and fellow peers. This flexible 'connectivist' approach to inquiry and discussion has many advantages, not the least of which is a capacity to accommodate diverse personal or cultural learning styles. Notwithstanding the potential merits of this design approach, it is imperative to consider the learner's capacity to undertake independent learning. That is, in order to manage high levels of autonomy and faculty, learners must be experienced in identifying the relationships that connect the available data and information and to apply the insights gained to the construction of models and strategies that will assist them to become adept constructors of knowledge.

9. Final Thoughts: Toward a New Perspective on Learning Design

Although the design strategies proposed above are speculative at this stage, some direction on the future of learning may be gained from current developments. Computer technologies have reached a point where they provide exciting, motivating environments in which students can direct their own learning strategies. As part of their everyday activities, students now use computers to communicate with a diverse audience of teachers, peers, family, and contacts located anywhere throughout the world, all of which encourage the development of collaborative learning skills. The interactive nature of computers means that lecturers can pay more attention to facilitating learning rather than sustain the more traditional expository teaching approach. Of greater significance, the technological changes that are occurring throughout the world at present mean that the hierarchical, pre-structured learning models of the past can soon be replaced with more innovative design strategies. For example, learning environments could be designed to prompt students to reflect on their thinking. Learners could also be encouraged to solve problems for themselves or with their peers, explore alternative solutions to problems, carry out additional research, analyse and plan their work, and evaluate their own progress. From a social standpoint, they need to participate in group-based activities, articulate their ideas to their lecturers and fellow students, and work cooperatively with team members located anywhere around the globe.

With careful planning and judicious choice of design strategy, technology-based teaching and learning can be effective. Students can learn from interaction with multimedia and from collaboration with other students. Because of the improved instructional strategies and enhanced materials facilitated by the various mediums, students are afforded an opportunity to learn more effectively and in many cases, more efficiently. While not denying that some media will suit some students and not others, the provision of alternative media has the potential to match varying learning styles. Thus, the task of choosing a technology becomes one of comparing it with the identified learning needs. Moreover, any concern about choice should be less about the age of a given technology and more about its usefulness as an educational tool. Once freed from the question of which form of technology is superior to another, lecturers can concentrate their efforts towards discovering the most effective means of using technology to facilitate learning. In essence, we should ensure the computer, its software programmes, and most important, the lecturer's instructional approaches function in unison as a bridge between the knowledge to be learned and the learner's need to learn. The technology must also be accessible to the learner and yet remain true to the knowledge it presents. In this sense therefore, it is not appropriate to conclude that the computer, in and of itself, is the only agent of change.

Despite their growing complexity and sophistication, educational technologies alone cannot influence student learning. Computers enable the storage and delivery of information and instructions, but in themselves do not determine the quality of learning. Most research evidence to date suggests that computer-based teaching and learning are not always more effective than traditional teaching and learning practices. However, comparing the classroom with a computer screen is not a straightforward task. The educational value of computers cannot simply be measured by the manner in which content is displayed onscreen as ultimately, it is the innate processes of teaching and learning that will determine the quality of the educational outcomes. Educational technologies, in whatever form they are applied, are tools that require meticulous, skilled planning. Furthermore, while acknowledging the power of technology, it is essential to be aware of the need to develop a complex matrix of integrated learning tools and teaching strategies based on a proven framework of learning theories, pedagogical practices, and evaluation techniques. Perhaps (and only) then, is it possible to achieve what most educators would regard as an 'enhanced learning outcome' in a future that will be marked by extraordinary technological change.

Given the tenor of the viewpoints raised in this chapter, I re-emphasise that all research studies that focus on learning in the future should demonstrate a clear pedagogical and technological capacity to interweave all aspects of the learning process within a loosely structured (flexible) environment where the focus is on the learning needs of the individual. That is, addressing the quality and effectiveness of learning are not the only factors to consider. Future learning environments, regardless of delivery mode, should be inherently flexible to facilitate support for the divergent needs of current, past, and future generations. These needs apply to the distinctly divergent attributes of; technology use and skills; influences, preferences, needs and aspirations; values, perceptions and attitudes; and, current and future concerns. Emphasis must also be given to identifying and allowing for variations in learner behaviours, inter-personal communication skills, and preferred learning styles relative to all the available modes of learning. In other words, the full potential of educational technology cannot be realized without a detailed analysis of the factors that influence the interplay between technology, communication, media, human behaviour, and cognitive development. In essence, the design of advanced learning environments requires an evolving programme of research, design, experimentation, and development augmented by distinctly identifiable, yet highly interconnected and adaptable forms of delivery, support and resources.

In the final analysis, it is argued that learning in the future should aim to support the lifelong learning and personal development needs of all individuals through the provision of 'intelligently' supported (both the lecturer/tutor and software agents) and self-directed learning environments characterised by flexible, ubiquitous, mobile delivery at any time and to any place. A focus on flexible, individualised learning redirects research towards the design and creation of new models of learning while recognising the emergent need for learners to develop knowledge skills that are in constantly tune with evolving perspectives on the purpose of learning. Finally, in light of the many complexities and issues covered in this chapter, it is fitting the last words are given to David Ward (2000, p. 5):

> ...the survivors will be those institutions of higher learning with the courage to re-imagine and reinvent themselves and so find a place of intellectual and societal relevance on the beachhead of the twenty-first century.

References

Anderson, T. (2004). *Toward a theory of online learning* [Online]. Chapter in 'Theory and Practice of Online Learning'. Anderson, T. & F. Elloumi (Eds.), Athabasca University. Canada. Available: WWW Ref: http://www.cde.athabascau.ca/online_book.

Candy, P. C. (2004). *Linking thinking: Self-directed learning in the digital age.* Commonwealth of Australia. Research Fellowship Scheme of the Department of Education, Science and Training (DEST). August.

Capra, F. (1996). *The web of life.* London, UK: Harper Collins.

Carmean, C. & Haefner, J. (2002). Mind over matter: Transforming course management systems into effective learning environments. *Educause Review.* November/December. 5.

Department of Education, Science and Training (DEST). (2002). *Higher education review process. Striving for quality: Learning, teaching and scholarship* [Online]. Report No. 6891HERC02A. Section 6: Accepting and Adapting to a New Teaching and Learning Context. Available: WWW Ref.
http://www.backingaustraliasfuture.gov.au/publications/striving_for_quality/default.htm#contents.

Greater Expectations National Panel. (2002). *Greater expectations: A new vision for learning as a nation goes to college* [Online]. The Association of American Colleges and Universities. Available: WWW Ref. http://www.greaterexpectations.org/.

Healy, J. M. (1991). Endangered minds. In D. Dickinson (Ed.), *Creating the future: Perspectives on educational change.* Aston Clinton, Bucks, UK: Accelerated Learning Systems Limited. 52-8.

Hill, J. R. & Hannafin, M. J. (2001). Teaching and learning in digital environments: The resurgence of resource-based learning. *Educational Technology, Research and Development, 49* (3).

Holland, J. H. (1998). *Emergence from chaos to order.* Reading, Berkshire, UK: Oxford University Press.

Leadbeater, C. (2004). *Learning about personalisation: How can we put the learner at the heart of the education system? Teachers transforming teaching* [Online]. Available: WWW Ref. http://www.standards.dfes.gov.uk/innovation-unit.

McCune, S. D. (1991). Restructuring education. In D. Dickinson (Ed.), *Creating the future: Perspectives on educational change* (pp. 162-182). Aston Clinton, Bucks, UK: Accelerated Learning Systems Limited.

McLean, N. & Lynch, C. (2004). *Interoperability between library information services and learning environments – Bridging the gaps* [Online]. A Joint White Paper on behalf of the IMS Global Learning Consortium and the Coalition for Networked Information. May 10. Available: WWW Ref. http://www.imsglobal.org/digitalrepositories/ CNIandIMS_2004.pdf.

Mask, T. (2002). Are *millennials smarter?* [Online]. Available: WWW Ref. http://www.millennials.com/CognitiveMask.html.

National Board of Employment, Education and Training. (1996). *Education and Technology Convergence: A Survey of Technological Infrastructure in Education.* Canberra, ACT: Employment and Skills Council, Commissioned Report No. 43.

Oliver, R., Omari, A., & Herrington, J. (1998). Investigating implementation strategies for WWW based learning environments. *International Journal of Instructional Media, 25* (2), 121.

Organisation for Economic Co-operation and Development (OECD). (2005). *E-Learning in tertiary education: Where do we stand?* [Online]. Report written by The OECD Centre for Educational Research and Innovation (CERI). 109 and 221. Available: WWW Ref. http://www.cudi.edu.mx/educacion/publicaciones/E_Learning_Tertiar y_Education.pdf.

Reid, I. (2002). *Distance education in a flexible learning environment: Trends and prospects for Edith Cowan University.* Perth, Western Australia: Edith Cowan University.

Resnick, M., (2002). *Rethinking learning in the digital age.* The Media Laboratory. Massachusetts Institute of Technology. Chapter 3. 32-37.

Schuur, K. (2003). *A holistic vision of the future of eLearning* [Online]. Paper presented to a seminar series on Exploring models and partnerships for eLearning in SMEs, held in Stirling, Scotland and Brussels, Belgium. Available: WWW Ref. http://www.theknownet.com/ict_smes_seminars/papers/Schuur.html.

Sheldrake, R. (1988). *The presence of the past*. London, UK: William Collins Sons and Co.

Siemens, G. (2004). *Connectivism: A learning theory for the digital age* [Online]. Available: WWW Ref. http://www.connectivism.ca.

Taylor, J. C. (2002). *Automating e-Learning: The higher education revolution* [Online]. Available: WWW Ref. http://www.usq.eud.au/users/taylorj.

Ward, D. (2000). Catching the waves of change in American Higher Education [Online]. *Educause Review.* January/February, 5th. Available: WWW Ref. http://www.educause.edu/pub/er/erm00/pp022031.pdf

Wenger, E. (2005). *Learning for a small planet – A research agenda* [Online]. Version 2.0, revised March-May. Available: WWW Ref. http://ewenger.com/research/LSPfoundingdoc.doc.

Chapter 24

COMPUTER-SUPPORTED COLLABORATIVE LEARNING FOR KNOWLEDGE CREATION

Ching Sing Chai
Seng Chee Tan
Nanyang Technological University
Singapore

Computer-Supported Collaborative Learning (CSCL) is an emerging field of research that has gained significant momentum in the past decade. For its relatively short history, it has been associated with three perspectives of learning: acquisition, participation, and knowledge creation. This chapter focuses on CSCL for knowledge creation, particularly the Knowledge Building approach proposed by Bereiter and Scardamalia. It includes the theoretical foundation of Knowledge Building, its relevance in the Knowledge Age, some key research directions and methodologies, and discussion on some key challenges.

1. Introduction

About two decades ago, Peter Drucker, a renowned management professor, predicted that knowledge workers would become the dominant group of the workforce in many countries (Drucker, 1985). He also believed that creativity and innovation should be pervasive among the masses in society rather than among a few privileged elites. This has become a reality as we move into the Knowledge Age where economy is based on knowledge and expertise rather than products (Trilling & Hood, 1999) and ability to create knowledge becomes the key asset of a society.

The change in global economy has real impact in schools. Higher-order learning objectives like problem solving skills, creative and critical thinking skills, and collaboration and communication skills are regarded as the 21st Century life skills (North Central Regional Educational Laboratory, 2003). From the learning psychology perspective, the acquisition model, where learners receive knowledge transmitted from the teacher, is under heavy criticism for its inadequacy in fostering higher order cognition. Constructivist approaches, which emphasize the importance of the learner's active cognitive construction of knowledge, have since gained greater momentum among the educators.

Constructivist learning, however, can be implemented in many ways. Lipponen, Hakkarainen, and Paavola (2004), for example, differentiated between the participatory approach and the knowledge creation approach. In the participatory approach, a novice is enculturated while moving from periphery to the central of a community. It is premised on situation cognition and the notion of identity creation as learning. However, the cultural capital of a society is at best preserved with this approach. To address this concern, a knowledge creation approach advocates collaborative knowledge building, with the constant goal of improving cultural artifacts and knowledge. This is epitomized by the Knowledge Building approach advocated by Scardamalia and Bereiter (2002).

One of the key factors that bring about the changes highlighted above is Information and Communication Technology (ICT). ICT unleashes the power of knowledge by making information easily shared and accessed. In fact, the advent of the Internet has "flattened" the world in that a knowledge product can be created in any part of the world, thus leveling the competition field (Friedman, 2005). It is hardly surprising that emerging technology like the *Computer-Supported Collaborative Learning* (CSCL) tool found its way into many progressive educational institutions.

This chapter focuses on a learning environment that leverages technology for knowledge creation: using CSCL for Knowledge Building in school settings. In this chapter, we review the theoretical foundations of Knowledge Building, CSCL and related research, and make recommendations for future research.

2. Theoretical Foundations of Knowledge Building Community

CSCL is a field of study that focuses on group-based collaborative learning supported by computers, where learning could take place either face-to-face, via computer networks, or through both modalities (Kirschner, Martens, & Strijbos, 2004). In the field of CSCL, the Knowledge Building Community (KBC) seems to be the one with the longest and most successful history (Miyake & Koschmann, 2001). Scardamalia and Bereiter (2003) argued that the emergence of the knowledge society requires schools to reconceptualize themselves as agencies that enculturate knowledge workers/producers whose key task is to add value to knowledge. They postulated that by immersing students in an environment that is anchored on knowledge production, students will naturally employ a range of cognitive, metacognitive and interpersonal skills to adapt to the environment (Scardamalia, 2000). They also argued that through knowledge building, other important goals such as foundational learning, creative and critical thinking will naturally ensue. In this section, we trace the advancement of learning psychology from a Vygotskian's social constructivist view, to identity building in a community of practice, and finally the knowledge creation perspective. Readers interested in the theory of building collaborative knowing can refer to Stahl (2004).

Vygotsky's (1978) sociocultural theory stresses the importance of social interaction for the development of cognitive ability. Interacting with more capable peers or experts creates for the learners a Zone of Proximal Development (ZPD), which is defined by Vygotsky as "the distance between the actual developmental level as determined by independent problem solving and the level of potential development as determined through problem solving under adult guidance or in collaboration with more capable peers" (p. 86). Interactions in ZPD give the learners opportunities to appropriate "ways of seeing" and problem solving (Hung, 1999) that are mediated through language. As such, the development of higher cognitive ability would be greatly hampered if social interactions were limited. However, the Vygotskian's view is narrowly focused on the internal cognitive structures of the learners at the price of neglecting the social structures that could facilitate knowledge advancement (Scardamalia, Bereiter, & Lamon, 1994).

Lave and Wenger's (1999) notion of Community of Practice (CoP) builds on the social constructivist view of learning with additional emphasis on the critical role of situated cognition. In the social setting of apprenticeship, apprentices are afforded opportunities to participate in the various activities that constitute the practice. Through such participation, the apprentice learns to be a practitioner. Lave and Wenger characterized the learning journey as one that moves from legitimate peripheral participation to central participation of the practice. Within this journey, an important aspect of participation is that of learning to talk professionally. Lave and Wenger distinguished the forms of talk that occur in an authentic CoP and that of school-based CoP. The former is talking within the practice, situated or contextualized by the practice. The latter is talking about the practice in a circumscribed environment, which may not help newcomers in appropriating the actual use of language and therefore the problem solving dispositions within the practice. This emphasis of situating talks within the context of a practice is partly addressed in a KBC by emphasizing the primary importance of initiating an inquiry with authentic problems within a discipline (Hewitt, 2001).

Another key idea forming the foundation of KBC is distributed cognition in a collaborative situation (Pea, 1993; Roth, 1999). In a KBC, learners can distribute the responsibilities of the difficult and complex learning tasks. This avoids cognitive overload of individual members and allows members to develop differential expertise (Roth, 1999). At the same time, learners with different backgrounds and abilities enter the learning environment with different ideas and perspectives. The diversity in ideas, abilities and perspectives forms the collective resources of the KBC that members can draw on. It creates multiple ZPDs where all members can support each other mutually towards the achievement of learning goals (Oshima, 1998). It also creates a natural social environment for the members to articulate and explain their ideas, which requires the members to be precise and concrete. In a nutshell, it enriches learning by creating opportunities for members to understand from others' points of view and expose them to diverse ways of conceptualizing and investigating a given phenomenon (Kolodner & Guzdial, 1996).

Bereiter (1997) extends the situated perspective of learning to emphasize critical and creative work on ideas, which has become the most distinctive characteristics of KBC. This emphasis shifts attention away from the internalization and appropriation of existing practices and knowledge to the co-construction of new knowledge. Learning about the practice and knowledge becomes a by-product of being a knowledge worker. In other words, it is not sufficient just to appropriate and preserve the cultural capital of a society, but to build the capacity and disposition of citizens in advancing knowledge. Bereiter holds that knowledge building can begin in elementary school and that learning is a by-product of knowledge building.

The epistemological belief underlying KBC is Popper's (1965) construct of World 3 objects. Other than World 1 (the physical world) and World 2 (the subjective world inside the mind), Popper suggested World 3 objects that are constituted of cognitive artifacts, for example, theories created by scientists. These theories, once created, are largely autonomous and can generate a range of possibilities as others interact with it. They are treated as tentative theory that should be subjected to error elimination under Popper's schema for the search for truth. In other words, all knowledge created is reified as "objects" that are open to further inquiry and improvement. This epistemological stance is translated into the practice of treating all knowledge as improvable ideas in a KBC (Scardamalia, 2002). Bereiter (1994) argues that school has focused on changing students' mind (i.e. World 2) but neglected the enculturation of students into World 3. In a KBC, students are empowered to produce cognitive artifacts such as explanations of phenomena they have encountered. These cognitive artifacts (or knowledge objects as Bereiter calls them) are then subjected to the community scrutiny for improvement. Bereiter (1997) argues that this process is similar to scientists' intellectual work. Engaging students in the improvement of knowledge objects will inevitably lead students to the examination of existing theories (i.e., the theories produced by established scientists). Bereiter (2002) posits that by engaging learners in a KBC, we are empowering learners to work constructively and creatively with ideas, that is, treating learners as knowledge producers.

3. Knowledge Building Community

Following the above theoretical discussion on KBC, this section operationalizes the concept of KBC by describing how KBC looks like in a classroom and the design principles of such an environment.

> Knowledge building may be defined as the production and continual improvement of ideas of value to a community, through means that increase the likelihood that what the community accomplishes will be greater than the sum of individual contributions and part of broader cultural efforts.
>
> Scardamalia and Bereiter (2003, p. 1371)

A Knowledge Building Community (KBC) is formed when a group of committed individuals jointly identify authentic problems and assume the responsibilities to advance each other's understanding with regard to the problems (Hewitt, 2001; Scardamalia, 2002). Unlike other

Communities of Practice, the primary goal of a KBC is to advance knowledge rather than merely solving problems. Examples of such communities include all forms of research and development teams from universities and private organizations (Scardamalia & Bereiter, 1999).

We consult several case reports to form an epitome of a KBC classroom (see Caswell & Lamon, 1998; Lamon, Reeve, & Scardamalia, 2001; Messina, 2001). In a classroom, KBC is usually initiated by the social negotiation of a broad theme of inquiry relevant to a discipline. Ideas and questions that the members have about the theme are then articulated and posted in the Knowledge Forum (a CSCL tool) as notes. The forum then acts as a communal database where the ideas are seeded. This initial stage promotes ownership and responsibility among community members and enhances the authenticity of the theme of inquiry (Scardamalia, Bereiter, Mclean, Swallow, & Woodruff, 1989). The notes are treated as improvable ideas. As the participants engage themselves in the various means of advancing understanding (for example, reading notes, conducting empirical research, reflecting, discussing, etc.), they improve each other's ideas through face-to-face interactions as well as through online building of new notes or revision of existing notes. This phase is essentially a social process mediated by knowledge-building discourse that focuses on sharing new knowledge, synthesizing new knowledge with prior knowledge, detecting gaps in understanding, co-construction of theory and so on. It leads naturally to the growth of the database which reflects the progress of the community as a whole (Scardamalia & Bereiter, 1994). As initial questions are being answered, participants are encouraged to ask further and deeper questions thereby creating an ever-deepening pursuit. They are also encouraged to take up the responsibility to organize and re-organize the databases through design features such as creating new views. The closure of a KBC is usually arbitrarily decided by school terms since knowledge building is iterative and potentially never ending.

Wells (1999) characterized the above processes of building better understanding as the "spiral of knowing" (p. 85). Individuals achieve advancements in knowing by first making meaning through personal experiences. They then move to enhance their understandings by a process of knowledge negotiation that is mainly constituted in comparing and refining one's ideas with others' ideas obtained from literature, empirical works and peers. The refined understanding then becomes the new interpretive framework for further understandings and actions.

Lamon (2005) summarizes the 12 design principles for KBC as shown in Table 24.1.

Table 24.1. Knowledge Building Principles

Knowledge building principles	Definitions
Real ideas and authentic problems	Real knowledge problems arise from efforts to understand the world; creative work with ideas supports faster and more reliable learning, whereas learning alone seldom leads to knowledge innovation.
Idea diversity	Different ideas create a dynamic environment in which contrasts, competition, and complementarity of ideas is evident, creating a rich environment for ideas to evolve into new and more refined forms.
Improvable ideas	All ideas are treated as improvable; participants aim to mirror the work of great thinkers in gathering and weighing evidence, and ensuring that explanations cohere with all available evidence.
Knowledge building discourse	Discourse serves to identify shared problems and gaps in understanding and to advance understanding beyond the level of the most knowledgeable individual.
Epistemic agency	Participants mobilize personal strengths to set forth their ideas and to negotiate a fit between personal ideas and ideas of others, using contrasts to spark and sustain knowledge advancement rather than depending on others to chart that course for them.
Democratizing knowledge	All participants are legitimate contributors to the shared goals of the community; all have a sense of ownership of knowledge advances achieved by the group.
Collective knowledge, community responsibility	Participants take responsibility for the overall advancement of knowledge in the community.
Embedded transformative assessment	The community engages in its own internal assessment, which is both more fine-tuned and rigorous than external assessment, and serves to ensure that the community's work will exceed the expectations of external assessors.

Table 24.1 (Continued)

Knowledge building principles	Definitions
Constructive use of authoritative sources	Participants use authoritative sources, along with other information sources as data for their own knowledge building and idea-improving processes.
Rise – above	The conditions to which people change because of the successes of other people in the environment. Adapting means adapting to a progressive set of conditions that keep raising standards.
Pervasive knowledge building	Creative work with ideas is integral to all knowledge work.
Symmetric knowledge advances	Interleaved communities provide successively more demanding contexts for knowledge work, and set into motion inner-outer community dynamics that serve to embed ideas in a broader social context.

(Lamon, 2005, p. 360; see also Scardamalia, 2002)

4. Technology Support for Knowledge Creation

As a pedagogical model, the KBC exploits both the social and the technological affordances of the communal database. On the social dimension, interactions with others' perspectives are vital to refining understanding. To activate the social dynamics that will lead to idea refinement, students are empowered to identify areas of interest to build expertise. They gain status and respect among their peers as they contribute to the database. As research teams are formed according to interest, the less knowledgeable members from other teams or weaker students within the teams contribute by asking questions about explanations or ideas that are not clear to them. They also benefit from participating in the KBC since the asynchronous platform prevents anyone from dominating the conversation. Diversity allows ideas to be challenged and improved. Also, ideas are accepted or rejected, not because the teacher says so but because the community has detected flaws in them. In short, it creates a more democratized classroom.

On the technological dimension, Knowledge Forum (www.knowledgeforum.com), a Computer-Supported Collaborative Learning (CSCL) tool, is specifically designed to support Knowledge

Building activities. It mediates the process of collaboration among learners; promote inquiry, sense-making and reflective thinking; facilitating knowledge building; and providing record keeping. Knowledge Forum (version 3.4), which is the second generation Computer-Supported Intentional Learning Environment (CSILE), makes use of a graphical interface to organize discussion (Figure 24.1). Each page is called a View, which can host messages pertaining to a topic, and links to other Views. Notes containing messages are linked graphically, which allow one to trace the development of ideas. Learners can post, reflect, link, relate and question ideas posted by themselves or others, thus making the knowledge-construction process overt and traceable.

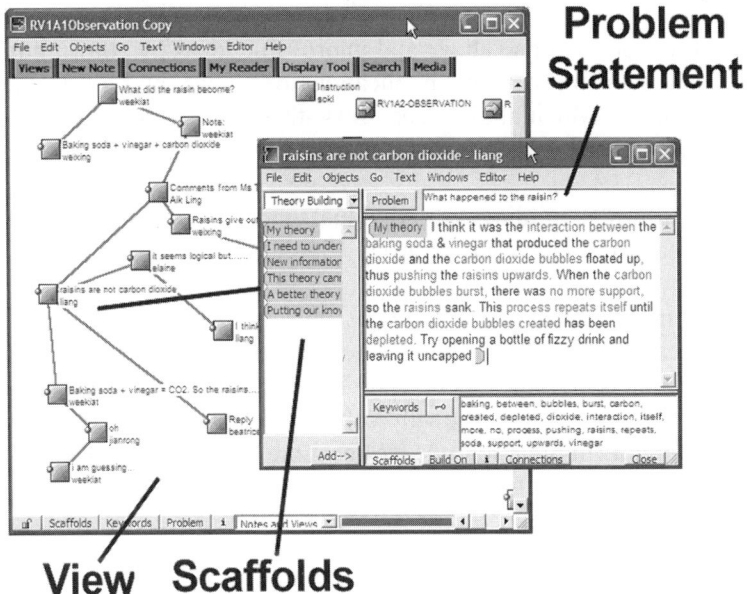

Figure 24.1. A discussion in Knowledge Forum.

Scardamalia (2004) summarizes the affordances of Knowledge Forum in supporting knowledge building process:

1. It provides various ways of connecting ideas: building on, citation, annotation, and references.

2. It provides customizable scaffolds that facilitate knowledge building discourse. For instance, to support inquiry-based knowledge building, student may be asked to post notes using the following labels: "My theory", "I need to understand", "My theory doesn't explain", or "A better theory is". These are metacognitive cues which model and encourage learners to engage in more in-depth inquiry rather than superficial chatting.

3. It provides graphical Views that host different topics of discussion foster multiple perspectives, multiple literacies, and team work by allowing the use of text, graphics, and multimedia to describe ideas and allowing individual or group design of Views and notes.

4. It encourages rise above and improvable ideas by allowing review and revision of notes, publications of Views, and a "rise above" function which allows users to synthesize or summarize ideas at a higher level.

5. It affords building of individual and group portfolios through creation of individual or group Views that can be linked.

6. It makes ideas and artifacts as objects of discussion. By putting ideas in Knowledge Forum, they are subject to review, critique or comment by other members. The historical interactions of these processes are automatically captured in the database. Thus ideas in mind (implicit knowledge) become "objects" that can be acted and improved upon.

7. It allows embedded and transformative assessment by allowing searching and tracking of contribution from individuals and groups.

In the following section, we review the key research approaches and outcomes in the field of knowledge creation with CSCL.

5. Research Approaches and Outcomes to Date

The review so far has highlighted that knowledge creation with CSCL is an emerging technology that is generally underpinned by social-cultural view of learning. This view of learning inevitably carries with it certain research orientations, typically a qualitative case study based on design research. Experimental designs that compare achievement scores of control and treatment groups are therefore not in abundance. In addition, the major research methods and findings can be grouped under two main categories: (1) learning outcomes as measured by some instruments including traditional assessment, and (2) interaction analysis and knowledge advancement.

5.1 Learning outcomes

In terms of learning outcomes as measured by traditional assessment such as standardized reading and vocabulary tests, students in KBC generally scored significantly higher than other students (Lamon et al. 1994; Oshima & Scardamalia, 1996; Scardamalia, & Bereiter, 1996; Scardamalia et al., 1992). Many of these studies were conducted in Canadian schools where teachers having substantial experience in fostering the KBC in a well-supported environment. Knowledge building was introduced to Singaporean schools in 2002. To date, research has found that in grade 7 and 8 classrooms, KBC enhanced students' scientific inquiry skills, fostered a positive perception towards science learning, and students in KBC were able to transfer the skills to solve daily life problems (Tan, Hung, & So, 2005; Tan, Yeo, & Lim, 2005). A case study in Singapore schools (Teo, Chiam, & Ng, 2004) has also shown that less academically inclined students, who were usually reticent in class, were found to contribute actively in Knowledge Forum and were cautious about validity of information posted. A study in an elementary school (Ow & Tan, 2005) showed that students were able to engage in Knowledge Building activities, resulting in a better performance in a class test and a change in perception of science among the students. In general, research in the dimension of knowledge acquisition is scarce. This could be due to the current emphasis towards investigating and understanding the constructive processes involved in learning rather than the learning outcomes (Suthers, 2005). However, some researchers hold that CSCL, in general, is still in need of substantiating its claim for better learning (Lipponen, 2002; Hendriks & Maor, 2004). It is therefore important that adequate attention should be focused on the dimension of knowledge acquisition to convince policy makers and practitioners about its effectiveness (see also Strijbos, Kirschner, & Martens, 2004).

5.2 Interaction analysis and knowledge advancement

Since knowledge creation with CSCL is premised on the socio-cultural view of learning, much of the research involves interaction analysis of online discourse. The general approach to analyzing the interaction data captured is content analysis, which involves segmenting online messages into unit of analysis and assigning categorical labels to the messages (Chi, 1997). One common approach is to quantify observable interactive behaviors such as number of posts and who responds to whose messages. It provides information about the participation and the social aspect of learning in CSCL environments. Another approach is to go beyond observable actions, and interpret the coded messages as an indicator of some cognitive/metacognitive actions. The third approach is to subject-specific code the level of knowledge, for example, the level of scientific reasoning in the messages.

One pioneer in formulating a content analysis model for online interactions is Henri (1992). She proposed a model that includes five dimensions of interactions: participation, social, interactivity, cognitive skills, and metacognitive skills. The participation dimension analyzes posting of online messages; the social dimension is concerned with online social talks; and the interactivity dimension classifies messages according to direct or indirect responses or commentary. The first three dimensions of Henri's model can be subsumed under the participation dimension as conceptualized by Lipponen, Hakkarainen, and Paavola (2004) since they are generally different types of participation. The cognitive and metacognitive dimensions are more akin to knowledge creation since they are targeted at examining the thinking skills exhibited and these skills, when absent, would clearly point to the failure in knowledge creation through online collaboration. Henri believes that the use of her model allows comprehensive understanding of the online learning processes.

Hara, Bonk, and Angeli (2000) adapted the model for a study of 20 students' online discussions in the area of cognitive psychology at the graduate level. The results indicated that students' participation was limited to an average of one posting average per week. For the dimension on interactivity, they devised message maps that depicted students' interaction clearly. At times, the maps showed that the learners were not well connected to each other. The study also revealed the difficulty in achieving high inter-rater reliability for the metacognitive dimension. This is important to note because questions about the validity and reliability of the cognitive and metacognitive dimensions of various coding schemes has started to surface (see later section).

While Henri's model has provided some indicators of learning for Hara et al.'s study, it remains silent about collaborative knowledge building. Coding online messages for cognitive and metacognitive skills could only provide indirect evidence for knowledge construction. The ability to co-construct knowledge is the behavior that many advocates of CSCL hope to cultivate among the learners. Hewitt (1996) proposed that the measure of the connectivity of the online forum could provide an indication of the extent of collaborative knowledge building. The connectivity of a forum is reflected mainly through the mean size of the note clusters and the mean depth of the note clusters. In other words, researchers could gain some indication of collaborative knowledge building by looking at the number of cluster of notes and isolated notes in the forum, the number of notes per cluster, and the level of depth achieved. Hewitt (1996) reported a maximum of 5.6 notes/cluster achieved by a teacher with a doctoral degree after four years of experimenting with KBC in an elementary classroom. His report cautions researchers that achieving in-depth discussion is not an easy task.

Another less rigorous but more common way of assessing collaboration is to compute the average length of the threads (Guzdial & Turns, 2000; Lipponen, Rahikainen, Lallimo, & Hakkarainen, 2003). The average thread length is equivalent to Hewitt's mean size of notes cluster. Although the computation of average length of threads is insufficient for full understanding of online interactions, it provides an indicator on how sustained the interactions are. Methodologically, the number of notes per cluster or the average length of threads provides simple and reliable measure of connectivity, but they do not account for links between messages that are references of other messages not in the same thread.

Guzdial and Turns (2000) assessed over 1,000 undergraduates who used online forum mainly from the participation dimension. The average number of postings, average length of threads, proportion of participants/non-participants and on/off task notes were the indicators they employed to assess learning. It is clear that their analysis focuses on the participation dimension. The strength of their study is in the great number of participants and forums that they analyzed. Guzdial and Turns's (2000) study of undergraduate online interactions yielded a result of about one note for every two weeks. They also reported an average of 7.2 notes per cluster when the discussion threads were anchored around examinations and homework assignments using CaMILE, another CSCL environment that has similar scaffolding feature as Knowledge Forum. They argued that the relevant topic (what they refer to as anchor) of discussion and technological facilitation features promote broad and sustained participation. However, their results show that not all students participated and the rate of posting is fairly low.

Noticing the gaps in Henri's model, Gunawradena, Lowe and Anderson (1997) developed an interaction analysis model (IAM) to examine meaning negotiation and co-construction of knowledge. The model describes co-construction of knowledge as five progressive phases. Table 24.2 provides a brief summary of the phases.

Table 24.2. The Five Phases of the Interaction Analysis Model (IAM)

Phase 1:	Sharing/Comparing of Information
Phase 2:	Discovering dissonance, gaps in understanding or areas for improvements among ideas or concepts
Phase 3:	Negotiation of meaning/ co-construction of knowledge
Phase 4:	Testing and modification of proposed synthesis or co-construction
Phase 5:	Agreement statements/ application of newly-constructed knowledge

Each phase consists of other sub-phases such as asking questions and proposing solution for problems. As the IAM was developed specifically to analyze knowledge construction, it has been employed in a number of studies (see Hendriks & Maor, 2004; Marra, Moore, & Klimczak, 2004; Schellens & Vackle, 2005; Chai & Khine, 2006). The IAM seems to be an instrument that could achieve high level of inter-rater reliability (Marra et al., 2004; De Wever, Schellens, Vackle & Van Keer, 2006). The four studies that employed the IAM have all documented that phase 4 and phase 5 interactions were very scarce. Most interactions in these studies were confined to phase 1. Gunawardena et al. (1997) reported similar phenomenon with their data. This highlights the problem that a higher level of knowledge construction is difficult to achieve.

Garrison et al. (2001) had also created a model for analyzing online interactions based on their conceptualization of online learning as practical inquiry for higher education. The model has four progressive phases, starting from a triggering event where the problems are presented. The learners then move through the exploration, integration and the resolution phases. They claimed that their model is consistent with that of IAM. Although the general progressions of knowledge construction for both models were parallel, there were some differences in terms of the sub-phases. As the model was only tested on three sets of online messages which amount to only 95 messages, it was less descriptive than the IAM.

Recent studies of online interactions roughly fall within the dimensions described above with adaptations to the specific contexts and purposes of the study. For example, Lipponen et al. (2003) categorized the students' postings as an on/off task, and further classified the functions of the postings as providing information, asking research/ clarification questions, and something else. They also measured the mean size of notes and the depth of notes and mapped out the social relations through case-by-case matrix. In the participation dimension, other than notes creation and responses/comments, they also made use of log files to study who-read-whose notes. The mapping of social relations at times provide important information that could explain why a community is not progressing in their knowledge-building Endeavour. A community where members do not read or build on each others' notes may have not reached a level of social cohesiveness that allows members to comment on each others' ideas. However, a socially cohesive community may on the other hand suffer from members' reservation on giving critical comments to peers. For example, Chai and Khine (2006) discovered that the teachers in the knowledge-building community that they studied were well connected to each other but they were not critical of each others' ideas. They speculated that it could be due to the cultural norm of the teaching profession that teachers do not pass on critical comment about each other's practices.

Schellens and Valcke's (2005) employed similar dimensions as Lipponen's study. For the cognitive dimension, their scheme of classification is geared towards knowledge building rather than learning.

They claimed that the scheme is parallel to Gunawardena et al.'s scheme. They have also differentiated between the use of theoretical and experiential information in the online messages for knowledge building. Analysis in this aspect is important, as one concern in CSCL is superficial exchange. The most recent application of IAM was conducted by Marra et al. (2004). They analyzed a small sample of 47 notes using IAM and Newman, Webb and Cochrane's (1996, in Marra et al.) model. They found that the IAM produced better descriptive data and inter-rater's agreement was more easily reached since the IAM was better defined.

The above approaches make use of generic coding of interaction and level of thinking. In order to trace development of ideas, subject specific coding of the level of knowledge is necessary. For example, to trace the progressive level of scientific inquiry, Hakkarianen (1998) classified students' scientific ideas into five levels: Separate pieces of facts, partially organized facts, well-organized facts, partial explanation, and explanation. This is premised on the design principles of knowledge building which encourage development of intuitive ideas into better ideas through progressive discourse and deepening level of inquiry. This coding scheme differs from those described in the previous section in that subject-specific knowledge (scientific knowledge) is necessary. Hakkarianen found that 10 and 11 year old students who engaged in knowledge building showed deepening level of inquiry over 3 years.

6. Concluding Remarks

Knowledge creation with CSCL is a move towards fostering 21st century skills among our students. It aims to develop students as knowledge producers, so that society as a whole can innovate and advance beyond cultural preservation and replication. Knowledge Building Community exploits both the social and the technological affordances of the CSCL communal database. It provides an environment which taps the distributed intelligence and multiple perspectives of a community, and an electronic platform which reifies knowledge artifacts so that they can be acted upon for improvement.

Research on KBC has shown some positive results in terms of measurable learning outcomes. To date, several content analysis models were developed to analyze the rich data captured in an online forum from different dimensions of learning. However, research studies have also revealed that low participation rate and insufficient depth of interaction and thinking are common issues in CSCL (Garrison, et al., 2001; Marra et al., 2004).

Although CSCL environments attempt to exploit technological affordances that would facilitate in-depth inquiry among its learners, its impacts on learning are mediated by a myriad of factors (Kirschner, Martens, & Strijbos, 2004). For example, the level of prior knowledge that an individual student has, the personality of the team members, and the moment-to-moment interactions that can not be predefined are just some factors that are not controllable. The pedagogical design such as the selection of an appropriate anchor to initiate authentic knowledge negotiation is crucial (see Gilbert & Driscoll, 2002). Facilitators' commitments and dispositions are also important variables as the time and skill demands on careful facilitation are great. Although KBC involves a learning community, research that examines interactions and process at the macro community level is scarce. For example, activity theory could be used to surface contradictions within a community, these contradictions which serve as the source of innovation within the system (Engeström, 1987). In terms of research methodology, the use of content analysis has also recently been questioned. Rourke and Anderson (2004) questioned the validity of using content analysis as a form of test. They were not convinced that the current practice of assigning scores to coded messages and performing inferential statistic on those scores is warranted. Similar attention to content analysis as a method for analyzing online messages is also apparent in the first issue of *Computers and Education* in 2006.

It is noteworthy that educational researchers from various parts of the world are forming communities that aim at advancing knowledge work and knowledge creation with CSCL. For example, led by Bereiter and Scardamalia, the Institute for Knowledge Innovation and Technology (www.ikit.org) is formed as a centre to conduct research, develop technology, and congregate international members from a variety of sectors who are actively engaged in pooling intellectual resources and participating in joint research projects. These communities serve as useful source of information and centers of innovation for researchers interested in the field of knowledge creation with CSCL.

References

Bereiter, C. (1994). Implications of postmodernism for science, or, Science as progressive discourse. *Educational Psychologist, 29* (1), 3-12.

Bereiter, C. (1997).Situated cognition and how to overcome it. In D. Kirshner & J. A. Whitson (Eds.). *Situated cognition: Social, semiotic, and psychological perspectives* (pp. 281-300). Hillsdale NJ: Lawrence Erlbaum.

Bereiter, C. (2002). *Education and mind in the knowledge age.* Mahwah, NJ: Lawrence Erlbaum.

Caswell, B. & Lamon, M. (1998). *Development of scientific literacy: The evolution of ideas in grade four knowledge-building classroom.* Paper presented at the Annual Meeting of the America Educational Research Association, San Diego, CA.

Chai, C. S. & Khine, M. S. (2006). An analysis of interaction and participation patterns in an online learning community. *Journal of Education Technology and Society, 9* (1), 250-261.

Chi, M. T. H. (1997). Quantifying qualitative analyses of verbal data: A practical guide. *The Journal of the Learning Sciences, 6* (3), 271-315.

De Wever, B., Schellens, T., Valcke, M. & Van Keer, H. (2006). Content analysis schemes to analyze transcripts of online asynchronous discussion groups: A review. *Computers & Education, 46* (1), 6-28.

Drucker, P. (1985). *Innovation and entrepreneurship: Practice and principles.* New York: Harper and Row.

Engeström, Y. (1987). *Learning by expanding: An activity theoretical approach to developmental research.* Helsinki, Finland: Orienta-Konsultit Oy.

Friedman, T. L. (2005). *The world is flat: A brief history of the twenty-first century.* NY: Farrar, Straus & Giroux.

Garrison, D. R., Anderson, T., & Archer, W. (2001). Critical thinking, cognitive presence, and computer conferencing in distance education. *American Journal of Distance Education, 15* (1), 7-23.

Gilbert, N. J. & Driscoll, M. P. (2002). Collaborative knowledge building: A case study. *Educational Technology, Research and Development, 50* (1), 59-79.

Gunawardena, C., Lowe, C., & Anderson, T. (1997). Analysis of a global online debate and the development of an interaction analysis model for examining social construction of knowledge in computer conferencing. *Journal of Educational Computing Research, 17* (4), 397-431.

Guzdial, M. & Turns, J. (2000). Effective discussion through computer-mediated anchored forum. *The Journal of the Learning Sciences, 9* (4), 437-469.

Hakkairaien, K. P. J. (1998). *Epistemology of scientific inquiry and Computer-Supported Collaborative Learning.* Unpublished PhD, University of Toronto.

Hara, N., Bonk, C. J. & Angeli, C. (2000). Content analysis of online discussion in an applied educational psychology course. *Instructional Science, 28,* 115-152.

Hendriks, V. & Maor, D. (2004). Quality of students' communicative strategies delivered through computer-mediated communications. *Journal of Interactive Learning Research, 15* (1), 5-32.

Henri, F. (1992). Computer conferencing and content analysis. In A. R. Kaye (Ed.). *Collaborative learning through computer conferencing* (pp. 117-136). Berlin, Heidelberg: Springer-Verlag.

Hewitt, J. (1996).Progress toward a knowledge-building community. *Dissertation Abstract International, 57* (8) pp. 3465, Feb 1997. (UMI No. AAT NN11743).

Hewitt, J. (2001). From focus on task to focus on understanding: The cultural transformation of a Toronto classroom. In T. Koschmann., R, Halls., & N. Miyake. (Eds.), *CSCL 2: Carrying forward the conversation.* (pp. 11-42). Mahwah, NJ: Lawrence Erlbaum.

Hung, D. (1999). Activity, apprenticeship, and epistemological appropriation: Implications from the writing of Michael Polanyi, *Educational Psychologist, 34* (4), 193-205.

Kirschner, P. A., Martens, R. L., & Strijbos, J. W. (2004). CSCL in Higher Education? In J. W. Strijbos, P. A. Kirschner, & R. L. Martens (Eds.), *What we know about CSCL and Implementing it in Higher Education*, (pp. 3-31). Dordrecht, Netherlands: Kluwer Academic Publishers.

Kolodner, J. & Guzdial, M. (1996). Effects with and of CSCL: Tracking learning in a new paradigm. In T. Koschmann (Eds.), *CSCL: Theory into practice of an emerging paradigm* (pp. 307-320). Mahwah, NJ: Lawrence Erlbaum.

Lamon, M., Secules, T., Petrosino, A. J., Hackett, R., Bransford, J. D., & Goldman, S. R. (1994). Schools for thought: Overview of the international project and lessons learned from one of the sites. In

L. Schauble & R. Glaser (Eds.), *Contributions of instructional innovations to understanding learning*. Hillsdale, NJ: Lawrence Erlbaum.

Lamon, M., Reeve, R., & Scardamalia, M. (2001, April). *Mapping learning and the growth of knowledge in a Knowledge Building Community*. Paper presented at the American Educational Research Association Meeting, Seattle, Washington.

Lamon, M. (2005). Information and communications technology and literacy development. In T. Koschmann, D. Suthers, & T. W. Chan (Eds.), *Computer supported collaborative learning 2005: The next 10 years*. (pp. 358-367). Mahwah, NJ: Lawrence Erlbaum.

Lave, J. & Wenger, E. (1999). Legitimate peripheral participation in the communities of practice. In R. McCormick, & C. Paechter (Eds.), *Learning and knowledge* (pp. 21-35). Thousand Oaks, CA: SAGE Publication.

Lipponen, P. (2002, Jan). Exploring foundations for computer-supported collaborative learning. Proceedings of CSCL 2002, Boulder, Colorado, USA. Retrieved Sep 23, 2003, from http://newmedia.colorado.edu/cscl/31.html.

Lipponen, L., Hakkarainen, K., & Paavola, S. (2004). Practices and orientations of CSCL. In J. W. Strijbos, P. A. Kirschner, & R. L. Martens (Eds.), *What we know about CSCL and Implementing it in Higher Education*, (pp. 34-50). Dordrecht, Netherlands: Kluwer Academic Publishers.

Lipponen, L., Rahikainen, M., Lallimo, J., & Hakkarainen, K. (2003). Patterns of participation and discourse in elementary students' computer-supported collaborative learning. *Learning and Instruction, 13*, 487-509.

Marra, R., Moore, J., and Klimczak, A. (2004). Content analysis of online discussion forums: A comparative analysis of protocols. *Educational Technology Research and Development. 52*, 23-40.

Messina, R. (2001). *Intentional learners, cooperative knowledge building, and classroom inventions*. Paper presented at the annual meeting of the American Educational Research Association, Seattle, WA.

Miyake, N. & Koschmann, T. (2001). Realizations of CSCL conversations: Technology transfer and the CSILE project. In T. Koschmann., R. Halls, & N. Miyake (Eds.), *CSCL 2: Carrying forward the conversation* (pp. 1-10). Mahwah, NJ: Lawrence Erlbaum.

North Central Regional Educational Laboratory. (2003). enGauge 21st Century skills: Literacy in the Digital Age. Retrieved 18 Oct, 2005, from http://www.ncrel.org/engauge/skills/skills.htm.

Oshima, J. & Scardamalia, M. (1996). Knowledge-building and conceptual change: An inquiry into student-directed construction of scientific explanations. In D. C. Edelson & E. A. Domeshek (Eds.), *Proceedings of the Second International Conference on the Learning Sciences*, Northwestern Univ., Evanston, IL.

Oshima J. (1998). Differences in knowledge-building between two types of networked learning environments: An information analysis. *Journal of Educational Computing Research, 19* (3), 329-351.

Ow, E. G. J. & Tan, S. C. (2005). *Learning of science in an elementary classroom through Knowledge Building.* Summer Institute 2005, Ontario Institute for Studies in Education, 9-12 August 2005.

Pea, R. D. (1993). Practices of distributed intelligence and designs of education. In M. Cole & Y. Engeström (Eds.),. *Distributed Cognition: Psychology and educational considerations*, Cambridge University Press.

Popper, K. R. (1965). *Conjectures and refutations: The growth of scientific knowledge.* New York, NY: Harper & Row.

Reeves, T., Herrington, J. & Oliver, R. (2004). A development research agenda for online collaborative learning. *Educational Technology, Research and Development, 52* (4), 53-65.

Roth, W. (1999). Authentic school science. In R. McCormick & C. Paechter (Eds.), *Learning and knowledge.* (pp. 6-20). Thousand Oaks, CA: SAGE Publication.

Rourke, L. & Anderson, T. (2004). Validity in qualitative content analysis. *Educational Technology, Research and Development, 52* (1), 5-18.

Scardamalia, M. (2000). Can school enter a knowledge society? In M. Selinger (Ed.), *Proceedings of educational technology and the impact on teaching and learning: A global research forum.* London, England.

Scardamalia, M. (2002). Collective cognitive responsibility. In B. Smith (Ed.), *Liberal Education in the Knowledge Age.* (pp. 76-98). Chicago: Open Court.

Scardamalia, M. (2004). CSILE/Knowledge Forum®. In *Educational technology: An encyclopedia*. Santa Barbara: ABC-CLIO.

Scardamalia, M. & Bereiter, C. (1994). Computer support for knowledge-building communities. *The Journal of the Learning Sciences, 3* (3), 265-283.

Scardamalia, M. & Bereiter, C. (1996). Computer support for knowledge-building communities. In T. Koschmann (Ed.), *CSCL: Theory and Practice of an emerging paradigm* (pp. 249-268). NJ: Lawrence Erlbaum.

Scardamalia, M. & Bereiter, C. (1999) Schools as knowledge-building organizations. In D. Keating & C. Hertzman (Eds.), *Today's children, tomorrow's society: The developmental health and wealth of nations* (pp. 274-289). New York: Guilford.

Scardamalia, M. & Bereiter, C. (2003). Knowledge Building. In James W. Guthrie (Ed.), *Encyclopedia of Education. (2nd ed.)* (pp. 1370-1373). New York: Mcamillan Reference, USA.

Scardamalia, M., Bereiter, C., Brett, C., Burtis, P. J., Calhoun, C., & Lea, N. S. (1992). Educational applications of a networked communal database. *Interactive Learning Environment, 2* (1), 45-71.

Scardamalia, M., Bereiter, C., & Lamon, M. (1994). The CSILE project: Trying to bring the classroom into world 3. In K. McGilly (Ed.), *Classroom lessons: Integrating cognitive theory and classroom practice* (pp. 201-228). Cambridge, MA: Bradford Books/MIT Press.

Scardamalia, M., Bereiter, C., McLean, R., Swallow, J., & Woodruff, E. (1989). Computer supported intentional learning environments, *Journal of Educational Computing Research, 5* (1), 51-68.

Schellens, T. & Valcke, M. (2005). Collaborative learning in asynchronous discussion groups: What about the impact on cognitive processing? *Computers in Human Behavior.* 21 Issue 6, p.957-975

Stahl, G. (2004). Building collaborative knowing: Elements of a social theory of CSCL. In J. W. Strijbos, P. A. Kirschner, & R. L. Martens (Eds.), *What we know about CSCL and Implementing it in Higher Education* (pp. 53-86). Dordrecht, Netherlands: Kluwer Academic Publishers.

Strijbos, J., Kirschner, P. A., & Martens, R. L. (2004). What we know about CSCL. In J. W. Strijbos, P. A. Kirschner, & R. L. Martens (Eds.), *What we know about CSCL and Implementing it in Higher Education*, (pp. 245-260). Dordrecht, Netherlands: Kluwer Academic Publishers.

Suthers, D. (2005). Technology affordances for intersubjective learning: A thematic agenda for CSCL. In T. Koschmann, D. Suthers, & T. W. Chan (Eds.), *Computer supported collaborative learning 2005: The next 10 years* (pp. 662-671). Mahwah, NJ: Lawrence Erlbaum.

Tan, S. C., Hung, D., & So, K. L. (2005). Fostering Scientific Inquiry in Schools through Science Research Course and Computer-Supported Collaborative Learning (CSCL). *International Journal of Learning Technology, 1* (3), 273-292.

Tan, S. C., Yeo, J., & Lim, W. Y. (2005). Changing epistemology of science learning through inquiry with Computer-Supported Collaborative Learning. *Journal of Computers in Mathematics and Science Teaching, 24* (4), 367-386

Teo, C. L., Chiam, C. L., & Ng, F. K. (2004). Fostering Knowledge Building among Low Achievers through Technologies: A Perspective from Singapore. *Teaching and Learning, 25* (1), 89-102.

Trilling, B. & Hood, P. (1999). Learning, technology, and education reform in the Knowledge Age or "We're Wired, Webbed, and Windowed, Now What?" *Educational Technology, 39* (3), 5-18.

Vygotsky, L. S. (1978). *Mind in society.* Cambridge, Massachusetts: Harvard University Press.

Wells, G. (1999). *Dialogic inquiry: Toward a sociocultural practice and theory of education.* New York, NY: Cambridge University Press.

Chapter 25

EVALUATING THE VIRTUAL LEARNING ENVIRONMENT

Susan M. Chard
Whitireia Community Polytechnic
New Zealand

There are many initiatives to build virtual learning environments to enable web-based learning. Once built a reliable evaluation method is required to develop an understanding of the utility of these environments, for both learners and teachers, and to facilitate the evolution of these environments. Learning environment research has established that there is a strong correlation between student outcomes and the learning environment, that the learning environment has a significant impact on student learning. Learning environment research is well established, with a history spanning three decades. Originating from investigations into the psychological aspects of social environments, learning environment research has evolved to include many instruments to evaluate different types of learning environments, measuring the effectiveness of a specific environment for the learners and teachers who participate in it. Recently, learning environment research has moved into distance and web-based learning environments, with new instruments being developed for the purpose of evaluating and improving these environments. This chapter discusses the development of learning environment instruments from their roots in psychosocial research to the current development of learning environment instruments for the evaluation of virtual learning environments including 3D virtual worlds designed for learning.

1. Introduction

There are many initiatives to build virtual learning environments to enable web-based learning. The rising popularity and subsequent wide-spread use of the web as an information distribution and communication medium in the late 1990s, has led to a change in the delivery of learning materials. The web has increasingly been seen as an attractive method of publishing learning materials, as it is significantly cheaper to publish material electronically than on paper. The convenience and flexibility of the web is attractive to both students and teachers as it enables ready access to learning material and a means of communicating with other course participants, at any time, from multiple locations as long as there is a connection to the web. The web has increasingly been seen as an effective alternative to face-to-face mode learning (Chang & Fisher, 1999; McMahon, 1997).

Current web-based learning environments usually consist of a means to deliver study material and one or more communication tools to enable student-teacher and student-student interaction. The web primarily facilitates the storage of information for asynchronous communication as was defined in the original proposal document for a distributed hypertext structure for information management (Berners-Lee, 1989). The information published is available to learners as required providing learning materials for a subject area. The materials may cover subject content, learning activities, research tasks, assessment tasks and links to textbook resources, references or supplementary materials. The standard browser-based web provides for different media, enabling information to be presented using text, images, video and sound.

More recently, web-based learning environments also offer communication tools that may be asynchronous or synchronous. As well as enabling communication in the process of learning, the communication tools enable students to share the resources and materials which become the products of learning (Chang & Fisher, 1999). These communication tools are able to facilitate both one to one and group communication. Asynchronous communication tools include email, on-line forums, and file sharing systems. Synchronous communication tools include on-line chat using one or more methods such as text, voice or video, shared whiteboards, shared documents and avatar based scenes.

Each of these communication tools is separate from the browser based materials and from each other. However the web is evolving as a communications medium to integrate the information publishing and communications tools into blended environments that incorporate multiple communications channels into one web page, using technologies that incorporate multiple media fro information publication and communications tools such as 3D scenes with embedded media, and chat facilities.

To facilitate the development of successful learning environments, it is important to gain an understanding of how effective the environments are for the learners and teachers using them and how well they are supporting the learning process. To develop this understanding, a reliable evaluation method is required. The virtual learning environments utility for both learners and teachers must be studied to develop an understanding of the effectiveness of these environments and guide future development to ensure the environments provide strong support for student learning. Learning environment research has established that there is a strong correlation between student outcomes and the students' perception of the learning environment, and that the learning environment has a significant impact on student learning outcomes. Learning environment research has now moved into the area of evaluation of virtual learning environments. Evaluation instruments have been designed and proven for web-supported and web-based learning environments (Chang & Fisher, 2003). These instruments are being used to give valuable feedback to the designers of web-supported and web-based distance learning environments.

2. Learning Environment Research

Since the late 1960s the field of learning environment research has generated a rich collection of instruments that are proven to provide an accurate picture of the effectiveness of the learning environments investigated. The concepts underlying learning environment research have their roots in psychosocial research that investigates the relationship between peoples perceptions of their environment and their behaviour. Research in the 1930s investigated the relationship between the environment and behaviour. This includes the work of Lewin in 1936 that stated behaviour is a function of personality and environment, expressed as the function $B = f(P,E)$ (Hall & Lindzey, 1978), and the work of Hartshorne and May (1928) that demonstrated that children will behave differently depending on the classroom situation.

In 1970, Stern developed a theory relating the degree of person–environment congruence to student outcomes, based on the needs press theory of Murray (1938). This has been used as the basis for learning environment studies that measure the congruence between the preferred environment and the perceptions of the actual environment and the relationship of this to student outcomes (Fraser & Fisher, 1994). Learning environment research has been further developed to correlate student perceptions of their learning environment with achievement. Learning environment research since the late 1960s, particularly in the field of science education, has documented that students perceptions of their environment are important social and psychological factors in classrooms (Chang & Fisher, 2003).

In the 1970s, Moos investigated the affect of students' environments on their ability to reach their potential. Moos (1974) identified a scheme for classifying human environments. This scheme identified three types of dimensions in the human environment: the Relationship dimension, which identifies and assesses the extent of peoples involvement in the environment and their support for each other; the Personal Growth dimension, which assesses the basic directions along which self enhancement and personal growth appear; and the System Maintenance and System Change dimension which involves orderliness of the environment, clarity of expectations, control, and responsiveness to change (Fraser, 1998).

The *Learning Environment Inventory* (LEI) (Fraser, Anderson, & Walberg, 1982) was developed and validated in the late 1960s. It is designed to measure the students' perceptions of the learning environment through 35 scales, each consisting of seven questions. These scales are designed to measure the three types of environment dimensions identified by Moos: the scales of Cohesiveness, Friction, Favouritism, Cliqueness, Satisfaction and Apathy are related to the Relationship dimension; the scales of Speed, Difficulty and Competitiveness are related to the Personal Development dimension; and the Scales of Diversity, Formality, Material Environment, Goal Direction, Disorganisation and Democracy are related to the System Maintenance and System Change dimension (Fraser, 1998). The LEI was developed for use with high school students studying physics. Initially, there was evolutionary change to these scales as they were refined to make them easier to administer or altered to tailor the instruments to a particular age group or culture, leading to a large number of studies and new instruments with small variations.

Gardner (1989) identified additional dimensions related to the environment, these are the dimensions of ecosphere, sociosphere and technosphere. This initiated the developments of new instruments designed to measure environmental variables associated with the ecosphere, such as the resources available and the technosphere, such as technical infrastructure.

Gardner described a general framework for thinking about the pressures that may be driving change in human environments. Gardiner's model consists of three overlapping spheres of influence that he describes as the ecosphere, the sociosphere, and the technosphere. The ecosphere relates to a person's physical environment and surroundings, whereas the sociosphere relates to an individual's interactions with all other people within that environment. Finally, the technosphere is described as the total of all the person-made things in the environment .

Gardiner described the individual person located in the centre of the model as the most complicated component in the system. Located at the intersection of these three spheres, people are subjected to all three influences. Learning environment studies in technological settings were further developed to utilize this conceptual model of competing environmental influences to increase understanding of the learning environment. This led to the development of instruments that include scales related to the physical and the psychosocial learning environment particularly when the classroom incorporated the use of information and communications technology (Zandvliet, 1999).

3. Online Learning Environment Instruments

Since 1995 several instruments have been developed aimed for use in distance and online learning environments: these include the *Distance and Open Learning Environment Survey* (DOLES), the *Constructivist On-Line Learning Environment Survey* (COLLES), the *Online Learning Environment Survey* (OLLES), the *Web-based Learning Environment Instrument* (WEBLEI) and the *Distance Education Learning Environments Survey* (DELES). These instruments have variously been developed to focus on student activities, interpersonal interaction, material design and organisation, technical environments and organisation issues.

The DOLES was developed in the 1995 for Web-delivered science courses. The DOLES measures student perceptions of their learning experience related to the eight components of effective learning environments: Interactivity, Institutional Support, Task Orientation, Teacher Support, Negotiation, Flexibility, Technological Support, and Ergonomics (Jegede, Fraser, & Fisher, 1995).

The COLLES was developed from its three-scale predecessor, the *Constructivist Virtual Learning Environment Survey* (CVLES), to measure questions about the quality of online learning environments from a social constructivist perspective. The purpose of the instrument was to ensure that technological determinism did not prevent sound educational judgment (Taylor & Maor, 2000). The COLLES is arranged in six scales of: Relevance, Reflection, Interactivity, Tutor Support, Peer Support, and Interpretation.

The DELES was developed in 2003 and is designed to examine distance education environments for tertiary education. The scales cover: Instructor Support, Student Interaction and Collaboration, Personal Relevance, Authentic Learning, Active Learning, Student Autonomy and Satisfaction (Walker, 2003).

The OLLES is being developed and validated in New Zealand for use with post secondary students. The OLLES consists of 61 questions in eight scales: Reflective Thinking, Information Design and Appeal, Order and Organization, Active Learning, Affective Support, Student Cohesiveness and Affiliation, Computer Anxiety and Competence, Material Environment, and Rule Clarity. These scales are nearly equally distributed across Moos' three social organization dimensions (Clayton 2005).

The WEBLEI was developed in 2003 for university level web based and web supported learning environments. The WEBLEI draws on the long history of research instruments and has four scales: Access which covers emancipatory activities in three categories convenience, efficiency, and autonomy; Interaction, co-participatory covering six categories of flexibility, reflection, quality, interaction, feedback, and collaboration; Response, qualia covering six categories of enjoyment, confidence, accomplishment, success, frustration, and tedium; and Results, information structure and design activities covering organization, relevance, accuracy, and balance of learning materials. This instrument was been validated as internally consistent although the scales are somewhat overlapping (Chang & Fisher, 2003). The WEBLEI has been selected as a suitable instrument for this study as it is targeted for web-based and web-supported learning environments and is designed for the tertiary level.

4. Developments in Online Learning

Taking learning outside the traditional classroom does not remove the necessity for student-teacher communication nor the need for student-student communication. It does however, make it harder to facilitate as the students are physically separated from both teachers and other students.

The web has developed from an information publishing space to an interactive communication space. The web now supports activities similar to those involved in online games which utilise the communicative and social aspects of computer-mediated interaction. Online games often use avatars to provision user embodiment within the virtual environment fulfilling several functions, including the means of interaction with the world, the means of communication including awareness of others, the visual/social embodiment of the user and the means of sensing various attributes of the scene.

Research investigating engagement associated with on-line gaming environments highlights the potential for these environments to be used for other purposes. Work in the field of knowledge management and knowledge representation highlights the role of discussion and interaction in the dissemination and acquisition of knowledge. Contemporary developments in gaming, particularly interactive stories, digital authoring tools, and collaborative worlds, suggest powerful new opportunities for educational media (Squire, 2003). Situating the development of educational environments in rich social contexts, combining powerfully-motivating digital environments with a rich interpersonal communications medium provides an environment that has vast potential for education and learning. This forms the basis for an emerging type of online education environment facilitating multiple interaction layers for the participants to create a compelling online learning environment.

The theories of learning that the 3D virtual environment is to support are those that emphasize communication between peers as a being a significant part of the learning process and those that emphasise the role of teacher as facilitator and knowledge creator. In the traditional classroom it has generally been the role of the teacher to impart knowledge to learners. Studies show that in this type of teacher-centric classroom, teachers talk more than students do (Relan & Gillani, 1997). The increasing use of Information and Communication Technologies (ICT) in classrooms and increase in influence of constructivism is changing the role of the teacher in the classroom from the expert dispensing knowledge, to the facilitator of student learning (Dwyer, Ringstaff, & Sandholtz, 1991; Hadley & Sheingold, 1993; Ravitiz, Becker et al., 2000).

The development of this 3D Online Learning Environment is based on the social constructivist theories of learning derived from the developmental theories of Vygotsky and Bruner, and the social cognitive theory of Bandura (Shunk, 2000). In social constructivist theory, learning is viewed as a social process, learning is not something that takes place within an individual, and it is not a passive development of behaviours that are shaped by external forces (McMahon, 1997). Vygotsky proposed the Zone of Proximal Development as "the distance between the actual development level as determined by independent problem solving and the level of potential development as determined through problem solving under adult guidance or in collaboration with more capable peers" and further proposed that for learning to take place it requires learners to apply knowledge to problems, that are in advance of those that they can solve independently, and that learners are able to solve these problems through interaction with more advanced peers or with teachers (Vygotsky, 1978, p. 86).

The 3D Online Learning Environment provides more opportunities than other web based learning environments for the social processes associated with learning by increasing the opportunities for learners to interact with each other through the presence of the avatars. The avatars promote awareness of other participants when they enter a scene to view the learning materials and the embedded text chat enables interaction between the participants.

Social constructivist learning environments must support communication and collaboration between peers as well as between learners and teachers as it is through these interactions that learning takes place. The environment must support social activities as well as task related activities as learning often takes place when individuals are engaged in social activities. Social constructivist approaches can include reciprocal teaching, peer collaboration, cognitive apprenticeships, problem-based instruction, anchored instruction and other methods that involve learning with others (Shunk, 2000). In addition, it has been proposed that heterogeneous grouping can assist in the creation of zones of proximal development (Walker & Lambert, 1995). To promote heterogeneous grouping the learning environment should encompass more than one class grouping, and the resulting heterogeneous grouping will maximise opportunities for the creation of zones of proximal development.

The prototype learning environments used to date have been narrowly focused on one small group of learners who are working in the field of Human Computer Interaction. The next iteration of the 3D

Virtual Learning Environment is being designed to facilitate the learning of all the Information Technology students learning to create computer applications in a polytechnic. It is envisaged that this will provide a heterogeneous group of learners and teachers who will be able to work collaboratively on problem-based learning tasks.

5. Design Process

Building an application with this software is a new process. The software being used was first released in December 2003. This software embodies a new means of interaction through web pages. There is very little literature on the design process for this type of environment for education or other community support activity. One published study is *Hutchworld* a study of the development of a community support centre for cancer patients developed using a similar product Microsoft V-Chat. This used a participatory approach and followed an iterative development methodology (Farnham, Cheng, Stone, Zaner-Godsey, & Clark, 2000, 2002). The participatory approach has been used successfully in both information technology projects (Bodker, Gronbaek, & Kyng, 1993) and community projects (Hasell, 1987).

　　Gould and Lewis (1985) described three principles for user-centred design of instructional systems: an early focus on typical users and actual tasks; the use of empirical methods to assess the ability of the intended users to perform real tasks in the target context; and a focus on iterative, participatory design, incorporating the results of pilot testing and feedback from typical users. This is very similar to the process described as participatory design. Another advocate of participatory design suggests that typical end users should be in direct contact with the developers of an instructional system during the development process (Grudin, 1991). Some of Grudin's suggestions for narrowing the gap between designers and end users include: including end users in the design/development teams; designers participating in the local culture of the end users; integrating pilot testing, prototyping, and formative evaluation into the design process; and encouraging users to take more responsibility for their own environments. Another study found that close collaboration between the design team and typical end users led to a high degree of local adaptation and re-invention of on-line supports for users (Sherry & Myers, 1998). Participatory design involves the inclusion of users within the development process actively helping in planning prototypes and setting design objectives. It contrasts with other development methods that seek user input after the initial concepts, visions, and prototypes exist. The participatory approach was pioneered and has been widely used in Europe since the 1970s, and now consists of a well-articulated and differentiated set of engineering methods in worldwide use (Greenbaum & Kyng, 1991; Muller, Haslwanter, & Dayton, 1997; Schuler & Namioka, 1993).

The development of systems for teaching is an area where a long term participatory approach is essential owing to the level of personal control and "invisible" nature of teachers work plus the loose coupling to organizational workflow (Carroll, Chin, Rosson, & Neale, 2001). Participatory approaches also underlie the development methodologies associated with Human Computer Interaction and are at the heart of participatory action research. To develop the initial design, a participatory design approach has been followed.

During the initial design phase, regular discussion sessions were conducted with a group of third year students over two semesters. The students were first asked to propose metaphors for scenes suitable for a virtual 3D learning environment, prototypes were developed and evaluated from the perspective of interaction design, and support for learning methods. All participants were encouraged to reflect on their experiences and refine the prototypes. The ideas generated fall into four broad groups: galleries; themed rooms; replications of physical environments and designs based on computer games. The most popular was the gallery concept, a large open space with surfaces to display images, text, video, and sometimes spaces for interactive objects and other information objects. These spaces resembled art galleries and interactive museums. The next most popular was the themed space usually a room or building consisting of an area surrounded by walls and ceilings, sometimes comprising several areas and usually following a cultural theme such as: futuristic spaceship; vampires; martial arts; and pacific island meeting house. The third in popularity was a replication of a physical learning environment such as a classroom or study, the detail for these scenes included computer workstations and whiteboards, floor rugs, clocks, lamps, pictures, chairs and tables. The fourth type of scene created was built to resemble a computer game; the type of game chosen ranged from mazes, through puzzles, building blocks, and even "first person shooter" games.

The feedback from discussions about the initial prototypes indicated the most popular design was the gallery museum concept, and this is being used as the basis for the 3D learning environment. It consists of a large multilevel scene with surfaces and places to display information using image, text, video and audio. There are also a number of quick loading scenes that are for social use and some of the trial scenes are available as additional meeting spaces.

6. Learning Material-Technology Limitations

The early prototypes have been used to experiment with different concepts to integrate information based learning material within the scenes. Many students have been using relatively slow speed dial up internet connections when using the scenes from home based computers. In the classroom the network has to support up to 30 computers with participants using the scene at once.

The prototypes that use text based information embedded in the scene are limited in the amount of information that can be displayed in a participants' view, text based information is displayed as a jpg image on a flat surface, such as a noticeboard. Each display board can clearly display a text image of 500 x 500 pixels at 12 point font which enables about 20 lines of 40 characters including spaces, which is about the size of this paragraph. Display boards can be created in any size however, as the display board becomes larger the whole board is not clearly visible to a participant. The maximum viewable size depends on the screen resolution, however at a screen resolution of 800 x 600 the maximum viewable size is as described above and at higher resolutions 40 lines of 80 characters is easily viewable.

When video-based information is embedded in the scene, the user experiences slow load times. Several different types of video have been tried: a slide presentation with a voice over; a slide presentation with no sound; and a recorded lecture streaming from an internet based streaming server. If a streaming server is used, all participants in a scene are seeing the same images at the same time. If archived video files are used each participant starts the video at the time they first view the playing surface and they must wait for the movie to load before it starts playing. To improve the slow load times, the movies were separated into booths so that only one would be visible to a participant at any one time. Controls were included to enable the participant to control the playing of the movies. These included pause, stop and rewind controls. It is not possible in this version of Atmosphere to prevent the movies automatically playing when the viewing surface is first visible to the participant. After trying scenes that included several video lectures in separate booths, it became apparent that it was not practical to have more than one movie in a scene with the current Internet bandwidth and computer configurations.

When audio files were embedded in a scene, the users also experienced slow load times, but this caused fewer problems than the video load times because the sound is set up to play only when a participant's avatar is in a certain proximity range of the object to where the sound is attached. This means a participant must move their avatar close to the object that has the sound associated with it before the sound starts to load and play, and the sound stops playing when the avatar moves out of range again. The sound track may be set to repeat indefinitely or play a limited number of times.

To identify the most effective methods to integrate the information content with the 3D Virtual Learning Environment, the next iteration will include different presentation methods in separate scenes and include tracking and logging to identify participants' preferred methods of moving between the information resources.

7. Results

The WEBLEI has been selected as a suitable instrument to study online learning environments, including the study of 3D scenes being used for online learning, as it is targeted for web-supported and web-based learning environments and is designed for a tertiary environment. In addition, it is designed to measure learning effectiveness in terms of a cycle that includes access to materials, interaction, students' perceptions of the environment, and students' determinations of what they have learned (Chang & Fisher, 2001). This cycle is appropriate to the 3D online learning environment, as the areas of study include the accessibility of the learning materials, the interactions that take place and the effectiveness of these interactions plus the students' perceptions of the environment and the learning that takes place. Minor changes have been made to the wording of the questionnaire after trials with local students highlighted a few areas of confusion, and several of the questions that named specific communication technologies such as email were altered to reflect the broader range of communication technologies available in the 3D Virtual Learning Environment.

The WEBLEI is being used in an iterative manner in the evaluation phase of each cycle of this action research project as part of the feedback to inform the development of the next iteration of the 3D virtual learning environment. The first evaluation has been conducted covering five groups of students, where only one of the groups has been using the prototype learning environment. All students have mixed-mode course delivery within person classroom components and web support via Blackboard resources. The questionnaires were administered as paper questionnaires in the classroom.

The first evaluation has been conducted covering five groups of students, where only one of the groups has been using the prototype learning environment. All students have mixed mode course delivery within person classroom components and web support via Blackboard resources. The paper-based questionnaires were administered in the classroom. Of the students in the group participating in the trial of the 3D Virtual Learning Environment, 100% replied to the survey. In the control group, students who had access to similar web based resources, but no access to the 3D Virtual learning Environment, overall there was a 70% response rate and the rate varied from 100% to 58% across the individual groups. The groups were very small, there were 55 responses in total and the number in the trial group was 17. There were 11 students in the control group who were new to using online learning resources. The results are limited by the small size of the sample, however, the mean scores for each group on each scale show that the participant group gave a response of sometimes often or always more frequently on all scales.

Table 25.1 shows that the mean scores on the Access scale were 4.23 for the participant group and 3.57 for the control group. This indicates that students in the participant group on average responded often to always to questions on the Access scale, which means they agree that they can access the online learning materials in their environment in a convenient and efficient way providing them with autonomy in their access to the materials. Students in the control group on average responded with sometimes to often indicating they were less in agreement but generally still satisfied with their access to the online learning materials in their learning environment and the autonomy in access to learning materials.

The mean scores on the Interaction scale were 3.18 for the participant group and 2.19 for the control group. This means that the participant group on average responded sometimes to often indicating that students believed they were able to participate and interact regularly with each other and the teacher enhancing their ability to be successful and effective learners in this environment. The control group on average responded seldom to sometimes indicating they did not believe that they were able to participate and interact regularly with each other and the teacher and this was detracting from their ability to be successful and effective learners in their learning environment.

The mean scores on the Response scale were 3.75 for the participant group and 2.90 for the control group. This means that the participant group on average responded sometimes to often indicating that the students felt a sense of satisfaction and achievement once they completed the course. The control group were less satisfied as on average they responded seldom to sometimes indicating they were less likely to feel a sense of achievement and satisfaction on completion of the course.

The mean scores on the Results scale were 3.77 for the participant group and 3.10 for the control group. This means that both groups on average responded often to always indicating that the students agree that the learning objectives and organisation of the online learning materials were important in guiding them through their studies.

Table 25.1. Mean and Standard Deviation Responses to Questions on Scales of the WEBLEI

	Mean participants	Standard deviation	Mean control	Standard deviation
Access	4.23	0.74	3.57	0.94
Interaction	3.18	1.39	2.19	1.36
Response	3.75	0.98	2.90	1.42
Results	3.77	0.83	3.10	1.64

The 3D Virtual Learning Environment trials to date have demonstrated that the environment has the potential to provide a rich learning experience for participants and that students perceive this enhanced online environment more favourably than students perceive the standard online learning environment. The environment has been enthusiastically received by the students who have been involved in the trials and after re-design to improve areas that have caused concern the project is being expanded to cover a heterogeneous group of learners involved in learning computer programming and applications development.

8. Conclusion

The WEBLEI has proved a valuable instrument to develop understanding of the 3D environment for learning and has given valuable feedback to further the design of the environment. The four scales of the WEBLEI measuring access, interaction, response and results have reported the students' ability to utilise the environment, the support for inter-group interaction within the environment, the students' satisfaction with the learning experience and the results they felt they were able to achieve in the environment.

The student responses clearly demonstrated that they perceived this enhanced online environment more favourably than the control group of students perceived the standard online learning environment. There is a question as to whether this is due to the novelty value of the environment or to the participating students investment in the development process of the environment through the use of participative design practices. To answer these questions, it is imperative to extend the trials to a wider group of students who have not been involved in its development. It is envisaged that this will provide a heterogeneous group of learners and teachers working across several levels in a vertical subject area. As the project is expanded to include more teachers, the teachers' perceptions of the environment must also be included in the study.

The 3D Virtual Learning Environment has been demonstrated to provide a rich learning experience that students perceive favourably and with further development the environment has potential to engage students in learning activities.

References

Berners-Lee, T. (1989). The original proposal of the WWW. from http://www.w3.org/History/1989/proposal.html.

Bodker, S., Gronbaek, K., & Kyng, M. (1993). *Cooperative design: Techniques and experiences from the Scandinavian scene.* Paper presented at the Participatory design: Principles and practices. Hillsdale: Erlbaum.

Carroll, J. M., G. Chin, G., Rosson, M. B., & Neale, D. C. (2001). The development of cooperation: Five years of participatory design in the virtual school. In J. M. Carroll (Ed.), *Human computer interaction in the new millennium* (pp. 373-393). Boston, MA: Addison-Wesley.

Chang, V. & Fisher, D. (1999). Students' perceptions of the efficacy of Web-based learning environment: the emergence of a new learning instrument. *Proceedings HERDSA Annual Conference -Cornerstones of Higher Education*, Melbourne.

Chang, V. & Fisher, D. (2003). The validation and application of a new learning environment instrument for online learning in higher education. In M. S. Khine & D. L. Fisher (Eds.), *Technology-rich learning environments: A future perspective* (pp. 1-18). Singapore: World Scientific.

Clayton, J. (2005). *The validation and application of an online learning environment instrument (OLLES).* Paper presented at World Conference on Educational Multimedia, Hypermedia and Telecommunications, Montreal, Canada.

Dwyer, D. C., Ringstaff, C., & Sandholtz, J. (1991). Changes in teachers' beliefs and practices in technology-rich classrooms. *Educational Leadership, 48* (8), 45-53.

Farnham, S., Cheng, L., Stone, L., Zaner-Godsey, M., & Clark, A. M. Hutchworld: Lessons learned. from http://research.microsoft.com/scg/papers/hutchvw2000.pdf.

Farnham, S., Cheng, L., Stone, L., Zaner-Godsey, M., & Clark, A. M. (2002). *HutchWorld: Clinical study of computer-mediated social support for cancer patients and their caregivers.* Paper presented at SIGCHI conference on human factors in computing systems.

Fraser, B. J. (1998). Classroom environment instruments: Development, validity and applications. *Learning Environments Research 1*, (1), 7-34.

Fraser, B. J., Anderson, G. J., & Walberg, H. J. (1982). *Assessment of learning environments: Manual for Learning Environment Inventory (LEI) and My Class Inventory (MCI) (3rd vers.).* Perth, Australia: Western Australian Institute of Technology.

Fraser, B. J. & Fisher, D. L. (1994). Assessing and researching the classroom environment. In D. Fisher (Ed.), *The study of learning Environment: Volume 9* (pp. 23-38). Perth: Curtin University of Technology.

Gardiner, W. L. (1989). Forecasting, planning, and future of information society. In P. Goumain (Ed.), *High technology workplaces:*

integrating technology, management, and design for productive work environments (pp. 27-39). New York: Van Nostrand Reinhold.

Gould, J. D. & Lewis, C. (1985). Designing for usability: Key principles and what designers think. *Communications of the ACM, 28* (3), 300-311.

Greenbaum, J. & Kyng, M. (Eds.). (1991). *Design at work: Cooperative design of computer systems.* Hillsdale, NJ: Erlbaum.

Grudin, J. (1991). Obstacles to user involvement in software product development, with implications for CSCW. *International Journal Man-Machine Studies, 34,* (3), 435-452.

Hadley, M. & Sheingold, K. (1993). Commonalities and distinctive patterns in teachers' integration of computers. *American Journal of Education, 101* (3), 261–315.

Hall, C. S. & Lindzey G. (1978). *Theories of personality (3rd ed).* New York: John Wiley & Sons.

Hartshorne, H. & May, M. A. (1928). *Studies in nature of character I. Studies in deceit. Book one: General methods and results. Book two: Statistical methods and results. (Vol 1).* New York: Macmillan.

Hasell, M. J. (1987). Community design and gaming/simulation: Comparison of communication techniques for participatory design session. *Simulations and Games, 18* (1), 82-115.

Jegede, O. J., Fraser, B. J., & Fisher, D. L. (1995). The development and validation of a distance and open learning environment scale. *Educational Technology Research & Development, 43* (1), 90-94.

Lewin, K. (1936). *Principles of topological psychology.* New York: McGraw.

McMahon, M. (1997). Social constructivism and the World Wide Web – A paradigm for learning. *Conference Proceedings of ASCILITE '97,* Perth, Australia.

Moos, R. H. (1974). *The social climate scales: An overview.* Palo Alto: Consulting Psychologists Press.

Muller, M. J., Haslwanter, J. H., & Dayton, T. (1997). Participatory practices in the software lifecycle. In M. Helander, T. K. Landauer, & P. Prabhu (Eds.), *Handbook of human-computer interaction* (Second edition) (pp, 225-297). Amsterdam, Elsevier.

Murray, H. A. (1938). *Explorations in personality.* New York: Oxford University Press.

Ravitz, J. L., Becker, H. J., & Wong, Y. T. (2000). *Teaching, learning and computing: 1998 national survey. Report #4,* University of

California, Irvine: Centre for Research on Information Technology and Organizations.

Relan, A. B. & Gillani, B. J. (1997). Web-based instruction and the traditional classroom: similarities and differences. In B. Khan (Ed.), *Web-based instruction* (pp. 25-37). New Jersey: Educational Technology Publications.

Schuler, D. & Namioka, A. (Eds.). (1993). *Participatory design: Principles and practices.* Hillsdale: Lawrence Erlbaum Associates.

Sherry, L. & Myers, K. M. M. (1998). The dynamics of collaborative design. *IEEE Transactions on Professional Communication, 41* (2): 123-139.

Shunk, D. H. (2000). *Learning theories: An educational perspective.* Upper Saddle River, NJ, Prentice-Hall.

Squire, K. (2003). Video games in education. *Journal of Intelligent Simulations and Gaming, 2* (1).

Stern, G. G. (1970). *People in context: Measuring person-environment congruence in education and industry.* New York: Wiley.

Taylor, P. C. & Maor, D. (2000, February). *Assessing the efficacy of online teaching with the Constructivist On-line Learning Environment Survey.* Paper presented at the 9th Annual Teaching Learning Forum, Perth, Western Australia.

Vygotsky, L. (1978). *Mind in society The development of higher psychological processes.* Cambridge, Mass: Harvard University Press.

Walker, R. A. & Lambert, P. E. (1995). *Designing electronic learning environments to support communities of learners: A tertiary approach.* from http://www.aare.edu.au/95pap/walkr95.220.

Walker, S. L. (2003). *Development and validation of an instrument for assessing distance education learning environments in higher education: The Distance Education Learning Environment Survey.* Unpublished doctoral thesis, Curtin University of Technology, Perth, Australia.

Zandvliet, D. B. (1999). *The physical and psychosocial environment associated with classrooms using new information technologies: A cross-national study.* Unpublished doctoral thesis, Curtin University of Technology, Perth, Australia.

Selected Bibliography

Alcorn, N. (1986). Action research: A tool for school development. *Delta, 37*, 33-44.

Aldridge, J. M. & Fraser, B. J. (2000). A cross-cultural study of classroom learning environments in Australia and Taiwan. *Learning Environments Research, 3*, 101-134.

Aldridge, J. M., Dorman, J. P., & Fraser, B. J. (2004). Use of multitrait-multimethod modelling to validate actual and preferred forms of the Technology-Rich Outcomes-Focused Learning Environment Inventory (TROFLEI). *Australian Journal of Educational and Developmental Psychology, 4*, 110-125.

Aldridge, J. M. & Fraser, B. J. (2000). A cross-cultural study of classroom learning environments in Australia and Taiwan. *Learning Environments Research, 3*, 101-134.

Aldridge, J. M. & Fraser, B. J. (2003). Effectiveness of a technology-rich outcomes-focused learning environment. In M. S. Khine & D. L. Fisher (Eds.), *Technology-rich learning environments, A future perspective* (pp. 41-69). Singapore: World Scientific Publishing.

Aldridge, J. M., Fraser, B. J., & Huang, T.-C. I. (1999). Investigating classroom environments in Taiwan and Australia with multiple research methods. *Journal of Education Research, 93*, 48-57.

Aldridge, J. M., Fraser, B. J., Taylor, P. C., & Chen, C.-C. (2000). Constructivist learning environments in a cross-national study in Taiwan and Australia. *International Journal of Science Education, 22*, 37-55.

Alva, S. A. (1991). Academic invulnerability among Mexican-American students: The importance of protective resources and appraisals. *Hispanic Journal of Behavioural Sciences, 13*, 18-34.

Anderson, G. J. (1982). The search for school climate: a review of the research. *Review of Educational Research, 52*, 368-420.

Anderson, L. W. & Burns, R. B. (1989). *Research in classrooms: The study of teachers, teaching, and instruction.* Oxford, England: Pergamon.

Anstine-Templeton, R. & Johnson, C. E. (1998). Making the school environment safe: Red Rose's formula. *Learning Environments Research: An International Journal, 1* (1), 35-57.

Anstine-Templeton, R. & Jensen, R. A. (1993). How exemplary teachers perceive their school environments. In D. L. Fisher (Ed.), *The study of learning environments, 7*, 94-100.

Ashton, P. & Webb, R. (1986). *Making a difference: Teacher's sense of efficacy*. New York: Longman.

Askew, M. & William, D. (1995). *Recent research in mathematics education 5-16*. London: Office for Standards in Education.

Astin, A. W. (1993). An empirical typology of college students. *Journal of College Student Development, 34*, 36-46.

Astin, A. W. (1993). *What matters in college: Four critical years revisited*. San Francisco: Jossey-Bass Publishers.

Astin, A. W. (2004). Why spirituality deserves a central place in liberal education. *Liberal Education, 90* (2) 34-41.

Atwool, N. (1999). Attachment in the school setting. New Zealand *Journal of Educational Studies, 34* (2), 309-322.

Bandura, A. (1997). *Self-efficacy: The exercise of control*. New York: Freeman.

Bain, J. D., McNaught, C., Mills, C., & Lueckenhausen, G. (1998). Describing computer-facilitated learning environments in higher education. *Learning Environments Research, 1*, 163-180.

Barksdale-Ladd, M. A. & Thomas, K. F. (2000). What's at stake in high-stakes testing: teachers and parents speak out. *Journal of Teacher Education, 51,* 384-397.

Barnette, J. J. (2000). Effects of stem and Likert response option reversals on survey internal consistency: If you feel the need, there is a better alternative to using those negatively worded stems. *Educational and Psychological Measurement, 60*, 361-70.

Beam, K. J. & Horvat, R. E. (1975). Differences among teachers' and students' perceptions of science classroom behaviors, and actual classroom behaviors. *Science Education, 59*, 333-344.

Beijaard, D., Verloop, N., Wubbels, T., & Feiman-Nemser, S. (2000). The professional development of teachers. In R. J. Simons, J., van der Linden & T. Duffy (Eds.), *New Learning* (pp. 261-274). Dordrecht/Boston/London: Kluwer Academic Publishers.

Ben-Chaim, D. & Zoller, U. (2001). Self-perception versus students' perception of teacher personal style in college science and mathematics courses. *Research in Science Education, 31*, 437-454.

Bentler, P. M. (1990). Comparative fit indexes in structural models. *Psychological Bulletin, 107*, 238-246.

Bentler, P. M. (1995). *EQS: Structural equations program manual*. California: Multivariate Software Inc.

Ben-Zvi, R., Hofstein, A., Kempa, R. F., & Samuel, D. (1977). Modes of instruction in high school chemistry. *Journal of Research in Science Teaching, 14*, 433-439.

Bereiter, C. (1994). Implications of postmodernism for science, or, Science as progressive discourse. *Educational Psychologist, 29* (1), 3-12.

Bereiter, C. (1997). Situated cognition and how to overcome it. In D. Kirshner & J. A. Whitson (Eds.), *Situated cognition: Social, semiotic, and psychological perspectives* (pp. 281-300). Hillsdale NJ: Lawrence Erlbaum.

Bereiter, C. (2002). *Education and mind in the knowledge age.* Mahwah, NJ: Lawrence Erlbaum.

Berry, J. M. (1987). *A self-efficacy model of memory performance.* Paper presented at the annual meeting of the American Educational Research Association, New York.

Bielaczyc, K. (2001). Designing social infrastructure: the challenge of building computer-supported learning communities. In P. Dillenbourg, A. Eurelings, & K. Hakkarainen (Eds.), *European perspectives on computer-supported collaborative learning. The proceedings of the First European Conference on Computer-Supported Collaborative Learning* (pp. 106-114). Maastricht: University of Maastrich.

Biemans, H. A., Jongmans, C. T., de Jong, F. P. C. M., & Bergen, T. C. M. (1999). Perceptions of teachers' instructional behavior in secondary agricultural education. *Journal of Agricultural Education and Extension, 5*, 231-238.

Biggs, J. B. (1987). *Student approaches to learning and studying.* Melbourne, Australia. Australian Council for Educational Research.

Black, P. & Wiliam, D. (1998). Assessment and classroom learning. *Assessment in Education, 5* (1), 7-74.

Blackburn, R. & Renwick, S. J. (1996). Rating scales for measuring the interpersonal circle in forensic psychiatric patients. *Psychological Assessment, 8* (1), 76-84.

Blaike, N. (1992). *Approaches to social enquiry.* Cambridge: Polity Press.

Bodgan, R. & Bilken, S. (1992). *Qualitative research for education.* Massachusetts: Allyn & Bacon.

Boekaerts, M. (1997). Self-regulated learning: a new concept embraced by researchers, policy makers, educators, teachers and students. *Learning and Instruction, 7* (1), 133-149.

Borg, W., Gall, J., & Gall, M. (1993). *Applying educational research.* New York: Longman.

Borich, G. D. (1992) (2nd Ed). *Effective teaching methods*. New York: Macmillan Publishing Company.

Boy, A. V. & Pine, G. J. (1988). *Fostering psychosocial development in the classroom*. Springfield, IL: Charles C. Thomas.

Boyle, E. A., Duffy, T., & Dunleavy, K. (2003). Learning styles and academic outcome: The validity and utility of Vermunt's inventory of learning styles in a British higher education setting. *British Journal of Educational Psychology, 73,* 263-290.

Brekelmans, M., Holvast, A., & van Tartwijk, J. (1992). Changes in teacher communication styles during the professional career. *Journal of Classroom Interaction, 27,* 13-22.

Brekelmans, M., Holvast, A., & van Tartwijk, J. (1993). Changes in teacher communication styles during the professional career. *Journal of Classroom Interaction, 27,* 13-22.

Brekelman. M., Levy, J., & Rodriquez, R. (1993). A typology of teacher communication style. In T. Wubbels & J. Levy (Eds.), *Do you know what you look like?* (pp. 46-55). London: The Falmer Press.

Brekelmans, M., Sleegers, P., & Fraser, B. J. (2000). Teaching for active learning. In P. R. J. Simons, J. L. van der Linden, & T. Duffy (Eds.), New learning (pp.227-242). Dordrecht: Kluwer.

Brekelmans, M. & Wubbels, T. (1991). Student and teacher perceptions of interpersonal teacher behavior: A Dutch perspective. *The Study of Learning Environments, 5,* 19-30.

Brekelmans, M., Wubbels, T., & den Brok, P. (2002). Teacher experience and the teacher-student relationship in the classroom environment. In S. C. Goh & M. S. Khine (Eds.), *Studies in educational learning environments: An international perspective* (pp. 73-100). Singapore: New World Scientific.

Borich, G. D. (1992) (2nd Ed). *Effective teaching methods*. New York: Macmillan Publishing Company.

Brislin, R. (1980). Translation and content analysis of oral and written material. In H. Triandis & J. Berry (Eds.), *Handbook of cross-cultural psychology: Methodology* (Vol. 2, pp. 389-444). London: Allyn & Bacon.

Brislin, R. W. (1983). Cross-cultural research in psychology. *Annual Review of Psychology, 34,* 363-400.

Brookover, W. B., Schweitzer, J. H., Schneider, J. M., Beady, C. H., Flood, P. K., & Weisenbaker, J. M. (1978). Elementary school social climate and school achievement. *American Educational Research Journal, 15,* 301-318.

Brooks, D. W., Nolan, D. E., & Gallagher, S. M. (2001). *Web-Teaching* (Second ed.). New York: Kluwer Academic/Plenum Publishers.

Brophy, J. E. & Good, T. L. (1986). Teacher behaviour and student achievement. In M. C. Wittrock (Ed.), *Handbook of research on teaching* (3rd ed., pp. 328-375). New York: Macmillan.

Brown, J. S., Collins, A., & Duguid, P. (1989). Situated cognition and the culture of learning. *Educational Researcher, 18*, 32-41.

Brown, J. S. & Duguid, P. (1994). Boderline issues: Social and material aspects of design. *Human-Computer Interaction, 9*, 3-36.

Brown, R. (1965). *Social psychology.* London: Collier-MacMillan.

Bruce, B. (1993). Innovation and social change. In B. Bruce, J. Peyton, & T. Batson (Eds.), *Networked-based classrooms: Promises and realities* (pp. 33-49). New York: Cambridge University Press.

Bryk, A. S. & Raudenbush, S. W. (1992). *Hierarchical Linear Models.* Newbury Park: CL: SAGE.

Busato, V. V., Prins, F. J., Elshout, J. J., & Hamaker, C. (1999). The relation between learning styles, the Big Five personality traits and achievement motivation in higher education. *Personality and Individual Differences, 26*, 129-140.

Byrne, B. M. (1998). *Structural equation modeling with LISREL, PRELIS, and SIMPLIS: Basic concepts, applications and programming.* Mahwah, NJ: Erlbaum.

Campbell, R. J., Kyriakides, L., Muijs, R. D., & Robinson, W. (2004). *Assessing teacher effectiveness: A differentiated model.* London: Routledge Falmer.

Candy, P. C. (1991). *Self-direction for lifelong learning.* San Francisco, CA: Jossey -Bass.

Carr, W. & Kemmis, S. (1986). *Becoming critical: Education knowledge and action research.* London: The Falmer Press.

Carroll, J. B. (1963). A model of school learning. *Teacher College Record, 64*, 723-733.

Carroll, J. M., G. Chin, G., Rosson, M. B., & Neale, D. C. (2001). The development of cooperation: Five years of participatory design in the virtual school. In J. M. Carroll (Ed.), *Human computer interaction in the new millennium* (pp. 373-393). Boston, MA: Addison-Wesley.

Cazden, C. B. (1986). Classroom discourse. In M. C. Wittrock (Ed.) *Handbook of research on teaching* (pp. 432-463). New York: MacMillan.

Chamberlain, V. M. & Cummings, M. N. (1984). Development of an instructor/course evaluation instrument. *College Student Journal, 18*, 246-250.

Chang, V. & Fisher, D. L. (2003). The validation and application of a new learning environment instrument for online learning in higher education. In M. S. Khine & D. L. Fisher (Eds.), *Technology-rich learning environments: A future perspective* (pp. 1-20). Singapore: World Scientific.

Chavez, R. C. (1984). The use of high inference measures to study classroom climates: A review. *Review of Educational Research, 54,* 237-261.

Chi, M. T. H. (1997). Quantifying qualitative analyses of verbal data: A practical guide. *The Journal of the Learning Sciences, 6,* (3) 271-315.

Ciborra, C. (2004). Encountering information systems as a phenomenon. In C. Avgerou, C. Ciborra, & F. Land (Eds.), *The social study of information and communication technology* (pp. 17-37). Oxford: University Press.

Clark, C. M. & Peterson, P. L. (1986). Teachers' thought processes. In M. C. Wittrock (Ed.), *Handbook of research on teaching* (3rd Ed.) (pp. 255-296). New York: MacMillan.

Clifton, R. A., Perry, R. P., Stubbs, C. A., & Roberts, L. W. (2004). Faculty environments, psychosocial dispositions and the academic achievement of college students. *Research in Higher Education, 45,* 801-828.

Cohen, D., Manion, L., & Morrison, K. (2000) (5th Ed). *Research methods in education.* London: Routledge/Falmer.

Collins, A., Brown, J. S., & Newman, S. E. (1989). Cognitive apprenticeship: Teaching the craft of reading, writing and mathematics. In L. B. Resnick (Ed.), *Knowing, learning and instruction: Essays in honor of Robert Glaser.* (pp. 453-494). Hillsdale: NJ: Erlbaum.

Cothran, D. J. & Ennis, C. D. (1997). Students' and teachers' perceptions of conflict and power. *Teaching and Teacher Education, 13,* 541-553.

Cox, M. (2001). Faculty learning communities: Change agents for transforming institutions into learning organizations. In D. Lieberman, & C. Wehlburg (Eds.), *To improve the academy* (pp. 69-93).

Creemers, B. P. M. (1994). *The effective classroom.* London: Cassell.

Creemers, B., Peters, T., & Reynolds, D. (1989). *School effectiveness and school improvement.* Lisse, The Netherland: Swets & Zeitlinger.

Creemers, B. P. M. & Reezigt, G. J. (1996). School level conditions affecting the effectiveness of instruction. *School Effectiveness and School Improvement, 7,* 197-228.

Creemers, B. P. M. & Scheerens, J. (1994). Developments in the educational effectiveness research programme. *International Journal of Educational Research, 21* (2), 125-140.

Cronbach, D. J. (1951). Coefficient alpha and internal structure of tests. *Psychometrika, 16* (3), 297-334.

Cronbach, L. J. (1990). *Essentials of psychological testing* (3rd ed.). New York: Harper and Row.

Crooks, T. J. (1988). The impact of classroom evaluation practices on students. *Review of Educational Research, 58,* 438-481.

Cruickshank, D. R. & Kennedy, J. J. (1986). Teacher clarity. *Teaching and Teacher Education, 2,* 43-67.

Cuban, L. (2002). *Oversold and underused: Computers in the classroom.* Cambridge, MA: Harvard University Press.

D'Apollonia, S. & Abrami, P. C. (1997). Navigating student ratings of instruction. *American Psychologist, 52,* 1198-1208.

Dart B., Burnett, P., Boulton-Lewis, G., Campbell, J., Smith, D., & McCrindle, A. (1999). Classroom environment and students' approaches to learning. *Learning Environments Research, 2,* 137-156.

De Corte, E., Verschaffel, L., Entwistle, N., & van Merriënboer, J. (Eds.), (2003). *Powerful learning environments: Unravelling basic components and dimensions. Advances in learning and instruction series.* Amsterdam/Boston/London: Pergamom.

Dempo, M. & Gibson, S. (1985). Teachers' sense of efficacy: An important factor in school achievement. *The Elementary School Journal, 86,* 173-184.

den Brok, P., Bergen, T., Stahl, R., & Brekelmans, M. (2004). Students' perceptions of teacher control behaviours. *Learning and Instruction, 14* (4), 425-443.

den Brok, P., Brekelmans, M., Levy, J., & Wubbels, T. (2002). Diagnosing and improving the quality of teachers' interpersonal behavior. *The International Journal of Educational Management, 4,* 176-184.

den Brok, P., Brekelmans, M., & Wubbels, T. (2003). Interpersonal teacher behaviour and student outcomes. *School Effectiveness and School Improvement, 15,* 407-466

den Brok, P., Fisher, D. L., Rickards, T., & Bull, E (2006). Californian science students' perceptions of their classroom learning environments. *Educational Research and Evaluation, 12* (1) 3-25.

den Brok, P., Levy, J., Rodriguez, R., & Wubbels, T. (2002). Perceptions of Asian-American and Hispanic-American teachers and their students on interpersonal communication style. *Teaching and Teacher Education, 18*, 447-467.

den Brok, P., Levy, J., Wubbels, T., & Rodriguez, M. (2003). Cultural influences on students' perceptions of videotaped lessons. *International Journal of Intercultural Relations, 27* (3), 355-374.

De Vellis, R. F. (1991). *Scale development: Theory and application.* Newbury Park: Sage Publications.

De Wever, B., Schellens, T., Valcke, M. & Van Keer, H. (2006). Content analysis schemes to analyze transcripts of online asynchronous discussion groups: A review. *Computers & Education, 46* (1), 6-28.

Diamond, R. M. (2002). Curricula and courses: Administrative issues. In R. M. Diamond (Ed.), *Field guide to academic leadership* (pp. 135-156). San Francisco: Jossey-Bass.

Docker, J, G., Fraser, B. J., & Fisher, D. L. (1989). Differences in psychosocial work environment of different types of schools. *Journal of Research in Childhood Education, 4*, 5-7.

Dorman, J. P. (2001). Associations between classroom environment and academic efficacy. *Learning Environments Research, 4*, 243-257.

Dorman, J. P. (2002). Classroom environment research: Progress and possibilities. *Queensland Journal of Educational Research, 18,* 112-140.

Dorman, J. P. (2003). Cross national validation of the What Is Happening In this Class questionnaire using confirmatory factor analysis. *Learning Environments Research, 6*, 231-245.

Dorman, J. P., Adams, J. E., & Ferguson, J. M. (2002). Psychosocial environment and student self-handicapping in secondary school mathematics classes: A cross-national study. *Educational Psychology, 22,* 499-511.

Dorman, J. P. & Ferguson, J. M. (2004). Associations between students' perceptions of mathematics classroom environment and self-handicapping in Australian and Canadian high schools. *McGill Journal of Education, 39, 68-86.*

Dorman, J. P. & Fraser, B. J. (1996). Teachers perceptions of school environment in Australian catholic and government secondary schools. *International Studies in Educational Administration, 24* (1), 78-87.

Doyle, W. (1986). Classroom organization and management. In M. C. Wittrock (Ed.), *Handbook of research on teaching* (3rd Ed.) (pp. 255-296). New York: MacMillan.

Drucker, P. (1985). *Innovation and entrepreneurship: Practice and principles.* New York: Harper and Row.

Dunkin, M. J. & Biddle, B. J. (1974). *The study of teaching.* New York: Rhinehart & Winston.

Dwyer, D. C., Ringstaff, C., & Sandholtz, J. (1991). Changes in teachers' beliefs and practices in technology-rich classrooms. *Educational Leadership, 48* (8), 45-53.

Edwards, C. H. (2000). *Classroom discipline and management* (3rd ed.). New York: John Wiley & Sons.

Emmer, E. T. & Everston, C. M. (1981). Synthesis of research on classroom management. *Educational Leadership, 38* (4), 342-347.

Engeström, Y. (1999). Activity theory and individual and social transformation. In Y. Engeström, R. Miettinen & R.-L. Punamäki (Eds.), *Perspectives on activity theory,* (pp. 19-38). Cambridge: Cambridge University Press.

Engeström, Y. (2004) New forms of learning in co-configuration work. Available: http://is.lse.ac.uk/events/ESRCseminars/engestrom.pdf. Retrieved 02.09.2005.

Entwistle, N. (1988). Motivational factors in students' approaches to learning. In R. R. Schmeck (Ed.), *Learning strategies and learning styles* (pp. 21-51). New York: Plenum Press.

Entwistle, N., & Ramsden, P. (1983). *Understanding student learning.* London: Croom Helm.

Entwistle, N. & Tait, H. (1990). Approaches to learning, evaluations of teaching and preferences for contrasting academic environments. *Higher Education, 19,* 169-194.

Erickson, F. (1986). Qualitative methods in research on teaching. In M. C. Wittrock (Ed.), *Handbook of research on teaching* (3rd ed.; pp. 119-161). New York: Macmillan.

Erickson, F. (1998). Qualitative research methods for science education. In B. J. Fraser & K. G. Tobin (Eds.), *International handbook of science education* (pp. 1155-1173).

Evans, H. & Fisher, D. L. (2000). Cultural differences in students' perceptions of science teachers' interpersonal behaviour. *Australian Science Teachers Journal, 46* (2), 9-18.

Everston, C. M., Anderson, C., Anderson, L., & Brophy, J. (1980). Relationships between classroom behaviour and student outcomes in junior high math and English classes. *American Educational Research Journal, 17,* 43-60.

Fabrigar, L. R., Visser, P. S., & Browne, M. W. (1997). Conceptual and methodological issues in testing the circumplex structure of data in personality and social psychology. *Personality and Social Psychology Review, 1,* 184-203.

Fabrigar, I. R., Wegener, D. T., MacCallum, R. C., & Strahan, E. J. (1999). Evaluating the use of exploratory factor analysis in psychological research. *Psychological Methods, 4*, 272-229.

Falloon, G. W. (1999). Developing exemplary practice: Why are some teachers better at IT than others? *Computers in New Zealand Schools, 11* (3), 19-23.

Fang, Z. (1996). A review of research on teacher beliefs and practices. *Educational Research, 38* (1), 47-65.

Ferguson, P. D. & Fraser, B. J. (1998). Changing in learning environment during the transition from primary to secondary school. *Learning Environments Research, 1*, 369-383.

Fisher, D. & Cresswell, J. (1998). Actual and ideal principal interpersonal behaviour. *Learning Environments Research, 1*, 231-247.

Fisher, D. L. & Fraser, B. J. (1982). Use of classroom environment scale in investigating relationships between achievement and environment. *Journal of Science and Mathematics Education in Southeast Asia, 5* (2), 5-9.

Fisher, D. L. & Fraser, B. J. (1983). A comparison of actual and preferred classroom environment as perceived by teachers and students. *Journal of Research in Science Teaching, 20*, 55-61.

Fisher, D. L. & Fraser, B. J. (1983). Validity and use of Classroom Environment Scale. *Educational Evaluation and Policy Analysis, 5*, 261-271.

Fisher, D. L. & Fraser, B. J. (1990). School Climate, (*SET Research information for teachers No.2*). Melbourne: Australian Council for Educational Research.

Fisher, D. F. & Fraser, B. J. (1991). Validity and use of school environment instruments. *Journal of Classroom Interaction, 26* (2), 13-18.

Fisher, D. L. & Fraser, B. J. (1991). School climate and teacher professional development. *South Pacific Journal of Teacher Education 19* (1), 17-32.

Fisher, D., Fraser, B., & Cresswell. J. (1995). Using the Questionnaire on Teacher Interaction in the professional development of teachers. *Australian Journal of Teacher Education, 20, 8-18*.

Fisher, D., Fraser, B., & Wubbels, T. (1993). Associations between school learning environment and teacher interpersonal behaviour in the classroom. In T. Wubbels & J. Levy (Eds.), *Do you know what you look like?* (pp.103-112). London: The Falmer Press.

Fisher, D. L., Fraser, B. J., Wubbels, T., & Brekelmans, M. (1993). Associations between school learning environment and teacher interpersonal behavior in the classroom. *The Study of Learning Environments, 7, 32-41.*

Fisher, D., Harrison, A., Henderson, D., & Hofstein, A. (1999). Laboratory learning environments and practical tasks in senior secondary science classes. *Research in Science Education, 28*, 353-363.

Fisher, D., Henderson, D., & Fraser, B. (1995). Interpersonal behaviour in senior high school biology classes. *Research in Science Education, 25*, 125-133.

Fisher, D., Henderson, D., & Fraser, B, J. (1997). Laboratory environments and student outcomes in senior high school biology. *The American Biology Teacher, 59*, 214-219.

Fisher, D. L. & Rickards, T. (2000). Teacher-student interpersonal behaviour as perceived by Science teachers and their students. In D. Fisher & J. Yang (Eds.), *Improving classroom research through international cooperation* (pp. 391-398). Taipei: National Taiwan Normal University.

Fisher, D. L., Rickards, T., Goh, S. C., & Wong, A. F. L. (1997). Perceptions of interpersonal teacher behaviour in secondary science classrooms in Singapore and Australia. *Journal of Applied Research in Education, 1* (2), 2-11.

Fisher, D. L. & Waldrip, B. G. (1999). Cultural factors of science classroom learning environments, teacher-student interactions and student outcomes, *Journal of Science Education and Technology, 17* (1), 83-96.

Fiske, S. T. & Taylor, S. E. (1991). *Social cognition.* New York: McGraw Hill.

Flanders, N. (1970). *Analyzing teacher behavior.* Reading, MA: Addison-Wesley.

Flavell, J. H. (1987). Speculations about the nature and development of metacognition. In F. E. Weinert & R. H. Kluwe (Eds.), *Metacognition, motivation and understanding* (pp. 21-29), Hillsdale, New Jersey: Erlbaum.

Foa, U. G. (1961). Convergence in the analysis of the structure of interpersonal behaviour. *Psychological Review, 68*, 341-353.

Fraser, B. J. (1981). *TOSRA: Test of Science-Related Attitudes Handbook.* Hawthorn: The Australian Council for Educational Research Limited.

Fraser, B. J. (1982). Differences between student and teacher perceptions of actual and preferred classroom learning environment. *Educational Evaluation and Policy Analysis, 4*, 511-519.

Fraser, B. J. (1986). *Classroom environment*. London: Croom Helm.

Fraser, B. J. (1990). Students' perceptions of their classroom environments. In K. Tobin, J. B. Kahle, & B. J. Fraser (Eds.), *Windows into science classrooms: Problems associated with higher-level cognitive learning* (pp. 199-221). Bristol, PA: Falmer.

Fraser, B. J. (1991). Two decades of classroom environment research. In B. J. Fraser & H. J. Walberg (Eds.), *Educational environments: Evaluation, antecedents and consequences* (pp. 3-27). Oxford, England: Pergamon.

Fraser, B. J. (1994). Research on classroom and school climate. In D. Gabel (Ed.), *Handbook of research on science teaching and learning* (pp. 493-541). New York: Macmillan.

Fraser, B. J. (1998). Science learning environments: Assessments, Effects and determinants. In B. J. Fraser & K. G. Tobin (Eds.), *International handbook of science education* (pp. 527-564). Dordrecht, The Netherlands: Kluwer.

Fraser, B. J. (1998). Classroom environment instruments: Development, validity, and applications. *Learning Environments Research, 1*, 7-33.

Fraser, B. J. (1999). Using learning environment assessments to improve classroom and school climates. In H. J. Freiberg (Ed.), *School climate: Measuring, improving and sustaining healthy learning environments* (pp. 65-83). London: Falmer Press.

Fraser, B. J. (2002). Learning Environment Research: Yesterday, today and tomorrow. In S. C. Goh & M. S. Khine (Eds.), *Studies in Educational learning Environments*. Singapore: World Scientific.

Fraser, B. J. & Deer, C. E. (1983). Improving classrooms through the use of information about learning environments. *Curriculum Perspectives, 3* (2), 41-46.

Fraser, B. J., Docker, J. G., & Fisher, D. L. (1988). Assessing and improving School Climate. *Evaluation and Research in Education, 2* (3). 109 – 122.

Fraser, B. J. & Fisher, D. L. (1982). Predicting students' outcomes from their perceptions of classroom psychosocial environment. *American Educational Research Journal, 19,* 498-518.

Fraser, B. J. & Fisher, D. L. (1983). Student achievement as a function of person-environment fit: A regression surface analysis. *British Journal of Educational Psychology, 53*, 89-99.

Fraser, B. J. & Fisher, D. L. (1983). Development and validation of short forms of some instruments for measuring student perceptions of actual and preferred classroom environment. *Science Education, 67*, 115-131.

Fraser, B. J. & Fisher, D. L. (1983). Use of actual and preferred classroom environment scales in person-environment fit research. *Journal of Educational Psychology, 75*, 303-313.

Fraser, B. J. & Fisher, D. L. (1986). Using short forms of classroom climate instruments to assess and improve classroom psychosocial environment. *Journal of Research in Science Teaching, 5*, 387-413.

Fraser, B. J., Malone, J. A., & Neale, J. M. (1989). Assessing and improving the psychosocial environment of mathematics classrooms. *Journal for Research in Mathematics Education, 20*, 191-201.

Fraser, B. & McRobbie, C. J. (1995). Science laboratory classroom environments at schools and universities: A cross-national study. *Educational Research and Evaluation, 1*, 289-317.

Fraser, B. J. & O'Brien, P. (1985). Student and teacher perceptions of elementary school classrooms. *Elementary School Journal, 85*, 567-580.

Fraser, B. J., Rennie, L., & Tobin, K. G. (1990). The learning environment as a focus in a study of higher cognitive learning. *International Journal of Science Education, 12*, 531-548.

Fraser, B. J . & Tobin, K. (1991). Combining qualitative and quantitative methods in classroom environment research. In B. J. Fraser & H. J. Walberg (Eds.), *Educational environments: Evaluation, antecedents and consequences* (pp. 271-292). Oxford, England: Pergamon Press.

Fraser, B., Treagust, D. & Dennis, B. (1986). Development of an instrument for assessing classroom psychosocial environment at universities and colleges. *Studies in Higher Education, 11*, 43-54.

Fraser, B. & Walberg, H. J. (Eds.). (1991). *Educational environments: Evaluation, antecedents and consequences.* Oxford: Pergamon Press.

Fraser, B. & Walberg, H. J., Welch, W. W., & Hattie, J. A. (1987). Synthesis of educational productivity research. *International Journal of Educational Research, 11, 145 – 252.*

Fraser, B. J. & Wubbels, T. (1995). Classroom learning environments. In B. J. Fraser & H. J. Walberg (Eds.), *Improving science education* (pp. 117-144). Chicago: National Society for the Study of Education.

Freiberg, H. J. (1998). Measuring school climate: Let me count the ways. *Educational Leadership, 56* (1), 22-26.

Galton, M. (1987). An ORACLE Chronicle: A decade of classroom research. *Teaching and Teacher Education, 3* (4), 299-313.

Garcia, J. A. & Floyd, C. E. (2002F). Addressing evaluative standards related to program assessment: How do we respond? *Journal of Social Work Education, 38*, 369-382.

Gardiner, W.L. (1989). Forecasting, planning, and the future of the information society. In P. Gourmain (Ed.), *High technology workplaces: Integrating technology, management, and design for productive work environments* (pp. 27-39). New York: Van Nostrand Reinhold.

Gardner, P. (1975). *Attitudes to science: A Review.* Studies in Science Education, 2, 1-41.

Gardner, P. & Gauld, C. (1990). Labwork and students' attitudes. In E. Hegarty-Hazel (Ed.), *The student laboratory and the science curriculum* (pp. 132-156). London: Routledge.

Garrison, D. R., Anderson, T., & Archer, W. (2001). Critical thinking, cognitive presence, and computer conferencing in distance education. *American Journal of Distance Education, 15* (1), 7-23.

Getzels, J. W. & Thelen, H. A. (1960). The classroom group as a unique social system. *National Society for Studies in Education Year Book, 59*, 53-82.

Gilbert, N. J. & Driscoll, M. P. (2002). Collaborative knowledge building: A case study. *Educational Technology, Research and Development, 50* (1), 59-79.

Gladieux, L. E. & Swail, W. S. (2000). Beyond access improving the odds of college success. *Phi Delta Kappan, 81*, 688-692

Godfrey, C. (2001). Computers in schools: Changing pedagogies. *Journal of the Australian Council for Computers in Education, 16* (2), 14-17.

Goh, S. C. & Khine, M. S. (Eds.). (2002). *Studies in educational learning environments: An international perspective.* Singapore: World Scientific.

Goldstein, H. (1995). *Multilevel statistical models.* London: Edward Arnold.

Good, T. & Brophy, J. (2003). *Looking in classrooms.* (9th ed.). Boston: Allyn and Bacon.

Goodrum, D., Hackling, M., & Rennie, L. (2001). *The status and quality of teaching and learning in Australian schools.* Department of Education, Training and Youth Affairs: Canberra.

Gore, J. M. (2001). Beyond our differences, a reassembling of what matters in teacher education. *Journal of Teacher Education, 52*, 124-135.

Gorham, J. & Millette, D. M. (1997). A comparative analysis of teacher and student perceptions of sources of motivation and demotivation in college classes. *Communication Education, 46*, 245-261.

Gorham, J. & Zakahi, W. R. (1990). A comparison of teacher and student perceptions of immediacy and learning: monitoring process and product. *Communication Education, 39*, 354-368.

Goumain, P. (1989). Changing environments for high-technology workplaces. In P. Goumain (Ed.), *High technology workplaces: integrating technology, management, and design for productive work environments* (pp. 1-23). New York: Van Nostrand Reinhold.

Greenwald, A. G. (1997). Validity concerns and usefulness of student ratings of instruction. *American Psychologist, 52*, 1182-1186.

Griffin, G.A. & Barnes, S. (1986). Using research findings to change school and classroom practice: Results of an experimental study. *American Educational Research Journal, 23* (4), 572-586.

Griffith, J. (2000). School climate as group evaluation and group consensus: Student and parent perceptions of the elementary school environment. *The Elementary School Journal, 101* (1), 35-61.

Grundy, S. (1995). Action research as on-going professional development. *Affiliation of Arts Educators (WA)*.

Guba, E. G. & Lincoln, Y. S. (1989). *Fourth generation evaluation*. Beverly Hills: Sage Publications.

Gunawardena, C., Lowe, C., & Anderson, T. (1997). Analysis of a global online debate and the development of an interaction analysis model for examining social construction of knowledge in computer conferencing. *Journal of Educational Computing Research, 17* (4), 397-431.

Gurtman, M. B. & Pincus, A. L. (2000). Interpersonal adjective scales: confirmation of circumplex structure from multiple perspectives. *Personality and Social Psychology Bulletin, 26*, 374-384.

Guskin, A. E. & Marcy, M. B. (2002). Pressures of fundamental reform: Creating a viable academic future. In R. M. Diamond (Ed.), *Field guide to academic leadership* (pp. 3-13). San Francisco: Jossey-Bass.

Guzdial, M. & Turns, J. (2000). Effective discussion through computer-mediated anchored forum. *The Journal of the Learning Sciences, 9* (4), 437-469.

Haertel, G. D., Walberg, H. J., & Haertel, E. H. (1981). Sociopsychological environments and learning: A quantitative synthesis. *British Educational Research Journal, 7*, 27-36.

Hannum, W. (2002). Technology in the learning process. In R. M. Diamond (Ed.), *Field guide to academic leadership* (pp. 175-192). San Francisco: Jossey-Bass.

Hanseth, O. (2004). Knowledge as infrastructure. In C. Avgerou, C. Ciborra, & F. Land (Eds.), *The social study of information and communication technology,* (pp. 103-118). Oxford: University Press.

Hanseth, O. & Lundberg, N. (2001). Designing work oriented infrastructures. *Computer Supported Cooperative Work, 10,* 347–372.

Hara, N., Bonk, C. J., & Angeli, C. (2000). Content analysis of online discussion in an applied educational psychology course. *Instructional Science, 28,* 115-152.

Harlen, W. (1998). Teaching for understanding in pre-secondary science, In B. J. Fraser & K. G. Tobin (Eds.), *International handbook of science education* (pp. 183-198). Dordrecht, The Netherlands: Kluwer.

Hattie, J. A. (1987). Identifying the salient facets of a model of student learning: A synthesis of meta-analyses. *International Journal of Educational Research, 11,* 187-212.

Henderson, D. & Fisher, D. (1998). Assessing learning environments in senior science laboratories. *Australian Science Teachers Journal, 44,* 57-61.

Henderson, D., Fisher, D. L., & Fraser, B. J. (2000). Interpersonal behaviour, laboratory learning environments and student outcomes in senior biology classes. *Journal of Research in Science Teaching, 37,* 26-43.

Hill, J. R. & Hannafin, M. J. (2001). Teaching and learning in digital environments: The resurgence of resource-based learning. *Educational Technology, Research and Development, 49* (3).

Hobden, P. (1998). The role of routine problems in science teaching. In B. J. Fraser & K. G. Tobin (Eds.), *International handbook of science education* (pp. 219-232). Dordrecht, The Netherlands: Kluwer.

Hofstein, A. & Lazarowitz, R. (1986). A comparison of the actual and preferred classroom in biology and chemistry as perceived by high-school students. *Journal of Research in Science Teaching, 23,* 189-199.

Hofstein, A., Lazarowitz, R., & Cohen, I. (1996). *Research in Science and Technological Education*, 14, 103-116.

Hofstein, A., Levi-Nahum, T., & Shore, R. (2001). Assessment of the learning environment of inquiry-type laboratories in high school chemistry. *Learning Environments Research, 4,* 193-207.

Hofstein, A. & Lunetta,V. N. (1982). The role of the laboratory in science teaching: Neglected aspects of research. *Review of Educational Research, 52* (2), 201-217.

Hofstein, A. & Lunetta, V, N. (2004). The laboratory in science education: Foundation for the 21st century. *Science Education, 88,* 28-54.

Hoftsein, A., Navon, O., Kipnis, M., & Mamlok-Naaman, R. (2005). Developing students ability to ask more and better questions resulting from inquiry-type chemistry laboratories. *Journal of Research in Science Teaching, 42* (7), 791-806.

Hofstein, A., Shore, R., & Kipnis, M. (2004). Providing high school chemistry students with opportunities to develop learning skills in an inquiry-type laboratory-a case study. *International Journal of Science Education, 26,* 47-62.

Hofstein, A. & Walberg, H. (1995). Effective instructional strategies in science. In: B. Fraser & H. Walberg (Eds.), *Improving science education.* The National Society for the Study of Education (NSSE) Yearbook.

Holland, J. H. (1998). *Emergence from chaos to order.* Reading, Berkshire, UK: Oxford University Press.

Hooper, S. (1992). Cooperative learning and computer-based instruction. *Educational Technology Research and Development, 40* (3), 21-38.

Howard, S., Dryden, J., & Johnson, B. (1999). Childhood resilience: Review and critique of literature. *Oxford Review of Education, 25,* 307-323.

Hox, J. J. (1995). *Applied multilevel analysis.* Amsterdam: TT Publicaties.

Hoy, W. K. & Hannum, J. W. (1997). Middle school climate: An empirical assessment of organisational health and student achievement. *Educational Administration Quarterly, 33* (3), 290-311.

Hoy, W. K., Tarter, C. J., & Bliss, J. R. (1990). Organizational climate, school health, and effectiveness: A comparative analysis. *Educational Administration Quarterly, 26* (3), 260-279.

Hunt, D. E. (1975). Person environment interaction: A challenge found wanting before it was tried. *Review of Educational Research, 45,* 209-230.

Iverson, B. (2001). *Transformation of teaching and learning through technology: It's about the teaching, not the tools.* Chicago: Columbia College. Retrieved June 16, 2003, from http://nexus.colum.edu/user/iverson/fipse/for%20printing/toprint.pdf.

Johnson, C. E. & Anstine-Templeton, R. (1999). Promoting peace in a place called school. *Learning Environments Research An International Journal, 2* (1), 65-77.

Johnson, D. W. & Johnson, R. T. (1996). Cooperation and the use of technology. In D. H. Jonassen (Ed.), *Handbook of research for educational communications and technology* (pp. 1017-1044). New York: Macmillan.

Jonassen, D. H. & Grabowski, B. L. (1993). *Handbook of individual differences in learning and instruction.* New Jersey/London: Lawrence Erlbaum Associates.

Jöreskog, K. G. & Sörbom, D. (1993). *LISREL 8: User's reference guide.* Chicago, IL: Scientific Software International.

Kelloway, E. K. (1998). *Using LISREL for structural equation modeling: A researcher's guide.* Thousand Oaks, CA: Sage.

Kember, D. (1997). A reconceptualisation of research into university academics' conceptions of teaching. *Learning and Instruction, 7* (3), 255-275.

Kember, D. & Gow, L. (1994). Orientations to teaching and their effect on the quality of student learning. *Journal of Higher Education. 65* (1), 59-74.

Kember, D. & Kwan, K. P. (2000). Lecturers' approaches to teaching and their relationship to conceptions of good teaching. *Instructional Science, 28*, 469-490.

Khalili, A. & Shashaani, L. (1994). The effectiveness of computer applications: A meta-analysis. *Journal of Research on Computing in Education, 27* (1).

Khine, M. S. (2001). Using the WIHIC Questionnaire to measure the learning environment. *Teaching & Learning, 22* (2) 54-60.

Khine, M. S. & Fisher, D. L. (Eds.). (2003). *Technology-rich learning environments: A future perspective.* Singapore: World Scientific.

Khine, M. S. (2003). Creating a technology-rich constructivist learning environment in a classroom management module. In M. S. Khine & D. L. Fisher (Eds.). *Technology-rich learning environments: A future perspective*, (pp. 21-39). Singapore: World Scientific.

Khine, M. S. & Fisher, D. L. (2003). Teacher-student interactions in science classrooms in Brunei. *Journal of Classroom Interaction, 38* (2), 17-28.

Khine, M. S. & Fisher, D. L. (2004). Teacher interaction in psychosocial learning environments: cultural differences and their implications in science instruction. *Research in Science and Technological Education. 22* (1), 99-111.

Kim, H., Fisher, D. L., & Fraser, B. J. (1999). Assessment and investigation of constructivist science learning environments in Korea. *Research in Science & Technological Education, 17* (2), 239-250.

Kim, H., Fisher, D. L, & Fraser, B. J. (2000). Classroom environment and teacher interpersonal behaviour in secondary science classes in Korea. *Evaluation and Research in Education, 14,* 3-22.

Kirschner, P. A., Martens, R. L., & Strijbos, J. W. (2004). CSCL in Higher Education? In J. W. Strijbos, P. A. Kirschner, & R. L. Martens (Eds.), *What we know about CSCL and Implementing it in Higher Education,* (pp. 3-31). Dordrecht, Netherlands: Kluwer Academic Publishers.

Kline, R. B. (1998). *Principles and practice of structural equation modeling.* New York: The Guilford Press.

Klopfer, L. E. (1976). A structure for the affective domain in relation to science education. *Science Education, 60,* 299-312.

Knight, S. L. & Waxman, H. C. (1990). Investigating the effects of the classroom learning environment on students' motivation in social studies. *Journal of Social Studies Research, 14,* 1-12.

Knight, S. L. & Waxman, H. C. (1991). Students' cognition and classroom instruction. In H. C. Waxman & H. J. Walberg (Eds.), *Effective teaching: Current research* (pp. 239-255). Berkeley, CA: McCutchan.

Kolb, D. A. (1984). *Experiential learning. Experience as a source of learning and development.* Englewood Cliffs, New Jersey: Prentice Hall Inc.

Kolodner, J. & Guzdial, M. (1996). Effects with and of CSCL: Tracking learning in a new paradigm. In T. Koschmann (Eds.), *CSCL: Theory into practice of an emerging paradigm* (pp. 307-320). Mahwah, NJ: Lawrence Erlbaum.

Korthagen, F. A. J. & Lagerwerf, B. (1996). Reframing the relationship between teacher thinking and teacher behavior: levels in learning about teaching. *Teachers and Teaching: Theory and Practice, 2,* 161-190.

Kulkarni, V. G. (1988). Role of language in science education. In P. Fensham (Ed.), *Development and dilemmas in science education* (pp. 150-168). The Falmer Press.

Kyriakides, L. (2005a). Extending the comprehensive Model of Educational Effectiveness by an empirical investigation. *School Effectiveness and School Improvement, 16* (2), 103-152.

Kyriakides, L., Campbell, R. J., & Gagatsis, A. (2000). The significance of the classroom effect in primary schools: An application of Creemers' comprehensive model of educational effectiveness. *School Effectiveness and School Improvement 11* (4), 501-529.

Laforgia, J. (1988). The affective domain related to science education and its evaluation. *Science Education, 72* (4), 407-421.

Lajoie, S. P. (1993). Computer environments as cognitive tools for enhancing learning. In S. P. Lajoie & R. Derry (Eds.), *Computers as cognitive tools* (pp. 261-288). Hillsdale, NJ: Erlbaum.

Lazarowitz, R. & Tamir, P. (1994). Research on using laboratory instruction in science, in D. L. Gabel. (Ed.), *Handbook of research on science teaching and learning* (pp. 94-130). New-York: Macmillan.

Leary, T. (1957). *An interpersonal diagnosis of personality.* New York: Ronald Press Company.

Lee, O. (1995). Subject matter knowledge, classroom management, and instructional practices in middle school science classrooms. *Research in Science Teaching, 32* (4), 423-440.

Leithwood, K. A. & Montgomery, D. J. (1980). Evaluating program implementation. *Evaluation Reviews, 4*, 193-214.

Levy, J., den Brok, P., Wubbels, T., & Brekelmans, M. (2003). Students' perceptions of interpersonal aspects of the learning environment. *Learning Environments Research, 6*, 5-36.

Levy, J., Wubbels, T., Brekelmans, M., & Morganfield, B. (1997). Language and cultural factors in students' perceptions of teacher communication style. International *Journal of Intercultural Relationships, 21*, 1, 29-56.

Levy, J., Wubbels, T., & Brekelmans, M. (1992). Student and teacher characteristics and perceptions of teacher communication style. *Journal of Classroom Interaction, 27*, 23-29.

Lewin, K. (1935). *A dynamic theory of personality.* New York: McGraw.

Lewin, K. (1936). *Principals of topological psychology.* New York: Ronald Press Co.

Lin, X. & Hatano, G. (2001*).* Cross-cultural adaptation of educational technology. In T. Koschmann & N. Miyake (Eds.), *CSCL2: Carrying forward the conversation.* Mahwah, NJ: Lawrence Erlbaum Associates.

Lipponen, L., Hakkarainen, K., & Paavola, S. (2004). Practices and orientations of CSCL. In J. W. Strijbos, P. A. Kirschner, & R. L. Martens (Eds.), *What we know about CSCL and Implementing it in*

Higher Education, (pp. 34-50). Dordrecht, Netherlands: Kluwer Academic Publishers.

Lipponen, L. & Lallimo, J. (2004). From collaborative technology to collaborative use of technology: Designing learning oriented infrastructures. *Educational Media International, 41*, 111-116.

Lipponen, L. & Lallimo, J. (2004). Assessing applications for collaboration: From collaboratively usable applications to collaborative technology. *British Journal of Educational Technology, 35*, 433-442.

Lonner, W. J. (1980). The search for psychological universals. In H. C. Triandis & W. W. Lambert (Eds.), Handbook of cross cul tural psychology (vol.1) (pp. 143-204). Boston: Allyn and Bacon.

Loughlin, C. E. & Suina, J. H. (1982). *The learning environment: An instructional strategy*. New York: Teachers College Press.

Luyten, H. & De Jong, R. (1998). Parallel classes: differences and similarities. Teacher effects and school effects in secondary schools. *School Effectiveness and School Improvement, 9* (4), 437-473.

Lyman, R. D., Prentice-Dunn, S. Wilson, D. R., & Bonfilio, S. A. (1984). The effect of success or failure on self-efficacy and task persistence of conduct-disordered children. *Psychology in the Schools, 21,* 516-519.

Maor, D. & Fraser, B. J. (1996). Use of classroom environment perceptions in evaluating inquiry based, computer assisted learning. *International Journal of Science Education, 18*, 401-421.

Marjoribanks, K. (2004). Learning environments, family contexts, educational aspirations and attainment: A moderation-mediation model extended. *Learning Environments Research, 6*, 247-265.

Marsh, H. W. & Roche, L. A. (1997). Making students' evaluations of teaching effectiveness effective. *American Psychologist, 52*, 1187-1197.

Maruyama, G. M. (1998). *Basics of structural equation modeling*. Thousand Oaks, California: SAGE.

Marx, A., Fuhrer, U., & Hartig, T. (2000). Effects of classroom seating arrangements on children's question-asking. *Learning Environments Research, 2*, 249-263.

McCombs, B. L. & Whisler, J. S. (1997). The learner-centered classroom and school: Strategies for increasing student motivation and achievement. San Francisco: Jossey-Bass.

McCune, S. D. (1991). Restructuring education. In D. Dickinson (Ed.), *Creating the future: Perspectives on educational change* (pp. 162-

182). Aston Clinton, Bucks, UK: Accelerated Learning Systems Limited.

McRobbie, C. J. & Fraser, B. J. (1993). Associations between student outcomes and psychosocial science environment. *Journal of Educational Research, 87,* 78-85.

Medley, D. (1979). The effectiveness of teachers. In P. Peterson & H. Walberg (Eds.), *Research on teaching: Concepts, findings and implications.* Berkeley, CA: McCutchan.

Merriam, S. B. (1990). *Case study research in education.* San Francisco: Jossey-Bass Inc.

Messick, S. (1989). Validity. In R. Linn (Ed.), *Educational measurement* (3rd ed.) (pp. 13-103). New York: Macmillan Publishing Co.

Middleton, D. (1981). *Observing classroom processes.* Milton Keynes: The Open University Press.

Midgley, C. & Urdan, T. (1995). Predictors of middle school students' use of self-handicapping strategies. *Journal of Early Adolescence, 15,* 389-411.

Moos, R. H. (1974). *The social climate scales: An overview.* Palo Alto: Consulting Psychologists Press.

Moos, R. H. (1979). *Evaluating educational environments: procedures, measures, findings and policy implications.* San Francisco: Jossey Bass.

Moos, R. H. (1981). *Manual for Work Environment Scale.* Palo Alto, CA: Consulting Psychology Press.

Moos, R. H. (1991). Connections between school, work, and family settings. In B. J. Fraser & H. J. Walberg (Eds.), *Educational environments: Evaluation, antecedents and consequences* (pp. 29-53). London: Pergamon.

Moos, R. H. & Trickett, E. J. (1987). *Classroom Environment Scale manual* (2nd Ed.). Palo Alto, CA: Consulting Psychologists Press.

Mucherah, W. M. (2003). The influence of technology on the classroom climate of social studies classrooms: A multidimensional approach. *Learning Environment Research, 6,* 37-57.

Muijs, D. & Reynolds, D. (2000). School effectiveness and teacher effectiveness in mathematics: Some preliminary findings from the evaluation of the Mathematics Enhancement Programme (Primary). *School Effectiveness and School Improvement, 11* (3), 273-303.

Multon, K. D., Brown, S. D., & Lent, R. W. (1991). Relation of self-efficacy beliefs to academic outcomes: A meta-analytic investigation. *Journal of Counselling Psychology, 18,* 30-38.

Muncey, D. E. & McQuillan, P. (1993). Preliminary findings from a five-year study of the coalition of essential schools. *Phi Delta Kappan, 74* (6), 486-489.

Munck, I. M. E. (1979). *Model building in comparative education: Applications of the LISREL method to cross-national survey data.* Stockholm: Almqvist & Wiksell.

Murray, H. A. (1938). *Explorations in personality.* New York: Oxford University Press.

Murdock, S. H. & Hoque, M. N. (1999). Demographic factors affecting higher education in the United States in the twenty-first century. In G. H. Gaither (Ed.), *Promising practices in recruitment, remediation, and retention* (pp. 5-13). San Francisco: Jossey-Bass.

Muthén, B. (1994). Multilevel covariance structure analysis. *Sociological Methods & Research*, 22, 338-354.

Newhouse, P. (1998). The impact of portable computers on classroom learning environments. *Journal of the Australian Council for Educational Computing, 13* (1), 5-11.

Nieto, S. (1996). Affirming diversity: *The sociopolitical context of multicultural education.* New York: Longman.

Nowicki, S. & Strickland, B. (1973) A locus of control scale for children. *Journal of Consulting and Clinical Psychology, 40* (1), 148-154.

Nunnally, J. (1967). *Psychometric theory.* New York: Mc-Graw Hill.

Nuthall, G. & Alton-Lee, A. (1990). Research on teaching and learning: Thirty years of change. *The Elementary School Journal, 90*, 546-570.

Oldfather, P. (1995). Songs "come back to most of them": Students' experiences as researchers. *Theory into Practice, 34*, 131-137.

Oliver, R., Omari, A., & Herrington, J. (1998). Investigating implementation strategies for WWW based learning environments. *International Journal of Instructional Media, 25* (2), 121.

Ornstein, A. C. (1991). Teacher effectiveness research: Theoretical considerations. In H. C. Waxman & H. J. Walberg (Eds.), *Effective teaching: Current research* (pp. 63-80). Berkeley, CA: McCutchan.

Oshima J. (1998) Differences in knowledge-building between two types of networked learning environments: An information analysis. *Journal of Educational Computing Research, 19* (3), 329-351.

Ouimet, J. A., Bunnage, J. C., Carini, R. M., Kuh, G. D., & Kennedy, J. (2004). Using focus group, expert advice and cognitive interviews to establish the validity of a college student survey. *Research in Higher Education, 45*, 233-250.

Pace, C. R. & Stern, G. G. (1958). An approach to the measurement of psychological characteristics of college environments. *Journal of Educational Psychology, 49*, 269-277.

Padrón, Y. N., Waxman, H. C., & Huang, S. L. (1999). Classroom and instructional learning environment differences between resilient and non-resilient elementary school students. *Journal of Education for Students Placed at Risk of Failure, 4* (1), 63-81.

Page, N. (1999). In search of a philosophy for ICT. *Computers in New Zealand Schools, 11* (3), 15-18.

Pajares, F. (1996). Self-efficacy beliefs and mathematical problem solving of gifted students. *Contemporary Educational Psychology, 21*, 325–344.

Papanastasiou, C. (2002). School, teaching and family influence on student attitudes toward science: Based on TIMSS data for Cyprus. *Studies in Educational Evaluation, 28* (1), 71-86.

Peterson, R. W. & Carlson, G. R. (1979). A summary of research in science education. *Science Education, 59*, 207-210.

Pickering, M. (1980) Are laboratory courses a waste of time? *Chronicle of Higher Education, 19*, 44-50.

Pierce, C. (1994). Importance of classroom climate for at-risk learners. *Journal of Educational Research, 88*, 37-42.

Printrich, P. R. & De Groot, E. V. (1990). Motivation and self-regulated learning components of classroom academic performance. *Journal of Educational Psychology, 82*, 33-40.

Pintrich, P. R., Smith, D. A. F., Garcia, T., & McKeachie, W. J. (1993). Reliability and predictive validity of the Motivated Strategies for Learning Questionnaire (MSLQ). *Educational and Psychological Measurement, 53*, 801-813.

Popham, W. J. (1997). Consequential validity: Right concern-wrong concept. *Educational Measurement: Issues and Practice, 16* (2), 9-13.

Powell, R. R. (1992). The influence of prior experiences on pedagogical constructs of traditional and non-traditional preservice teachers. *Teacher & Teacher Education, 8* (3), 225-238.

Radnor, H. (1996). *Evaluation of key stage 3 assessment in 1995 and 1996.* Exeter: University of Exeter.

Redfield, D. & Rousseau, E. (1981). A meta-analysis of experimental research on teacher questioning behaviour. *Review of Educational Research, 51*, 237-245.

Reeves, T., Herrington, J., & Oliver, R. (2004). A development research agenda for online collaborative learning. *Educational Technology, Research and Development, 52* (4), 53-65.

Reigeluth, C. M. (1999). Visioning public education in America. *Educational Technology, 39* (5), 50-55.

Rentoul, A. J. & Fraser, B. J. (1980). Predicting learning from classroom individualization and actual-preferred congruence. *Studies in Educational Evaluation, 6*, 265-277.

Rentoul, A. J. & Fraser, B. J. (1983). Development of a school-level environment questionnaire. *Journal of Educational Administration, 21*, 21-39.

Resnick, M. (2002). *Rethinking learning in the digital age.* The Media Laboratory. Massachusetts Institute of Technology. Chapter 3. 32-37.

Reyes, O. & Jason, L. A. (1993). Pilot study examining factors associated with academic success for Hispanic high school students. Journal of Youth and Adolescence, 22, 57-71.

Reynolds, D. & Packer, A. (1992). School effectiveness and school improvement in the 1990s. In D. Reynolds & P. Cuttance (Eds.), *School effectiveness: Research, policy and practice* (pp. 171-187). London: Cassell.

Rickards, T. (1998). *The relationship of teacher-student interpersonal behaviour with student sex, cultural background and student outcomes.* Unpublished doctoral dissertation, Curtin University, Perth, Australia.

Rickards, T. (2003). Technology-rich learning environments and the role of effective teaching. In M. S. Khine & D. L. Fisher (Eds.). *Technology-rich learning environments: A future perspective* (pp. 97-113). Singapore: World Scientific.

Rideng, I. M., & Schibeci, R. A. (1984). The development and validation of a test of biology-related attitudes. *Research in Science and Technological Education, 2*, 21-29.

Rigdon, E. E. (1998). Structural equation modeling. In G. A. Marcoulides (Ed.), *Modern methods for business research* (pp. 251-294). Mahwah, NJ: Lawrence Erlbaum Associates.

Roeser, R. W., Midgley, C., & Urdan, T. (1996). Perceptions of the school psychological environment and early adolescents' self-appraisals and academic engagement: The mediating role of goals and belonging. *Journal of Educational Psychology, 88,* 408-422.

Rogoff, B. (2001, September 14). Student assessment for the information age. *The Chronicle of Higher Education, 48* (3), p. B17.

Roschelle, J. M., Pea, R. D., Hoadley, C. M., Gordin, D. N., & Means, B. M. (2001). Changing how and what children learn in school with computer-based technologies. *The Future of Children: Children and Computer Technology, 10* (2), 76-101.

Rosenshine, B. (1971). *Teaching behaviours and student achievement.* London: NFER.

Rosenshine, B. & Furst, N. (1973). The use of direct observation to study teaching. In R. M. W. Travers (Ed.), *Second handbook of research on teaching.* Chicago: Rand McNally.

Rosenshine, B. & Stevens, R. (1986). Teaching functions. In M. C. Wittrock (Ed.), *Handbook of research on teaching* (3rd. ed., pp. 376-391). New York: Macmillan.

Rossum, E. J. Van & Schenk, S. M. (1984). The relationship between learning conception, study strategy and learning outcome. *British Journal of Educational Psychology, 54,* 73-83.

Rutter, M. (1983). School effects on pupils progress: Research findings and policy implications. *Child Development, 54,* 1-29.

Sadler-Smith, E. (1996). Approaches to studying: Age, gender and academic performance. *Educational Studies, 22* (3), 367-379.

Säljö, R. (1979). Learning about learning. *Higher Education, 8,* 443-451.

Salomon, G. (2002). Technology and pedagogy: Why don't we see the promised revolution? *Educational Technology, 42,* 71-75.

Samdal, O., Wold, B., & Bronis, M. (1999). Relationship between students' perceptions of school environment, their satisfaction with school and perceived academic achievement: An international study. *School Effectiveness and School Improvement, 10* (3), 296-320.

Santos, J. R. A. & Clegg, M. D. (1999). Factor analysis adds new dimension to extension survey. *Journal of Extension, 37*(5), 1-7.

Scardamalia, M. (2000). Can school enter a knowledge society? In M. Selinger, (Ed.), *Proceedings of educational technology and the impact on teaching and learning: A global research forum.* London, England.

Scardamalia, M. & Bereiter, C. (1994). Computer support for knowledge-building communities. *The Journal of the Learning Sciences, 3* (3), 265-283.

Scardamalia, M. & Bereiter, C. (1996). Computer support for knowledge-building communities. In T. Koschmann (Ed.), *CSCL: Theory and Practice of an emerging paradigm* (pp. 249-268). NJ: Lawrence Erlbaum.

Scardamalia, M. & Bereiter, C. (2003). Knowledge Building. In James W. Guthrie (Ed.), *Encyclopedia of Education. (2ⁿᵈ ed.)* (pp. 1370-1373). New York: Mcamillan Reference, USA.

Scheerens, J. (1993). Basic school effectiveness research: items for a research agenda. *School Effectiveness and School Improvement, 4,* (1), 17-36.

Schmidt, K. (1998). Applying the four principles of total quality management to the classroom. *Tech Directions, 58,* (1) 16-18.

Schofield, J. W., Eurich-Fulcer, R., & Britt, C. L. (1994). Teachers, computer tutors, and teaching: The artificially intelligent tutor as an agent for classroom change. *American Educational Research Journal, 3,* 579-607.

Schultz, R. A. (1979). Student importance ratings as indicator of structure of actual and ideal sociopsychological climates. *Journal of Educational Psychology, 71,* 827-839.

Schumacker, R. E. & Lomax, R. G. (1996). *A beginner's guide to structural equation modeling.* Mahwah, NJ: Erlbaum.

Schunk, D. H. (1989). Self-efficacy and cognitive skill learning. In C. Ames & R. Ames (Eds.), *Research on motivation in education. Vol. 3, Goals and cognitions* (pp. 13-44). San Diego, CA: Academic.

Schunk, D. H. (1995). Self-efficacy and education and instruction. In J. E. Maddux (Ed.), *Self-efficacy, adaptation, and adjustment: Theory, research, and application* (pp. 281-303). New York: Plenum.

Shavelson, R. J. (1973). What is "the" basic teaching skill? *Journal of Teacher Education, 14,* 144-151.

Shrigley, R. L. (1983). The attitude concept and science teaching. *Science Education, 67,* 425-442.

Shrigley, R. L., Koballa, T. R., & Simpson, R. D. (1988). Defining attitude for science educators. *Journal of Research in Science Teaching, 25,* 659-678.

Shuell, T. J. (1993). Towards an integrated theory of teaching and learning. *Educational Psychologist, 28,* 291-311.

Shuell, T. J. (1996). Teaching and learning in a classroom context. In D. C. Berliner, & R. C. Calfee (Eds.), *Handbook of educational psychology* (pp. 726-764). New York: Macmillan.

Shulman, L. (1986). Paradigms and research programs in the study of teaching: a contemporary perspective. In M.C. Wittrock (Ed.) *Handbook of research on teaching* (pp. 3-36). New York: MacMillan.

Shulman, L. S. & Tamir, P. (1972). Research on teaching in the natural sciences. In R. M. W. Travers, (Ed.), *Second handbook of research on teaching* (pp. 1098-1148). Chicago, IL: Rand McNally.

Simons, P. R. J. & de Jong, F. P. C. M. (1992). Self-regulation and computer-aided instruction. *Applied Psychology: An International Review, 41,* 36-346.

Smith, N.L. (1991). Evaluation reflections: The context of investigations in cross-cultural evaluations. *Studies in Educational Evaluation, 17,* 3-21.

Smith, P. (2004, January/February). Curricular transformation: Why we need it: How to support it. *Change, 36* (1), 28-35.

Smith, L. & Land, M. (1981). Low-inference verbal behaviors related to teacher clarity. *Journal of Classroom Interaction, 17,* 37-42.

Snijders, T. & Bosker, R. (1999). *Multilevel analysis: An introduction to basic and advanced multilevel modeling.* London: Sage.

Stallings, J. A. & Mohlman, G. G. (1988). Classroom observation techniques. In J. P. Keeves (Ed.), *Educational research, methodology, and measurement: An International handbook* (pp. 469-474). Oxford, England: Pergamon.

Star, S. L. (1999). The ethnography of infrastructure. *American Behavioral Scientist, 43,* 377–391.

Stern, G. G. (1970). *People in context: Measuring person-environment congruence in education and industry.* New York: Wiley.

Stern, G. G., Stein, M. I., & Bloom, B. S. (1956). *Methods in personality assessment.* Glencoe, IL: Free Press.

Sternberg, R. J. (1988). Mental self-government: A theory of intellectual styles and their development. *Human Development, 31,* 197-224.

Stevens, J. (1992). *Applied multivariate statistics for the social sciences.* Hillsdale, NJ: Lawrence Erlbaum Associates.

Stockard, J. & Mayberry, M. (1992). *Effective educational environment.* Newbury Park, CA: Corwin.

Stodolsky, S. S. (1990). Classroom observation. In J. Millman & L. Darling-Hammond (Eds.), *The new handbook of teacher evaluation: Assessing elementary and secondary school teachers* (pp. 175-190). Newbury Park, CA: Sage.

Stofflett, R. & Stoddart, T. (1994). The ability to understand and use conceptual change pedagogy as a function of prior content learning experience. *Journal of Research in Science Teaching, 31* (1), 31-51.

Stolarchuk, E. & Fisher, D. L. (2001). First years of laptops in science classrooms result in more learning about computers than science. *Issues In Educational Research, 11* (1), 25-39.

Stringfield, S. (1994). The analysis of large data bases in school effectiveness research. In D. Reynolds, B. P. M. Creemers, P. S, Nesselrodt, E. C. Schaffer, S. Stringfield & C. Teddlie (1994). *Advances in school effectiveness research and practice* (pp. 55-72). Oxford: Pergamon.

Suchman, L., Blomberg, J., Orr., J. E., & Trigg, R. (1999). Reconstructing technologies as social practice. *American Behavioral Scientist, 43*, 392-408.

Svinicki, M. (2002). Faculty development: An investment for the future. In R. M. Diamond (Ed.), *Field guide to academic leadership* (pp. 211-221). San Francisco: Jossey-Bass.

Sweetland, S. R. & Hoy, W. R. (2000). School characteristic and educational outcomes: Toward organisational model of student achievment in middle schools. *Educational Administration Quarterly, 36* (6), 703-729.

Tamir, P. (1972). The practical mode a distinct mode of performance, *Journal of Biological Education, 6*, 175-182.

Tashakkori, A. & Teddlie, C. (2003). *Handbook of mixed methods in social & behavioral research.* Thousand Oaks/London/New Delhi: Sage Publications.

Taylor, P. C., Fraser, B. J., & Fisher, D. (1997). Monitoring constructivist classroom learning environments. *International Journal of Educational Research, 27* (4), 293-302.

Templeton, R. A. & Johnston, C. E. (1998). Making the school environment safe: Red Rose's formula. *Learning Environments Research, 1* (1), 35-77.

Thomas, G. P. (2003). Conceptualisation, development and validation of an instrument for investigating the metacognitive orientation of science classroom learning environments: The metacognitive orientation learning environment scale – Science (MOLES-S). *Learning Environments Research, 6*, 175-197.

Tobin, K. G. (1990). Research on science laboratory activities; In pursuit of better questions and answers to improve learning. *School Science and Mathematics, 90*, 403-418.

Tobin, K. G. (1998). Qualitative perceptions of learning environments on the world wide web. *Learning Environments Research, 1*, 139-162.

Tobin, K. G. & Fraser, B. J. (1998). Qualitative and quantitative landscapes of classroom learning environments. In B. J. Fraser & K. G. Tobin (Eds.), *International Handbook of Science Education* (pp. 623-640). Dordrecht, The Netherlands: Kluwer Academic Publishers.

Tracey, T. J. (1994). An examination of complementarity of interpersonal behaviour. *Journal of Personality and Social Psychology, 67*, 864-878.

Tracey, T. J. & Schneider, P. L. (1995). An evaluation of the circular structure of the checklist of interpersonal transactions and the checklist of psychotherapy transactions. *Journal of Counseling Psychology*, 42, 496-507.

Tyler, R. W. (1949). *Basic principles of curriculum and instruction.* Chicago: University of Chicago Press.

Uguroglu, M. E. & Walberg, H. J. (1986). Predicting achievement and motivation. *Journal of Research and Development in Education, 19* (3), 1-12.

Umbach, P. D. & Wawrzynski, M. R. (2004). Faculty do matter: The role of college faculty in student learning and engagement. *Research in Higher Education, 46* (2), 153-184.

Van de Grift, W., Houtveen, T., & Vermeulen, C. (1997). Instructional climate in Dutch secondary education. *School Effectiveness and School Improvement, 8* (4), 449-462.

Veenman, S. (1984). Problems of beginning teachers. *Review of Educational Research, 54*, 143-178.

Vermetten, Y. J., Vermunt, J. D., & Lodewijks, H. G. (2002). Powerful learning environments? How do university students differ in their response to instructional measures. *Learning and Instruction, 12*, 263-284.

Vermunt, J. D. (1998). The regulation of constructive learning processes. *British Journal of Educational Psychology, 68*, 149-171.

Vermunt, J. D. (2005). Relations between student learning patterns and personal and contextual factors and academic performance. *Higher Education, 49,* 205-234.

Vermunt, J. D. & Minnaert, A. (2003). Dissonance in student learning patterns: when to revise theory? *Studies in Higher Education, 28* (1), 49-61.

Vermunt, J. D. & Verloop, N. (1999). Congruence and friction between learning and teaching. *Learning and Instruction, 9*, 257-280.

Vermunt, J. D. & Verschaffel, L. (2000). Process-oriented teaching. In R. J. Simons, J. van der Linden, & T. Duffy (2000). *New learning* (pp. 209-225). Dordrecht/Boston/London: Kluwer Academic Publishers,.

von Glasersfeld, E. (1981). The concepts of adaption and viability in a radical constructivist theory of knowledge. In I. E. Sigel, D. M. Brodinsky, & R. M. Golinkoff (Eds.), *New directions in Piagetian theory and practice.* New Jersey: Lawrence Erlbaum Associates.

von Glasersfeld, E. (1988). The reluctance to change a way of thinking. *The Irish Journal of Pyschology, 9* (1), 83-90.

von Glasersfeld, E. (1989). Cognition, construction of knowledge, and teaching. *Synthese, 80*, 121-140.

Vygotsky, L. S. (1978). *Mind in society*. Cambridge, Massachusetts: Harvard University Press.

Walberg, H. J. (1976). The psychology of learning environments: Behavioural, structural or perceptual? *Review of Research in Education, 4*, 142-178.

Walberg, H. J. (1979). *Educational environments and effects: Evaluation, policy, and productivity*. Berkely: McCutchan.

Walberg, H. J. (1981). A psychological theory of educational productivity. In N. J. Gordon (Ed.), *Psychology and education: the state of the union* (pp. 81-108). Berkeley, CA: McCutchan.

Walberg, H.J. (1986). Synthesis of research on teaching. In M. C. Wittrock (Ed.), *Handbook of research on teaching* (3rd ed.). New York: Macmillan.

Walberg, H. J. & Anderson, G. J. (1968). Classroom climate and individual learning. *Journal of Educational Psychology, 59*, 414-419.

Wang, M. C., Haertel, G. D., & Walberg, H. J. (1993). Toward a knowledge base for school learning. *Review of Educational Research, 63*, 249-294.

Ward, J. H. (1963). Hierarchical grouping to optimise an objective function. *Journal of the American Statistical Association, 58*, 236-244.

Watzlawick, P., Beavin, J. H., & Jackson, D. (1967). *The pragmatics of human communication*. New York: Norton.

Waxman, H. C. (1991). Investigating classroom and school learning environments: A review of recent research and developments in the field. *Journal of Classroom Interaction, 26* (2), 1-4.

Waxman, H. C. (1992). Reversing the cycle of educational failure for students in at-risk school environments. In H. C. Waxman, J. Walker de Felix, J. Anderson, & H. P. Baptiste (Eds.), *Students at risk in at-risk schools: Improving environments for learning* (pp. 1-9). Newbury Park, CA: Corwin.

Waxman, H. C. (1995). Classroom observations of effective teaching. In A. C. Ornstein (Ed.), *Teaching: Theory into practice* (pp. 76-93). Needham Heights, MA: Allyn & Bacon.

Waxman, H. C. & Huang, S.-Y. L. (1996). Motivation and learning environment differences in inner-city middle school students. *The Journal of Educational Research, 90*, 93-102.

Waxman, H. C. & Huang, S.-Y. L. (1997). Classroom instruction and learning environment differences between effective and ineffective urban elementary schools for African American students. *Urban Education, 32,* 7-44.

Waxman, H. C. & Huang, S.-Y. L. (1998). Classroom learning environments in urban elementary, middle, and high schools. *Learning Environments Research, 1,* 95-113.

Waxman, H. C. & Huang, S. L. (1999). Classroom observation research and the improvement of teaching. In H. C. Waxman & H. J. Walberg (Eds.), *New directions for teaching practice and research* (pp. 107-129). Berkeley, CA: McCutchan.

Waxman, H. C., Huang, S. L., & Padrón, Y. N. (1995). Investigating the pedagogy of poverty in inner-city middle level schools. *Research in Middle Level Education, 18* (2), 1-22.

Waxman, H. C., Huang, S. L., & Wang, M. C. (1997). Investigating the multilevel classroom learning environment of resilient and nonresilient students from inner-city elementary schools. *International Journal of Educational Research, 27,* 343-353.

Waxman, H. C. & Padrón, Y. N. (2002). Research-based teaching practices that improve the education of English language learners. In L. Minaya-Rowe (Ed.), *Teacher training and effective pedagogy in the context of student diversity* (pp. 3-38). Greenwich, CT: Information Age.

Waxman, H. C. & Padrón, Y. N. (2004). The uses of the Classroom Observation Schedule to improve classroom instruction. In H. C. Waxman, R. G. Tharp, & R. S. Hilberg (Eds.), *Observational research in U. S. classrooms: New approaches for understanding cultural and linguistic diversity* (pp. 72-96). Cambridge, United Kingdom: Cambridge University Press.

Webster, B. J. & Fisher, D. L. (2004). School-level environment and student outcomes in mathematics. *Learning Environments Research, 6,* 309-326.

Weinstein, C. S. (1979). The physical environment of the school: A review of the research. *Review of Educational Research, 49* (4), 577-610.

Weinstein, C. E., Zimmerman, S. A., & Palmer, D. R. (1988). Assessing learning strategies: the design and development of the LASSI. In C.E. Weinstein, P.A. Alexander & E.T. Goetz (Eds.). *Learning and study strategies: Issues in assessment, instruction and evaluation* (pp.25-40). New York: Academic Press.

White, R. T. (1989). *Learning science.* Oxford: Basil Blackwell.

Wierstra, R. F. A., Kanselaar, G., Van der Linden, J. L., Lodewijks, H. G., & Vermunt, J. D. (2003). The impact of the university context on

European students' learning approaches and learning environment preferences. *Higher Education, 45* (4), 503-523.

Winne, P. H. & Marx, R. W. (1982). Students' and teachers' views of thinking processes for classroom learning. *Elementary School Journal, 82*, 493-518.

Winne, P. H. & Marx, R.W. (1997). Reconceptualizing research on teaching, *Journal of Educational Psychology, 69*, 668-678.

Wittrock, M. (1986). Students' thought processes. In M. Wittrock (Ed.), *Handbook of research in teaching* (3rd ed., pp. 297-314). New York: Macmillan.

Witty, J. P. & DeBarysch, B. D. (1994). Student and teacher perceptions of teachers' communication of performance expectations in the classroom. *Journal of Classroom Interaction, 29*, 1-8.

Wong, A. F. L. & Fraser, B. J. (1996). Environment-attitude associations in the chemistry laboratory classroom. *Research in Science and Technological Education, 14*, 91-102.

Woodson, W. E., Tillman, B., & Tillman, P. (1992). *Human factors handbook: Information guidelines for the design of systems, facilities, equipment, and products for human use* (2nd Ed.). New York: McGraw-Hill.

Wubbels, T. & Brekelmans, M. (1997). A comparison of student perceptions of Dutch Physics teachers' interpersonal behavior and their educational opinions in 1984 and 1993. *Journal of Research in Science Teaching, 34* (5), 447-466.

Wubbels, T. & Brekelmans, M. (1998). The teacher factor in the social climate of the classroom. In B. J. Fraser, & K. G. Tobin (Eds.), *International Handbook of Science Education* (pp. 565-580). London: Kluwer Academic Publishers.

Wubbels, T., Brekelmans, M., & Hermans, J. (1987). Teacher behaviour: an important aspect of the learning environment. In B. J. Fraser (Ed.), *The study of learning environments, Volume 3* (pp.10-25). Perth: Curtin University.

Wubbels, T., Brekelmans, M., & Hooymayers, H. (1991). Interpersonal teacher behaviour in the classroom. In B. J. Fraser & H. Walberg (Eds.), *Educational environments: Evaluation, antecedents and consequences* (pp. 141-160). Oxford: Pergamon Press.

Wubbels, T., Brekelmans, M., & Hooymayers, H. P. (1992). Do teacher ideals distort the self-reports of their interpersonal behavior? *Teaching and Teacher Education, 8* (1), 47-58.

Wubbels, T., Créton, H. A, & Hooymayers, H. P. (1987). A school-based teacher induction programme. *European Journal of Teacher Education, 10,* 81-94.

Wubbels, T., Creton, H. A., & Hooymayers, H. P. (1992). Review of research on teacher communication styles with use of the Leary model. *Journal of Classroom Interaction, 27* (1), 1-12.

Wubbels, T., Creton, H., Levy, J., & Hooymayers, H. (1993). The model for interpersonal behaviour. In T. Wubbels & J. Levy (Eds.), *Do you know what you look like? Interpersonal relations in education.* (pp. 13-28) London: The Falmer Press.

Wubbels, T. & Levy, J. (1991). A comparison of interpersonal behaviour of Dutch and American teachers. *International Journal of Intercultural Relations, 15,* 1-18.

Wubbels, T. & Levy, J. (1993). *Do you know what you look like?* London: The Falmer Press.

Yair, G. (1997). When classrooms matter: Implications of between-classroom variability for educational policy in Israel. *Assessment in Education, 4* (2), 225-248.

Yelland, N. (1995). Collaboration and learning with Logo: Does gender make a difference? *Proceedings of the Conference on Computer-Supported Cooperative Learning* (pp. 197-410). Bloomington, IN.

Yin, R. K. (1984). *Case study research: Design and methods.* Newbury Park, CA: Sage.

Zandvliet, D. (2000). *Designing productive learning environments for tomorrow's teachers.* In D. L. Fisher & J.-H. Yang (Eds.), *Proceedings of the Second International Conference on Science, Mathematics and Technology Education* (pp. 489-502). Perth: Curtin University of Technology.

Zandvliet, D. B. (2003). Learning environments in new contexts: Web-capable classrooms in Canada. In M. S. Khine & D. L. Fisher (Eds.), *Technology-rich learning environments: A future perspective* (pp. 133-156). Singapore: World Scientific.

Zeldin, A. L. & Pajares, F. (2000). Against the odds: Self-efficacy beliefs of women in mathematical, scientific and technological careers. *American Educational Research Journal, 37,* 215–246.

Zimmerman, B. J. (1995). Self-efficacy and educational development. In A. Bandura (Ed.), *Self-efficacy in changing societies* (pp. 202-231). Cambridge, UK: Cambridge University Press.

Zimmerman, B. J. (2001). Theories of self-regulated learning and academic achievement: An overview and analysis. In B. J. Zimmerman & D. H. Schunk (Eds.), *Self-regulated learning and academic achievement. Theoretical perspectives* (pp. 1-37). Mahwah, NJ: Lawrence Erlbaum.

Index

3D virtual world, 603

academic achievement, 409
academic efficacy, 1–3, 5–11, 13–17, 20–22
achievement, 76, 80, 82, 83
action research, 247, 248, 250–252, 256, 257, 269
actual, 224, 230–234, 297, 298, 300, 302–306, 308, 409, 415–423, 497, 502, 504, 507–513
advanced learning models, 543
AEI, 179, 182–184
affective outcomes, 369, 378, 380, 382, 393–395, 397–399
assessing patterns, 93
association, 425–428, 442
attitude, 77, 80, 87, 517–525, 527, 529–537, 539
attitude to science, 1, 3, 7–11, 13–17, 20–22
attitudinal data, 161
Australia, 51–53, 55, 56, 61–63, 65, 425, 427, 429, 443

Belgium, 93, 99
blended learning, 465, 477

CCEI, 161, 177, 179
CCEW, 161, 177
CCI, 500
CCL, 464
CES, 249
CFA, 433, 435
CIC, 313, 328, 329
class size, 51, 55, 57, 62, 63, 66–69

classroom environment, 1–3, 7–10, 13–16, 20–22, 247–251, 253–259, 261, 262, 265, 269
classroom organisational systems, 337
CLES, 297, 299–308, 427
COEHS, 313, 314, 317, 318, 320–325, 328–332
cognitive achievement, 290–292
cognitive outcomes, 378, 398, 399
collaborative learning environment, 297
college environment, 314, 322, 323, 325–327 479–483
COLLES, 607, 608
COM, 208, 209
communications technologies, 543, 547, 551, 558, 565, 570
complex learning environments, 449, 450
computer, 337–340, 342–344, 346, 347, 349, 352–354, 358, 359, 361–366, 543, 545, 549, 551, 553, 555, 559, 562, 565, 570, 573, 574
computer classroom, 297–299, 308
computer course, 297, 298, 302, 303
computer-supported collaborative learning, 579, 580, 586
Computer-Supported Cooperative Work (CSCW), 455
construct validity, 369, 382, 383, 385, 392
constructivist learning environment, 297, 299, 300, 303, 305